THE ROUTLEDGE COMPANION TO BRITISH MEDIA HISTORY

The Routledge Companion to British Media History provides a comprehensive exploration of how different media have evolved within social, regional and national contexts.

The 50 chapters in this volume, written by an outstanding team of internationally respected scholars, bring together current debates and issues within media history in this era of rapid change, and also provide students and researchers with an essential collection of comparable media histories.

The first two parts of the *Companion* comprise a series of thematic chapters reflecting broadly on historiography, providing historical context for discussions of the power of the media and their social importance, arranged in the following sections:

- Media history debates
- Media and society

The subsequent parts are made up of in-depth sections on different media formats, exploring various approaches to historicizing media futures, divided as follows:

- Newspapers
- Magazines
- Radio
- Film
- Television
- Digital media

The Routledge Companion to British Media History provides an essential guide to key ideas, issues, concepts and debates in the field.

Contributors: Jane Bentley, Adrian Bingham, Timothy Boon, Jilly Boyce Kay, Jonathan Cable, Andrew Calcutt, Lily Canter, Deborah Chambers, James Chapman, Hugh Chignell, Martin Conboy, Lez Cooke, John Corner, Theresa Cronin, Stephen Cushion, Tristan Donovan, Scott Eldridge II, David Finkelstein, Joanne Garde-Hansen, Victoria E. M. Gardner, Peter Golding, Jean-Baptiste Gouyon, Ann Gray, Philip Hammond, Richard Haynes, Matt Hills, Su Holmes, Tim Holmes, Daniel Kilvington, Peter Lee-Wright, Tim Luckhurst, Rachel Matthews, Kaitlynn Mendes, Brett Mills, Caroline Mitchell, Graham Murdock, Marcus Nevitt, Siân Nicholas, Tom O'Malley, Bill Osgerby, Jussi Parikka, Julian Petley, Michael Pickering, Richard Rudin, Tom Ryall, Amir Saeed, Jonathan Silberstein-Loeb, Clarissa Smith, Guy Starkey, John Steel, Mick Temple, Karin Wahl-Jorgensen, Tim Wall, Nick Webber, Joel H. Wiener, Kevin Williams.

Martin Conboy is Professor of Journalism History in the Department of Journalism Studies at the University of Sheffield and co-director of the Centre for the Study of Journalism and History. He is the author of seven single-authored books on the language and history of journalism. He is on the editorial boards of *Journalism Studies*; *Media History*; *Journalism: Theory, Practice and Criticism*; and *Memory Studies*.

John Steel is a lecturer in Journalism Studies at the University of Sheffield. He is the author of *Journalism and Free Speech* (Routledge, 2012) and is published in the areas of media history, journalism studies and political communication. He has recently edited a special collection of articles in *Media History* on digital newspaper archives. He is currently working on 'normativity' in journalism.

THE ROUTLEDGE COMPANION TO BRITISH MEDIA HISTORY

Edited by
Martin Conboy and John Steel
(With editorial assistance from Scott Eldridge II)

LONDON AND NEW YORK

First published 2015
by Routledge
2 Park Square, Milton Park, Abingdon, Oxon, OX14 4RN

and by Routledge
711 Third Avenue, New York, NY 10017

Routledge is an imprint of the Taylor & Francis Group, an informa business

© 2015 Martin Conboy and John Steel for selection and editorial matter; individual contributions the contributors

The right of Martin Conboy and John Steel to be identified as authors of the editorial material, and of the authors for their individual chapters, has been asserted in accordance with sections 77 and 78 of the Copyright, Designs and Patents Act 1988.

All rights reserved. No part of this book may be reprinted or reproduced or utilised in any form or by any electronic, mechanical, or other means, now known or hereafter invented, including photocopying and recording, or in any information storage or retrieval system, without permission in writing from the publishers.

Trademark notice: Product or corporate names may be trademarks or registered trademarks, and are used only for identification and explanation without intent to infringe.

British Library Cataloguing in Publication Data
A catalogue record for this book is available from the British Library

Library of Congress Cataloging in Publication Data
The Routledge companion to British media history / edited by Martin Conboy and John Steel.
pages cm
Includes bibliographical references and index.
1. Mass media--Great Britain--History--20th century . 2. Mass media--Great Britain--History--21st century . I. Conboy, Martin, editor. II. Steel, John, 1966- editor.
P92.G7R68 2014
302.230941--dc23
2014009981

ISBN: 978-0-415-53718-6 (hbk)
ISBN: 978-1-315-75620-2 (ebk)

Typeset in Goudy
by Taylor & Francis Books

Printed and bound in Great Britain by
TJ International Ltd, Padstow, Cornwall

CONTENTS

List of contributors — x
Acknowledgments — xvii

Introduction: British media and mediations of the past — 1
MARTIN CONBOY AND JOHN STEEL

PART I
Media history debates — 7

1 The devaluation of history in media studies — 9
   MICHAEL PICKERING

2 Media products as historical artefacts — 19
   ADRIAN BINGHAM

3 Doing media history: The mass media, historical analysis and the 1930s — 29
   KEVIN WILLIAMS

4 Media studies in question: The making of a contested formation — 41
   GRAHAM MURDOCK AND PETER GOLDING

5 Media archaeology: From Turing to Abbey Road, Kentish radar stations to Bletchley Park — 60
   JUSSI PARIKKA

PART II
Media and society — 73

6 The political economy of media — 75
   JONATHAN SILBERSTEIN-LOEB

7	Historicizing the media effects debate THERESA CRONIN	85
8	Citizen or consumer? Representations of class in post-war British media MICK TEMPLE	100
9	Inscriptions and depictions of 'race' DANIEL KILVINGTON AND AMIR SAEED	111
10	Home comforts? Gender, media and the family JILLY BOYCE KAY AND KAITLYNN MENDES	122
11	Sex and sexuality in British media CLARISSA SMITH	133
12	This sporting 'life-world': Mediating sport in Britain JOHN STEEL	147
13	Social conflict and the media: Contesting definitional power JONATHAN CABLE	160
14	The media and armed conflict PHILIP HAMMOND	171

PART III
Newspapers — 181

15	Ballads and the development of the English newsbook MARCUS NEVITT	183
16	Eighteenth-century newspapers and public opinion VICTORIA E. M. GARDNER	195
17	The nineteenth century and the emergence of a mass circulation press JOEL H. WIENER	206
18	Tabloid culture: The political economy of a newspaper style MARTIN CONBOY	215
19	The regulation of the press TOM O'MALLEY	228
20	The provincial press in England: An overview RACHEL MATTHEWS	239

21 Online and on death row: Historicizing newspapers in crisis TIM LUCKHURST	250
PART IV **Magazines**	261
22 The role of the literary and cultural periodical DAVID FINKELSTEIN	263
23 Specialist magazines as communities of taste TIM HOLMES AND JANE BENTLEY	273
24 Contexts and developments in women's magazines DEBORAH CHAMBERS	285
25 Mapping the male in magazines BILL OSGERBY	297
26 Magazine pioneers: Form and content in 1960s and 1970s radicalism ANDREW CALCUTT	309
PART V **Radio**	321
27 The Reithian legacy and contemporary public service ethos SIÂN NICHOLAS	323
28 Pirates, popularity and the rise of the DJ RICHARD RUDIN	334
29 Breaking the sound barrier: Histories and practices of women's radio CAROLINE MITCHELL	345
30 Radio drama HUGH CHIGNELL	356
31 Radio sports news: The longevity and influence of 'Sports Report' RICHARD HAYNES	366
32 Radio's audiences GUY STARKEY	380

PART VI
Film
                                                                    391

33 The British cinema: Eras of film   393
    TOM RYALL

34 British cinema and history   404
    JAMES CHAPMAN

35 'The Horror!'   414
    MATT HILLS

36 The documentary tradition   425
    PETER LEE-WRIGHT

37 The censors' tools   437
    JULIAN PETLEY

PART VII
Television
                                                                    449

38 The television sitcom   451
    BRETT MILLS

39 Drama on the box   460
    LEZ COOKE

40 The origins and practice of science on British television   470
    TIMOTHY BOON AND JEAN-BAPTISTE GOUYON

41 History on television   484
    ANN GRAY

42 'Reality TV'   493
    SU HOLMES

43 Journalism and current affairs   504
    STEPHEN CUSHION

PART VIII
Digital Media
                                                                    515

44 Technology's false dawns: The past of media futures   517
    LILY CANTER

45	Change and continuity: Historicizing the emergence of online media SCOTT ELDRIDGE II	528
46	Personal listening pleasures TIM WALL AND NICK WEBBER	539
47	Futures of television JOHN CORNER	550
48	Video games and gaming: The audience fights back TRISTAN DONOVAN	561
49	From letters to tweeters: Media communities of opinion KARIN WAHL-JORGENSEN	571
50	Digital memories and media of the future JOANNE GARDE-HANSEN	582
	Index	594

LIST OF CONTRIBUTORS

Jane Bentley is a Lecturer at Cardiff University's School of Journalism, Media and Cultural Studies. She teaches magazine reporting and writing on the PTC accredited MA in Journalism as well as other postgraduate and undergraduate programmes. She previously worked in specialist magazine publishing for ten years.

Adrian Bingham is Reader in Modern History at the University of Sheffield. He is the author of two monographs: *Gender, Modernity and the Popular Press in Inter-War Britain* (OUP, 2004) and *Family Newspapers? Sex, Private Life, and the British Popular Press 1918–1978* (OUP, 2009).

Timothy Boon is Head of Research & Public History at the Science Museum, London and specializes in the history and current practice of the public culture of science. His book *Films of Fact: A History of Science in Documentary Films and Television* was published by Wallflower in 2008.

Jilly Boyce Kay is a PhD student at De Montfort University whose research focuses on the history of television debate programmes and feminist political and media theory. Additionally, she has published on *Question Time*, journalistic framing of the austerity agenda and student protest.

Jonathan Cable works as a researcher and lecturer at Cardiff University, having completed his PhD in Journalism Studies there in July 2012. His thesis examined the different media strategy and protest tactics choices made by protest groups and their impact on press coverage.

Andrew Calcutt is Principal Lecturer in Journalism at the University of East London and Co-Director of the London East Research Institute. Before academia, he was a B2B editor (*Tenders & Contracts Journal*), television reporter (*Clarke TV* for Channel 4), political commentator (*Living Marxism*) and online commissioner (*Channel Cyberia*). His books include *Journalism Studies: A Critical Introduction* (Routledge, 2011).

Lily Canter is BA Journalism course leader at Sheffield Hallam University. She previously worked in regional newspapers before working as a freelance journalist for print and online publications. Her research interests are regional newspapers, digital journalism, hyperlocal journalism and social media. She is also an NCTJ examiner.

Deborah Chambers is Professor of Media and Cultural Studies at Newcastle University. Intersecting media and cultural studies and sociology, her research areas include media cultures; media technologies, families and households; and changing intimate relationships. Her latest book is *Social Media and Personal Relationships* (Palgrave 2013).

James Chapman is Professor of Film Studies at the University of Leicester and editor of the *Historical Journal of Film, Radio and Television*. His books include *The British at War: Cinema, State and Propaganda, 1939–1945* (I. B. Tauris, 1998) and *Licence To Thrill: A Cultural History of the James Bond Films* (I. B. Tauris, 2nd edn, 2007).

Hugh Chignell is Professor of Media History and Director of the Centre for Media History at Bournemouth University. He has published mainly in the field of radio history and has a particular interest in radio talks, news and current affairs.

Martin Conboy is Professor of Journalism History in the Department of Journalism Studies at the University of Sheffield and co-director of the Centre for the Study of Journalism and History. He is the author of seven single-authored books on the language and history of journalism. He is on the editorial boards of *Journalism Studies*; *Media History*; *Journalism: Theory, Practice and Criticism*; and *Memory Studies*.

Lez Cooke is a Senior Research Officer in the Department of Media Arts at Royal Holloway, University of London and Co-Investigator on the AHRC research project, 'The History of Forgotten Television Drama in the UK'. He is the author of *British Television Drama: A History* (BFI, 2003), *Troy Kennedy Martin* (MUP, 2007), *A Sense of Place: Regional British Television Drama, 1956–82* (MUP, 2012) and *Style in British Television Drama* (Palgrave, 2013).

John Corner is Visiting Professor at the University of Leeds and Emeritus Professor of the University of Liverpool. He has written widely on media theory and forms and his most recent books are *Theorising Media: Power, Form and Subjectivity* (Manchester University Press, 2011) and, with Kay Richardson and Katy Parry, *Political Culture and Media Genre* (Palgrave, 2012).

Theresa Cronin is a Lecturer in Media and Cultural Studies at Middlesex University. Her areas of expertise include film regulation, media effects, film cultures, and audience and reception studies. Her research publications include 'Media Effects and the Subjectification of Film Regulation' (*Velvet Light Trap: A Critical Journal of Film & Television – Special Issue on Censorship*, No 63, Spring 2009).

Stephen Cushion is a Senior Lecturer at the School of Journalism, Media and Cultural Studies, Cardiff University. He has recently published *The Democratic Value of News: Why Public Service Media Matter* (Palgrave, 2012) and *Television Journalism* (Sage, 2012).

Tristan Donovan is the author of *Replay: The History of Video Games* (Yellow Ant Media Ltd, 2010) and a freelance journalist who has written about games for *Stuff*, *The Times*, *Eurogamer* and *Gamasutra* among others. He is also the author of *Fizz: How Soda Shook up the World* (Chicago Review Press, 2013).

LIST OF CONTRIBUTORS

Scott Eldridge II is a Lecturer in Journalism Studies at the University of Sheffield and researches WikiLeaks, new media and journalism's reactions to emerging *interloper media*. He has authored several journal articles on changing journalism dynamics and is Reviews Editor for the journal *Digital Journalism*.

David Finkelstein is Dean of the School of Humanities and Professor of Print Culture at the University of Dundee. Recent publications include *The Edinburgh History of the Book in Scotland, Vol. 3, 1880–2000* (Edinburgh University Press, 2007) and *Print Culture and the Blackwood Tradition* (University of Toronto Press, 2006), which was awarded the Robert Colby Scholarly Book Prize in 2007.

Joanne Garde-Hansen is Associate Professor, Culture, Media and Communication in the Centre for Cultural Policy Studies, University of Warwick. She is author of *Media and Memory* (Edinburgh University Press, 2011) and, with Kristyn Gorton, *Emotion Online* (Palgrave, 2013). She is currently working on a British Academy-funded project – Inheriting British Television: Memories, Archives and Industries.

Victoria E. M. Gardner is a Lecturer in economic and social history at the University of Edinburgh. Her research interests are in business, communities and communication in industrializing Britain. She is the author of several chapters and articles on the book trade and newspapers. Her monograph, *The Business of News in England, 1760–1820*, is due out in 2015.

Peter Golding is Pro-Vice Chancellor for Research and Innovation at Northumbria University, and chaired the panels assessing media research in the national research evaluation exercises in both 2008 and 2014. His recent books include, as co-editor with Graham Murdock, *Digital Dynamics: Engagements and Disconnections* (Hampton Press, 2010).

Jean-Baptiste Gouyon is currently a post-doctoral research associate at the Science Museum in London, where he conducts research on the history of television science, and a teaching fellow at UCL STS, where he teaches a course on science in the mass media.

Ann Gray is Professor of Cultural Studies in the Lincoln School of Media, University of Lincoln, UK and co-director of the Centre for European Cultural Studies. She was the Principal Investigator for the AHRC-funded research project, 'Televising History 1992–2010'. She is a founding editor of the *European Journal of Cultural Studies*.

Philip Hammond is Professor of Media & Communications and Head of the Centre for Media & Culture Research at London South Bank University. Recent books include the edited volume *Screens of Terror* (Abramis, 2011) and, with Andrew Calcutt, *Journalism Studies: A Critical Introduction* (Routledge, 2011).

Richard Haynes is Professor of Communications, Media and Culture at the University of Stirling. He has published widely on the subject of the media and sport and has written several books on the subject including *Power Play: Sport, the Media & Popular Culture*, written with Raymond Boyle (Edinburgh University Press, second edition, 2009). He has also published numerous articles on the history of sports broadcasting in the UK.

LIST OF CONTRIBUTORS

Matt Hills is Professor of Film and TV Studies at Aberystwyth University. He is the author/editor of six books including *The Pleasures of Horror* (Bloomsbury, 2005) and *New Dimensions of Doctor Who* (I. B. Tauris, 2013). Matt's recent work on horror includes chapters in *A Companion to the Horror Film* (John Wiley & Sons, 2014) and *Merchants of Menace* (Bloomsbury, 2014).

Su Holmes is Reader in Television at the University of East Anglia. She is the author of *British TV and Film Culture in the 1950s* (Intellect, 2005), *Entertaining TV: The BBC and Popular Programme Culture in the 1950s* (MUP, 2008) and *The Quiz Show* (EUP, 2008). She is also the co-editor of *Understanding Reality TV* (Routledge, 2004), *Framing Celebrity* (Routledge, 2006), *Stardom and Celebrity: A Reader* (Sage, 2007) and *In the Limelight and Under the Microscope: Forms and Functions of Female Celebrity* (Continuum, 2011).

Tim Holmes is a Senior Lecturer at Cardiff University's School of Journalism, Media and Cultural Studies. He is course director of the PTC accredited MA in Journalism and magazine pathway leader for the MA in International Journalism. Publications include *Magazine Journalism* (Sage, 2012) and *The 21st Century Journalism Handbook* (Pearson, 2013).

Daniel Kilvington lectures in Media and Cultural Studies at the University of Sunderland. He completed his PhD in January 2013 and has published several titles, including a co-authored book with Routledge in 2012. His areas of expertise include 'race', racisms, social media, sport and exclusion.

Peter Lee-Wright is a Senior Lecturer in Media and Communications at Goldsmiths, University of London. He was a documentary filmmaker for the BBC and Channel 4, filming over 100 films in 40 countries, and is the author of *The Documentary Handbook* (Routledge, 2009).

Tim Luckhurst is Professor of Journalism at the University of Kent and a former editor of *The Scotsman*. He researches newspaper history. Recent publications include 'Excellent but Gullible People: The Press and the People's Convention' (*Journalism Studies*, 2013) and *Responsibility Without Power: Lord Justice Leveson's Constitutional Dilemma* (Abramis, 2012).

Rachel Matthews worked in the regional news industry for 15 years, reaching the role of deputy editor before joining academia. She is now Principal Lecturer in Journalism at Coventry University. Her journalistic background continues to inform her research into the history of the provincial press.

Kaitlynn Mendes, PhD, is a Lecturer in Media and Communication at the University of Leicester. Her research focuses on representations of feminism, feminist activists and feminist goals in mainstream, alternative and social media. She is author of *Feminism in the News* (Palgrave, 2011) and *Representing SlutWalk* (forthcoming).

Brett Mills is a Senior Lecturer in the School of Film, Television and Media Studies at the University of East Anglia. He is the author of *Television Sitcom* (BFI Publishing, 2005) and *The Sitcom* (Edinburgh University Press, 2009), and the Principal

Investigator on the AHRC-funded research project, 'Make Me Laugh: Creativity in the British Television Comedy Industry' (makemelaugh.org.uk).

Caroline Mitchell has been active in production, teaching and research about women and radio since 1988. She combines work as a Senior Lecturer in Radio at the University of Sunderland, UK with consultancies in community media evaluation and training.

Graham Murdock is Professor of Culture and Economy at the Department of Social Sciences at Loughborough University. His recent books include, as co-editor, *The Idea of the Public Sphere* (Lexington, 2010), *The Blackwell Handbook of Political Economy of Communication* (Wiley-Blackwell, 2011) and *Money Talks: Media, Markets, Crisis* (Intellect, 2014).

Marcus Nevitt is a Senior Lecturer in Renaissance Literature at the University of Sheffield. He is author of *Women and the Pamphlet Culture of Revolutionary England* (Ashgate, 2006) and numerous articles on early modern news. The book he is currently working on is called *Poetry and the Art of English News Writing*.

Siân Nicholas is Reader in Modern British History at Aberystwyth University and Co-Director of the Aberystwyth Centre for Media History. Her publications include *The Echo of War: Home Front Propaganda and the Wartime BBC* (Manchester University Press, 1996) and, co-edited with Tom O'Malley, *Reconstructing the Past: History in the Mass Media 1890–2005* (Routledge, 2008).

Tom O'Malley is Professor of Media at Aberystwyth University. He writes on press and broadcasting history and policy. His publications include, with Clive Soley, *Regulating the Press* (Pluto, 2000). He is co-founder and co-editor of the journal *Media History*.

Bill Osgerby is Professor of Media, Culture and Communications at London Metropolitan University. His research focuses on twentieth-century British and American cultural history, and his books include *Youth in Britain Since 1945* (Wiley-Blackwell, 1997), *Playboys in Paradise: Youth, Masculinity and Leisure-Style in Modern America* (Berg 3PL, 2001) and *Youth Media* (Routledge, 2004).

Jussi Parikka is Reader at the Winchester School of Art, University of Southampton. He is the author of several media theory and history books, including *Digital Contagions* (Peter Lang Publishing, 2007), *Insect Media* (University of Minnesota Press, 2010) and *What is Media Archaeology?* (Polity Press, 2012). He is currently writing a book on *Geology of Media* (University of Minnesota Press, 2015).

Julian Petley is Professor of Screen Media in the School of Arts at Brunel University. His most recent publications are the edited collections *The Media and Public Shaming* (I. B. Tauris, 2013) and *Moral Panics in the Contemporary World* (Bloomsbury, 2013). He is chair of the Campaign for Press and Broadcasting Freedom and a member of the advisory board of Index on Censorship.

Michael Pickering is Professor of Media and Cultural Analysis at Loughborough University. He has published extensively in cultural history and the sociology of culture, as well as media analysis and theory. His most recent book is, with Emily Keightley, *The Mnemonic Imagination* (Palgrave, 2012).

Richard Rudin is a Senior Lecturer in Journalism at Liverpool John Moores University. He has worked for BBC, commercial and British forces' broadcasting. His main research interest is in the development of UK commercial radio. His most recent book is *Broadcasting in the 21st Century* (Palgrave Macmillan, 2011).

Tom Ryall is Emeritus Professor of Film History at Sheffield Hallam University with research interests in British and American cinema. His recent work is included in *Modern British Drama on Screen* (Cambridge University Press, 2013), *A Companion to Film Noir* (Wiley-Blackwell, 2013) and *A Companion to Alfred Hitchcock* (Wiley-Blackwell, 2011).

Amir Saeed has researched 'race', racism and media influence for 15 years. His recent publications focus on Islamophobia, racism after 9/11, Muslim hip hop, Malcolm X and social media in relation to the Palestinian occupation.

Jonathan Silberstein-Loeb is a Senior Lecturer in History at Keble College, Oxford. His latest book, *The International Distribution of News: The Associated Press, Press Association, and Reuters, 1848–1949* (Cambridge University Press, 2014), investigates how cooperation among newspapers and international news organizations subsidized the collection of news and how governments around the world regulated the extent and nature of their joint efforts.

Clarissa Smith is Professor of Sexual Cultures at the University of Sunderland. Her publications include *One for the Girls! The Pleasures and Practices of Pornography for Women* (Intellect, 2007) and, with Niall Richardson and Angela Werndly, *Studying Sexualities: Theories, Representations, Practices* (Palgrave, 2013). She is co-editor of the journal *Porn Studies*.

Guy Starkey, a former radio producer and presenter, is Professor of Radio and Journalism at the University of Sunderland, UK. His publications include *Radio in Context* (Palgrave, 2013), *Local Radio, Going Global* (Palgrave, 2011) and, with Professor Andrew Crisell, *Radio Journalism* (Sage, 2009).

John Steel is a Lecturer in Journalism Studies at the University of Sheffield. He is the author of *Journalism and Free Speech* (Routledge, 2012) and has recently edited a special collection of articles in the journal *Media History* on digital newspaper archives. He is currently working on 'normativity' in journalism.

Mick Temple is Professor of Journalism and Politics at Staffordshire University. His books include *The British Press* (OUP, 2008) and *How Britain Works: From Ideology to Output Politics* (Palgrave, 2000). He has published many academic articles on politics and the media and is co-editor of *Journalism Education*.

Karin Wahl-Jorgensen is a Professor in the Cardiff School of Journalism, Media and Cultural Studies. She is the author or editor of five books, most recently, with Mervi Pantti and Simon Cottle, *Disasters and the Media* (Peter Lang Publishing, 2012) and is currently completing *Emotions, Media and Politics* (Polity).

Tim Wall is Professor of Radio and Popular Music Studies and Director of the Birmingham Centre for Media and Cultural Research. His research focuses on the production and consumption cultures around music and media. His *Studying Popular Music Culture* is published by Sage (2013).

Nick Webber is Associate Director of the Birmingham Centre for Media and Cultural Research. His research focuses on the contemporary relationship between technology and culture. His co-authored chapter on the history of the transistor radio appears in the *Oxford Handbook of Mobile Music Studies* (OUP, 2014).

Joel H. Wiener is Emeritus Professor of History at the City University of New York. He has written widely on aspects of modern press history. His most recent book is *The Americanization of the British Press, 1830s–1914* (Palgrave, 2011).

Kevin Williams is Professor of Media and Communication in the Department of History and Classics at Swansea University. His research interests include: the history of war reporting; newspaper and media history; European media and history and the mass media; and national identity in small nations.

ACKNOWLEDGMENTS

A volume such as this draws on the talents, energies and expertise of many people. We would firstly like to thank the authors of each chapter of this book for their hard work and commitment to the project and for their patience and diligence in dealing with our queries and comments on their work. We would also like to thank Natalie Foster at Routledge for entrusting such a significant project to us and Sheni Kruger, editorial assistant at Routledge, who has ensured that the administration of the project, from inception to final production, has been smooth and efficient. The effort involved in liaising with authors on various drafts of chapters has been a major component of this project and we are indebted to the hard work, organisational nous and professionalism of our editorial assistant here at Sheffield – Scott Eldridge II. In addition to producing a chapter for the volume, Scott has committed a significant amount of time and effort to this project and we are very grateful for all his work. Finally, we would like to thank the 'kindred spirits' in the Department of Journalism Studies at Sheffield University for their encouragement, advice and inspiration. They know who they are.

Martin Conboy and John Steel
Sheffield, March 2014

Introduction
British media and mediations of the past

Martin Conboy and John Steel

History is big news in the media at the moment. Over the past few decades we have seen a steady rise in the representation of historical events as either documentary or fictional entertainment even before the media saturation of the centenary commemorations of the outbreak of the First World War began in 2014. What is also on the rise, although with less immediate attraction for the mainstream media, is the historicization of the media themselves. Yet there is a noticeable increase in the quantity as well as the quality of such studies in the academy. Sometimes these studies have emerged for traditional contextual reasons but at other times they are driven by the need to be able to understand how emerging media technologies differentiate themselves or duplicate communication patterns from the past and, as Peters reminds us, there is much work to do in exploring his maxim that history, viewed reflexively, is communication history (Peters, 2008: 32).

Contemporary fascination with mediations in and of the past should come as no surprise since the media are the central conduit for many of our public celebrations of past achievements as well as commemorations of tragedies and horrors of the past. Such interest arguably reflects a desire to reconnect with and therefore make sense of our national and cultural identity in all its manifestations. Media therefore partly serve as forms of national popular memory. Inevitably, all these aspects raise familiar questions over the ownership of and access to processes of remembering. Such questions, of course, are overtly political and contested and, as this volume highlights, multifaceted.

The 'cultural turn' in historiography has served media history well and promises still more productive engagements in the future. History as a discourse can be profoundly cultural in its illumination of how the world, including the media world, has been created by human intervention. History allows us insights into the formulation of the narratives and symbols of the past as well as the formation and mutation of those channels of communication we term the media. To an extent, media history is not simply about transmission, it is also about translation into the present. Steiner (1975) extends our understanding of translation in a broader cultural sense to include the flow between preserving the distinctiveness of the past and the transformations which are imposed over time; history as a dialectic of continuity and rupture with media history acting as a work of cultural translation.

This book will continue to assert the media as cultural in their orientation and to demonstrate in a wide variety of expert contributions how this has been evident over centuries and in different technological epochs; against teleology but in favor of providing a series of accounts of moments in the formation of media history. We also assert that such an emphasis should not dissolve into relativism, nor does it come at the expense of more overt political or economic analyses as many of the chapters highlight the centrality of political and economic forces in the transformations and adaptations of British media history. Moreover, we do not seek to suggest that in recalling the specific histories of various media practices and products we are using historical approaches merely to illuminate the present, nor simply to reflect upon the continuities with the past; our approach is one which seeks to problematize the past–present axis in order to appreciate the specificity of the past.

We assert these points at a time when history is becoming one of the most important genres within British media, adding both commercial and cultural value. We suggest that such historical contextualization is particularly valuable and sought after as it offers respite from the economically induced pressures of time and space so evident in an increasingly diverse digital media market, which arguably limits opportunities for an appreciation of and reflection on historical context. As media are by definition tied into technologies of communication it is important to stress, particularly in the present era, that media have been developed, spurred on or curtailed by human activity. It is this fundamental truth that enables us to explore the reservoir of understandings/potential knowledge (Pöttker, 2012: 19) that the past of the media provides in the present.

Despite the purported globalization of mass media, it remains the case that our media consumption is predominantly rooted within national boundaries especially as components of the ritual of identity formation (Carey, 1989). Inevitably perhaps, considerations of the particular national aspects to the histories of media systems are of increasing prominence. Developing a national narrative allows the critical reader to be better able to critique its constructed nature and its dependence on the tensions between exclusivity and international influences especially in its quotidian banality (Billig, 1995). Although it would be foolish to assert that any history can be rooted in one geo-political space, likewise it would be difficult to begin our exploration without respect for the national specifics of media development, even as we place them within wider international, cross-cultural and imperialist settings. This is particularly the case with Britain intrinsically constructed as an 'old country' (Wright, 1985). This volume is therefore very much a national account while acknowledging that national developments have always emerged as a part of broader cross-national, international, imperial and even neo-imperialist forces.

In preparing this book, we were confident that there was significant potential for a companion on British media history in Routledge's series of collected essays on media themes. This confidence was based on the number of examples of critical reflection on the history of the media that we had observed over recent years. Media Studies continues to develop as a subject area in the UK as well as abroad and media history is clearly emerging as one of its most fertile and important sub-fields. Scholars from a range of disciplinary areas are using historical approaches to study a wide range of media to ensure that contemporary students are equipped with the historical literacy to fully understand and appreciate their chosen area. Such scholarship has come through regular conferences in the UK focusing on the history of the media (e.g. at Aberystwyth University and the University of Sheffield), the editorial efforts of the journal *Media History* and, at the same time, historians' increasing preoccupation with language, discourse and identity, which has encouraged them to draw increasingly upon a broader range of media texts than ever before. The digitization of print and visual media archives is, moreover, significantly extending the opportunities for such historical research (Steel, 2014). We have sought to develop this trend by incorporating established and emergent scholarship on the changing historical and political contexts of media production, structures and reception. Likewise, scholarship on the ways in which culture and identity have been historically mediated adds to the rich texture of British media history that this volume seeks to capture. This study, we hope, provides scholars with opportunities to explore how different media have evolved – and sometimes been arrested – within social, regional and national contexts. It also offers a space for scholars to explore and critique the range of ways in which we use media to construct our historical understandings.

This volume was planned with the needs of the widest possible range of readers in mind. These readers may be media and communication students at undergraduate or postgraduate levels, or researchers, policy makers or activist researchers. Its chapters will, we hope, serve as required reading on media, journalism studies and communication courses and across an array of humanities, social science and particularly history modules. At the same time it should secure a strong secondary readership on degrees in critical theory, cultural studies, politics and sociology. Many current publications in the field are either too media specific, in that they concentrate only on journalism history, television history and the history of film, or they provide an aspect of historical reflection within a narrow assessment of the current state of one particular medium. Others arguably do not provide sufficient scope with which to appreciate the range of different methods and conceptual approaches to the study of media history within particular historical and social contexts. As such, one benefit to the reader is that the literature which pertains to each section and each era of media history is available here in one volume for cross-reference. This book provides a range not found in other texts currently on the market. Having made a case for its distinctiveness, however, it is only fair to mention some of the exemplary texts which have served as inspiration for this book. Three stand out. Bailey's *Narrating Media History* (2009) is a fine collection of various strands of thinking on the historiography of the media. Briggs and Burke's *A Social History of the Media: From Gutenberg to the Internet* (2009), now in its third edition, is the closest to ours in terms of its thematic ambition to address mass media more specifically over time. Last but by no means least, Curran and Seaton's book *Power Without Responsibility: Press, Broadcasting and the Internet in Britain* (2010) is a classic. Having done much to establish media history on its first appearance, it is now in its seventh edition and an excellent account of the emergence of mass media in Britain with a clear emphasis on news media. It has most notably contextualized contemporary developments within this historical frame.

This volume is different from even the best of its precursors to the extent that, as a carefully constructed edited collection, it provides aspects of historiographic context while adding more specific historical accounts of various aspects of a wide range of media formats. Despite a clear historical drive, its edited nature releases it from the need so often evident in other media histories to provide an overarching narrative at all costs. Drawing on experts in the field of media history, it provides readers with a thorough exposition of many of the inter-relating themes within the historiography of mass media in Britain as well as providing insights into challenges for individual areas. We aim therefore to present here some of the range and vitality of work emerging from studies of the media of the past and their social and political contexts. Its distinctiveness is that its remit is not restricted to chronologies of media history as usually conceived – although that will comprise a substantial part of its content – but seeks to set up more ambitious dialogues about using the media as sources for both understanding the past and clarifying ideas about the relationships between the public sphere – and society and culture more broadly – media format, technology and discourse.

Media is a plural noun and the history of British media is certainly a pluralistic activity. This observation drove our selection of contributors from a wide range of professional and academic backgrounds. They are characteristic of our interdisciplinary approach since many of them would not describe themselves as 'historians of the media' although they all contribute to the history being presented here. Contributors have been selected from among the leading researchers and commentators in their fields. Given the national emphasis of the book, they are predominantly drawn from British university and media environments. The editors have also done their best to blend well-known names with some emerging talents in the range of subject matter dealt with.

The book is organized into three sections. The first part of the book is comprised of a series of thematic chapters reflecting broadly on historiography, providing historical context for discussions of the power of the media and their social importance. This section therefore implicitly asserts a fundamental requirement to adequately contextualize media history since such contextualization ensures that the reader is not drawn towards an overly technocentric conceptualization of the subject. These chapters then offer insights into methods of media history as well as assessments of the broader cultural and intellectual environment in which the study of media history takes place. Chapters here also emphasize particular power dynamics which, in our view, the study of media history must acknowledge. As such, issues of conceptualization and representation are prominent. The second part of the book consists of five separate sections which focus on different media formats: newspapers, magazines, radio, film and television. These chapters assess a range of formats either within distinctive or important historical periods or through the prism of a much longer historical view. Though formats and technologies are prominent, we have sought contributions that again stress the wider social significance and importance of these formats as well as those that reflect upon the broader political and cultural context in which they are situated. The final section asserts powerfully the need to assess the contemporary media environment with due regard for those contours of the past which flow into present media technologies, exploring various approaches to historicizing media futures from the false dawns to the utopian. Here we seek to reassert the importance of historical reflection and analysis in our evaluations of contemporary technologies and their histories. We suggest then a greater sense of caution from those claiming technologies' purported 'impact' on society.

The sections all highlight the essential social, political and economic fluctuations which have informed media developments over time. The benefit of constructing an approach to media history which draws on such a wide range of contributions is that it avoids the sweeping overview approach and at the same time provides accounts which pay due respect to the unevenness of debate and technological development over time. Our approach also provides space to acknowledge important debates about media regulation, taste, morality and, of course, the range of roles that media have hitherto fulfilled in British life. Genre as well as mode of delivery demonstrate some of the potential range of media from print as news to the extension of communities of interest in magazines; from television as deliverer of information to an entertainer; from periodicals as shapers of political and literary taste to periodicals as consumer magnets; from film as document to film as entertainment; from media in general as communicative functions to media as symbolic consensus on levels as complex as class, 'race', national identification and gender. In addition to providing a range of contributions which stand up to scrutiny as individual accounts of specific moments in British media history, the book aims to provide something more ambitious in terms of the historiography and educational potential of this aspect of history. It is therefore intended to act in a variety of ways including as a compendium, a portal and a spur to further innovation in our range and depth of research. This book may not be the integrated media history that Dahl called for as long ago as 1994 but in assembling a collection of essays which explore different facets of media history in pluralistic fashion we are at least, in a modest way, inviting readers to consider media history in conversation across genres and between eras of influence.

We hope that you enjoy it and that it takes you further in your historical explorations of British media.

Martin Conboy and John Steel, Sheffield, February 2014

Bibliography

Bailey, M. (2009) *Narrating Media History*. Abingdon, Oxon: Routledge.
Billig, M. (1995) *Banal Nationalism*. London: Sage.
Briggs, A. and Burke, P. (2009) (eds.) *A Social History of the Media: From Gutenberg to the Internet*. 3rd edition. Cambridge: Polity.
Carey, J. W. (1989) "A Cultural Approach to Communication". In *Communication as Culture*. Boston, MA: Unwin Hyman (pp. 13–36).
Curran, J. and Seaton, J. (2010) *Power Without Responsibility: Press, Broadcasting and the Internet in Britain*. 7th edition. Abingdon, Oxon: Routledge.
Dahl, H.-F. (1994) "The Pursuit of Media History". *Media, Culture and Society*, 16(4), 551–63.
O'Malley, T. (ed.) (2012) "The Historiography of the Media in the United Kingdom". *Media History* Special Issue, 18(3–4).
Peters, J. D. (2008) "History as a Communication Problem". In B. Zelizer (ed.) *Explorations in Communication and History*. Abingdon, Oxon: Routledge (pp. 19–34).
Pöttker, H. (2012) "A Reservoir of Understanding: Why Journalism Needs History as a Thematic Field". In M. Conboy (ed.) *How Journalism Uses History*. Abingdon, Oxon: Routledge (pp. 15–32).
Steel, J. (ed.) (2014) "Digital Newspaper Archive Research". *Media History* Special Issue, 20(1), 1–3.
Steiner, G. (1975) *After Babel: Aspects of Language and Translation*. Oxford: Oxford University Press.
Wright, P. (1985) *On Living in an Old Country*. London: Verso.

Part I
MEDIA HISTORY DEBATES

1
The devaluation of history in media studies

Michael Pickering

In the early 1980s, I reviewed a book by Peter Golding and Sue Middleton (1982) entitled *Images of Welfare*, recommending it for its general historical range and praising its use of historical evidence in showing that the 'scroungerphobia' moral panic of the late 1970s was an extension of a long tradition of public hostility to the poor in English society.[1] By developing a historical perspective, Golding and Middleton clearly established the resilience of particular assumptions, myths and stereotypes about poverty and welfare. These, as they put it, have "lengthy pedigrees in popular consciousness" (1982: 48). I start with this example not only because of its relevance to the issue of welfare in contemporary British politics, particularly around the cynically labelled 'something for nothing' culture, but also because it is a historical perspective of this kind that is lacking in much of the media studies work of the past 30 years.[2] The devaluation of history in the field is an entrenched problem that has been identified and remarked upon at various times, and the periodic complaints that have been made of it clearly demonstrate that it is a recurrent characteristic, if not endemic, then certainly persistent within the field. James Curran, for example, has called history the "neglected grandparent of media studies"; John Corner has referred to the "frantically contemporary agenda" of media studies; and Nick Garnham has described the bulk of media studies as "enraptured by the new and the ephemeral", exhibiting "an almost willed amnesia that amounts to what one might call a nostalgia for the future" (Curran, 1991: 27; Corner, 1999: 126; Garnham, 2000: 24). Despite such criticism, little has changed across or since the various times it has been made.

The purpose of this chapter is to discuss this problem and call for an end to, or at least a diminution of, history's devaluation in media studies. This has not been consistently evident and indeed those just cited have themselves engaged in important historical work, but such work figures minimally in the field's roll of achievements. The lack of historical reference and scope in media studies has a number of causes, but certainly the postmodernist attack on history's credentials as a form of knowledge and the relentless adoption in media studies of resolutely synchronic methodologies, along with a continual skewing of attention towards the latest issues and developments in communications, have encouraged an assumption of the past as settled and over, and so of little relevance to what is happening today.[3] This assumption provides the rationale for present-centredness, an adjacent problem stemming from researching and studying communications and media culture in the short term, in a narrow temporal ambit of recency or even immediacy.

Present-centredness is manifest in an obsession with the waves just breaking at our feet, regardless of how long those waves have travelled in their movement towards the present. Its watchwords are newness and nowness. When these watchwords command analytical practice in the field, amnesia is induced by a process which seizes on what is, or what seems, emergent; hustles it into greater prominence than it would deserve in the longer term; and pronounces upon its epochal significance, sometimes endorsing this with a claim for an irrevocable break with the past. The historical irony is that if this claim is true, it can only be made once, at least within specific historical periods, yet perversely, trend-spotting in media and cultural studies is by definition recurrent and so continually runs the risk of becoming a reflex academic imitation of that which it identifies as replete with the alluring qualities of newness and nowness.

There is always a grandiloquent appeal in such claims, despite the fact that they are usually empirically unsubstantiated and the grounds on which they are being made are hazy and unclear. This is hardly surprising. Over 30 years ago, Raymond Williams (1977: 123) referred to the difficulty in distinguishing between what is truly emergent and what is merely novel. In a frequent iteration, that which seems truly emergent turns out, in time, to be merely novel. This happens because what is already established sets limits and conditions for how the emergent is able to develop, or because of the subsequent incorporation of emergent alternatives into what is already established, but the source of the confusion between what is emergent and what is novel lies most of all in the lack of investigation into their development in the longer term, and their place in a more abiding pattern. The broad historical framework needed for discerning either development or location within the pattern is absent, and that absence is central to the syndrome of newness and nowness. The syndrome justifies itself by reference forwards, with a strident emphasis on gauging the future, the way things are currently turning for good or ill. An example of this occurs at the start of what has been hailed as a contemporary classic, with Ulrich Beck announcing that what "is to follow does not at all proceed along the lines of empirical social research. Rather, it pursues a different ambition: to move the future which is just beginning to take shape into view against the still predominant past" (1992: 9). This approach can easily descend into sociological soothsaying and it is closely related to the prevalent tendency in media studies of trying to move the future into view on the basis only of recent trends and developments. The still predominant past is a token acknowledgement; it is attended to only in a vague, gestural manner. That is why there is such readiness to claim that nowness and newness represent some unheralded rupture with what has gone before. It is this which creates a condition of being haunted by the future, a condition which doesn't require empirical social research because it dances to a different ambition.

Radical claims for newness depend upon an abrupt dichotomizing between 'then' and 'now', with what is claimed as new being held in stark contrast to what is claimed to be old. The sense conveyed in this common rhetorical strategy is that 'new' media have broken with the past and we are entered into a new age – Mark Poster (1995) presumptuously called it the Second Media Age – in which the internet and interactive media totally alter the ground rules of social communication. This is what being dazzled by newness and nowness entails: not only an exaggeration of any shift or change that is occurring, but also a distortion of historical development, as if all that has happened in the past has been leading up to this New Age, this whiggish culmination of all previous movement. When new media are seen only in terms of their alleged newness, the lack of any cross-temporal perspective leads to a fixation on media themselves. We then stand just one step away from technological determinism, paying little if any attention to the broader historical contexts in which media develop because of an underlying assumption that it is the technology which drives such development. Communications technologies are seen not as an integral feature of change but its impelling force. The consequence of such a view is always an abbreviation of historical process as well as an abnegation of human responsibility for social transformations.[4]

The establishment of a communications medium around the manufacture of its associated hardware and software, along with the ensuing patterns of consumption and usage, does not mark the historical beginning of that medium. It marks its historical consolidation. But even seeing it as a historical consolidation is to point our understanding too much in the direction of the technology. Communications technologies do not create their institutional forms or their social uses. They have to be understood instead in the ways they operate as historically specific resources for, say, cultural processes of encounter, exchange and representation, or political structures of surveillance, power and control. They may indeed be diverted away in their social uses from their intended application, as was famously the case with the phonograph, which, among other things, Edison considered would be adopted as early forms of the dictaphone, audiobook and speaking clock. "Even though it would remain largely in the grip of corporate interests", phonography "was a medium deeply defined by its users and the changing conditions of use" (Gitelman, 2008: 83–84). Communications technologies have also to be understood for the ways they are adapted to existing social practices and cultural conventions, and for how continuities as well as changes are negotiated through them, so that while there is short-term displacement and replacement, there is also on the one hand antecedent occurrence and prefiguring, as for example in the widely recognized lines of continuity between telegraphy and the internet or the barely acknowledged anticipation of the basic elements of digitization in the paper rolls of player-pianos, and on the other hand long-term extension and renewal, as for example with radio moving from its initial communicative form as wireless broadcasting to "forms such as AM and FM technologies, maritime navigation, Radar, the microwave oven, low-power broadcasting and mobile telephony" (Standage, 1998: 193–98; Suisman, 2010: 24; Peters, 2009: 23).[5]

Assuming acceptance of these various points, and bearing in mind that it is always individuals, groups and institutions who create and use any communications technology, we can agree that "what is new about new media comes from the particular ways in which they refashion older media and the ways in which older media refashion themselves to answer the challenges of new media" (Bolter and Grusin, 1999: 15, 78). This two-way influence may of course be superseded as the distinctiveness of new media becomes more fully realized over the course of time, while older media may over time come to seem quite obsolete or definitely relegated to the past, as with wax cylinders or silent film, but this can never be guaranteed, for what seems to have been so relegated may in time be conceived anew, moving into some different configuration of application or intent.[6] The mutualism of 'old' and 'new' then becomes temporally more extensive, as dimensions of evolving tradition and more sharply identifiable change:

> Old media rarely die; their original functions are adapted and absorbed by newer media, and they themselves may mutate into newer cultural niches and new purposes. The process of media transition is always a mix of tradition and innovation, always declaring for evolution, not revolution.
> (Thorburn and Jenkins, 2003: 12)

So it is always a question of how the established and emergent interact at any particular time, whether this involves the responses of painterly art to photography, the modelling of steam-driven railway coaches on horse-driven stage coaches, or the adaptation of theatrical traditions in early cinema. This is one important perspective which a historical approach can bring to media studies, but of course at times it can and should be turned around, for just as important as seeing the old in the new is finding the new in the old. It is the task of historical cultural analysis to do both, for it is only when we move in both ways that we shall be able to fully grasp the dynamics of cross-temporal relations.

Developing a concerted historical perspective means that we change our approach to any contemporary media phenomena by asking not only about their constitutive features and conditions but also how they came to be this way over the course of time. Answering this question may include attending to their political, economic, technological, cultural and aesthetic dimensions, but primarily it means looking at 'old' and 'new' media, and more broadly at past unfoldings and present issues, through the prism of each other, as for example in thinking about the past when it was present, the old when it was new, so that they can be made to cross-refer and cast light on each other across a series of temporal folds and loops, rather than in terms of linear chronological progression. The work of Carolyn Marvin (1988) and Lisa Gitelman (2008) is exemplary in this respect, encouraging us to move beyond simplistic narratives of media development from primitive progenitors to their culmination in classic forms. Another interesting example of this is Siegfried Zielinski's (1999) conception of cinema and television – the predominant industries for audio-visual media in the twentieth century – as *entr'actes*, rather than finished stages, in a longer *durée* of mediated ways of looking. This allows us to see anew such pre-twentieth-century optical devices and instruments as the panorama, diorama, zoëtrope, magic lantern and stereoscope, rather than having them relegated to shadowy positions within a vaguely outlined period prior to the advent of cinematography. Historically, they are far too differentiated and significant for that, and in any case the apparatus of optical communications which accumulated across the nineteenth century testifies to the gradual shift to a more visually oriented everyday culture. Both cinema and television need to be understood as part of this larger pattern, and in themselves as historically delimited, finite and in their times only relatively new as cultural forms. This is especially so now that the heyday of television is over, superseded by new media just as television superseded, but did not supplant, the preceding visual medium of cinematography. This in turn suggests that the story of convergence stretches back a good deal further than is commonly presumed.[7]

Contrary to the entire spirit of this, the tendency that follows from a blinkered focus on the unadulterated newness of new media technologies is to see change as inherent in them rather than being contingent upon a wider social, cultural, economic and political context, or being embedded within a matrix of longer-term historical forces. The claim, implicit or otherwise, is that 'new' media can only be understood in terms of their newness. All previous development leads to this point, but this point is utterly new. Such a conception is not only historically illiterate; it is also conceptually naïve. If anything was ever utterly new, recognition of it would be impossible. New and old are temporally relative notions. They require and necessitate each other, and if as temporally relative terms they are to acquire any analytical traction, what is meant by new and old needs to be empirically identified and investigated, in particular contexts and in particular periods of time. Change is only meaningful in terms of prefigurations, antecedents and continuities. When it is viewed primarily in terms of ruptures and radical breaks, such temporal phenomena as persistence, durable influence, inheritance in cultural traditions and episodic recurrence in social processes cannot be explained, or explained adequately. The tendency to see change only or mainly in terms of dramatic rifts and ruptures makes it difficult to get a critical purchase on the different rates and rhythms of temporal movement. Change, even when radical, only makes sense in relation to lines of relative continuity; it only becomes properly intelligible and able to be evaluated alongside what doesn't change, or change at the same pace or in the same direction. Radical presentism can only explain and understand what is new on an analogy with the jack-in-the-box: it springs up out of a historical nowhere. So being preoccupied by newness and nowness means being driven by current products and fashions and not being able to see beyond the event horizons that they represent. It makes for a historical myopia which forestalls any conception of how such developments are invariably part of longer processes of historical movement or of how change is often curtailed or compromised by durable institutional structures. Being preoccupied by newness and nowness is to share in fashion's "refusal to inherit", to borrow a phrase from Barthes (2006: 116).

There are of course certain widely shared assumptions and values supporting the sense of historical change within modernity as exceeding and even cancelling out all other temporal processes. The cultural historian Michael Steinberg cites a prevalent example of this in referring to "the very American conceit wherein the sense of having arrived riding a wave of historical transformation justifies the sense of having been liberated from history altogether" (1996: 110). It might be expected that those engaged in the critical analysis of media and modern culture would dissent from this image of the past endlessly disappearing in the wake of a continuously rising wave of innovation in which the ever-new rapidly becomes the ever-extinct, but many seem seduced and so run the risk of reproducing it in their own conceptions of historical process. To give just one instance of this awe in the face of relentless movement and supersession, Lawrence Grossberg describes the post-Second World War period in the United States as "characterised by a steadily rising rate of change", and then in the light of this goes on to claim that "what is unique" in what this rise inaugurates "is that change increasingly appears to be all that there is ... Both the future and the past appear increasingly irrelevant; history has collapsed into the present" (1997: 33–34). Rhetorically, this may seem appealing, providing the sense of an old social order swiftly fading, particularly in the view of contemporary youth, but as a statement about the consequences of an accelerating rate of social change, it is plain nonsense. It means that we can no longer have any sense of history, or of its various legacies as potential resources for the future, because they have now disappeared into the present; it means that we can have no perspective from which to understand nostalgia, in its specifically modern temporal forms; and it means that we are unable to relate at all to the slowness, as opposed to the speed, with which some things change.[8] Even in modernity, some things change slowly, or are only slowly negotiated, resolved, or come to terms with. Even in modernity, or rather, especially in modernity, time has different rhythms, tempos and paces. Historical processes operate according to different timescales, sometimes seeming to accelerate because of sharp transitions and shifts, sometimes appearing to move sluggishly, but we neither inexorably leave the past nor do we ever experience anything but change even when caught headlong in the very flurry of it. It is not only that uncritical acceptance of the notion of change accelerating to a state of timelessness supports the loss of a historical perspective in media and cultural analysis, but also that, when looked at in the longer term, we can see the period following the Second World War in quite a different way, as "one of unusual stability" very much in contrast to the first half of the century, "in which there were wars and revolutions of global dimensions and the establishment of novel socio-political configurations, notably socialism and fascism" (Wagner, 2001: 160). It was a period characterized by a surfeit of upheaval and eventfulness, very much in contrast to the immediate post-war period.

The example shows, once again, that failure to develop or deploy a sufficiently extended historical scale of analysis leads to present-centredness and by this process to the devaluation of history – the irrelevant state from which we have been liberated. As David Edgerton (2006) has pointed out in his book *The Shock of the Old*, present-centredness occurs when attention is fixed on invention and innovation, on singular defining moments that seem to inaugurate a new age (as with Poster's [1995] Second Media Age). Invention and innovation become inflated as values and determinist as forces. Edgerton argues that if we think instead of technology-in-use, we gain a quite different view of historical processes to one based on innovation-based timelines. We see old and new technologies and cultural forms co-existing within time, with adaptations and synergies occurring between long-established media and recently developed media. Innovation-centricism of the kind Edgerton critiques is characteristic of a good deal of the fatuously named 'new media studies'. The title is fatuous because of all the unanswered historical questions which it begs. For example, the internet and mobile communication technologies have now been around for 25 years or so, so when do they stop being new? Would it have made any sense to refer to radio in the Second World War as a new medium? It had by then been around on a widespread scale for roughly the equivalent span of time. A similar point applies to 'new media studies'. Do they make research into anything in existence before the 1990s fall into what would have to be called 'old media studies'? That of course would be an equally fatuous title, not least because it would simply mirror the other, and fall into the same trap of temporal dichotomizing.

Prefacing media studies with 'new' carries the same danger as prefacing reference to some period or condition with 'post'. In a recent article, Andrew Thacker (2011) claims that for many researchers working in university humanities departments, the cry is now: "Postmodernism is dead, long live Modernism!" Hey presto, we might say – the mists of historical myopia have suddenly blown away and we can now see much further back, so recognizing that we are living in an extended modernity and with an extended modernism. Thacker refers to postmodernism as a "craze of the 1980s" and says that "our sense of what constitutes late modernism now seems to get later and later" (2011: 41–42). What is the lesson in this? It is clear enough, in terminology if nothing else: as with the term 'new', use of the term 'post' as a prefix to something apparently superseded necessarily has a short historical shelf life. 'Posting' older historical processes, institutions, formations and systems exaggerates and reifies the changes involved and the degree to which those changes contribute to a disappearing past. It creates a relentless forward drive and a wilful amnesia as to what has been accomplished in the past and what has been inherited in the present. It leads to one-dimensional work which highlights the apparent contemporary distinctiveness of a form of cultural representation or technologically mediated communication and fails to recognize how it coexists with various features from different, overlapping pasts. Of course we need to study what is recent and contemporary, and try to assess what is new, but we also need to check the rush to pronounce on the 'posts' by attending to the 'pre-s' – all that precedes and yet also anticipates, all that has cumulatively developed and led into the present. Among the many values of attending to the 'pre-s' are that it clarifies awareness of how the present is a complex mix of what is continuing and what is changing, what is ephemeral and what is enduring; it sharpens awareness of how processes of change have been generated and have a certain logic of unfolding; and it not only enriches awareness of our sense of possibilities, but also makes our sense of possibilities possible.

An obvious objection to the charge that historical approaches are devalued in media studies is to say that media history exists as a sub-field, and it is easy to find historical accounts of various media, such as the press and broadcasting. There are even journals and occasional conferences devoted to media history. All that is true, but it doesn't affect the charge simply because of its 'sub-ness' within media studies. History is the 'neglected grandparent of media studies' because it is left isolated in its own residential home, attended to only by specialists, and visited by few from outside. Shunted off to the margins of the field, it hardly informs what goes on at the centre, as, for example, is shown by various media studies textbooks that pay little, if any, attention to the historical development of the media and its continuing legacies. Media studies has developed its own rationale much more around its ability to deliver knowledge of current developments in both cultural production and consumption, and provide explanations of the 'new' in those developments. This is equally true of cultural studies, the field with which it is often paired, and it is because of this that the *Dictionary of Cultural and Critical Theory* can define it as being based upon "the critical analysis of cultural forms and processes in contemporary and near-contemporary societies" (Payne and Barbera, 2010: 163). This simply fudges the issue (how 'near' is 'near' and how far do you have to go before you become 'distant'?) because you cannot understand what is contemporary without understanding what created it as contemporary and how it is differentiated from what came before. Critical analysis in media and cultural studies requires comparative criteria, and since no one is able to travel to the future and report back to us, secure in the knowledge of what will happen, where else can we go for such criteria than to the past? This is not a rhetorical question. We may only ever be able to retain or regain an approximate knowledge of the past, but it is all we have. That is why history provides the vital measure of difference against which any sense of contemporary distinctiveness can be assessed.

Even where the historical development of the media is attended to, this in itself is at times too narrow, for we need to see such development far more broadly within the context of social, cultural, economic and political history, with the view that this brings informing our approach. The problem is therefore not just one of the marginalization and neglect of media history itself, for media studies so often proceeds without an integral historical perspective informing its key questions and preoccupations, and without an active historicizing impulse generating major research questions and methods of enquiry. That is precisely why, against the strident emphasis on newness and nowness, we need to be more sceptical of claims about the revolutionary impact of communication technologies and more receptive to slower processes of cultural change and adaptation, longer-term institutional formations and resilient structural continuities. Only in that way will we avoid the oscillation between utopian pronouncements and dystopian pessimism that has characterized responses to new media over the past 20 years or so, which radical temporal dichotomizing both fosters and reinforces. As Philippe Ariès once pointed out, it is difficult to distinguish the leading characteristics of the present "except by means of the differences which separate them from the related but never identical aspects of the past" (1973: 7). When absolute conceptions of newness and nowness prevail, we have no scope for seeing how newness is often a matter of reconceiving aspects of the past in new situations or realigning them in new relations. That is why the devaluation of history must be reversed. What I have been arguing is that, if we are to avoid being transfixed by the steady glare of an insistent present and the siren call of an insistent future, we need to rethink how we may use the resources of the past. We have had the linguistic turn and the cultural turn, so perhaps now it is time for the historical turn. If that happens, then the example with which I started, *Images of Welfare*, will finally be given its due and acknowledged as an unjustly neglected classic in its field.

Further reading

Briggs and Burke in their *A Social History of the Media* (2010) provide one of the best introductions to media history, covering every significant wave of development from the print revolution to the internet. Two recent edited collections on communications history to be recommended are *Explorations in Communication and History* (2008) and *Narrating Media History* (2009), while *Rethinking Media Change* (2003) offers an excellent set of discussions on media change and cultural transformation. Pickering (2008) argues for the benefits of historical understanding for media and cultural studies.

Notes

1. The review appeared in the *Journal of Communication*, 33:1, Winter 1983.
2. For example, a report published in late 2012 by the University of Kent's social policy team revealed that a quarter of claimants had "delayed or avoided asking for" welfare payments because of "misleading news coverage" and "the perceived stigma generated by false media depictions of 'scroungers'" (Ramesh, 2012: 17).
3. In his synthetic account of modern historiography, Michael Bentley refers to postmodernism as having shaken the discipline of history to its foundations (1999: ix). For a couple of critical responses to this challenge, including its relation to poststructuralism, see Appleby, Hunt and Jacob (1994) and Pickering (1997).
4. One of the best critiques of technological determinism and the media remains that of Raymond Williams (1974, chapter one).
5. In arguing that more than a century before the advent of MP3s, "the technology of the player-piano was essentially indistinguishable from the modern digital computer", Suisman criticizes the casting of the player-piano merely as "a foil to the more dramatic advent of the phonograph" and argues that the tendency to see the triumph of the latter over the fading of the former is a historically myopic view of the complex set of changes associated with the development of sound recording (2010: 13 and 24).
6. With silent film, for example, this point is illustrated by the huge success of Michael Hazanavicius's 2011 romantic comedy *The Artist*.
7. Two other examples of historical studies which place visual media in a more general stream of innovation and transformation are provided by Laurent Mannoni's archaeology of the cinema, *The Great Art of Light and Shadow* (2000), and Lynda Nead's *The Haunted Gallery* (2007).
8. For discussion of both critical and regressive forms of temporal nostalgia in modernity, see Keightley and Pickering (2012, chapters 4 and 5).

References

Appleby, J., Hunt, L. and Jacob, M. (1994) *Telling the Truth About History*. New York and London: W.W. Norton.
Ariès, P. (1973) *Centuries of Childhood*. Harmondsworth: Penguin.
Bailey, M. (ed.) (2009) *Narrating Media History*. London and New York: Routledge.
Barthes, R. (2006) *The Language of Fashion*. Oxford: Berg.
Beck, U. (1992) *Risk Society*. London: Sage.
Bentley, M. (1999) *Modern Historiography: An Introduction*. London and New York: Routledge.
Bolter, J. D. and Grusin, R. (1999) *Remediation*. Cambridge, MA and London: The MIT Press.
Briggs, A. and Burke, P. (2010) *A Social History of the Media*. Cambridge: Polity.
Corner, J. (1999) *Critical Ideas in Television Studies*. Oxford: Clarendon Press.
Curran, J. (1991) "Rethinking the Media as a Public Sphere". In P. Dahlgren and C. Sparks (eds.) *Communication and Citizenship: Journalism and the Public Sphere in the New Media Age*. London: Routledge (pp. 27–57).

Edgerton, D. (2006) *The Shock of the Old: Technology and Global History since 1900*. London: Profile Books.
Garnham, N. (2000) *Emancipation, the Media, and Modernity*. Oxford and New York: Oxford University Press.
Gitelman, L. (2008) *Always Already New: Media, History, and the Data of Culture*. Cambridge, MA and London: The MIT Press.
Golding, P. and Middleton, S. (1982) *Images of Welfare: Press and Public Attitudes to Poverty*. Oxford: Martin Robertson.
Grossberg, L. (1997) *Dancing in Spite of Myself*. Durham and London: Duke University Press.
Keightley, E. and Pickering, M. (2012) *The Mnemonic Imagination: Remembering as Creative Practice*. Basingstoke and New York: Palgrave Macmillan.
Mannoni, L. (2000) *The Great Art of Light and Shadow*. Exeter: University of Exeter Press.
Marvin, C. (1988) *When Old Technologies Were New*. Oxford and New York: Oxford University Press.
Nead, L. (2007) *The Haunted Gallery: Painting, Photography, Film c. 1900*. New Haven, CT and London: Yale University Press.
Payne, M. and Barbera, J. R. (eds.) (2010) *A Dictionary of Cultural and Critical Theory*. Malden, MA and Oxford, UK: Wiley-Blackwell.
Peters, B. (2009) "And lead us not into thinking the new is new: A bibliographic case for new media history". *New Media and Society*, 11(1&2), 13–30.
Pickering, M. (1997) *History, Experience and Cultural Studies*. Basingstoke and London: Macmillan/ New York: St Martin's Press.
——(2008) "Engaging with History". In M. Pickering (ed.) *Research Methods for Cultural Studies*. Edinburgh: Edinburgh University Press (pp. 198–213).
Poster, M. (1995) *The Second Media Age*. Cambridge: Polity.
Ramesh, R. (2012) "'Scrounger' Rhetoric Putting Off Claimants". *The Guardian*, 21 November, p. 17.
Standage, T. (1998) *The Victorian Internet*. London: Weidenfeld & Nicolson.
Steinberg, M. (1996) "Cultural History and Cultural Studies". In C. Nelson and D. P. Gaonkar (eds.) *Disciplinarity and Dissent in Cultural Studies*. New York and London: Routledge (pp. 103–29).
Suisman, D. (2010) "Sound, Knowledge, and the 'Immanence of Human Failure'". *Social Text*, 28(1), 13–33.
Thacker, A. (2011) "Making It New All Over Again". *Times Higher Education*, 11 August, pp. 41–42.
Thorburn, D. and Jenkins, H. (eds.) (2003) *Rethinking Media Change*. Cambridge, MA and London: The MIT Press.
Wagner, P. (2001) *Theorising Modernity*. London: Sage.
Williams, R. (1974) *Television, Technology and Cultural Form*. London: Fontana/Collins.
——(1977) *Marxism and Literature*. Oxford and New York: Oxford University Press.
Zelizer, B. (ed.) (2008) *Explorations in Communication and History*. London and New York: Routledge.
Zielinski, S. (1999) *Audiovisions*. Amsterdam: Amsterdam University Press.

2
Media products as historical artefacts

Adrian Bingham

The media industry, more than almost any other, is based on ephemerality. We browse newspapers and magazines and then discard them with little thought; we tune in and out of television and radio channels with a casual press of a button. In the world of the internet and 24-hour news and entertainment, this ephemerality has intensified, as journalists insistently pursue the next scoop on the assumption that there is little interest in 'yesterday's news.' There is a frenetic pace to the modern media environment. Beneath this surface preoccupation with the present and the immediate future, however, there is an awareness, at least in some sections of the media, of broader and deeper perspectives. It is most evident in the traditional cliché that journalism provides the 'first draft of history', or the bold self-definition of certain titles that they are 'newspapers of record', with the implicit assumption that citizens and scholars of the future will find it essential to consult their archives. With new technologies and digital storage capabilities, moreover, broadcasts no longer disappear into the ether, newspaper articles have a life beyond the library shelves, and films and television serials are endlessly recycled on a multitude of satellite and digital channels. The products of the media are at once disposable and durable; instant commodities and historical artefacts.

This chapter explores the work of scholars who have regarded media content as valuable evidence that can reveal much about the development of British society. It addresses in turn the three main approaches to the historical study of media sources. The first section examines the uses of the media as a record of events or as a repository of information; the second discusses the ways in which the media have been studied in terms of helping to construct the 'public sphere' and shaping British political life; and the third considers how media sources have been used to analyze the formation and evolution of social and cultural identities such as class, gender and ethnicity. The first two of these approaches inevitably focus on the products of the news media; the final approach has drawn on a wider range of media content, including films and broadcast entertainment. The chapter will conclude with a brief overview of the impact of digitization on historical scholarship into the media.

The disposability of media products for a long time inhibited their use as evidence by historians. Newspapers might occasionally be used as a source of colour and incidental detail, but they were rarely the subject of sustained analysis, except in the histories of the press that began to appear in the second half of the nineteenth century (Vella 2009). Newspapers were not deemed to be sufficiently reliable and authoritative; they were hastily produced, partisan, and inevitably made compromises to appeal to the market. Before the availability of convenient means of recording and storing films, radio or television programmes, moreover, it was difficult to place these media under close scrutiny. For many scholars, in any case, cinema, radio and television were trivial products of an entertainment-obsessed mass society, making little noteworthy contribution to the deeper structures of politics, culture and society. Serious and conceptually sophisticated writing about film, in particular, did emerge, but it was not as prominent in Britain as elsewhere in Europe and, during its infancy as a media form, there was little focus on patterns of change over time.

The emergence of cultural studies from the late 1950s, and the rise of social history in the following decade, brought the potential value of media products for understanding social change more sharply into focus. Richard Hoggart's seminal *The Uses of Literacy* (1957) used mass-market newspapers, magazines, advertisements and songs as evidence to support the author's argument that the modern media, operating under conditions of growing affluence and consumerism, were undermining traditional class cultures. E. P. Thompson's similarly influential *The Making of the English Working Class* (1963), which stimulated a significant growth in 'history from below', drew in places on radical weekly and monthly publications to demonstrate the rise in class consciousness in the early nineteenth century. The study of contemporary media forms blossomed far more quickly, however, than their use as historical artefacts. Even while cultural studies flourished within such institutions as the Birmingham Centre for Contemporary Cultural Studies (founded by Hoggart in 1964), most historians retained their scepticism about the value of the media as sources. Practical considerations were important too: with rare exceptions, newspapers were not indexed, and locating specific issues and themes could be very time-consuming. By the early 1980s, a number of valuable histories of different media forms and institutions had emerged (Boyce, Curran and Wingate, 1978; Curran and Seaton, 1981; Briggs, 1961/1965/1970/1979; Curran and Porter, 1983) but these had a relatively limited impact on the broader historiographies of political and social change in Britain.

Only really in the wake of the 'cultural turn' of the 1980s and 1990s, and with the heightened scholarly interest in language, meaning and identity, have historians reassessed the value of media products as historical artefacts and started to engage with them in a more sophisticated and critical way to explore and illuminate important historiographical questions. As media and journalism studies expanded and matured as disciplines, moreover, there was inevitably pressure to understand the evolution of media over time. This has been a slow and uneven process. Writing in 2002, James Curran, who has done so much to develop the study of media history, could still describe the subject as the "neglected grandparent of media studies" (Curran, 2002: 3). Over a decade later, though, the situation looks very different, and the field has blossomed; with the rapid digitization of media sources, moreover, many of the practical difficulties of media history have been removed, and the future looks bright.

Recording society

> The newspapers are making morning after morning the rough draft of history. Later, the historian will come, take down the old files, and transform the crude but sincere and accurate annals of editors and reporters into history, into literature.
> (*The State*, 5 December 1905, cited in Pettinato, 2010)

The notion that newspapers provided a 'rough draft of history' was a popular one among many British and American journalists by the early twentieth century. It lent legitimacy and prestige to the profession, suggesting that the press was performing a serious role for posterity as well as informing its immediate audience; adherence to it was also a way for 'respectable' titles to distance themselves from the 'sensationalism' of the cheaper publications. (A *Daily Express* sub-editor told the Royal Commission on the Press in 1949, by contrast, that "we as newspapers are not concerned with what will appear important to posterity … to the man in the street the daffodils in Regent's Park are often more important … than a massacre in Chungking" [Royal Commission on the Press 1947–49, 1949: 104].) The belief that the media could represent and report society with a certain degree of accuracy and 'impartiality' underpinned the development of the BBC's 'public service broadcasting' ideal after 1922. Many outside the media world, including most scholars, have been sceptical about this self-appointed role to chronicle society. These critics have questioned the reliability and comprehensiveness of much reporting, pointing to the speed at which most journalism is produced, the difficulty of verifying facts in the required timeframe, and the journalist's lack of specialized knowledge about many of the subjects he or she is covering. There were, and are, also numerous internal and external actors – editors and proprietors, governments, state officials, politicians, advertisers – who had the power to intervene to influence, distort or suppress news stories. In times of war or national crisis, in particular, when governments insist on a combination of secrecy and morale-boosting propaganda, press and broadcast reporting often bears little resemblance to reality (Carruthers, 2011). More substantially, decades of scholarship on the media have highlighted the ways in which news is always a construction or framing of reality: the selection, presentation and content of news about the world are heavily influenced by institutional norms, social discourses and relations of power. 'Objectivity' and 'impartiality', despite the claims of journalists, is not achievable.

These critiques of journalism are so familiar that it is easy to overlook the ways in which the media can still be useful sources of historical information. Historians, after all, almost inevitably face an imperfect evidence base and rarely have reliable and comprehensive sources for all the questions they are seeking to answer. The media may be more trustworthy and detailed than the alternatives, especially the further one moves back in time. Newspapers in particular are so valuable because they offer evidence on a scale, and of a diversity, that other sources simply cannot match. Newspapers have evolved to be miscellanies, containing reports on such diverse topics as politics, business, international affairs, crime, fashion, sport, literature and the weather. As daily or weekly publications, they provide more detailed coverage of their societies than almost any other source. From the eighteenth century, moreover, the market sustained a range of titles with varying local, regional and national coverage, different political slants, and different readerships. Even if we need to be cautious about their accuracy and, where possible, cross-reference their claims with other evidence, newspapers still provide a treasure trove of information about all aspects of public and private life. They report speeches, meetings and court proceedings, describe unusual and surprising events, record fluctuations in prices and exchange rates, announce births, marriages and deaths, and act as a marketplace for goods and services. When the literary historian Ronald Schuchard was researching T. S Eliot, for example, he came across, in the pages of the *Salisbury and Winchester Journal*, a full report of a previously unknown lecture the author gave to a local audience about the influence of the work of the poet George Herbert on his own *Four Quartets*. "That wondrous newspaper page," Schuchard observes, "changes our view of Eliot's intellectual and poetic development in the 1930s and greatly enhances our comprehension of his great poem" (Schuchard, 2001). Newspaper archives contain many such nuggets which can provide anything from a colorful but incidental detail to vital new perspectives on the topic in hand.

For historians of the twentieth and twenty-first centuries, radio and television broadcasts, films, newsreels and internet sites can be similarly rich sources of evidence. These newer media forms are, of course, just as 'constructed' and partial as newspapers, and have to be treated with the same care. Nevertheless, they can provide a store of sounds and moving images that are difficult to retrieve from other sources. It is through our media archives that we can hear, for example, Winston Churchill or J. B. Priestley's wartime speeches and understand for ourselves their rhetorical power; that we can capture echoes of the voices, glimpses of the clothing and the self-presentations of ordinary people recorded or interviewed on camera; that we can see long-demolished buildings and dramatically changed landscapes, and obtain unparalleled insights into the material culture of the past. Historical training has traditionally tended to focus on the evaluation of written texts but, for historians of modern societies in particular, it is becoming increasingly difficult to ignore the wealth of aural and visual material that is now available through media sources.

Media, politics and the public sphere

Viewing media products as (imperfect) records of society or as repositories of information, to be raided for facts, examples and images to add detail or context to broader scholarship, is only one, rather limited, perspective on their use to the historian. Most scholars of the media are more interested in the ways in which the media are implicated in patterns of political, social and cultural change: how they shape the world around them, how they influence their audiences, how they encourage institutions and social actors to react and respond to their content. The most established, and perhaps most keenly debated, area for investigation is the relationship between the media and political life. The earliest histories of the press, such as Frederick Knightley Hunt's *The Fourth Estate: Contributions Towards a History of Newspapers and of the Liberty of the Press* (1850), were preoccupied with the political role of newspapers, and particularly their function in scrutinising the activities of the state, thereby helping to guarantee the precious liberties of 'the people' (Raymond, 1999). More recent scholarship is usually heavily influenced by the conceptual apparatus provided by Jürgen Habermas, the German social philosopher, and Benedict Anderson, a political scientist and historian. Habermas argued that in the eighteenth century newspapers played an important role in the construction of a 'public sphere', an arena for rational political debate in which an increasingly broad section of the public could participate. The press both helped to inform political debate and represented public opinion to those in power; over time, though, Habermas argued, the 'public sphere' was corrupted by the commercialization of the media and the encroaching power of the state (Habermas, 1989). Anderson, meanwhile, highlighted the role of newspapers in shaping and consolidating the nation as "an imagined political community." Daily newspaper reading, Anderson suggested, was a "mass ceremony" which enabled individuals to learn about, and imagine, the broader nation of which they formed a part (Anderson, 1991: 35). The newspaper, in short, enabled the political communication and debate that was central to the emergence of the modern, liberal nation state. In the twentieth century, moreover, radio and television broadcasting increasingly took up the role previously performed by the newspaper, with regular news bulletins providing the basis for 'mass ceremonies' of a different form.

There is now an extensive scholarship on the interconnections between the media and political activity in Britain. Historians have, for example, examined how newssheets and newsbooks represented the bitter conflicts of the Civil War in the mid-seventeenth century (Raymond, 1996); demonstrated how radical publications stimulated the political reform movements of the late eighteenth and early nineteenth centuries (Thompson, 1963; Stedman-Jones, 1983: ch. 3); and studied how 'respectable' papers in London and the provinces played a key role in consolidating party identities in the evolving political system (Koss, 1981/4; Barker, 1998). Scholars of the twentieth century have investigated the political interventions of newspaper proprietors, from the 'press barons' such as Northcliffe, Rothermere and Beaverbrook to modern moguls such as Rupert Murdoch (Boyce, 1987; Seymour-Ure, 2003); scrutinized the pressures and influences shaping the output of supposedly 'impartial' news providers such as the BBC and ITN (Schlesinger, 1978; Eldridge, 1995); considered the explicit and implicit ideologies shaping cinema films and newsreels (Pronay and Spring, 1982; Richards, 1984); and traced the changing representation of oppositional groups, reforming organizations and social movements (Atton, 2002). In each case, scholars study media products to see how they frame and represent political issues, the language and images they use to describe political actors and institutions, and the sources of authority and expertise to which reporters and filmmakers refer and defer.

Underlying this body of scholarship is, however, a fundamental tension between those who argue that the media have played a broadly democratizing role by providing the public with essential political information and holding the powerful to account, and those who contend that the media have consistently defended the interests of those in power and have distorted the nature of the political system in order to mislead or mystify ordinary people. This is the conflict between what James Curran has characterised as the "liberal" and "radical" narratives of media history (Curran, 2002: ch. 1). The liberal narrative was for many years the dominant interpretation of British media history, and was initially based on accounts of the freeing of the press from the shackles of state censorship and the 'taxes on knowledge', and the powerful idea of the press as a 'Fourth Estate' exposing the inadequacies and misdeeds of ruling institutions. In the twentieth century, the BBC presented itself as the true heir to this tradition, and this liberal narrative has had a significant influence on histories of broadcasting as well as the press. For some commentators, the internet is encouraging a further democratization of society, both by allowing access to information on an unprecedented scale and by providing new opportunities for individuals and organizations to have their voices heard (Castells, 2010).

Since the 1970s, however, the radical tradition has challenged this interpretation, and arguably now represents the new orthodoxy in British media history; it certainly structures what remains the most influential history of the British media environment, James Curran and Jean Seaton's *Power without Responsibility* (originally published in 1981, and now in its seventh edition). Many writers in this tradition highlight how the market operated as a 'system of control' rather than a guarantor of freedom. The classic case study, highlighted in Curran's work, is the decline of the radical press after the ending of the 'taxes on knowledge' in the mid-nineteenth century: as the newspaper industry became characterized by high levels of investment and dependent on commercial advertising, smaller independent operators struggled to compete and the market was dominated by right-wing titles (Curran and Seaton, 1981/2010: Part 1). Given the intense competition for a mass audience, it is often suggested that media outlets have prioritized entertainment, celebrity and consumerism rather than pursuing the complexities of politics or accepting the costs of investigative journalism. Other writers in this tradition point to the ways in which media output has been shaped by state regulation and official pressure, the apparatus of public relations, or the personal ideologies of proprietors; still others have examined the socialization of journalists into working patterns that defer to authority and official expertise (Curran, 2002: ch. 1).

Scholars in these two traditions tend to approach media products as historical artefacts in rather different ways. Historians in the liberal tradition tend to take the content of newspapers and broadcast programmes largely on their own terms, exploring the detail of the reporting and making comparisons between titles and programmes or across times. They view media producers as operating in a pluralistic society, thereby having a certain degree of independence of thought and action. Writers in the radical tradition are more interested in exposing the gaps and silences in the content, trying to show how media producers seek to encourage certain patterns of thinking and closing off alternative ways of understanding politics. They see journalists and broadcasters as being largely tied into existing power structures, either colluding with elites or being socialized into patterns of deference. The debates and disagreements between these two schools of thought are inevitably heated, because so much is at stake – for the understanding not just of the past but also of the present.

Media and the formation of identities

Implicit in the early histories of the press, and in many of the histories of the media more broadly, was the assumption that the most important function of any media form was to provide information about politics and the public sphere; the focus was on the provision of news and other types of content were often overlooked or dismissed as trivial. In recent years, however, scholars have embraced a far wider range of material in their studies of the media. This has been largely driven by two related developments. The first is the blossoming of feminist scholarship since the 1970s. Many feminists of the 1970s were concerned with the cultural obstacles to equality, and particularly with the ways in which certain stereotypes and definitions of femininity operated to restrict or undermine women's activities in society. The media were, and are, central to the circulation of ideas about gender, and the high-profile feminist activism against sexism in the media encouraged scholars to explore the representation of women (and sometimes men) in the past. Women's magazines – which date as a genre back to the 1690s and have traditionally been very explicit about the appropriate roles and behaviour of women – provided a popular source for study (White, 1970; Beetham, 1996); there was also significant feminist scholarship on cinema (Mulvey, 1975). By the 1990s, gendered perspectives had become mainstream in the academy, and studies of masculinity and femininity have now become one of the most vibrant areas of media history. In recent years, there has been significant work in this tradition on national newspapers (Bingham, 2004), girls' magazines (Tinkler, 1995), feminist periodicals (Tusan, 2005), and radio and television broadcasting (Andrews, 2012).

The 'cultural turn' in the humanities, of which feminist scholarship was one part, has also encouraged a much greater use of media sources. Historians in recent decades have become much more interested in language, representation and meaning, and have found media products to be particularly valuable as a means of examining the images and narratives that circulated through society and the interpretative frameworks with which readers made sense of the world. A rich scholarship has developed, for example, on the ways in which the media helped to forge national, imperial or ethnic identities, whether through the repeated use of particular national stereotypes or images in films (Richards, 1997), racialized representations in advertising (Ramamurthy, 2003), the broadcasting of rituals of national or imperial celebration and commemoration (Hajkowski, 2010), or the reporting of immigration in the popular press (Van Dijk, 1991). There is a similarly detailed and diverse literature on the representation and discussion of a range of sexual identities. Scholars have mined newspaper court reports to provide insights into the lives and identities of individuals defying moral codes (Oram, 2007), examined the changing portrayal of gay, lesbian and transgender individuals in films and television broadcasting (Howes, 1993); and explored the battles over obscenity and vulgarity in the mainstream media, from topless pin-ups in the tabloid press to the simulation of sex at the cinema (Bingham, 2009; Aldgate and Robertson, 2005). While significant gaps remain, especially in terms of broad overviews, there is now a scholarship on the media representation of most forms of identity, including class, age, region and religion. Precisely how powerful the media are, or have been, in shaping those identities remains a contested question.

Social and cultural historians often have to be creative in their use of media products as historical artefacts. They often have to read 'against the grain', using categories – such as gender, sexuality and ethnicity – which the producers and consumers of the time may not have recognized or fully understood. Scholars pay close attention to particular forms of language use and how they changed over time – studying, for example, the varying ways in which terms such as 'homosexual', 'queer', 'deviant' and 'gay' were deployed. Silences and euphemisms are often as important as the explicit content: it is revealing that in many periods, for example, journalists and broadcasters were very reluctant to address sexual issues. Considerable effort is also expended in decoding and explaining images and visual representations – from the sexualization of the female body to the visual stereotyping of supposedly lesser races. Frank Mort has recently encouraged social and cultural historians to move beyond studies of content to develop a firmer grasp of the "genres through which the press codified cultural and political change for popular consumption, within the confines of their operation as marketable commodities" (Mort, 2011: 215). This will enable scholars to take up James Curran's challenge to integrate their work on media history into broader analyses of social and cultural change (Curran, 2002).

Conclusions

The rapid digitization of media sources in recent years has encouraged, and will likely sustain, a boom in historical research into the media. Digitization is enabling more ambitious and more rigorous projects that seek to map changing patterns of content over considerable stretches of time. Increasingly sophisticated tools are becoming available for 'text-mining' – searching and comparing very large quantities of text using algorithms, statistical formulae and language processing techniques. Digitization makes it much easier to trace flows of ideas and information between different media forms and across national boundaries. Commercially produced digital archives remain expensive, however, and even leading British universities are often able to subscribe only to a few of the available databases; outside of the UK, the take-up is even slower. The full promise of digitization will not be realized until archives become more accessible to scholars inside and outside of the academy.

Yet even where they are available, digital resources certainly do not solve all the issues associated with the study of the media. Indeed, there is the danger that scholars will be seduced by the surfeit of media products available to read or watch at the click of a button. We cannot properly assess the political, social and cultural significance of the media simply by studying their content: we need to place them in their proper historical context and understand how they were produced and received. We need to explore the ways in which media organizations were connected to political, social and legal power structures; and if we are making claims about the media shaping the views or attitudes of their audiences, we also need to consider how newspapers are read and understood by actual readers. Evidence about production and reception is often very sketchy, but the search is worthwhile if we are to capture and understand the lasting impact of these ephemeral products.

Further reading

James Curran's "Rival Narratives of Media History" in his collection *Media and Power* (2002) is a masterly survey of the field from the leading exponent of media history. The piece is updated in Michael Bailey's *Narrating Media History* (2008), which also provides a useful and diverse set of chapters based around Curran's six narratives. The two most accessible and informative recent introductions to the history of the British media are Martin Conboy's *Journalism in Britain: A Historical Introduction* (2011) and Kevin Williams' *Get Me a Murder a Day! A History of Media and Communication in Britain* (2010).

References

Aldgate, A. and Robertson, J. (2005) *Censorship in Theatre and Cinema*. Edinburgh: Edinburgh University Press.
Anderson, B. (1991) *Imagined Communities: Reflections on the Origin and Spread of Nationalism* (revised edn). London: Verso.
Andrews, M. (2012) *Domesticating the Airwaves: Broadcasting, Domesticity and Femininity*. London: Continuum.
Atton, C. (2002) *Alternative Media*. London: Sage.
Bailey, M. (ed.) (2008) *Narrating Media History*. London: Routledge.
Barker, H. (1998) *Newspapers, Politics, and Public Opinion in Late Eighteenth-Century England*. Oxford: Oxford University Press.
Beetham, M. (1996) *A Magazine of her Own? Domesticity and Desire in the Woman's Magazine 1800–1914*. London: Routledge.
Bingham, A. (2004) *Gender, Modernity, and the Popular Press in Inter-War Britain*. Oxford: Oxford University Press.
——(2009) *Family Newspapers? Sex, Private Life, and the British Popular Press, 1918–78*. Oxford: Oxford University Press.
Boyce, D. G. (1987) "Crusaders Without Chains: Power and Press Barons 1896–1951". In J. Curran, A. Smith and P. Wingate (eds.) *Impacts and Influence: Essays on Media Power in the Twentieth Century*. London: Methuen & Co (pp. 97–112).
Boyce, G., Curran, J. and Wingate, P. (eds.) (1978) *Newspaper History from the Seventeenth Century to the Present Day*. London: Constable.
Briggs, A. (1961/1965/1970/1979) *The History of Broadcasting in the UK*: Vols 1–4. Oxford: Oxford University Press.
Carruthers, S. (2011) *The Media at War* (2nd edn). London: Routledge.
Castells, M. (2010) *The Rise of the Network Society* (2nd edn). London: Wiley-Blackwell.
Conboy, M. (2011) *Journalism in Britain: A Historical Introduction*. London: Sage.
Curran, J. (2002) "Rival Narratives of Media History". In J. Curran, *Media and Power*. London: Routledge (pp. 3–54).
Curran, J. and Porter, V. (eds.) (1983) *British Cinema History*. Totowa, NJ: Barnes and Noble Books.
Curran, J. and Seaton, J. (1981/seventh ed. 2010) *Power Without Responsibility: The Press, Broadcasting and New Media in Britain*. Abingdon: Routledge.
Eldridge, J. (1995) *Glasgow Media Group Reader, Vol. 1: News Content, Language and Visuals*. London: Routledge.
Habermas, J. (1989) *The Structural Transformation of the Public Sphere: An Inquiry into a Category of Bourgeois Society* (T. Burger, Trans.). Cambridge: Polity.

Hajkowski, T. (2010) *The BBC and National Identity in Britain, 1922–53*. Manchester: Manchester University Press.

Hoggart, R. (1957) *The Uses of Literacy*. London: Chatto & Windus.

Howes, K. (1993) *Broadcasting It: An Encyclopaedia of Homosexuality on Film, Radio and TV in the UK 1923–1993*. London: Cassells.

Hunt, F. (1850) *The Fourth Estate: Contributions Towards a History of Newspapers and of the Liberty of the Press*. London: David Bogue.

Koss, S. (1981/4) *The Rise and Fall of the Political Press, Vol. 1, The Nineteenth Century; Vol. 2, The Twentieth Century*. London: Hamish Hamilton.

Mort, F. (2011) "Intellectual Pluralism and the Future of British History". *History Workshop Journal*, 72(1), 212–21.

Mulvey, L. (1975) "Visual Pleasure and Narrative Cinema". *Screen*, 13(3), 6–18.

Oram, A. (2007) *Her Husband Was a Woman! Women's Gender-Crossing in Modern British Popular Culture*. London: Routledge.

Pettinato, T. (2010) "Newspapers: 'the rough draft of history'". Retrieved from http://www.readex.com/blog/newspapers-rough-draft-history

Pronay, N. and Spring, D. (eds.) (1982) *Propaganda, Politics and Films 1918–45*. London: Macmillan.

Ramamurthy, A. (2003) *Imperial Persuaders: Images of Africa and Asia in British Advertising*. Manchester: Manchester University Press.

Raymond, J. (1996) *The Invention of the Newspaper: English Newsbooks, 1641–1649*. Oxford: Oxford University Press.

——(1999) "The History of Newspapers and the History of Journalism: Two Disciplines or One?". *Media History*, 5(2), 223–32.

Richards, J. (1984) *The Age of the Dream Palace: Cinema and Society in Britain 1930–1939*. London: Routledge and Kegan Paul.

——(1997) *Films and British National Identity: From Dickens to Dad's Army*. Manchester: Manchester University Press.

Royal Commission on the Press 1947–49 (1949) *Report*. London: HMSO, Cmd. 7700.

Schlesinger, P. (1978) *Putting "Reality" Together: BBC News*. London: Constable.

Schuchard, R. (2001) "Why I Go To Colindale". Retrieved from http://w01.ies.wf.ulcc.ac.uk/events/conferences/2001/Newspapers/schuch.htm

Seymour-Ure, C. (2003) *Prime Ministers and the Media: Issues of Power and Control*. Oxford: Blackwell.

Stedman-Jones, G. (1983) *The Languages of Class: Studies in English Working-Class History*. Cambridge: Cambridge University Press.

Thompson, E. P. (1963) *The Making of the English Working Class*. London: Victor Gollancz.

Tinkler, P. (1995) *Constructing Girlhood: Popular Magazines for Girls Growing Up in England 1920–1950*. London: Taylor & Francis.

Tusan, M. (2005) *Women Making News: Gender and Journalism in Modern Britain*. Urbana and Chicago, IL: University of Illinois Press.

Van Dijk, T. (1991) *Racism and the Press*. London: Routledge.

Vella, S. (2009) "Newspapers". In M. Dobson and B. Ziemann (eds.) *Reading Primary Sources: The Interpretation of Texts from 19th and 20th Century History*. Abingdon: Routledge (pp. 192–208).

White, C. (1970) *Women's Magazines 1693–1968*. London: Michael Joseph.

Williams, K. (2010) *Get Me a Murder a Day! A History of Media and Communication in Britain* (2nd edn). London: Bloomsbury.

3
Doing media history
The mass media, historical analysis and the 1930s

Kevin Williams

Introduction

Historical accounts of mass communication are criticized for their media-centric focus. They are often directed at the examination of the content and organization of a specific medium. This focus means media history tends "not to illuminate the links between media development and wider trends in society" (Curran, 2002: 135). The historiography of the mass media is primarily concerned with "parallel histories of individual mediums which only fleetingly acknowledge the existence of other media" (Nicholas, 2012: 381). The failure to consider them as a whole has resulted in "fractured and incomplete understandings of the historical role of the media" (Curran, 2002: 135). It excludes the complex interactions and exchanges between different media at different stages in their growth (Bastiansen, 2008). It neglects the wider social context in which the media operate and media technologies are developed. Calls have been made for integrated histories of the mass media which highlight the interplay between media and address the social context within which this takes place. Considerable problems confront media history of this kind.

Sian Nicholas (2012) has already examined some of the obstacles to producing an integrated history of the media. She describes the problems that arise from the different characters of media, the different ways they are addressed, the different modes of engagement with their audiences and their very different archival records. Nicholas (2012: 382) argues that what is required is "simply to note the existence of other media; to contextualise developments in one mass medium in relation to other media; and/or identify a range of media responses to a particular issue." Her case study documents the interrelatedness of the media during the interwar years by identifying the extent and nature of the connections between individual media practitioners and between media institutions. She describes how the convergence of style, language and personnel led to "an increasingly sophisticated and integrated mass information and entertainment culture" (Nicholas, 2012: 387). She argues that 'intermediality' led to the emergence in the 1930s of a 'common culture' which was underpinned by an entertainment-driven mass media community.

Nicholas demonstrates how an integrated approach helps us to understand the historical role of the media in a more complete sense but her discussion raises questions about what we mean by interconnectedness. This chapter asks what types of connections and interactions constitute interconnectedness. Like Nicholas it draws on the example of the 1930s[1] to discuss whether the interrelatedness of the media adds up to anything more than a superficial and shared exposure to media technologies. In particular does interconnectedness form a common media culture? Some of the methodological and conceptual issues presented by the sheer magnitude of the challenge that confronts historians in documenting interrelatedness are touched on. The chapter begins by exploring a problem that confronts every media historian – the relationship between media history and history. Understanding the historical context within which we want to study the media presents an interpretative challenge to efforts to document and describe the nature of mass communication.

Media history and history

Integrated media history requires an understanding of the historical conditions within which media texts and messages are produced and received. The approach taken to a particular historical period will lay down a framework for understanding and evaluating the performance, practice and power of the media and ultimately shape the interpretation put forward to account for their role. That the past is a matter of dispute and only accessed through the concerns of the present are established components of the historian's analytical tool kit. Recent trends in historiography suggest that reproducing an accurate picture of what happened in the past is impossible. What we have are different accounts produced by different groups with different concerns and at different times. This poses a particular challenge to media history. How a period in history is conceptualized shapes the effort to describe and discuss the role of the media. Dissimilar and sometimes contradictory evaluations confront the media historians with interpretative difficulties. This is apparent with the 1930s.

Historians agree that the 1930s were a "peculiarly heightened and potentially transformative moment" in British history (McKibbin, 1994: 518). There is a relatively high degree of scholarly consensus that British society underwent dramatic and far-reaching change. Disagreement exists over the nature of the change. It was a matter of controversy amongst those who lived through the 1930s and has remained ever so. Many historians[2] and much popular history[3] represent the decade in terms of a society bitterly divided between the haves and have-nots, between classes and peoples, Left and Right, a nation at war with itself. Images of hunger marches, unemployment, idleness, poverty, slums, ill health, political extremism, the rise of fascism, civil war in Spain and appeasement illustrate these divisions. Revisionist historians[4] challenge this interpretation, painting a different picture. They draw attention to the uneven distribution of unemployment and hardship around the country; it was concentrated mainly in the old industrial areas of the North, Scotland and Wales. Outside these regions the 1930s were boom years. They witnessed the birth of consumerism, the development of the suburbs and technological innovations such as the motor car, washing machine and gramophone which changed most people's lives, many would say for the better. For those in work the 1930s were not 'wasted years'; they were years of prosperity. Longer holidays, shorter working hours and higher real income are seen as more typical of the experience of ordinary British men and women.

Both these perspectives are partial; as Andrew Thorpe (1992: 126) notes, the 1930s "have suffered too much from people using them for their own purposes." Interpretations of the decade have changed as the time that has elapsed since the period has grown (Smith, 1998). According to John Baxendale and Chris Pawling (1999) "the ever changing constructions of the 1930s have reflected the conflicts and concerns of the world that came afterwards." The 1930s throw up "so many paradoxes about Britain's experience of the depression years that it is possible to credibly put forward interpretations which are wholly at odds with each other" (Smith, 1998: 1). With so many constantly changing accounts, accessing the 'real' Thirties is far from straightforward if at all possible.

Matters are further complicated by the part the media play in constructing the past. How they report and represent what happened are important sources of historical information. Accounts produced at the time by *Picture Post*, the Documentary Film Movement, the newsreels and popular newspapers amongst others are drawn on to piece together the history of 1930s. How historians make sense of competing and contradictory media reports is often shaped by the emphasis they place on their sources of information. There is a hierarchy of sources with a tendency to attribute more attention and credence to certain accounts. There is an emphasis in some quarters on media with the greatest reach. Historians justify their focus on the press, or wireless or cinema in quantitative terms, neglecting the role of smaller but perhaps more influential media in shaping the style and nature of representation. Within these broad categories greater reliability is accorded to factual forms *and* media of record. This conforms to the conventional approach of a discipline wedded to high politics and the socio-economic conditions that demarcate its practice. It is reinforced by the commitment made by news organisations to produce 'objective' accounts of reality and the 'first rough draft of history'. The practical advantages of the detailed archival records of established organizations such as the BBC and *The Times* further attract the historian. Integrated media history runs the risk of giving preference to particular media. For example, despite the tremendous demand for newsreels in the 1930s, which drove the legendary rivalry between the companies and their camera workers, there is relatively little examination of their content and how they shaped the output and practices of the rest of the media (see Aldgate, 1979). This reflects not only the disposition of historians and the problems of accessing archives and material but also the concerns as to whether newsreels were real news or part of show business.[5]

Interconnectedness

Focusing on the interconnectedness of media institutions and personnel neglects the media's interaction with other social and political actors. The media on a daily basis work closely with representatives of the State. The interaction between the State and the media not only shapes institutional practices and output but also frames perceptions of the media as an interrelated whole. In the 1930s the media were seen as a catalyst for political tension and a threat to the authority of the State. This was expressed in a number of ways such as Baldwin's outburst about the 'power without responsibility' of the press barons and the Committee for Imperial Defence's warning about the 'incalculable significance for political stability' of the wireless. The State had to adjust to new problems of political, social and cultural management in the era of mass democracy. The threat posed by mass communication, however, was matched by the opportunity the media presented as a means for managing public and political discourse and moulding popular taste.

A range of formal and informal mechanisms of information control were embedded in British society in the 1930s. The coming of sound provided an impetus for the extension of the ability of the British Board of Film Censorship (BBFC) to censor what people saw in British cinemas. In 1937 the President of the Board could boast that "there is not a single film showing in London today which deals with any of the burning issues of the day" (Street and Dickinson, 1985: 8). Pressure from government, politicians and local authorities diminished the capacity of the newsreel companies to convey independent and informed opinion (see Aldgate, 1987). The BBC exercised caution and self-censorship; for example, "independent expressions of views" on the European situation were discouraged (see Scannell and Cardiff, 1981). Even the press suspended its critical faculties on some of the pressing issues of the day: the non-reporting of King Edward VIII's affair with Mrs Simpson and the Abdication crisis as well as the reluctance of many newspapers to criticize Nazi Germany for fear of offending government are examples (see Cockett, 1989). The process of embedding censorship and control across the media draws attention to the close connections between the media and the State.

During the 1930s the relationship between the media and politics was institutionalized. In the wake of the Great War various government and political organizations had developed apparatus to 'sell' information. On a daily basis they sought to manage the environment in which the media gathered news and information. Press officers, public relations advisors and information officers became a feature of government in the 1930s.[6] Government used mass media to pioneer innovative techniques of propaganda. For example, the Empire Marketing Board (EMB), set up in 1926 to promote trade with the Empire, employed documentary filmmakers such as John Grierson to communicate its message. Such organizations fuelled the interaction with the media. BBC officials served on the publicity committee of the EMB and the man who headed up the Board went to the BBC as head of publicity. Filmmakers such as Grierson moved between government, media and corporate sectors to obtain the backing for their documentaries. In the case of the press and later broadcasting, the daily interactions between media practitioners and government personnel were institutionalized in the Parliamentary Lobby. The news cartel which has shaped the reporting of politics in Britain until today was formally established in the late 1920s even though its roots go back to the 1880s (see Sparrow, 2003). The network of informal and personal contacts that had permeated the daily relationship between government, official bodies and the media in the nineteenth century was formalized. The interrelatedness of media practitioners and agents of the State in the

1930s contributed to the shaping of the output and perceptions of the media as much as the interactions between practitioners themselves.

The synthetic whole

The search for interconnectedness threatens to downplay the contested nature of media representation and the variety of ways in which class, gender, region, political power and 'race' find expression in the media. Take the issue of locality and the regions. A fundamental shift took place in the British media in the 1930s. At the start of the 1920s Britain's media were highly localized. Sound broadcasting had started as a local service based on relay stations in different parts of the country. Film-making could be found in a variety of regions outside of London and the newspaper industry was provincial in character and production. By the eve of the Second World War media production had become highly concentrated on London and the south east of England and output had become 'national' in outlook. Britain had one of the most centralized and metropolitan-centred media systems in the western world. Regionalized film production gave way to the establishment of studios in the London region, at Elstree, Pinewood and Denham. Under John Reith the BBC had been transformed from a regional network exchanging programmes to a national network, with regional opt outs, located in London. Finally the provincial press experienced a significant decline with the number of regional morning newspapers falling from 41 in 1920 to 23 in 1937 accompanied by a severe contraction in circulation of regional newspapers. At the same time the London press, through the extension of the rail network, extended itself into local newspaper markets throughout the country, with the exception of Scotland.

Integrated media history's search for interconnectedness will focus study on the centralization of production and the range of media responses but in the process it risks losing sight of the story of local resistance. In the 1930s BBC nationalization was opposed by local stations, most notably Sheffield which fought a campaign bringing together unions, the Chamber of Commerce, the press and members of the public to oppose closure of its station in 1928. Cinemas across the UK had to adapt their programmes to respond to the social and cultural needs of their local consumers (see James, 2010). An increasingly commercial world emphasized that consumer tastes varied not only by region but also by gender, age and class. Locality was most acutely expressed in the form of the provincial press. Provincial morning and evening newspapers resisted the encroachment of Fleet Street in the 1930s. An example is the *Yorkshire Post*, a bastion of conservatism and the North of England. Under editor Arthur Mann it warned of becoming too close to government, discouraging contact with politicians altogether (Cockett, 1989: 62–64). The paper was more outspoken against appeasement and was the first title to break the Abdication story. This stance led to the paper merger and Mann's departure in 1939 when diminishing financial returns undermined its independence (Cockett, 1989: 128). In the search for what has been called the 'synthetic whole' integrated media history might reinforce totalizing narratives. For example, telling the story of the British media in the 1930s in terms of the development of 'national' British institutions can lose sight of the struggle to maintain regional and local media and identities.

Nature of interconnectedness

The issue of which actors and institutions to focus on is accompanied by the problem of what types of interaction to investigate. Historians have traditionally considered the media as sources of information. Even historians of the cinema have tended to analyze films in terms of the extent to which they inform, or not, politics and society. The so-called 'cultural turn' has seen more attention on the media as sources of entertainment and in recent years the pleasure and diversion they provide have been examined in more detail. Yet the importance of the media as a leisure and recreational activity is still not fully recognized in spite of the media's increasing dominance of people's leisure time. In the 1930s spare time generated a significant amount of attention and unease. How ordinary people made use of their increased leisure time was the subject of numerous conferences, books, articles, columns and broadcasts. These often reflected the view expressed by *The Times* in 1929 that "spare time" was "that serious thing, a 'problem'" (Langhamer, 2000: 19). Speculation about the consequences of excessive spare time abounded and many social ills were attributed to its growth. The extent of State intervention in the provision and organisation of leisure and recreation at local and national level to manage people's spare time attests to the strength of the perception that leisure was a problem.

Historians have concentrated more on 'enforced leisure' as a result of unemployment in the 1930s than 'spare time'. The range of meaning people made out of their spare time has largely been neglected. Historical analysis tends to focus on the politics of leisure. The growth of leisure and entertainment is usually associated with the de-politicization of the working class, a recurrent theme is the study of the popular press, cinema, broadcasting and other popular media forms. Blame is attached to the commercialization of leisure which is considered as detrimental in that it distracted people from the contemplation of contemporary issues and perpetuated public ignorance.[7] The media and leisure industries provided escapism from the problems of everyday life in a country beset by economic and political problems.

The effects of commercialized leisure have been subject to a re-evaluation, for example Adrian Bingham (2013) and James Nott (2002) have suggested that in spite of their use for escapism the popular media made the interwar generation "better informed" (Nott, 2002: 228). This re-evaluation seeks to refute the view that there was a de-politicization or trivialization of the media. Integrated media history shows that the balance between 'education' and 'entertainment' was a matter of struggle across the media in the 1930s. It highlights that established opinion believed that media consumption encouraged political education. More leisure time allowed people, and in particular working people, more time to read, think and learn and enhance their political awakening. For some this was a positive development as it enabled people to better fulfil their roles as citizens. However, there were many more who believed that such activity was de-stabilizing and a threat to the established political and social order. The issue of de-politicization and trivialization has been explored primarily through the examination of media content. Historians have discussed the extent to which political coverage declined or changed in the 1930s, the misrepresentation of politics or the degree to which 'human interest' and fictional representation informed the public. Less attention has been paid to the study of what people learned from the media. The assumption of much media history, integrated or not, is that audiences are passive consumers with no individual agency (James, 2010: 2). The reluctance to engage with the messy world of audiences means historians have not fully engaged with the complexities of how meaning has been constructed.

Audiences and reception

One of Nicholas' most telling points is that the audience experience the media "as thoroughly interrelated and overlapping phenomena" (Nicholas, 2012: 389). History has not found it easy to differentiate between 'newspaper readers' or 'radio listeners' or 'cinema goers' or 'newsreel watchers' as "engagement in one medium routinely overlapped with others" (Nicholas, 2012: 390). Excavating basic quantitative material about audiences in the past, let alone their experiences, is, as we know, a challenge. Unearthing how they make sense of what they consume from different media outlets further complicates matters. In the 1930s the fact that audience surveys were in their infancy emphasizes this obstacle. Gaining insights into working people's views and attitudes is handicapped by the lack of printed recollections. However, audience dispositions to media offerings can be deduced from other sources. Robert James (2010) in a compelling study documents the regional variations in cinema viewing and popular reading habits drawn from the booking practices of cinema hall managers and the acquisition policies of libraries and working class institutes. The letters pages of newspapers and specialist magazines such as *The Listener* and *Kineweekly* as well as the correspondence of broadcasters and wireless societies are also useful sources. Oral histories can provide impressionistic glimpses into how people experienced the media and how they integrated their knowledge and understanding from different media sources.

Understanding audiences in history is more than an appreciation of the aggregate of individual views, feelings and dreams. Consumers interpret what is represented to them but what appears in the media is influenced by producers who inscribe their audiences with particular characteristics. Producers construct their audiences out of notions of what they believe their viewers, listeners or readers should be told and their interpretation of what research tells them about people's interests, likes and dislikes. People's wants and desires were a feature of public discussion in the 1930s. British society to paraphrase Bernard Bergonzi (1978) had to come to terms *directly* with what has come to be described as 'mass society' and there was considerable debate and scrutiny about the impact and influence of the 'masses' on British culture and society. The creation of Mass Observation in 1937 in some ways crystallizes the obsessive concern with the views, opinions and behaviour of ordinary men and women. From art to literature, media to social research, intellectuals in Britain were 'discovering' ordinary people and trying to document and interpret their lives.

Historical knowledge of what ordinary people believed and desired draws heavily from contemporaneous cultural and media representation. Daniel Le Mahieu (1988) draws heavily on the views and interpretations of the intellectual and primarily metropolitan minority of the interwar years to support his argument that a common culture emerged.

Whether or not these views accurately represented people's cultural and media experience they highlight the importance attached by historical analysis to the beliefs and observations of cultural producers. Proponents of the emergence of a common culture in the 1930s often cite examples of the presence of certain individuals across the range of media. Nicholas, like Le Mahieu before her, refers to J. B Priestley's appearance in film production, radio, the press, popular literature, theatre and magazines as "the epitome of the common culture of the time" (Nicholas, 2012: 389). Priestley's struggle to make his voice heard, as well as the compromises he made, raise questions about popular culture between the wars as a contested terrain (see Baxendale, 2007). There is a need to understand the social context of cultural production in different periods of media history. In the 1930s a "complex crisis of representation" took place as the "small, compact and closely linked group" that constituted Britain's intellectual class began to lose its "coherence and authority" (Baxendale and Pawling, 1999: 28). New cultural producers were created by the advertising, media and leisure industries. Less well educated and drawn from different sections of society, most earned their living from cultural production; there was a rapid increase in those describing themselves as "authors, editors and journalists" between 1891 and 1931 (Baxendale and Pawling, 1999: 3). They were more likely as a result of the growing commercialization of cultural production to respond to what they perceived as their audiences' wants than to impose their values from above. There were also significant divisions between cultural producers concerning the response to the rise of mass society and mass culture.[8] Historical accounts of the 1930s tend to pit 'intellectuals' against journalists, film directors and popular novelists, and media practitioners in general, ignoring their interconnectedness in an environment in which a high level of media professionalism had not established clear boundaries.

Emotional environment

One aspect of understanding the production process is through the personal tastes, prejudices and talent of individual media practitioners. An emphasis on political, economic and social structures has often led historians of the media to neglect the role of individuals in the creative process. David Hendy (2012) has recently drawn attention to the need to understand the role of media practitioners in history, placing emphasis on the emotional 'communities' or environment within which they operate. Historians have been reluctant to address the psychological motivations of actors in history (Rosenwein, 2002). Joanna Bourke (2003: 114) states: "although fear, hate, joy and love might be at the very heart of historical experience, they still tend to be regarded as by-products in historical scholarship." Cultural historians have embraced the social-psychological dimension of history and several historians have taken a psychoanalytical approach to excavating the past. However, emotion and conventional historical scholarship remain uneasy bedfellows.

Introducing emotion adds complications to understanding the past. It is difficult to assess and verify the psychology of individual historical actors. Yet emotion is integrated into history in a number of ways and plays a significant part in shaping the relationships that contribute to the interconnectedness of the media. In the 1930s we can talk about emotion at a number of levels. There is the public mood. Assessing the impact of the Great War on British society between the wars is fraught with problems but it is possible to argue that the rise of mass media took place in a society characterized by deep disenchantment and uncertainty. The extent to which the certainties of Edwardian Britain were swept away by the war is disputed but the efforts of families and communities across the country to come to terms with the grief produced by the huge loss of life and suffering of the war is not. The grieving found the established order wanting in a variety of ways. There was, for example, an acute decline in religious faith and church attendance accompanied by a huge growth in spiritualism (Hazelgrove, 1999). Public trust in the political establishment decreased with the failure of post-war governments to deliver on pledges to produce "a country fit for heroes to live in". This was imbued with strong emotion highlighted by the notion of a "Lost Generation" (Winter, 2003: 99). Concerns about the influence and impact of the media have to be seen in the context of an acute sense of irrationality in public thought between the wars.

The personal battles that take up the time of individual media practitioners influence their attitude to their work. The role of individuals in making the history of the media has concentrated on the 'good and the great'; only a few studies have attempted to explore the variety of actors who participate in the production process. There is "an enormous historical deficit to be tackled: beyond the upper ranks much cultural activity remains uncharted" (Hendy, 2012: 362). The focus of organizational studies is on the workplace, on how people participate in the world of media work and the institutional cultures they confront. Hendy focuses on how exploration of the private life histories of media practitioners contributes to our understanding of media institutions as 'emotional communities'. Personal feelings and institutional sentiments also have to be seen as part of a broader creative culture. One is struck by the emotional commitment expressed by many media practitioners in the 1930s in relation to the audience. There was a strong motivation to document the lives of ordinary men and women across the media, to the extent that documentation could be seen as an important part of their work as information or entertainment.

Conclusion

There are a number of methodological and conceptual issues and problems that arise from 'doing' integrated media history. The magnitude of the practical problems of drawing out and documenting the range and variety of interconnections between media and the media and society threatens to turn integrated media history like social history before it into descriptive history. Interconnectedness as this chapter has tried to show has many dimensions. Further connections could be identified; for example, there is an international dimension – many of the features of the British media system in the 1930s drew from experiences and interactions with other media systems, in particular the United States. It is important to be aware of the multifaceted nature of interconnectedness and the problems it presents for the writing and researching of media history. For the interrelatedness to add up to something more than shared exposure, integrated media history has to include a variety of relationships at a number of levels, from production to reception, and draw on the accounts of the experience of a range of actors including audiences. However, in spite of the problems of such an approach to the study of history it is invaluable as it enables us to understand more fully the broad communication environment in which the media function.

Further reading

Sian Nicholas (2012) and Henrik Bastiansen (2008) provide excellent discussions of the need for and problems of developing integrated media history. James Curran's (2002) groundbreaking article "Media and the Making of British Society c 1700–2000" advocates more media history and media histories of different kinds. John Baxendale and Chris Pawling's *Narrating the Thirties: A Decade in the Making: 1930 to the Present* (1999) examines the changing construction of the 1930s in professional and popular history, while David Hendy's "Biography and the Emotions as a Missing 'Narrative'" (2012) provides insight into the role of personality and emotion in programme making in the BBC in the 1930s. Robert James' *Popular Culture and Working Class Taste in Britain 1919–39: A Round of Cheap Diversion?* (2010) is a compelling account of regional differences in the consumption of film and popular literature in the 1930s. Daniel Le Mahieu's *A Culture for Democracy: Mass Communication and the Cultivated Mind in Britain Between the Wars* (1988) is required reading for anyone wishing to understand mass communication and popular culture in the years between the wars.

Notes

1 For a discussion of the common problems and themes facing the media in 1930s Britain see Williams (2006).
2 This is reflected in the titles of some of the leading texts on the period: *The Dark Valley* (2000), *The Morbid Age* (2009), *The Twenty Years Crisis* (1939), *Borrowed Time* (2007), *The Long Weekend* (1940), *The Age of Illusion* (1963), *Britain on the Breadline* (1990) and *The Devil's Decade* (1973).
3 For example see the BBC series *People's Century* (1995) and *The Making of Modern Britain* presented by Andrew Marr (2009).
4 The most cited example is Stevenson and Cook's (1994) *Britain in the Depression: Society and Politics 1929–39*. For a discussion of their arguments see Howkins and Saville (1979).
5 For a discussion of news value of the newsreels see Young (2005).
6 In 1935 the national government set up the National Publicity Bureau which "carried through the first, modern large scale propaganda campaign on a national basis in the history of British politics, yet it worked so unobtrusively and anonymously that few outside the ranks of the professional politician and organisation men has any appreciation of its potency" (Casey, 1939: 624).
7 See, for example, essays in Day Lewis (1937).
8 See Williams (1994), Baxendale and Pawling (1999), Baxendale (2007).

References

Aldgate, A. (1979) *Cinema and History: British Newsreels and the Spanish Civil War*. London: Scolar Press.

——(1987) "The Newsreels, Public Order and the Projection of Britain". In J. Curran, A. Smith and P. Wingate (eds.) *Impacts and Influences: Essays on Media Power in the Twentieth Century*. London: Methuen (pp. 145–56).

Bastiansen, H. (2008) "Media History and the Study of Media Systems". *Media History*, 14(1), 95–112.

Baxendale, J. (2007) *Priestley's England: J. B. Priestley and English Culture*. Manchester: Manchester University Press.

Baxendale, J. and Pawling, C. (1999) *Narrating the Thirties: A Decade in the Making: 1930 to the Present*. London: Macmillan.

Bergonzi, B. (1978) *Reading the Thirties: Texts and Contexts*. London: Macmillan.

Bingham, A. (2013) "'An Organ of Uplift?': The Popular Press and Political Culture in Interwar Britain". *Journalism Studies*, 14(5), 651–62.

Blythe, R. (1963) *The Age of Illusion: England in the Twenties and Thirties*. London: Faber & Faber.

Bourke, J. (2003) "Fear and Anxiety: Writing about Emotion in Modern History". *History Workshop Journal*, 53(1), 111–33.

Brendon, P. (2000) *The Dark Valley: A Panorama of the 1930s*. London: Jonathan Cape.

Carr, E. H. (1939) *The Twenty Years Crisis*. London: Macmillan.

Casey, R. (1939) "The National Publicity Bureau and British Party Propaganda". *The Public Opinion Quarterly*, 3(4), 623–34.

Cockburn, C. (1973) *The Devil's Decade*. London: Sidgwick & Jackson.

Cockett, R. (1989) *Twilight of Truth: Chamberlain, Appeasement and the Manipulation of the Press*. London: Palgrave Macmillan.

Curran, J. (2002) "Media and the Making of British Society c. 1700–2000". *Media History*, 8(2), 135–54.

Day Lewis, C. (ed.) (1937) *The Mind in Chains: Socialism and the Cultural Revolution*. London: Frederick Muller.

Graves, R. and Hodge, A. (1940) *The Long Weekend: A Social History of Great Britain 1918–1939*. London: Faber and Faber.

Hattersley, R. (2007) *Borrowed Time: The Story of Britain Between the Wars*. London: Abacus.

Hazelgrove, J. (1999) "Spiritualism after the Great War". *Twentieth Century British History*, 10(4), 404–30.

Hendy, D. (2012) "Biography and the Emotions as a Missing 'Narrative' in Media History: A Case Study of Lance Sieveking and the Early BBC". *Media History*, 18(3–4), 361–78.

Howkins, A. and Saville, J. (1979) "The Nineteen Thirties: A Revisionist History". *The Socialist Register*, 16(1), 89–110.

James, R. (2010) *Popular Culture and Working Class Taste in Britain 1919–39: A Round of Cheap Diversion?* Manchester: Manchester University Press.

Langhamer, C. (2000) *Women's Leisure in England 1920 60*. Manchester: Manchester University Press.

Laybourn, K. (1990) *Britain on the Breadline: A Social and Political History of Britain Between the Wars*. Gloucester: Sutton Publishing.

Le Mahieu, D. L. (1988) *A Culture for Democracy: Mass Communication and the Cultivated Mind in Britain Between the Wars*. Oxford: Clarendon Press.

McKibbin, R. (1994) *Classes and Cultures 1918–1951*. Oxford: Oxford University Press.

Nicholas, S. (2012) "Media History or Media Histories? Re-Addressing the History of the Mass Media in Interwar Britain". *Media History*, 18(3–4), 379–94.

Nott, J. (2002) *Music for the People: Popular Music and Dance in Interwar Britain*. Oxford: Oxford University Press.

Overy, R. (2009) *The Morbid Age: Britain and the Crisis of Civilisation 1919–1939*. London: Penguin.

Rosenwein, B. (2002) "Worrying about Emotions in History". *The American Historical Review*, 107, 3, pp. 821–45. Retrieved from http://www.historycooperative.org/journals/ahr//107.3/ah0302000821.html

Scannell, P. and Cardiff, D. (1981) *A Social History of Broadcasting*. London: Blackwell.

Smith, M. (1998) *Democracy in a Depression: Britain in the 1920s and 1930s*. Cardiff: University of Wales Press.

Sparrow, A. (2003) *Obscure Scribblers: A History of Parliamentary Journalism*. London: Politicos Publishing.

Stevenson, J. and Cook, C. (1994) *Britain in the Depression: Society and Politics 1929–39*. London: Longman.

Street, S. and Dickinson, M. (1985) *Cinema and State: the Film Industry and the British Government 1927–84*. London: BFI Publishing.

Thorpe, A. (1992) *Britain in the 1930s: The Deceptive Decade*. London: Wiley-Blackwell.

Williams, K. (1994) *British Writers and the Media 1930–45*. London: Macmillan.

Williams, K. (2006) "The Devil's Decade and Modern Mass Communication: The Development of the British Media during the Inter-war Years". In B. Moore and H. Nierop (eds.) (2006) *Twentieth-Century Mass Society in Britain and the Netherlands*. Oxford: Berg (pp. 93–114).

Winter, J. M. (2003) *The Great War and the British People* (2nd edition). London: Palgrave.

Young, C. (2005) "The Rise and Fall of the News Theatres". *Journal of British Cinema and Television*, 2, 2, 227–41.

4
Media studies in question
The making of a contested formation

Graham Murdock and Peter Golding

Hiding in the light

In January 2014, the popular writer and philosopher Alain de Botton appeared on the BBC flagship current affairs programme *Newsnight* to promote his new book *News: A User's Manual* (de Botton, 2014). He argued, unchallenged, that schools and universities ought to teach critical thinking on news, neglecting to mention that this project has been a mainstay of media studies in the classroom for over 50 years, supported by a substantial body of university-based research on the politics of news production and representation. This refusal to acknowledge the growth of media studies as an academic field is unusual. Public debate has more often been dominated by two other reactions. A swelling chorus of commentators has dismissed the area as trivial and lightweight, the resort of the second-rate, unwilling or unable to cope with the rigors of traditional disciplines in the social sciences and humanities, labeling it, in a much over-used phrase, a 'Mickey Mouse' subject. A second response elevates training above critical reflection and disinterested analysis and insists that media studies should focus on the acquisition of the practical skills and professional disciplines required to work effectively in the media industries.

Against these dismissals, the account presented here is grounded in the conviction that media studies is indispensable to any full understanding of the organization of modern life, the play of power and the dynamics of change. This is so for three reasons. First, communication systems constitute the basic infrastructure of modernity. The networks of connection they provide allow military, security, political and economic activity to operate across time and space. Second, media command the key arenas of public culture where the images, explanations and emotional states that provide the major resources for everyday understanding and action are recycled and contested. Third, media have come to play an increasingly central role in the organization and performance of daily routines, social relations and styles of self-presentation.

As even this bald outline of its scope makes clear, media studies is not a discipline in the conventional sense, occupying a designated academic territory with fixed boundaries. It is a space of encounter and debate. Its concerns overlap with the cognate areas of cultural and information studies and draw on traditions of inquiry and debate from across the entire range of the social and human sciences. This diversity defined the initial phase of the field's expansion in Britain out of necessity. Since there were no established degrees in the subject, the first wave of academic researchers mobilized interests and methods they had brought with them from a range of established disciplines, most notably sociology, social psychology, history and English literature. There were convergent concerns with the organization and operation of media systems and the ways they were reshaping social and imaginative life and pressures from political and public debates around 'effects'. But there was no agreed definition of the field. This initial push, which gathered momentum from the mid-1960s onwards, was concentrated mainly in dedicated research centres, supplemented by individual 'outlier' researchers scattered across other locations within the university system and by the first wave of doctoral students, who were attracted to the openness of the new field and its relevance to contemporary concerns (cf. Chibnall, 1977; Tracey, 1977; Schlesinger, 1978). Together these diverse researchers established a body of work that spoke to specifically British conditions. The results began to be anthologized and codified alongside American materials (see Tunstall, 1970a; McQuail 1972) providing resources for teaching that fed into optional modules on degrees in established disciplines and into the first dedicated undergraduate degrees in the field, starting with the launch of the programme at the then Polytechnic of Central London in 1975. The years since then have seen an accelerating process of institutionalization. Research has expanded, degrees have proliferated, dedicated journals have been launched and professional associations have been formed.

This chapter outlines the major moments in the establishment of media studies as a field of research and teaching within the British university system and examines the challenges to its legitimacy posed first by persistent attacks on its claims to seriousness and second by the utilitarian turn towards training for employment. It emerges from this account as a field that remains continually 'in question' with detractors denying its importance and value and its practitioners arguing over its boundaries and priorities.

Formations

The period between the two world wars witnessed an explosion of popular media with the consolidation of the popular press and the rapid growth of the advertising, radio, cinema and record industries. In the United States and continental Europe these developments generated a significant body of empirical research and conceptual debate among scholars both inside and outside the university system (see Murdock, 2002) but in Britain there was only a scattered response. The major exceptions were the studies of popular literature (Leavis, 1932) and advertising (Thompson, 1943) developed in the group gathered around F. R. Leavis, doyen of the Cambridge English Faculty. These were rooted in the distinctive style of critical textual reading which he had energetically promoted in *Culture and Environment*, a broadside against commercial media written with Denys Thompson, a working teacher, and aimed specifically at adult education students (Leavis and Thompson, 1933). In contrast, the operations of the media industries and the grounded dynamics of audience responses attracted less attention. Cinema, the leading medium of popular entertainment, was a partial exception, with the Marxist sociologist of art F. D. Klingender producing a political economy of the industry (Klingender and Legg, 1937), the German emigré J. P. Mayer employing audience accounts of their film experiences to develop an interpretive account of the making and taking of meaning (Mayer, 1948) and the Mass Observation group collecting first-hand records and testimonies of cinema going as part of their general project of mapping everyday life and popular leisure (Richards and Sheridan, 1987; Hubble, 2006).

The concern with cinema continued after the end of the war. In 1948, the British Film Institute, which had been launched in 1933, was given particular responsibility for promoting the appreciation of film art. Its existing educational activities and outreach activities in schools expanded (see Bolas, 2009) and in 1957 Paddy Whannel was appointed Education Officer, later collaborating with Stuart Hall to produce the first major British critical evaluation of popular media, *The Popular Arts* (Hall and Whannel, 1964). Under Whannel's stewardship the BFI Education Department became a significant centre for the development of film studies and film theory, a movement that found an influential platform with the launch of the BFI-sponsored journal *Screen* in 1969 and the subsequent importation of new conceptual frameworks organized around semiotic and psychoanalytic categories. By the time *The Popular Arts* was published, however, the focus of public and political debate had already shifted substantially to television and its impact on social life and attitudes, particularly among children and young people.

In 1958, the German-born social psychologist Hilde Himmelweit and her collaborators at the LSE published *Television and the Child* (Himmelweit, Oppenheim and Vince, 1958), the first comprehensive research study conducted in Britain, funded by the Nuffield Foundation. With 'Teddy Boys' brawling in the streets, however, political attention was becoming increasingly preoccupied with the possible links between television and teenage delinquency. In 1961 the Home Secretary convened a conference to discuss the issue. This led to the formation of a committee to investigate further, chaired by the Vice Chancellor of Leicester University who then asked James Halloran, teaching in the University's adult education department and having just published a critical evaluation of the media (Halloran, 1963), to act as Secretary. Alongside collating existing materials, Halloran directed an original research study that opposed the simple direct 'effects' model and reasserted that delinquency was rooted in social conditions and inequalities (Halloran, Brown and Chaney, 1970). When the committee completed its work in 1966, the University launched the Centre for Mass Communication Research under Halloran's directorship, to look more generally at the organization and impact of contemporary media.

The Centre's first major study examined the production, organization and reception of news coverage of the major anti-Vietnam War demonstration in London in October 1967 (Halloran, Elliott and Murdock, 1970), presenting it as an interlocking process of textual and social construction. The analysis of newsroom routines drew on Phillip Elliott's pioneering ethnography of the making of a television documentary series (Elliott, 1972) and laid the ground for a major comparative study of news making (Golding and Elliott, 1979). Work on the social and class basis of audience interpretation was followed up in studies of youth cultures (Murdock and Phelps, 1973) and racism (Hartmann and Husband, 1974), while analysis of media constructions of contentious events and groups was later developed in research on representations of welfare claimants (Golding and Middleton, 1982) and terrorism (Schlesinger, Murdock and Elliott, 1983).

The changing relations between the media and political culture were also a major focus of the work being done in the second foundational research center, though from a different direction. In 1958, the Granada Group, which had secured one of the first wave of franchises to operate commercial television in the north of England, funded a Television Research Fellowship at Leeds University to explore the medium's political influence. The General Election of 1959, the first to allow television coverage of campaigning, was an obvious choice of topic and in collaboration with Denis McQuail, the inaugural Fellow, Joseph Trenaman, drew on his experience of conducting empirical research in the BBC's Further Education department to produce the first British study of mediated politics (Trenaman and McQuail, 1961). The issues raised were pursued by his successor, Jay Blumler, again in collaboration with McQuail, in a study of the next General Election, held in 1964 (Blumler and McQuail 1969). This study went beyond questions of influence to foreground the ways in which voters interacted with and deployed televised information. This version of the 'active audience' was later codified as the 'uses and gratifications' approach and became an important current in the Leeds Centre's future work (Blumler and Katz, 1974).

While the Leeds and Leicester centers provided institutional bases for research, interest in the organization and impact of media was also gathering momentum elsewhere in British academia, particularly within sociology. First, it was attracting scholars interested in the sociology of organizations and occupations with Jeremy Tunstall's successive investigations of advertising workers (1964), lobby correspondents (1970b) and specialist journalists (1974), and Tom Burns' (1977) interview-based study of BBC culture. Second, the connections between the 'manufacture of news', the demonization of delinquency and the creation of 'moral panics', which Stanley Cohen had opened up in his pioneering work on the media coverage of the Mod–Rocker riots (Cohen, 1972), became a central focus within the re-analysis of policing and justice being developed by the critical criminologists grouped around the National Deviancy Conference (see Cohen and Young, 1973). Third, in 1974, the group around John Eldridge in the sociology department at Glasgow University embarked on a sustained interrogation of news as a system of misrepresentation. The first outcome, *Bad News* (Glasgow Media Group, 1976), a controversial analysis of the coverage of trade unions, was followed by a succession of studies of other areas and the creation of the Glasgow Media Group as an organizational umbrella.

The other major tradition of work feeding into the first phase of media studies' development came from literary studies and found its main institutional base in the Centre for Contemporary Cultural Studies which Richard Hoggart had established in 1964 within the English Department at Birmingham University. It was launched to pursue the project announced in his landmark book, *The Uses of Literacy* (Hoggart, 1957), of exploring the sources, direction and meaning of cultural change in contemporary Britain. Under the intellectual leadership of Stuart Hall, who had been appointed to the staff and became Director on Hoggart's departure to UNESCO, investigating the media's role in change took the Centre's work in several directions. First, it explored the dynamic encounters between media artefacts and everyday practices. This was pursued both through text-based analysis, exemplified by early work on the *Daily Mirror's* construction of its readers (Smith, 1975) and more ethnographically grounded studies of youth subcultures (Willis, 1978; Hall and Jefferson, 1975) and the role of experiential resources in structuring viewers' responses to television (Morley, 1980). Second, building on the analysis of 'moral panics', center members investigated the way a series of street 'muggings' had been handled in the local Birmingham press, focusing on the structural relations between the media and its 'powerful' sources and opening up "the neglected question of the *ideological role* of the media" in a society confronting the politics of 'race' and the legacy of empire (Hall et al., 1978: 59). With the translation of the influential Marxist reformulations of Antonio Gramsci and Louis Althusser, both of which appeared in 1971 (Gramsci, 1971; Althusser, 1971), questions of ideology became a major focus of debate. These conceptual reorientations coincided with the arrival in translation of Roland Barthes' *Myth Today* (Barthes, 1971). His attractive and powerful semiotic approach to uncovering the ideological constructions concealed below the surface of popular media forms was greeted by enthusiasm as an alternative to the home-grown variant of close reading and became hugely influential.

The resurgence of Marxism also coincided with the growth of critiques of popular media informed by the feminist and anti-racist movements, fueling a renewed interest in the mediated reproduction of stereotypical conceptions of femininity and ethnic difference. Angela McRobbie's pioneering work on the culture of teenage girls' magazines at the Birmingham Centre (McRobbie, 1991) and Charles Husband's work on 'race' and media at Leicester (Husband, 1975) joined a growing body of research that established work on the stereotyping and denigration of minorities as a central and continuing focus within media studies.

At the same time, a re-engagement with Marxism was shaping the emerging current of work around a critical political economy of media being developed by Graham Murdock and Peter Golding (1974) at the Leicester Centre and by Nicholas Garnham, who had moved from the BBC to head the media studies programme at the then Polytechnic of Central London, later to become the University of Westminster (Garnham, 1979). Critical political economy was already well established in North America, but the British variant was distinguished by its greater attention to public cultural investment as a counter to commercialization and corporate reach, a position that produced a qualified defence of public service broadcasting rooted conceptually in Jürgen Habermas' theory of the public sphere (Garnham, 1986) and models of cultural citizenship (Murdock, 1999).

The Westminster group also played a leading role in developing a critical re-reading of British media history with analyses of the capitalist control of the press (Curran, 1977) and a 'people's' history of the BBC (Scannell and Cardiff, 1991).

Grounding the critique of contemporary media historically was also central to the work of Raymond Williams who, though working largely alone, was a major influence on the early development of both cultural studies and media studies. His interest in media came from his years working as an adult education tutor (McIlroy and Westwood, 1993) and his major survey of Britain's transition to modernity, the *Long Revolution* (Williams, 1961), assigned popular communication a central role in cultivating a mass democratic culture. But he saw this promise repeatedly stalled by the interests of advertising and the concentration of commercial power, themes he returned to in the detailed analysis he presented in *Communications* (Williams, 1962) published the following year. He returned to these themes a decade later in arguably his most influential book within media studies, *Television: Technology and Cultural Form* (Williams, 1974). Written during a sabbatical stay in the United States, it grappled with the full force of a commercialized media culture, introducing the idea of 'flow' to signal the seamless integration of promotion messages into the experience of viewing. He also insisted, in a powerful critique of technological determinism, that analysis must always start not from the properties of new machines but from the social conditions and power relations which shape their development and deployment.

Although the foundational phase of British media studies focused primarily on national issues and concerns, there was also a growing engagement with the mounting international debate around the role of media as an agent of cultural domination and 'Americanization'. Oliver Boyd-Barrett, at the Open University, built on his doctoral work on the role of the major western news agencies in reproducing a highly asymmetric global flow of news and information (Boyd-Barrett, 1976) to develop an influential general conception of media imperialism (Boyd-Barrett, 1977). Peter Golding, at the Leicester Centre, drew on his empirical study of news organizations in Nigeria to develop an analysis of development communication (Golding, 1974) and Jeremy Tunstall entered the debate on cultural imperialism initiated in the United States by Herbert Schiller's influential *Mass Communications and American Empire* (Schiller, 1969) with a critical riposte, *The Media are American* (Tunstall, 1977), presenting popular media made in the USA in a more positive light. These concerns came to a head in the acrimonious debate within UNESCO around the committee chaired by the veteran Irish politician Sean MacBride, which began working in December 1977, pitching American corporate interests against calls for a new and more equitable 'world information order'. James Halloran of the Leicester Centre acted as a consultant to the committee, contributing position papers summarizing the available research (UNESCO, 1980). The *Financial Times* articulated a wide consensus within the media industries in dismissing the commission's final report as "gobbledygook". Its truculent restatement of the entrenched commercial 'free press' position that "attacking the idea of profit-making media is attacking the diversity of information and opinion" (Rutherford, 1980: 12) underlined the distrust of the critiques being developed in academic analysis that was already prevalent among media practitioners.

Consolidations

Whereas the formative phase in media studies growth as an area of research and postgraduate activity had been centered in the solid provincial 'red brick' universities, the major movement into undergraduate teaching occurred in the second tier of the higher education system, the Polytechnics.

Initial expansion took place under the auspices of the Council for National Academic Awards (CNAA), launched in 1965 to supervise the provision of degrees within the polytechnic sector. The traditional universities were slow to recognize either the potential or the legitimacy of emerging areas of study, a disaffection buttressed in the case of media studies by the continuing recognition that broadcasting persistently preferred Oxbridge graduates, or at least those grounded in traditional disciplines. The resulting gap in undergraduate provision offered polytechnics an opportunity to capitalize on the sheer enthusiasm for the subject matter among students.

The first undergraduate media studies degree in Britain was launched at the Polytechnic of Central London in 1975. It was headed by Nicholas Garnham who had followed a well-worn path from English at Cambridge to BBC producer and assembled other renegades from public school and Oxbridge backgrounds attracted by the relative openness of the new field and its resistance to established disciplinary boundaries. They drew on their diverse intellectual trainings to forge a distinctive 'school' of research (Curran, 2004) which provided the starting point for the first dedicated British journal in the field, *Media, Culture and Society*, launched in 1979 under Garnham's editorship. The Westminster initiative was followed by a succession of programmes in the field approved by the CNAA, installing media studies as a distinctive feature in the higher education provided by polytechnics.

Other leading figures in establishing media studies followed Garnham in moving from the industry to the academy. Roger Silverstone had been a researcher and producer at the BBC and London Weekend Television before returning to the LSE in his late twenties to write a doctorate on television's narrative structures (Silverstone, 1981). He went on to draw on his practical experience of working in the industry to produce a major ethnography of science programme making (Silverstone, 1985) and later built on his interest in the media in everyday life to direct a research group at Brunel University that played a key role in launching work on the social impact of new technologies (Silverstone and Hirsch, 1992). He later moved back to the LSE as the founding head of the newly established media programme. After graduating in law from Oxford, Brian Winston worked on Granada Television's current affairs series *World in Action* before becoming Research Director on the first 'Bad News' study. In 1985 he won an Emmy Award for documentary scriptwriting and went on to write widely cited books on the history and ethics of documentary film (Winston, 1995, 2000). He has headed both the Westminster and Cardiff departments and was an early contributor to the debate on the dynamics of technological change with an influential analysis of successive innovations in media (Winston, 1998). This pattern, of gamekeepers turning poachers, did little to allay the industries' distrust of the field.

Outside the undergraduate system, media studies has long been a popular option with students attending evening and weekend classes offered by university extra mural departments. Like Raymond Williams, a number of the key figures in establishing the field had begun their careers in adult education: Hoggart at Hull, Blumler at Ruskin College and Halloran at Leicester. But in 1971 the launch of the Open University opened a new national avenue for adults wishing to study at home in their spare time, taking courses that led to a degree. In 1977 the OU launched a major course in media studies, 'Mass Communication and Society' (Open University, 1997). The course materials were supplemented by two major 'readers' offered on general sale, by Curran, Gurevitch and Woollacott (1977) and by Gurevitch, Bennett, Curran and Woollacott (1982). Both carried contributions from leading British figures in the field (including Stuart Hall and Jay Blumler) alongside chapters written by the course team. Their appearance was followed by the publication of two textbooks that codified the distinctive characteristics of the field as it was emerging in Britain. *Power Without Responsibility*, co-authored by James Curran, offered a critical account of the history of the British press and broadcasting (Curran and Seaton, 1981). *Mass Communication Theory*, authored by Denis McQuail (1983), provided a comprehensive review of research evidence and conceptual debate. McQuail, who had moved to the University of Amsterdam, was also instrumental in launching the second major dedicated British journal, the *European Journal of Communication*, in 1986. Despite being joined by a growing library of competitors, both these founding texts have gone through multiple editions and updates and remain in print as obligatory fixtures on degree reading lists.

The sense that a distinctive new area was emerging with its own unique intellectual configuration was further cemented by the creation of a national subject association for cultural, communication and media studies in the early 1990s, a move fostered by the CNAA.

The CNAA was abolished when the polytechnics and the universities were fused into a single sector in 1992, ceding control over the introduction of new degrees in the 'new' universities (as the polytechnics had been renamed) to individual institutions, accelerating decisions and giving an extra push to the expansion of the field.

Faced with the continued vitality of the field, some of the 'old' universities, who had initially been reluctant to add media studies to their roster of general undergraduate degrees, belatedly entered the field, a move cemented by the establishment of the programme at the London School of Economics in 2003. Resistance remained, however, with the elite Russell Group of universities issuing guidance in 2011 advising schools and parents not to encourage their children to take up media studies (Young, 2011). At the same time, belatedly recognizing the centrality of communication systems to economic, political and social life, Oxford University established major research centers in core areas of debate – the Oxford Internet Institute in 2001 and the Reuters Institute for the Study of Journalism in 2006.

Data on the number of academic staff now working in the field is hard to determine precisely. However, figures published after the last national Research Assessment Exercise in 2008 showed that 425 academic staff were submitted in communication, cultural and media studies, though this figure excludes staff specializing in the field submitted to other panels. Even so, compared to the 2,354 staff submitted in biological sciences and the more than 4,000 submitted for both engineering and business and management, media studies remains a small component of the university system.

Salutary also is data about research funding in the field. Unlike some other countries, little funding for media research within UK academia is provided by the industries, leaving researchers heavily dependent on public money from the research councils and the EU and funding from charities. Again precise figures are hard to

Table 4.1 Students Enrolled in Media Studies and Journalism in UK Universities

	Media Studies	*Journalism*
1996/7	5918	1687
2001/2	14045	3665
2006/7	24160	6935
2012/13	24850	10640

Source: Research Assessment Exercise (RAE) 2008, *Report Data, Panel* O: http://www.rae.ac.uk/pubs/2009/ov

obtain but the same RAE data for the period 2001–2008 showed that communication, cultural and media studies attracted a total of £17.6 million, as against £45.4 million in English and £294.5 million in psychology, both important contributors to the field (see Table 4.2). The annual £2.51 million average spend on academic research in cultural and media studies in this period was however dwarfed by the amounts spent outside the universities, with the main regulator, Ofcom, spending £5.06 million on audience research, and turnover in the market research industry in 2007 reaching £1,800 million.

These figures point to a relatively modest institutional base within the academy but this has not silenced long-standing political attacks on media studies, amplified by popular media commentary that dismisses media studies as an area that has no legitimate place in a university.

Dismissals

Much of this commentary has assumed, without argument, that because some of the objects of media analysis are ephemeral and of contestable aesthetic value, their systematic study must be both trivial and easy. This position was put with particular force in 1993 by the then Minister for Education, John Patten, who announced that:

> I have ordered an enquiry within the Department of Education to try and find out why some young people are turned off by the laboratory, yet flock to the seminar room for a fix of one of those contemporary pseudo-religions like media studies … For the weaker minded, going into a cultural Disneyland has an obvious appeal.
>
> (Patten, 1993: 14)

Almost two decades on, Michael Gove, the Secretary of State for Education (and a former *Times* journalist), restated this position, arguing that:

> The current problem with subjects like media studies relates to the way … They encourage schools to push a subject which, currently, actually limits opportunities … some schools still steer students towards subjects such as media studies because they know it is easier to secure a pass.
>
> (Gove, 2010)

Table 4.2 Research Funding in Selected Different Subject Areas 2001–8 (£m)

Subject	Research Council Funding	Industry Funding	Total Funding
Communication, Cultural and Media Studies	7.3	0.9	17.6
English Language/Literature	28.8	0.8	45.4
Art and Design	26.3	15.7	110.7
Psychology	119.3	16.5	294.5
Biological Sciences	787.1	69.3	1,959
Civil Engineering	77.6	25.6	1,946

Source: *The Times*, February 2008

This supposed 'push' towards media studies has not however produced large numbers of entrants for school examinations. In 2013, of 850,000 students who sat the GCSE A level examinations for those who stay on after the compulsory leaving age, just 1,767 (0.2%) took communication studies while 29,112 (3.4%) sat media studies. Nor is the assumption that media studies is an easy option within the school curriculum supported by the evidence. Of the 862,000 school students who sat A levels in 2013, 53% obtained the highest grades (A*, A or B). This figure drops to 42.4% among media studies students and comparison with other subjects, as illustrated in Table 4.4, suggests that obtaining these highest grades is more difficult in this field than in many others, undermining popular claims in headlines that, "A-level media studies is soft option for students, exam watchdog reports" (*The Times*, Feb 2008).

Nor is media studies attracting the 'floods' of undergraduates portrayed in popular and political commentary. The number of university students enrolled in media studies or journalism courses is shown in Table 4.1.

Growth has been substantial, with media studies showing a four-fold increase between 1996 and 2012, and Table 4.1 does not include the 30,485 students enrolled in 'Mass Communications and Documentation' degrees in 2012, one of many categorization difficulties posed in understanding such data since many of these enrollments are in librarianship and information sciences. But in a higher education student population of about two and a half million, these are not large numbers. The biggest growth areas have been in business and administration studies and in biological sciences, each growing at twice the rate of media and communications studies.

Table 4.3 Numbers Employed in UK as in 2011 Census

Occupation Group	Numbers
Advertising and Public Relations Directors	27.5
Journalists, Newspaper and Periodical Editors	82.8
Public Relations Professionals	47.4
Artists	54
Authors, Writers and Translators	77.3
Actors, Entertainers, Presenters	60.1
Photographers, Audio-Visual and Broadcasting Equipment Operators	81.6

Source: Office of National Statistics (2011) *EMP16, Employment by Occupation*: http://www.ons.gov.uk/ons/rel/lms/labour-force-survey-employment-status-by-occupation/index.html

Table 4.4 Results for Students sitting GCSE A levels in Various Subjects, 2013

Subject	% with A*, A or B
Art & Design	57.8
Biology	52.8
Business Studies	43.0
Chemistry	60.7
Classics	65.3
Computing	36.8
Design and Technology	43.3
Economics	61.6
English	48.6
French	68.8
Geography	57.9
History	56.3
Mathematics	65.2
Media, Film/TV Studies	42.4
Physics	54.6
Political Studies	58.6
All Subjects	52.9

Source: Joint Council for Qualifications: http://www.jcq.org.uk/examination-results/a-levels

Nonetheless, political commentary has frequently asserted that there are too many media studies graduates and that the courses they have followed do not equip them for employment.

This argument sits uneasily alongside figures for the expansion of the 'cultural industries' which a recent government study suggests now employs 8.5% of the working population and grew by 9.4% in 2012 alone (DCMS, 2014). The 'cultural industries' are wider than the 'media industries' and cover IT software and computer services, but they also include 465,000 jobs in advertising and marketing, 266,000 in film, TV, video, radio and photography and 255,000 in publishing. The range and extent of media-related occupations open to media studies graduates is confirmed by figures from the UK 2011 census, shown in Table 4.3.

The decade since the 2001 census has seen a 42% rise in PR professionals and an equivalent 41% rise in journalists, though, as commentators have pointed out, this figure obscures important shifts in the nature of employment. The economic downturn has led to major job losses, especially in provincial journalism, and many of the new jobs are, on closer inspection, part-time, casualized, and involve a high proportion of unpaid overtime and large numbers of low or unpaid internships (see Ponsford, 2014).

Intensified competition for graduate-level jobs and the precarious nature of many of the jobs on offer is increasingly characteristic of employment in the media industries as a whole, but it is not confined to them. Securing employment is becoming more difficult for all students in a period of economic downturn and rapidly increasing graduate numbers in the population. Nonetheless, a report issued in 2013 showed that media and information studies graduates had an employment rate second only to medicine and ahead of, among others, graduates in technology, business and finance, engineering and computer science (ONS, 2013). These figures suggest that far from being ill-fitted to the demands of the modern economy, the interdisciplinary nature of media studies, with its requirement to work across boundaries and create innovative configurations of knowledge and application, is better able to develop the skills that employers value than subjects with more resilient borders and a narrower focus. The cultivation of general intellectual and analytical capacities, which can be applied to a range of occupations outside the media as well within them, has, however, always sat uneasily alongside demands for more precisely tailored vocational training. This demand has long roots.

Practices

The rapid rise in the number and circulations of newspapers in the late nineteenth century generated a rising demand for journalists, prompting continuous dispute about their professional status and demeanor and the training required to prepare them for their central role as essential brokers of public information and knowledge in a democratic polity. Concern was fueled by the rise of new, cheap dailies and their perceived drift towards trivialization. In response, the Institute of Journalists (formed in 1888), promoted a high-minded sense of the vocational aspirations for its members and proposed an examination which would require candidates to have a knowledge of English history and literature and an understanding of the first book of Euclid. The tension between the requirements of professional training and the need for media practitioners to be generally knowledgeable and analytically able embedded in this project has characterized debates ever since. The challenge was met first at London University which launched a Diploma in Journalism in 1919 that continued for 20 years, with examinations for it introduced in 1927. Such was the authority of the course that the part-time lecturer F. J. Mansfield, of *The Times*, turned his lecture notes into two books that remained in print as training primers for 40 years (Herbert, 2000). By the 1930s London University was providing facilities for a degree course in the subject, interrupted only by the war (Bainbridge, 1984: 55–57).

In 1952, following a critical Royal Commission on the Press, the National Council for the Training of Journalists (NCTJ) was launched to manage and accredit professional qualifications. Training was initially concentrated at post-graduate level, with an intensive course giving graduates, who had studied general subjects for their first degrees, a certificate of proficiency attesting to their mastery of practical professional skills. The influential Cardiff postgraduate course began in 1970. Like that at City University, begun in 1976, it was propelled initially by the involvement of a major figure from the industry but, as Herbert notes, "even at this stage the emphasis was not on preparing students for jobs but giving them an academic introduction to journalism studies" (Herbert, 2000: 114).

Graduates were still a minority of the journalistic workforce then, most practitioners having trained 'on the job', starting out on local and provincial papers and hoping to work their passage to Fleet Street and a position on a national title. With the introduction of undergraduate degrees in journalism, however, the number of graduates aiming to enter the profession increased significantly. By 2000 there were four universities (Bournemouth, Staffordshire, Central Lancashire and Sheffield) with BA Journalism programmes accredited by the NCTJ. There are now 21 courses at 15 universities and, as Table 4.1 shows, in 2012 they were enrolling over 10,000 students, a more than four-fold increase on 1996. This development has not been universally welcomed within the profession. A number of senior journalists have dismissed extended undergraduate study as surplus to requirements, with the BBC Radio 4 *Today* programme presenter John Humphrys denigrating the "idea of three years at university doing journalism [as] utterly barmy" and the former Sun editor, Kelvin McKenzie, claiming that, "There's nothing you can learn in three years studying the media at university that you can't learn in just one month on a local paper" (Curran, 2013; see also Thornham and O'Sullivan, 2004; Barker 1997).

As we noted earlier, this dismissive rhetoric runs directly counter to governmental promotion of the 'creative industries' as one of the key nodes of future growth and innovation in a post-industrial economy. This push has placed media studies at the center of a more general reconstruction of universities around economic priorities and business interests.

Utilitarian turns

The traditional view of the university has presented it as "a place in which the pursuits of truth and understanding are given special protection, not to the exclusion of useful or socially relevant subjects, but not principally in their service either" (Graham, 2002: 165). At the heart of this conception is a spirited defence of independent inquiry and critical analysis against the claims of immediate applicability (Collini, 2012: 55). A New Labour government report in 2009, however, saw the role of universities very differently, arguing for a "much greater use of universities for management and leadership training [and] enhanced support for … skills that underwrite this country's competitive advantages … [and are] central to this country's economic performance in the twenty-first century." (BIS, 2009: 12). This vision was reaffirmed in the Wilson Report on university–business co-operation, which argued that since "the economic and social prosperity of the UK depends upon a healthy knowledge-based economy" universities need to be "an integral part of the skills and innovation supply chain to business" (Wilson, 2012: 1). The following year, the Witty Report reaffirmed that "universities should assume an explicit responsibility for facilitating economic growth" and that all universities should have stronger incentives to embrace this "enhanced Third Mission" alongside teaching and research (BIS, 2013: 6). These statements point to a fundamental antithesis between a view of universities as "driven by the demands of humanity" and the struggle to understand better the forces reshaping contemporary lives and collective futures, and funding policies directed to "the conformities necessary to the efficiencies that maximise industrial growth" (Docherty, 2011: 161)

This tension has become increasingly evident within media studies. On the one hand, as we argued at the outset, a properly critical understanding of the organization and impact of changing communications systems is essential to any comprehensive analysis of economic, political and social change. On the other hand, recent years have seen this commitment to open inquiry come under increasing pressure from the utilitarian turn in government policy. In part this has been fostered by the interests of the Sector Skills Councils, anxious to influence curricula in a more vocational direction and to accredit appropriate programmes and training. As one such body put it in their annual report, "We have worked closely with employers and training providers to ensure training meets the needs of our industries ... We invested £6.5m directly into creative media training programmes to nurture the skills and talent and business leaders of the future" (Creative Skillset, 2012/13: 41). Yet, as many commentators point out, even the most vocational and utilitarian of conceptions of media education recognize that the very rapid changes under way in all of the industries likely to employ such graduates render skills-specific training of very short-term value. And, as we argued earlier, the diversity of employment directions taken by media studies graduates suggests that an unduly focused or skills-based higher education would short-change them on even the most utilitarian of terms.

The future of media studies as a general university subject is also under challenge from the government decision to privilege teaching in the STEM subjects (science, technology, engineering and mathematics). While financial support in these areas has been ring-fenced, public funding for degrees in arts, humanities and social sciences has been withdrawn, leaving media studies degrees reliant on student fees, which have been increased to unforeseen levels, with most now hovering around £9,000 a year for undergraduates. There are fears that this new market economy will reproduce the general dynamics of markets, with students coming to see themselves as consumers and customers and gravitating towards courses that promise the best prospects of immediate employment.

Engagements

Media studies has sought to not only understand communication systems but also, on occasion, to change them. Much British work has questioned prevailing practices but some scholars in the field have gone beyond academic critique to look for ways of influencing public policy. This has taken a variety of forms. Some have organized manifestos advancing alternatives (see e.g. Curran, 1978). Others have accepted invitations to contribute to governmental inquiries, a strategy exemplified by Jay Blumler's trenchant critique of American commercial television, prepared in 1985 for the Peacock Committee on Financing the BBC, which was actively considering alternatives to public funding (Blumler, 1991). Others again have taken advantage of new political spaces opening up to become involved in developing alternative policies. Nicholas Garnham played a leading role as a consultant on cultural policies to the radical, Labour-led, Greater London Council in the early 1980s (see Garnham, 2005). Still others have moved from academia to regulatory agencies. Guy Phelps, an early member of the Leicester Centre, drew on his scholarly interest in film censorship (Phelps, 1975) in his later role as Assistant Director of the British Board of Film Classification, where he was involved in debates around the Board's perceived 'over permissiveness'. Others again have aligned themselves with movements to established alternative media or joined lobby and campaigning groups. What unites these diverse initiatives is a practical commitment to the critical and questioning stance that has informed the development of British media studies more generally but which has also played a central role is sustaining the suspicion of the field frequently displayed by media professionals and conservative politicians.

Futures

The account offered here presents a paradox. On the one hand, media studies in Britain continues to be defined by its intellectual dynamism. The formative phase in its development mapped out a distinctive general orientation that saw communication as an indelibly social and relational process in which mediated meanings are continually being constructed, reconstructed and challenged by producers and audiences in conditions profoundly shaped by wider patterns of power, inequality and contest. This basic conception has been elaborated on and refined as new frameworks and methodological approaches have emerged and research has grappled with the issues presented by the transformative processes set in motion by the convergence of digitalization, marketization and globalization. The results have commanded worldwide currency. At the same time, as we have seen, commitment to open inquiry has come under increasing pressure from the new utilitarianism and the push to commercialize universities, ensuring that the future of media studies will continue to be contested.

Acknowledgments

The authors wish to acknowledge the assistance of Karen Williamson in the preparation of this chapter.

Further reading

For additional work in these areas, Martin Conboy's *Journalism: A Critical History* (2004) offers an exploration of the historiography of media developments that correspond with the advancement of media studies in this chapter. James Curran's edited volume *Media and Society* (2010) collects together recent scholarship in key areas of contemporary concern. Roger Silverstone's (1999) *Why Study the Media?* demonstrates the value of media scholarship; Graeme Turner does the same for cultural studies in his book *British Cultural Studies: An Introduction* (2002). Finally, Janet Wasko, Graham Murdock and Helena Sousa's edited volume *The Handbook of Political Economy of Communications* (2011) offers an authoritative survey of one of the most influential strands within British work.

References

Althusser, L. (1971) *Lenin and Philosophy and Other Essays*. New York: Monthly Review Press.
Bainbridge, C. (ed.) (1984) *One Hundred Years of Journalism: Social Aspects of the Press*. London: Macmillan.

Barker, M. (1997) "On the Problems of Being a Trendy Travesty". In M. Barker and J. Petley (eds.) *Ill Effects: The Media/Violence Debate*. London: Routledge (pp. 202–24).

Barthes, R. (1971) *Myth Today*. London: Fontana.

BIS (Department of Business, Innovation and Skills) (2009) *Higher Ambitions: The Future of Universities in a Knowledge Economy*. London: BIS.

——(2013) *Encouraging a British Invention Revolution: Sir Andrew Witty's Review of Universities and Growth*. London: BIS.

Blumler, J. G. (1991) "Television in the United States: Funding Sources and Programming Consequences". In J. G. Blumler and T. J. Nossiter (eds.) *Broadcasting Finance in Transition: A Comparative Handbook*. Oxford: Oxford University Press (pp. 41–94).

Blumler, J. G. and Katz, E. (eds.) (1974) *The Uses of Mass Communication*. London: Sage Publications.

Blumler, J. G. and McQuail, D. (1969) *Television in Politics: Its Uses and Influence*. London: Faber and Faber.

Bolas, T. (2009) *Screen Education: From Film Appreciation to Media Studies*. Bristol: Intellect Books.

Boyd-Barrett, J. O. (1976) *The World-Wide News Agencies*. Ph.D Thesis, Open University.

——(1977) "Media Imperialism: Towards an International Framework for the Analysis of Media Systems". In J. Curran, M. Gurevitch and J. Woollacott (eds.) *Mass Communication and Society*. London: Edward Arnold (pp. 116–35).

Burns, T. (1977) *The BBC: Public Institution and Private World*. Basingstoke: Macmillan.

Chibnall, S. (1977) *Law and Order News: An Analysis of Crime Reporting in the British Press*. London: Tavistock Publications.

Cohen, S. (1972) *Folk Devils and Moral Panics: The Creation of the Mods and Rockers*. London: MacGibbon and Kee.

Cohen, S. and Young, J. (eds.) (1973) *The Manufacture of News: Deviance, Social Problems and the Mass Media*. London: Constable.

Collini, S. (2012) *What Are Universities For?* London and New York: Penguin Books.

Conboy, M. (2004) *Journalism: A Critical History*. London: Sage.

Creative Skillset (2012/13) Annual Report. Retrieved from http://www.creativeskillset.org/creativeskillset/publications/article_9083_1.asp

Curran, J. (1977) "Capitalism and Control of the Press,1800–1975". In J. Curran, M. Gurevitch and J. Woollacott (eds.) *Mass Communication and Society*. London: Arnold (pp. 195–230).

——(ed.) (1978) *The British Press: A Manifesto*. Basingstoke: Macmillan.

——(2004) "The Rise of the Westminster School". In A. Calabrese and C. Sparks (eds.) *Toward a Political Economy of Culture: Capitalism and Communication in the Twenty-First Century*. Oxford: Rowman and Littlefield Publishers Inc. (pp. 13–40).

——(ed.) (2010) *Media and Society* (Fifth Edition). London: Bloomsbury Academic.

——(2013) "*Mickey Mouse Squeaks Back: Defending Media Studies*". Keynote paper at the Annual Conference of Media, Communication and Cultural Studies Association, Derry 2013. Retrieved from http://www.meccsa.org.uk/news/mickey-mouse-squeaks-back-defending-media-studies/

Curran, J. and Seaton, J. (1981) *Power Without Responsibility: The Press and Broadcasting in Britain*. London: Fontana.

Curran, J., Gurevitch, M. and Woollacott, J. (eds.) (1977) *Mass Communication and Society*. London: Edward Arnold.

DCMS (Department for Culture, Media and Sport) (2014) *Creative Industries Economic Estimates*. London: DCMS.

de Botton, A. (2014) *The News: A User's Manual*. London: Hamish Hamilton.

Docherty, T. (2011) *For The University: Democracy and the Future of the Institution*. London: Bloomsbury.

Elliott, P. R. (1972) *The Making of a TV Series: A Case Study in the Sociology of Culture*. London: Constable.
Garnham, N. (1979) "Contribution to a Political Economy of Mass Communciation". Originally published in the first issue of *Media, Culture and Society*. Reprinted in N. Garnham, *Capitalism and Communication*. London: Sage.
——(1986) "The Media and the Public Sphere". In P. Golding, G. Murdock and P. Schlesinger (eds.) *Communicating Politics: Mass Communication and the Political Process*. Leicester: Leicester University Press (pp. 37–53).
——(2005) "From Cultural Industries to Creative Industries: An Analysis of the Implications of the 'Creative Industries' Approach to Arts and Media Policy in the United Kingdom". *International Journal of Cultural Policy*, 11(1), 15–29.
Glasgow Media Group (1976) *Bad News Volume 1*. London: Routledge and Kegan Paul.
Golding, P. (1974) "Media Role in National Development". *Journal of Communication*, 24(3), 39–53.
Golding, P. and Elliott, P. (1979) *Making the News*. London: Addison-Wesley Longman.
Golding, P. and Middleton, S. (1982) *Images of Welfare*. London: Martin Robertson.
Gove, M. (2010) Response to questions on Matthew Taylor blog. Retrieved from http://www.matthewtaylorsblog.com/public-policy/michael-goves-response
Graham, G. (2002) *Universities: The Recovery of an Idea*. London: Imprint Academic.
Gramsci, A. (1971) *Selections From the Prison Notebooks*. London: Lawrence and Wishart Ltd Co.
Gurevitch, M., Bennett, T., Curran, J. and Woollacott, J. (eds.) (1982) *Culture, Society and the Media*. London: Methuen.
Hall, S. and Jefferson, T. (eds) (1975) *Resistance Through Rituals: Youth Subcultures in Post-War Britain*. London: Hutchinson.
Hall, S. and Whannel, P. (1964) *The Popular Arts*. London: Hutchinson.
Hall, S., Chritcher, C., Jefferson, T., Clarke, J. and Roberts, B. (1978) *Policing the Crisis: Mugging, the State and Law and Order*. Harmondsworth: Macmillan Education.
Halloran, J. (1963) *Control or Consent: A Study of the Promise of Mass Communication*. London: Sheed and Ward.
Halloran, J. D., Brown, R. L. and Chaney, D. (1970) *Television and Delinquency*. Leicester: Leicester University Press.
Halloran, J. D., Elliott. P. and Murdock, G. (1970) *Demonstrations and Communication: A Case Study*. Harmondsworth: Penguin Books.
Hartmann, P. and Husband, C. (1974) *Racism and the Mass Media: A Study of the Role of the Mass Media in the Formation of White Beliefs and Attitudes in Britain*. London: Davis-Poynter.
Herbert, J. (2000) "The Changing Face of Journalism Education in the UK". *Asia Pacific Media Educator*, 1(8), 113–23. Retrieved from http://ro.uow.edu.au/apme/vol1/iss8/10
Himmelweit, H. T., Oppenheim, A. N. and Vince, P. (1958) *Television and the Child: An Empirical Study of the Effect of Television on the Young*. Oxford: Oxford University Press.
Hoggart, R. (1957) *The Uses of Literacy*. Harmondsworth: Penguin Books.
Hubble, N. (2006) *Mass-Observation and Everyday Life*. Houndsmill, Basingstoke: Palgrave Macmillan.
Husband, C. (ed.) (1975) *White Media and Black Britain*. London: Arrow Books.
Klingender, F. D. and Legg, S. (1937) *Money Behind the Screen*. London: Lawrence and Wishart.
Leavis, F. R. and Thompson, D. (1933) *Culture and Environment: The Training of Critical Awareness*. London: Chatto and Windus.
Leavis, Q. D. (1932) *Fiction and the Reading Public*. London: Chatto and Windus.
McIlroy, J. and Westwood, S. (eds.) (1993) *Border Country: Raymond Williams in Adult Education*. Leicester: National Institute of Continuing Education.

McQuail, D. (1972) *Mass Communication Theory: An Introduction*. London: Sage.

McRobbie, A. (1991) *Feminism and Youth Culture: From Jackie to Just Seventeen*. Basingstoke: Macmillan.

Mayer, J. P. (1948) *British Cinemas and Their Audiences: Sociological Studies*. London: Denis Dobson.

Morley, D. (1980) *The 'Nationwide' Audience: Structure and Decoding*. London: BFI.

Murdock, G. (1999) "Rights and Representations: Public Discourse and Cultural Citizenship". In J. Gripsrud (ed.) *Television and Common Knowledge*. London: Routledge (pp. 7–17).

——(2002) "Media, Culture and Modern Times: Social Science Investigations". In K. Bruhn Jensen (ed.) *A Handbook of Media and Communication Research: Qualitative and Quantitative Methodologies*. London: Routledge (pp. 40–57).

Murdock, G. and Golding, P. (1974) "For a Political Economy of the Mass Media". In R. Miliband and J. Saville (eds.) *The Socialist Register 1973*. London: Merlin (pp. 205–34).

Murdock, G. and Phelps, G. (1973) *Mass Media and the Secondary School*. Basingstoke: Macmillan.

ONS (Office for National Statistics) (2013) *Graduates in the UK Labour Market 2013*. London: ONS.

Open University (1977) *Mass Communication and Society*. Milton Keynes: The Open University.

Patten, J. (1993) "Must Think Harder". *The Spectator*, 1 October, pp. 14–15.

Phelps, G. (1975) *Film Censorship*. London: Gollancz.

Ponsford, D. (2014) "Labour Force Survey suggests surge of 12,000 in number of journalists since 2009". Retrieved from http://www.pressgazette.co.uk/content/labour-force-survey-suggests-surge-12000-number-uk-journalists-2009

Richards, J. and Sheridan, D. (eds.) (1987) *Mass-Observation and the Movies*. London: Routledge and Kegan Paul.

Rutherford, M. (1980) "Newspeak with NWICO". *Financial Times*, 8 August, p. 12.

Scannell, P. and Cardiff, D. (1991) *A Social History of Broadcasting 1922–1939: Serving The Nation*. Oxford: Basil Blackwell.

Schiller, H. I. (1969) *Mass Communications and American Empire*. Boston, MA: Beacon Press.

Schlesinger, P. (1978) *Putting 'Reality' Together: BBC News*. London: Constable.

Schlesinger, P., Murdock, G. and Elliott, P. (1983) *Televising 'Terrorism': Political Violence in Popular Culture*. London: Comedia Publishing Group.

Silverstone, R. (1981) *The Meaning of Television: Myth and Narrative in Contemporary Culture*. London: William Heinemann.

——(1985) *Framing Science: The Making of a BBC Documentary*. London: BFI Publishing.

——(1999) *Why Study Media?* London: Sage.

Silverstone, R. and Hirsch, E. (1992) *Consuming Technologies: Media and Information in Domestic Space*. London: Routledge.

Smith, A. C. H. (1975) *Paper Voices: The Popular Press and Social Change 1935–1965*. London: Chatto and Windus.

Thompson, D. (1943) *Voice of Civilisation: An Enquiry into Advertising*. London: F. Muller.

Thornham, S. and O'Sullivan, T. (2004) "Chasing the Real: Employability and the Media Studies Curriculum". *Media, Culture & Society*, 26(5), 717–36.

Tracey, M. (1977) *The Production of Political Television*. London: Routledge and Kegan Paul.

Trenaman, J. M. and McQuail, D. (1961) *Television and the Political Image: A Study of the Impact of Television on the 1959 General Election*. London: Methuen.

Tunstall, J. (1964) *The Advertising Man in London Advertising Agencies*. London: Chapman Hall.

——(ed.) (1970a) *Media Sociology: A Reader*. London: Constable.

——(1970b) *The Westminster Lobby Correspondents: A Sociological Study of National Political Journalism*. London: Routledge and Kegan Paul.

——(1974) *Journalists at Work*. London: Sage.

——(1977) *The Media are American: Anglo-American Media in the World*. London: Constable.
Turner, G. (2002) *British Cultural Studies: An Introduction* (Third Edition). London: Routledge.
Wasko, J., Murdock, G. and Sousa, H. (eds.) (2011) *The Handbook of Political Economy of Communications*. Oxford: Wiley-Blackwell.
Williams, R. (1961) *The Long Revolution*. London: Chatto and Windus.
——(1962) *Communications*. Harmondsworth: Pelican Books.
——(1974) *Television: Technology and Cultural Form*. London: Fontana.
Willis, P. E. (1978) *Profane Culture*. London: Routledge and Kegan Paul.
Wilson, T. (2012) "A Review of Business-University Collaboration". London: Department for Business Innovation and Skills.
Winston, B. (1995) *Claiming the Real: The Griersonian Documentary and its Legitimation*. London: BFI Publishing.
——(1998) *Media,Technology and Society: A History From the Telegraph to the Internet*. London: Routledge.
——(2000) *Lies, Damn Lies and Documentaries*. London: BFI Publishing.
UNESCO (1980) *Many Voices, One World: Towards a More Just and More Efficient World Information and Communication Order*. London: Kogan Page.
Young, T. (2011) "It's official: If you do A-levels in Media Studies or Law you won't get into a top university". *The Daily Telegraph*, 4 February. Retrieved from http://blogs.telegraph.co.uk/news/tobyyoung/100074686/its-official-if-you-do-a-levels-in-media-studies-or-law-you-wont-get-into-a-top-university/

5
Media archaeology
From Turing to Abbey Road, Kentish radar stations to Bletchley Park

Jussi Parikka

British media history has many great stories to tell. It has been one of the biggest inspirations for a range of narratives and for scholars that have tried to decipher the main trends of the media of modernity; from the nineteenth-century establishment of standardized mail to the twentieth century Britain of the BBC that, for instance, for this author became a central symbol when he turned on the television in 1980s Finland. BBC content traveled across national boundaries, both in the structural form it provided for public broadcasting and through Bergerac and the FA Cup Finals over the years. British exports from television to microcomputing continued and have established such a status that writing Britain into media history is rather redundant. It is already there, and always was there; even before actual media technologies became subsumed into the consolidated consensus about media as mass media. Indeed, Britain was already there with its investment in transatlantic cables as well as its pioneering scientific inquiries in electricity and electromagnetism and its prehistories of computing from Babbage to Turing and so forth. Early on, British media history was already transnational, like the transatlantic cables and telegraph clicks. It is irreducible to a simple national story, and is more like something that presents an interesting case for consideration in relation to both the master narratives and the minor themes of media history.

In this chapter I will focus on the 'minor' aspect of media history and present a case for a different sort of narrativization of the past of media technologies. This is 'minor' media history – or, as I will use the term, 'media archaeology' – that brands the Britain of technical media and hence acts as an underbelly of the more standardized narratives. This is the Britain of quirky media archaeology that ranges from nineteenth-century cultures of invention to the birth of computing in the midst of the Second World War to the misuse of abandoned military technologies for the benefit of pop cultural mobilization of teenagers since the 1960s, of Pink Floyd as the key to understand technical media, and other stories that fall outside the usual histories of media.

This perspective offers an interest in the neglected ideas that are only being discovered *a posteriori*; a fantastic example is the Oramics project at the Science

Museum. Involving not only the museum but also artists and other stakeholders, the project commemorates the pioneering projects in electronic music of Daphne Oram. She developed a unique musical instrument, which represented a sort of early synthetiser, the Oramics machine (c. 1959). Working in her studio in Kent, she was also part of the wider circuit of the BBC Radiophonic Workshop and other 1960s and 1970s British experimental electronic music studios. In this fresh context, we are asking questions that make the neglected projects and work relevant once more, spurred by the discovery of the machine and highlighting its possibilities to trigger new ideas in media art practice.

This chapter is meant to illustrate an alternative way of understanding media history, namely media archaeology. In order to establish this theoretical and methodological provocation in a fruitful way in relation to the volume in which this chapter is situated, I will continue to establish the case for British media archaeology: a media archaeology of Britain underpinned by its media technological innovations and networks. I will discuss some media archaeological theories and focus first on Friedrich A. Kittler in order to illustrate how Britain has been included in novel ways in recent media theory. In addition, I want to discuss a range of media artistic projects of recent years that show another face of media archaeology; to excavate British media history through creative practice and hence connect to another sort of a public-facing aspect of histories of technology and science.

What is media archaeology?

Media archaeology has grown slowly over the past years as a methodology to excavate the losers of media history. That, however, is not all. It is not merely a 'search and rescue' operation into media history, but a field of multiple, diverse theoretical approaches which in differing ways questions the newness of new media cultures and aims to resurrect new forms of old media culture in the new. The terms 'new' and 'old' can be considered poor ways of understanding the complex nature of media historical change. Media archaeology can be seen as a practice that extends to theory as well as for instance to curation and artistic contexts. In the words of Erkki Huhtamo, one of the leading writers in the field, it is indeed

> a critical practice that excavates media-cultural evidence for clues about neglected, misrepresented, and/or suppressed aspects of both media's past(s) and their present and tries to bring these into a conversation with each other. It purports to unearth traces of lost media-cultural phenomena and agendas and to illuminate ideological mechanisms behind them. It also emphasizes the multiplicity of historical narratives and highlights their constructed and ideologically determined nature.
>
> (Huhtamo, 2011: 28)

Media archaeology's historically inclined theoretical work has opened up archives of the more surprising sides of media history from the neglected innovation of moving panorama to prehistories of gaming before digital computers made it into a mass craze since the 1980s and such seemingly unimportant features as noise. Media archaeology partly borrows its name from Michel Foucault's critique of historical knowledge. As is so well known in the discipline of history, Foucault branded this inquiry into the conditions of knowledge as an 'archaeology' that was interested in the various forces that constitute objects and statements. For Foucault, the archaeology of knowledge poses a question concerning how statements are distributed and what techniques and institutions support their preservation (Foucault, 2002: 139). Indeed, there is more of the archival than the archaeological in Foucault's emphasis: "The archive is first the law of what can be said, the system that governs the appearance of statements as unique events" (ibid.: 145). His interest is in the *a priori* that conditions statements and objects.

Such pioneering media scholars as Friedrich A. Kittler argued that Foucault's dictum should be updated to take into account that we live in the midst of a technical media culture. With tones that at times remind one of a mix of Marshall McLuhan, Harold Innis and also Friedrich Nietzsche, Kittler claims that Foucault's archaeology of knowledge was too focused on the role of the material techniques of books and institutions such as libraries in its excavation of the conditions of knowledge. For Kittler, this should be considered a media technological question in a more wide-reaching sense. It is not only in books that power resides, "[a]rchaeologies of the present must also take into account data storage, transmission, and calculation in technological media" (Kittler, 1990: 369). In other words, Kittler is saying that we need to realize that besides books, power resides in computers and related 'new' technologies.

Besides the inspiring ideas of media archaeology such as excavating how media technologies condition cultural statements and habits, and the often quoted sentence from Nietzsche – "Our writing tools are also working on our thoughts" (quoted in Kittler, 1999: 200) – we can focus on its innovative contribution to the historical nature of the media. In order to understand new media cultures and the emerging technological situations we are faced with, we must look back. Carolyn Marvin's (1990) insight that "old technologies were once new" is one such guideline, as is McLuhan's idea of driving towards the future with an eye on the rear-view mirror (McLuhan and Quentin, 1967/2008). We can in this way start to understand the complexities of influences of media archaeology that remain irreducible to Foucault.

As a way to account for multiple temporalities, we need to investigate the new in the old, or how the past has become a fruitful archive (in a metaphorical and literal sense) of 'cheap R&D' (Hertz, 2009) for media artistic and design inquiry. Such a discourse is of course not exclusively media archaeology but resonates with the interest in 'history in the present' and is what brings a certain liveliness and dynamism into play when considering the persistence – the distribution – of media historical ideas, statements, objects, practices and discourses.

Do mention the war

A curious and important detail of Kittler's work has to do with a relation to Britain. It is interesting to observe how British media history has been partly 'preserved' or at least highlighted in German media theory of the past 20 years in ways that have been able to open up new aspects of analysis. Partly this might have to do with the status Kittler has enjoyed as a theorist and a media historian. His provocative, against-the-grain histories of the media in Europe have highlighted often marginal names from science as much as from literature, but also at times British case studies that have to do with the Second World War as well as its after effects. Indeed, British media history seen through a German periscope looks at different aspects than mass media. The focus turns to war and the wider refashioning of media as an extension of the military interests and wartime innovations of science and engineering. As Geoffrey Winthrop-Young (2002) critically outlines, this is an extended focus on media as the *a priori* of culture and the 'martial' as the *a priori* of media. As someone dipping into the media theoretical landscape of such ideas in the 1990s, it seemed to make complete sense. Even popular media adopted the rhetoric of the first Gulf war in the early 1990s as a technological war of simulations. And even French theorists of the era when Minitel was still seen as a viable model for a networked society were picking up on this point. Jean Baudrillard and Paul Virilio acquired a lot of their international fame in the midst of these hi-tech war efforts. But Kittler does not merely offer footnotes to the most recent wars. Instead he insists that this is a characteristic feature of modernity. We have different phases of technologization stemming from wars:

> Phase 1, beginning with the American Civil War, developed storage technologies for acoustics, optics, and script: film, gramophone, and the man-machine system, typewriter. Phase 2, beginning with the First World War, developed for each storage content appropriate electric transmission technologies: radio, television, and their more secret counterparts. Phase 3, since the Second World War, has transferred the schematic of a typewriter of predictability per se; Turing's mathematical definition of computability in 1936 gave future computers their name.
>
> (Kittler, 1999: 243)

From the perspective of our contemporary computer society, we can appreciate this link between the mobilization of scientific and technological resources although, to be honest, Kittler goes beyond historical facts. Even if, for instance, the Arpanet came to fruition because of heavy military investment, with the British computing industry lagging behind, it still is just one particular cause contributing to the emergence of networks, personal computers and so forth. In most cases, there are good reasons to be critical of his perspective in terms of historical details but its benefits lie elsewhere. Kittler's theory lessons teach us how to think media history differently. So if we stay in the Kittlerian U-Boat for the ride (see Winthrop-Young, 2002 for an elaboration of the Yellow Submarine in this context), we can expand to an interesting view of Britain. Kittler's archaeologies of technical media place a lot of emphasis on Alan Turing's inventiveness and his specific work on computing. It could, without exaggeration, be said that in the same way that McLuhan (1962) indexed the media change of print to a specific proper name – a shift to Gutenberg Galaxy – for Kittler the Turing Age remained the horizon of media history becoming archaeology. As the translators of the volume *Gramophone, Film & Typewriter* note, this relates to Kittler's appreciation of the work of engineers in a history that has become more than human history: "Edison, Muybridge, Marey, the Lumière brothers, Turing, and von Neumann have left behind a world – or, rather, have made a world – in which technology, in more senses than one, reigns supreme" (Kittler, 1999: xxxvii). Figures such as Turing are seen, then, as forefathers not merely of one particular industry (the computing industry as we just noted did not really take off in Britain with the force it did in the US) but of a more McLuhan-type periodization of an era: The Turing Age. Britain was inscribed as a focal point for the whole new scene that emerged with the symbol processing contraptions called 'Turing Machines'.

Kittler might work through such human inventors and engineers, but this is for ulterior motives. They jumpstart a mode of history where machines also gain agency. Indeed, this is the reason why his theories of media archaeology at times get labeled 'posthumanism', even if for Kittler this is just a matter of technical descriptions. The Turing machine was conceived both as a machine that can simulate any other machine and as one that sits as the blueprint for any subsequent computer built. For Kittler it set itself as a model in an epistemological sense too, which demands a new way of understanding writing and, in general, cultural symbolism when machines can automate processes which had previously existed as exclusively human domains:

> Unlike the history to which it put an end, the media age proceeds in jerks, just like Turing's paper strip. From the Remington via the Turing machine to microelectronics, from mechanization and automatization to the implementation of a writing that is only cipher, not meaning one century was enough to transfer the age-old monopoly of writing into the omnipotence of integrated circuits.
>
> (Kittler, 1999: 18–19)

Kittler has a certain European bias in his narratives. His analysis remains absorbed in Germany and Britain. There is more of Mick Jagger than Neil Young in his interests and more of Alan Turing than Ronald Reagan in his exposition of the technologies that constitute our culture – including pop culture (Winthrop-Young, 2002: 831). Indeed, despite the seemingly odd mix of French philosophy and British computing pioneers, Kittler's brand of media archaeology (which surely is not the only way to approach media archaeology) jumps as easily to rock music as it does to computer programming languages. This again illuminates the relation to war. If Turing's computational thinking, which stemmed from a certain Cambridge culture of the 1930s, is such a jumpstart for a different mode of cultural production – and not ignoring the fact that these deciphering machines were essential to the war effort which is conversely branded by the computations of rocket trajectories like the V2 – the rock music that followed is a continuation of technological development too. This of course has not been left unnoticed by others. London's famous Abbey Road studio's magnetic recording technology was developed at least partly thanks to some audio engineers' visits to Berlin just after the war had ended, in 1946. (On the origin of the Abbey Road magnetic tapes, see Southall, 1982: 37). For the German military powers, the magnetic tapes were part of their code-breaking efforts, but here they became a form of war-to-rock remediation. Indeed, the BTR series (British Tape Recorders) were then passing on only messages by the Beatles instead of the enemy armed troops, to paraphrase Kittler (1999: fn. 26: 282–83).

Kittler's huge historical sweeps are entangled with his love for the minutest of details. In this case it relates to odd examples of 'German–British Technology Transfer', although in rather forced circumstances. Kittler's perspective on British media history seems to adopt Thomas Pynchon's fictional work *Gravity's Rainbow* as its guideline. Media history is connected to the history of technological development as well as to a psychotechnics of manipulation in which communication technologies are responsible for the short-circuiting of human senses, and are in this Pynchon-Kittler world even characteristic of a connection to illicit drugs. The jump to rock music is, in this context, one of the technological misuses of war technologies as the idea made famous by Kittler goes (1999: 96–97). Besides this aspect of Pynchon, the other one relates to 'technology transfer' which for Kittler is the true focus of Pynchon's novel; the projects started in Peenemünde and Nordhausen in terms of rockets and jets are continued in Huntsville and Baikonur as part of the US post-war efforts to produce a list of things essential to waging later wars – and media: audio tapes, color film, VHF, radar, UHF, computers and so forth (Kittler 1997: 102).

And what about Britain? Well, it is a bit of a similar story even if it proceeds less through Pynchon and more through Kittler. Military technologies and pop music rather than the production of new computer technologies are the main thrust of technological Britain; even recent governments have had to face the economic puzzle of how best to kickstart a British version of Silicon Valley without the same massive level of American investment from governmental military budgets. Hence, what by 2010 was being touted across British policy and governmental business strategy as the 'digital economy' was, from one media archaeological angle, a mourning of how things could have been different. This conveniently coincided with the centenary of Alan Turing's birth in 2012 as well as the earlier allocation of Lottery Funds to the restoration of Bletchley Park in 2009. And yet there remained the sense that the British history of computing was merely a good rhetorical vehicle to justify another sort of discourse, namely the import of Silicon Valley as an economic dream now rhetorically rebranded as 'the Silicon Roundabout' of tech companies in Shoreditch, London. The misuse of technologies of war that produced the technological spark for New Labour's enthusiasm for the creative industries was also the other side of why the later emphasis on the digital was never embedded in such a way despite, for instance, the strong openings in the field of computers from BBC Micro to Sinclair in the 1980s.

This is why Kittler is left with rock music, ignoring a range of other technological developments in Britain since the Second World War. He is not interested in a full narrative of European media technological development after the war but works through case studies, such as recording technologies. Hence, Abbey Road is the parallel version to what took place in Cologne in the late 1950s at the Westdeutscher Rundfunk. With Karlheinz Stockhausen at the helm, discarded US army technologies were put to use in an assemblage of pulse generators, amplifiers, band-pass filters and oscillators (Kittler, 1999: 97).

For Kittler, such archaeologies of media – experimental and pop – become a stubbornly war-oriented enterprise. In the British context, his close reading of Pink Floyd might be a slight exception as it introduces a different angle. Nonetheless, it insists on rock music as a way to understand media technological development. While war might be the main thrust of new innovations, at least Pink Floyd developed their own version of psychotechnical manipulation of the senses. For Kittler, it is implicitly about Pink Floyd revealing in more detail what such later theorists as Baudrillard never really discussed in such media-specific terms as media archaeologists have. This refers to yet another innovation that, through its association with Syd Barrett, has its Cambridge roots – just like Turing did. The Azimuth Coordinator was one of the audio innovations that enabled extra control of speakers and quadraphonic sound across acoustic space, providing a striking example of what can happen to physical sensation in the age of technical media. Technology invades the sense of self and becomes part of the subject's constitution, just like when Pink Floyd sing in the track *Brain Damage*: "the lunatic is in my head." Close readings of rock lyrics become a way to meditate on the advances of technological culture and in exaggerated but still provocative accounts. Yet, one has to be more accurate with details. For instance, it was not Syd Barrett behind the Azimuth Coordinator but someone from the Abbey Road engineer team: Bernard Speight (Winthrop-Young, 2011: 55; V&A Collection, n.d.).

Such insights as Kittler's open up new avenues of inquiry. Indeed, one could in this way start excavating alternative media histories of Britain across a range of examples that move from engineers to pop music and, indeed, taking the war into account. As part of some of the media archaeological heritage of theorists such as Kittler, places like Peenemünde (infamous as the site of V1 and V2 rocket engineering) have almost reached a cult status. But similarly one could expand that interest to the space- and place-specific excavations on the Kentish coast for instance. The various radar systems that formed the early warning system of the 1930s and 1940s are definitely examples of what is left out of the usual media history books; the various 'giant ears' or acoustic mirroring systems which signaled the era just before technical systems of distance perception, such as radar, were introduced. International media relations between Germany and Britain were during the war conducted through the technological means of rocket trajectories, signal interception, radar-enhanced mapping and the back and forth prehistory of computing: ciphering and deciphering military messages.

In terms of British media history the place-specific and location-related media dynamism of the past is important. From the Kentish coast to Bletchley Park, not only the legacy of the war but also the possibility of rewiring past media to contemporary concerns is what enables new perspectives. Such places and spaces are where media history is alive and contemporary to the current media cultural revisiting of the past in the light of emerging technological cultures. This is why I want to turn next to a different sort of emphasis that relates to bringing media history alive as part of installation and reconstruction projects and how this relates to a media archaeological interest in knowledge which is executed by artistic means. How can we recursively rewire narratives and examples of neglected media into a new image of media history?

Present archaeologies: Media arts of media pasts

What are the soundscapes of the technologies of war? How are the instances, described above, mixing nowadays into media artistic appropriations of the technologies of war, such as submarines and torpedoes? Walking into the installation space of British artist Aura Satz's Impulsive Synchronization (2013) at the Hayward Gallery transmits the visitor into a weird mix of audiovisual experience and war technologies. It seems that a Kittlerian spirit is haunting the media archaeological excavations of the past and also the creative practice interests that surround the use of media technologies in technological arts. The science and technologies of war, as well as extending audiovisual arts to grasp history in new ways, return it to our current concerns too. This is the area where media artistic practice meets with historical concerns and the practices of heritage.

One can say that recent years have seen a wide array of artistic projects that execute an interest in alternative histories of British technology and media. These have ranged from installation projects by British artists (even if the subject topic is not always *exclusively about* Britain) to novels such as Tom McCarthy's (2010) much hailed C, which took as its focus the era of technological development from the late nineteenth century to the Second World War as a regime of intensive changes. This interest also includes the alternative sides of technologies, for instance those related to spiritualism (as part of the cultural history of the telegraph) and other paranormal phenomena that escorted old new media discourses on both sides of the Atlantic (Sconce, 2000). Indeed, such minor histories and cultural historical aspects of technology have been activated in various projects. One already mentioned, and which works on a very different level to that of novels like C, is the Science Museum Oramics project, which rediscovers female media histories and archaeologies of technological sound arts.

The Oramics project was important in that it did not only involve the backroom excavation of a lost musical instrument by experts and the media archaeologically inspired considerations of its significance. It also included front-end activities that besides exhibiting such lost artifacts of media art history also produced interesting rewirings that demonstrate an active sense of the production of cultural memories of technical media. In other words, the Science Museum exhibition and project (from July 2011 to December 2013) involved different groups, from theatre students to female writers, contributing to monologues, dialogues and a play that related to Daphne Oram and the Oramics project. It was perfectly suited to engage people in considering issues of technology and gender. The media artist mentioned above, Aura Satz, was also invited to collaborate on such Public History projects. Satz's film engaged with Oram's voice (and writings) as well as the sounds of the Oramics machine which itself was an odd mixture of technologies of film (35mm film) and sound. The sound was painted on the film as the 'script'. In Satz's poetic formulation, accompanying her film *Oramics: Atlantis Anew*:

> We're going to enter a strange world and we're going to find composers will be mingling with capacitors, transistors are going to be transmuting triplets,

and, perchance, metaphysics may creep in, to mate memory, music and magnetism in some strange sort of eternal triangle.

(Satz, n.d.)

These artistic and in general public-facing projects are themselves producing such living forms of media history, where the connections to the past are at times 'non-linear' (see Huhtamo and Parikka, 2011a). By this we mean a temporary neglecting of narratives of continuity and a traditional telling of media historical events, inventions and contexts. It instead encourages us to see how such discoveries of the forgotten, the ruins (in the Benjaminian sense) can activate our thoughts and creative minds. The past becomes a reservoir for creative activity and British media history itself becomes an active part of a constitution of 'cultures of history' in the present. Media archaeology relates to this sort of understanding of history where artifacts as well as practices link pasts, presents and futures (see Aronsson, 2005). For instance the Media Archaeological Fundus in Berlin, at the Humboldt University Institute of Media Studies, is such an archive of operational old technology which is used for pedagogical purposes and to demonstrate principles of liveness in past media history (See Ernst, 2013; Parikka, 2011).

With the Science Museum Public History project, the themes of co-curation and participation by a wide range of stakeholders in *staging media history* have presented an interesting way to broaden both the scope of media technological history as well as the traditional areas of media archaeology. Workshops by Aleks Kolkowski (sound art and technology) and Katy Price (creative writing) are a good example. Kolkowski is a London-based composer and musician who had for a long time performed with such technologies as Stroh instruments, wind-up gramophones, shellac discs and wax-cylinder phonographs. His interest in techniques and technologies of sound recordings was tuned in with a wider artistic focus on creative clashes between the old and the new.

Kolkowski pitches his interest as part of the physicality of media cultures of sound (cf. Demarinis, 2011). This is of course spurred by the increasing obsolescence of analogue technologies of inscription, in the midst of digital technologies. This juxtaposition and investigation of media technological devices was also part of the Oramics project as a sort of archaeology of the groove; inscription technologies in British media history that preceded even the Oramics machine. With a youth group and part of the Science Museum Youth and Public Engagement programme, Kolkowski and Price organized in February 2011 a workshop to investigate this in person, producing a living form of sonic history and engagement exploring how we think about historical sound instruments and how such sound instruments themselves form a basis of history, by recording, storing and hence feeding back to future sounds of the past. Implicitly, the workshops investigated the mediatic conditions of history as well. In Kolkowski's words:

In this case it was to show that the origins of Daphne Oram's sound painting can be traced back to 19th-century advances in capturing, visualising and reproducing sound through the phonoautograph and subsequently the

> phonograph and gramophone. We were also treating groove-based sound recording as a form of inscription, as sound-writing.
>
> (Kolkowski, 2011)

Kolkowski's collaboration with Price combined creative writing workshops with staging a media historical event in order to experience first-hand such historical technologies as phonoautographs and gramophones on an experiential level:

> The fundamentals and science of sound recording are vividly demonstrated through mechanical devices, through objects you can touch and sound inscriptions you can see and hear played back via styli, vibrating diaphragms and horns. As well as showing how our forefathers experienced recorded music, it also offers us a different kind of listening experience as I've mentioned before. It helps us to examine our relationship to recorded sound, the antiquated sound-engraving processes add distance to the newly recorded voices, allowing us to reflect more profoundly on what we hear.
>
> (ibid.)

The same idea could be felt with another restaging of audio media history that involved Kolkowski. The Babble Machine sound and device installation at the Science Museum (2012) was developed together with Price and researcher Alison Hess and involved a media archaeological twist to the mass media history of the BBC. Babble Machine-installation room was coined after H. G. Wells' transmitter device in *When The Sleeper Wakes* (1898–99 and 1910) and in this installation was a polyphonic experience space of old sound archive recordings collaged into a multi-layered experience of BBC history.

Through devices and textual ideas, we can here point out the central role of renarrativizing the past in creative ways and creative spaces, and imagining alternative media presents through summoning the neglected aspects of the past. Beside the projects at such central institutions as the Science Museum, consider for instance J. R. Carpenter's (2011) digital generative text-based piece and performance *Transmission [A Dialogue]*, which investigates telegraphic trans-Atlantic communication through the means of generative text scripts. It summons a philosophical meditation, executed through computer scripts, on the questions of transmission between Cornwall, UK and Newfoundland, US as a distance of telecommunication that tied national media histories to transnational concerns.

As already mentioned above, computers and war occupy a central position in the international interest in British media history. For sure, in relation to computers the pioneering role of Turing and the immediate years after the Second World War are of interest to a lot of researchers who want to find alternative stories to that of the teleology of US success that tends to brand the narratives of the emergence of digital culture. For instance, David Link's work is exemplary in this regard. His reconstruction of the Manchester Mark computer's (the 'Manchester Baby') 'loveletters' program can be seen as a media archaeological work of excavating the specific technological moments that are of interest to current software culture. Besides winning a major prize for this reconstruction work, Link's explicitly media archaeological work has toured various art festivals; it demonstrates where cultural heritage meets media arts and a way to short-circuit media history with current concerns and technological arts.

Conclusion

In short, and by way of concluding, media archaeology can be seen as an excavation of the *other* stories of media history. It is characterized by an interest in including such stories in contemporary evaluations of the role of science and technology in society. Various theorists have elaborated new temporal ways of understanding media history which have had major methodological effects on what sort of sources we use and how we see their relevance; media history is not just history, but always recurring (Huhtamo, 2011) and at times recursively (Winthrop-Young, forthcoming). Writers such as Kittler have offered a refreshing twist to the usual stories of media, war and the emergence of technological culture as well as contributing to a rather singular way of seeing British media innovators, from Turing to Syd Barrett, as focal points in a wider epochal story. And yet a major part of media archaeology is not executed only in theoretical and historical mappings of the media but also in creative practices. These are not always necessarily about the national borders of media industries or practices, but can always be tracked back to their situations of invention, to their use, but also, as we can understand being part of a fruitful and living relation to history, their misuse. Hence, the focus on media artistic (re)appropriations of old ideas as well as concrete archival work is one important way in which we can think 'media archaeologically'. The British heritage of media technology, grounded as it is in scientific innovations and the engineering of devices from Babbage to the cybernetic tortoise of William Grey Walter in the 1950s, for example (Pickering, 2010), provides us with ways of understanding the conditions of existence of new ideas within creative media arts and a living cultural heritage of technological quirkiness.

Further reading

A good way to deepen understanding of the media archaeological methodology is to have a look at the edited volume *Media Archaeology: Approaches, Applications and Implications* (Huhtamo and Parikka, 2011b) which includes several articles by leading scholars introducing case studies and methodological choices in media archaeological theory. Similarly, Parikka's recent monograph *What is Media Archaeology?* (2012) is an introduction to the major debates and key themes in the field, including artistic practice. Speaking of artistic media archaeology, Siegfried Zielinski's *Deep Time of the Media* has been available since 2006 in English and represents one major example of how to conduct deep time analysis in a slightly different way than is usual in media history. One can get an insight into other issues and historical themes from collections such as *Multimedia Histories: From the Magic Lantern to the Internet* (Lyons and Plunkett, 2007) which might not use the term 'media archaeology' but is a good example of the British context of engaging with new media through old media. If one wants to get a deeper understanding of Kittler's work, one book to start with is

Gramophone, Film, Typewriter (1999) where one can encounter some of the arguments regarding Alan Turing and Pink Floyd for instance. Geoffrey Winthrop-Young's *Kittler and the Media* (2011) is an excellent introduction to the controversial German thinker.

References

Aronsson, P. (2005) "En forskningsfält tar form". In P. Aronsson and M. Hillström (eds.) *Kulturarvens dynamik. Det institutionaliserade kulturarvets förändringar*. Tema Kultur of samhälle, Skriftserie 2005: 2. Linköping: Linköpings universitet (pp. 9–24).

Carpenter, J. R. (2011) "Transmission [A Dialogue]-project website". Retrieved from http://luckysoap.com/generations/transmission.html

DeMarinis, P. (2011) "Erased Dots and Rotten Dashes: How to Wire Your Head for a Preservation". In E. Huhtamo and J. Parikka (eds.) *Media Archaeology: Approaches, Applications and Implications*. Berkeley, CA: University of California Press (pp. 211–38).

Ernst, W. (2013) *Digital Memory and the Archive* (J. Parikka, ed.). Minneapolis, MN: University of Minnesota Press.

Foucault, M. (2002) *The Archaeology of Knowledge*. London and New York: Routledge.

Hertz, G. (2009) "Dead Media Laboratory". Retrieved from www.conceptlab.com/deadmedia/

Huhtamo, E. (2011) "Dismantling The Fairy Engine: Media Archaeology as Topos Study". In E. Huhtamo and J. Parikka (eds.) *Media Archaeology: Approaches, Applications and Implications*. Berkeley, CA: University of California Press (pp. 27–47).

Huhtamo, E. and Parikka, J. (2011a) "Introduction: An Archaeology of Media Archaeology". In E. Huhtamo and J. Parikka (eds.) *Media Archaeology: Approaches, Applications and Implications*. Berkeley, CA: University of California Press (pp. 1–21).

——(eds.) (2011b) *Media Archaeology: Approaches, Applications and Implications*. Berkeley, CA: University of California Press.

Kittler, F. A. (1990) *Discourse Networks 1800/1900*. Stanford, CA: Stanford University Press.

——(1997) *Literature, Media, Information Systems* (edited with an introduction by John Johnston). Amsterdam: G+B Arts.

——(1999) *Gramophone, Film, Typewriter*. Stanford, CA: Stanford University Press.

Kolkowski, A. (2011) "Sonic Alchemy: An Interview with Aleks Kolkowski". Retrieved from http://jussiparikka.net/2011/04/11/%E2%80%9Csonic-alchemy%E2%80%9D-an-interview-with-aleks-kolkowski/

Lyons, J. and Plunkett, J. (eds.) (2007) *Multimedia Histories: From the Magic Lantern to the Internet*. Exeter: University of Exeter Press.

McCarthy, Tom. (2010) *C*. London: Jonathan Cape.

McLuhan, M. (1962) *The Gutenberg Galaxy. The Making of the Typographic Man*. Toronto: University of Toronto Press.

McLuhan, M. and Quentin, F. (1967/2008) *The Medium is the Massage: An Inventory of Effects*. New York: Penguin Classics.

Marvin, C. (1990) *When Old Technologies Were New: Thinking About Electric Communication in the Nineteenth Century*. Oxford: Oxford University Press.

Parikka, J. (2011) "Operative Diagrammatics: Wolfgang Ernst's Materialist Media Diagrammatics". *Theory, Culture & Society*, 28(5), 52–74.

——(2012) *What is Media Archaeology?* Cambridge: Polity.

Pickering, A. (2010) *The Cybernetic Brain. Sketches of Another Future*. Chicago, IL and London: Chicago University Press.

Satz, A. (n.d.) "Oramics: Atlantis Anew". Retrieved from http://www.sciencemuseum.org.uk/visitmuseum/galleries/oramics/satz_video.aspx

Sconce, J. (2000) *Haunted Media. Electronic Presence from Telegraphy to Television*. Durham: Duke University Press.
Southall, B. (1982) *Abbey Road: The Story of the World's Most Famous Recording Studio*. Cambridge: Patrick Stevens.
V&A Collection (n.d.) Azimuth Co-ordinator. Retrieved from http://collections.vam.ac.uk/item/O76817/azimuth-co-ordinator-sound-equipment-bernard-speaight/ (accessed April 28, 2013).
Winthrop-Young, G. (2002) "Drill and Distraction in the Yellow Submarine: On the Dominance of War in Friedrich Kittler's Media Theory". *Critical Inquiry*, 28(4), 825–54.
——(2011) *Kittler and the Media*. Cambridge: Polity.
——(forthcoming) "Kittler's Siren Recursions". In S. Sale and L. Salisbury (eds.) *Kittler Now*. Cambridge: Polity.
Zielinski, S. (2006) *Deep Time of the Media*. Cambridge, MA: MIT Press.

Part II
MEDIA AND SOCIETY

6
The political economy of media
Jonathan Silberstein-Loeb

A principal concern of political economy is the relationship between the state and the market, but historians of the British news media have not adequately defined the parameters of the market or how it operated or overlapped with politics. There is a body of published historical work concerned with the political economy of the British media (e.g. Garnham, 1979; Curran and Seaton, 2009), but whichever approach to political economy one prefers, one must start with a clear understanding of the market and its structure and dynamics. Key to understanding any market is the nature and degree of competition. Thinking about competition is a helpful way in which to approach issues of political economy, but economic analysis need not determine the course of one's inquiry. For example, one might consider the way in which competition affected the provision of news and in turn influenced how readers understood the media they consumed, as well as how media producers sought to attract them. Thinking about competition, and the regulation of it, is also an effective way in which to grapple with how people thought about the role of the media in the past. Historians are also well placed to ascertain the extent to which, and conditions in which, competition has helped or hindered the creation of the media (Lacy, 1990).

Comprehending competition

There is frustratingly little consensus as to how newspapers compete. Part of the difficulty lies in determining the geographical extent of the relevant market. Economists have devised so-called 'umbrella' models to explain how newspapers in different circulation territories compete with each other (Rosse, 1980; Lacy, 1984). Umbrella competition refers to newspapers headquartered in different cities and with varying publication cycles competing in overlapping circulation areas for news, readers and advertising (Bridges, Litman and Bridges, 2007). Competition among these overlapping layers varied according to region. Communications technology, which permitted more rapid distribution of newspapers and news, affected competition and government regulation of both influenced the contours of newspaper markets.

Newspapers attract particular audiences partly by appealing to readers' political preferences, socioeconomic status and other interests. The degree of competition between newspapers, inasmuch as it existed, depended on the extent to which consumers found them to be acceptable substitutes for each other. Today, when like products occupy different market segments, economists call it 'monopolistic competition', since producers in such a market do not compete directly (Rosse, 1967). Think of *The Guardian*, a left-leaning liberal newspaper, the *Daily Telegraph*, which appeals to readers to the right of the political spectrum, and the *Financial Times*, which avoids party politics by focusing on business. Each of these publications occupies a different market segment and none of them compete directly with each other for readers. That said, even if their political interests are disparate, the broader consumer habits of readers may overlap, which obliges publishers to compete directly for advertising.

The fact that newspapers compete simultaneously for readers and advertising makes understanding competition more complicated. First, consider readers. In the eighteenth and nineteenth centuries, when most readers' disposable income was constrained, substitutable newspapers may have competed on newsstand or circulation price. Once most readers could afford a daily, small changes in price presumably had less effect on sales. Historically, journalists made an educated guess about what their readers wanted to read, so competition over content was an inexact science at best. Until the age of market studies in the 1930s, reader demand was a black box. Journalists wrote what they thought their readers ought to read, or they wrote for themselves and sought to appeal to a like-minded audience. Some market segments, such as the audience for a socialist daily, dried up and newspapers closed. Economic depression, education, financial inequality, increasing gender and racial equality, immigration, increased literacy and urbanization are a few of the many factors that altered demand. One strategy for coping with changes in demand was to provide content that appealed to a broad church, but not so broad as to compete with other newspapers. Publishing a newspaper that catered to an established political group was one way in which to pursue this strategy.

Unlike the market for readers, the advertising market is more sensitive to price. Fluctuations in advertising rates affect who purchases space in a publication, but newspaper publishers have historically set advertising rates collusively (Silberstein-Loeb, 2011). In any event, it was difficult to value advertising space in newspapers because circulation statistics were unreliable. Similarly, advertisers and publishers had only a vague sense of who read newspapers. Admittedly, when the press is partisan, it is easier to guess who is reading what, but historically, when publications were tied to political parties they had little in the way of advertising, in part because circulation was low but also because advertising was not then big business (Nevett, 1982). For certain publications, the quality of the circulation was more important than the quantity, so historical circulation statistics, advertising figures or data respecting reader demand may be misleading (Wadsworth, 1955). The absence of reliable circulation figures before the establishment of the Audit Bureau of Circulations (ABC) in 1931 makes it an unsolved question of media history how publishers and advertisers valued advertising space, and why, despite the absence of an established system for pricing it, advertising expenditure grew.

In addition to competition among newspapers, one must take into account competition between forms of media, such as between newspapers, on the one hand, and radio, television and the internet on the other. Market segmentation and monopolistic competition occurred within the newspaper market and across media markets. The newspaper, as a medium, enjoyed something of a monopoly until the advent of the internet, since both radio and television are imperfect substitutes for the printed word. The internet approximates the written word, which helps to explain why it has brought such hard times to publishing industries. Broadcasting, television and the internet may have usurped readers and advertising revenue from newspaper publishers, but over time the supply of readers and advertising expenditure has changed. The relative availability of readers and advertisers influenced the extent to which alternative forms of media, such as broadcasting and television, ate into newspaper circulation and advertising revenue.

Market segmentation affected inter-media competition as well as intra-media competition. Although the British press has always complained bitterly about the monopoly the BBC possesses over the licence fee, a dominant radio and television provider is arguably more benign than a competitive radio and television market. To justify its monopoly over the licence fee paid formerly by radio and now by television users, the BBC aims to appeal to a wide audience and avoids appealing to a particular economic, political or social class. The market for politically partial news is consequently left open to the press.

An oblique approach

As opposed to looking at newspapers and attempting to ascertain whether and how they competed with each other, it may be more effective to look at the barriers to entry that made it difficult to enter or operate in a given market. This approach does not preclude detailed accounts of individual publications but does favor the bigger picture. Barriers to entry may be economic, geographic and technological, political or cultural and social. It is artificial to consider these categories in isolation, but for ease of organization, and to convey more clearly the approach adopted, it is best to start with cultural and political barriers and then to move on to technological ones, since culture and politics have had such a significant influence on the structure of telecommunications, before turning to the way in which culture, politics and technology affected business practice.

At the beginning of the eighteenth century, information was perceived as a luxury and a danger to the stability of the commonwealth, but by the nineteenth century it was thought to be a democratic necessity. This shift was part of a change in thinking about politics. The heroic story of Thomas Erskine and Thomas Paine is widely known, but it is worth highlighting that the argument for a free press depended not only on an appeal to the 'rights of man', but also on an appeal to reason and to the reasonableness of the public generally. In his defense of Paine against charges for libel in 1792, Erskine argued that "every man, not intending to mislead, but seeking to enlighten others with what his own reason and conscience, however erroneously, have dictated to him as truth, may address himself to the universal reason of a whole nation ... " (quoted in Siebert, 1952: 392). Erskine's presumption that authors and readers were sufficiently reasonable and responsible to deserve a free press marked a departure from late seventeenth and early eighteenth-century thought. It appeared to contradict Bernard Mandeville's sentiment, expressed at the outset of the Hanoverian Succession, that "should a Horse know as much as a Man, I should not desire to be his Rider" (Mandeville, 1732: 331).

If the people and their press were to be free, preserving the status quo required shifting from restrictions on the press to reforming its consumers. As Roy Porter has observed, during the late eighteenth century the accent moved from prosecution to prevention and from punishment towards reform. The "restraining forces of traditional society", such as scarcity, paternal discipline, community opinion, dependency, and hostility to strangers and foreigners no longer functioned effectively (Porter, 2001). Instead, by providing them with a suitable education, urban moneyed interests acting in the name of charity hoped to ensure that the lower orders successfully met the test of freedom. By 1834, Lord Brougham could testify before the Select Committee on Libel Reform that *contra* Mandeville but *pace* Alexander Pope, the danger lay not in 'the people reasoning too much' but in them 'knowing too little.' If the content available to the public could not be actively censored by the state, then the people would have to be educated, socialized and reformed to know 'good' content from 'bad'.

Would-be reformers of the early nineteenth century turned to free trade as a way in which to ensure that the 'humble classes', if they did read, had access to 'useful' publications. The Society for the Diffusion of Useful Knowledge led this movement (Wiener, 1969; Hollis, 1970). Achieving the diffusion of useful knowledge required removing the economic impediments stymieing its flow. This explains why Edwin Chadwick, the radical Victorian social reformer, named the stamp on newspapers and the duty on advertisements the "taxes on knowledge". Working-class reformers such as Thomas Cooper and William Lovett agitated for repeal as well, but it is important to recognize that the concept of ideas competing freely was fundamentally a conservative notion. In 1831, Francis Place, one of the principal agitators for removal of the taxes, remained fearful that it was too late to prevent revolution in England, but he was certain "that every man who has property to lose, is bound to do all he can to avert it; and sure I am, that if it can be averted, a free press must be one of his main instruments" (Place, 1831: 2). Mill's *On Liberty*, published in 1859, was the apotheosis of this logic.

The policies pursued in the name of free trade in information and ideas extended beyond the abolition of the 'taxes on knowledge' to the means by which information was distributed. In theory this meant extending the rules of common carriage to communication. In practice it was utopian to hope that communication networks could be neutral. During the eighteenth century, certain forms of post, such as newspapers, and certain customers, such as Members of Parliament, received special economic treatment. A group of postal officials called the Clerks of the Road could frank newspapers for domestic and foreign distribution, which were then free from postage (Whyman, 2006). "Clerks of the Road, carrying on the business of newsmen," observed William Cobbett, "have it in their power to add to the sale of one newspaper and to diminish that of another" (Cobbett, 1802). When, in 1834, an act of parliament (4 & 5 Gul. IV, c. 44) prohibited Post Office officials from selling newspapers and allowed them to pass free from postage the practical effect of the statute was principally to make law correspond with usage.

There was a clear connection between the newspaper stamp and newspaper postage, so that reforming the former influenced the latter. When, in 1836, the government reduced the newspaper stamp from 4d to a penny, the remaining tax was seen as payment for the circulation of information. According to advocates of total abolition of the stamp, a universal tax of a penny, as opposed to a scale of postal charges, benefited the London papers, which could consequently circulate from one end of the country to the other, and back, as well as to any place thereafter, having paid only for a newspaper stamp. Local newspapers, which had a comparatively smaller territory of circulation, received less in terms of circulation for the stamp duty. Some form of graded postage, or price discrimination, would have privileged provincial papers. Under a postal regime, as opposed to a stamp regime, local papers could copy news from London publications and then circulate freely by hand delivery, thereby underselling London papers that had to pay postage. Although the penny stamp remained in place, after the passage of penny postage in 1840, parliament attempted to compensate for the advantages accruing to the London papers by allowing newspapers to travel from one town to another in Britain free of charge and for one penny each by the post within the limits of the same town from which it was posted (3 & 4 Victoria, cap. 96; s. 42). Newspapers received a considerable subsidy from the Post Office. In 1860, the average cost of transmission for a newspaper was 1.25d and for a letter it was 1/36th of a penny, yet they were charged alike. Daily packet lists, shipping lists, daily bills of entry, weekly prices current, Lloyds list twice a week and certain lottery lists all received similarly privileged treatment from the Post Office. Policy-makers contended that these forms of communication deserved subsidizing because they contributed more than normal letters to the development of the nation's commerce (Place and Watson, 1849: 69).

The advent of telegraphy presented similar difficulties for free trade in news. Private telegraph companies, which formed a cartel in the 1850s, provided a telegram service and supplied news reports to the press. Provincial publishers and other reformers argued that the combination of the means of distribution and newsgathering in the hands of several companies limited free trade in news. Edwin Chadwick, who had campaigned for repeal of the 'taxes on knowledge', argued that nationalization of telegraphy was part of a program that would promote efficient competition and free trade (Perry, 1992: 102). According to Frank Ives Scudamore, the Post Office official responsible for telegraph nationalization, one of the principal results the government sought to obtain through purchase of the telegraphs was "free trade in the collection of news for the press" (Scudamore, 1871: 2). By nationalizing telegraphy, Parliament sought to create and maintain through the Post Office a level playing field for competition among provincial publishers while subsidizing their newsgathering collectively. The Post Office lost considerable sums supplying a cheap service for the press that had to be set off against revenue from other sources. Additionally, free and equal access to telegraphy amongst the press also required the creation of a monopolistic news organization to moderate relationships among newspapers in the provinces and to coordinate the creation of news reports. This led to the creation of the Press Association (PA). The PA was open to all provincial newspapers but not the London press. The PA extracted a high charge from the

London press, which was used to subsidize the news report provided to the provincial papers (Silberstein-Loeb, 2009).

During the eighteenth century, and until the late nineteenth century, copying news from existing publications was the norm. For much of the eighteenth century, the provision of news was incidental to the supply of other services and it was often taken from other publications (Slauter, forthcoming). Although newspaper operations were more developed by the end of the eighteenth century, copying the news was not regarded as 'pilfering' or 'pirating' until the nineteenth century. In 1851, Thomas Milner Gibson, chairman of the parliamentary Select Committee on Newspaper Stamps, asked the great New York newspaper publisher Horace Greeley whether he had cause to "complain of piracy in the United States; for instance, of one publisher who has not himself been at the expense of obtaining news, copying immediately from another?" To which Greeley replied: "It is talked of for effect's sake; yet, on the whole, I would rather that those who do not take it should copy than not … the evening journals all copy from us, and we rather like it" (Report, 1851: 393). The exchange between Gibson and Greeley suggests that even in the 1850s so-called piracy was not cause for concern among New York publishers, although it may have been a source of irritation for their English counterparts. Once the value of news came to reside in its exclusivity, the business of newspapers changed materially. After the value of news was linked to its exclusivity, it was of great importance not only to have exclusive scoops but also to maintain exclusivity for as long as possible. Maintaining exclusivity was difficult because no legal protection was afforded to published news. To reinforce exclusivity publishers sought to develop extra-legal mechanisms to prevent copying and to restrict competition from those newspapers that did.

Although there are numerous instances in the historical record of isolated battles for valuable exclusives before the 1880s, the age of the scoop appears to have arrived in England between the first and second Boer Wars, which perhaps explains why, according to the *OED*, the word 'scoop', which originated in the Untied States in the 1870s, did not make its way across the Atlantic until the 1880s. It makes sense that the 1880s and 1890s marked the birth of the scoop in England. It was then that the cost of newsgathering and the value of exclusivity dramatically increased. The increased cost was partly attributable to burgeoning use of the telegraph to obtain news from abroad (Read, 1999). Newspaper production and circulation also grew rapidly after the introduction of wood-pulp paper, which made it possible to sell large sheets at two pennies and even one penny a copy. The invention of the linotype machine in 1885 undermined the control that the compositing trade held over the development of the London press and vastly increased the speed of newspaper production. The cost of starting a newspaper grew due to the need to purchase expensive presses and other machinery (Starr, 2004; O'Malley, 1981). This made it more difficult for potential publishers to enter the market since the greater the capital required, the greater the risk incurred. Similarly, the increasingly high fixed costs associated with publishing a newspaper meant that printing more newspapers increased the efficiency of production. Changes in the economics of newspaper publishing led to changes in newspaper ownership and content provision. It was during the 1880s that Harmsworth got his start and by 1896 he owned *The Evening News*, the *Edinburgh Daily Record*, and the *Daily Mail*.

As the cost of newspaper production grew, it became prohibitively expensive for publications with small circulations to maintain parity of performance with successful London dailies or those from other major cities, such as Manchester, which could rely on larger circulation and greater advertising revenue. Publishers who could not afford to obtain news of the Boer wars copied it from London newspapers. In 1888, the Belfast *News-Letter* copied Reuters' news from evening editions of London papers and sent it by rented private telegraph wire to its headquarters. When the *News-Letter* ignored demands to desist, Reuters published its telegrams in a journal entitled *The Epoch*, which was subject to statutory copyright. In March 1890, Reuters advised the *News-Letter* that its telegrams were copyrighted. Despite these precautions, the second Boer War, and the increased demand for news that it precipitated, caused a significant growth in the use of privately rented wires to telegraph published news from the capital to the provinces. In 1899, the Manchester *Evening News* hired a private wire and engaged in independently collecting and wiring Reuters' news from London, much to the dismay of the Manchester *Evening Mail*, which continued to pay for its report of Reuters' news. A bill to amend and consolidate the law relating to literary copyright was read in the House of Lords that April.

No legal protection for news was forthcoming, so publishers had to seek out alternative methods to protect the value of exclusivity. By nationalizing the telegraph and vesting a monopoly over news collection in the hands of the PA, officials had sought to maintain a level playing field among the publishers of the provinces by granting them equal access to telegraphy at the expense and displeasure of the London press. This situation only lasted so long as the postal telegraphs were the quickest way to transmit news. Once the telephone and private telegraph wires were available for transmitting news, the level playing field afforded to the provincial press broke down (Silberstein-Loeb, 2014). Although the First World War interrupted developments, after the war the British press increasingly adopted private solutions to protect their access to the news. The PA made increased use of a private network of telegraph wires and moved off the public postal telegraph system. It also purchased Reuters, the principal supplier of foreign news to the British Isles. A great part of the motivation behind the 'rationalization' of the newsgathering business was the threat presented by the rise of the BBC. Although newspaper interests had attempted to stave off competition from radio by successfully insisting that the BBC take its news from Reuters and the PA, and only air it after the London evening papers had had time to circulate, these limitations were gradually eroded and completely collapsed with the onset of the Second World War (Nicholas, 2007). The state's long-standing policy of subsidizing the press had shifted to radio (Silberstein-Loeb, 2014).

The supply of advertising had been no less collusive. Since the eighteenth century, advertising had been a source of newspaper revenue (Boyce, Curran and Wingate, 1978). As advertising became big business, the opportunism of both publishers and advertisers increased proportionately. Would-be advertisers sought to place fraudulent advertisements intended to dupe readers into various rouses including purchasing stock in non-existent corporations. Publishers likewise threatened advertisers with libel if they did not pay higher rates for their insertions. The Newspaper

Society, the principal trade association of the provincial press established in 1836, consequently set rates for advertisements and admonished members to hold fast against demands for lower rates since to do so, said the Society, would adversely affect all publishers in the long run. Circulation figures were carefully guarded trade secrets, which precluded potential advertisers from valuing the space they purchased. Advertising agents, who began during the 1880s to procure deals between newspapers and potential advertisers, were no less opportunistic. Agents misled advertisers about the extent of publicity they could provide, so the Society encouraged its members to patronize only agents it had vetted. Such difficulties eventually led to the creation of additional self-regulatory associations, such as The Advertisers Protection Society (1900), but only in 1931, after considerable back and forth before the First World War, did newspaper proprietors and advertisers finally manage to form an ABC. In 1914, a comparable organization had formed in the United States. Only after verified circulation figures were available did it become possible for advertisers to attempt to value the advertising space they purchased from the press, but it would take still more time to ascertain which readers read which articles and what impact if any advertising had on their consumption (Silberstein-Loeb, 2011).

Conclusion

The analysis above provides some indication of the extent to which the British newspaper market was competitive during the eighteenth and nineteenth centuries and some of the ways the state shaped the degree of competition. Barriers to entry were low during the eighteenth century but so was competition. In the late nineteenth century, competition, insofar as it existed, was not so much local as it was regional. It existed among newspapers of the provinces and between the provincial and the London press. Through telecommunications policy the state moderated this relationship. Much more research on the political economy of the media in Britain is required and the question of competition ought at least to inform any study, but it is safe to say that the market for newspapers was never freely competitive. There are numerous conclusions one may draw from this finding (see Baker, 2002), but in any event historians ought to avoid assuming that the market is to blame for whatever ails the media (e.g. Curran and Seaton, 2009) and instead entertain the possibility that the absence of an effective and competitive market may be the cause.

Further reading

Baker's (2002) *Media, Markets, and Democracy* is an excellent introduction to how markets affect the provision of news. Curran and Seaton's (2009) *Power Without Responsibility* is still the textbook account of British media history told from a political-economic perspective. Although Starr's (2004) *The Creation of the Media: Political Origins of Modern Communications* is principally about American media, it raises important questions for British journalism historians.

References

Baker, C. E. (2002) *Media, Markets, and Democracy*. Cambridge: Cambridge University Press.

Boyce, G., Curran, J. and Wingate, P. (1978) *Newspaper History from the Seventeenth Century to the Present Day*. London: Constable.

Bridges, J. A., Litman, B. R. and Bridges, L. W. (2007) "Rosse's Model and the Ring Model: Explaining Newspaper Competition in the Millennium." In P. E. Grossmark (ed.) *Advances in Communications and Media Research*, vol. 3. New York: Nova Science (pp. 1–21).

Cobbett, W. (1802, November 27) *Cobbett's Political Register*, p. 2.

Curran, J. and Seaton, J. (2009) *Power Without Responsibility*. London: Routledge.

Garnham, N. (1979) "Contribution to a Political Economy of Mass-communication." *Media, Culture and Society*, 1(1), 123–46.

Hollis, P. (1970) *The Pauper Press: A Study in Working-Class Radicalism of the 1830s*. London: Oxford University Press.

Lacy, S. (1984) "Competition among Metropolitan Daily, Small Daily and Weekly Newspapers." *Journalism Quarterly*, 61(3), 640–44.

——(1990) "A Model of Demand for News: Impact of Competition on Newspaper Content." *Journalism Quarterly*, 67(4), 40–48, 128.

Mandeville, B. (1732) *The Fable of the Bees* (6th ed.). London: J. Tonson.

Mill, J. S. (1859) *On Liberty*. London: J. W. Parker and Son.

Nevett, T. R. (1982) *Advertising in Britain: A History*. London: Heinemann.

Nicholas, S. (2007) "Keeping the News British: Reuters, the British United Press and the BBC in the 1930s." In M. Hampton and J. Wiener (eds.) *Anglo-American Media Interactions*. Basingstoke: Palgrave Macmillan (pp. 195–214).

O'Malley, P. (1981) "Capital Accumulation and Press Freedom, 1800–850." *Media, Culture, and Society*, 3(1), 71–83.

Perry, C. R. (1992) *The Victorian Post Office: The Growth of a Bureaucracy*. London: Royal Historical Society.

Place, F. (1831) *A Letter to a Minister of State, Respecting the Taxes on Knowledge*, 2nd ed. London: Innes.

Place, F. and Watson, J. (1849, August) "The Newspaper Stamp Abolition Committee." *The Reasoner*, p. 5.

Porter, R. (2001) *English Society in the Eighteenth Century*. London: Penguin.

Read, D. (1999) *The Power of News: the History of Reuters*. Oxford: Oxford University Press.

"Report from the Select Committee on Newspaper Stamps" (1851) *Parliamentary Papers* 558.

Rosse, J. N. (1967) "Daily Newspapers, Monopolistic Competition, and Economies of Scale." *The American Economic Review*, 57(2), 522–33.

——(1980) "The Decline of Direct Newspaper Competition." *The Journal of Communication*, 30(2), 65–71.

Scudamore, F. I. (1871) "Report by Mr. Scudamore on the re-organization of the telegraph system of the United Kingdom." *Parliamentary Papers*, 304.

Siebert, F. S. (1952) *Freedom of the Press in England, 1476–1776*. Urbana, IL: University of Illinois Press.

Silberstein-Loeb, J. (2009) "The Structure of the News Market in Britain, 1870–1914." *The Business History Review*, 83(4), 759–88.

——(2011) "Puff Pieces and Circulation Scams: Middlemen and the Making of the Newspaper Advertising Market, 1881–1901." *Business Archives*, 103.

——(2014) *The International Distribution of News: the Associated Press, Press Association, and Reuters, 1848–1947*. Cambridge: Cambridge University Press.

Slauter, W. (forthcoming) "Making the Newspaper Work, 1688–1775." In R. John and J. Silberstein-Loeb (eds.) *Making News*. Oxford: Oxford University Press.

Starr, P. (2004) *The Creation of the Media: Political Origins of Modern Communications*. New York: Basic Books.

Wadsworth, A. P. (1955) *Newspaper Circulations, 1800–1954*. Manchester: Norbury, Lockwood & Co.

Wiener, J. H. (1969) *The War of the Unstamped: the Movement to Repeal the British Newspaper Tax, 1830–1836*. London: Cornell University Press.

Whyman, S. E. (2006) "Postal Censorship in England 1635–1844." Retrieved from web.princeton.edu/sites/english/csbm/./postal_censorship_england.doc

7
Historicizing the media effects debate

Theresa Cronin

Introduction

'Media effects' are perhaps one of the most frequently discussed and hotly debated topics in media studies. From debates over the effects of playing violent video games on children, through concerns over young women accessing pro-anorexia websites, to questions about the possible damaging effects of online pornography, potential media effects are of enduring interest to media students and the general public alike. As we shall see, these are perennial debates that appear to resurface with the invention and proliferation of each new media form. This chapter will therefore place the question of media effects within the context of a long history of public concern for the moral welfare of children and young people. It will demonstrate a clear link between media effects and regulation in the UK. However, it will also argue that the very real epistemological problems that underpin media effects research means that these laws are not necessarily founded on a secure evidence base. Rather, the move toward greater regulation of media in the UK has instead been driven by high-profile media stories that have naturalized the relationship between violent media and violent crime.

Media effects and the rise of mass entertainment

Looking back over the last two centuries it would seem that debates over media effects are inextricable from the rise of mass media. As far back as the 1850s lurid popular fictions, sensationalized newspaper coverage and blood-soaked, spectacular and thrilling entertainments had all found purchase within a growing urban culture. Social commentators of the era saw these ever more sensational popular entertainments as a clear symptom of social and moral decline and argued that such depictions were likely to incite further instances of immorality and crime (Murdock, 2001).

However, it was the arrival of cinema that prompted the development of media effects research as we know it today. So while in the early days of cinema public fears circulated around the potential for the darkness of the movie theatre itself to lead to crime and immoral behavior (Currie, 1907; Fosdick, 1911; Kuhn, 1988; Butsch, 2002), and the very real danger presented by the highly inflammable film stock (Kuhn, 1988; Czitrom, 1992; Merritt, 1976; Vorspan, 2000), these soon gave way to a perception that the films themselves might be "injurious to public morality ... to encourage or incite to crime, or ... lead to disorder" (Kuhn, 1988: 20). Indeed many writers at the time claimed that moviegoers were likely to imitate the crimes they witnessed on screen (Butsch, 2002). For example, Hugo Münsterberg, a professor at Harvard, argued that

> the intensity with which the plays take hold of the audience cannot remain without social effects ... it is evident that such a penetrating influence must be fraught with dangers. The more vividly the impressions force themselves on the mind the more easily they must become starting points for imitation and other motor responses.
>
> (Münsterberg, 1916: 217–18)

In the UK, social commentators argued that the effects of cinema on children and young people were of particular concern since "the senses of the adolescent, now open at their widest, are opened not to Art, but to cheap and tawdry pantomime" (Freeman, 1914: 151). Similarly, campaigners in the US contended that cinema led to "the corruption of the minds of children" and to "degeneracy and in some instances actual crime", and was thus a threat to religious, familial and moral order (*The New York Times*, 1908: 3, cited in Grieveson, 2001). As a result, social reformers began researching movies, documenting the numbers of unchaperoned children in attendance and reporting on their behavior both in and out of the theatres (Butsch, 2001). Such research led one social reformer in the US to conclude that "while the occasional child is driven distraught, a hundred children permanently injure their eyes watching the moving films, and hundreds more seriously model their conduct upon the standards set before them on this mimic stage" (Addams, 1909: 92–93).

Such declarations only served to fuel parental fears that their children might be psychologically and socially damaged by what they saw at the cinema but it took until 1928 before Rev. William H. Short, executive director of the National Committee for the Study of Social Values in Motion Pictures, called upon a group of researchers led by Dr. W. W. Charters to investigate "the harmfulness of the influence exerted by the movies upon the American public and particularly upon the children and youth of the nation" (Charters, 1932: 196). The group was financed by the Payne Fund, an organization dedicated to researching matters related to children and young people, and between 1929 and 1933 they conducted 13 separate studies. Some of this work focused exclusively on the content of commercial films and hence the kinds of messages children were exposed to while visiting the movie theatre. The remainder concentrated on the effects of the films on children in five key areas: the types of knowledge they were exposed to; the effects on children's attitudes to society; the effects upon children's health; the impact movies might have on their emotions; and the influence of films on conduct, particularly in relation to sexual behavior (Charters, 1933).

Charters concluded that some of the studies showed "specific and significant differences [...] between those children who go often to the movies and those who attend infrequently." For him it was clear that "the motion picture ... is a potent medium of education" and, particularly in relation to the cinema's capacity to stir the emotions of the viewer, "the evidence of their influence is massive and irrefutable." Moreover, "these impartial studies indicate" that "there is too much sex and crime and love" than is healthy for children and as such "the power flows too much in dangerous directions" (Charters, 1933: 60–61). However, other studies failed to replicate this finding, leading Charters to suggest that "the motion-picture situation is very complicated" and that commercial films were "one among many influences which mold the experience of children. How powerful this is in relation to the influence of the ideals taught in the home, in the school, and in the church, by street life and companions or by community customs these studies have not canvassed" (Charters, 1933: 61).

Despite their inconclusive nature, the Payne Studies were sensationalized in the popular press of the time and the more inflammatory findings were emphasized. As a result, the studies produced an enduring 'legacy of fear' in which media were seen by the general public to be powerful agents of social and moral change with the capacity to damage the individual moviegoer and through them society at large (Lowery and DeFleur, 1995). Moreover, the particular concern about the effects of media on children and young people has recurred frequently since that time (Wartella and Reeves, 1985). Indeed it appears that with each new technological development the fear that a new form of media might bring lasting harm to the most vulnerable is seemingly reignited, and so current concerns over the influence of violence in computer games or the effects of exposure to sexual content on the internet appear to replicate the issues and concerns that have been raised in relation to previous forms of media. Buckingham et al. (2007: 8) suggest that such persistent public concerns about the possibility of profound media effects may have less to do with media technologies themselves than they have to do with the public's "broader fears about the future direction of society." Perhaps more importantly, they point out that fears about dangers of new technologies and anxieties about the welfare of the young can be easily "exploited by 'moral entrepreneurs' seeking to gain assent for arguments that might otherwise seem illiberal or unduly censorious" (Buckingham et al., 2007: 8).

Media effects in the popular press

Writers such as Murdock (2001) and Pearson (1984) have shown that the history of media effects in the UK has been characterized by a series of 'moral panics' which have led almost inevitably towards a stricter regulation of media content. The 'video nasties' debacle in the early 1980s is a case in point. In this instance, a group of very loosely defined 'video nasties', consisting mostly of low-budget American and Italian horror films, including *I Spit on Your Grave* (1978), *The Texas Chainsaw Massacre* (1974) and *The Toolbox Murders* (1978), which relied heavily on the presentation of horror and graphic violence, provoked outrage within the British tabloid press.

Concern circulated around the potential of these (as yet) unregulated videos to fall into the hands of children and young people leading inexorably, it was asserted, to an increase in violent crime.

The 'moral panic' initiated with the aid of the British press over the effects of these videos on the nation's youth led directly to the introduction of the Video Recordings Act (1984). The Act granted the British Board of Film Classification (BBFC) statutory powers for the first time in its history and required the Board to make classification and censorship decisions with "special regard to the likelihood of video works ... being viewed in the home" (section 4(1)(a)) as well as to consider whether a particular film was "suitable for viewing by persons who have not attained a particular age" (section 4(3)(b)). For while the cinema box office had functioned as a statutory age bar since the passing of the Cinematograph Act (1952), the same could not be guaranteed within the unregulated space of the home; especially, it was argued, within working-class homes (Petley, 2001). The Video Recordings Act (1984) therefore placed the possibility of children viewing works intended for an adult audience right at the heart of the BBFC's regulatory agenda and as a result the BBFC was legally required to make much stricter regulatory decisions with regard to video works than it did for films shown within the cinema.

While the passing of the Video Recordings Act temporarily assuaged the pro-censorship campaigners, the 'video nasties' debate re-emerged a decade later in the wake of the murder of the toddler James Bulger in February 1993 by two ten-year-old boys. Summing up the case at the end of the boys' trial, the presiding judge suggested that the boys' crime could be at least partly explained by their exposure to violent videos. Although video violence had not been discussed at the trial, and despite a dearth of evidence, the UK press claimed that the crime was almost exclusively attributable to the fact that the two boys had watched *Child's Play 3* (1991). The case reinvigorated public concern over 'media effects' and led directly to the strengthening of the Video Recordings Act (1984). The amendment required the BBFC to take particular account of the "harm that may be caused to potential viewers or, through their behavior, to society" (section 4A(1), inserted 3.11.1994) – a test of harm which for the first time enshrined in UK law the idea promoted by media effects research that watching certain kinds of films can directly damage a viewer and/or be causally linked to antisocial behavior.

This idea that the consumption of certain kinds of images may lead to deviancy and crime, a notion that has by no means been proven by media effects research, not only lies at the root of the statutory definition of harm, but recently formed the basis of a law designed to criminalize the consumption of extreme pornography in the UK. The Criminal Justice and Immigration Act, which came into effect in May 2008, made it "an offence for a person to be in possession of an extreme pornographic image" (section 63(1)). The law was prompted by the trial of Graham Coutts for the murder of Jane Longhurst in 2003, where the prosecution placed a great deal of emphasis on the discovery of a large number of violent pornographic images on Coutts' computer. Although no evidence was presented to prove a causal link between his consumption of these images and the murder of Jane Longhurst, the prosecution contended that this material had "'fostered' his bizarre and macabre fantasies", prompting Jane's mother to lead a campaign "to close down or filter out these pornographic sites, so that people like Jane's killer may no longer feed their sick imaginations and do harm to others" (BBC News, 2004).

Like the Video Recordings Act (1984) before it, this legislation is clearly born out of public anxiety about the unregulated circulation of images, facilitated by the development of new technologies, despite the fact that distribution of hardcore and illegal pornography predates the development of both the internet and video tape. Indeed, as Petley (2001) points out, in the early 1970s large numbers of 8mm films were sold via mail order and under the counter in Soho and East End sex shops. Moreover, such films were not restricted to the UK's flourishing black market. Until 1982 a loophole in British law allowed a limited range of pornography to be screened in private cinema clubs, always assuming that such films did not contravene laws of obscenity or indecency. Nevertheless, despite the fact that it was already illegal to publish such material under the Obscene Publications Act (1964), "the global nature of the internet means that it is very difficult to prosecute those responsible who are mostly operating from abroad" making it necessary to "take a different approach" (Home Office and Scottish Executive, 2005: 1) in which it is the consumer rather than the producer or distributor of extreme pornography who is criminalized.

Debates about how we might define 'extreme' pornography, and growing concern about the impact of this law on minority sexual practices notwithstanding, the Criminal Justice and Immigration Act (2008) is symbolic of a more general shift within UK regulatory policy which places an increasing emphasis on the notion of harm. Within broadcasting, for example, the Communications Act (2003) marks a distinct shift from regulation through notions of 'taste and decency' to regulation through concepts of 'harm and offence'. Similarly, the European Directive on Audio-visual and Media Services (2007) legislates for the protection of children and young people from harmful or offensive material across multiple forms of media, including television, the internet, mobile telephony and video-on-demand services. However, as Livingstone and Millwood Hargrave argue, "while norms of taste and decency can be tracked with some reliability through standard opinion measurement techniques, methods for assessing harm", that is media effects research, "are much more contested and difficult" (2006: 22).

Video games and violence

In the current era, however, it is violence within computer and console games that attract the greatest amount of public concern. The interactive nature of the media brings with it particular fears about how children and young people understand and relate to the violence on screen. Here, too, such public anxiety has been fueled by high-profile media reports that lay the blame for acts of horrific violence at the door of particular types of digital games. In February 2004, for example, Warren Leblanc, a 17-year-old boy from Leicester, lured his friend, Stefan Pakeerah, to a local park and murdered him with repeated blows from a claw hammer. After the trial Stefan's parents were convinced that the murder had been motivated by Warren's obsession with the game *Manhunt* (2003). The game was described by some news reports as a 'sado-masochistic' 'murder simulator' in which players are rewarded for the viciousness and brutality of their killings. The incident garnered headlines across the UK – such as, in the the *Daily Mail*, "Murder by Playstation: Horror images on computer drove teenager to kill his friend aged 14" (29 July 2004) – and led several leading stores to withdraw the game from its shelves. All of this was in spite of Leicestershire Constabulary's insistence that the motive for the attack had been robbery and that the game itself had been found in the possession of the victim rather than the perpetrator of the crime.

While the controversy had little impact on regulation in itself, the issue was reignited just three years later with the release of *Manhunt 2* (2007). The BBFC refused to classify the work on the grounds that:

> There is sustained and cumulative casual sadism in the way in which these killings are committed, and encouraged, in the game ... [The] unrelenting focus on stalking and brutal slaying and the sheer lack of alternative pleasures on offer to the gamer ... [suggests] that to offer a certificate to *Manhunt 2* ... would involve a range of unjustifiable harm risks to both minors and adults.
>
> (BBFC, 2007)

Rockstar Games modified and resubmitted the game to the BBFC only to find that it was rejected for a second time and so they took up an appeal with the Video Appeals Committee (VAC), an independent body set up under the terms of the Video Recordings Act (1984) to adjudicate any appeal against the BBFC's decisions. In December 2007 the VAC upheld the complaint and overturned the BBFC's decision. The BBFC responded by taking the matter to the High Court in the UK where the matter was considered by Mr Justice Mitting, who suggested that the VAC's decision had been based on errors of law. The VAC were compelled to reconsider but again granted the appeal, pushing the BBFC to classify the work as an 18 certificate and release the game.

The classificatory struggle left a lasting mark on UK law, however. For in Mr Justice Mitting's concluding statements he sought to clarify the legal definition of harm. So where harm had been understood in a relatively narrow sense up until that point, resting on the issue of whether certain works might be seen to influence the behavior of potential viewers, Mr Justice Mitting urged the VAC to consider not only

> the behaviour of potential viewers, but also any 'moral harm' ... for example, desensitising a potential viewer to the effects of violence, degrading a potential viewer's sense of empathy, encouraging a dehumanised view of others, suppressing pro-social attitudes, encouraging anti-social attitudes, reinforcing unhealthy fantasies, or eroding a sense of moral responsibility.
>
> (BBFC, 2009: 4)

The judge's statement therefore not only reasserted a moral obligation for media producers, but ensured that the findings of media effects researchers would remain central to censorship debates in the UK for decades to come.

These concerns, of course, are not unique to Britain. In the US video games have been linked to a number of massacres, including the Columbine High School massacre in 1999, which was linked directly to the game *DOOM* (1993); the massacre at Virginia Tech University in 2007, which was alleged to have been inspired by *Counter-strike* (1999); and the shootings at Sandy Hook Elementary School in 2012, where press on both sides of the Atlantic speculated about the shooter Adam Lanza's time spent playing *Call of Duty* (2007) – although a report released by the State's Attorney in November 2013 suggests that Lanza's computer game obsession was rather more fixated on the game *Dance, Dance Revolution* (1998) which he played almost "every Friday through Sunday … for four to ten hours" (Office of the State's Attorney Judicial District of Danbury, 2013). This is not to mention the case of Anders Breivik, who killed 75 people in Norway in 2011 and afterwards claimed to have trained for the event using the game *Call of Duty: Modern Warfare* (2007). However, given the popularity of such games in the US it is not actually surprising to find that these particular young men owned or played such games, so, as Karen Boyle (2005) argues, such 'common-sense' reasoning is based on a flawed logic in which certain aspects of these young men's lives have come under intense scrutiny at the expense of other perhaps more meaningful incidents, events and/or social contexts. Moreover, there are more likely causes of violence in our society, such as familial abuse, bullying, social deprivation or undiagnosed mental health issues, but these may be extremely difficult to solve at the level of policy, at least without a significant investment in social infrastructure. Imposing ever stricter regulations on media content can therefore be a way of appearing to act without ever having to address more complicated and entrenched social problems.

Criticisms of the field

While a thorough review of the thousands of media effects studies conducted over the previous decades is beyond the scope of this chapter, it is pertinent here to highlight some of the more profound weaknesses in the evidence presented by this body of research. For as Gauntlett suggests, "so often is the possibility – or rather, supposed *likelihood* – of television [and media more generally] having direct effects pushed into the public eye that it can seem naïve, even perverse, to argue against the contention" (2005: 5). Despite the long history of effects research, however, the evidence remains at best inconclusive (Fowles, 1999). Far-reaching claims are often made on the basis of limited evidence and studies often contradict one another (Buckingham et al., 2007: 21), although after comprehensive reviews of the literature authors such as Freedman have concluded unequivocally that "the scientific evidence does not support [the hypothesis that] media violence causes aggression" (2002: 210).

Nevertheless, effects studies have focused predominantly on trying to establish a direct causal link between media exposure and the particular behavioral or attitudinal effects they are testing for. In relation to computer and console games, for example, researchers such as Craig Anderson have argued a strong case for the potential harmful effects of computer games. In one recent paper, Anderson (2004:

114) suggests that there are "a number of negative behavioral, cognitive, and affective consequences of exposure to violent entertainment media, in both the immediate context as well as developmentally across time." These include higher levels of aggressive behavior, aggressive cognition, aggressive affect, physiological arousal and lower levels of pro-social behavior (Anderson et al., 2010: 152).

These meta-analytic studies have come in for significant criticism, partly on the grounds of the relatively small effects sizes indicated (Cumberbatch, 2004), as well as for their publication bias (Ferguson, 2007); that is, work that demonstrates a positive link between media and aggression is more likely to be put forward for publication, thereby skewing the results of any meta-analytic study. More recently, Ferguson and Kilburn (2010: 176) have criticized Anderson et al. (2010) not only for their methodological flaws, but also for the substantial omission that since the mid 1990s, as violent video games have become more popular, violent crime rates in both the US and the UK have fallen to lows that have not been seen since the 1960s. Moreover, as Buckingham et al. (2007: 27) suggest, media effects researchers in the US tend to argue much more vehemently for a direct causal relationship between media and their purported effects, whereas those researching in the UK appear to be "much more cautious and circumspect when reviewing the same evidence" and more generally critical of the research techniques and approaches adopted in the field.

Behaviorist models

Crudely framed, research studies often rely on a classic behaviorist model which conceives of the viewer's relation with the text as a simple question of stimulus and response. As a result, effects research has consistently neglected the social factors that might underpin the committing of a crime. Furthermore, Boyle argues that by framing interpersonal violence in terms of cause and effect in this way, research not only ignores the fact that individuals make active choices about how they behave, but also suggests individuals are not entirely accountable for their actions (2005: 17). For Boyle, this forms part of a wider problem in which the mobilization of debates over media effects provides a way of excusing male violence against women. Although the cause and effect logic of much effects research may simply be indicative of behaviorism's overly simplistic and reductionist approach to the social world, it is imperative that we challenge the basic theoretical assumptions that underpin this research. That is, we must question how both 'stimulus' and 'response' are conceived within such studies.

In the first instance, researchers often present the stimulus material – 'violence' or 'pornography' – as though these were self-evident and objective categories, free from the value judgment of the researchers. Many studies simply do not explain what is meant by violence, or what kind of media violence was used in the process of the research, and it is simply assumed that the participants, not to mention the reader, share their perception and definition of the material under scrutiny. However, work by Morrison and Millwood (2007) suggests that definitions of what counts as 'violence' on the screen will vary, at least in part, depending on the life experience of the individual. In studies of screen violence, this kind of gross over-simplifications can lead to a total elision of the question of context. Within those studies that conduct content analyses, for example, there is an assumption that violence is a simple category with a singular fixed meaning that can ultimately be quantified. However, such approaches neglect issues such as how such violence is represented, who commits it, what their motivations are, who it is perpetrated against and why (Barker, 2001)? Indeed some studies neglect even the most basic issues of genre, leading to definitions of violence that are so broad that they make programs like *Tom and Jerry* appear to be one of the most violent shows on television (Cumberbatch and Howitt, 1989). As a result, Barker and Petley suggest that

> claims about the possible 'effects of violent media' are not just false, they range from the daft to the mischievous ... different kinds of media use different kinds of 'violence' for different purposes ... without asking where, when and in what context they are used ... it is stupid simply to ask 'what are the effects of violence?'
>
> (Barker and Petley, 2001: 1–2)

But while on the one hand definitions of what counts as violence appear so broad that they seem to encompass depictions that are of little or no concern to the public at large, on the other hand this same set of studies appear remarkably specific in their focus on fictional violence. As Gauntlett (1998) points out, the range of violent acts that are featured in news programs is almost always exempt from criticism. Condemnation of screen violence, it would seem, is reserved for those genres whose purpose is to entertain rather than edify, despite the obvious fallacy of assuming that depictions of fictional violence and depictions of violence on the news will differ in their effects.

In the second instance, it is also important to question how such studies conceive of the issue of 'response'. Effects research very often assumes its subjects to be passive and uncritical. This often leads researchers to assume that while children are inherently 'vulnerable', other groups of viewers are potentially dangerous and might be led to commit violent and/or sexual offences simply by virtue of witnessing them on the screen. Research suggests, however, that this is simply not the case and that children are in fact remarkably sophisticated in their handling of media texts (Buckingham, 1996). Similarly, work by Barker et al. (2007) suggests that viewers of sexual violence bring a range of interpretations to bear on what they see and in the process create a variety of ways in which these texts might be understood. Indeed, as Gauntlett so succinctly puts it,

> since the effects model rides roughshod over both the meanings that actions have for characters in dramas and the meanings which those depicted acts may have for the audience members, it can retain little credibility with those who consider popular entertainment to be more than just a set of very basic propaganda messages flashed at the audience in the simplest possible terms.
>
> (Gauntlett, 2005: 151)

Problems with laboratory testing

However, there is a more general problem with effects research insofar as many studies make use of laboratory-based experiments that might be seen to contain 'demand characteristics' which present the participant with a defined role to play. In this respect, Cumberbatch (2004) recounts the tale of an experiment based on the famous study by Bandura, Ross and Ross (1963). In the original experiment children were exposed to either a real adult, a film of an adult or a cartoon of a cat all of whom were aggressive towards a large plastic Bobo doll. Compared to a control group who had not witnessed this kind of aggression, the experimental group exhibited nearly twice as much aggression towards the Bobo doll, suggesting that aggression could be actively modeled through the viewing of mediated violence. However, in the later study, "one shrewd four-year-old ... arriving at the laboratory for a modelling experiment was heard to whisper to her mother "Look Mummy! There's the doll we have to hit!" (Cumberbatch, 2004: 28). As Cumberbatch suggests, "if four-year-olds can guess what an experimenter wants them to do" then one needs to ask serious questions about whether adult participants may also "behave as 'good' participants, providing the experimenter only with the results they think s/he wants", results which are "arguably more likely with controversial and well-publicized issues such as video violence" (ibid.: 30).

What these issues suggest is that while laboratory-based studies may be among the most influential in policy debates over the regulation of pornography and violence (Boyle 2005), the artificial character of these studies means that they lack ecological validity. The kinds of texts encountered, as well as the manner of presentation, are unlikely to be representative of what subjects would choose to view outside the lab, or the way media texts may be used in more natural settings. The artificial nature of the most common test for aggression, for example – giving another party an electric shock within a laboratory setting – leads one to seriously question whether those studies that report increases in aggression in response to viewing violence can be applied to behavior in the outside world, since choosing to administer an electric shock to a woman who has usually deliberately annoyed you in the context of a laboratory is rather different to an act of assault (Cumberbatch and Howitt, 1989: 49). Moreover, in the real world acts of violence have myriad consequences for both the victim and the perpetrator, and individuals also have a range of more or less legitimate ways of dealing with their aggression, like phoning a friend or hitting a pillow, which are simply not available to them in the laboratory (Boyle, 2005).

The passive viewer

In addition, media effects research often fails to account for the psychological processes that lie behind the behaviors witnessed in the laboratory. For example, where studies seek to demonstrate that viewing sex or violence on screen might lead to desensitization or attitudinal effects, their conclusions can completely cut across alternative explanations for the subjects' responses. For example, Howitt (in Cumberbatch and Howitt, 1989) discusses research conducted by Zillman and Bryant

(1982) on the effects of watching pornography on 'sexual callousness'. Howitt suggests that while these researchers claim that the lowering of a subject's support for the Women's Liberation Movement after viewing pornography is indicative of a more general increase in 'sexual callousness', they wholly neglect the possibility that the subject's lower support might be because the films were not as extreme as feminist campaigners had led them to believe.

Similarly, a study by Linz, Donnerstein and Penrod (1988) claimed to show that viewing sexualized violence in R-rated films led subjects to become desensitized toward issues of rape and violence. The researchers suggested that after watching ten hours of feature films subjects reported feeling less anxious, seeing less 'offensive scenes' within the films, perceived the films to be 'less graphic and gory', and by the last day "men were rating the material as significantly less debasing and degrading to women, more humorous, more enjoyable, and claimed a greater willingness to see this type of film again" (Donnerstein and Linz, 1998: 188). Within the study these findings were construed as evidence that the subjects had become desensitized. However, these responses may just as easily be interpreted as the men's growing familiarity with the specific narrative conventions that define the genre of the films they saw. The interpretation was therefore based on the notion that subjects ought to find the material offensive, demonstrating not only the researchers' own value judgements about the films being screened, but also the power relationship implicit within the research. That is, the nature of the research design did not allow the subjects to offer their own interpretations of the films and nor did it allow subjects to account for the change in their own responses. As such these viewers are presented as passive and ignorant victims of media texts, rather than rational agents actively involved in a process of interpreting these texts.

Conservative social judgements are also a feature of studies conducted on the effects of pornography on attitudes. For example, Zillman and Bryant have published a series of papers that suggest that the consumption of pornography might lead to a greater acceptance of promiscuity; a lower evaluation of the value of marriage; a greater acceptance of pre or extra-marital sex; and a belief that sexual practices like oral sex, anal sex and sadomasochism are more common amongst the population (Zillman and Bryant, 1982; 1984; 1988). Even if we concede that these findings are an accurate reflection of the direct effects of viewing pornography, we must still question the ideological agenda that underpins the tests. The suggestion that harm can be measured in terms of conformity to a prescribed set of normative 'family values' is a matter for some serious debate.

Similarly, laboratory-based studies that have sought to demonstrate the media's capacity to produce desensitization in the viewer have also shown that post-exposure debriefing sessions can not only significantly ameliorate desensitization and/or attitudinal effects produced by the research, but can also lead to greater sensitivity to issues of rape (see Donnerstein, Linz and Penrod, 1987). Taken at face value this undermines the premise that watching sexual or sexualized violence on screen causes harmful effects in any simple way, suggesting instead that interpretations of these depictions are profoundly influenced by the social and ideological climate in which they are viewed. In which case, the question becomes less about the regulation of film works and more about the information and attitudes that circulate within our culture more generally.

Conclusion

While it is clear that the question of media effects has been a persistent one, it is also beyond doubt that the many thousands of research studies published since the first Payne Fund studies have failed to bring about consensus within the academic community. So while some psychologists, such as Anderson (2004) and Anderson et al. (2010) argue vehemently for the direct causal effects that media might have on their audience, others, particularly UK-based scholars more aligned with the cultural studies tradition, have argued just as vociferously that the very premise of the media effects tradition is flawed. For scholars such as Boyle (2005), Gauntlett (1998; 2005) and Barker and Petley (2001) media effects researchers are simply asking the wrong questions. Add to that the significant epistemological flaws that underpin the key methodologies within the field and the case for media effects begins to look very tenuous indeed.

For these scholars the only way to overcome issues of researcher demand, the lack of ecological validity, the problems with interpretation, and assumptions about the passivity, vulnerability and lack of critical faculties amongst research subjects it to abandon laboratory-based research in favor of more ethnographic work, wherein subjects are recruited as informants in the research process rather than guinea pigs to be tested. It is only then that we can begin to recognize and understand the conscious and willing decisions that viewers must make in face of the messages included within media texts, and therefore begin to question how viewers make use of media content in the course of their everyday lives. Such a project demands that we recognize the audience, even of violent media, as active interpreters and users of such media, and that we privilege the voices of users when attempting to describe the meaning and function of media texts in the context of social and cultural life. And for those concerned with the issue of violence within society it is imperative that such studies are complemented by sociological work that attempts to broaden the question in terms of the causal factors that underpin violent crimes within our societies. It is only then that we will fully be able to comprehend the complexity of the social causes of crime and the media's place within that network of relations. Such sociological work may then provide a more suitable evidence base on which to found social policy on the one hand and media regulation on the other. For while increasing regulation of media texts and, in the case of the Criminal Justice and Immigration Act (2008), media users, may provide a quick fix for politicians looking to assuage public fears in the wake of high-profile media stories that assume links between media and violence, it does little to help us understand the real causes of violent crime in our communities.

Further reading

Potter's (2012) *Media Effects* and Carter and Weaver's (2003) *Violence and the Media* are two excellent introductions to the range of studies conducted in the field. Similarly, Bryant and Oliver's (2008) *Media Effects: Advances in Theory and Research* gives a good overview of those who argue for a direct causal relationship between media and behavior. Anderson, Gentile and Buckley's (2007) *Violent Video Game Effects on Children and Adolescents* argues strongly for the link between violent video games and aggression. On the other hand, Barker and Petley's (2001) *Ill Effects: The Media Violence Debate* and Gauntlett's (2005) *Moving Experiences* offer valuable critical perspectives on the debate. Boyle (2005) in her *Media and Violence* concerns herself with the relationship between media effects and gender, and as such is a useful intervention in the discussion of media effects as a form of discourse.

References

Addams, J. (1909) *The Spirit of Youth and the City Streets*. New York: The Macmillan Company.

Anderson, C. A. (2004) An update on the effects of playing violent video games. *Journal of Adolescence*, 27(1), 113–22.

Anderson, C. A., Gentile, D. A. and Buckley, K. E. (2007) *Violent Video Game Effects on Children and Adolescents*. Oxford: Oxford University Press.

Anderson, C. A., Shibuya, A., Ihori, N., Swing, E. L., Bushman, B. J., Sakamoto, A., Rothstein, H. R. and Saleem, M. (2010) Violent video game effects on aggression, empathy, and prosocial behavior in eastern and western countries: A meta-analytic review. *Psychological Bulletin*, 136(2), 151–73.

Bandura, A., Ross, D. and Ross, S. A. (1963) Imitation of film-mediated aggressive models. *The Journal of Abnormal and Social Psychology*, 66(1), 3–11.

Barker, M. (2001) "The Newson Report: A case study in 'common sense'". In M. Barker and J. Petley (eds.) *Ill Effects: The Media Violence Debate*, 2nd ed. London: Routledge (pp. 27–46).

Barker, M. and Petley, J. (eds.) (2001) *Ill Effects: The Media Violence Debate*, 2nd ed. London: Routledge.

Barker, M., Mathijs, E., Sexton, J., Egan, K., Hunter, R. and Selfe, M. (2007) *Audiences and Receptions of Sexual Violence in Contemporary Cinema*. [report] London: BBFC.

BBC News Online (2004, February 5) UK police seek web porn crackdown. Retrieved from http://news.bbc.co.uk/1/hi/uk/3460855.stm

BBFC (2007, June 19) BBFC Rejects Video Game Manhunt 2. Retrieved from http://web.archive.org/web/20071012145910/http://www.bbfc.co.uk/news/press/20070619.html

——(2009) BBFC Guidelines. [report] London: BBFC.

Boyle, K. (2005) *Media and Violence*. London: Sage Publications.

Bryant, J. and Oliver, M. B. (eds.) (2008) *Media Effects: Advances in Theory and Research*. London: Routledge.

Buckingham, D. (1996) *Moving Images*. Manchester: Manchester University Press.

Buckingham, D., Whiteman, N., Willett, R. and Burn, A. N. (2007) The impact of the media on children and young people with a particular focus on computer games and the internet: Prepared for the Byron Review on children and new technology. [report] London: Department for Children, Schools and Families.

Butsch, R. (2001) Class and audience effects: A history of research on movies, radio, and television. *Journal of Popular Film and Television*, 29(3), 112–20.

——(2002) "The celluloid stage: Nickelodeon audiences". In S. Ross (eds.) *Movies and American Society*. London: Blackwell (pp. 15–31).

Carter, C. and Weaver, C. K. (2003) *Violence and the Media*. Buckingham: Open University Press.

Charters, W. (1932) A technique for studying a social problem. *The Journal of Educational Sociology*, 6(1), 196–203.

Charters, W. W. (1933) *Motion Pictures and Youth: A Summary*. New York: The MacMillan Company.

Child's Play 3. (1991) [film] USA: Jack Bender.
Cumberbatch, G. (2004) *Video Violence: Villain or Victim?* [report] London: Video Standards Council.
Cumberbatch, G. and Howitt, D. (1989) *A Measure of Uncertainty*. London: J. Libbey.
Currie, B. W. (1907, August 24) The nickel madness: The amazing spread of a new kind of amusement enterprise which is making fortunes for its projectors. *Harper's Weekly* (pp. 1246–7).
Czitrom, D. (1992) The politics of performance: From theater licensing to movie censorship in turn-of-the-century New York. *American Quarterly*, 44(4), 525–53.
Donnerstein, E. I., Linz, D. and Penrod, S. (1987) *The Question of Pornography*. New York: The Free Press.
Donnerstein, E. and Linz, D. (1998) "Mass media, sexual violence, and male viewers". In M. E. Odem and J. Clay-Warner (eds.) *Confronting Rape and Sexual Assault*. Oxford: SR Books (pp. 181–98).
Ferguson, C. J. (2007) Evidence for publication bias in video game violence effects literature: A meta-analytic review. *Aggression and Violent Behavior*, 12(4), 470–82.
Ferguson, C. J. and Kilburn, J. (2010) Much ado about nothing: The misestimation and over-interpretation of violent video game effects in eastern and western nations: Comment on Anderson et al. (2010). *Psychological Bulletin*, 136(2), 174–78.
Fosdick, R. B. (1911) Report on motion picture theatres of Greater New York. [report] New York: City of New York.
Fowles, J. (1999) *The Case for Television Violence*. Thousand Oaks, CA: Sage Publications.
Freedman, J. L. (2002) *Media Violence and its Effect on Aggression*. Toronto: University of Toronto Press.
Freeman, A. J. (1914) *Boy Life and Labour*. London: PS King and Son.
Gauntlett, D. (1998) "Ten things wrong with the 'effects model'". In R. Dickinson, R. Harindranath and O. Linné (eds.) *Approaches to Audiences: A Reader*. London: Arnold (pp. 120–30).
——(2005) *Moving Experiences* (2nd ed.). Eastleigh: J. Libbey.
Grieveson, L. (2001) "A kind of recreative school for the whole family": Making cinema respectable, 1907–9. *Screen*, 42(1), 64–76.
Home Office and Scottish Executive (2005) Consultation: On the possession of extreme pornographic material. [report] London: HMSO.
I Spit On Your Grave (1978) [film] USA: Meir Zarchi.
Kuhn, A. (1988) *Cinema, Censorship, and Sexuality, 1909–1925*. London: Routledge.
Linz, D., Donnerstein, E. and Penrod, S. (1988) Effects of long-term exposure to violent and sexually degrading depictions of women. *Journal of Personality and Social Psychology*, 55(5), 758–68.
Livingstone, S. and Millwood Hargrave, A. (2006) "Harmful to children? Drawing conclusions from empirical research on media effects". In U. Carlsson (ed.) *Regulation, Awareness, Empowerment: Young People and Harmful Media Content in the Digital Age*. Goteborg: The International Clearing House of Children (pp. 21–48).
Lowery, S. A. and DeFleur, M. L. (1995) *Milestones in Mass Communication Research*. White Plains, NY: Longman.
Merritt, R. (1976) "Nickelodeon theatres 1905–14: Building an audience for the movies". In T. Balio (ed.) *The American Film Industry*. Wisconsin: University of Wisconsin Press (pp. 59–82).
Morrison, D. E. and Millwood, A. (2007) The meaning and definition of violence. *International Journal of Media & Cultural Politics*, 3(3), 289–305.
Münsterberg, H. (1916) *The Film: a Psychological Study*. London: D. Appleton and Company.
Murder Set Pieces (2008) [DVD] USA: Nick Palumbo.
Murdock, G. (2001) "Reservoirs of dogma: An archaeology of popular anxieties". In M. Barker and J. Petley (eds.) *Ill Effects: The Media Violence Debate*. London: Routledge (pp. 150–69).

Office of the State's Attorney Judicial District of Danbury (2013) Report of the State's Attorney for the Judicial District of Danbury on the Shootings at Sandy Hook Elementary School and 36 Yogananda Street, Newtown, Connecticut on December 14, 2012. [report] Danbury: State of Connecticut, Division of Criminal Justice.

Pearson, G. (1984) "Falling standards: A short sharp history of moral decline". In M. Barker (ed.) *The Video Nasties: Freedom and Censorship in the Media*. London: Pluto Press (pp. 88–103).

Petley, J. (2001) "There's something about Mary..." In B. Babington (ed.) *British Stars and Stardom: From Alma Taylor to Sean Connery*. Manchester: Manchester University Press (pp. 205–17).

Potter, W. J. (2012) *Media Effects*. London: Sage.

The Texas Chainsaw Massacre (1974) [film] USA: Tobe Hooper.

The Video Recordings Act. (1984) [Online]. Available at http://www.legislation.gov.uk/ukpga/1984/39.

Vorspan, R. (2000) Rational recreation and the law: The transformation of popular urban leisure in Victorian England. *McGill Law Journal*, 45(1), 891–973.

Wartella, E. and Reeves, B. (1985) Historical trends in research on children and the media: 1900–1960. *Journal of Communication*, 35(2), 118–33.

Zillmann, D. and Bryant, J. (1982) Pornography, sexual callousness and the trivialisation of rape. *Journal of Communications*, 32(4), 10–21.

——(1984) "Effects of massive exposure to pornography". In N. M. Malamuth and E. Donnerstein (eds.) *Pornography and Sexual Aggression*. Orlando, FL: Academic Press (pp. 115–41).

——(1988) Effects of prolonged consumption of pornography on family values. *Journal of Family Issues*, 9(4), 518–44.

8
Citizen or consumer?
Representations of class in post-war British media

Mick Temple

This chapter critically examines the relationship between changing media representations of class and views of the audience as 'consumers', 'citizens' or 'citizen-consumers'. After a brief historical overview of the relationship between the concepts, we focus on the post-Second World War decades. Representations of class and patterns of consumption in the British national press are complemented by an analysis of the class orientations of the British Broadcasting Corporation (BBC) and, from 1955, the Independent Television (ITV) channels. The ways in which changing media representations of class have influenced the public and the role played by post-war British newspapers and television in challenging and changing perceptions of class and citizenship are the main elements of the chapter, which concludes by assessing the potential of the citizen-consumer to assert political power in a world dominated by global mass media.

Citizen, consumer and class

There is no space here to explore the intricacies of the British class system nor to examine the various means by which class has been codified. Non-Marxist, empirical definitions of class use a combination of elements of social status including wealth, income and occupation. In 2011, the BBC helped develop a system with seven basic classifications, but I propose to use 'working', 'middle' and 'upper' class, terms utilized by most research into viewing and consumption patterns. In a society still obsessed with class, these distinctions (whatever the difficulties of deciding precise boundaries) are quite clearly understood by the population who still tend to use such broad definitions of class as a means of understanding who they are (Roberts, 2001: 224).

While Scammell notes that the distinction between 'citizen' and 'consumer' is also far from clear cut, she characterizes the citizen as "politically interested, informed and outward-looking" and the consumer as "self-interested, isolated and inward-looking" (2000: 352). The belief that the public is now overwhelmingly addressed by the media and the state as consumers rather than citizens is widespread (see Jackson,

2008), leading to many concerns about democratic participation. However, Scammell argues that the traditional model of citizenship, with public-spiritedness at its core, is "an increasingly apt description of consumer behavior" and that the "citizen-consumer" is aware of his/her political power "and increasingly willing to use it" (2000: 352).

Habermas (1989) argues that modern capitalism has seen the demise of the 'public sphere', arguing that the capitalist mass media encourage a conception of the people as passive consumers rather than active citizens. Complementing this, British governments since 1979 have largely seen their role as facilitating and even mimicking markets. However, democratic governance must be about more than satisfying consumer preferences. In his 2009 BBC Reith lectures, the philosopher Michael Sandel maintains that market-mimicking governance does "nothing to make us democratic citizens" and has contributed to a deeper class divide. The concentration on private consumption means not only that inequality deepens but also that the "rich and poor live increasingly separate lives" (Sandel, 2009). So, contrasting with Scammell's idea that we might all now be defined as 'citizen-consumers', Sandel argues the need for us to be primarily citizens because free market consumerism has failed.

Class and the consumer: The rise of the popular press

While this chapter will concentrate on media representations of class during the post-war years, notions of consumer-citizenship have been 'forever in flux': it is argued that the process stretches back to at least the beginning of the modern British press (Hilton, 2002: 103). The spread of the national and provincial press in the eighteenth century corresponded to an expansion of the 'middle classes', with the press playing an important role in the "commercialization of culture and society" (Harris, 1998: 1). The capitalist economy was a "market structure favored by an expanding middle class pleased to embrace an ideology that legitimated their rising social and political influence" (Hilton, 2000: 656). Hilton argues that the eighteenth-century expansion of newspapers paralleled the "birth of consumer society", with consumption helping forge a middle-class identity across Britain (ibid.: 658). The role of 'consumer' was still largely incidental to that of 'citizen'. However, Kidd and Nicholls (1999) suggest that the primacy of civic culture as evidencing one's position in society was superseded by a more consumerist culture in the Victorian age; that is, 'class' remained vitally important but became increasingly characterized by consumption patterns rather than by one's public activities.

The spread of radical newspapers in the first half of the nineteenth century, encouraging the growth of trade unionism, ensured a lively and potentially inclusive public sphere. The collapse of that press from the mid nineteenth century (see Conboy, 2004: 106) led to an expansion of cheap, popular, 'capitalist' newspapers, filled with advertisements aimed at the emerging middle classes – and later, with the introduction of the *Daily Mail* (1896) and the *Daily Mirror* (1903), at the lower middle and 'respectable' working class. This new mass national press played a primary role in establishing new ideas and divisions of class which were closely related to patterns of consumption. Those radical papers which survived the avalanche of new publications failed to attract advertisers, as they were unlikely to be receptive to attacks on capitalism and so either went out of business or abandoned their radical sentiment and embraced the consumers of new branded products (Temple, 2008: 18).

The process continued into the twentieth century. After the First World War, "an unstable middle class defined itself through what it bought" (Hilton, 2000: 661). Many middle and upper class privileges, such as the plentiful availability of cheap servants, were eroding and a range of new magazines promoted a form of middle-class identity based on consumption (Greenfield, O'Connell and Reid, 1999). Conboy (2010: 110–11) notes the success of the 1930s popular press at attracting "the broadest range of lower middle-class readers". Indeed, prime minister Stanley Baldwin heralded those readers responding to the *Daily Mail* and *Daily Express*'s use of explicit consumerist rhetoric as the "new citizens of the public" (Hilton, 2000: 661). The working class consumer was also catered for. Conboy argues that the re-launching of the *Daily Mirror* in 1934 created the first popular paper to "redefine and then dominate the market with a proletarian language of specifically commercial appeal." The *Mirror* articulated the broad interests and aspirations of its working-class readers, crucially in an "intensely commercialized form" (Conboy, 2010: 110–12).

Consumption and class: Post 1945

That move from citizen to consumer has accelerated during the post-war years and most research agrees that the public is now overwhelmingly addressed as consumers rather than citizens (Jackson, 2008). For Whiteley, 1951 signifies the moment when the balance shifted "from social idealism to consumerism". He maintains that, "symbolically, if not materially", the consumer society arrived in Britain when the Conservatives won that year's general election with the slogan *Set the People Free* (Whiteley, 1985: 32–33). He further argues that in the early 1950s consumption patterns were still a reliable indicator of social class but the effect of prosperity and consumerism was an increase in social mobility, "particularly amongst the young" (ibid., 1985: 33–34).

The influence of American mass culture was crucial. American mainstream ideology sees consumption as a civic duty; there is no ideological divide between being a consumer and being a citizen (Cohen, 2003: 7–8). That message was embraced by British youth and quickly popularized in a new breed of youth magazines and movies. The emergence of 'teenagers' as a new consuming class in the 1950s potentially blurred class divides among the young. The message that the new medium of 45 rpm pop records promulgated – whatever you do, 'don't step on my blue suede shoes' – not only signaled the dawn of a young generation's obsession with consumer goods, it also challenged many existing notions of 'class'.

At that time, the dominant view of the consumer was as a middle-class housewife and within British official channels "working-class groups were marginalized in state consumer politics [and] an expanding group of professional men posited themselves as the spokesmen of the affluent consumer" (Hilton, 2002: 103). The political impact of that 1950s affluence was "a new consumer movement concerned more with value for money of [luxury] goods ... than with the rights to consume through collective provision of goods classified as necessities" (ibid., 2002: 107). Approved patterns of consumption in the media followed middle-class prejudices, as 'consumers', on luxury cars and expensive consumer goods, as 'citizens', on the collapse of 'traditional values', with the consumption patterns and values of the working class often parodied and ridiculed (Kirk, 2007: 206–7). The famous 'class sketch' from *The Frost Report* (BBC, 1966) – "I know my place" – while satirizing the entrenched British views on social class also noted that the increased buying power of the middle class was challenging the innate sense of superiority of an often financially straitened 'upper class'.

Newspapers, class and consumption

Shrubsole's (2012) analysis of broadsheets in the post-war years argues that the increasing use of 'consumer' rather than 'citizen' helped to normalize the broader shift towards a consumerist identity. Something similar appears to have taken place in the tabloid press. Rooney's examination of red tops from 1968 to 1992, a time when the corporatist structures of the British post-war consensus were challenged by neo-liberalism, identifies a comparable trend. He argues that as working-class consumption grew, "editorial content moved away from matters of the public sphere in favor of material which encouraged acts of consumption" (Rooney, 1998: 95). Rooney argues that both the *Mirror* and the *Sun* educated their publics to become consumers through editorial content encouraging readers to "define themselves by what they consumed." Rooney believes television companies colluded with newspapers to increase interest in programs – such as the soaps – aimed largely at working-class viewers. Indeed, research into early commercial television audiences indicates that viewing stimulated readership of the popular press while having a negative impact on the purchase of upmarket titles (Murdock and Golding, 1978: 133). The tabloids moved away from material in the public interest towards material that interested the public, a crucial distinction. Rooney suggests that competition for advertising revenue helped drive this editorial agenda and argues that the *Sun* and the *Mirror* "abandoned the public sphere" (Rooney, 1998: 102).

So, despite competition from other media, newspapers remained a key medium in changing attitudes. For example, Thatcherism was sold to the public largely by right-wing newspapers keen to embrace new ideas of 'citizenship' and anxious to break down traditional patterns of voting along class lines by supporting this share-owning, home-owning message. While it may be that the popular press has always 'bolstered capitalism' by encouraging materialistic values, the *Sun* went beyond this by specifically highlighting "the perceived interests of a newly empowered blue-collar conservatism' (Conboy, 2010: 115). The paper's unswerving support for Thatcherism (along with the vast majority of Fleet Street) had major political ramifications. New Labour's ability to sell itself to a more aspirational electorate was enhanced by a press which applauded Tony Blair's acceptance of Thatcherite reforms and his party's conversion to this new characterization of the voter as 'stakeholder' rather than citizen. For Rooney, the *Daily Mirror's* commitment to collective action by the working class as citizens was forgotten in the working class's apparent embracing of consumerist values. Unger (2010) argues that the challenge to the post-war settlement by the spread of 'privatization', where the media have stressed the importance of 'consumption' in forging a sense of 'class identity', helped signal a fundamental shift in our attitudes to social class. If there was a fundamental shift, it was also aided by a challenge to the BBC's broadcasting (and cultural) hegemony.

ITV arrives: Consumerism flourishes, class differences fade?

The creation of ITV initially divided the television audience on largely class lines, with the mass working class seduced by the new advertising medium while the BBC held onto a more traditional 'middle class' their previous 30 years of broadcasting monopoly had to a large extent created. From 1922, first as the British Broadcasting Company and later Corporation, the BBC's monopoly gave it enormous cultural power and despite its famous mission to 'inform, educate and entertain', its programs sought to educate the masses more than entertain them. The BBC's location outside the influence of advertisers and the requirement to make a profit created the impression that it could build a 'neutral' national consensus on political issues to serve as "a guide to citizens in their decision making" (Conboy, 2011: 24). In reality, a narrow moral view and a commitment to high culture – in essence the overt values of an upper-middle-class elite – predominated. During the 1930s its listening figures were challenged by foreign commercial radio stations such as Radio Luxemburg which, despite poor reception, attracted those dissatisfied with the BBC's output. The American Forces Network wartime broadcasts also captivated British audiences. Ang (1991) notes that the BBC's response to commercial radio was to gradually adopt a more American style of broadcasting, a process that BBC television also followed (eventually) after the creation of ITV in 1955. She argues that in the post-war years, the BBC stopped defining "the audience as public" and succumbed to an environment in which ratings were paramount (Ang, 1991: 111–12) a move from paternalism to populism also noted in its news coverage (Conboy, 2011: 41).

On its re-launch in 1947, the BBC's television audience was overwhelmingly middle class (Terramedia, 2001) but by 1954, boosted by the televising in 1953 of both the FA Cup Final and the Coronation, 59 percent of TV sets were in working-class homes (Emmett, 1956: 294). ITV's introduction encouraged even more lower income households to buy or rent televisions and the post-war consumer boom meant more money was available (Hand, 2007: 69–70). For Emmett (1956: 291) the powerful urge to "keep up with the Joneses" perhaps contributed to the rapid growth in television possession. The independent channels provided manufacturers with a ready and willing mass audience, eager to spend after decades of restraint, and advertisements helped fuel materialism by creating a desire for new consumer goods (Whiteley, 1985: 34).

Acknowledging elite fears of Americanization and rampant commercialism, and in a conscious nod to the BBC's remit, the Television Act of 1954 required ITV "to inform, educate and entertain" (Johnson and Turnock, 2005: 18). From the start, it was clear that entertaining was the dominant aim. In 1957, Roy Thompson of Scottish Television famously declared that owning a television franchise was a "license to print money" (ibid.: 21). By then, two-thirds of a predominantly working-class audience which had the choice were watching ITV rather than the BBC (Bignell, 2005: 62). ITV styled itself 'the people's channel' and cleverly contrived to be "both firmly capitalist and proudly working-class in character: hand in hand with big business but vaunting an anti-establishment stance" (Wickham, 2005). Its news service provided more entertaining news than the BBC, and ITV's success at gaining a mass, general audience eventually had an impact on BBC television, which had to adopt a more populist approach (Conboy, 2004: 198–200).

The renowned cultural commentators Richard Hoggart and Raymond Williams both saw television, and in particular commercial television, as in large part responsible for the loss of good working-class values (Whiteley, 1985: 36). The BBC's first director general, Lord Reith, said the introduction of ITV was akin to importing the "bubonic plague" into Britain (Temple, 2008: 68). As feared by Reith and others, the aura of 'Americanness' in ITV programs attracted British consumers. From the very start, quizzes such as *Double Your Money* and *Take Your Pick* (the first UK shows with big cash prizes) established a difference from BBC quiz shows, highlighting the class divide between the cerebral nature of BBC shows and the 'vulgarity' of working-class aspirations, and quiz shows soon dominated ITV prime-time (Hills, 2005: 178). Within a few years, some of ITV's required public service output was being broadcast outside peak hours, with the justification that high ratings were needed to generate sufficient advertising revenues (Medhurst, 2005: 99).

As Johnson and Turnock (2005: 4) note, assessing the differences between ITV and BBC programs over time is a difficult "if not impossible" task, so that "common-sense notions of the differences ... tend to be perpetuated". Despite the fact that by the end of the twentieth century it was becoming increasingly difficult to characterize the ITV viewer (Svennevig, 1998: 100), the stereotype of a middle-class BBC 'citizen' contrasting with a working-class ITV 'consumer' persisted – and ITV's forays into the world of the upper classes, from *Upstairs Downstairs* (1971–75) to *Downton Abbey* (2010–present), display a stereotypical 'working-class deference' to upper-class taste and lifestyles. Against this, there was also a belief that the working class had become more like the middle classes, in terms of both aspirations and behavior, with the mass media's emphasis on consumption breaking down class divisions (Benson, 1994). By the mid 1970s, researchers were arguing that the convergence between manual and white collar lifestyles, first seen in the 1950s, had become more explicit (Piepe, Emerson and Lannon 1975: 159). The authors maintained that the new working class had:

> culturally and materially converged with the middle class. They are consumption oriented, have a middle-class pattern of television use and tend to be Conservative voters ... Some internalization of middle-class values has clearly occurred ... [television's role] has been 'as a source of values and attitudes to those in search of new models of behavior'.
>
> (ibid.: 165–66)

In contrast, other observers argue that the middle class discursively asserts itself as opposed to the 'vulgarities' of commercial (working-class) values exemplified by the 'tabloid culture' of much ITV output. The rise of reality television shows, primarily on commercial television, illustrates the relationship between 'tabloidism' and the working class, and are seen as opposed to middle-class values (Wilson, 2005: 160–61). For many, the 'classlessness' of the 1960s "turned out to be an image, not a reality" (Whiteley, 1985: 45). The working class may aspire to be middle class but their viewing habits and consumption patterns reveal their differences.

Consumerism and working-class aspirations

Opinion polls regularly show that a majority of the British people now identify themselves as middle class. In the post-war years, there appears to have been a fundamental shift from a two-thirds working-class society to one which sees itself as two-thirds middle class (Toynbee, 2011). Many writers have noted the role of the media in promoting consumption to an audience aspiring to greater status, and consumption patterns are arguably the dominant way people now fix their position in society (see Aldridge, 2003: 3). But owning the right consumer goods is not, in itself, a sign of discrimination or social class – the apparent equality is only an illusion of culture. As Baudrillard has famously noted, "consumption ... is a class institution ... in short, not everyone has the same objects." More deeply, "there is radical discrimination" in the sense of a "sharper, subtler, cultural segregation" in that the better educated and informed have the knowledge and culture to recognize the "fetishistic logic" of an ideology of consumption. So, the newly affluent consumer may call themselves middle class but their aping of those consumption patterns is clear to the "better educated and informed" (Baudrillard, 1998: 59; see also Hall, 1980).

Similarly, McGuigan (2000: 298) disputes the idea of 'consumer sovereignty', at least for the masses, because without money or cultivation (which includes "a postmodernist picking and mixing of tastes, high and low") consumption choices are limited. Class differences are arguably reinforced by consumption patterns rather than challenged. As Bourdieu argues, "taste classifies – and it classifies the consumer" (1984: 88). Someone's social class is revealed by the media they consume and 'culture' becomes a mechanism of class differentiation and contributes to maintaining existing power structures. The idea that consumption patterns lead the working class to adopt a middle-class outlook and values is dismissed by Roberts (2001) as simplistic – inequalities in income, the types of items consumed and contrasts in occupations and life experience remain. Roberts (2001: 224) points out that social mobility is roughly the same at the beginning of the twenty-first century as it was at the beginning of the twentieth, hardly an indication that the mass media and their emphasis on consumption have introduced a more equitable and classless society.

There is, however, evidence that a stress on consumerism can impact on political leanings. Buijzen & Valkenburg found that increased exposure to commercial advertising increased materialistic values and that "campaigns which appeal to particular values serve both to strengthen those values and to weaken opposing values" (2003: 15–21). Advertisements tend to appeal to social status and conspicuous consumption rather than the public good. In addition, it has been asserted that the political role of television has generally been "to promulgate and reinforce conservative social values" (Piepe, Emerson and Lannon, 1975: 166) and to "glorify and support" the status quo (in Brasted, 2004: 7–9). Others agree that advertisements appearing to encourage adventure and experimentation are more realistically a participation in consumption characterized by "acquiescence and conformity" (Andersen, 1995: 104).

Conclusion: Consumerism, class and politics

It is argued that the media's representations of the public do little to encourage politically active and informed 'citizens' (Lewis, Inthorn and Wahl-Jorgensen, 2005). The political power being credited to consumers is partly "a reflection of the primacy given to the consumer in the post-Fordist era since the 1970s in particular", when Margaret Thatcher's policies attempted to increase the power of private and corporate enterprise (Littler, 2009: 4). But whether consumers are sovereign or respond to desires implanted by the mass media is disputed. We *may* be more self-aware and more media literate, but the overwhelming dominance of the economic system makes it difficult to know whether what we think we want is really what we want – or need. Middle-class consumers may console themselves that they are consuming rationally (Aldridge, 2003: 155) and behaving ethically in their consumer choices. But exercising such 'political' power via spending decisions requires that citizen-consumers are both knowledgeable enough and wealthy enough to be able to engage in consumer activism.

So, Scammell's argument that corporate reputations count as never before, thereby offering the possibility of a "power shift to the citizen-consumer" (Scammell, 2000: 355), needs to be critically assessed. Scammell agrees that the "marketing utopia" of a "virtuous circle of citizen-consumers, ethical business and profits" is just that, a utopia (Scammell, 2000: 352). While there is little doubt that consumer action can be a significant lever for change (Littler, 2009: 5), the possibility for action is limited by the information provided by the media – and also confined by social class. As well as perhaps lacking the knowledge and wealth for effective citizen action as consumers, the working class also tend to be more "fatalistic" than the middle class in their consumption patterns and less certain of their capacity to effect change (Sassatelli, 2007: 85).

Despite the widespread use of 'citizen-consumer' to describe the modern 'citizen', Sandel emphasizes a dichotomy between the 'citizen' and the 'consumer'. And for Sandel neither the state's mimicking of the market nor the idea of the citizen-consumer addresses the problems of collective political action. He argues the need for a new kind of politics – "a politics of the common good' – which invites us to think of ourselves "less as consumers, and more as citizens" (Sandel, 2009):

> When we deliberate as citizens, when we engage in democratic argument, the whole point of the activity is critically to reflect on our preferences, to question them, to challenge them, to enlarge them, to improve them.
> (Sandel, 2009)

However, his noble concept requires not only governments prepared to engage at more than a superficial level; it also needs a mass media that takes its responsibilities in the public sphere seriously, addressing us primarily as citizens rather than consumers. But mass media are predominantly global capitalist organizations and their main aim is to sell us things on behalf of themselves and other global capitalist organizations.

That said, it is constantly argued that the internet has 'changed everything', introducing new patterns of consumption so that people need to assert their rights as "citizens of a globally connected internet" (MacKinnon, 2012: 201). In an online environment where genuine consumer choice is a possibility and where e-commerce has been predicted to eventually kill the multinationals, and despite her acknowledgement of the utopian nature of the concept, perhaps Scammell (2000: 355) is correct in suggesting that the 'citizen-consumer' may be an informed public's only effective weapon against the overwhelming power of multinational capitalist organizations and mass media, which have arguably contributed to deepening class divisions rather than challenging them (Sandel, 2009). The age old political question of "who writes the rules and in whose interests?" (Savigny, 2013: 21) is rarely addressed by the mainstream media. When we contemplate the widespread acceptance of such an economic system by a 'working class' and a 'middle class' who have largely not benefitted from it themselves, the ability of the media to influence beliefs is apparent. And the belief that we are now all 'middle class' operates in the interests of a political system in which continuous, conspicuous and largely unquestioning consumption is essential for its survival.

Further reading

The seminal theoretical analysis of the relationship between class and consumerism is Jean Baudrillard's (1998) *The Consumer Society: Myths and Structures*. For a very useful review article, see Matthew Hilton's (2000) "Class, consumption and the public sphere." Margaret Scammell's (2000) "The internet and civic engagement: The age of the citizen-consumer" is a short and accessible introduction to the important concept of the citizen-consumer. For an up-to-date examination of the changing relationship between the media, citizens and audiences in contemporary politics, Richard Scullion et al.'s (2013) edited collection of new writings, *The Media, Political Participation and Empowerment*, is invaluable.

References

Aldridge, A. (2003) *Consumption*. Cambridge: Polity.
Andersen, R. (1995) *Consumer Culture and TV Programming*. Boulder, CO: Westview Press.
Ang, I. (1991) *Desperately Seeking the Audience*. New York: Routledge.
Baudrillard, J. (1998) *The Consumer Society: Myths and Structures*. London: Sage.
BBC (1966) *The Frost Report*, 7 April. Retrieved from http://www.bbc.co.uk/programmes/p00hhrwl
Benson, J. (1994) *The Rise of Consumer Society in Britain: 1880–1980*. London: Longman.
Bignell, J. (2005) "And the rest is history: Lew Grade, creation narratives and television historiography". In C. Johnson and R. Turnock (eds.) *ITV Cultures: Independent Television Over Fifty Years*. Maidenhead: Open University Press (pp. 57–70).

Bourdieu, P. (1984) *Distinction: A Social Critique of the Judgement of Taste*. Abingdon: Routledge.

Brasted, M. (2004) "Through the looking glass: Class and reality in television". *Electronic Journal of Sociology*. Retrieved from http://www.sociology.org/content/2004/tier2/brasted.html

Buijzen, M. and Valkenburg, P. M. (2003) "The effects of television advertising on materialism, parent-child conflict and unhappiness: A review of the research". *Applied Developmental Psychology*, 24(4), 437–56.

Cohen, L. (2003) *A Consumer's Republic: The Politics of Mass Consumption in Postwar America*. New York: Arthur A. Knopf.

Conboy, M. (2004) *Journalism: A Critical History*. London: Sage.

Conboy, M. (2011) *Journalism in Britain: A Historical Introduction*. London: Sage.

Emmett, B. P. (1956) "The television audience in the United Kingdom". *Journal of the Royal Statistical Society*, 113(3), 284–311.

Greenfield, J., O'Connell, S. and Reid, C. (1999) "Fashioning masculinity: Men Only, consumption and the development of marketing in the 1930s". *Twentieth Century British History*, 10(4), 457–76.

Habermas, J. (1989) *The Structural Transformation of the Public Sphere*. Cambridge: Polity Press.

Hall, S. (1980) "Encoding/decoding". In S. Hall, D. Hobson, A. Lowe and P. Willis (eds.) *Culture, Media, Language*. London: Longman (pp. 51–61).

Hand, C. (2007) "The advent of ITV and television ownership in lower income households: Correlation or causation?" *Journal of British Cinema and Television*, 4(1), 67–79.

Harris, B. (1998) "Praising the middling sort? Social identity in eighteenth-century British newspapers". In A. Kidd and D. Nicholls (eds.) *The Making of the British Middle Class? Studies of Regional and Cultural Diversity Since the Eighteenth Century*. Stroud: Sutton Publishing (pp. 1–18).

Hills, M. (2005) "Who wants to be a fan of *Who Wants To Be A Millionaire?* Scholarly television criticism, 'popular aesthetics' and academic tastes". In C. Johnson and R. Turnock (eds.) *ITV Cultures: Independent Television Over Fifty Years*. Maidenhead: Open University Press (pp. 177–95).

Hilton, M. (2000) "Class, consumption and the public sphere". *Journal of Contemporary History*, 35(4), 656–66.

——(2002) "The female consumer and the politics of consumption in twentieth-century Britain". *The Historical Journal*, 45(1), 103–28.

Jackson, D. (2008) "Citizens, consumers and the demands of market-driven news". In D. Lilleker and R. Scullion (eds.) *Voter as Consumer: Imaging the Contemporary Electorate*. Cambridge: Cambridge Scholars Publishing (pp. 141–61).

Johnson, C. and Turnock, R. (2005) "From start-up to consolidation: Institutions, regions and regulation over the history of ITV". In C. Johnson and R. Turnock (eds.) *ITV Cultures: Independent Television Over Fifty Years*. Maidenhead: Open University Press (pp. 15–35).

Kidd, A. and Nicholls, D. (eds.) (1999) *Gender, Civic Culture and Consumerism: Middle-Class Identity in Britain 1800–1940*. Manchester: Manchester University Press.

Kirk, J. (2007) *Class, Culture and Social Change*. Basingstoke: Palgrave.

Lewis, J., Inthorn, S. and Wahl-Jorgensen, K. (2005) *Citizens or Consumers? What the Modern Media Tell Us About Political Participation*. Maidenhead: Open University Press.

Littler, J. (2009) *Radical Consumption: Shopping for Change in Contemporary Culture*. Maidenhead: Open University Press.

McGuigan, J. (2000) "Sovereign consumption". In M. J. Lee (ed.) *The Consumer Society Reader*. Oxford: Blackwell (pp. 294–9).

MacKinnon, R. (2012) "The netizen". *Development*, 55(2), 201–4.

Medhurst, J. (2005) "Mammon's television? ITV in Wales, 1959–63". In C. Johnson and R. Turnock (eds.) *ITV Cultures: Independent Television Over Fifty Years*. Maidenhead: Open University Press (pp. 88–107).

Murdock, G. and Golding, P. (1978) "The structure, ownership and control of the press 1914–76". In G. Boyce, J. Curran and P. Wingate (eds.) *Newspaper History: From the 17th Century to the Present Day*. London: Constable (pp. 130–48).

Piepe, A., Emerson, M. and Lannon, J. (1975) *Television and the Working Class*. Farnborough: Saxon House.

Roberts, K. (2001) *Class in Modern Britain*. London: Palgrave Macmillan.

Rooney, D. (1998) "Dynamics of the British tabloid press". *The Public*, 5(3), 95–107.

Sandel, M. (2009) A new citizenship: A new politics of the common good. BBC Reith Lectures, 30th June, BBC Radio Four.

Sassatelli, R. (2007) *Consumer Culture: History, Theory and Politics*. London: Sage.

Savigny, H. (2013) "Media, politics and empowerment: In whose interests?" In R. Scullion, R. Gerodimos, D. Jackson and D. G. Lilleker (eds.) *The Media, Political Participation and Empowerment*. Abingdon: Routledge (pp. 13–23).

Scammell, M. (2000) "The internet and civic engagement: The age of the citizen-consumer". *Political Communication*, 17(4), 351–55.

Scullion, R., Gerodimos, R., Jackson, D. and Lilleker, D. G. (eds.) (2013) *The Media, Political Participation and Empowerment*. Abingdon: Routledge.

Shrubsole, G. (2012) "Consumers outstrip citizens in the British media". *Our Kingdom*, 5 March. Retrieved from http://www.opendemocracy.net/ourkingdom/guy-shrubsole/consumers-outstrip-citizens-in-british-media

Svennevig, M. (1998) *Television Across the Years: the British Public's View*. Luton: University of Luton Press.

Temple, M. (2008) *The British Press*. Maidenhead: Open University Press.

Terramedia (2001) "Social composition of early UK television audiences". Retrieved from http://www.terramedia.co.uk/media/change/early_tv_audiences.htm

Toynbee. P. (2011) "Viewpoint: Why the class struggle is not dead", 1 September, BBC Online. Retrieved from http://www.bbc.co.uk/news/uk-politics-14721315

Unger, S. (2010) "Social class and citizenship". *Cultural Anthropology*, editorial overview. Retrieved from http://www.culanth.org/?q=node/303

Whiteley, N. (1985) "Pop, consumerism and the design shift". *Design Issues*, 2(2), 31–45.

Wickham, P. (2005) "ITV: Broadcaster". BFI Screen Online. Retrieved from http://www.screenonline.org.uk/tv/id/1139047/

Wilson, S. (2005) "Real people with real problems? Public service broadcasting, commercialism and *Trisha*". In C. Johnson and R. Turnock (eds.) *ITV Cultures: Independent Television Over Fifty Years*. Maidenhead: Open University Press (pp. 159–76).

9
Inscriptions and depictions of 'race'

Daniel Kilvington and Amir Saeed

Introduction

This chapter will explore 'race' in British media history. The historical trajectory of 'race' will be critically investigated with specific reference to media examples. The aim of this discussion is to first, draw attention to the persistent nature of 'race' in media discourse and second, highlight how this concept has mutated, advanced and survived over time. Before we begin to apply 'race' within a media context, it is important that we first discuss 'race'. Following this, we will explore early media accounts of 'Others'. Third, representations of non-European groups will be analyzed within a colonial context. The work will then investigate twentieth-century news media representations of Commonwealth migrants before examining inscriptions and depictions of 'race' in film and television. Finally, we will explore Islamophobia, thus locating 'race' within a contemporary media context.

The shifting nature of 'race'

Although the concept of 'race' has been rigorously analyzed ever since its first recorded appearance in 1508 (Husband, 1987), we still cannot provide a single definition for what 'race' really is (Malik, 1996). Although Montagu (1974: 62) notes that 'race' should be dropped from our vocabulary because of its unjustifiable generalizations, this would prove almost impossible as it has become so entwined within elements of biology, culture, religion, politics and nation. In short, ever since the European explorations of the late fifteenth century, 'race' thinking has permeated the consciousness of human groups. As the category of 'race' developed, it worked to separate 'them' from 'us' (Said, 1981) and consequently 'race' science was used to justify slavery, colonialism and imperialism.

We now live in a binarized world where complex socio-cultural phenomena are commonly represented in terms of civilized/uncivilized and superior/inferior (Said, 1981). These binarized representations play a crucial role in perpetuating our racialized preoccupations. Arguably, the media have helped retain the hegemonic position of 'race' within public consciousness as, according to Hartmann and Husband (1974: 163), "there is a strong connection between race reporting and racial attitudes among the public." Because the media play a key role in our understanding of 'race', one could suggest that they must approach it with extreme care.

Although journalists must avoid mentioning a person's 'race' unless it is deemed "genuinely relevant" to the story (Farrington et al., 2012: 4), we commonly observe stories that label rioters as Asian, fundamentalists as Islamic and gangs as black. Conversely, can you remember reading stories about English rioters, Christian extremists and white knife crimes? For Dyer, this highlights the invisibility of the white 'race' in media discourse. He suggests: "As long as race is something only applied to non-white peoples, as long as white people are not racially seen and named, they/we function as a human norm. Other people are raced, we are just people" (Dyer, 1997: 1). For Solomos, the media therefore plays a significant part in "shaping public images of racial and ethnic minorities" (2003: 30). As this chapter notes, 'race' has been, and still is, used to decipher in- and out-groups across various media platforms.

Early accounts of 'Others' in the media

Between the sixteenth and eighteenth centuries, the term 'race' was rarely employed explicitly in the writings of clerics, historians, authors of fiction, early anthropologists or travellers (Malik, 1996). However, non-white groups were racialized as 'Other' and deemed to represent a mirror image of the civilized West or white norm. This mirror image was constructed as not only capturing external difference of skin colour and facial features but also internal character differences. "[B]lack was associated with paganism, savagery, barbarism and evil; white with purity and goodness" (Ratcliffe, 2004: 16). Europeans who travelled in pursuit of trade carried with them "expectations about what and whom they might meet which were derived from extant verbal and written accounts of the Other" (Miles, 1989: 20).

The influence of travel writers during the sixteenth century onwards was noteworthy as the narratives of their voyages went hand in hand with the development of printing which resulted in books becoming commodities with a wide social reach. The ruling classes and literate members of the lower orders could therefore turn to such writers to learn of the 'new world' and its peoples. Sir Thomas Herbert, a seventeenth-century traveller and writer, summarizes the pre-modern image of Africans:

> Their language is apishly rather than articulately formed, with whom 'tis thought they have unnatural mixture ... Having a voice 'twixt humane and beast, makes that supposition to be of more credit, that they have a beastly copulation or conjuncture. So as considering the resemblance they bear with Baboons, which I could observe kept frequent company with the women, their speech ... rather agreeing with beasts than men ... these may be said to be the descendants of Satyrs.
>
> (quoted in Malik, 1996: 44)

These accounts were published throughout Europe but proved extremely popular in England. Miles (1989: 21) states: "They were published for profit and, secondarily, to educate and entertain." At a time when slavery was an unproblematic practice for many, "European travellers to Africa were only too happy to support the growing prejudice against Africans by exaggerating what they observed in an effort to gain the public's attention" (Bernasconi, 2009: 93). The fascination of the African physicality, language and culture captured European imaginations and so accounts, or stereotypes, of their 'strangeness' and 'Otherness' developed. Yet it was not just Africans who were racialized, but all non-white groups.

South Americans were represented as savages and/or cannibals (Dickason, 1984). The explorer Thomas Cavendish commented on a population on the South American mainland: "In this river there are great store of savages which we saw, and had conference with them: they were man eaters, and fed altogether upon raw flesh and other filthy food" (Hakluyt, 1972: 279). Non-white groups were reported to contrast physically, socially and culturally to superior whites.

During the pre-Enlightenment era, "differences between individuals and groups were the result of God's will. The serf, the slave, the peasant, the artisan, the lord, the king – all were allotted their place in the world by divine sanction" (Malik, 1996: 43). Travel writers played a major role in exaggerating this thinking which upheld the hierarchical structure of human groups. For Ratcliffe (2004: 18), "Common-sense constructs of white and black were central to the discourse surrounding the enslavement of Africans and the development of colonialism." Pilkington (2003: 3) adds: "The idea of race could thus be routinely drawn upon to account for the observed physical and cultural differences between people and the assumed superiority of the West."

In the case of the British Empire, the dark-skinned people of Asia, and elsewhere, were seen as a biologically determined 'race' of inferior people in need of civilizing, a process which came to be known as 'the white man's burden'. Yet underlying these motives were political and economic imperatives.

'The white man's burden'

The period of colonial expansion began in the sixteenth century and lasted until the mid twentieth century. As suggested, whites were seen to take on the 'burden' in an attempt to civilize and moralize inferior peoples. It has been noted that imperial values were projected throughout Britain by diverse means such as "music halls, missionary societies, Churches, book publishers, magazines and juvenile literature, school texts [and] cinema" (Kaul, 2003: 8). The media played an important role in advocating this mission. Back and Solomos add that because most Britons during Victorian times had little or no contact with exotic peoples, "their opinions were formed according to the sources of their information, and these sources were for the most part the popular press and literature" (1996: 147).

Works of Modernist literature of the late nineteenth and early twentieth centuries were influenced by 'race' thinking, none more so than H. G. Wells' *The Time Machine* in 1895. Childs (2008: 50) suggests that: "The Time Machine is an example of a novel about degeneracy because it is a story about the loss of mental and physical strength." This apocalyptic text warns of a future in which 'Others' have not been 'civilized' (Miles, 1989), meaning whites have not carried out their 'burden-like' duties successfully. Set in the future, the 'Traveller' encounters two tribes: the Eloi and the Morlocks. While the Morlocks are depicted as "a queer little ape-like figure" (Wells, 1972: 46–47, cited in Childs, 2008: 48), the Eloi are described as follows:

> One of them suddenly asked me a question that showed him to be on the intellectual level of one of our five-year-old children – asked me ... if I had come from the sun in a thunderstorm! It let loose the judgement I had suspended upon their clothes, their frail light limbs, and fragile features.
> (Wells, 1972: 25, cited in Childs, 2008: 48)

This suggests that the Eloi, a synonym for 'Others', have the mental capacity of children while they are also physically inferior. Literature at that time was fascinated by new ways of thinking and Darwin's theory of evolution certainly influenced the writings of many authors during this time. *The Time Machine*, among other texts, buoyed the idea that 'civilization' processes were necessary for non-European groups.

Moreover, Kaul (2003) notes that British newspapers such as the *Daily Chronicle*, *Daily Express*, *Daily Mail*, *Daily Telegraph* and *Morning Post* were not only pre-occupied by this imperialistic mission, but they (notably the popular press) also learned the value of it. Alfred Harmsworth, for example, the founder and proprietor of the *Daily Mail* from 1896, realized the commercial potential of imperialism. The *Daily Mail* became the "embodiment of empire" as reports touched upon all aspects of colonial life, such as fashion, while human-interest stories were "fully exploited" (Kaul, 2003: 73–74). Fleet Street thus provided the speaking link for empire during the nineteenth and twentieth centuries. Put simply, imperial values, or 'race-thinking', were notably reinforced by Fleet Street to help construct and preserve power structures (MacKenzie, 1986).

'Race' was largely unquestioned during colonial times but by the mid twentieth century, 'race' had been discredited from a biological and scientific standpoint. Nevertheless, Commonwealth migration during the mid twentieth century re-energized 'race' thinking and this paved the way for new racisms. Balibar (1991b, cited in Burdsey, 2007: 82) observes the shifting reconstructions of 'race', nation and culture across twentieth-century Western Europe. Burdsey summarizes this shift, explaining that "external racism", as popularly embraced ideologies consistent with the age of empire, was replaced with notions of "internal racism" which, in opposition, "involved prejudice against a recently constituted minority within one's own national collectivity" (Burdsey, 2007: 82). It has been suggested that the UK press framed Commonwealth migrants in stereotypical and negative contexts (Hartmann and Husband, 1974).

Commonwealth migration and news media representation

Commonwealth migration, or mass migration, occurred after the Second World War as peoples from former colonies were 'pulled' to Britain for paid work. The furore that surrounded immigration throughout the post-war era, though, was focused almost exclusively on the dangers associated with 'coloured' immigration, not the white Australians, South Africans and Canadians who were received unproblematically by both the State and the media. In contrast, blacks and Asians had to suffer a barrage of hostility and prejudice in which the media played a significant role.

Throughout the years, Britain's non-white contingent were portrayed in terms of a limited repertoire of representations and within contexts characterized by conflict, controversy and deviance. In the 1960s and 1970s, studies observed how immigrants were reported in relation to problems of 'numbers' and to the tensions caused by 'race relations' (Hartmann and Husband, 1974). In politics, this notion of fear was similarly articulated, and can be observed through Enoch Powell's 1968 "Rivers of Blood" speech (Saeed, 2007a), in which he famously quoted one of his constituents to have remarked that the "black man will have the whip hand over the white man" (Powell, 1969). Dockers in East London marched in his support, newspaper editors who criticized him were besieged by letters supporting him and one opinion poll even suggested that as many as 75 percent of the population agreed with him (Greenslade, 2005). Given the stereotype of black people as lazy, unemployed and predisposed to criminality, such hostility to 'coloured' immigration was hardly surprising. There is little doubt that the media played some role in cultivating the negative stereotypes which had such austere consequences for immigrants and minorities.

Immigration and social problems were redefined as a 'race' problem. Minority groups were not represented as being part of British society, but as outsiders who should be kept out. In the build-up to the 1979 general election, soon-to-be Prime Minister Margaret Thatcher told viewers of ITV's *World in Action* programme:

> People are really rather afraid that this country might be rather swamped by people with a different culture ... the British character has done so much for democracy, for law, and done so much throughout the world that if there is any fear that it might be swamped people are going to react and be rather hostile to those coming in. So, if you want good race relations, you have got to allay people's fears on numbers.
> (Thatcher, 1978)

Thatcher's comments paved the way for further policy clampdowns on 'coloured' immigration once in office. The message was clear: the number of immigrants coming in was desperately in need of halting before Britain was 'swamped' and its democratic, law-abiding culture undermined by the uncivilized hordes from beyond its shores.

In the 1980s, representations tended to criminalize Britain's black population, ignoring social inequalities and growing anger at police tactics. The 1990s witnessed attacks on anti-racist groups, vilifications of black representatives and the seeming endorsement of 'new racism' by prominent politicians, actively disparaging attempts to further multicultural and anti-racist agendas (Van Dijk, 1991). Other studies have also noticed how the growing number of British-born second and third-generation minorities have been subjected to representations of the 'alien within'.

This began with the so-called "criminalisation of black youth" (Hall et al., 1978). Hall et al. (1978), by employing the notion of the "moral panic", argue that 'race' and 'crime' news converged. They note that the causes of crime were rarely mentioned or discussed, with focus only on the outcomes. Van Dijk (1991), who discusses the 1985 Brixton riots, argues that 'race' was positioned in both tabloid and broadsheet headlines to imply that it was a contributing factor. Take for instance these headlines, both published on the same day by the *Daily Telegraph*, in the aftermath of the disturbances, when participants in the 'riots' had been taken to court:

Second black on murder charge (*Daily Telegraph*, 14 December 1985)
Black Brixton looters jailed (*Daily Telegraph*, 14 December 1985)

Note that when black people are accused or jailed they are described as "blacks" (Van Dijk, 1991: 64). In short, the violence was highlighted and it was suggested that this was inherent to West Indian culture (Gilroy, 1992). These somewhat dated views were expressed again in recent times when, following the London Riots of 2011, the historian David Starkey rather simplistically noted that "whites have become black" (Quinn, 2011). Starkey alluded to a "profound cultural change" (Merrick, 2011) which, in turn, appeared to excuse white rioters as they were simply imitating the 'problem' culture – 'black culture'.

The news media have represented black people as troublesome while immigrants are believed to 'swamp' the nation. Ultimately, these narrow representations influence our perceptions of minority groups. But not only are the news media guilty of essentializing 'Others', so too are films, soap operas, sitcoms, etc.

'Raced' representations on television

Although 'whiteness' is believed to dominate Britain's televisual landscape, black people have appeared on British screens ever since the first transmission in 1933. Although this inclusion sounds positive, Hall (1981) observes "television's basic grammar of race" which, he states, consists of three basic types: the slave-figure, the native and the entertainer.

Traditionally, ethnic minorities have been presented as socio-cultural outsiders within British soap operas. Often represented as intolerant and traditional, the ethnic 'Other' struggles with British values and norms. According to MacDonald (2011: 416), Asians, notably Muslims, are commonly represented as social 'problems' within film and documentaries. Within the crime drama, non-white characters are regularly stereotyped as victims or criminals and are framed in sexual, transgressive and dangerous contexts. Sitcoms are equally important to consider although they have been neglected by academic investigations which have tended to concentrate on more 'serious' genres such as documentaries and the news. That said, sitcoms must not be dismissed as this popular genre is one of the longest running on British television.

Gledhill's (1997) analysis of verisimilitude is relevant here as it refers to what dominant audiences believe is credible and suitable. In order for audiences to laugh at certain sitcom characters and situations, they must comply with our beliefs of what is and what is not acceptable. Dyer's (1977) work on *typing* and *stereo-typing* therefore complies. He suggests that without *types*, we could not intelligibly make sense of the world. However, Hall (2013: 247) adds that *stereo-types* differ as they reduce, essentialize, naturalize and fix "difference" while they divide "the normal and the acceptable from the abnormal and the unacceptable". Those who do not fit are positioned as outsiders and face exclusion.

Till Death Us Do Part (BBC1, 1966–68, 1972, 1974–75), written by Johnny Speight, centres on lead character Alf Garnett, a "flawed, bigoted and reactionary character" who openly displays his controversial views on "race, sex, religion and politics" (Malik, 2002: 92–93). Although Speight intended to ridicule, through Alf, the ignorant and politically incorrect views of many Britons, his preferred reading backfired as "the nation fell in love with him" (*The Life & Times of Alf Garnett*, BBC, 1997, cited in Malik, 2002: 93). As the previous section noted, Enoch Powell arguably legitimized or authorized Alf's claims of a 'whiter' Britain.

Speight's next project, *Curry and Chips* (LWT, 1969) provided a more multicultural setting. He used stock characters such as the overt racist (Norman), the black worker (Kenny) and the tolerant factory foreman (Arthur). The show attempted to tackle issues of multiculturalism and notions of belonging and it even highlighted the socio-cultural differences between ethnic minority groups, such as blacks and Asians. The most shocking aspect was that of Spike Milligan, who played a blacked-up Irish Pakistani (Kevin, or 'Paki Paddy'). This inclusion was both surreal and insulting as Milligan, a blacked-up white actor, was often "mocked for his foreignness by a genuinely black actor" (Malik, 2002: 95).

Love Thy Neighbour (ITV, 1972–76), which focused on a white (Booth) and a black (Reynolds) family, attempted to highlight the culture clash between natives and newcomers, indicating that 'reciprocal racism' was a natural response. Yet Reynolds' 'blackness' was often presented as being backwards and un-British. Moreover, the show appeared to reinforce the belief that blacks and whites reflected binary opposites as 'blackness' became synonymous with trouble, as witnessed in the news media.

By the mid 1980s, comedies such as *No Problem!* (1983–85) and *Tandoori Nights* (1985–87) offered a "more integrated mode of Black production" as "Black artists were now actively involved as writers, actors and producers" (Malik, 2002: 99). During the 1990s, *Chef* (BBC, 1993–96) and *Goodness Gracious Me* (BBC2, 1998–2001) similarly represented significant comedy landmarks.

That said, stereotypes have by no means disappeared. *Citizen Khan* (2012–present), which employs consistent stereotypes, is the latest BBC sitcom to tackle multiculturalism, shifting Asian identities and Islamophobia (Huq, 2013; Saha, 2013). Despite gathering mixed reviews and hundreds of complaints (Hayday, 2012), its second series aired in October 2013.

In sum, stereotypes have been present on television for decades. These stereotypes, often considered 'harmless', help maintain the "social and symbolic order" (Hall, 2013: 248). We are, as an audience, invited to laugh at racialized regimes of representation (Hall, 1997) but are we laughing "*with* or *at*" raced characters (Malik, 2002: 92)? In early sitcoms, non-white characters were the butt of the joke but now audiences are perhaps invited to laugh with characters. However, television representations continue to essentialize outsiders which upholds dominant positions of power and inequality. Character dimensions are limited, narrow and replicate hegemonic thinking. As MacDonald (2011: 423) notes, "Across television's fictional and documentary output, scant attention to the memories of British Muslims of South Asian origin compounds a general lack of specificity in the historical positioning of those represented."

As with racialized representations in fiction genres, some sections of the news media have reified Islamophobia and framed Muslims in narrow and negative contexts.

British Muslims and the media

Since the events of 9/11 and the subsequent 'war on terror', it could be argued that Muslims are now treated as the dominant threat to British society. Various authors contend that the media represent Muslims as one homogenous uncivilized group, similar to other racialized groups, but with supplementary mass generalizations that often depict Muslims as terrorists or Islamic extremists (Saeed, 2004, 2007a, 2007b).

To an equal extent, Muslims are also portrayed in opposition to Western values and social integration (Modood, 1997). Solomos (2003: 186) suggests that this follows a wider tradition of media representations that depict ethnic minority communities as "endangering the cultural and political values of the nation". To illustrate this, the headline published by *The Sun*, "Muslims win toy pigs ban" (21 May 2007), arguably implies that Muslims are insisting on challenging the 'British way of life'.

In 1997, the Runnymede Trust published a report which suggested that anti-Muslim prejudice was becoming increasingly dominant, rendering Muslims extremely vulnerable to physical violence and harassment by racist attackers. Significantly, the Runnymede Trust also appeals to the media to acknowledge their role in the reproduction of Islamophobia. An ever increasing body of research has argued that images, representations and discourses relating to Islam/Muslims in mainstream Western media tend to be negative and hostile (Poole and Richardson, 2006). Various studies have examined the specific relationship between media and Islam (Ahmed, 1993; Runnymede Trust, 1997); the representations of Muslim minorities in the West (Poole, 2002) and Muslims/Islam in the global media (Poole and Richardson, 2006). Ideologically, these constructions can be traced back to the expansion of Western imperialism where a dichotomy of 'west' versus 'east' was constructed (Drainville and Saeed, 2013; Said, 1981).

Recent years have seen mainstream media debate the merits of a multicultural society. Much of this discourse challenges the need for immigration, questioning the value and even validity of minority communities (Modood, 1997). Fekete (2002: 38) draws attention to the difficult situation which ensued after the passing of legislation against terrorism:

> What has finally set the seal on xeno-racism, legitimising even further its populist appeals and inflammatory expression in the press, is the passing of

the Terrorism Act 2000. This, the first permanent anti-terrorism law in twenty-five years, directly targets exile organisations. Even as Macpherson in his report into the death of Stephen Lawrence warned of the danger of stereotyping black communities as criminal, the government gave legitimacy to a new set of stereotypes: asylum seekers are phonies and fraudsters; refugees are terrorists and the enemy within.

The news media's focus on non-white immigration into the UK and other parts of Europe has re-awakened debates on 'Otherness' and 'culture clash'. Too often, these debates ignore the reality of the existence of the marginalized groups and concentrate on the 'fear of the outsider' rather than on the contribution immigrants can make. This homogenization of 'Otherness' and stereotyping, however, generates fear, contempt and hatred of the groups deemed the 'Other', such as, for example, non-whites, Muslims or asylum seekers.

Conclusion

We have explored the shifting nature of 'race' in British media discourse. We have specifically alluded to key historical periods including exploration, colonization and Commonwealth migration. But, as we argue throughout, 'race' must be treated with sensitivity and care as, unfortunately, media consumers have traditionally been relayed information that places 'un-belonging' groups in narrow, negative contexts. Even now, racist discourses can still resemble the biological arguments employed to justify slavery and imperialism. Simultaneously, cultural racism is evident within politicians' questioning the validity of a multicultural society. The moral panic surrounding 9/11 and 7/7 has led to a right-wing-led debate under the guise of community cohesion that has suggested a return to 'core national values/culture' but we must note that this debate indicates a lack of precise meanings for terms such as national and culture. Such debates have been aired at the same time as stricter immigration and policing controls have been introduced. It is certainly worth stressing that it is essential that media critics, academics and practitioners join together to critically examine 'race', a term which Miles (1989: 72) argues "should be explicitly and consistently confined to the dustbin of analytically useless terms".

In summary, the words of Fanon (1986: 53) seem particularly relevant even now: "Hate is not inborn; it has to be cultivated, to be brought into being." There can be little doubt that through the detrimental representation of the 'Other' in the press and wider media, this 'hate' has almost demanded to come into existence.

Further reading

Before applying theories of 'race' and racism to media discourse, reading the works of Malik (1996) and Miles (1989) should provide a firm conceptual understanding. Hartmann and Husband's (1974) seminal publication, although somewhat dated, is essential for anyone interested in media power and minority representations in the press. In a similar vein, Hall et al. (1978), Poole and Richardson (2006) and Van Dijk (1991) have focused on the media portrayal of black, Muslim and ethnic minority groups, respectively. MacKenzie (1986) is essential if interested in the representation of 'Others' during imperialism, while Malik (2002) and MacDonald (2011) are of use in exploring minority representations on television. Penultimately, Stuart Hall's (2013) chapter in his most recent edition of *Representation* provides an excellent but simplified analysis of how 'Others' have been racialized and stereotyped in the media, across various platforms. And finally, Nakamura's (2008) *Digitizing Race* is key in investigating 'race' online.

References

Ahmed, A. (1993) *Living Islam: From Samarkand to Stornoway* London: BBC Books.
Back, L. and Solomos, J. (1996) *Racism and Society*. London: Macmillan.
Bernasconi, R. (2009) "Who invented the concept of race?". In L. Back and J. Solomos (eds.) *Theories of Race and Racism: A Reader*, 2nd edition. Oxon: Routledge (pp. 83–100).
Burdsey, D. (2007) *British Asians and Football: Culture, Identity, Exclusion*. Oxon: Routledge.
Childs, P. (2008) *Modernism*, 2nd edition. London: Routledge.
Dickason, O. P. (1984) *The Myth of the Savage and the Beginnings of French Colonialism in the Americas*. Edmonton: University of Alberta Press.
Drainville, E. and Saeed, A. (2013) "A Right to Exist. A Palestinian Speaks". In *Feminist Media Studies*, 13(5), 830–39.
Dyer, R. (1977) *Gays and Film*. London: British Film Institute.
——(1997) *White*. London: Routledge.
Fanon, F. (1986) *Black Skin, White Masks*. London: Pluto Press.
Farrington, N., Kilvington, D., Price, J. and Saeed, A. (2012) *Race, Racism and Sports Journalism*. London: Routledge.
Fekete, L. (2002) *Racism, the Hidden Cost of September 11*. London: Institute of Race Relations.
Gilroy, P. (1992) "The End of Antiracism". In J. Donald and A. Rattansi (eds.) *Race, Culture and Difference*. London: Routledge (pp. 49–61).
Gledhill, C. (1997) "Genre and Gender: The Case of Soap Opera". In S. Hall (ed.) *Representation*. London: Sage (pp. 337–87).
Greenslade, R. (2005) *Seeking Scapegoats: The Coverage of Asylum in the UK Press*. London: Institute for Public Policy Research.
Hakluyt, R. (1972) *Voyages and Discoveries*. Harmondsworth: Penguin.
Hall, S. (1981) "The whites of their eyes". In R. Brunt (ed.) *Silver Linings*. London: Lawrence & Wishart (pp. 28–52).
——(1997) *Representation: Cultural Representations and Signifying Practices*. London: Sage.
——(2013) "The Spectacle of the 'Other'". In S. Hall, J. Evans and S. Nixon (eds.) *Representation*, 2nd edition. London: Sage (pp. 223–34).
Hall, S., Critcher, S., Jefferson, T., Clarke, J. and Roberts, B. (1978) *Policing the Crisis*. London: Constable.
Hartmann, P. and Husband, C. (1974) *Racism and the Mass Media*. London: Dans-Poynter.
Hayday, G. (2012) "Citizen Khan: How did Twitter react?". *Guardian Online*, 31 August. Retrieved from http://www.theguardian.com/media/2012/aug/31/citizen-khan-twitter-reaction
Huq, R. (2013) "Situating *Citizen Khan*: Shifting representations of Asians onscreen and the outrage industry in the social media age". *South Asian Popular Culture*, 11(1), 77–83.
Husband, C. (1987) "Introduction: 'Race', the continuity of a Concept". In C. Husband (ed.) *'Race' in Britain – Continuity and Change*, 2nd edition. London: Hutchinson Education (pp. 11–23).

Kaul, C. (2003) *Reporting the Raj*. Manchester: Manchester University Press.

MacDonald, M. (2011) "British Muslims, Memory and Identity: Representations in British Film and Television Documentary". *European Journal of Cultural Studies*, 14(4), 411–27.

MacKenzie, J. (1986) *Imperialism and Popular Culture*. Manchester: Manchester University Press.

Malik, K. (1996) *The Meaning of Race*. London: Macmillan.

Malik, S. (2002) *Representing Black Britain: Black and Asian Images on Television*. London: Sage.

Merrick, J. (2011) "Starkey raving bonkers! Historian accused of racism on riots". *The Independent*, 14 August. Retrieved from http://www.independent.co.uk/news/uk/crime/starkey-raving-bonkers-historian-accused-of-racism-on-riots-2337441.html

Miles, R. (1989) *Racism*. London: Routledge.

Modood, T. (1997) *Ethnic Minorities in Britain: Diversity and Disadvantage*. London: Policy Studies Institute.

Montagu, A. (1974) *Man's Most Dangerous Myth: The Fallacy of Race*. New York: Oxford University Press.

Nakamura, L. (2008) *Digitizing Race: Visual Cultures of the Internet*. Minneapolis, MN: University of Minneapolis Press.

Pilkington, A. (2003) *Racial Disadvantage and Ethnic Diversity in Britain*. Basingstoke: Palgrave Macmillan.

Poole, E. (2002) *Reporting Islam: Media Representations of British Muslims*. London: I. B. Tauris.

Poole, E. and Richardson, J. (2006) *Muslims and the News Media*. London: I. B. Tauris.

Powell, E. (1969) *Freedom and Reality*. Kingswood: Elliot Right Way Book.

Quinn, B. (2011) "David Starkey claims 'the whites have become black'". *The Guardian*, 13 August. Retrieved from http://www.guardian.co.uk/uk/2011/aug/13/david-starkey-claims-whites-black

Ratcliffe, P. (2004) *Race, Ethnicity and Difference: Imagining the Inclusive Society*. Maidenhead: Open University Press.

Runnymede Trust (1997) *Islamophobia: A Challenge For Us All*. London: Runnymede Trust.

Saeed, A. (2004) "9/11 and the Consequences for British-Muslims". In J. Morland and D. Carter (eds.) *Anti-Capitalist Britain*. Manchester, UK: New Clarion Press (pp. 70–81).

——(2007a) "Northern Racism: A Pilot Study of Racism in Sunderland". In C. Ehland (ed.) *Thinking Northern: Textures of Identity in the North of England*. Amsterdam/New York: Rodopi Press (pp. 163–92).

——(2007b) "Media, Racism and Islamophobia: The Representation of Islam and Muslims in the Media". *Sociology Compass*, 1(2), 443–62.

Saha, A. (2013) "*Citizen Smith* more than *Citizen Kane*? Genres-in-progress and the cultural politics of difference". *South Asian Popular Culture*, 11(1), 97–102.

Said, E. W. (1981) *Covering Islam*. London: Routledge.

Solomos, J. (2003) *Race and Racism in Britain*, 3rd edition. Basingstoke: Palgrave Macmillan.

Thatcher, M. (1978) TV Interview for Granada *World in Action* ("rather swamped"), April 2013. Retrieved from http://www.margaretthatcher.org/speeches/displaydocument.asp?docid=103485

Van Dijk, T. (1991) *Racism and the Press*. London: Sage.

10
Home comforts?
Gender, media and the family
Jilly Boyce Kay and Kaitlynn Mendes

In this chapter, we examine the emergence of various media in Britain since 1850, and explore their impact on, and gendered relationship with, the category of the 'family'. Following a broadly chronological structure, we discuss the intersections between mass media, gender and the family in two parts: print media (including newspapers and magazines) and broadcast media (including television and radio). These historical narratives are interwoven with scholarship relating to media, gender and the family, and we additionally discuss the range of debates that have animated this field.

Whilst our key analytical emphasis is on the 'family', a direct discussion of this category will come in and out of focus because of the different orientations and methodologies of the media scholarship we survey. As such, our analysis often broadens out to address related themes such as: the ideological division between public and private spheres; the gendered address of media; employment practices and discrimination; and the relationships between the media, women, men and children.

Much scholarship on media and the family has been concerned with the 'effects' of media content on children (for a critical overview see Messenger Davies, 2010). However, this is beyond the scope of our analysis. Similarly, whilst there is a range of excellent scholarship on the *representation* of the family in the mass media (see Chambers, 2001; Douglas, 2003; Tincknell, 2005), this chapter will instead focus on the historiography of the production and reception contexts of media in relation to 'the family'.

Print media, gender and the family

Britain has a long and fascinating history of the commercial printed press, including newspapers and magazines, dating back to the nineteenth century (Beetham, 1996; Conboy, 2011; Curran and Seaton, 2010). Although printed material long predates this period, it is with the shift to a commercialized model from the 1850s onwards, aided by the repeal of various press taxes and stamp duties, that this chapter is able to explore the (re)positioning of gender and the family within British media history.

Women and newspapers

Despite women's long involvement in the creation and consumption of newspapers, such enterprises have been and remain male dominated (Beetham, 1996; Chambers, Steiner and Fleming, 2004; Conboy, 2011; GMMP, 2010). In the late nineteenth century, assumptions about women's 'proper' place in the private sphere, as well as laws which prevented women from legally owning property, inheritance or money, resulted in their widespread but not total exclusion from newspaper production (Chambers, Steiner and Fleming, 2004). While men were considered the most desirable audience, the fact that household budgets were usually in the hands of women meant that they became increasingly targeted as consumers of news from the 1850s onwards.

This was particularly evident in the 1880s with the rise of 'new' journalism – a commercially driven shift away from politics towards sport, crime, entertainment and human interest. As Conboy (2011) writes, rather than providing information to educate and inform readers, as the non-commercial radical press largely aimed to do, newspapers sought to satisfy audience interests to increase commercial gain (see also Curran and Seaton, 2010). This 'new' journalism not only discussed previously ignored issues relating to the 'private' sphere, but also prompted the recruitment of women as professional writers in an attempt to attract a larger female audience (Chambers, Steiner and Fleming, 2004). By 1903, women were considered an important enough market that the *Daily Mirror*, the first "paper for gentlewomen, written by gentlewomen", was established (Chambers, Steiner and Fleming, 2004: 21). Unfortunately it failed as a commercial entity and was converted into a much more successful illustrated publication in 1904 (Williams, 1998).

In the twentieth century, both world wars provided women with unprecedented opportunities to enter a variety of professions, including journalism. However, although women were "kicked out of the workforce and into the hen house" upon men's return from battle (Fraser, 1997: 165), their contributions to the public sphere challenged a range of restrictive gendered ideologies. It would take until the 1960s and 70s before women journalists began to reach critical mass and 'women's issues' were regularly reported outside of the 'women's pages'. While women's pages might have begun as a commercial ploy to attract female audiences, they provided women with both an entry point into the profession and important spaces for feminist critiques of society (Chambers, Steiner and Fleming, 2004). Although few newspapers today maintain separate women's pages in their printed versions (such as the *Daily Mail's* 'Femail' section), others have women's sections on their websites (see *The Guardian*, *Mail Online*, and *The Telegraph*), and there remain noticeably gendered sections within the paper (such as Fashion/Lifestyle for women and Motoring for men).

Despite women's clear progress, they continue to be outnumbered and outranked by men in print, radio and television news (Byerly, 2013; Croteau and Hoynes, 1991; GMMP, 2010; Skillset, 2011), notwithstanding the fact that women outnumber men on journalism courses (Ross, 2010). Furthermore, when women do produce the news, international research has indicated that, just as was the case in the late nineteenth century, they are continually relegated to the 'softer' news items (GMMP 2010;

Women in Journalism, 2012). Research consistently demonstrates that women news workers face a 'glass ceiling' (GMMP, 2010; Mendes, 2013; Robinson, 2005) and although incremental gains have been won, "what we see, read and hear is mostly news [by and] about men" (Ross, 2010: 89). Despite this, however, women (and men) continue to campaign for reforms, greater awareness of gender imbalances and the institutionalization of equality programmes at news organizations.

Women's alternative press

Britain has a long and successful history of alternative newspapers, providing women with an opportunity to hone their editing and managerial skills, writing about and engaging with 'public' *and* 'private' affairs. Some of the most prolific and successful alternative publications in Britain revolved around the suffrage movement (see DiCenzo, Delap and Ryan 2011; Smith, 2003), but other papers engaged in a wide variety of other 'political campaigning' and activism dating back to the 1850s (see Delap, DiCenzo and Ryan, 2006; DiCenzo, 2010; Tusan, 2005). These papers allowed women to engage with politics as producers, audiences and distributors. Middle-class women often sold suffragette newspapers on the streets at a time when most news-sellers were men (DiCenzo, 2003) and this "appropriation of public space" came to be seen as an important component of suffragette campaigning (Finnegan, 1999, cited in DiCenzo, 2003: 21).

Scholarship on more contemporary women's alternative publications has focused on the 1960s and 70s, particularly the prominence of feminist zines, newsletters, magazines and journals (see Chambers, Steiner and Fleming, 2004). Although most feminist publications were short lived, some, such as *Jus Suffragii* (1906–29), *Votes for Women* (1907–18) and *Spare Rib* (1972–93) had longer-term success, reaching tens of thousands of readers. While there is still an abundance of alternative women's publications, the internet has also opened up a new platform to reach a wider audience.

The family, newspapers and youth

Unlike other media, newspapers have had a peculiar relationship with the 'family', initially targeting men and women separately, before recognizing that a broader audience would lead to greater commercial success. This has led to what is known as the 'family newspaper' (Bingham, 2009). While men and women were clearly targeted as consumers, it is unclear to what extent children or youth were addressed, as few scholars have investigated the structure, content and reception of children's news. Instead, research has focused almost exclusively on television and online news (Buckingham, 2000; Mendes, Carter and Messenger Davies, 2010). This is perhaps a result of the historic dearth of news (particularly print) aimed at children. Two exceptions include the long-running *Children's Newspaper* (1919–65) and the short-lived *Boys' and Girls' Picture Newspaper* (1923–24) (Briggs, Butts and Grenby, 2008). The surprising lack of academic research on either publication indicates the extent to which this field remains underexplored.

Women's magazines

Women's magazines have long provided fruitful ground for studying production, consumption and gender representations (see Adburgham, 2012; Hermes, 1995; McRobbie, 1991). Although the earliest magazines targeted men, they soon became regarded as a specifically feminine genre (Jackson, Stevenson and Brooks, 2001). This, however, did not prevent men from entering the world of women's magazines, as editors, writers and even readers (Beetham, 1996). Just as newspapers had done towards the end of the nineteenth century, women's magazines began to emphasize women's roles as consumers through advice columns and other editorial content (Beetham, 1996). Although much scholarship has focused on middle-class women's magazines, others acknowledge those aimed at working-class women and girls (see Bingham, 2009). Women's magazines boomed from the 1930s to the 1950s, when research indicates that five out of every six British woman read at least one woman's magazine per week (Pugh, 1992). However, it was not until the 1950s that advertisers really clued into women's potential as a growing consumer market and 'lifestyle magazines' began to flourish (Gough-Yates, 2003). Although sales dipped in the 1970s as a result of economic hardship and increased competition from TV, a series of new 'glossy' magazines emerged in the 1980s, finding success with the increasing number of (middle-class) women in paid employment (Gough-Yates, 2003). Other older magazines such as *Cosmo* and *Honey* rebranded themselves in order to attract professional women. While some magazines, such as *Working Woman*, began to include more politics, 'intellectual' articles and a focus on professional women's lives, these were ultimately unsuccessful and magazines re-focused on consumerism and femininity/sexuality (Gough-Yates, 2003). There also exists a thriving body of work on adolescent girls' magazines, though most focus on content rather than consumption or production (for exceptions, see Frazer, 1987; McRobbie, 1991).

Men's magazines

As the number of women's lifestyle magazines boomed from the 1930s onwards, there was no equivalent for men, whom it was assumed were well catered for by newspapers and magazines on specific hobbies such as motoring, sport and photography (Bingham, 2009; Jackson, Stevenson and Brooks, 2001). Boys were similarly well catered for in commercial magazines and some of the more popular titles included *The Boy's Own Paper* (1879–1967) and *Chums* (1892–1934). Despite this, most academic research has focused on men's rather than adolescents' magazines (see Benwell, 2003; Beynon, 2004; Jackson, Stevenson and Brooks, 2001). In particular, there has been a growing body of research on the rise of men's lifestyle magazines of the 1980s and the 'lad' magazines of the 1990s. As masculinity became increasingly commodified in the 1980s, a range of magazines emerged, such as *Arena*, *The Face* and *Esquire*, focusing on the narcissistic and sensitive 'new man' – a fashion-conscious, ostensibly pro-feminist version of masculinity, which emerged in response to feminism (Beynon, 2004). While such magazines continue to remain popular, the 1990s witnessed the booming success of the new 'lad' magazines such as *Loaded*, *Maxim* and *FHM*, which rejected the 'new man' and instead focused on football, beer, women and music (Beynon, 2004). Feminist scholars have been highly critical of these magazines, arguing that 'laddism' is an attempt to override feminism and revert back to a world where women are sex objects (Whelehan, 2000). Others argue that these magazines present unrealistic images of what 'normal' sex and sexuality looks like (Mooney, 2008), creating confusion for the young men (and women) who read them. Although circulation for lad magazines soared in the late 1990s and early noughties, they have been in steep decline for several years now (Reynolds, 2012). Reynolds suggests that the availability of sexual imagery for free online is the main driver of this decline.

Broadcasting in Britain: Gendered production context

The public service framework of broadcasting in Britain that was instituted in 1922 has had a different set of implications for gender than those of the more 'individualized' press. The first Director General of the BBC, John Reith, famously operated according to a "strict Presbyterian moral code" (Chambers, Steiner and Fleming, 2004: 29). Morley (2000) identifies the Reithian impulse to symbolically model national broadcasting on an idealized family, replicating this conservative, heteronormative model at the macro level of the BBC. Reithian paternalism has had lasting implications for both the BBC's employment of women and its gendered address to audiences. For example, "divorced and married women were not allowed to work for the BBC until the 1960s … [and w]omen were banned from reading news bulletins … right up to the 1970s" (Chambers, Steiner and Fleming, 2004: 29).

Whilst the paternalistic, patriarchal culture of the BBC precluded women's full participation in early broadcasting, many scholarly and popular media histories have tended to marginalize the contributions of the women who *were* key figures at the BBC. Hilmes has argued that, in this respect, "it is history writing that has consigned women to the sidelines, not historical events themselves" (1997: 132). One of the tasks for feminist media historians, then, has been to restate the importance of women personnel and women's genres in broadcasting histories, from which they have too often been absent. For example, see Leman's work on 1950s television for women (1987); Irwin's work on Doreen Stephens, the BBC's first editor of women's television programs (2011); Collie et al.'s historical research on television for women (2013); and Skoog's work on the relationship between women and radio history (2009).

Constructing the family: Broadcasting's gendered address

From the outset of licensed broadcasting in Britain, the 'family' was the key prism through which individuals were understood and addressed (Morley, 2000). Early children's radio programme presenters referred to themselves as 'Aunties' and 'Uncles' and a transmission break between 6 and 7pm in the 1950s came to be called the 'toddlers' truce' to "allow parents (mothers) to get their children to bed before the evening's entertainment commenced" (Thumim, 2002: 210).

Oswell argues that in the early days of radio "the child audience was constituted not as a distinct audience of children but as a family audience" (2002: 25); children's programming was conceived of as "a miniature of broadcasting as a whole" (McCulloch, 1946: 229). By contrast, with the increasing social individualization from the 1950s onwards, programmes addressed children as autonomous individuals, more often physically dispersed around the home than gathered around the hearth.

Broadcasting and anxieties about the family

Broadcasting in Britain has often been the focus for wider public (and counterpublic) debates and conflicting anxieties about 'the family', which are difficult to conceptualize within conventional understandings of left- and right-wing politics. The family has long been identified by feminists, and especially within second-wave feminism, as a patriarchal institution that functions as a key site of the oppression of women. In these particular feminist arguments, the hegemonic, patriarchal family ideal has been incessantly reproduced through media representations – specifically through the naturalization and valorization of particular roles for women as heterosexual wives, mothers and homemakers (see Friedan, 1997[1963]; Rowbotham, 1973; Tuchman, Kaplan Daniles and Benit, 1978).

On the other hand, for social conservatives, broadcasting technologies and their increasing popularity throughout the twentieth century – and into the twenty-first – have carried a different threat: one that does not maintain the ideological power of the family, but rather threatens the existence of the institution itself. This position is most famously embodied by the campaigner Mary Whitehouse and her 'Clean up TV' campaign of 1964, which became the National Viewers and Listeners Association in 1965 (see Tracey and Morrison, 1979). This pressure group held that broadcasting was the key facilitator of the 'permissive society' that was perceived to be undermining 'traditional' family life in Britain. As such, the histories of broadcasting, and of the contested gender politics of the twentieth century, are tightly bound up with one another. However, DiCenzo (2004) has pointed out that the contribution of the women's movement to the history of the media is often ignored or underplayed in media scholarship.

Broadcasting, the family and domesticity

Within both academic and popular discourse, British radio and especially television have long been conceived of as *domestic* technologies (Andrews, 2012; Ellis, 1982; Gillis and Hollows, 2009). Unlike print media, which has historically had a public orientation (consumed by active citizens within a public realm), radio and television have largely been characterized by their address to a domestic audience within the context of the home. As such, they have often been discursively constructed as 'feminine'.

Radio, for example, had initially been seen as a 'masculine' technology requiring technical skill to operate; however, it soon became associated with passivity, domesticity and femininity (Andrews, 2012). In the 1930s, fears abounded about the ability of radio to enter the home – and so to destabilize the boundaries between the public and private spheres (ibid.). Later, television became an object of cultural fear and censure for its supposed stupefying (feminising) effects on its audiences; this specifically gendered discourse intensified in 1955 with the introduction of the commercial broadcaster ITV. Thumim (1998) has pointed out how television critics in the 1950s often used sharply gendered language in their treatment of the medium.

For Bailey (2009), early radio content played a powerful role in maintaining the hegemonic power of the patriarchal state in Britain. It did this first by accommodating women's newly acquired civic roles, achieved in the wake of universal suffrage, but then neutralizing the threats this posed to patriarchy by "addressing them as mothers and housewives located in the private sphere, thus amplifying Victorian idealizations of women" (ibid.: 53). Other research, discussed below, considers the relationships between women, domesticity and the media to have been more complex.

Gender and the family in media scholarship

Ellis argues that the "particular ideological notion of the nuclear family in its domestic setting provides the overarching conception within which broadcast TV operates" (1982: 115). Much scholarly work on broadcasting, then, has been concerned with audiences and the *context* of consumption within the unequal but shifting gendered space of the household (see Brunsdon, 2000; Gillespie, 1995; Gray, 1992; Hobson, 1980; Lull, 1990; Modleski, 2008; Morley, 1986; Sullivan, 1991; Spigel, 2001).

In Morley's *Family Television* (1986), a study of television viewing conducted within the social context of the family, he found that the remote control device was obsessively appropriated by male family members and, as such, functioned as a "highly visible symbol of condensed power relations" (1986: 148). Similarly, Gray's (1992) study of women's use of VCR technology paid attention to the gendered power context of the family. According to van Zoonen, these findings suggest that, "within the context of the traditional western nuclear family, watching television is a leisure activity for husbands, but an extension of domestic labour for wives" (1994: 116). Such research indicates how media consumption has been shaped by the structural gender inequality it takes place within.

The focus on gender and audience was driven in large part by feminist scholars' critical reaction to existing media scholarship in the 1970s, which "disregarded femininity, gender and sexuality in discussions of the 'political' … [and so argued] for a broadening of the meaning of the term 'political' to include a general interest in everyday life, especially the female-associated spheres of domesticity and consumerism" (Brunsdon and Spigel, 2008: 7). In keeping with the second-wave feminist premise that 'the personal is political', feminist television criticism has paid particular attention to genres coded as 'feminine' – especially soap operas (see Ang, 1985; Hobson, 1980) and daytime talk shows (see Wood, 2009; Livingstone and Lunt, 1994). As such, feminist media analyses form an important historiographical body of work – one that offers valuable, historically specific insights into the contested gender politics of the family sphere.

Conclusion

Curran (2002, 2009) argues that the most productive and engaging media histories might be those which 'insert' the media into existing social histories; this, he suggests, "is liable to produce a more contingent view of ebb and flow, opening and closure, advances in some areas and reverses in others" (Curran, 2009: 149). The contested histories of gender and the family provide one such opening for media studies. Existing research, whilst rich and diverse in nature, has nonetheless developed in such a way that 'masculine' and 'feminine' genres tend to be studied separately and within different methodological traditions. In particular, we suggest that more research into the gendered dimensions of news and current affairs, and the implications that this has for the constitution of the normative 'family' – as well as actually existing ones – would extend the scope of an already rich body of feminist work on the mass media.

Further reading

Deborah Chambers, Linda Steiner and Carole Fleming's *Women and Journalism* (2004) provides an ambitious and valuable historiography of the roles, status and experiences of women journalists in the US and Britain from the nineteenth century to the present. Maria DiCenzo, Lucy Delap and Leila Ryan's *Feminist Media History: Suffrage, Periodicals and the Public Sphere* (2011) offers a compelling analysis of the British feminist press in the late nineteenth and twentieth centuries, as well as an excellent section discussing the challenges and contributions of feminist media history. Stacy Gillis and Joanne Hollows' edited collection *Feminism, Domesticity and Popular Culture* (2009) includes interesting discussions of feminism's complex relationship with domestic femininities through historical and contemporary case studies of popular media. Carolyn Byerly's *Palgrave International Handbook of Women and Journalism* (2013) considers women's position in the journalism industry in Britain and around the world, analyzing how far they have come and what improvements are still needed. Karen Ross' *Gendered Media: Women, Men and Identity Politics* (2010) examines a range of contemporary media phenomena and analyzes them in relation to masculinity and femininity, and queer, lesbian and gay identities.

References

Adburgham, A. (2012) *Women in Print: Writing Women and Women's Magazines From the Restoration to the Accession of Victoria*. London: Faber & Faber.

Andrews, M. (2012) *Domesticating the Airwaves*. London and New York: Continuum.

Ang, I. (1985) *Watching Dallas: Soap Opera and the Melodramatic Imagination*. London and New York: Routledge.

Bailey, M. (ed.) (2009) *Narrating Media History*. Abingdon and New York: Routledge.
Beetham, M. (1996) *A Magazine of Her Own: Domesticity and Desire in the Woman's Magazine, 1800–1914*. London and New York: Routledge.
Benwell, B. (2003) *Masculinity and Men's Lifestyle Magazines*. Oxford and Malden: Blackwell.
Beynon, J. (2004) "The commercialisation of masculinities: From the 'new man' to the 'new lad'". In C. Carter and L. Steiner (eds.) *Critical Readings: Media and Gender*. Maidenhead: Open University Press (pp. 198–217).
Bingham, A. (2009) *Family Newspapers? Sex, Private Life and the British Popular Press 1918–1978*. Oxford and New York: Oxford University Press.
Briggs, J., Butts, D. and Grenby, M. O. (2008) *Popular Children's Literature in Britain*. Hampshire and Burlington, VI: Ashgate Publishing.
Brunsdon, C. (2000) *The Feminist, the Housewife and the Soap Opera*. Oxford: Oxford University Press.
Brunsdon, C. and Spigel, L. (2008) *Feminist Television Criticism: A Reader*, 2nd edition. Maidenhead and New York: Open University Press.
Buckingham, D. (2000) *The Making of Citizens: Young People, News and Politics*. London: Routledge.
Byerly, C. (2013) *The Palgrave International Handbook of Women and Journalism*. New York: Palgrave Macmillan.
Chambers, D. (2001) *Representing the Family*. London, Thousand Oaks, CA and New Delhi: Sage.
Chambers, D., Steiner, L. and Fleming, C. (2004) *Women and Journalism*. London and New York: Routledge.
Collie, H., Irwin, M., Wheatley, H. and Wood, H. (2013) "Researching the history of television for women in Britain, 1947–89". *Media History*, 19(1), 107–17.
Conboy, M. (2011) *Journalism in Britain: A historical introduction*. London, Thousand Oaks, CA and New Delhi: Sage.
Croteau, D. and Hoynes, W. (1991) "Men and the news media: The male presence and its effect". In S. Craig (ed.) *Men, Masculinity and the Media*. London: Sage (pp. 154–68).
Curran, J. (2002) "Media and the making of British society". In M. Bailey (ed.) *Narrating Media History*. Abingdon and New York: Routledge.
——(2009) "Media and the making of British society, c. 1700–2000". In *Media History*, 8(2), 135–54.
Curran, J. and Seaton, J. (2010) *Power Without Responsibility*, 7th edition. Abingdon: Routledge.
Delap, L., DiCenzo, M. and Ryan, L. (2006) *Feminism and the Periodical Press. 1900–1918* (3 Volumes). London and New York: Routledge.
DiCenzo, M. (2003) "Gutter politics: Women newsies and the suffrage press". *Women's History Review*, 12(1), 15–33.
——(2004) "Feminist media and history: A response to James Curran". *Media History*, 10(1), 43–49.
——(2010) "Pressing the Public: Nineteenth Century Feminist Periodicals and 'the Press'". *Nineteenth-Century Gender Studies*, 6(2). Retrieved from http://ncgsjournal.com/issue62/dicenzo.htm#note2
DiCenzo, M., Delap, L. and Ryan, L. (2011) *Feminist Media History: Suffrage, Periodicals and the Public Sphere*. London & New York: Palgrave.
Douglas, W. (2003) *Television Families: Is Something Wrong in Suburbia?* London and New York: Routledge.
Ellis, J. (1982) *Visible Fictions*. London and New York: Routledge.
Fraser, S. (1997) *A Woman's Place: Seventy Years in the Lives of Canadian Women*. Toronto, ON: Key Porter Books.

Frazer, E. (1987) "Teenage Girls Reading *Jackie*". *Media, Culture and Society*, 9(4), 407–25.

Friedan, B. (1997[1963]) *The Feminine Mystique*. New York and London: Norton.

Gillespie, M. (1995) *Television, Ethnicity and Cultural Change*. Abingdon and New York: Routledge.

Gillis, S. and Hollows, J. (eds.) (2009) *Feminism, Domesticity and Popular Culture*. Abingdon and New York: Routledge.

GMMP (Global Media Monitoring Project) (2010) "Who Makes the News?" World Association for Christian Communication. Retrieved from http://whomakesthenews.org/images/stories/restricted/national/UK.pdf

Gough-Yates, A. (2003) *Understanding Women's Magazines: Publishing, Markets and Readerships*. London: Routledge.

Gray, A. (1992) *Video Playtime: The Gendering of a Leisure Technology*. London: Routledge.

Hermes, J. (1995) *Reading Women's Magazines: An Analysis of Everyday Media Use*. Cambridge: Polity Press.

Hilmes, M. (1997) *Radio Voices: American Broadcasting 1922–1952*. Minneapolis, MN: University of Minnesota Press.

Hobson, D. (1980) "Housewives in the mass media". In S. Hall, D. Hobson, A. Lowe and P. Willis (eds.) *Culture, Media and Language*. London: Hutchinson (pp. 105–14).

Irwin, M. (2011) "What women want on television: Doreen Stephens and BBC television programmes for women, 1953–64". *Westminster Papers in Communication and Culture*. Retrieved from http://www.westminster.ac.uk/__data/assets/pdf_file/0011/124886/007What-women-want-on-television-Mary-Irwin.pdf

Jackson, P., Stevenson, N. and Brooks, K. (2001) *Making Sense of Men's Magazines*. Cambridge: Polity Press.

Leman, J. (1987) "'Programmes for women' in 1950s British television". In H. Baehr and G. Dyer (eds.) *Boxed In: Women and Television*. London and New York: Pandora Press (pp. 73–88).

Livingstone, S. and Lunt, P. (1994) *Talk on Television: Audience Participation and Public Debate*. London: Routledge.

Lull, J. (1990) *Inside Family Viewing: Ethnographic Research on Television's Audiences*. London: Routledge.

McCulloch, D. (1946) "Entertaining the young listener". *BBC Quarterly*, 1(1).

McRobbie, A. (1991) *Feminism and Youth Culture: From Jackie to Just Seventeen*. Basingstoke: MacMillan Education.

Mendes, K. (2013) "The UK: Equal Opportunities in Theory, but Not Practice". In C. Byerly (ed.) *The Palgrave International Handbook of Women and Journalism*. New York: Palgrave Macmillan (pp. 176–90).

Mendes, K., Carter, C. and Messenger Davies, M. (2010) "Young citizens and the news". In S. Allan (ed.) *The Routledge Companion to News and Journalism*. London: Routledge (pp. 450–9).

Messenger Davies, M. (2010) *Children, Media & Culture*. Maidenhead: Open University Press.

Modleski, T. (2008) "The search for tomorrow in today's soap operas: Notes on a feminine narrative form". In C. Brunsdon and L. Spigel (eds.) *Feminist Television Criticism*. Maidenhead and New York: Oxford University Press (pp. 36–47).

Mooney, A. (2008) "Boys will be boys: Men's magazines and the normalisation of pornography". *Feminist Media Studies*, 8(3), 247–65.

Morley, D. (1986) *Family Television: Cultural Power and Domestic Leisure*. London and New York: Routledge.

——(2000) *Home Territories: Media, Mobility and Identity*. London: Routledge.

Oswell, D. (2002) *Television, Childhood and the Home: A History of the Making of the Child Audience in Britain*. Oxford: Clarendon Press.

Pugh, M. (1992) *Women and the Women's Movement in Britain 1914–59*. Basingstoke: Macmillan.

Reynolds, J. (2012) "Magazine ABCs: *Men's Health* and *Men's Fitness* lead lifestyle charge". *Brand Republic*, August 16. Retrieved from http://www.brandrepublic.com/news/1145887/magazine-abcs-mens-health-mens-fitness-lead-lifestyle-charge

Robinson, G. J. (2005) *Gender, Journalism and Equity: Canadian, US, and European Perspectives.* Cresskill, NJ: Hampton Press Inc.

Ross, K. (2010) *Gendered Media: Women, Men and Identity Politics.* Lanham, Boulder, New York, Toronto, and Plymouth, UK: Rowman & Littlefield.

Rowbotham, S. (1973) *Hidden from History.* London: Pluto.

Skillset (2011) "Tuning out: Women in the UK radio industry". *Skillset*. Retrieved from http://www.skillset.org/radio/industry/article_8511_1.asp

Skoog, K. (2009) "Focus on the housewife: The BBC and the post-war woman, 1945–55". *Networking Knowledge: Journal of the MeCCSA Postgraduate Network*, 2(1), 1–12.

Smith, A. K. (2003) "The Pankhursts and the War: Suffrage magazines and First World War propaganda". *Women's History Review*, 12(1), 103–18.

Spigel, L. (2001) *Welcome to the Dreamhouse: Popular Media and Postwar Suburbs.* Durham, NC: Duke University Press.

Sullivan, T. (1991) "Television memories and cultures of viewing 1950–65". In J. Corner (ed.) *Popular Television in Britain: Studies in Cultural History.* London: BFI (pp. 158–81).

Thumim, J. (1998) "'Mrs Knight *must* be balanced': Methodological problems in researching early British television". In C. Carter, G. Branston and S. Allan (eds.) *News, Gender and Power.* London: Routledge (pp. 91–104).

——(2002) "Women at work: Popular drama on British television c1955–60". In J. Thumim (ed.) *Small Screens, Big Ideas: Television in the 1950s.* London and New York: I. B. Tauris (pp. 207–22).

Tincknell, E. (2005) *Mediating the Family: Gender, Culture and Representation.* London: Hodder Education.

Tracey, M. and Morrison, D. (1979) *Whitehouse.* London and Basingstoke: Macmillan.

Tuchman, G., Kaplan Daniles, A. and Benit, J. (eds.) (1978) *Hearth and Home: Images of Women in the Mass Media.* New York: Oxford University Press.

Tusan, M. E. (2005) *Women Making News: Gender and Journalism in Modern Britain.* Urbana and Chicago, IL: University of Illinois Press.

Van Zoonen, L. (1994) *Feminist Media Studies.* London, Thousand Oaks, CA and New York: Sage.

Whelehan, I. (2000) *Overloaded: Popular Culture and the Future of Feminism.* London: Women's Press.

Williams, K. (1998) *Get Me A Murder A Day!: A History of Mass Communication in Britain.* London: Arnold.

Women in Journalism (2012) "Seen but not heard: How women made the front page news". *Women in Journalism*. Retrieved from http://womeninjournalism.co.uk/wp-content/uploads/2012/10/Seen_but_not_heard.pdf

Wood, H. (2009) *Talking with Television: Women, Talk Shows and Modern Self-Reflexivity.* Urbana and Chicago, IL: University of Illinois Press.

11
Sex and sexuality in British media

Clarissa Smith

Increased visibility and the seemingly diverse nature of representations of sex and sexuality in contemporary media might suggest that British society has become more liberal and tolerant of expressions of different sexual interests. However, the mediatization of sex (whether depictions of actual acts; talk about identities, practices or problems; humorous or serious references to sex) continues to provoke great anxiety and controversy. Indeed the media are often accused of harboring and promoting sexual, and therefore social, disorder. Representations across television, music video and magazines are increasingly 'pornographic' – encouraging 'over-sexualized' behaviors in boys and young men and the over-enthusiastic embrace of 'sexiness' in girls and young women; fostering 'bad body-image', depression, promiscuity; contributing to marriage breakdown, divorce and general unhappiness; and trivializing art and storytelling. Yet at the same time, it seems clear that sexual content can make an important, albeit controversial, contribution to the vibrancy of media output, whether that is fictionalized drama, or educational, reality or documentary programing (Attwood, 2006; Arthurs, 2004; McNair, 2002, 2013).

Thus, the mediatization of sex presents us with a number of interesting problems and contradictions. The media offer up representations of a diverse range of sexual desires, encounters and practices, for which they are both praised and vilified and, at the same time, the media are the key means by which calls for a 're-moralization' of culture are repeatedly aired and disseminated. The adage 'sex sells' seems ever more apposite at this time, although for some media commentators, life would be better if 'sex' was not so ubiquitous and if people would keep their private lives private. Yet, it is precisely this idea that 'sex' is an entirely private matter that renders sex and sexuality so important to studies of contemporary culture. Mediatized sex exists in a variety of spaces – it is both *in* the media and *about* the media. This paradox will be central to the discussion of contemporary and historical examples in this chapter. Hence, this chapter will seek to capture some of the complex topographies of representations and discussions of sex and sexuality within and across the media.

The importance of narratives: Not your father's *Playboy*

Contemporary sexualities are often constructed as forms of consumer lifestyle. In the popular newspaper and magazine press, readers are exhorted to seek out and try the necessary therapeutic and commercial products which give access to 'good' or 'better' sex. Television, particularly Channel 4 (C4), has also played its part in the 'extension of sexual consumerism' (McNair, 2002: 87) with reality programming such as *The Sex Inspectors* (2004–6), *The Sex Education Show* (2008–11) and most recently *Sex in a Box* (2013–), and some dramas which make sex and sexuality a primary focus such as *Queer as Folk* (1999–2000), *Shameless* (2004–13) and *Skins* (2007–13). We should also note that some productions studiously avoid explicit sexual themes, while others attempt nuanced explorations of changing mores. C4's *A Very British Sex Scandal* (TX: 2007), for example, attempted to demonstrate the cruelty of the criminalization of homosexuality. Documentaries have also explored the problems of sexual grooming (BBC3's *Exposed: Groomed for Sex*, TX: 15 December 2011), trafficking (BBC1 East Midlands, *Inside Out*, TX: 12 December 2011), prostitution (C4's *WI Lady's Guide to Brothels*, TX: 3 August 2008) and pornography (C4's *The Dark Side of Porn*, Series 1 TX: April 2005; Series 2 TX: April 2006) whilst others have examined 'naughty' practices, especially those which can still be treated light-heartedly (C4's *Dogging Tales*, TX: 4 April 2013).

Complaints about TV's sexual content often focus on questions of explicitness, or that sex scenes are simply gratuitous as per Mary Whitehouse's complaints during the 1980s, but there are also complaints about the 'unnecessary promotion' or normalization of alternative (non-heterosexual) sexualities. The *Daily Mail*'s right-wing Richard Littlejohn is a key commentator on what he sees as a media 'agenda' to liberalize sex. The BBC's *Doctor Who* spin-off *Torchwood* (BBC1, TX: 28 July 2011) caused him particular offence. Claiming many viewers were outraged by a gay sex scene, Littlejohn demanded to know "what on earth has sex got to do with a science fiction show? Why does the lead character have to be a 'pansexual'? They'll be telling us next that the Daleks all wore bondage gear under their tinfoil armour." Littlejohn went on to argue that "prime time BBC had no *purpose* to air gay themes – prime time is *family* time and therefore not a space for homosexuality" (Littlejohn, 2011). But it is not just commentary on the right which finds there is too much sex on television; stalwart of 'intelligent media' Joan Bakewell also found the BBC straying beyond proper boundaries in a scene in *Sherlock* featuring a nude dominatrix (BBC1, TX: 1 January 2012). As a one-time champion of 60s liberation, Bakewell was aware of the contradictions in her critique but explained that her worries about "too much raunch, too young" were caused by access and availability:

> The media explosion brought on by the internet brings performances within the reach of anyone, children included. And today's smartphone-savvy youth think nothing of forwarding explicit images and video clips to others' handsets. This week, a new set of contestants entered the *Celebrity Big Brother* house to take part in Channel Five's fly-on-the-wall show whose audience is mostly millions of young people. Prior to his incarceration, one

housemate proudly boasted of his intent to have sex on screen – 'and none of this under-the-covers'.

(Bakewell, 2012)

The widespread preoccupations with 'self-revelation' and 'public intimacy' which characterize 'striptease culture' (McNair, 2002) mean that the separations between sex as 'intimate relations' and 'commercial sex' are perhaps no longer as clear as they once (if ever) were. Increased visibility might suggest increasingly liberal attitudes towards groups and practices which do not conform to the heteronormative ideal. However, calls for increased regulation are a constant feature of media headlines, even as those same media spaces are themselves presenting their readers and viewers with 'sexy' and 'sexual' content. The *Daily Mail* surely merits a special award for this kind of double-speak with its constant refrains of 'not in front of the children' while on another page lasciviously exclaiming over teen stars who are 'all grown up' (e.g. Cogan and Strang, 2013). Moreover, the *Daily Mail* has been a key voice in calls to end the 'sexualization' of mainstream cultural output, from prime-time TV through teen magazines and music videos.

In many accounts, including reports produced for the UK Government – Bailey (2011), Horvath et al. (2013) and Papadopoulos (2010) – sexualization is conceptualized as a force working on individuals and on society as a whole, but most especially on girls and women – providing scripts, molding their bodies into particular forms of 'sexy' and encouraging forms of self-objectification – and boys are "a 'guinea pig generation … ' growing up addicted to hardcore pornography" (Peev, 2012: 1). Opportunistically drawing on feminist theorizations in their calls for regulation of music videos and magazines but most particularly pornography, these stories offer a complex narrative of nostalgia and futurology. Apparently while parents have been otherwise occupied, the media that their children are accessing has become increasingly explicit, if not absolutely pornographic. The subheading for this section – 'not your father's *Playboy*' – comes from an article written by Gail Dines (2011) laying out the particular ways in which adults blithely assume that internet pornography is simply an e-copy of the glossy and non-explicit *Playboy* centerfold. A Google search for the phrase turns up more than 12,000 hits, demonstrating its widespread adoption by journalists, politicians and other cultural commentators and its particular resonance as a call-to-arms for a generation of adults ignorant of the trajectory porn has taken. While the phrase 'not your father's *Playboy*' invokes the playful permissiveness of 1950s and 1960s soft-core publishing to bemoan the current state of affairs, other authors have looked even further back for the halcyon days when things were so much better. Penny Marshall looked to Jane Austen's world of chaperones and 'precious' reputations to declaim contemporary mores where "teenage boys watching hours of internet pornography every week are treating their girlfriends like sex objects" (Marshall, 2010).

The 'things-were-better-when' narrative was in full effect when Channel 4 kicked off its autumn season with the documentary *Porn on the Brain* (TX: 30 September 2013) investigating how teenagers' relationship with pornography is changing in the internet age. Hopes of a nuanced and cool investigation were dashed as presenter Martin Daubney, one-time editor of lads' magazine *Loaded*, exclaimed, "But *now* [pornography] is turning our kids into psychopaths!" Over camera-friendly scenes of family kitchens and brain scans, hyperbole and claim was laid on thick producing a picture of lost innocence, brain change and addiction. Establishing spurious connections, the documentary explicitly likened pornography to heroin, claiming that it was damaging kids' brains because the "nature of the teenage brain ... makes it especially vulnerable to addiction"; one expert was wheeled in to intone "we have a great difficulty in proving the connection between violent imagery and violent behavior but clinically it is clear there is a connection."

Porn on the Brain joins the myriad pages of newssheet narrating young peoples' obsessions with sex and sexual representations. Headlines have shouted "How internet porn turned my beautiful boy into a hollow, self-hating shell" (Martin, 2012) and "So, Minister, since when were the civil liberties of porn users more important than those of children?" (Phillips, 2012). Writing for *Psychologies* magazine as part of its campaign against pornography in 2010, Decca Aitkenhead describes boys sitting "in silence, staring at hardcore pornography on their phones, swapping images of astonishing sexual violence as if they were Pokémon cards" (2010). This depiction of porn as a narcotic has been supplemented by claims that it is linked to child abuse and coercive sex work; porn and 'sexualized' media have been said to act "as a de facto pimp for the prostitution and pornography industries" (Tankard Reist, 2009: 20), with men being victims of "grooming" by pornographers – "abused" and "consumed" (Whisnant, 2010: 115) and the "target for ruthless commercial exploitation" (ibid.: 132). Gail Dines (2010) describes young men experiencing the downward spiral of addiction as unstoppable, neglecting schoolwork and spending money they don't have, suffering depression and feeling out of control.

Here, innocence and childhood are talked of as a protected period of life, under threat from outside forces – the forces of unbridled sex, perverse acts, degradation and humiliation which take a physical toll in almost direct replication of nineteenth-century masturbation panics. Almost a decade ago, Henry Jenkins suggested we know less about the audiences of pornography than "probably any other genre of popular entertainment" (2004: 2). Indeed, what little we do know often comes from representations in mainstream media where two stereotypes predominate. For example, in men's magazines like *Loaded* or in films like *American Pie*, the porn consumer may be represented as "a normal bloke, having a bit of fun", but elsewhere he (and it is usually a he) is more likely to be presented as "deviant, slightly suspect and probably addicted" (McKee, Lumby and Albury, 2008: 25) and as "pimply teenagers, furtive perverts in raincoats, and asocial compulsively masturbating misfits" (Kipnis, 1996: 161). In the past the "falsely innocent adolescent female" and a "truly depraved adult male" (Kendrick, 1996: 261–62) have also featured, but the traumatized child and addicted adult male are currently the most frequently depicted figures of contemporary porn consumption, the focus for much 'concerned' press discussion of pornography illustrated with photographs of a pale child or harassed-looking man hunched over a computer keyboard, making clear the unwholesome connection between body and screen.

In May 2013, the UK Children's Commissioner released its Rapid Evidence Assessment on the state of research into children's experiences of pornography (Horvath et al., 2013) following up the widely reported claims by deputy commissioner Sue

Berelowitz that children were grooming other children and that thousands were at risk of sexual abuse and exploitation. The Children's Commissioner report into pornography presents a series of deeply embedded assumptions, which are revealed, as Martin Barker has observed, "by its insistent use of the word 'exposed'. Children are 'exposed' to pornography – a wording carried no less than 66 times in the REA" (Barker, 2014). In the following November, the government announced that its representations to Internet Service Providers had succeeded with the big four ISPs (Sky, BT, Talk Talk and Virgin) who would introduce 'family friendly' internet filters. By the end of 2014, 20 million homes – 95 percent of all homes in Britain with an existing internet connection – will be required to choose whether to switch on a whole-home family-friendly internet filter. Any opposition to this picture is framed as the interests of a few strange, sad, unpleasant individuals against the needs of the innocent child and the wider well-being of society.

These twenty-first-century narratives about pornography posit the idea of 'something new' occurring but a broader examination of media and its reporting, depictions and representations of sex indicate that in fact there is very little that is absolutely new. In researching this chapter it became apparent that a key characteristic of work on media and sex, sexuality and sexual identity is that it is often focused on examination of the present, the here and now, and dependent upon the politics of the author, an elaboration of fears for the future, as media are understood to have considerable effects upon attitudes towards sexuality and on actual practices. In such accounts, history only seems to be important for its rhetorical function; representations and practices in previous decades operate as simple contrasts to demonstrate that the current era accepts ever more explicit or more liberal (again depending upon the politics of the individual authors) representations. Interestingly, while there is a sense that things have moved on from the past there is seemingly little acknowledgement that representations of sex and sexuality are always seemingly 'too advanced' for the particular age.

James Curran has suggested that histories of media are often incomplete: "Media history tends not to illuminate the links between media development and wider trends in society because it is often narrowly focused on the content or organization of the media" (2002: 135). He concludes his short overview of the variety of approaches taken to media history with an admonition that media histories ought to be inserted into a broader engagement with the development of British society "in favour of complexity" (ibid., 149). I have considerable sympathies with such an ambitious approach although it is impossible to do that within the confines of this short piece. However, I do wish to avoid the linear narrative of media development, of a trajectory from 'buttoned-up' Victorian values through to increasing liberalization as we move forward in the twenty-first century. Thus in what follows, I offer an impressionistic account of particular flashpoints. There is no doubt that archival work on newspapers and other media forms gives plenty of scope for amusement. Researching this chapter uncovered a story in the *Western Morning News and Daily Gazette* from 1935 reporting a speech given by a Dr Leonard Williams who expounded on the need for "Maidenly Education", that "girls should be brought up as girls" (the discursive similarities to Mumsnet's call to "Let girls be girls"[1] is remarkable) and their education should not include molding by "embittered, sexless or homosexual hoydens." Williams thought that girls' engaging in games was no more than coercion by "thin-lipped, flat-chested, sadistic creatures." Mothers also came under his fire, with the recommendation that manganese be used to improve maternal attachment and to "induce them [mothers] to forsake the cocktail bar, the cigarette box and the bridge table for the nursery" (Girls Forced to Play Games, 1935).

While it can be tempting to look back to earlier periods with wry bemusement, if not horror, at the ignorance and/or unenlightened attitudes expressed, it is also important to recognize that the picture is more complicated. There are particular nostalgias for earlier decades which may lead to politicized historicism which smoothes out the complex ideological terrains of sexuality across centuries and individual decades. As in the phrasing 'not your father's *Playboy*', other historical periods are used as means of 'reimagining' and working through the dilemmas of the present – the 1950s as a period of repression/shame which flowered into the 1960s period of hedonistic liberation; the 1980s as a period of calm before the storm of AIDS; and our present as an era in which media operate in an unfettered and potentially catastrophic free-for-all, at least as far as sex is concerned. Histories of sex and its representations are not so even as we might like to believe.

If we were to gauge by sales figures alone, reportage of sex has been and remains incredibly popular. As Alison Oram points out, paying attention to newspaper stories is important because they are:

> Highly sensitive to what is topical and what will be acceptable to readers and hence ... useful barometers of social change. Yet, they are not straightforward reflections of popular views and knowledge, nor an accurate record of events.
>
> (2012: 42)

There is, for instance, a long history of media offering sexual advice and doing so in ways which avoid some of the controversies attendant on, for example, book publishing or clinics. Marie Stopes reached a large audience through her books, but she also reached an even wider one through her columns in the mass-circulation *John Bull* (Bashford and Strange, 2004: 78). Advice columns brought quite explicit discussion into mass media forms such as daily newspapers and laid down the foundations for the range of sexual health reportage and programming in our contemporary period which still privileges 'expert', often medical, advice dispensed with friendly concern, constituting both new audiences and new interpretive possibilities. Early advice columns must take their place in any periodization of the increasingly informal social manners in western societies (Wouters, 2004, 2007); of the development of recreational understandings of sex as part of a broader 'therapeutic' culture of self-development and self-fulfillment (Plummer, 1995: 124–25) and fascinations with revelation and "public intimacy" (McNair, 2002: 98).

Yet what is also clear is that the media are often significant vehicles for the circulation of stories of doom and degradation. It is tempting to label these 'moral panics', in which 'a threat' is uncovered, its main characters are stereotyped as 'monsters' and discovered in what ought to be 'safe places', leading to increasingly absolutist demands in the mass media for 'something to be done', followed by regulation and eventual subsidence of the original anxieties. Simon Watney has suggested that when it comes to sex it might be better to recognize that they are not so much *moral* as *sexual* panics. Stories bemoaning, for example, the widening of representation to include LGBTQ persons or highlighting the perils of 'risky' sexual practices are simply "the latest variation in the spectacle of the defensive ideological rearguard action which has been mounted on behalf of 'the family' for more than a century" (Watney, 1997: 43).

Arguably the media come in for so much concerned commentary because their interests in sexual matters are often in conflict with the institutional address of news and broadcast to the 'family' (Cocks, 2004), offering a double-structured narrative, "nurtured by Puritanism, of exposing sexual transgression in order to condemn it" (Arthurs, 2004: 55). Narratives of sexual deviance offer space for vicarious thrills whilst at the same time giving opportunities for condemnation.

Magnifiers of deviance[2]

Historians of sexuality have tended to regard the press "as another key partner in the containment and vilification of homosexuality" but Justin Bengry suggests that perhaps press treatment of queer men in the 1950s "was more complicated and fraught than a simple history of intolerance" (2012: 167). Bengry seeks to open up questions about the capitalist impulses of newspapers that drove their interests in "the intersection of sexual aberration and criminal offence" precisely because "press commodification of queer scandal grew so lucrative … that it contributed to the creation of homosexuality as a public issue attracting government concern and ultimately requiring state intervention" (ibid., 168).

Examining 1950s newsprint about the problem of homosexuality (especially in urban spaces) it is clear that intolerance *is* a defining feature (Houlbrook, 2006). Homosexuality was described in ways which invited readers to respond as 'ordinary men and women' (i.e. heterosexual) offering contrasts of moral and immoral behaviors, the good man and 'perverts', 'degenerates', 'pansies', 'freaks', 'sick men' and the 'abnormally sexed':

> Most people know there are such things – 'pansies' – mincing, effeminate young men who call themselves queers. But simple, decent folk regard them as freaks and rarities.
> ('Evil men', *Sunday Pictorial*, 25 May 1952)

Stories emphasized the disregard of properly masculine codes as the homosexual man acted and dressed like a woman:

> I watched effeminate-looking men disappear into the 'ladies' to titivate their appearance and tidy their waved, dyed hair before going into the back room to dance and cuddle with their 'boyfriends'.
> ('Do we need pubs like this?' *The People*, 24 March 1968)

Along with their transgressions of strict gender norms, homosexuals were also accused of paying little heed to class divisions – in 1954 Peter Wildeblood, Lord Montague and his cousin Michael Pitt-Rivers were condemned for mixing with their 'social inferiors'. In the *Sunday Pictorial*'s 'Evil Men' reportage it was suggested that, "In Swansea police consider the vice most rampant among the 'socially elevated classes', although they take their unnatural desires down to the dockland" (*Sunday Pictorial*, 1 June 1952). Homosexuality was also understood as a kind of infection: less condemnatory commentary would discuss homosexuals as "sick", requiring help, so long as they did not offend public decency, but in descriptions of homosexuality as a kind of "cancer" and "spreading fungus" (Gordon, 1953), its potentials to corrupt others were made abundantly clear:

> They offer them bed and breakfast, and that, in case after case, is a young man's introduction to perversion. Inevitably he drifts to the clubs that male prostitutes frequent! Furthermore, many men who are not homosexuals go to prison and come out tainted in this way, making them even more of a social menace than they were before.
> ('Evil men', *Sunday Pictorial*, 4 June 1952)

The narrative of youth peril should be clear. The possibility of impressionable young people coming into contact with a predatory man is also very similar to late nineteenth-century newspaper accounts which saw the city as a space of degeneracy and danger and to our contemporary times which view the internet as a gateway to predators and corrupters of the innocent. The decriminalization of homosexuality which came in 1967 ought to have put paid to lurid stories of disease and corruption, but later panics during the 1980s over AIDS and the 'vile' book *Jenny Lives with Eric and Martin* (Smith, 2010a; Watney, 1997; Weeks, 1985, 2007) should remind us that tolerance of sexual minorities too often has its limits. In the intervening decades, between the 1950s and now, homosexuality as 'perverse practice' has not entirely disappeared (Hennelly, 2010).

Scandal

Explorations of scandals in Victorian Britain (Cohen, 1996; Fisher, 1995; Israel, 1997) and later (Davenport-Hines, 2013; Tumber, 2004) abound, although these tend, as Cohen observes, "to ignore the fact that scandal even *has* a history, treating each new case as if it sprang up sui generis" (1996: 2). Continuing interest in scandal from the Wilde affair, through Profumo to the current trials of Dave Lee Travis and Bill Roache illustrates Lull and Hinerman (1997) and Thompson's (1997) suggestions that scandals are a cultural genre distinct and familiar across media-scapes and time. As Cohen notes, "While the discursive status of sexuality has indisputably changed in this period [Victorian to present], sexual transgressions still provoke the most sensational media spectacles" (1996: 7–8). He also suggests that the narrative patterns of scandal have remained remarkably familiar, based on the "juridical model of plaintiff, defendant and jury … an accuser exposes an indiscretion or iniquity in the life of an accused and broadcasts that secret for public consumption and the accused responds with denial" (ibid.).

Even so, Gamson draws our attention to the ways in which the actual details of a scandal are rarely the focus of sociological inquiry – partly because of their "apparent transparency" and their appearance as simple "barometers of sexual moralities, moments in which a society reminds itself what is and is not acceptable sexual behaviour by punishing with public humiliation and the risk of status loss those highly visible people caught doing the unacceptable stuff" (Gamson, 2001: 186). Too often the importance of scandal to British newspaper reporting has tended to be seen as a form of 'dumbing down', a betrayal of the radical roots of early news media. And "sensational reporting was sometimes used as part of the radical propaganda of the Sunday papers with personal revelations and scandals often reinforcing a radical analysis of society" (Williams, 1998: 53). Yet Gamson suggests that the sex in the scandal is often "strikingly banal" and that perhaps the *sex* might be the least important element of the scandal: "What is revealed in sex scandal discourse is not simply societal norms – sexual or other, institution-specific, or not – but also the institutional operations and relations of news media" (Gamson, 2001: 187). Thus sex scandal narratives are not just lessons about individual sexual transgressions but are primarily "*institutional morality tales*" where complex "sexual 'sins' reveal not individual but institutional pathologies; not a normative order, but institutional decay" (op. cit.: 188).

Hypocrisy tales, disloyalty and betrayals of trust of the individual might start out as the key features of the scandal but these quickly become tales of the institutions which allow these behaviors to flourish, markers of a social scene or workplace in which sexual shenanigans are simply a small part of the overall license to transgress enabled by the particular institution: the rottenness of politics or the corruption of the Church; the differences between public face and real life – "a crisis of image management" (Gamson, 2001: 192); and the problems of living with fame.

When Lull and Hinerman argue that scandals are really stories about "individuals who privilege their personal desires over the rules of society" (1997: 29), they seem to be missing the potentially more important ways in which scandals are rarely about the individuals (see Lucy Bland's [2012] exploration of the 'Virgin Mother' divorce case which effectively put 'motherhood on trial' as well as the idea of the 'family' and issues of women's proper behaviors); stories of politicians caught in priapic excess are not just about the 'adulterer' but about the corruption of power, the gap between the public and private faces of politics and even crises in the monarchy. Whilst these are at some level held up to us as "the most extreme example of how, in practice, individuals are held to an imagined, idealized standard of social conduct" (Lull and Hinerman, 1997: 5), there is more to them than the lessons for the individual – "rather than proving the normal with the deviant, mass-mediated scandals show the perversions of ... institutional habitats, which, in the end, seem to make the sinner more normal than not" (Gamson, 2001: 199).

It's more fun in the sun

Scandals and panics about sex in the popular press also invite a very particular kind of rapport between publication and reader. British tabloids have adopted a kind of 'ventriloquism' in their reportage. It is, as Smith (1975) suggests, an adoption of the idiom and language of the working class, and an 'us against them' view of the world which, when it comes to sex, expresses itself in both a raucous enjoyment of saucy stories and a prowling of the boundaries of the acceptable. The modern incarnation of the *Sun* launched in 1969 is surely the most obvious exponent "of the direct and vicarious pleasures of sexuality ... within a language of vulgar celebration best epitomized by the descriptions of the Page 3 Girl: 'Cor!'; 'Wot a Scorcher!'; 'Stunner!' (Conboy, 2006: 129).

The *Sun*'s combination of 'booze, birds and the box' brought a particularly working-class hedonism to the newsstands. Sex was used as an important element in marketing the paper from the start, from the 1970 launch of the Page 3 girl who needed no other justification to bare her breasts than that it was 'fun' (Holland, 1983), the *Sun* dispensed with coy excuses for sexually explicit feature articles. Interestingly, the newspaper was not aiming for an exclusively male audience, rather to provide "a language appealing to women as part of a broader celebration of heterosexual pleasure for ordinary people. "We Enjoy Life and We Want You To Enjoy It With Us" announced the first 'Pacesetters' section for women (the *Sun*, 17 November 1969: 14; Conboy, 2006: 129).

With its simple, direct and memorable language, the *Sun* plays a game around the cultural position of its readers and the importance of sex to them. The *Sun* established itself as not just a newsgatherer or mediator, but as a newsmaker and a kind of agent through which ordinary people's voices are expressed. Outcry at the *Sun*'s overtly sexual character contributed to the further sense of the newspaper's iconoclasm, feeding into its complex personality as enabling enjoyment of fun and sensuality while inviting readers to be horrified by what it terms 'evil'. Of note are the seeming inconsistencies of reportage focused on, for example, 'twisted' male teachers and their 'sordid sex' with pupils (Sharpe, 2010) or female teachers as "Miss mucky: Teacher asked boy for romp and urged pupils to mime sex" (West, 2013) or "Lesbian teacher who had kinky sex with a pupil is behind bars – after being reported by victim when she reached uni" (the *Sun*, 2013). The salacious style of reporting enables a frisson of pleasure while also condemning the abuse of institutional powers. Recent stories focused on celebrity arrests in the wake of Operation Yewtree give a further handle on this. The *Sun* has always been interested in the sexual peccadillos of TV and pop stars and has decried the 'bad behaviours' of certain celebrities. Interestingly, as noted above, their take on stories about Jimmy Savile went beyond his outrages to emphasize the rottenness at the core of the institution that is the BBC: "BBC Covered up Paedo Scandal No. 2: Simpson exposed radio 'Uncle' ... but was ignored" (White, 2012); "Savile: BBC's abuse of your license fee" (Moyes and Holmwood, 2012); "Does BBC stand for Blame-dodging Backstabbing Cover-up? Savile report 'whitewash' fury as Beeb chaos exposed" (Holmwood and Sales, 2013). If scandal in earlier periods had focused on the true face behind the façade of respectability of politicians and public office, and even royalty, it is 'celebrity', and the media industries which sustain it, that is now under fire.

Conclusion

Understandings of sex as orientations, practices and experiences have shifted in the twenty-first century, becoming matters of individual duty and responsibility. While sex has become a project of the self (Giddens, 1992) and is increasingly about possessing sexual value (Hakim, 2011), media talk about sex-in-the-media is still offered in proscribed ways – as scandal, confession, an object of medical, regulatory, or criminal concern. Normative notions of what constitutes 'proper' sexual interests still hold sway and in recent years, despite the much vaunted liberalization of culture, religious and feminist campaigns such as Safermedia and Object in the UK, and Stop Porn Culture in the USA, have reinvigorated previous doubts and suspicions about representations of sex, especially those which run counter to the ideal of the family. Previous figures of deviant sexuality – the sexless hoyden and the reptilian homosexual – may have dropped from view to be replaced by the celebrity pervert, the porn-addicted man, the traumatized child and the sexting teen (Egan and Hawkes, 2010). Commentary remains "saturated in the languages of concern and regulation" (Smith, 2010b: 104) while failing to illuminate the contradictory experiences of sex in the modern era. Sex and sexuality will remain key commodities for media producers and there seems little reason to assume that the issues will become any less complex or contradictory.

Further reading

For those interested in the cultural studies of sexuality in everyday culture, Feona Attwood's *Mainstreaming Sex: The Sexualization of Western Culture* (2009) offers a thorough study. Likewise, Danielle Egan's (2013) *Becoming Sexual: A Critical Appraisal of the Sexualization of Girls* contributes to the understanding of sexualization in modern culture, as does Brian McNair's (1996) *Mediated Sex: Pornography and Postmodern Culture*. For theoretical and analytical approaches, both Basil Glynn, James Aston and Beth Johnson's (2012) *Television, Sex and Society: Analyzing Contemporary Representations* and Niall Richardson, Clarissa Smith and Angela Werndly's (2013) *Studying Sexualities: Theories, Representations, Practices* provide further work in cultural studies specific to sexual representations, sexuality and sexualization.

Notes

1 The campaign was launched in 2010 out of "concern that an increasingly sexualised culture was dripping, toxically, into the lives of children" (http://www.mumsnet.com/campaigns/let-girls-be-girls).
2 Weeks, J. (1977) *Coming Out*. London: Quartet Books (p. 162).

References

Aitkenhead, D. (2010) "Are teenagers hooked on porn?" *Psychologies*. Retrieved from http://www.psychologies.co.uk/family/are-teenagers-hooked-on-porn
American Pie (1999) [film] USA: Paul Weitz.
Arthurs, J. (2004) *Television and Sexuality: Regulation and the Politics of Taste*. Maidenhead: Open University Press.

Attwood, F. (2006) "Sexed up: Theorizing the sexualization of culture." *Sexualities*, 9(1), 77–94.

Attwood, F. (2009) *Mainstreaming Sex: The Sexualization of Western Culture*. London: I. B. Tauris.

Bailey, R. (2011) "Letting children be children: The report of an independent review of the commercialisation and sexualisation of childhood." London: Department for Education, June.

Bakewell, J. (2012) "Sex in society: Too much raunch, too young." *The Telegraph*, January 6. Retrieved from http://www.telegraph.co.uk/news/celebritynews/8998434/Sex-in-society-too-much-raunch-too-young.html

Barker, M. (2014) "The 'problem' of sexual fantasies." *Porn Studies*, 1(1), 143–60.

Bashford, A. and Strange, C. (2004) "Public pedagogy: Sex education and mass communication in the mid-twentieth century." *Journal of the History of Sexuality*, 13(1), 71–99.

Bengry, J. (2012) "Queer profits: Homosexual scandal and the origins of legal reform in Britain." In H. and M. Cook (eds.) *Queer 1950s: Rethinking Sexuality in the Postwar Years*. London: Palgrave Macmillan (pp. 167–82).

Bland, L. (2012) "'Hunnish scenes' and a 'virgin birth': A 1920s divorce case of sexual and bodily ignorance." *History Workshop Journal*, 73(1), 118–43.

Cocks, H. G. (2004) "Saucy stories: Pornography, sexology and the marketing of sexual knowledge in Britain, c. 1918–70." *Social History*, 29(4), 465–84.

Cogan, J. and Strang, F. (2013) "Elle Fanning, 15, raises eyebrows as she dresses way beyond her years in sheer frock with very risqué cut-out keyhole detail." *Daily Mail*, 29 October. Retrieved from http://www.dailymail.co.uk/tvshowbiz/article-2478796/Elle-Fanning-15-raises-eyebrows-risque-cut-keyhole-dress.html#ixzz2zGcfwVvF

Cohen, W. A. (1996) *Sex Scandal: The Private Parts of Victorian Fiction*. Durham, NC: Duke University Press.

Conboy, M. (2006) *Tabloid Britain: Constructing a Community Through Language*. Abingdon: Routledge.

Curran, J. (2002) "Media and the making of British society, c.1700–2000." *Media History*, 8(2), 135–54.

Davenport-Hines, R. (2013) *An English Affair: Sex, Class and Power in the Age of Profumo*. London: William Collins.

Dines, G. (2010) *Pornland: How Porn Has Hijacked Our Sexuality*. Boston, MA: Beacon Press.

Dines, G. (2011) "How the hardcore porn industry is ruining young men's lives." *Sydney Morning Herald*, May 18. Retrieved from http://www.smh.com.au/opinion/society-and-culture/how-the-hardcore-porn-industry-is-ruining-young-mens-lives-20110517-1erac.html#ixzz23kFcaGSP

Egan, R. D. (2013) *Becoming Sexual: A Critical Appraisal of the Sexualization of Girls*. Cambridge: John Wiley & Sons.

Egan, R. D. and Hawkes, G. (2010) *Theorizing the Sexual Child in Modernity*. New York: Palgrave Macmillan.

Fisher, T. (1995) *Scandal: The Sexual Politics of Late Victorian Britain*. London: Alan Sutton Publishing.

Gamson, J. (2001) "Normal sins: Sex scandal narratives as institutional morality tales." *Social Problems*, 48(2), 185–205.

Giddens, A. (1992) *The Transformation Of Intimacy: Sexuality, Love and Eroticism in Modern Societies*. Cambridge: Polity Press.

"Girls forced to play games, teachers criticized, plea for maidenly education." (1935) *Western Morning News and Daily Gazette*, 5 September.

Glynn, B., Aston, J. and Johnson, B. (2012) *Television, Sex and Society: Analyzing Contemporary Representations*. London: Continuum.

Gordon, J. (1953) "Our sex-sodden newspapers." *Sunday Express*, 23 August, p. 4

Hakim, C. (2011) *Honey Money: The Power of Erotic Capital*. London: Penguin.
Hennelly, S. (2010) "Public space, public morality: The media construction of sex in public places." *Liverpool Law Review*, 31(1), 69–91.
Holland, P. (1983) "The Page 3 Girl speaks to women too." *Screen*, 24(3), 84–102.
Holmwood, L. and Sales, D. (2013) "Does BBC stand for blame-dodging backstabbing cover-up? Savile report 'whitewash' fury as Beeb chaos exposed." *The Sun*, 23 February 2013. Retrieved from http://www.thesun.co.uk/sol/homepage/showbiz/tv/4808862/BBC-chiefs-frenzy-to-dodge-fallout-from-Jimmy-Savile-scandal.html
Horvath, M. A. H., Alys, L., Massey, K., Pina, A., Scally, M. and Adler, J. R. (2013) *"Basically ... porn is everywhere" – A rapid evidence assessment on the effects that access and exposure to pornography has on children and young people*. London: Children's Commissioner, May 2013. Retrieved from http://www.childrenscommissioner.gov.uk/content/publications/content_667
Houlbrook, M. (2006) *Queer London: Perils and Pleasures in the Sexual Metropolis, 1918–1957*. Chicago, IL: University of Chicago Press.
Israel, K. (1997) "French vices and British liberties: Gender, class and narrative competition in a late Victorian sex scandal." *Social History*, 22(1), 1–26.
Jenkins, H. (2004) "Foreword: So you want to teach pornography?" in P. Church Gibson (ed.) *More Dirty Looks: Gender, Pornography and Power*. London: BFI Publishing (pp. 1–7).
Kendrick, W. (1996) *The Secret Museum: Pornography in Modern Culture*. Berkeley, CA: University of California Press.
Kipnis, L. (1996) *Bound and Gagged: Pornography and the Politics of Fantasy in America*. Durham & London: Duke University Press.
Littlejohn, R. (2011) "The Daleks are doing what, darling?" *Daily Mail*, 1 September. Retrieved from http://www.dailymail.co.uk/debate/article-2031514/Danny-Cohen-says-BBC1-cater-older-viewers-The-Daleks-doing-darling.html#ixzz1XfYo1cxe
Lull, J. and Hinerman, S. (eds.) (1997) *Media Scandals: Morality and Desire in the Popular Culture Marketplace*. Oxford: Polity Press.
McKee, A., Lumby, C. and Albury, K. (2008) *The Porn Report*. Melbourne: Melbourne University Publishing.
McNair, B. (1996) *Mediated Sex: Pornography and Postmodern Culture*. London: Arnold.
——(2002) *Striptease Culture: Sex, Media and the Democratisation of Desire*. London & New York: Routledge.
——(2013) *Porno? Chic!: How Pornography Changed the World and Made it a Better Place*. London & New York: Routledge.
Marshall, P. (2010) "Teenage boys watching hours of internet pornography every week are treating their girlfriends like sex objects." *Daily Mail*, 8 March.
Martin, L. (2012) "How internet porn turned my beautiful boy into a hollow, self-hating shell." *Daily Mail*, 20 April. Retrieved from http://www.dailymail.co.uk/news/article-2132342/How-internet-porn-turned-beautiful-boy-hollow-self-hating-shell.html
Moyes, S. and Holmwood, L. (2012) "Savile: BBC's abuse of your license fee." *The Sun*, 23 October. Retrieved from http://www.thesun.co.uk/sol/homepage/news/4604080/Jimmy-Savile-BBCs-abuse-of-your-licence-fee.html
Oram, A. (2012) "Love 'off the rails' or 'over the teacups?' Lesbian desire and female sexualities in the 1950s British popular press." In Bauer, H. and Cook, M. (eds.) *Queer 1950s: Rethinking Sexuality in the Postwar Years*. London: Palgrave Macmillan (pp. 41–58).
Papadopoulos, L. (2010) "Sexualisation of young people review." Retrieved from http://webarchive.nationalarchives.gov.uk/20100418065544/http://homeoffice.gov.uk/documents/Sexualisation-of-young-people2835.pdf?view=Binary
Peev, G. (2012) "Children grow up addicted to online porn sites: Third of 10-year-olds have seen explicit images." *Daily Mail*, 18 April. Retrieved from http://www.dailymail.co.uk/news/

article-2131799/Children-grow-addicted-online-porn-sites-Third-10-year-olds-seen-explicit-images.html#ixzz2gTOmwcgy

Phillips, M. (2012) "So, Minister, since when were the civil liberties of porn users more important than those of children?" *Daily Mail*, 24 April. Retrieved from http://www.dailymail.co.uk/debate/article-2133640/So-Minister-civil-liberties-porn-users-important-children.html

Plummer, K. (1995) *Telling Sexual Stories: Power, Change and Social Worlds*. London & New York: Routledge.

Richardson, N., Smith, C. and Werndly, A. (2013) *Studying Sexualities: Theories, Representations, Practices*. London: Palgrave Macmillan.

Sharpe, N. (2010) "Sir struck off for sex with pupil." The *Sun*, 26 November. Retrieved from http://www.thescottishsun.co.uk/scotsol/homepage/news/3246513/Thomas-Docherty-struck-off-for-sex-with-pupil.html

Smith, A. C. H. (1975) *Paper Voices: The Popular Press and Social Change 1935–1965*. London: Chatto & Windus.

Smith, C. (2010a) "British sexual cultures." In M. Higgins, C. Smith and J. Storey (eds.) *The Cambridge Companion to Modern British Culture*. Cambridge: Cambridge University Press (pp. 244–61).

Smith, C. (2010b) "Pornographication: A discourse for all seasons." *International Journal of Media and Cultural Politics*, 6(1), 103–8.

Tankard Reist, M. (ed.) (2009) *Getting Real: Challenging the Sexualisation of Girls*. Melbourne: Spinifex.

The *Sun* (2013) "Miss gets 2yrs after sex with girl pupil." The *Sun*, 23 November. Retrieved from http://www.thesun.co.uk/sol/homepage/news/5280119/Teacher-gets-two-years-for-lesbian-sex-with-pupil.html

Thompson, J. B. (1997) "Scandal and social theory." In Lull, J. and Hinerman, S. (eds.) *Media Scandals: Morality and Desire in the Popular Culture Marketplace*. Oxford: Polity Press (pp. 34–64).

Tumber, H. (2004) "Scandal and media in the United Kingdom from Major to Blair." *American Behavioral Scientist*, 47(8), 1122–37.

Watney, S. (1997) *Policing Desire: Pornography, AIDS and the Media*. London: Continuum.

Weeks, J. (1985) *Sexuality and Its Discontents: Meanings, Myths and Modern Sexualities*. London: Routledge & Kegan Paul.

——(2007) *The World We Have Won: The Remaking of Erotic and Intimate Life*. London: Routledge.

West, A. (2013) "Miss mucky: Teacher asked boy in her class for romp and urged other pupils to mime sex." The *Sun*, 7 November. Retrieved from http://www.thesun.co.uk/sol/homepage/news/5247674/newport-teacher-asked-pupil-for-sex.html

Whisnant, R. (2010) "From Jekyll to Hyde: The grooming of male pornography consumers." In K. Boyle (ed.) *Everyday Pornography*. London: Routledge (pp. 114–33).

White, R. (2012) "BBC covered up paedo scandal No. 2: Simpson exposed radio 'Uncle' … but was ignored." The *Sun*, 17 October. Retrieved from http://www.thesun.co.uk/sol/homepage/news/4593435/BBC-covered-up-childrens-radio-paedo-scandal.html

Williams, K. (1998) *Get Me A Murder A Day! A History of Mass Communication in Britain*. London: Arnold.

Wouters, C. (2004) *Sex and Manners: Female Emancipation in the West 1890–2000*. London: Sage.

——(2007) *Informalization: Manners and Emotion Since 1890*. London: Sage.

12
This sporting 'life-world'
Mediating sport in Britain

John Steel

Introduction

It has long been recognized that British sport has played a significant role in the historical maintenance of British cultural identity. In addition it has been deeply implicated in a complex pattern of contestation and transformation therein. Whether this recognition has been examined in relation to studies concerned with the history of sport, which have gained increasing prominence amongst historically centred studies of British society (Holt, 1989; Polley, 1998), or the relationship between sport, media and culture (Whannel, 2008; Boyle and Haynes, 2009; Kennedy and Hills, 2009; Horne et al., 2013), the mediation of sport and its relationship to the 'fabric' of British society has gained increasing attention amongst scholars in recent years. In acknowledging these interventions, this chapter will look to capture some of the myriad ways in which scholarship on the mediation of sport has reflected an increasing awareness that sport is an important site of continuity and contestation within British history, politics and identity and, for this reason, is worthy of serious study. Moreover, via an exploration of the way in which the mediation of sport has become a significant feature of the public sphere, this chapter asserts that many of the debates that scholarship on the media and sport have spawned are gaining in importance as sport becomes of even greater significance to contemporary life.

Mediating the 'life-world' of sport

Let me begin by framing sport within the communicative realm, as a mediated aspect of our society and history. This focus is demarcated from the sporting activities that ordinary people engage in for their recreation. Instead I wish to focus mainly on what could be termed elite sport in Britain. In order to do this, however, some initial conceptual sketching is required and I will be drawing on Jürgen Habermas's concept of the public sphere as a starting point. The public sphere is of course a contested concept. It was first identified by Habermas (1989) as an imagined space which came into being during the early eighteenth century in Europe and which facilitated discussion and debate in matters of social and political importance (Crossley and

Roberts, 2004). Habermas suggests that such a space was dominated by a bourgeoisie which sought to advance its commercial and political power and, as a consequence, altered the social and economic landscape of Europe. Of crucial importance to the constitution of the pubic sphere then are the communicative capacities that individuals and constituencies possess and the shifting dynamics of these constituencies. For Habermas, the key communicative spaces in the eighteenth and nineteenth centuries were the print media as well as coffee houses and debating societies. From the late nineteenth century onwards, particularly with the growth of the mass press (Chalaby, 1998), such communicative capacities have expanded. Of course debate about the historical and contemporary composition and status of the public sphere is significant (see Crossley and Roberts, 2004). Whether we should consider multiple public spheres (Fraser, 1992); gendered public spheres (McLaughlin, 1993) or even the validity of the concept itself (Schudson, 1992), all are worthy of debate. However, this chapter, while acknowledging the multiplicity of perspectives on Habermas's concept, does not wish to delve too deeply into the complexities of the term. Instead I wish to appropriate the term 'life-world' and apply it here in order to explore the mediation of elite sport in British society and culture. The 'life-world' so important to Habermas's analysis of the public sphere relates to the idea that the lived experiences and realms of understanding which constitute an individual's social environment are reflected in the public sphere. As such it is within the context of the public sphere that societies and individuals make sense of themselves through their 'life-world' (Stevenson, 2002) and, it will be argued here, the mediation of sport is increasingly prominent within such 'sense making'.

Sport, media and history

In discussing the relationship between sport, media and British society it would be tempting to focus explicitly on specific media and offer a technological overview of sport and its development. Such an approach of course would be folly. As Curran (2002) reminds us we should not look solely at technological innovation as the main driver of social and political change. Rather, "probably the best way to develop a new history of British media is to offer a general account of the development of modern British society, in which the history of the British media is inserted" (Curran, 2002: 149). Being mindful of the potential drift towards techno-centrism, I would assert that it is impossible to assess the centrality of sport to British history and culture without giving consideration to the ways in which sport has been mediated. Sport's role in the fabric of British social and cultural history is significant. As Richard Holt has suggested, "the games we have played and our ways of playing them can be properly understood only in terms of the development of British society and the British Empire" (Holt, 1989: 2). Here Holt asserts that sport should be seen as integral to our social and cultural history, a history which is not blind to class nor to the perspectives of those who participated in or watched sport for leisure. Holt's analysis is one which draws on the cultural and political as well as the social and economic (Holt, 1989: 3) and offers a nuanced analysis of the role that sport has played in the development of Britain's national identity as well as its contribution to debates concerning class, gender, race and ethnicity (see Polley, 1998). As such this chapter acknowledges that while it would be impossible to provide a comprehensive analysis of the interplay between sport, media and society which spans British history, it does explicitly recognize that understanding

> the role of the media in sport involves the complex relationship between media institutions, the programmes they make and the audience itself. [...] In Britain exploring this triangular relationship requires an appreciation of how press and radio coverage provided a model for BBC television sport [in which] from the 1950s to the 1980s BBC sport acquired a special kind of national authority through its distinctive broadcasting style and the personalities it chose to put before the nation to speak to and for 'us'.
>
> (Holt and Mason, 2000: 93)

Accordingly, it is necessary to recognise that "the media, television and the press in particular, are playing a central role in producing, reproducing and amplifying many of the discourses associated with sport in the modern world" (Boyle and Haynes, 2009: 7). Moreover, the authors go on to pay particular attention to emphasizing "some of the major transformations in the historical relationship between sport and the media: from the emergence of the popular press to the beginnings of an international sports-media nexus" (ibid.: 19). In doing so they stress the ways in which "mediated versions of sport are one of the key areas of culture which give us a sense of a lived history" which acts as a "bridge between the present and the past" (ibid.). As a consequence, we can see that sport and its mediation is fundamental to modern British cultural history.

The mediation of sport

The mediation of sport is a relatively recent phenomenon as modern sport became absorbed into industrialized society and its enlarged print culture by the mid Victorian era. Nevertheless, it would be a mistake to suggest that pre-Victorian life had no space for sport or leisure as villages and towns had long had their variations on popular sports and games (Holt, 1989). Yet the industrial revolution did bring with it a more formalized demarcation between work and leisure, which was reflected and reinforced through print media. Though sport was 'marginal' in the pages of both the 'respectable' and 'radical' press during the late eighteenth and early nineteenth centuries, a specialist sporting press "emerged to cater for genteel interests in horse racing, prize fighting and blood sports" (Boyle and Haynes, 2009: 21). Such a specialist press also served to "communicate and help legislate the organisation of sport" with the publication of rules and regulations, and the administration of large-scale sports, particularly in horse racing, reflecting the economic and industrial changes taking place in society more broadly at that time (Boyle and Haynes, 2009: 21). What could be described as specialist sports publications such as the *Sporting Life* (1859–1998) and the *Sporting Chronicle* (1871–1983) reflected an increasingly economic dimension of sports coverage in print with gambling in particular playing a pivotal role in its developing commercialization.

The commercial priorities of newspaper proprietors also generated a recognition that sports coverage would broaden the popular appeal of their products, an appeal that would by the 1930s diminish the circulation figures of the sporting press irrevocably (Boyle and Haynes, 2009). Specialist publications aside, the relationship between sport and journalism emerges from a nineteenth-century tradition of popular journalism which would seek to reflect the interests of a range of constituencies in the latter part of the century. It is particularly the relationship between social class and newspaper readership at this time that enables us to emphasize the significance of sport to the social and cultural life of Britain as class identity was reinforced through the pages of a popular press which sought to connect with an essentially working-class readership (Conboy, 2002). It is therefore via the press in the later nineteenth century and into the early twentieth century that we see sport beginning to occupy a place in the consolidation of class identity in Britain through a process of ritual identification and reaffirmation (Anderson, 1991; Carey, 1992; Conboy, 2006). James Carey has emphasized the role of newspapers in their 'symbolic construction' (Carey, 1992) of notions of community and identity and the growth of the popular press during the early twentieth century in particular seemed to emphasize this particular dynamic as newspaper proprietors such as Pearson and Harmsworth recognized that coverage of sport broadened their appeal and augmented their advertising and commercial potential. Such a recognition of the appeals of coverage of popular sports – football, cricket, rugby and horseracing in particular – meant that sports news in both serious and popular newspapers became an established part of newspaper journalism during the twentieth century. Moreover, popular newspapers such as the *Daily Mail* and the *Daily Mirror* and weeklies such as the *News of the World* developed a style of sports journalism which would articulate notions of nation, class and gender through their particular vernacular style (Conboy, 2006). Popular newspapers spoke to their readership in ways that did not patronize them. Rather, they sought to connect with them, speaking their language and deploying a tone which reinforced a close relationship between newspaper and reader. Humour in the popular press, in particular, has also enabled such popular identification as it is expressed in ways which reinforce this constructed community. As Conboy asserts, "one of the more obvious rhetorical strategies through which the tabloids attempt to reinforce their relationship with their readership is by employing colloquial expressions and slang" (Conboy, 2013: 198) particularly when discussing nation and national identity. Such an expression also reinforces claims to a shared historical experience which seeps into articulations of the present. Though such articulations may seem benign, they have always been able to "disguise their reactionary tendencies with regard to issues of ethnicity, nation and gender" (Conboy, 2013: 194). As such, in the popular press "humour is not the key to unlocking the past; more likely it is an acceptable way of maintaining populist prejudices in the present" (Conboy, 2013: 207).

Popular culture and sport

It is worth reflecting upon the relationship between popular culture and sport, as this allows us to appreciate the complex ways in which sport and its mediation has become ingrained within British cultural life more generally. As Gary Whannel has suggested, popular culture should be understood not as a set of practices emerging from 'below' nor as being imposed by institutions and structures from above through mass produced commercial product, but "rather as a result of processes of struggle and contestation between cultural practices generated from below and imposed from above (Whannel, 2008: 130). Here Whannel is keen to assert his concern for sports that "can be considered more centrally part of popular culture, by virtue not simply of their popularity but also because of the degree to which they are part of the cultural fabric of the everyday life of the people" (ibid.: 134). Sport's centrality to everyday life is of course also reflected in the forms in which sport is mediated. In his analysis of sport as popular culture Whannel usefully highlights the ways in which both performance and spectatorship draw together the participant and the viewer to produce (negotiate) sport as a specific cultural form. In his analysis of elite sport, Whannel draws attention to the ways in which the performative elements of elite sports connect with the audience and reflect a myriad of emotive, utopian and communitarian sensibilities which entertain but also help to explain popular sports culture more expansively. For example, the range of emotions which watching sport can engender, from elation to despair, astonishment to downright boredom, speaks to the palette of responses negotiated as sport is mediated.

Another aspect of how sport connects with our cultural life is how sports foreground the ideas of being the best, of physical perfection, of striving to go beyond the average. These tap into our utopian sensibilities which contrast starkly with our everyday experiences of life. As such "the utopian sensibility in [the] representation [of sport] is set up precisely in opposition to, and establishing a distance from, the grim realities of everyday life" (Whannel, 2008: 134). Sport and its mediation therefore provides people with a means of escape and the promise of a glimpse of near perfection. It also requires heroes and villains through which we can play out this utopian escapism and who can capture the audience by defying expectations (Whannel, 2008). Whether it is Ian Botham fighting against the odds and winning against Australia in the 1981 Ashes or Andy Murray, a British man finally winning Wimbledon after more than 77 years of waiting, sport's utopian sensibilities are part of how sports culture becomes manifest.

The cultural significance of sport is also reinforced via the ways in which the audience experiences the spectacle of sport. As such the communitarian element of sports culture is prominent and indeed a necessary part of its mediation. Whether it is with regard to a 'community' of invested spectators watching a match, or via the collective 'witnessing' of a sporting event, the collective spectatorship of mass mediated sport emphasizes the drawing together of event and audience which adds to the cultural capital of a sporting event. Professional football matches played behind closed doors in empty stadia, as sometimes occurs when clubs are sanctioned, lack not only atmosphere but also the authenticity which the presence of the crowd bestows. As a consequence the absence of the viewing audience from the representation of sport undermines the significance or import of the event itself. Again, therefore, we see that the audience is important in this regard. Watching sport therefore instils notions of identification which are fundamental. Even if one is nonpartisan, this remains a fundamental element of the mediation of sport. Therefore such connections are not solely based around inscribing particular notions of identity, though these are of course significant, but reflective of a requirement for us to associate or empathize with those participating, as such "identification is absolutely central to the consumption of sport" (Whannel, 2008: 138).

Notions of belonging are of course fundamental to the collective audience, but it is not just via the broadcast media that such belonging is negotiated. As we have seen, newspapers strive to connect with their readers' expectations. Similarly, then, newspapers and particularly the popular press have to draw on such notions of identification in order to reach their readership. Where broadcast media are more easily able to convey the intensity of the crowd and the emotional dynamics of the sporting spectacle, newspapers have to draw on a different set of narrative parameters in order to secure their audience. Yet of course this does not diminish the emotive or the spectacular. Whether it is via the broadcast media or print aspects of community the relationship between audience and team or individual reinforces a 'belongingness' which is a necessary feature of popular sports culture.

Journalism and sport

The ways in which sport is mediated through sports journalism is, as Rod Brookes (2002) reminds us, relatively conventional and 'fixed'. The first television broadcast of sport in the UK was in 1937 and this subsequently "developed in a relatively short space of time in the late 1940s and 1950s" into a set of standardized formats and procedures (Brookes, 2002: 24). Though technical and economic transformations have necessitated some modification, arguably these conventions have altered very little. Brookes, however, highlights the point that such conventions were established in order to "reconcile conflicting tensions" between accurately representing the sporting event and entertaining the audience (Brookes, 2002: 24). Entertainment is a dominant feature of popular journalism and Brookes highlights how the spectacular and sensational aspects of sport, particularly the sporting scandal, gain attention in popular newspapers. Whether with regard to the off-field exploits and personal tragedies of former England footballer Paul Gascoigne or the high-profile downfall of disgraced cyclist Lance Armstrong, popular tabloid news values dictate the terrain of tabloid sports coverage which emphasizes personalization and conflict (Brighton and Foy, 2007). High-profile public confessions of wrongdoing by sports personalities not only signal the ways in which specific news values continue to be salient across broadcast and print media, but also emphasize how male athletes in particular can "disrupt the ideological association of male athletes as glorified icons of hegemonic masculinity" (Messner, 2012: 117) as their public downfall symbolically, and literally, strips them of their sporting glories. At the same time, such media exposure frames transgressors as villains while also exploiting their very public humiliation. The disciplinary power of the media (Steel, 2012: 191–3; Petley, 2013) is particularly evident in this context.

Though clearly the spectacular and the extraordinary are key components in the mediation of sport as popular culture, it would be wrong to suggest that mediated sport always conforms to these parameters. Indeed as Brookes (2002) points out in his discussion of sports journalism, the mundane and banal are in fact the norm. Putting aside the scandalous and the sensational, he emphasizes the routine elements of sports journalism which also help to "define the relationship between sports journalism and its readers" (Brookes, 2002: 40). Brookes highlights, for example, the formulaic and routine presentation of players, managers and coaches to the media who are obliged to face a predictable format of questions from journalists and are expected also to provide a set of pat answers to these formulaic and well-rehearsed questions. Though we must acknowledge the increased professionalization of communication within sport and the media more generally and the role that social media play increasingly in the 'disintermediation' (Hermida, 2010) of sport, there is still a high level of predictability and routine in the mediation of sport. Significantly, however, it is also worth highlighting (as Brookes does) that these exchanges conform to the expectations of the audience, a specifically 'male' orientation which clearly prioritizes men's sport over women's.

Identity and the mediation of sport

The significance of mass mediated sports for the formation of identity is central to an understanding of how sports culture takes shape. Again the notion of identification becomes salient as not only is the audience confronted with an expectation to declare its support for a particular team or individual but the weight of national identification also transcends that of the regional, at least in terms of mass mediated sport. Such a weight is inscribed within structures of socialization far beyond the scope of this chapter. However, it is necessary to recognize the significant role that the mediation of sport has played in the construction of identities whether national, gendered or racial.

Sport clearly provides an opportunity for nationhood to be 'flagged' up (Bilig, 2005: 8) not only in major international sporting events such as the Olympics or the football World Cup, but also in less 'global' international competitions such as the Rugby Six Nations Cup or the Test Match in cricket. It should be noted however that national identity is not fixed but is negotiated and subject to challenges and modifications over time. Benedict Anderson (1991) has suggested that nations are 'imagined' and emerge from a collective reflection on the past in the present. As Brookes notes, "Anderson's comments are important in understanding how sport, and media coverage of sport, have contributed to the formation of national identity through making a psychological connection between the everyday life of the individual and the wider abstract category of the nation" (2002: 87). However, it is also worth echoing Brookes' concerns that Anderson's theory cannot account for the dynamic nature of national identity as configured through the mediation of sport. For this, he contends, there is a need to draw more broadly on debates within cultural studies which stress multiplicities of identity which are subject to contestation and competing categorization. Therefore, in order for us to have an understanding of the process of national identity construction, it is necessary to appreciate the ways in which the categories of nation compete with other identifiers, whether gendered, racial or regional. In other words we need to recognize the distinction between the representation *and* renegotiation of sporting identities. It is worthwhile expanding upon this point. As Brookes notes, sport plays a significant role in foregrounding tradition in the public psyche be it through boxing, horse racing, football, rugby or cricket, and as a consequence we can see that such sports have very strong traditions and myths which also feed into our understandings of who we are as a nation. Such narratives of history tend to be relatively fixed. However, particularly in the context of the emergence of identity politics and globalization, dominant narratives of nation are challenged and renegotiated as competing conceptions of identity, be they gender, class or ethnically orientated, vie for salience within the public sphere. The issues of gender and race and their representation are particularly helpful in exploring these processes and it is to these aspects of identity politics in sport that I shall now turn.

The mediation of sport in Britain and globally draws extensively on discursive repertoires which emphasize the "way in which nature is invoked to legitimise different types of representation" thereby providing a rationalization of "the institutional structures that continue to produce racism and sexism in sport" (Brookes, 2002: 107). The scholarly analysis of media coverage of gender in sport is significant, spanning, over 30 years, numerous geographical locations and a variety of methodological and conceptual approaches (Bruce, 2012). As Toni Bruce has suggested, much of this work "has been dedicated to content analyses and textual readings of media texts which focus on how mediasport reproduces, legitimates, and occasionally challenges ideologies of gender" (Bruce, 2012: 128). The ways in which women have been hitherto represented through sport has largely reflected the traditional gender roles within British society. Sport is and always has been predominantly male-centred, moreover, Bruce contends that the mediation of sport

> valorizes elite, able-bodied, heterosexual and professional sportsmen, especially those who bring glory to the nation. Simultaneously it excludes, marginalizes, or trivializes athletes who do not fall into this narrow realm, such as sportswomen, veterans, amateurs, children and sports unaligned to nationalism. Through its narratives and images, mediasport reinforces and amplifies the historical connection of sport to men and masculinity.
> (Bruce, 2012: 128)

As Bruce eloquently asserts, women have been and continue to be marginalized in the representation of sport within the media as participants and actors. Such marginalization of course not only diminishes the broader significance of women's participation in elite sport, it also reinforces much more deeply embedded notions of gender divisions within society. Men's sports are overwhelmingly better represented in the media than women's (Toft, 2011; Markula, 2009). Such a paucity of coverage is reflected in the relatively limited financial rewards for women athletes compared to men. The British triathlete Chrissie Wellington won four 'Iron Man' triathlon world championships between 2007 and 2011 yet was all but ignored in the mainstream British media. Wellington was not even recognized in the popular BBC Sports Personality of the Year awards, despite her global dominance in women's long course triathlon. This is in stark contrast to the coverage the Brownlee brothers received following their similar successes in world triathlon, including world championship medals and Olympic gold in 2012. 'Jonny' and 'Ali' have enjoyed a much higher profile in the media and therefore greater opportunities for financial rewards through sponsorship and endorsements than Wellington. Even though the representation of women's sport in the media has come some way since the highly gendered representations of the twentieth century, there is still some distance to travel before the mediation of women's sport gains parity with men's and reverses the 'symbolic annihilation' of women in sport. Where women are represented in sports they are often depicted in highly sexualized ways (Houck, 2006; Carmichael Aitchison, 2007). Yet, as Horne et al. (2013: 93) suggest, "one trend in the past twenty years is very striking. It is not just women's sporting bodies that are now sexualised but also male bodies." Though this might indeed be the case, it would be naïve to think that the gender imbalance in women's sports can be overcome by giving more air time to women's sports or gaining parity with men in terms of sexualizing the athletic body. Unfortunately whilst there remain more fundamental and deeper structures of gender discrimination in wider society, the representation of women in sport is likely to remain in the margins and highly stereotyped.

As with gender, the mediation of sport reflects and reinforces particularly negative and stereotyped representations of race and ethnicity. This is particularly the case with regards black athletes and "has played a fundamental role in the reproduction in unequal power relations" (Brookes, 2002: 107). Despite the fact, as Horne et al. (2013) note, that we often see black sports stars providing positive role models for younger people, the reality of course is that very few youngsters reach such heights. More significantly, however, representations of black athletes generally serve to entrench specific racist categorizations in which biological attributes are ascribed to different racial groups. Drawing on the work of Cashmore (1982), Horne et al. emphasize the way in which the myth of black athletes' racial superiority is inscribed within media representations as in references to their "silky skills, natural rhythms and natural ability" (Horne et al., 2013: 95). Biology is therefore used to 'explain' differences between black and white athletes despite the fact that race is a social rather than biological construction. As Brookes points out, despite the fact that 'race' has no biological or genetic basis, racism in sport persists, as it does in wider society.

Politicizing sport

The platitude that sport and politics should not mix misses the point about the centrality of sport within the social and cultural fabric of British society. This is also true of politics. We should acknowledge that sport is often utilized for political or strategic gain by governments whether this is on a global stage or within national contexts. One of the most stark examples of such politicization on the global level was the boycott by US athletes of the 1980 Moscow Olympics and the subsequent Soviet boycott of the games in Los Angeles in 1984 (see Guttmann, 1988). The playing out of Cold War tensions during the 1980s when relations between the capitalist West and communist East were at their most strained emphasizes the point about the way in which sport itself can become politicized. As Allen Guttmann

(1988: 554) has suggested, "propagandists on both sides of the Iron Curtain have presented the competition between Russian and American athletes as a portentous symbolic struggle between two ideological systems." Britain, which had been involved in the Cold War power play since the Second World War (see Beck, 2007), offered support to its US allies when it decided to boycott the 1980 Moscow Olympics in protest against the Soviet invasion of Afghanistan in 1979. Corthorn (2012) notes that despite pressure on the athletes and the British Olympic Association to boycott the games, a British boycott was avoided as broader diplomatic debate concerning human rights issues and détente were seen to be of greater concern. Corthorn highlights how the complexities of domestic and international politics starkly butted up against "a pronounced trend [of successive governments] to present the autonomy of sport as a liberal British value", moreover the issues resonated with broader public debate which was founded on "long-standing notions of the amateur spirit of fair play (on and off the sports field)" (Corthorn, 2012: 61). "Hands off, Maggie" was the call from the *Daily Mirror* (1980) which expressed its dissatisfaction with the government's position on the proposed Olympic boycott. The *Mirror's* letters pages also resonated with contempt for the government's attempts to pressure British athletes to boycott the games. "When will these fumbling politicians learn to keep their hands off sport?" asked Mr J. D. Clarke on the *Mirror's* letters page (1980: 27).

Another particularly significant example of how sport can become explicitly politicized on a global level can be seen in the public debate about the economic, cultural and sporting boycott of South Africa in the 1970s and 1980s. The South African government's racist policy of apartheid had long been subject to international scrutiny and condemnation and had led to the International Olympic Committee banning South Africa from the 1964 Olympic Games (Holt and Mason, 2000: 162). However, South Africa's attempts to use sport as a method of demonstrating a process of gradual reform in the late 1960s did not convince the international community and led to South Africa being "excluded from nine international sporting associations including the Olympics, weightlifting, swimming, athletics and football" by 1974 (Merrett, 2005: 5). Policing the effectiveness of South Africa's segregation policies as they applied to sport was not even, as from the early to mid 1970s, segregation rules were applied inconsistently. For example, as Merrett (2005: 5) suggests, "for a brief period during 1976–77, South African cricket abolished its racial structures and played under one umbrella." As Holt and Mason (2000) observe, the issue of race was a significant debate in Britain during the late 1960s and 70s. Enoch Powell's 'Rivers of Blood' speech in 1968 along with difficult questions about Britain's Imperial role ensured that the politics of race and sport during the 70s was never far from the headlines. With a South African rugby team touring Britain in 1969 and a South African cricket tour planned for 1970, it became impossible for politicians to avoid becoming publicly embroiled in the debate. As Holt and Mason suggest, Britain's relations with the Commonwealth as well as Anglo-American relations would be placed under significant pressure unless the British government failed to step in and prevent the South African cricket tour from taking place, which it duly did in 1970. This official intervention, however, did not prevent a number of 'rebel' tours of South Africa during the 1970s and 80s (Holt and Mason, 2000: 163).

One of the key players on the wider public stage was the Anti-Apartheid Movement in Britain which developed a number of high-profile media campaigns against the policies of the South African government. Such campaigns helped place the issue of apartheid more widely on the public's agenda. Media campaigns which included encouraging British citizens to boycott Barclays Bank and other British companies who had commercial dealings with the Republic played a leading role in forcing a national boycott of South African imports. The Anti-Apartheid Movement was also instrumental in its role of pressuring government to pull the aforementioned Springbok cricket tour in 1970. During the 1980s politicians too become involved in the Anti-Apartheid Movement with opposition politicians including the Labour leader Neil Kinnock and David Owen of the recently formed SDP calling for sanctions against the government in Pretoria. It is generally considered that sports boycotts did not affect the fundamental structural foundations of South African society "because the pressures it could exert were insignificant compared with the social changes that the boycotters demanded" (Booth, 2003: 492). Yet of course such boycotts, which were highly mediated, played an important 'symbolic role' (Holt and Mason, 2000) in the undermining of apartheid as a political system.

Conclusion

Historically, the life-world of sport within the broader public sphere in Britain has tended to exist at the margins. However, relatively recent transformations, both in society and from within the media, have witnessed sport shifting from the periphery of the public sphere towards a more central role in mainstream media culture. It is this reorientation of sport within the public sphere that has provided the central focus of this chapter and with it a reconsideration of aspects of politics, culture and identity in British media history and society. I have attempted to show both the centrality of sport and its mediation within British culture and the ways in which it raises important questions and problems for scholars of media history, cultural studies, sociology and journalism studies. In recent years scholarship on sport within these disciplines has grown significantly and it is hoped that such growth will continue to illuminate how mediated sport feeds into our collective 'life-world'.

Further reading

Boyle and Haynes' (2009) *Power Play: Sport, the Media and Popular Culture* provides an excellent overview and theoretical analysis of the role of sport and its contribution to popular culture. In *Understanding Sport: A Socio-Cultural Analysis* John Horne, Alan Tomlinson, Garry Whannel and Kath Woodward (2013) offer a revised and updated analysis of the ways in which sport plays a significant role in contemporary life, particularly with regards identity, globalization and politics. Grant Jarvie's (2006) excellent *Sport, Culture and Society: An Introduction* has a broad ranging introduction to the debates and literature on sport in society. Eileen Kennedy and Laura Hills' (2009) *Sport, Media and Society* provides a comprehensive analysis of the relationship between sport, media, politics and culture with particularly strong chapters on visual culture, advertising, branding and the internet. Finally, Richard Holt's (1989) *Sport and the British: A Modern History* provides the classic social history of sport in Britain from the late eighteenth century to the 1980s.

References

Anderson, B. (1991) *Imagined Communities*. London: Verso.
Beck, P. (2007) "Britain and the Cold War's 'cultural olympics': Responding to the political drive of Soviet sport, 1945–58." *Contemporary British History*, 19(2), 169–85.
Bilig, M. (2005) *Banal Nationalism*. London: Sage.
Booth, D. (2003) "Hitting apartheid for six? The politics of the South African sports boycott." *Journal of Contemporary History*, 38(3), 477–93.
Boyle and Haynes (2009) *Power Play: Sport, the Media and Popular Culture* (2nd ed.). Edinburgh: Edinburgh University Press.
Brighton, P. and Foy, D. (2007) *News Values*. London: Sage.
Brookes, R. (2002) *Representing Sport*. London: Arnold.
Bruce, T. (2012) "Reflections on communication and sport: On women and femininities." *Communication & Sport*, 1(1/2), 125–37.
Carey, J. (1992) *Communication as Culture*. New York: Routledge.
Carmichael Aitchison, C. (ed.) (2007) *Sport and Gender Identities, Masculinities, Femininities and Sexualities*. Abingdon: Routledge.
Cashmore, E. (1982) *Black Sportsmen*. London: Routledge & Kegan Paul.
Chalaby, J. (1998) *The Invention of Journalism*. Basingstoke: Macmillan.
Conboy, M. (2002) *The Press and Popular Culture*. London: Sage.
——(2006) *Tabloid Britain*. London: Routledge.
——(2013) "Geoff Hurst's ball: Popular tabloids and humour on the dark side." In B. Kore and D. Lechner (eds.) *History and Humour: British and American Perspectives*. Bielefeld: Transcript Verlag (pp. 193–209).
Corthorn, P. (2012) "The Cold War and British debates over the boycott of the 1980 Moscow Olympics." *Cold War History*, 13(1), 43–66.
Crossley, N. and Roberts, J. M. (2004) *After Habermas: New Perspectives on the Public Sphere*. Oxford: Blackwell.
Curran, J. (2002) "Media and the making of British society, c. 1700–2000." *Media History*, 8(2), 135–54.
Daily Mirror (1980) "Hands off, Maggie!" *Daily Mirror*, Friday 21 March, p. 27.
Fraser, N. (1992) "Rethinking the public sphere: A contribution to the critique of actually existing democracy." In C. Calhoun (ed.) *Habermas and the Public Sphere*. Cambridge, MA: MIT Press (pp. 109–42).
Guttmann, A. (1988) "The Cold War and the Olympics." *International Journal*, 43(4), 554–68.
Habermas, J. (1989) *Structural Transformation of the Bourgeois Public Sphere*. Cambridge: Polity.
Hermida, A. (2010) "Twittering the News." *Journalism Practice*, 4(3), 297–308.
Holt, R. (1989) *Sport and the British: A Modern History*. Oxford: Clarendon Press.
Holt, R. and Mason, T. (2000) *Sport in Britain 1945–2000*. Oxford: Blackwell.
Horne, J., Tomlinson, A., Whannel, G. and Woodward, K. (eds.) (2013) *Understanding Sport: A Socio-Cultural Analysis* (2nd ed.). London: Routledge.
Houck, D. W. (2006) "Sporting bodies." In A. A. Raney and J. Bryant (eds.) *Handbook of Sports and Media*. London: Routledge (pp. 586–604).
Jarvie, G. (2006) *Sport, Culture and Society: An Introduction*. London: Routledge.

Kennedy, E. and Hills, L. (2009) *Sport, Media and Society*. Oxford: Berg.

McLaughlin, L. (1993) "Feminism, the public sphere, media and democracy." *Media, Culture Society*, 15(4), 599–620.

Markula, P. (ed.) (2009) *Olympic Women and the Media: International Perspectives*. New York: Palgrave.

Merrett, C. (2005) "Sport and Apartheid." *History Compass*, 3(1), 1–11.

Messner, M. (2012) "Reflections on communication and sport: On men and masculinities." *Communication and Sport*, 1(1/2), 113–24.

Petley, J. (ed.) (2013) *Media and Public Shaming: Drawing the Boundaries of Disclosure*. London: I. B. Tauris.

Polley, M. (1998) *Moving the Goalposts: A History of Sport and Society Since 1945*. London: Routledge.

Schudson, M. (1992) "Was there ever a public sphere? If so, when? Reflections on the American case." In C. Calhoun (ed.) *Habermas and the Public Sphere*. Cambridge, MA: MIT Press (pp. 143–63).

Steel, J. (2012) *Journalism and Free Speech*. London: Routledge.

Stevenson, N. (2002) *Understanding Media Cultures*. London: Sage.

Toft, D. (2011) "News sports press survey: Newspapers focus narrowly on sports results." Play the game. Retrieved from http://www.playthegame.org/news/detailed/new-sports-press-survey-newspapers-focus-narrowly-on-sports-results-5248.html

Whannel, G. (2008) *Culture, Politics and Sport: Blowing the Whistle Revisited*. Abingdon: Routledge.

13
Social conflict and the media
Contesting definitional power

Jonathan Cable

The technological advances that have occurred in the last 50 years have dramatically changed how moments of social conflict become defined. This is nowhere more evident than in the coverage of the English riots in the summer of 2011. It was not just about 24-hour rolling news bringing the fire into people's living rooms. The internet played a massive part in shaping the coverage. Social media and mobile phone technology in particular (i.e. Facebook, Twitter, Blackberry Messenger) were partly blamed for the organization of the rioting but it was also a significant aspect of journalists' armory for reporting the riots as well as acting as a source for public information (LSE/Guardian, 2011: 30–33; see also Allen, 2013: 120–51). This stands in direct contrast to the world of the early 60s with its two television channels and a small number of radio stations.

With this in mind, this chapter aims to demonstrate how the media have reported social conflict, with a particular focus on protest and demonstrations since the 1960s. This will show that advances in technology over this time have not been matched by developments in the reporting of social conflict. This will be achieved by examining the media coverage of protests, mass demonstrations, direct action and 'violence' at protests. The chapter begins by presenting a broad examination of the attraction and news value of social conflict to the media and will then move on to examine specific case studies to demonstrate the common themes throughout the media coverage of social conflict.

The attraction of social conflict to the media

Before talking about protest events, it is worth looking closely at some of the base elements of media attraction to social conflict, which is to talk about deviance, crime and violence. The sources of the discussion around these particular facets of social conflict are drawn from classic studies that have interrogated these issues in relation to the media, and are still relevant today. Taking the first of these three topics, deviance, is to examine Stanley Cohen's ideas around 'moral panics' and the media's role in contributing to and covering them. Cohen sets out the following three main roles of the media in relation to moral panics:

1   Setting the agenda
2   Transmitting the images
3   Breaking the silence, making the claim

(Cohen 1972: xxviii–xxix)

How this works in practice is through the media process of first, selecting events that are newsworthy and which have an element of deviance to them; second, reproducing the assertions of claims-makers to either heighten or diminish the level of moral panic; and finally, the media may become claims-makers themselves and attempt to produce a moral panic (ibid.: xxviii-xxix). The second point in the list is particularly important in relation to protest as it involves the views of the media towards their sources and who is allowed to make claims. Cohen points out that our ideas about the world have been filtered through the mass media and, in addition, the information that leads to these ideas is open to a plethora of perspectives (ibid.: 9). The power to define introduces a hierarchy of subordinate and superordinate groups. Becker illustrates this point using deviance as an example:

> In the case of deviance, the hierarchical relationship is a moral one. The superordinate parties in the relationship are those who represent the forces of approved and official morality; the subordinate parties are those who, it is alleged, have violated that morality.
>
> (Becker 1967: 240)

If we take this hierarchy and apply it to social conflict the superordinate group is composed of those entities with the power for change, for example a politician with the ability to transform political policy. The subordinate, on the other hand, is the protest group who are challenging the superordinate to make change happen. In other words, they do not have the necessary power to achieve change by themselves. How the relationship between these different actors affects the definition of protest events and issues is what Becker terms a "hierarchy of credibility". What the hierarchy refers to is "any system of ranked groups, [where] participants take it as given that members of the highest group have the right to define the way things really are" (ibid.: 241). In political situations such as protest politics, an alternative way of referring to the hierarchy of credibility would be to talk about political standing. Public officials, for instance, will have a higher standing than challenger groups simply due to what they do.

Moving on from deviance and bringing crime and violence into the argument, Hall et al. note that there is a certain societal consensus which defines the legitimate and illegitimate ways for people in society to behave (1977: 64). Crime, they note, is the interruption of societal consensus based upon the rule of law and perceptions of what is acceptable and unacceptable (ibid.: 66). They go on to state that crime's place in the news can be explained because the way it is reported "evokes threats to but also reaffirms the consensual morality of the society" (ibid.). The consensus mentioned here also applies and extends to politics and challenges to consensus politics again raise the specter of a division between legitimate and illegitimate politics. For protest groups, this is reflected in the perception of their politics and protest actions, where actions can be seen as "illegitimate and 'deviant'" and any challenge to the political consensus is seen as "potentially violent" (Murdock, 1973: 156–57). What this chapter will now demonstrate, using historical examples of protest movements, is that protest fits into the event-based nature of news as follows:

1. There is a news threshold – in other words a protest needs to meet some particular characteristics before being reported
2. News attention is concentrated on what form a protest takes, what happened, who was involved and this is to the detriment of explanations of why a protest is happening
3. The focus on the event makes media attention short-lived and transitory
4. Finally, explanations of the issues coincide with mainstream political consensus.

(Murdock, 1973: 163–64)

These characteristics of the news coverage of protest are at the very heart of academic debates where the common argument is that the more spectacular the protest activity the more media attention a social movement receives. However, the spectacle causes the media to critically divorce protest activities from their corresponding politics and this, in turn, removes the overriding context of why people are protesting (Rosie and Gorringe, 2009a; Wykes, 2000; Gitlin, 1980; Wahl-Jorgensen, 2003). This goes further than just a negative portrayal of the protest action, it also leads to disapproving media coverage of the protesters themselves (Gitlin, 1980; Wahl-Jorgensen, 2003). Furthermore, the media coverage of social conflict tends to follow Hall et al.'s "signification spiral", which is a self-amplifying sequence around a set of events or people (1977: 223).

Bearing in mind the list already presented (see Murdock, 1973: 163–64) the following should be added to the general characteristics of the reporting of social conflict: escalation and amplification where something or someone is made to seem more threatening; identification of an issue or concern to include the identification of potential threats (Hall et al., 1977: 223); convergence where two acts are linked together (ibid.: 223); prediction of what is going to happen at an event (Cohen, 1972: 31); finally, symbolization with particular reference to stereotypes (ibid.: 35). To show how these common threads have manifested themselves in the reporting of protest over time, this chapter will now explore several specific protest events and actions.

Anti-Vietnam protest, 1968, London

On 27 October 1968 anti-war activists held a mass demonstration in London to protest against the Vietnam War and this event attracted approximately 100,000 protesters (Nehring, 2008: 131). Previous large-scale protests had been held in London in the previous year in July and October of 1967. These protests, as well as the demonstration in March of 1968, were characterized by protesters confronting the police, violence and numerous arrests (ibid.: 130). It was, however, the mass student protests which occurred in Paris in May 1968 that would be instrumental in fomenting the political and press preconception of the 27 October demonstration, predicting it would be inherently violent (Halloran et al., 1970: 92). The protests in Paris, in particular, sent a schism through mainstream political consensus. As Halloran et al. mention, the political and media bewilderment about the anti-war protests up until this moment was turned into anxiety:

> [T]he mid-sixties witnessed the first rupturing in the fabric of cultural hegemony so effectively woven since the war, as groups appeared at the margins of the political spectrum to challenge dominant definitions of social and political issues.
>
> (Halloran et al., 1970: 89)

Against this backdrop, the reporting of the protest in the press before the demonstration occurred was filled with concern about potential violence. What Murdock found when analyzing the press was the reporting of suspected violent plots in the run up to the demonstration which served to juxtapose the peaceful nature of the march with an expectancy of violent behavior (Murdock, 1973: 160). This type of coverage is then coupled with the contextualizing of a demonstration from within this theme of anticipated violence, and in so doing, it helps to transform the protesters into an 'outsider' group and create an opposition narrative where 'us versus them' becomes the societal consensus against militant outsiders (ibid.: 161–62). As a consequence, the participants at the protest are presented as actors in a spectacle of violence and therefore the press coverage empties the protest actions of their political content (ibid.: 165). Similarly, Halloran et al. (1970: 90) found that when the protest did not turn as violent as the press had predicted, the majority of peaceful protesters were effectively contrasted to the minority who were violent. These themes, as already mentioned, have characterized the reporting of protest ever since and will be detailed further in the following examples.

The miners' strikes of the 1970s and 1980s

The miners' strikes that hit Great Britain in the 1970s and 1980s were backdropped by an era of rapid economic change. The traditional industries that the British economy was built upon were gradually contracting from the 1960s onwards, and when

> the process of structural economic change accelerated, particularly after the election of Thatcher's Conservative government in 1979, the implications for trade unions of the decline of their manufacturing and public sector strongholds became clear.
>
> (Phillips, 2006: 206)

The militancy of the strikes as perceived by the press and politicians implied that the miners were laying down a substantial challenge to political consensus (ibid.: 201).

There were, however, big differences between the media treatment of the strikes in the 1970s and those of the 1980s. According to Routledge, the miners were able to obtain a lot more favorable press coverage in the 1970s and were sought after to give comment on events (2009: 157). The coverage changed when it came to the strikes in the 1980s where the majority of the press was supportive of the Conservative government of Margaret Thatcher (ibid.: 157). Press hostility was fueled by the strong, combative leader of the National Union of Miners, Arthur Scargill, who became a figurehead of the strikes (Williams, 2009: 38). This press focus on these two strong personalities reduced the arguments to a battle between two people, rather than dealing with the deeper issues affecting the miners (ibid.: 38, 40). The detailed concentration on conflict, a hostile media environment and attention to personalities are aspects which would be repeated during the protest camps at the Greenham Common missile base.

Anti-nuclear protest at Greenham Common

The protests at the missile base at Greenham Common were a slightly different challenge to political consensus when compared to the examples already mentioned. What made the Greenham Common protests different is that the camp developed into a women-only camp, which meant that the challenge to the political order came from 'ordinary women' who were not necessarily prevalent in undertaking acts of this type (Couldry, 1999: 338). In its formative years, however, between 1981 and late 1982, the base protest received very little media coverage (Glasgow University Media Group, 1985: 197). Then, in April 1983, the Campaign for Nuclear Disarmament held protests at the military bases of Burghfield, Greenham and Aldermaston (ibid.: 265).

These protests featured heavily in news coverage in both the press and broadcast media and protesters briefly had access to the news where their actions were highlighted (ibid.: 270–71). After the 1983 protests, according to Couldry (1999: 342), the camp was relatively ignored. Instead, the "women's refusal to tailor their activities to the needs of the media" (Glasgow University Media Group, 1985: 202) meant that it was their challenge to societal norms that became the focus. Women during this time period were not generally seen to be involved in this kind of publicly mediated protest action and the Greenham camps were a challenge to the "'common sense' expectation of 'ordinary women'" (Couldry, 1999: 339). Again, what this shows is that being represented as outside of the perceived political and social consensus becomes a point where the media can focus their attention, using it as a means of deconstructing and divorcing protest from its politics.

Mass mediated protests from the 1990s and 2000s

It would be naïve however to suggest that social movements are unaware of these reactions to their activities. Quite the opposite, the use of spectacular protest strategies both recognizes and exploits news values at the same time and it is this spectacle that Gamson and Mayer argue as the primary news value of protest:

Spectacle means drama and confrontation, emotional events with people who have fire in the belly, who are extravagant and unpredictable. This puts a high premium on novelty, on costume, and on confrontation. Violent action in particular has the most of these media valued elements. Fire in the belly is fine, but fire on the ground photographs better. Burning buildings and burning tires make better television than peaceful vigils and orderly marches.

(Gamson and Meyer, 1996: 288)

The spectacle in this respect is what appeals most to the visual requirements of news reporting. This means that protesters are blurring the lines between political expression and media spectacle. What follows as a consequence is that the major news values of protest revolve around four particular aspects of spectacle:

1. Size of protest, i.e. the number of people participating
2. Degree of disruptiveness or radicalness
3. Creativity or newness of the form of action and its accompanying symbolic elements
4. The political weight or public prominence of individuals or groups supporting or actually participating in the protest.

(Rucht, 2013: 257)

It is the use of protest as theatre which turns activists from political individuals into actors on the media stage, and which brings attendant dangers. Wall goes as far as comparing protest action to a 'performance', where "activism, even in its most serious form, is a method of performance that must be developed and improvised" (1999: 96). Sticking with the theater metaphor, one way of losing the interest of the media is by not staying in character but this very emphasis on the theatrical also raises the specter of activists being turned into celebrities.

This is one of the major disadvantages of spectacular protest tactics, as, Gitlin argues, "celebrated radicals become radical celebrities; four-star attractions in the carnival of distracting and entertaining international symbols" (1980: 162). The environmental activist 'Swampy' from the mid to late 1990s is a good example of this. He was involved in protesting against the expansion of Manchester's airport in 1997 by tunneling underneath the roads surrounding it (Wykes, 2000: 73). In doing so, his actions caused him to become a by-word for environmental direct action and, over the course of his protest, the media coverage moved from being about the protest into a focus on the lives and lifestyles of its young activists. This shift in focus was able to remove the political angle of the protest because it "dislocated the debate from the public to the private" (ibid.. 85). The key point that should be taken from this section is that protesters are not using the spectacle merely as a political photo opportunity which can be interpreted as a symbolic gesture. The next part of the chapter will look more closely at a specific social movement, the Global Justice Movement, their use of symbolic direct action and 'disruptive protest'.

The global justice movement

The Global Justice Movement is responsible for protest actions all around the world against issues ranging from government trade policies to transnational corporations. It is most noted for its mass demonstrations against international government and monetary summits such as those by the Group of 20 (G20), the International Momentary Fund (IMF) and the World Trade Organization (WTO). The movement gained international prominence when it made its North American debut at the WTO's Third Ministerial Conference in December 1999 in Seattle. The event has been considered the "coming out party of a movement" (Klein, 2002: 3). The main reasons for the vast amount of attention that caught the mainstream media, police and political elite unawares were the sheer scale and sophistication of the protests. The size and diversity of the protest groups were the biggest surprise, justifying them being considered a 'movement'. The participants ranged from trade unions, religious groups and Non-Governmental Organizations to autonomous non-hierarchical anarchists.

The Seattle protests were characterized by human blockades, running battles between the police and protesters and symbolic acts of vandalism against corporate icons of Nike, Starbucks and McDonalds (DeLuca and Peeples, 2002: 138). Violence in this instance served a paradoxical role. In DeLuca and Peeples' research into the demonstrations at the World Trade Organization (WTO) meeting in Seattle 1999, they found that instead of protesters becoming divorced from the issues, the violence gave a voice to the voiceless and opened up debates about WTO policy and public order policing (ibid.). They state that the disruptive protest contained all the "necessary ingredients for compelling the whole world to watch" (ibid.: 130). Most importantly, they argue that the violence did not succeed in "stealing the limelight of legitimate protest, the compelling images of violence and disruption increased the news hole and drew more attention to issues" (ibid.: 139–42). Therefore, this is not to say that activists have no control over their media representations but, on the contrary, that activists can use the media for their own ends.

How these types of protest actions are reported in the news media, especially in the build-up to a mass demonstration, has a telling impact on the construction of how a protest is perceived. In a similar vein to the other protest events already mentioned, Rosie and Gorringe argue that: "anticipatory coverage is, if anything, more important than how an event itself is reported" (2009b: 2.9). The creation of a dominant media narrative which anticipates violence decreases the amount of attention paid by the media to the issues under protest and shifts focus onto the protesters themselves. As has been shown in this chapter the prevalence of this type of constructed anticipation of violence is nothing new. Halloran et al.'s research into the coverage of the 1968 anti-Vietnam War protests in London demonstrated that the press in particular focused on a small minority and expected the kind of violence which had been seen at other protests in 1968 (1970: 139). The use of comparable demonstrations in the construction of media coverage of an imminent protest is an attempt at negatively contextualizing a mass demonstration.

However, this context is constructed as unfavorable to the majority of peaceful protesters because the protest references selected by the media are often events that were heavily characterized by violence (Rosie and Gorringe, 2009b: 2.9). Wahl-Jorgensen looked at the dominant themes of media coverage surrounding the 2001 May Day protests in London and found that these themes could be divided up into three categories:

1. Law and order – Protesters as a problem of policing
2. Economy – The negative impact of protest on the national economy
3. Spectacle – Focus on the irrational and spectacular aspects of Global Justice activism.

(Wahl-Jorgensen, 2003: 131)

Furthermore, it was found that the emphasis of the coverage was the systemic belittling, ridiculing, depoliticizing and preoccupation with the consequences of protest (ibid.: 142). The issues under protest became divorced from the protest itself because the spectacle of protest attracted the most attention and conflict or violence is especially effective at generating coverage. To exemplify this point, following the Group of 20 (G20) protests in London, Rosie and Gorringe wrote an article which stated that the majority of peaceful protesters were ignored in favor of what the media termed 'extreme' elements (2009b: 3, 9). These representations, however prevalent, are now heavily contested thanks to digital technology and the capabilities of the internet. These platforms allow an electronic platform to challenge these portrayals and transmit differing perspectives on protest events.

The internet, social media and social conflict

Before concluding this chapter it is worth taking a look at the influence which contemporary media technologies and practices have on the coverage of social conflict. To conceptualize what this means in practice it is useful to bring DeLuca and Peeples' research back into the argument. In their research into the WTO protests in 1999 they introduced the idea of the 'public screen' which took the Habermas concept of the public sphere and updated it for new technologies and a changing societal landscape (DeLuca and Peeples, 2002). They define it as a "metaphor for thinking about places of politics and possibilities of citizenship in our present moment." The 'screens' in this case refer to television, the internet and newspaper front pages (ibid.: 121). Nine years after this original conceptualization they returned to the concept to argue that the advent of Web 2.0, smartphones, digital cameras and tablets has fundamentally led to new forms of social organization and brand new ways of perceiving events (DeLuca, Sun and Peeples, 2011: 145).

There are several positives and negatives that can be associated with the internet and social conflict. In the realm of activism it is clear that there is much potential for the organization of protest. That said, the audience for activist websites and social media outputs tends to be mostly activists and to reach the wider public, protesters need to enter the more traditional media of print and broadcast (Rucht, 2013: 261). The internet also allows for the challenging of the dominant perspectives of an event presented by the mainstream news media. This occurred during the G20 protests when the newspaper seller Ian Tomlinson died. The initial reports in the press however were unclear as to whether Tomlinson was a protester or a member of the general public. For example, the *Daily Telegraph* wrote: "Protester dies after a day of violent clashes" (Edwards et al., 2009: 6). This type of narrative changed when a week later *The Guardian* published a mobile phone video of Tomlinson being pushed over by a member of the police (Lewis, 2009: 1). This led to debates and a questioning of the police public order tactics around protest.

The inquiry that was instigated into police tactics by Her Majesty's Inspectorate of Constabulary (HMIC) revealed a perhaps underappreciated result of protester internet communications. The HMIC document "Adapting to Protest" talks about activist online sources as being central to the gathering of police intelligence (2009: 42). The report goes further to state that it had observed, "unprecedented levels of communication between disparate protest groups" (ibid.: 42). Finally, the police document explains that intelligence for what protests were going to happen was garnered from "open source materials" (ibid.: 101). This underlines something of the positive and negative impacts of the internet on protest events.

Conclusion

What this chapter has shown is that the common thread running through the media coverage of social conflict over time is that the antagonists have been consistently demonized, depoliticized and depicted as deviant. However, this is not always the case. There are sometimes instances which present a balance to this portrayal and the changing technological landscape has increased the ability of social actors to challenge the dominant news frames and narratives. This has meant that the 'official' line from powerful centralized institutions such as politics, corporations and the police is constantly being challenged by alternative forms of media. This was never more starkly evidenced than in the death of the newspaper seller Ian Tomlinson as asserted above. These developments have also meant that accountability and definition of events can be contested almost instantly. It is the advent of these technologies that requires social conflict research to go beyond what is in newspapers or on broadcast media and delve into the world of social media to fully understand the range of different perspectives and interpretations of social conflict that exist in contemporary society.

Further reading

The first four recommendations set the initial groundwork for the research into social conflict ever since. First Cohen's (1972) *Folk Devils and Moral Panics* examines the way in which the media defines groups as a threat to society. This is complimented by Hall et al.'s (1977) *Policing the Crisis* which takes Cohen's ideas and applies it to street crime in the UK. In doing so Hall et al. uncover the definitional power of authoritative social and political actors to control the debates around contentious issues. The next two are specifically about anti-Vietnam War protests, one concerning the UK, the other America. Halloran, Elliott and Murdock's (1970) *Demonstrations and Communication* was one of the first in-depth accounts of the media coverage of a major protest event, and showed the levels of predictive violence, depoliticizing and sensationalizing of mass demonstrators in the media. Gitlin's (1980) *The Whole World is Watching* on the other hand shows the trajectory that the American anti-war movement took and is an influential text on the construction, actions and deconstruction of the anti-war movement in America. For more recent work about contemporary research in this area, Cammaerts, Mattoni and McCurdy's (2013) *Mediation and Protest Movements* and Cottle and Lester's (2011) *Transnational Protests and the Media* provide a broad range of chapters across a variety of subjects.

References

Allen, S. (2013) *Citizen Witnessing*. Cambridge: Polity Press.
Becker, H. S. (1967) "Whose side are we on?" *Social Problems*, 14(3), 239–47.
Cammaerts, B., Mattoni, A. and McCurdy, P. (2013) *Mediation and Protest Movements*. Bristol: Intellect.
Cohen, S. (1972) *Folk Devils and Moral Panics: The Creation of the Mods and Rockers*. Abingdon: Routledge Classics.
Cottle, S. and Lester, L. (eds.) (2011) *Transnational Protests and the Media*. New York: Peter Lang Publishing.
Couldry, N. (1999) "Disrupting the media frame at Greenham Common: A new chapter in the history of mediations?" *Media, Culture Society*, 21(3), 337–58.
DeLuca, K. M. and Peeples, J. (2002) "From public sphere to public screen: Democracy, activism, and the 'violence' of Seattle." *Critical Studies in Media Communications*, 19(2), 125–51.
DeLuca, K. M., Sun, Y. and Peeples, J. (2011) "Wild public screens and image events from Seattle to China: Using social media to broadcast activism." In S. Cottle and L. Lester (eds.) *Transnational Protests and the Media*. New York: Peter Lang Publishing (pp. 143–58).
Edwards, R., Gammell, C., Allen, N. and Bingham, J. (2009) "Protester dies after a day of violent clashes." *Daily Telegraph*, 2 April, p. 6.
Gamson, W. A. and Meyer, D. S. (1996) "Framing political opportunity." In D. McAdam, J. D. McCarthy and M. N. Zald (eds.) *Comparative Perspectives on Social Movements: Political Opportunities, Mobilising Structures, and Cultural Framings*. New York: Cambridge University Press (pp. 275–90).
Gitlin, T. (1980) *The Whole World is Watching: Mass Media in the Making and Unmaking of the New Left*. London: University of California Press.
Glasgow University Media Group (1985) *War and Peace News*. Maidenhead: Open University Press.
Hall, S., Critcher, C., Jefferson, T., Clarke, J. N. and Roberts, B. (1977) *Policing the Crisis: Mugging, the State and Law and Order*. Basingstoke: Macmillan.
Halloran, J. D., Elliott, P. and Murdock, G. (1970) *Demonstrations and Communication: A Case Study*. Harmondsworth: Penguin Books Ltd.
HMIC (2009) "Adapting to Protest." [pdf] Her Majesty's Inspectorate of Constabulary, 5 July. Retrieved from http://www.hmic.gov.uk/media/adapting-to-protest-20090705.pdf
Klein, N. (2002) *Fences and Windows: Dispatches from the Front Lines of the Globalization Debate*. London: Flamingo.

Lewis, P. (2009) "Revealed: Video of police attack on man who died at G20 protest: Footage shows man thrown to ground by officer: *Guardian* hands dossier to police watchdog." *The Guardian*, 8 April, p. 1.

LSE/Guardian (2011) *Reading the Riots: Investigating England's Summer of Disorder*. London: The Guardian/LSE.

Murdock, G. (1973) "Political deviance: The press presentation of a militant mass demonstration." In S. Cohen and J. Young (eds.) *The Manufacture of News: Social Problems, Deviance and the Mass Media*. London: Constable and Co Ltd (pp. 156–75).

Nehring, H. (2008) "Great Britain." In M. Klimke and J. Scharloth (eds.) *1968 in Europe: A History of Protest and Activism, 1956–1977*. Basingstoke: Palgrave Macmillan (pp. 125–36).

Phillips, J. (2006) "The 1972 miners' strike: Popular agency and industrial politics in Britain." *Contemporary British History*, 20(2), 187–207.

Rosie, M. and Gorringe, H. (2009a) "The 'anarchist world cup': Respectable protest and media panics." *Social Movement Studies*, 8(1), 35–53. Retrieved from http://www.socreson line.org.uk/14/5/14.html.

——(2009b) "What a difference a death makes: Protest, policing and the press at the G20." *Sociological Research Online*, 14(5).

Routledge, P. (2009) "Trade unions, public relations and the media." In G. Williams (ed.) *Shafted: The Media, the Miners' Strike and the Aftermath*. London: Campaign for Press & Broadcasting Freedom (pp. 155–62).

Rucht, D. (2013) "Protest movements and their media usages." In B. Cammaerts, A. Mattoni and P. McCurdy (eds.) *Mediation and Protest Movements*. Bristol: Intellect (pp. 249–69).

Wahl-Jorgensen, K. (2003) "Speaking out against the incitement to silence: The British press and the 2001 May Day protests." In A. Opel and D. Pompper (eds.) *Representing Resistance: Media Civil Disobedience, and the Global Justice Movement*. Westport, CT: Praeger Publishers (pp. 130–48).

Wall, D. (1999) *Earth First! and the Anti-Roads Movement*. London: Routledge.

Williams, G. (2009) "Media and the Miners." In G. Williams (ed.) *Shafted: The Media, the Miners' Strike and the Aftermath*. London: Campaign for Press & Broadcasting Freedom (pp. 36–46).

Wykes, M. (2000) "The burrowers: News about bodies, tunnels and green guerrillas." In B. Adam, S. Allan and C. Carter (eds.) *Environmental Risks and the Media*. London: Routledge (pp. 73–90).

14
The media and armed conflict
Philip Hammond

In the course of a generation, media coverage of war seems to have changed beyond recognition. Twenty-first-century audiences expect news to be instantly available 24/7, enlivened with satellite link-ups to the battlefield, reporter blogs and participant video footage. Moreover, they expect such coverage to be presented in several globally available varieties, not just CNN or the BBC, but Russia Today and Al Jazeera, and they may encounter it via social media rather than a conventional news outlet. It is a world away from the 1982 Falklands conflict, when only a limited number of journalists, all hand-picked by the Ministry of Defence (MoD), could get anywhere near the warzone. News did not 'roll', it came in restricted, daily bulletins, with the media's communications dependent on the military's infrastructure, their news images often delayed for days and their stories vetted before transmission back to London. Yet at the same time it often appears that little has changed. Many critics have noted the steady stream of propaganda and misinformation that has flowed through coverage of recent conflicts. Support for 'our boys' and near-hysterical demonization of enemies are still routine features of war journalism.

There is some uncertainty about what is new and distinctive about the media's role in armed conflict today. Some aspects of recent coverage (such as the 'embedding' of reporters with coalition troops in the 2003 Iraq war) have been treated as exceptionally novel even though there were clear precedents, while real and important changes have often been discussed in narrow, technical terms which do little to clarify their significance. Although this brief overview does not attempt to summarize the entire history of war correspondence (see Knightley, 2004 for an excellent account), it does endeavor to take a broader view of the changing social and political context and suggests that in order to understand the contemporary picture we need to take account of the past. Two earlier turning points in particular are important for the contrasts they offer: the Vietnam war and the end of the Cold War. While the lesson mistakenly learned from the former was that journalists must be tightly controlled, lest unfavorable coverage should undermine support for war, after 1989 the perception of a fundamental antagonism between the news media and the military began to be modified, as reporters increasingly understood their role in terms of encouraging an 'ethical' turn in western foreign policy. This chapter argues that coverage is now shaped by two contradictory trends: on the one hand, a disproportionate emphasis on image and presentation; on the other, an uncertainty about the content of the message.

After Vietnam

The guidelines issued by the MoD to correspondents covering the Falklands conflict sum up an enduring view of journalism in wartime: "The essence of successful warfare is secrecy. The essence of successful journalism is publicity" (in Harris, 1983: 16). The idea that the media/military relationship is one of inevitable and irreconcilable opposition can be traced back to the 1850s, when one of the first war correspondents, William Howard Russell, reported the Crimean war for *The Times*, revealing the incompetence of British commanders and the suffering of their men. In 1982, however, a closer and more pertinent historical reference point for Britain's conflict with Argentina was the US experience in Vietnam. The lesson learned by western militaries in that war was that journalists had been allowed too much freedom and should in future be kept on a tight leash in order to prevent them producing stories which would undermine domestic support.

The myth of the Vietnam war was that the military was stabbed in the back by disloyal media, as shocking images and anti-war voices were broadcast to American homes, sapping morale and sabotaging the war effort. It was a myth that suited the military/political authorities, for whom it provided a convenient scapegoat for defeat, and also many journalists, since it fostered an image of reporters as fearless champions of truth. While in some cases that glamorous professional image was well deserved – famous investigative reporters such as John Pilger and Seymour Hersh first came to prominence in Vietnam, for example – in general the media did not challenge or question the war until it became safe to do so. This point has been decisively demonstrated by Daniel Hallin (1986), who showed that news coverage was initially highly supportive and only began to give serious consideration to anti-war views when the elite pro-war consensus broke down. As the war started to go badly for the US, critical media coverage reflected increasing division and dissent at the top of American society, rather than causing popular opposition to the war.

The US military eventually acknowledged that the media were not to blame for losing the Vietnam war (Skoco and Woodger, 2000: 79), but for many years afterwards that traumatic defeat was held to show that reporters had to be restricted. The British authorities implemented that lesson in the Falklands, not only by attaching reporters to military units, thereby encouraging journalists' close identification with the forces on whom they were reliant for day-to-day survival, but also by assigning them official 'minders' to check their copy. In one case, when a correspondent complained that he was being censored, the word 'censored' was itself censored (Harris, 1983: 121). In turn, the US took the Falklands as a successful model of media management, one American officer noting in 1983 that "the Falklands War shows us how to make certain that government policy is not undermined by the way a war is reported" (in MacArthur, 1993: 138). The model was put into effect immediately in the 1983 US invasion of Grenada and again in the 1989 invasion of Panama. Journalists were simply excluded altogether, allowed in only after the fighting was over.

While such restrictions frequently brought journalists into conflict with the military/political authorities, this did not imply a critical or questioning outlook on the part of the media. The complaint of TV news executives after the Falklands War, for example, was that official constraints had hampered their ability to produce a "nightly offering of interesting, positive and heart-warming stories of achievement and collaboration born out of a sense of national purpose" (Glasgow University Media Group, 1985: 174). Notwithstanding government criticism of broadcasters for treating Argentine and British claims too even-handedly (Harris, 1983: 75), the media's performance in the Falklands was, with a few honorable exceptions, one of loyal propaganda service. It is also worth noting that throughout this period the British state was engaged in an armed conflict within its own borders, with the Provisional Irish Republican Army (IRA). The British news media joined in the accompanying propaganda offensive, sometimes by circulating crude racist stereotypes of the Irish as sub-human (Curtis, 1984), or, more subtly and significantly, by depicting a national liberation struggle as simple criminality. Nevertheless, in 1988 the government sought to restrict news of the conflict and deny the IRA the 'oxygen of publicity' by imposing a ban on broadcasting statements by its political leaders. Although this was an unusual and extreme measure (the ban was lifted in 1994), it typifies the post-Vietnam framework, in which the authorities attempted to control and censor news reporting, while the news media, despite their generally dependable patriotic outlook, were understood as potentially disloyal, untrustworthy and liable to challenge war efforts.

After the Cold War

The first major conflict of the post Cold War era, the 1990–91 Gulf war, in some ways seemed to continue the restrictive pattern of the past, assigning reporters to military units with whom they were supposed to 'bond', and instituting pool arrangements whereby the media had to rely on the shared copy of 'accredited' correspondents. The US even attempted to impose a 48-hour news blackout at the start of ground operations. In other respects, however, the conflict signaled the beginning of some important changes in the media's wartime role.

We can already see in 1991 the beginnings of an official shift from simply controlling and censoring the media toward an emphasis on proactively shaping the message. Rather than just trying to starve the media of information, greater priority was given to feeding their appetite for stories and images. In 1991 this was evident in the regular press briefings given by US generals Colin Powell and Norman Schwarzkopf, often accompanied by arresting footage from the nose-cones of 'smart' munitions flying towards their targets. The deluge of imagery and information did not necessarily mean that news audiences were better informed. The emphasis on 'precision bombing' and 'surgical strikes' disguised the fact that only 7 percent of the bombs dropped by coalition forces were 'smart' and that most bombs actually missed their intended targets (Knightley, 2004: 495). It did, however, mean that the war looked impressive on television. Although, as in past conflicts, journalists complained afterwards about the constraints placed on them, the Gulf war marked the beginning of mutual efforts to establish a more cooperative relationship (Skoco and Woodger, 2000). The results of this process could be seen in the second war with Iraq just over a decade later, when the US Department of Defense promised that "media will have long-term, minimally restrictive access ... through embedding"

(DoD, 2003). Although reporters were still being attached to military units as the UK had done in the Falklands, there had been a genuine shift in approach since 1982. In the words of one British officer in the 2003 Iraq war, the news media were now seen as "a tool, a weapon, a battle-winning asset" (in Franks, 2003).

Perhaps one obvious explanation for this shift is that the media environment was itself changing, so that by 2003 the Pentagon was saying: "We need to tell the factual story – good or bad – before others seed the media with disinformation and distortions, as they most certainly will continue to do" (DoD, 2003). Again the beginnings of the change might be traced back to the 1991 Gulf War, when the US cable news channel CNN first came to international prominence and we glimpsed the new possibilities and problems that round-the-clock, real-time global news might produce. With a satellite link from Baghdad to its headquarters in Atlanta, Georgia, CNN could show what the bombing looked like from the receiving end (Arnett, 2001). CNN's Peter Arnett, who had achieved some notoriety in Vietnam for reporting the remark of a US officer that "It became necessary to destroy the town to save it", was heavily criticized by American politicians in 1991 for 'unpatriotic journalism' in reporting civilian casualties and interviewing the Iraqi leader Saddam Hussein. It would no longer be possible simply to stifle reporting, or fully to control the sorts of messages that might appear.

The Gulf conflict – or, rather, its messy aftermath – also provided one of the earliest examples of what soon became known as the 'CNN effect', the idea that the media can set the western foreign policy agenda, as governments are forced to respond to the crises caught in the news spotlight. Just after the 1991 war, it appeared to be news coverage which prompted the west to intervene again in Iraq, to set up 'safe havens' and 'no-fly zones' in order to protect Kurds and other persecuted minorities. The following year, it seemed to be distressing images of suffering that prompted United Nations military intervention in Somalia. Former US Defense Secretary James Schlesinger expressed the elite's unease at the thought that "policies seem increasingly subject … to the images flickering across the television screen" (in Livingston, 1997: 1); while others welcomed what they saw as a positive sign of the news media's potential to promote a "global civil society" by creating pressure for humanitarian military intervention (Shaw, 1996). Subsequent research has found little evidence to support the existence of the CNN effect; news coverage is generally led by official policy rather than vice versa (Robinson, 2002). Yet while the extent of the media's actual influence is questionable, it surely was the case that in the 1990s journalists increasingly understood their role in terms of attempting to affect western policy.

In retrospect, it is this shift towards an active advocacy role, rather than any 'CNN effect', which is the more significant change in post Cold War conflict journalism. Former BBC correspondent Martin Bell coined the term "journalism of attachment" to describe a new style of reporting which "cares as well as knows" and which would "not stand neutrally between good and evil, right and wrong, the victim and the oppressor" (Bell, 1998: 16). What prompted this explicit rejection of journalistic impartiality was the 1992–95 Bosnian war, when many journalists felt compelled to take sides – encouraging public sympathy for the Bosnian Muslims, vilifying the Serbs, and agitating for forceful western intervention (Hume 1997). Such 'attached' journalists were often sharply critical of what they saw as the pusillanimity of political leaders, but this was criticism of a new sort. In the post Cold War era, campaigning, partisan journalists were more likely to criticize the Western powers for *not* intervening militarily in weaker states (Hammond, 2002). Hence, the emergence of a 'critical' advocacy journalism in the 1990s was perfectly consistent with a more cooperative media/military relationship. As Nik Gowing (1994: 15) notes, in Bosnia western reporters "willingly submitted to a UN pool system" in contrast to their "principled complaints … [about] pool arrangements and news management during the Gulf war" – no doubt in part because journalists wanted to encourage greater military involvement in the Balkans. CNN's Christiane Amanpour, for example, bemoaned the official restrictions that had been placed on reporters in 1991 (Amanpour, 2003) but berated President Bill Clinton on live television in 1994 for not articulating a tough policy on Bosnia (Ricchiardi, 1996).

Ultimately, despite striking a critical pose, the journalism of attachment proved quite compatible with the military's view of the media as "a tool, a weapon, a battle-winning asset." By the end of the 1990s, Bell's declaration of the need to take sides between "good and evil, right and wrong, the victim and the oppressor" had become Prime Minister Tony Blair's explanation of the Kosovo conflict as "a battle between good and evil; between civilization and barbarity; between democracy and dictatorship" (Blair, 1999). *The Guardian*'s Maggie O'Kane, who had belatedly complained that during the Gulf war "we, the media, were harnessed like … beach donkeys and led through the sand to see what the British and US military wanted us to see" (O'Kane, 1995), boasted in 1999 that "it was the press reporting of the Bosnian war and the Kosovar refugee crisis that gave [Blair] the public support and sympathy he needed to fight the good fight against [Serbian President Slobodan] Milosevic" (in Glass, 1999). The BBC's Mark Laity, who had covered the Kosovo conflict from Brussels, reporting the daily press conferences held by NATO spokesman Jamie Shea, identified so closely with the cause that after the war he quit his post as defense correspondent and went to work for NATO as Shea's deputy. Though unusual, Laity's poacher-to-gamekeeper journey was emblematic of the changing relationship between the military and the media in the post Cold War era.

Continuity and change since 9/11

The 'war on terror' pursued after the terrorist attacks of 11 September 2001, including the invasion of Afghanistan in 2001 and Iraq in 2003, has prompted several critics not only to argue that contemporary war is different from the past, but also to put the media at the center of their analysis of that change (de Franco, 2012). It is claimed that we live in an age of 'mediatized' conflict (Cottle, 2006), whereby rather than simply reporting on a discrete sphere of war and foreign policy, the media now constitute the ground on which conflict is enacted, and that, in today's new and unpredictable media ecology, war has become chaotic or "diffused" (Hoskins and O'Loughlin, 2010), as clear patterns of cause and effect break down. As noted at the beginning of this chapter, the media environment has indeed continued to develop rapidly in recent years. Yet such development always takes place within a larger political context – from the sharp divisions and counter-cultural challenges of the Vietnam era, through to the rise of the cosmopolitan 'ethical' interventionism which followed the collapse of the Left/Right politics of the Cold War.

Despite a widespread feeling at the time that 9/11 had changed the world, there turned out to be considerable continuity between the 'war on terror' and the 'humanitarian' interventions of the 1990s. The war in Afghanistan entailed dropping aid packages as well as bombs; the invasion of Iraq was justified in terms of 'liberating' the Iraqi people as well as dealing with the supposed threat of 'weapons of mass destruction'. The continuity in specific propaganda themes indicated a deeper connection. Both 'humanitarian intervention' and the 'war on terror' were attempts by western political leaders to reframe international relations for the post Cold War era. Again one might trace this back to the 1991 Gulf war, when President George Bush Sr. proclaimed the inauguration of a "New World Order", declaring that America had "kicked the Vietnam Syndrome once and for all" (in Chesterman, 1998). These grandiose claims were a response to the fact that after the end of the Cold War, with established political reference points no longer available, it became very difficult to articulate what Bush clumsily called 'the vision thing.' The response that was attempted in 1991, larding on moralistic rhetoric to portray a one-sided war against a weaker state as an epic battle against a 'new Hitler', was repeated many times: against Somali 'warlords', Haitian generals, Serbian 'Nazis', and back to Saddam. The problem was not simply to find new enemies to replace the Soviets: it was to address the far larger challenge of a "world without meaning" (Laïdi, 1998). Much like the crusading journalists who went to Bosnia and elsewhere in an attempt to "discover some sense of purpose – first for themselves, and then for their audience back home" (Hume, 1997: 18), western politicians looked to military interventionism as a way to give meaning and purpose to societies in which traditional political loyalties no longer made sense. As this suggests, post Cold War conflict and military intervention has been essentially *narcissistic* for western powers. Though usually justified in terms of saving vulnerable others, it is more about shoring up a sense of self (Hammond, 2007a).

The epochal political change of the end of the Cold War is the context for the phenomena that analysts have discussed in terms of 'mediatized' or 'diffused' conflict. On the one hand, the narcissistic orientation has meant that the media presentation of war has assumed an inordinate importance. Yet on the other hand, the same political shift which makes international affairs virtually the only arena in which some kind of common purpose and values can be conjured up and enacted also gives rise to doubt and uncertainty about what the content of propaganda messages should be. There is consequently both an awkward self-consciousness about the manufacture of images and an acute anxiety about the 'wrong' messages coming out.

In the 2003 Iraq war, for example, the coalition went to extraordinary lengths to create feel-good media stories and photo opportunities. The Pentagon advised that the use of helmet-mounted cameras on combat sorties was "approved and encouraged to the greatest extent possible" (DoD, 2003), apparently applying the advice not only to 'embedded' journalists but also to its own troops, who produced such memorable episodes as the rescue of Private Jessica Lynch from al-Nasiriyah. The story of the rescue, complete with video footage, was released to the media at 'Centcom', the coalition press center in Doha which was designed by a Hollywood art director. Professional set designers were also drafted in for President George W. Bush's announcement of the "end of major combat operations" on 1 May 2003. Bush co-piloted a fighter jet to land on an aircraft carrier before delivering the speech in front of a banner proclaiming 'Mission Accomplished'. Such attention to self-presentation was matched by nervousness over the dissemination of enemy images, with careful scrutiny of broadcasts by Saddam and attempts to suppress videos released by Osama bin Laden. In the end, though, the coalition's credibility was undermined more by its own publicity-conscious approach than by the amateurish efforts of its opponents. The very fact that so much attention was given to crafting the 'right' messages made the results appear contrived and unconvincing, virtually inviting a cynical response. Mainstream news organisations poured scorn on the "staged operation" to rescue Jessica Lynch (Lloyd Parry, 2003), derided Bush's "stage-managed" victory speech (BBC1, 2 May 2003) and exposed behind-the-scenes media arrangements for the first "choreographed" delivery of humanitarian aid (Buncombe, 2003).

In part, of course, the coalition's propaganda troubles were due to the nature of the contemporary media environment, which made trying to control the image of the conflict a hopeless task. No sooner had coalition troops secured what appeared, fleetingly, to be a fitting image of liberation – emancipated Iraqis toppling a statue of Saddam in Firdos Square in Baghdad, reminiscent of scenes of post Communist celebrations in 1989 – than alternative shots of the scene were circulating on the internet and on Arab satellite channels, showing the 'crowd' to be rather small and unimpressive (naturally, the mainstream soon began ridiculing that media stunt as well). And those same troops who carried cameras on combat sorties also took them into the torture chambers of Abu Ghraib prison, sharing squalid camera-phone snaps of degradation and abuse. The global circulation of such pictures via networked digital media seems almost inevitable, making official attempts to impose a single, defining image of the war futile.

Yet a more fundamental issue was that coalition governments were unsure what a 'defining image' of victory ought to look like. The sort of 'elite dissensus' which Hallin describes in Vietnam was part of the problem in 2003, and this helps to explain why some sections of the British media, notably the popular *Daily Mirror* tabloid, went beyond the kind of cynical attitude described above and adopted an explicitly anti-war stance. Elite disagreements and reservations about the war were compounded, though, by the fact that today's political culture is light on principle and short on big ideas. Old loyalties have weakened or disappeared but nothing has yet replaced them. This means that traditional, standby wartime themes are now as likely to cause embarrassment as to elicit support. Whereas once the military prowess of soldiers might have been a source of pride, for instance, in 2003 British journalists were "not allowed to take any pictures or describe British soldiers carrying guns" and were told to avoid portraying coalition troops as "fighters" (BBC, 2003). Similarly, the troops themselves were reportedly instructed not to "wave the Union flag" (Watt, 2003). Whilst in the past one could expect war to generate a degree of jingoistic fervor, in Iraq coalition forces who did raise their own national flags were quickly told to haul them down again. Such uncertainties speak to exactly the sort of incoherence and emptiness that western leaders have repeatedly attempted to address through war and intervention since the 1990s.

Conclusion

The Iraq war was such a debacle, in terms of its bloody aftermath as well as its propaganda blunders, that it appeared it might discredit western military intervention for years to come. Yet war and intervention have continued, of course. The most that might be said to have changed since 2003 is that Western governments are, for now, more downbeat and cautious about making political and media capital out of foreign interventionism. In parallel, contemporary scholarship on the media and conflict pursues variations on the theme of the CNN effect but with less optimism about potential 'cosmopolitan' outcomes and greater uncertainty about unpredictable media flows in a networked world in which non-western states and non-state actors exercise greater influence (Livingston, 2011). Researchers are attuned to the emergent potential of new communications technologies and to the fact that leaders have become increasingly mindful of how their actions might play out in the mediasphere. Yet, as this chapter has argued, the context for such changes is the larger historical transformation of the post Cold War era. The commonsense appeal of the CNN effect thesis was that it seemed to offer an explanation for western governments' apparent departure from *Realpolitik* and narrow national self-interest by seeing states as swayed by the vicissitudes of the media. Yet perhaps the unhappy truth is that policy is simply incoherent and opportunistic.

The most often invoked intellectual framework for making sense of the post Cold War role of western powers has been what Piers Robinson et al. (2010: 170) call the "humanitarian warfare ideology". Its continuing importance after its highpoint during the 1999 Kosovo conflict is indicated by its codification in doctrines such as the "Responsibility to Protect" (ICISS, 2001), its institutionalization in bodies such as the International Criminal Court, its use even when incongruous (as during the 'war on terror') and its sheer longevity (it was invoked in the NATO intervention in Libya in 2011 and subsequent discussions of intervention in Syria in 2012–13). Even during the 2003 Iraq war, some US activists simultaneously called for a withdrawal from that conflict while demanding humanitarian military intervention in the Darfur region of Sudan, adopting the slogan "Out of Iraq, into Darfur" (Mamdani, 2007). In the UK, there was immediate discussion of how to "revive the ethical foreign policy" in the wake of Iraq so that Britain could "act as a moral entrepreneur in terms of mobilizing domestic and international support for a worthy cause" (Wheeler and Dunne, 2004: 36). Yet it cannot plausibly be claimed that all this is a sign of success as such. The repeated invocation of the 'humanitarian war' narrative is more a symptom of the west's ongoing crisis of meaning than a solution to it.

We are indeed a world away from the Falklands, a war fought under the conventional banner of British nationalism, in defence of sovereign territory. There was certainly no embarrassment then about 'waving the union flag' nor about celebrating the armed forces' fighting capabilities. It was the last occasion when a British conflict ended with a traditional victory parade, complete with heavy artillery, tanks and armored vehicles. Back in the 1980s, the 'Falklands factor' could readily be mobilized as a domestic political weapon. The government used the defeat of the Argentine 'enemy without' to rally support for its battle against militant workers during the 1984–85 miners' strike, whom it characterized as the 'enemy within'. Since the 1990s, in contrast, western political life has been characterized by the absence of ideological contestation and, rather than pursuing a definite political vision, leaders have found it difficult to say what they stand for.

Further reading

Susan Carruthers (2011) provides an excellent overview of the field in *The Media at War*. Philip Hammond's (2007b) *Framing Post Cold War Conflicts* offers an empirical study comparing news coverage of several recent conflicts. Donald Matheson and Stuart Allan (2009) develop a critical analysis of war reporting in the digital age in *Digital War Reporting*.

References

Amanpour, C. (2003) "The Gulf War pool system." Reporting America at War. Retrieved from www.pbs.org/weta/reportingamericaatwar/reporters/amanpour/poolsystem.html

Arnett, P. (2001) "A look back at Operation Desert Storm." CNN.com, 16 January. Retrieved from http://edition.cnn.com/COMMUNITY/transcripts/2001/01/16/arnett

BBC (British Broadcasting Corporation) (2003) Correspondent, BBC2, 18 May. Retrieved from http://news.bbc.co.uk/nol/shared/spl/hi/programmes/correspondent/transcripts/18.5.03.txt

Bell, M. (1998) "The journalism of attachment." In M. Kieran (ed.) *Media Ethics*. London: Routledge.

Blair, T. (1999) "We must keep bombing to save the refugees." *Sunday Telegraph*, 4 April, p. 34.

Buncombe, A. (2003) "Long wait for help is over as 'Sir Galahad' docks." *Independent*, 29 March, p. 8.

Carruthers, S. (2011) *The Media at War*. London and Basingstoke: Palgrave.

Chesterman, S. (1998) "Ordering the new world." *Postmodern Culture*, 8(3). Retrieved from www.iath.virginia.edu/pmc/text-only/issue.598/8.3chesterman.txt

Cottle, S. (2006) *Mediatized Conflict*. Maidenhead: Open University Press.

Curtis, L. (1984) *Nothing But The Same Old Story*. London: Information on Ireland.

de Franco, C. (2012) *Media Power and The Transformation of War*. Basingstoke: Palgrave Macmillan.

DoD (Department of Defense) (2003) "Public affairs guidance on embedding media." Retrieved from www.defenselink.mil/news/Feb2003/d20030228pag.pdf

Franks, T. (2003) "Not war reporting – just reporting." *British Journalism Review*, 14(2). Retrieved from www.bjr.org.uk/data/2003/no2_franks.htm

Glasgow University Media Group (1985) *War and Peace News*. Milton Keynes: Open University Press.

Glass, C. (1999) "Hacks versus flacks." *Z Magazine*, 1 August. Retrieved from www.charlesglass.net/archives/1999/08/hacks_versus_fl.html

Gowing, N. (1994) "Real-time television coverage of armed conflicts and diplomatic crises." (Working Paper 94–1). Cambridge, MA: Harvard University. Retrieved from http://shorensteincenter.org/wp-content/uploads/2012/03/1994_01_gowing.pdf

Hallin, D.C. (1986) *The "Uncensored War:" The Media and Vietnam*. Oxford: Oxford University Press.

Hammond, P. (2002) "Moral combat." In D. Chandler (ed.) *Rethinking Human Rights*. Basingstoke: Palgrave (pp. 176–95).

——(2007a) *Media, War and Postmodernity*. Abingdon: Routledge.

——(2007b) *Framing Post Cold War Conflicts*. Manchester: Manchester University Press.

Harris, R. (1983) *Gotcha!* London: Faber.

Hoskins, A. and O'Loughlin, B. (2010) *War and Media*. Cambridge: Polity.

Hume, M. (1997) *Whose War is it Anyway?* London: InformInc.

ICISS (International Commission on Intervention and State Sovereignty) (2001) *The Responsibility to Protect*. Ottawa: International Development Research Centre.

Knightley, P. (2004) *The First Casualty* (Revised Edition). Baltimore, MD: Johns Hopkins University Press.

Laïdi, Z. (1998) *A World Without Meaning*. London: Routledge.

Livingston, S. (1997) "Clarifying the CNN effect." (Research Paper R-18). Cambridge, MA: Harvard University. Retrieved from www.genocide-watch.org/images/1997ClarifyingtheCNNEffect-Livingston.pdf

——(2011) "The CNN effect reconsidered (again)." *Media, War and Conflict*, 4(1), 20–36.

Lloyd Parry, R. (2003) "So who really did save Private Jessica?" *The Times*, 16 April, p. 11.

MacArthur, J. R. (1993) *Second Front*. Berkeley, CA: University of California Press.

Mamdani, M. (2007) "The politics of naming." *London Review of Books*, 29(5), 5–8.

Matheson, D. and Allan, S. (2009) *Digital War Reporting*. Cambridge: Polity.

O'Kane, M. (1995) "Bloodless words bloody war." *The Guardian*, 16 December, p. T12.

Ricchiardi, S. (1996) "Over the Line?" *American Journalism Review*, 18(7), 25–30.

Robinson, P. (2002) *The CNN Effect*. London: Routledge.

Robinson, P., Goddard, P., Parry, K. and Murray, C. with Taylor, P. M. (2010) *Pockets of Resistance*. Manchester: Manchester University Press.

Shaw, M. (1996) *Civil Society and Media in Global Crises*. London: Pinter.

Skoco, M. and Woodger, W. (2000) "The military and the media." In P. Hammond and E. S. Herman (eds.) *Degraded Capability: The Media and the Kosovo Crisis*. London: Pluto Press.

Watt, N. (2003) "Americans raise hackles by flying Stars and Stripes in Iraq." *The Guardian*, 22 March, p. 4.

Wheeler, N. J. and Dunne, T. (2004) *Moral Britannia?* London: The Foreign Policy Centre. Retrieved from http://fpc.org.uk/fsblob/233.pdf

Part III
NEWSPAPERS

15
Ballads and the development of the English newsbook

Marcus Nevitt

When the most brilliant journalist of seventeenth-century England launched the slickest, most informative newsbook of the era, he did so with a clear sense of aesthetic and political purpose. Marchamont Nedham announced *Mercurius Politicus*'s arrival in June 1650 with the swagger of a writer whose copious talent was backed by government subsidy; he represented his new professional identity in the service of Oliver Cromwell's Commonwealth government as a repudiation of both monarchical politics and contemporary journalistic fashions:

> Why should not the *Common-wealth* have a Fool, as well as the King had? 'Tis a point of State ... But you'll say, I am out of fashion, because I make neither *Rimes* nor *Faces*, for *Fidlers* pay, like the *Royal Mercuries*; Yet you shall know I have authority enough to create a fashion of my own, and make all the world to follow the humour.
> (*Mercurius Politicus*, 1650: 1)

Nedham's confidence in his editorship of this groundbreaking venture was well-placed as *Politicus* – underwritten by its editor's sharp eye for sources of advertising revenue and successive revolutionary governments' will to censor all competition – continued for the best part of a decade. At its inception, though, *Politicus* sought to distinguish itself from its rivals, particularly royalist newsbooks, by asserting its status as the Commonwealth's licensed fool who might speak truth to power and provoke the mirth of its readers. And this information and entertainment, Nedham contended, would be offered in sinuous prose, never lapsing into those passages of prefatory verse which had adorned the title pages of practically every unlicensed royalist newsbook published since late 1647. His disparagement of those poems and their fugitive authors' "Fidlers pay" is only partly a graceless boast about his own comfortable annual editor's salary of £100; it is also a careful attempt to position and ennoble *Politicus* as a newsbook worthy of careful reading rather than some multi-modal production which might be part-performed through "Rimes and Faces", embodied, spoken or sung to accompaniment.

As a former author-editor of Mercurius Pragmaticus, one of the "Royal Mercuries" he now denounced, Nedham was in a very good position to remember the performative dimensions of such serials and their prefatory ballads. It was he who had actually invented the convention of printing four quatrains in ballad meter at the head of a news pamphlet in the first issue of Pragmaticus in September 1647. Over the course of his editorship he wrote 64 of them and even if, like other news writers, he affected a certain anti-populist disdain for such "Tavern jingle[s]", he still saw them as a crucial means of maximizing potential audience share, an opportunity to appeal beyond a learned or literate readership and "tickle and charme the more vulgar phant'sies who little regard Truths in a grave and serious garb" (Mercurius Mastix, 1652; Mercurius Pragmaticus, 1648). Given the significance of ballads to Nedham's own account of his development as a journalist, it is surprising to see their occlusion from most recent accounts of the professionalization of the seventeenth-century news business, a process in which, everyone agrees, Nedham played a transformative role (Frank, 1961; Raymond, 1996, 2011: 377–97). An emphasis on scripted precursors to the seventeenth-century newsbook – whether printed or chirographic – in classic narratives of the development of news in the early modern period has meant that the continuing vitality of oral modes of news transmission has largely gone unexamined in the stories we have told ourselves about the rise of print journalism in the period (McShane, 2005). This chapter is an attempt to follow Marchamont Nedham's lead and situate ballads dead centre in one aspect of this story. Since both ballads and news were, as Fox (2000) has demonstrated, crucial nodal points between oral and literate cultures in early modern England, it is only by attending to their interaction and, in particular, to the connections between the topicality and performativity of ballads that we can fully appreciate, like Nedham, their place in revolutionary news culture. As we shall see, ballads were used by royalist journalists, for a combination of commercial and political reasons, to extend the reach of their serials into the acoustic and auditory worlds of street, marketplace and tavern. They became a vital means of informing, entertaining and mobilizing different audiences potentially loyal to the Stuart cause during and after the civil war. In order to appreciate how royalist news writers exploited their possibilities we must first consider the longstanding relationship between performance and topical balladry in early modern England.

Topical ballads and early modern news culture

As Shaaber (1966), Livingstone (1991) and McShane (2011) have shown, topical ballads were a key component of English news culture throughout the early modern period. Though most modern commentators are sceptical about the degree to which topical ballads might be regarded as journalism *per se* (rather than as a parasitically journalistic phenomenon which needed pre-existing systems of documentary or oral reportage and rendered them poetic) evidence exists to suggest that contemporaries did see ballads and news pamphlets as existing in competition or dialogue (Shaaber, 1966: 193; McShane, 2005: 144–45). When, in October 1621, news reached England of a prodigious battle of starlings over the Irish city of Cork, one of the foremost publishers of printed news in the period, Nicholas Bourne, issued a pamphlet account of the event which lamented the prior publication of several ballads on the subject and the effects on his trade; fearing the damage that the poems had done to truth-telling as much as the diminution of his own profits he complained that "so many poeticall fictions haue of late passed the print, that [book buyers] haue some cause to suspect almost euery extraordinary report that is printed" (Bourne, 1622: sig. A3^r). More commonly news pamphlets and ballads on the same topic were produced simultaneously, often by the same publisher. However, whereas Shaaber (1966: 196) presumed a hierarchical relationship between such items, where the pamphlet was always prior to the ballad in every sense, the dialogue between the prosaic and the poetic could be much more fluid than that. Topical broadside ballads, printed on one side of a folio sheet and running anywhere from 14 to 24 stanzas in either gothic (black-letter) or roman (white-letter) type, were severely restricted in the amount of journalistic detail they could provide. Frequently, therefore, with space short, those ballads could suspend principles of poetic organization altogether and reprint bare lists of war casualties, felons, traitors or, in the case of *The Arraignment of John Flodder* (1615), an extract from James I's 'Letters Patent' authorizing named individuals to collect money for the rebuilding of Wymondham, Norfolk, which had been recently damaged by fire (Anon, 1581; Nelson, 1586; Parker, 1640). One licensed broadside about the 1654 Anglo-Dutch peace negotiations spliced the poetic and the prosaic together on the same sheet supplementing a ballad entitled *Ioyfull Newes from England* set "to The Tune of Lord Willoughby" with a short prose account of "the manner how, the place and the time when" the treaty took place (Rollins, 1923: 342–47). Another ballad advertised the concurrent appearance of a more expansive prose pamphlet on the same topic. The Peace, concluded between the King of Denmark and the King of Sweden (1613), having lavished multiple stanzas on a precise description of the terms, six articles of a peace treaty and the role of James I in their negotiation, advised those readers "desirous to see this matter more at large" to consult "the new booke newly come forth according to the Dutch copy". Nothing in this ballad suggests that it regarded itself as secondary or inferior to the contemporary pamphlet account, merely that it was shorter.

If topical ballads interacted with the printed news discourses of the day, they went to even greater lengths to show how they were steeped in the more quotidian dynamics of oral news transmission. Part of their great success when delivered by ballad mongers in streets and public places was the way they quickened and fed an appetite for news gleaned through conversation, gossip and the chance encounter. "Now whispering fellowes, that walke every wheare … / I will tell ye, for troth, what newes I heare", began the Tudor ballad virtuoso William Elderton in his *Newes from Northumberland*, palming off a poem with the thrill of a wicked whisper. In a similar vein he attempted to secure an audience for his verse by styling his steady production of occasional poems as if he were delivering a rolling street news broadcast: "You shall haue more newes er Candelmas come/ Their be matters diffuse yet lookte for of some, / Look on, and look still, as ye longe to here newes" (Elderton, 1570). The other great balladist of the period, Martin Parker, used similar techniques to emphasize the speech-orientation of his work. He presented a 1639 poem on the

Battle of the Downs as a contribution to a pan-European homosocial conversation about naval conflict which filled an information gap in his own nation's talk:

> In euery place where men did meet,
> The talk was of the Spanish Fleet,
> Which the stout Dutchmen with great boast,
> Besieged upon our English coast:
> Now every severall expectation
> Is satisifi'd by this relation.
>
> (Parker, 1639)

Whilst Parker rhymed as if he were trying to drown out the braying of the Dutch, the urgent opening of another ballad expressed an anxiety that its unique insights were actually common knowledge, that the poem might be superseded by chat at any moment: "For, ere you heare it, I must tell/ my newes it is not common" (Chappell and Ebsworth, 1869–99: vol. 2, 367).

Topical ballads: Performance and community

That topical ballads and oral news culture could become practically indistinguishable was due in no small part to the performance orientation of the verse itself. Whilst they were sold by hawkers and booksellers and posted up as single-sheet printed texts, a key dimension of their immense popularity was the public declamation or singing of the text by specialist ballad-mongers (Marsh, 2004; Würzbach, 1990: 39–104). Even though historians and literary critics frequently neglect this fact, treating ballads as if they were primarily legible sources or texts, some recognition of the ways in which ballads in general, and topical ballads in particular, were transformed by live delivery in the public spaces of early modern England is vital for an understanding of the way in which they might operate in the period's news trade. Song or performance propelled the ballad beyond the confines of a literate audience and made it, in one sense, community property; it also transformed the enunciating 'I' into an embodied presence in front of a knowable audience before it became an enigmatic or anonymous subject circulating amongst an anonymized reading public. Würzbach (1990: 17) has discussed the ways in which this contributed to an anti-ballad prejudice in the period – according to which performance at the point of sale transformed the literary into wares – but there has been little analysis of the effects of the performance of news discourse in ballads. As we shall see, whilst the performance of a topical ballad could contribute much to the immediacy and realism of news communication, it was also a means of brokering loyalty and community amongst a heterogeneous audience.

One need only think of the interpellation of topical ballad listeners as the addressees of direct speech to see how the form encouraged collective affective engagement with (as well as providing information about) the topic under discussion. This was most noticeable in the balladist's use of prosopopoeia, allowing inanimate or abstract entities to address a public to suggest that particular interpretations of events were part of a collective conscience rather than personal deduction. For instance, following the conflagration which destroyed "fourescore dwelling houses, besides a great number of other houses" "to the value of tweenti thousande pounds" in the Suffolk market town of Beckles in 1586, one ballad writer had the town itself sing its woes to the tune of Labandalashotte:

> My loving good neighbours, that comes [sic] to beholde,
> Me sillie poore Beckles, in care manyfolde …
> Say thus my good neighbours that god in his ire:
> For sinne hath consumed poore Beckles with fire …
> O daye most unluckie, the winde lowde in the skie
> The water harde frosen, the houses so drye,
> To see such a burning, such flaming of fire
> Such wayling, such crying, through scourge of Gods ire.
>
> (Sterrie, 1586)

Despite the ballad's journalistic enumeration of environmental factors which might have triggered the disaster, the ballad-monger's assumption of a corporate identity to deliver providential news in a familiar tune encouraged individual listeners, hailed as a gathering of "good neighbours", to assume that the only proper response to catastrophe was the shared repentance of the faithful.

The great Elizabethan balladeer Thomas Deloney was particularly skilled at bringing his audiences together. During the Armada crisis, he not only offered them news from the front but was also adept at mobilizing anti-Catholic sentiment by addressing his auditors directly as if they were combatants in the field. One ballad turned the civic public spaces of London, where the poem was first performed and sold, into Tilbury camp in Essex as he ventriloquized Elizabeth I reviewing her troops before the anticipated Armada invasion: "My loving friends and countriemen … / Neuer let your stomackes faile you./ For in the midst of all our troupe,/ We our selues will be in place," the ballad-monger-as-queen declared, arrogating the power of the royal plural (Deloney, 1588b). The first-person speaker of another Deloney ballad staggered back from defeating the Spanish naval commander Don Pietro de Valdez to rally his potential customers as if they were veterans who might bear arms as well as the loose change to buy a broadside poem:

> And you dere breatheren
> Which beareth Armes this ay:
> For safeguard of your natiue soile,
> Marke well what I shall say.
> Regard your duetties,
> Think on our countries good;
> And feare not in defense thereof,
> To spend your dearest bloud.
>
> (Deloney, 1588a)

The anxious injunction to attend to the ballad-monger's performance, to "marke" what is being declaimed as it is uttered – a common illocutionary feature of ballads in the period – is transformed into the confident admonition of the war hero who has seen and known and demands similar sacrifices from his audience on behalf of the nation. The live recital of such speeches gave balladists an extra level of credibility in their accounts as the ballad-monger's physical presence enabled the performer to work as "guarantor of the truth" of the text at the point of delivery (Würzbach, 1990: 49). More than this, though, the performance of topical ballads gave their writers access to an immediacy and affective appeal denied the news pamphleteer; as the audience are hailed from the first person as comrades in arms, the speech seems more a report *at* the front rather than *from* it. Prose writers of occasional news pamphlets, without the performative dimension of topical ballads, might quote from their sources or their subjects but they could never become them.

Such community-brokering properties were especially valuable at times of intense political crisis. When the nation was perceived to be threatened from without or within, writers of topical ballads would routinely conclude their poems with a loyal prayer which bound speaker, audience, monarch and a divine addressee together against a common enemy. During the Northern Rebellion of 1569–70, William Kirkham wrote a ballad outlining the events of the unsuccessful Catholic uprising led by the Earls of Northumberland and Westmoreland, appending a refrain to each stanza which sang of the vertiginous hierarchies of Elizabethan England and the force that might be used to ensure subservience: "Come humble ye down, come humble ye down/ Perforce now submyt to the Queen and the Crowne". By the end of the poem, Kirkham has his audience praying for their own subjection:

> God graunt euery one after this vocation
> To remember the accompt he must laye downe:
> And that we may all in this Englysh Nation
> Be true to God, the Queene and the Crowne.
> Come humble ye down, come humble ye downe.
> God graunt Queene Elizabeth longe to weare ye crowne.
>
> (Kirkham, 1570)

This manipulation of the consensual logic of the refrain, the 'altogether now' camaraderie of a shared and repeated line, so that pious conformity to authoritarian order is at once as natural and unavoidable as a closed couplet, is an extreme example of the godly and loyalist tenor of early modern topical balladry. Whether they recorded regional conspiracies or European threats to English Protestantism, witnessed foreign calamity or domestic conflict, topical ballads typically concluded by praying that God "blesse", "defende", or "preserue" the long life of the monarch, "in plentie, health and peace" (Anon, 1570; Elderton, 1570; G., 1570; Nelson, 1586). That this formula could prove inescapable can be seen in something as apparently diverting or trivial as an early sports report. Having described the tense finale to an archery match in Yorkshire, William Elderton prayed for Queen, country, tidy darts and prayers that continually hit the spot: "God saue our Queene, and keepe our peace/ That our good shooting maie increase/ And praying to God, let us not cease" (Elderton, 1584). When such prayers were sung or declaimed by a ballad-monger before the public the effect was to transform what might read as singular devotion into a ritualistic act of community worship and corporate loyalty amongst the faithful. Thus Martin Parker's ballad about the siege of Protestants in La Rochelle in 1628, sung 'to the tune of In the dayes of old', reported details of the atrocity and ended by imploring God to protect Charles I, the "Royall King, who is true faiths defender". He also prayed to ensure that his topical poem prompted in his audience an empathetic recognition of the plight of their co-religionists in France: "God grant that we here dwelling/ May haue a fellow feeling of those Christians misery" (Parker, 1628).

Ballads and the royalist newsbook

It was the topical ballad's capacity to prompt such "fellow feeling" amongst its audience, to broker community amongst disparate groups with a loyal prayer for the preservation of the monarch, that led to its widespread adoption by the writers of royalist newsbooks during the English civil war. Though Marchamont Nedham, as we have seen, derided the innovation as "Rimes" and "Faces" for "Fidlers pay", the overwhelming majority of the 530 issues of 51 different newsbook titles produced in London by groups loyal to the Stuart cause from late 1647 until their extirpation by the Cromwellian administration in 1650 followed a convention of printing a short lyric or ballad as a preface to the week's news reports (McElligott, 2007: 1). Broadside topical ballads continued to appear unabated throughout this period, written by people from a surprising range of politico-religious positions; quite why, then, they also started appearing on the title pages of certain serials in the autumn of 1647, six years after the advent of the newsbook in 1641, and quite why only royalist titles adopted the convention, requires some investigation. One reason is the well-known politicization of different song styles during the conflict: parliamentary forces such as the New Model Army were famed for singing psalms as a preparation for battle, whereas, with the odd exception, the less restrained singing styles and subject matter of ballads meant that they quickly became associated with the cavalier soldiery (Rollins, 1923: 26–30). As one Tory commentator on the conflict reflected later in the century, those loyal to Charles I heard "Truth in a Song ... and were charmed into obedience" (McElligott, 2007: 19). This politicization of song was witnessed in some of the legislation outlawing royalist serials in 1647. When the parliament agreed to ban all unlicensed books and pamphlets, the activities of the ballad singer who would sing of his loyalty to the king were also criminalized, punishable by public flogging and the confiscation of stock (Rollins, 1923: 26, 36–37). Such strong associations between loyal balladry and the opposition or threat to parliamentary politics meant that they were almost inevitably drawn into the repertoire of royalist serials. As McElligott and Raymond have shown the efflorescence of these newsbooks was related to the rebellions and propaganda battles known as 'the second civil war' (1648–49), when royalist groups unsuccessfully attempted to forge an oppositional consensus to resist and wrest power back from parliament and its forces in the capital (McElligott, 2007: 43–44; Raymond, 1996: 61). Royalist serials printed in London played a central role in this pamphlet war and the popularity of ballads, their appeal across the broadest social spectrum of auditors and readers, certainly fitted with the coalition-building goals of such newsbooks; by contrast, earlier influential royalist serials, such as *Mercurius Aulicus* ("The Court Mercury"), which were published from the king's headquarters in Oxford between January 1643 and September 1645, could be more self-consciously courtly in emphasis, and were thus less obviously congenial hosts for popular balladry.

The first royalist newsbook to use a title-page poem as a consistent design feature was *Mercurius Melancholicus*. Even though the great Stuart balladist Martin Parker, along with John Hackluyt, was probably involved in the production of certain issues of this title, it only began using specifically balladic verse from issue 10, imitating a convention established by *Mercurius Pragmaticus*, under Marchamont Nedham's editorship, a month or so earlier. Outlawed, hounded and frequently short of high-end intelligence, *Melancholicus* printed more verse than any other newsbook of the period almost as if it were a ready supply of risk-free copy at a time of information scarcity. As the second civil war raged, it sought to mobilize "all Loyal subjects" in defence of the king's cause; it called its audience to arms, sounding notes that had animated popular topical balladry since its first appearance in the 1570s:

> Cheer up your hearts brave Englishmen,
> the time is now at hand,
> A Lyon rouzed from his Den
> with Peace shall crown your Land.
>
> The Saints are grown so odious
> in all good Peoples eyes
> They can no longer cozen us
> with Forgeries and lies.
>
> Prince Charles for Scotland's on his way,
> Irish with [Colonel] Poyre joyne,
> Most happy needs must prove the Day,
> Where Charles his Son doth shine.
>
> Arm, arm, brave laddes, True Subjects all,
> redeem your KING and Land,
> Men, Women, Children, great and small,
> as ONE man for him stand.
>
> (*Mercurius Melancholicus*, 1648)

Informing its audience of recent military developments at the same time as it united them against a common enemy who threatened English monarchy, the opening to this *Melancholicus* made its plea for partisan political intervention sound as if it were simply a return to historic ballad values.

Whether this poem was actually sung, like so many of its generic predecessors, is unclear since no royalist newsbook detailed a catch or tune on its title page. (This need not argue against performance since many well-known white-letter ballads from the period did not cite tunes in their titles, either.) Royalist newsbooks regularly did, however, invoke their ballad's performative dimensions, suggesting at least the possibility of occasional live delivery. The 1648 Christmas edition of *Melancholicus*, for instance, ridiculed the puritan Lord Mayor of London, John Warner, by offering him a mock carol as a seasonal gift:

> Listen a while, and you shall heare,
> so he does, so he does
> Ile sing you a song, my good Lord Major,
> my honest Cuz, my honest Cuz.
>
> The Lord Mayor rides on a bob-tayled horse,
> so he does, so he does,
> Whil'st another rides his Wife that's worse,
> how now Cuz? how now Cuz?
>
> (Mercurius Melancholicus, 1647: 100)

The radical potential of this ballad is only fully realized in performance, where the resistance to a puritan hostility to traditional forms of festive ritual, as well as the allegation of mayoral cuckoldry, is voiced and shared by a community committed to monarchy and good cheer. In the 1650s *Mercurius Fumigosus* and *Mercurius Democritus*, edited by the royalist John Crouch, adopted much the same approach to encourage their readers to think irreverently about the puritanical basis of the Cromwellian Commonwealth and Protectorate. Closely scrutinized by the authorities, these titles though offering themselves to the public as newsbooks were more like jestbooks; containing less than a page of 'weekly news', they were swamped by bewildering paragraphs of 'merry intelligence', a surreal miscellany of character satire, learned nonsense, paeans to sack and invitations to enjoy embedded ballads set to instantly recognizable catches such as "Ayme not too high" or "Fortune my foe" (*Mercurius Fumigosus*, 1654: 110–12). Their ludic, celebratory tone, coupled with the repeated invitation to sing old ballad tunes – whilst containing little that was straightforwardly or transparently seditious – was profoundly political, entailing a thoroughgoing rejection of sensible, authoritarian or puritanical ways of being (McElligott, 2004).

Even though he was to become one of the foremost polemical defenders of successive Cromwellian governments, it was Marchamont Nedham who first saw the promise that the union of ballad and newsbook held for royalist politics in revolutionary England. Whilst editor of *Mercurius Pragmaticus* he could, unlike every other underground royalist serial in the capital, boast excellent and exclusive intelligence sources in the army, the exiled court and even parliament itself. Yet from the very first issue of his editorship he sought to frame his prose exposés of parliamentarian hypocrisy, greed or bad faith with a more participatory mode of news communication. In order to engage the widest circle of political friends and to antagonize his enemies as publicly and convivially as he possibly could, he always used the four quatrain topical ballad as a prelude to his prose reportage and polemic. Thus one issue which reported the king's imprisonment in Carisbrook Castle and detailed the disquiet provoked in households forced to give quarter to parliamentarian troops, began by reminding its audience of the traditional pleasures of drink and song:

> Come let us Live, and laugh away
> The Follies of this Age:
> Treason breeds Care; Wee'll sing and play
> Like Birds within a Cage.

> Fetters are the only favours now
> The Houses give (we see,)
> And since the King them weares, I vow
> 'Twere basenesse to be free.
>
> Then let us all our Sorrowes drowne
> In Sack and merry glee
> Ye Citizens of London Towne
> What jolly Slaves are wee!
>
> For Common-Prayer, yee have Excise,
> Free Quarter too is coming,
> To pay you for your Mutinies
> Feasts, Covenants and Drumming.
>
> (*Mercurius Pragmaticus*, 1647b: sig N^r)

As well as glossing the news content of the issue, Nedham here engaged his audience by manipulating one of the period's most famous pieces of balladic verse: Richard Lovelace's 'To Althea from Prison'. The oppositional logic of Nedham's adaptation of this poem demands that we read defeat as victory, the oblivion of sorrows drowned as the enlivened camaraderie of a common cause with its signature texts and tunes. Though Nedham indicated no tune on his title page, the fact that Lovelace's poem had been in manuscript circulation in royalist circles since 1642 and appeared as a licensed broadside set to its own tune in 1656, indicated that it evidently had some popularity as a sung text (Rollins, 1924: 179; Wilkinson, 1930: 276–86).

In his Pragmaticus phase, Nedham was indeed keen to advocate the singing of his verses; in the conclusion to one issue he enjoined his audience to "sing, sing on, thou bonny Royallist" and, imagining the death of the king's fool, Archie Armstrong, and John Warner, Lord Mayor of London, refused to speculate about an uncertain political future in a poem with what sounds like a sung refrain:

> Who shall be Foole when Archees dead?
> Or who Lord Mayor in fifty three?
> I were a Foole if it should be said
> That that should trouble me, Boyes,
> That that should trouble me.
>
> (*Mercurius Pragmaticus*, 1647a: 1)

Conclusion

Even though the news at this time was grim for royalists, the insouciance of such a song arises from the ballad's capacity to carry topical information and, in performance, bear a shared voice and collective will. Such rhymes and their accompanying faces might well, as Nedham later scoffed, have drawn only a fiddler's fee, but they were a vital means of transmitting information and rallying those beleaguered, fugitive groups who remained true to a particular vision of the nation and its monarchy during violent political crisis. Topical ballads, as we have seen, had been doing such work, informing and bonding loyal audiences, for the best part of a century. It was this rich heritage which made them so useful for royalist journalists, yet so antipathetic to parliamentarian or republican news serials like *Mercurius Politicus* trying to map an uncharted political course out of civil war. *Politicus* may well have been the most professional news publication of the revolutionary decades, a venture which cemented Nedham's reputation as one of greatest pioneers in the history of English journalism, but it, too, became a text to forget with the Restoration of the Stuarts in 1660. When the time came for Nedham to pay rather than deride the fiddler, to repudiate his Cromwellian past and demonstrate a rediscovered loyalty and usefulness to monarchy, he collected all of the poems he had written for *Mercurius Pragmaticus* and published them as *A Short History of the English Rebellion Compiled in Verse* (1661). Politically expedient though Nedham's recovery of his poetic oeuvre undoubtedly was, it should also remind us of the vital but frequently occluded place of topical ballads in the early modern news trade.

References

Anon (1570) *A Ballad reioycinge the sodaine fall, of Rebels that thought to devower vs all.* London.
——(1581) *A Triumph for True Subjects.* London.
——(1613) *The Peace, concluded between the King of Denmarke, and the King of Sweden.* London.
Bourne, N. (1622) *The Wonderfvll Battell of Starelings: Fought at the Citie of Corke in Ireland, the 12 and 14 of October last past, 1621.* London.
Chappell, W. and Ebsworth, J. W. (eds.) (1869–99) *The Roxburghe Ballads*, 9 vols. Hertford: The Ballad Society.
Deloney, T. (1588a) *A ioyful new Ballad, declaring the happy obtaining of the great Galleazzo.* London.
——(1588b) *The Queenes visiting of the campe at Tilburie with her entertainment there.* London.
Elderton, W. (1570) *A Ballad Intituled, a Newe well a daye/ As plaune maister Papist, as Donstable waye*, London.
——(1584) *A New Yorkshyre Song.* London.
Fox, A. (2000) *Oral and Literate Cultures in Early Modern England, 1500–1700.* Oxford: Oxford University Press.
Frank, J. (1961) *Beginning of the English Newspaper, 1620–1660.* Cambridge, MA: Harvard University Press.
G., F. (1570) *The End and Confession of John Felton.* London.
Kirkham, W. (1570) *Ioyfull Newes for true Subiectes, to God and the Crowne: The Rebelles are cooled, their Bragges be put downe.* London.
Livingstone, C. R. (1991) *British Broadside Ballads of the Sixteenth Century: A Catalogue of the Extant Sheets and an Essay.* New York and London: Garland.
McElligott, J. (2007) *Royalism, Print and Censorship in Revolutionary England.* Woodbridge: The Boydell Press.
——(2004) "John Crouch: A royalist journalist in Cromwellian England." *Media History*, 10(3), 139–55.
McShane, A. J. (2011) *Political Broadside Ballads of Seventeenth-Century England: A Critical Bibliography.* London: Pickering and Chatto.
——(2005) "The gazet in meter or the rhiming newsmonger: The English Broadside ballad as intelligencer. A new narrative." In W. K. Joop (ed.) *News and Politics in Early Modern Europe.* Leuven: Peeters (pp. 131–50).

Marsh, C. (2004) "The sound of print in early modern England: The broadside ballad as song." In J. Crick and A. Walsham (eds.) *The Uses of Script and Print, 1300–1700*. Cambridge: Cambridge University Press (pp. 171–90).

Mercurius Fumigosus 12 (1654) 16–23 August.

Mercurius Mastix 1 (1652) 20–27 August.

Mercurius Melancholicus 17 (1647) 18–25 December.

——34 (1648) 17–24 April.

Mercurius Politicus 1 (1650) 6–13 June.

Mercurius Pragmaticus 2 (1647a) 21–28 September.

——13 (1647b) 7–14 December.

——29 (1648) 28 March–4 April.

Nedham, M. (1661) *A Short History of the English Rebellion Compiled in Verse by Marchamont Nedham, and Formerly Extant in his Weekly Mercurius Pragmaticus*. London.

Nelson, T. (1586) *A Proper New Ballad*. London.

Parker, M. (1628) *Rochell her Yeelding to the Obedience of the French King*. London.

——(1639) *A Lamentable Relation of a fearfull fight at Sea*. London.

——(1640) *Good Newes from the North*. London.

Raymond, J. (1996) *The Invention of the Newspaper: English Newsbooks, 1641–1649*. Oxford: Oxford University Press.

——(2011) "News." In J. Raymond (ed.) *The Oxford History of Popular Print Culture*. Oxford: Oxford University Press (pp. 377–97).

Rollins, H. E. (1923) *Cavalier and Puritan: Ballads and Broadsides Illustrating the Period of the Great Rebellion, 1640–1660*. New York: New York University Press.

——(1924) *An Analytical Index to the Ballad Entries (1557–1709) in the Registers of the Company of Stationers of London*. Chapel Hill: University of North Carolina Press.

Shaaber, M. (1966) *Some Forerunners of the English Newspaper in England, 1476–1622*. New York: Octagon Books.

Sterrie, D. (1586) *A Briefe Sonet declaring the lamentation of Beckles, a Markt Towne in Suffolke which was in the great winde vpon S. Andrewes eue pitifuly burned with fire to the value of tweenti thousande pounds. And to the number of fourescore dwelling houses, besides a great number of other houses*. London.

Wilkinson, C. H. (ed.) (1930) *The Poems of Richard Lovelace*. Oxford: Clarendon Press.

Würzbach, N. (1990) *The Rise of the English Street Ballad, 1550–1650*. Cambridge: Cambridge University Press.

16
Eighteenth-century newspapers and public opinion

Victoria E. M. Gardner

Following the lapse of the Licensing Act in 1695, the newspaper press came to provide a new and powerful communication network and medium for influence across Britain. Newspapers' immediate and extensive interest in foreign and domestic politics, their regular production and their commercial character positioned them as ideal mediators between parliament and the people. Over the eighteenth century, contemporaries came to recognize that public opinion was becoming an integral part of Britain's political machinery, although they differed in the role and value they accorded it and in their assessments of whom exactly 'the public' comprised. An emerging rhetoric of press liberty and appeals to public opinion did not necessarily develop along a Whiggish trajectory to democracy but was dependent upon a changeable political and legislative climate.

The historiographical landscape of eighteenth-century politics and the press was transformed in 1989 with the translation of Jürgen Habermas's *Structural Transformation of the Public Sphere*. Habermas provided a new theoretical model for the interaction between newspapers and readers by assigning the press an institutional role in the emergence of public opinion (Habermas, 1989). For Habermas, later seventeenth and eighteenth-century Britain hosted the emergence of a new kind of public space that enabled 'rational-critical debate', in which individuals outside of parliament cast aside class distinctions and came together to form a critical public. The coffee house typified this new physical public sphere and the newspaper was its literary analogue. The Habermasian public sphere has attracted extensive criticism, not least for being largely populated by white middle-class males but also for the openness of coffee-house culture. More recent studies suggest that instead multiple public spheres existed and were characterized by conflict (Calhoun, 1992; Robbins, 1993). In Habermas's own revision of the model, he suggests that there were two public spheres: the 'strong' public sphere, associated with decision-making, and a 'weak' counterpublic, which was important in the dissemination of alternative information and the formation of collective identity (Habermas, 1996). This binary mirrors wider debates on the character of eighteenth-century Britain and the role of the press in it.

Changes in historical understanding of the eighteenth century had already encouraged a review of the press in instigating and facilitating change by the 1980s. Brewer describes the press as one component of the "alternative structure of politics" in which the emerging – and largely disenfranchised – middle class engaged (Brewer, 1976; Langford, 1989). Post Habermas, historians have continued to argue that newspapers increased readers' political awareness, alerting them and politicians to the public's role in the formation of public opinion. In this way, newspapers contributed to political change (Barker, 1998, 2000; Harris, 1997). Conversely, some historians continue to emphasize the nature of eighteenth-century Britain as an ancien regime in which an aristocratic elite dominated politics and society (Clark, 2000). In this analysis, the press played a peripheral role, primarily mirroring society's views rather than acting as a catalyst for change (Aspinall, 1949). Key to this debate is the disconnect between the value that politicians, newspapers and others *professed* to attach to public opinion as a political force and that which they genuinely attached to it. Measuring impact and locating the real motivations of individuals and groups, however, is problematic. Moreover, while newspapers themselves exist in abundance, sources relating to their production or impact are in short supply. This essay reviews the evidence for the relationship between public opinion and the newspaper press and considers why the two became so entwined in the eighteenth century.

Newspapers were not new in form, political content or partisanship in 1695. Licensing had lapsed previously in England in 1641–42 (during the English Civil War) and 1679–80 (during the Exclusion Crisis), during both of which times newspapers had flourished (Raymond, 1996). In 1695 three London newspapers were immediately established: the *Post Boy*, associated with the Tories, the *Flying Post*, which became increasingly Whig, and the *Post-Man*, focusing on foreign news. Published tri-weekly in time for the posts that left London, they had a national audience. In 1701 the first provincial newspaper (either the *Norwich Post* or the *Bristol Post Boy*) was issued and in 1705 the first Scottish title, the *Edinburgh Courant*, was launched. Thereafter the press grew at a tremendous rate. In 1770 there were 17 London newspapers and 42 English provincial weeklies. By 1790, there were 23 London titles (by now published daily, bi-weekly, tri-weekly and weekly) and 60 weekly provincial titles. Circulation grew from a few hundred copies per issue to around 5,000 daily at the largest London titles, the *Daily Advertiser* and the *Gazetteer*, by 1770; successful provincial titles saw circulation rise from around 200 to 2,000 (Ferdinand, 1997: 19). These increases were in spite of stamp duties paid on every copy of each newspaper, introduced in 1712 and not abolished until 1855.

Public opinion and press liberty

Interest in the exercise of public opinion as part of the political process, and as refereed by the newspaper press, was bound up with a rhetoric of press freedom (Barker, 2000: 9–28). Early discussions on the liberty of the press were literal, referring to the freedom of the printing press and of print in general following the lapse of the Licensing Act. As the freedom of print became established by the second quarter of the eighteenth century, the definition of press liberty refocused, referring specifically to the newspaper press in its role as a check on politics and protector of the people. In 1739, the Lord Chancellor, Lord Hardwicke, argued that the "liberty of the press is what I think ought to be sacred to every Englishman" (Barker, 2000: 16). By the 1740s, according to Bob Harris, the notion that the press was vital to "the exercise of the people's alleged right to examine 'the measures of every administration'" was "near commonplace" (Harris, 1993: 32). By the 1760s and the Wilkes affair, the term was bound up in popular rhetoric and increasingly connected to radical ideas of historic English freedoms. William Blackstone was therefore able to argue in his *Commentaries on the Laws of England* that "The liberty of the press is indeed essential to the nature of a free state ... Every freeman has an undoubted right to lay what sentiment he pleases before the public; to forbid this, is to destroy the freedom of the press." Newspapers, of course, were not entirely free to do so, for Blackstone made clear that if a newspaper printer were to publish "what is improper, mischievous, or illegal, he must take the consequences of his own temerity" (Dickinson, 1995: 169; Barker, 2000: 14). By the end of the eighteenth century newspapers were thus viewed, and promoted to varying degrees, as protectors of the constitution and bound up with the essential freedoms guaranteed by the Glorious Revolution and Bill of Rights, despite the latter not having mentioned the press at all.

Press freedom became vital to ensure good governance because newspapers came to act as mediators between parliament and people, enabling the exercise of public opinion. Public opinion can be defined as a body of opinion or argument to whom the press and elite referred and appealed in order to claim legitimacy in the decision-making process, and to which the public increasingly laid claim. The public consisted of those outside of parliament and the governing elite who were considered part of the political nation and thus held a legitimate right to critique affairs of the state. Similar to the liberty of the press, the term 'public opinion' also had a literal meaning in the early eighteenth century, referring to general opinion expressed about a range of issues and not simply politics. In the 1712 *Memoirs of the Chevalier de St. George*, for example, the author describes how the Chevalier was "complimented by the Principal of the Court of *France*; for the Mareschal *de Villars* had likewise given such an account, as serv'd to heighten the public Opinion of him" (James, Prince of Wales, 1712 [2010]: 208). Over the century, however, newspapers increasingly made reference to 'the public' or 'the people' and to 'public opinion' or 'the sense of the people' as a legitimate body of opinion on political matters.

From the 1760s, the concept of public opinion was promoted by newspapers and by reform groups in the light of radical MP John Wilkes' challenges to parliament and the freedoms engendered by the American and French Revolutions. In the 1780s, reform groups even suggested that parliamentary reform should be dealt with by the public rather than parliament (Barker, 1998: 80). While it failed to change the parliamentary constitution, the movement nevertheless encouraged debates that "acted to change the ways in which political life was perceived and actually functioned, as 'the people' and public opinion played an increasingly influential part in the nation's politics" (Barker, 1998: 94). Politicians increasingly referred to public opinion in order to claim legitimacy in their decision-making, especially after 1771 when reports of parliamentary proceedings were published in the papers – a development to which we will return later. The newspaper press was also commercially motivated to refer to itself as the arbiter of public opinion and representative of the people since, in order to appeal to as many people as possible, newspapers had to claim to represent a wider body. Regardless of their politics, all newspapers emphasized the importance of public opinion as a legitimate social and political force, although the degree to which a newspaper supported the exercise of public opinion varied according to its political sympathies (Barker, 1998: 91–92).

The uniqueness of newspapers

The form and funding of newspapers made them an especially suitable type of print for the expression of public opinion. Of course, newspapers were not entirely divorced from other channels of communication, complementing and becoming part of other circuits of information, relayed through print, manuscript and word-of-mouth. London newspapers relied on, among other communications, European newspapers and correspondence, diplomatic dispatches, merchants and the captains of ships, printed scaffold speeches, and Royal Exchange and coffee-house gossip. Provincial English and Scottish newspapers "cut and pasted" their news from the London papers, leading earlier historians to describe them as parasitic (Fox Bourne, 1887). Provincial proprietors, however, had control over what they placed in the paper and what they left out, and offered expanding levels of original local copy over the century (Cranfield, 1962; Wiles 1965). What *was* unique was the newspaper press's periodicity: metronomically regular appearance that enabled the creation of communities of readers and the development of regular columns and content that fed back to parliament the views of 'the public'.

The periodicity of the newspaper press had a significant impact on the production of news, for it meant that events were fitted artificially into a regular publishing schedule (Raymond, 2011). Periodicals were also a particularly visible form of print, requiring fixed weekly production and a place of publication that made them detectable to government authorities, thus providing them almost with an officially sanctioned aspect. For Benedict Anderson, the date on the page tied together an "imagined community" of readers underpinning national identity (Anderson, 1983). Reading communities were also specific to individual newspapers and developed a loyalty to a particular newspaper, which could then represent their particular views.

Readers

The restricted readership of newspapers encouraged the close relationship between press and public opinion, for it chimed with conceptions of 'the public' in the eighteenth century. At times, 'the public' or 'the people' could refer to everybody other than those in power. More usually, contemporaries were referring to the political nation, itself limited by the franchise and largely defined by property ownership. By the 1790s, Edmund Burke could declare the size of the political nation to be 400,000 (Barker, 2000: 23). For the radical John Jebb, it constituted all adult males, although this would have been far too wide in most contemporaries' estimation; the conservative press "suggested a more propertied, respectable definition of the people" (Barker, 1998: 92).

The core readership of newspapers also consisted of the 'respectable' middling ranks of society and upwards. It is problematic to assess accurately the number of readers of any newspapers for accurate records exist for only a handful of papers. Stamp duties limited readership from 1712 by inflating the cost of newspapers and limiting regular purchase of a newspaper to anyone other than the middling ranks and upwards. Nevertheless, whereas early nineteenth-century campaigns argued that stamp duties were purposely 'taxes on knowledge', stamp duties were introduced and subject to successive hikes because they were classed as luxuries and therefore subject to taxation in a period of almost constant warfare. Evidence for the middling-rank constituency of newspapers can be found in the newspapers themselves, which have been identified as middling rank in moral tone, drawing "on the major cultural themes of the middling orders ... Christian conduct, polite behaviour, and moral improvement. Many items ... served as secular sermons and were clearly intended as such" while attacks on popular superstitions, drunkenness, profanity and cruelty to animals indicate a "socially specific moral resonance, appropriate for a medium with restricted circulation" (Black, 2002: 177). Despite this, it is likely that readers from lower down the social scale also regularly accessed newspapers. Newspapers could be borrowed, shared, exchanged, hired or purchased at a reduced cost a day or two after publication. They were often freely available in coffee houses, taverns, alehouses and inns, where readers could also listen to the news read out aloud. Estimates of the number of readers per newspaper thus vary from ten to forty per copy (Heyd, 2011: 22).

Public opinion also had a national dimension, and was used interchangeably with the 'political nation' or the 'sense of the people'. Benedict Anderson argues that the newspaper press plays a key role in the development of the "imagined community" of nation (Anderson, 1983). The press operated as a cultural counterpart to the political creation of the nation under the Act of Union in 1707, binding and promoting a shared sense of Britishness and, for those inhabitants of the nation beyond the metropolis, a proximity to Westminster (Colley, 1992; Wilson, 1995; Harris, 1996). As a result, the national news network facilitated a means by which public opinion could be expressed on metropolitan matters and filtered to parliament.

In the light of expanding literature on geographical identities, the eighteenth-century press has been recognized as sustaining competing regional identities alongside national and imperial ones (Gardner, 2013). The articulation and representation of public opinion also varied according to location. Thanks to its size (eighteen times larger than its nearest provincial rival), London was more politically diverse and divided and this was played out in the press. Its readership has been estimated to have been significantly higher than the rest of the country, potentially reaching 250,000 in 1782 – one-third of London's population (Barker, 2000: 47). Readers could consume news more regularly in London than in other parts of the country; contemporaries described a daily buzz around news acquisition in the metropolis as Londoners pounded the streets from one coffee house to the next, searching for up-to-date news. Reading frequency varied accordingly, some readers consuming news infrequently or weekly, others daily and others still hourly. Contemporary descriptions of a new kind of voracious news glutton, the Quidnunc, emerged in the metropolis (Heyd, 2011: 195–230). As news swirled across different fora, it was also more immediate and fast-changing in character; by implication, therefore, metropolitan public opinion was also fast-changing. London dominated the British press by providing the largest number of newspapers and supplying the majority of news. Its politics was therefore frequently presented in national terms, whereas provincial opinion was often presented in provincial terms. Indeed, with less political diversity in provincial towns, the provincial press tended to define the public more narrowly and according to a more propertied definition (Barker, 1998: 159–78). This was also the result of provincial proprietors' more intimate knowledge of their reading communities (Gardner, 2013).

Content and public opinion

Beyond the news-reading community, the regular production of newspapers enabled regular ongoing content. From the lapse of the ban on parliamentary reporting in 1771, newspapers contained parliamentary reports. Printers and publishers had attempted to insert parliamentary news into papers and periodicals since the early eighteenth century, but in 1738, following the publication of a speech made by the king, parliament banned reporting proceedings in print from either House. Subsequent breaches were subject to fines, court cases and reprimands, which meant that after the 1750s, reporting was no longer attempted. Parliament ended the ban on reporting after a legal battle with MP John Wilkes, following attempts to arrest several printers for publishing debates. This new transparency of government, made by committing reports to paper and thus to consumption outside of parliament, meant that politicians changed the style and focus of their oratory inside parliament. From the early 1780s, with a defeat in America seemingly inevitable, movements for reform at home were pressing for change and the press was paying closer attention to parliament, where "orators consciously spoke within the context of a culture of print" (Reid, 2000: 126); or, as Habermas described the speeches of Charles James Fox, they "were made with the public in mind" (Habermas, 1989: 66). The change indicated recognition on the part of parliament that their decisions had to be visible to, and could be interrogated by, the public.

The new permanent transparency of parliamentary reporting spawned other innovations, namely editorials and an increase in published letters to the editor. Some of the earliest editorials, or 'leaders', appeared in the London *Star* in 1789 and the *Cambridge Intelligencer* in the early 1790s (Werkmeister, 1963; Black, 1987: 281). It is notable that both were supporters of Fox and had a national circulation, thus seeking to persuade readers of the vital role of the people in the parliamentary process. Rather than speaking from individual proprietors, editorials spoke as though from the newspaper itself, thus aiming to accrue gravitas from a supposedly representative position. Published letters to the editor enabled readers to comment directly on politics or on the paper's views and to galvanize support on particular issues. Letter writers usually used pseudonyms, which were themselves frequently representative, such as 'the freeman' or 'Alfred'. They were also written by journalists or by agents for particular groups or parties. Perceptions that letters in newspapers offered more effective fora for propaganda, it has been argued, resulted in newspapers eclipsing essay papers and political pamphlets after the American Revolution (Harris, 1996: 38–39).

Commercial power

A final reason that the newspaper was such a suitable vehicle for the articulation and influence of public opinion was in its commercial nature. Earlier studies of the press emphasized its dependence upon political bribes for funding thanks to stamp duties, which controlled circulation and therefore profit from sales (Aspinall, 1949; Werkmeister, 1963). However, it is now well-recognized that profits from advertising freed newspapers from total dependence on political subsidies (Barker, 1998: 47–53). Certainly some politicians bribed the press throughout the century, as will be seen in the following section, but they were not wholesale, for advertising profits were so substantial and the newspaper press so large that politicians' pockets could not match them. By the end of the century, between one-third and one-half of a newspaper was filled with advertisements and although advertisements were taxed too, they comprised a far smaller proportion of the revenue they brought in compared to stamp duties. As a result, while newspapers were bound by libel and other laws, and some were in the pay of some politicians, they had greater freedom to express the opinions of their editors and readers because they were not dependent upon political parties or others for profits.

Politicians and public opinion

Turning towards parliament and politicians' attitudes towards the press and public opinion, throughout the eighteenth century politicians viewed the press as an opportunity to promote themselves and control their image to an ever important public. Robert Harley, a minister of Queen Anne, employed Daniel Defoe, Jonathan Swift and others to defend his policies. Robert Walpole, the first Prime Minister, purchased the *London Journal* and spent over £40,000 bribing others extensively in the 1730s. London newspapers, Michael Harris argues, were accepted as a constituent part of the political system by this time, for "no other medium offered such ease of dispersal and range of regular access to the nation at large" (Harris, 1987: 113). Over the century, the numerical expansion of the press coupled with profits from advertising meant that this type of wholesale bribery probably reduced, although Secret Service payments to newspapers continued, especially in periods of national crisis, including during the American War of Independence when individual newspaper editors and writers were paid to insert particular items in their papers (Barker, 1998: 48). Even after the American War, in 1784, the Pitt ministry paid London's *Public Ledger, London Evening Post, Morning Herald, Whitehall Evening*

Post, and *St James Chronicle* £100 each, probably for placing paragraphs into the newspapers (Aspinall, 1949: 68). This was negligible and suggests that many newspapers were relatively free from substantial subsidies, but it has also been calculated that during the early years of the French Revolution, the Pitt ministry spent nearly £5,000 per annum on bribes, including £400 per annum to the London *Diary* and £600 per annum to the *Morning Herald* (Aspinall, 1949: 68–69). This may well have been paid to the editors or proprietor, for recruiting or positioning sympathetic editors may have been the most effective means by which politicians could promote their own politics.

That politicians felt bound to at least acknowledge public opinion during the eighteenth century suggests growing recognition that a cursory level of public consultation was necessary to the political process. Even so, a rhetoric of press liberty did not equate to absolute freedom and the press was controlled through the laws on treason, seditious libel and blasphemy. Prosecutions for seditious libel could be scattershot, although exemplar prosecutions appear to have been considered an effective means of controlling printers. As early as 1693, shortly before the lapse of the Licensing Act, the Jacobite printer William Anderton was tried and executed for treason, which underlined to other printers that they should take care in what they published. Nathaniel Mist was also prosecuted several times in the 1710s and 1720s for comments in his anti-ministerial *Weekly Journal*. When he published the allegorical 'Persian Letter', an allegory for the state of the nation under a usurper king, he was successfully prosecuted for a "false, infamous, scandalous, seditious and treasonable Libel" (Clark, 2004: 53). To underline its point, the administration prosecuted a further twenty people involved in the publication, including the woman who sold the paper on the streets.

Where newspaper proprietors and printers were viewed as a threat but where seditious libel, treason or blasphemy were not immediately apparent to prosecutors, prosecutions were brought on related charges. During the French Revolution at least ten British newspapers, including the London *Argus*, *Sheffield Register* and *Manchester Herald*, were involved in calls for radical parliamentary reform. With Thomas Paine's *Rights of Man* calling for radical action, a number of radical proprietors were prosecuted for selling it, including Richard Phillips of the *Leicester Herald* in 1795. Radical proprietors were brought down in succession. Richard Flower of the radical *Cambridge Intelligencer* was prosecuted for breach of privilege in 1799. Again, the mere threat of imprisonment succeeded in neutralizing the hardiest of radicals. In 1792, Joseph Gales of the *Sheffield Register* fled the country for the United States before he could be arrested for his supposed involvement in a plot to carry out an armed revolt. James Montgomery, Gales's successor at the later *Sheffield Iris*, experienced two spells in prison but made a conscious decision after the second that he could not face a third and instead muted his newspaper.

Despite successful prosecutions and a century of seemingly expanding press freedom, by the close of the eighteenth century there were more restrictions on newspapers than there had been at the beginning. The Newspaper Regulation Act of 1798, one of a raft of measures to restrict the spread of radicalism in the aftermath of the French Revolution, established a licensing system for newspaper proprietors, printers and any other persons with a connection to the trade, and demanded that if items had been copied from foreign newspapers that intended to incite contempt or hatred towards the King, it was the printer or proprietor's responsibility to prove that this was the case. Even so, by 1798, the radical elements of the press had been quelled, not simply through prosecutions but also because a heightened risk of invasion in 1797 had meant that loyalty to the nation took precedence over domestic reform (Barker, 2000: 189–90). This process, by which the press itself had already neutralized in response to the invasion threat, suggests that newspapers were responding to wider public opinion – and to commercial concerns.

Conclusion

The development of the newspaper press as the representative of public opinion and guardian of the people emerged over the eighteenth century thanks to the unique form and periodicity of the newspaper. It was facilitated by the commercial freedom of the press and simultaneous changes to Britain's political culture, which increasingly recognized the right of the middling ranks of society to have a say in politics. Even so, the freedom of the press was not a given and neither did it follow a trajectory of emerging liberty over the eighteenth century. On the contrary, politicians as a whole were perhaps more wary of the press – and its potential to reach the unrespectable elements of society – by the century's end than at its beginning.

Tensions in the emergence of public opinion were bound up in competing motivations between the multiple actors involved in the creation and publication of news. Those actors included politicians and readers as well as newspaper proprietors, editors and advertisers. Politicians in particular recognized that they had to engage with the press, although responses varied between individuals and across parties. Perhaps the most potent evidence of many politicians' recognition of the importance of public opinion is the way in which they sought surreptitiously to create good press through the insertion of items purportedly from the public. Public opinion was by its nature free and the most powerful influence on public opinion was public opinion itself.

Further reading

The majority of work on the eighteenth-century press and public opinion was written in the late 1990s, following Habermas's (1989) *Structural Transformation of the Public Sphere*. Of these, Hannah Barker's (2000) *Newspapers, Politics and English Society 1695–1855* provides a thorough and concise overview of the key issues. New work is emerging and turning towards the networked nature and cultural impact of news. Of these, Uriel Heyd's (2011) *Reading Newspapers: Press and Public in Eighteenth-Century Britain and America* explores the role of the press in transforming contemporaries' perceptions of time and space and Victoria Gardner's (2013) "The communications broker and the public sphere: John Ware and the *Cumberland Pacquet*" examines the impact of business networks on regional and imperial identities.

References

Anderson, B. (1983) *Imagined Communities: Reflections on the Origin and Spread of Nationalism*. London and New York: Verso.

Aspinall, A. (1949) *Politics and the Press, c. 1780–1850*. London: Home and Van Thal.

Barker, H. (1998) *Newspapers, Politics and Public Opinion*. Oxford: Oxford University Press.

——(2000) *Newspapers, Politics and English Society 1695–1855*. Harlow: Pearson.

Black, J. (1987) *The English Press in the Eighteenth Century*. Philadelphia, PA: University of Pennsylvania Press.

——(2002) "The press and politics in the eighteenth century." *Media History*, 8(2), 175–82.

Brewer, J. (1976) *Party Ideology and Popular Politics at the Accession of George III*. Cambridge: Cambridge University Press.

Calhoun, C. (1992) *Habermas and the Public Sphere*. Cambridge, MA: MIT Press.

Clark, B. (2004) *From Grub Street to Fleet Street: An Illustrated History of English Newspapers to 1899*. Aldershot: Ashgate.

Clark, J. C. D. (2000) *English Society 1660–1832*. Cambridge: Cambridge University Press.

Colley, L. (1992) *Britons: Forging the Nation, 1707–1837*. New Haven, CT: Yale University Press.

Cranfield, G. A. (1962) *The Provincial Newspaper, 1700–1760*. London: Oxford University Press.

Dickinson, H. T. (1995) *The Politics of the People in Eighteenth-Century Britain*. Basingstoke: Palgrave Macmillan.

Ferdinand, C. Y. (1997) *Benjamin Collins and the Provincial Newspaper Trade in the Eighteenth Century*. Oxford: Oxford University Press.

Fox Bourne, H. R. (1887) *English Newspapers: Chapters in the History of Journalism*. London: Chatto and Windus.

Gardner, V. (2013) "The communications broker and the public sphere: John Ware and the *Cumberland Pacquet*." *Cultural and Social History*, 10(4), 533–57.

Habermas, J. (trans.) (1989) *The Structural Transformation of the Public Sphere*. Cambridge, MA: MIT Press.

——(1996) *Between Facts and Norms*. Cambridge, MA: MIT Press.

Harris, B. (1996) *Politics and the Rise of the Press: Britain and France, 1620–1800*. London: Routledge.

——(1997) *A Patriot Press: National Politics and the London Press in the 1740s*. Oxford: Clarendon Press.

Harris, M. (1987) *London Newspapers in the Age of Walpole: A Study in the Origins of the Modern English Press*. London: Associated University Presses.

Harris, R. (1993) *A Patriot Press: National Politics and the London Press in the 1740s*. Oxford: Clarendon.

Heyd, U. (2011) *Reading Newspapers: Press and Public in Eighteenth-Century Britain and America*. Oxford: Voltaire Foundation.

James, Prince Of Wales (1712 [2010]) *Memoirs of the Chevalier de St. George: With Some Private Passages of the Life of the Late King James II. Never Before Published*. London: Gale ECCO Print Editions.

Langford, P. (1989) *A Polite and Commercial People: England 1727–83*. Oxford: Oxford University Press.

Raymond, J. (1996) *The Invention of the Newspaper: English Newsbooks, 1641–1649*. Oxford: Clarendon Press.

——(2011) "News." In J. Raymond (ed.) *The Oxford History of Popular Print Culture. Vol. 1: Cheap Print in Britain and Ireland to 1660*. Oxford: Oxford University Press (pp. 377–97).

Reid, C. (2000) "Whose Parliament? Political Oratory and Print Culture in the Later Eighteenth Century." *Language and Literature*, 9(2), 122–34.

Robbins, B. (1993) *The Phantom Public Sphere*. Minneapolis, MN: University of Minnesota Press.

Werkmeister, L. (1963) *The London Daily Press, 1772–1792*. Lincoln, NE: University of Nebraska Press.

Wiles, R. M. (1965) *Freshest Advices: Early Provincial Newspapers in England*. Columbus, OH: Ohio State University Press.

Wilson, K. (1995) *Sense of the People: Politics, Culture and Imperialism in England 1715–1785*. Cambridge: Cambridge University Press.

17
The nineteenth century and the emergence of a mass circulation press

Joel H. Wiener

British journalism underwent a dramatic series of changes during the nineteenth century that led to the creation of a mass circulation press. The shift from a traditional form of journalism with a limited circulation to a daily and Sunday press encompassing millions of readers is one of the significant events of the century. It solidified the integration of newspapers into the cultural and social life of Britain and introduced many of the features of modern journalism with which we are familiar today. It transformed the publication of newspapers from a series of small-scale commercial undertakings into corporative financial structures that served the reading needs of a large portion of the population. The rise of mass circulation journalism has engendered many important questions about literature, politics, culture and economics, as well as issues regarding the purpose and nature of the popular press and the extent to which it has been a force for good or ill in the lives of millions of readers.

General profile of the press

During the early decades of the century daily newspapers mostly sold for seven pence or more, a price well beyond the purchasing power of poorer readers. They were markedly sober in appearance, featuring unbroken columns of print and few illustrations. Small advertisements ('personals') appeared on the front page in place of news and these ads often dominated the inside pages as well. Little use was made of bright typography or crossheads, while headlines (or decked headings) in the modern sense did not exist. Publishers were mostly content to secure the loyalties of their upper and middle-class readership by means of a conservative layout. They relied on a subscription system for circulation and had little financial incentive to enliven their products in the expectation of attracting large numbers of readers.

A similar pattern of restraint is discernible in the area of content. Lengthy accounts of political and parliamentary speeches appeared in the news pages, which also featured court proceedings, reports of public meetings, letters from correspondents, a smattering of financial information, and some Continental and overseas news. There was relatively little information to be found regarding the United States or distant parts of the empire. Press agencies did not come into existence until later in the century, and in the absence of copyright protection it was a common practice for newspapers to reprint material without acknowledgement from their competitors. A small number of London-based daily newspapers such as the *Morning Chronicle* and the *Times*, which was the most influential newspaper of the period, made a determined effort to collect and distribute news efficiently by hiring special boats and trains. But the printing of news accounts in most papers tended towards discontinuity in the absence of professional teams of reporters. There was little consensus among newspaper publishers as to the advantage of spicing up a good news story or carrying it over into the next day's edition so as to attract more readers. Leading articles ('leaders') continued to be "the most important, authoritative, and characteristic mode of British journalism" (Liddle, 1999: 5). The chief London and provincial papers printed three or more leaders per day, generally taking up several columns of space. Not surprisingly, leader writers occupied a prestigious position on daily newspapers since they were expected to compose lengthy analyses of parliamentary debates and speeches at short notice. Nineteenth-century newspapers also included some crime reports, as well as accounts of sporting events and divorce proceedings. However, relatively little space was allotted to feature articles, or to news that might even tangentially be characterized as constituting entertainment or sensationalism. Daily newspapers generally maintained close ties to political parties and their financial viability depended on the subsidies these produced rather than an ability to independently generate profits by means of sales or advertising.

Not surprisingly, the chief objective of early nineteenth-century daily newspapers was to transmit selected morsels of information and preferred views to small numbers of educated, well-to-do readers. In the words of a leading editor, they sought "to enlighten the minds, and to elevate the character of mankind in general" (Grant, 1871: ii, 456). The editorial page was key to this mission and has been characterized as a pulpit from which a "journalism of opinion" might effectively be conveyed (Steed, 1938: 169). By virtue of position, the editor of a successful morning newspaper was a powerful figure in journalism. John T. Delane, who edited the *Times* from 1841 to 1877 and maintained a number of important political relationships, epitomized the traditional Victorian editor. Yet neither he nor other nineteenth-century editors were able to draw upon the expertise of specialized teams of paid reporters, or editors, who for the most part did not yet exist. Newspapers depended primarily for news on freelance correspondents, known as 'specials', such as William H. Russell, who covered the Crimean War, the Indian Mutiny of 1857 and other overseas military conflicts for the *Times*. Day to day reporters, whether paid on a regular basis or not, occupied a much lower place on the ladder of journalism; they were derided as mere compilers of facts rather than interpreters of events. Lowest of all among those aspiring to a role in journalism were 'penny-a-liners', who frequented the environs of Fleet Street and other press neighborhoods, searching for news stories in the hope of eking out a living.

By the final decades of the century, a mass circulation press was emerging whose characteristics were very different from those to be found in newspapers a generation or two earlier. However, the seemingly dramatic shift from an 'old' to a 'new' journalism did not take place overnight, and a number of historians emphasize the evolutionary, unspectacular nature of this change (Wiener, 1988: 47–72; Conboy, 2002: 87–96). For example, a key event underplayed in many histories of journalism was the struggle in the 1830s to dismantle the 'taxes on knowledge', a series of imposts that placed financial constraints on the press and made it almost impossible for newspapers to amass large circulations. By 1855, working- and middle-class supporters of this War of the Unstamped succeeded in their goal of repealing the tax on newspapers, which stood at four pence in 1815; this was complemented by the removal of the duties on advertisements (1853) and paper (1861). The ending of these restraints on popular journalism gave a pronounced impetus to the expansion of cheap newspapers (Hollis, 1970; Wiener, 1969). The price of papers fell rapidly and a number of daily newspapers began to experience an exponential growth. The London *Daily Telegraph*, which appeared for the first time in June 1855, broke new ground when it reduced its selling price to a penny three months later; within a short time it had achieved an unprecedented circulation of 270,000, supposedly the largest in the world. Other London papers, including the *Morning Star* (1856) and the *Echo* (1868), followed suit. At the same time hundreds of provincial papers came into existence, mostly in urban industrial cities in the north, and began to circulate at prices affordable to poorer readers. By the 1860s a market for daily readers of newspapers representing a much wider social spectrum was in the process of being established (Lee, 1976: 68).

Some of the cheap newspapers began to make use of the 'London Plan' of distribution, which had been introduced during the War of the Unstamped and was now popular in American cities. This involved the sale of papers outside a traditional subscription network. Newsboys were hired to vend papers in the streets, especially the rapidly expanding number of evening newspapers, which from the outset relied on commuters for circulation and printed sensational, eye-catching news on the front page. Daily newspapers began to feature multi-column display, or star, advertising, an innovation that further tilted the economic foundations of journalism away from reliance on a limited, subscription-based readership. By the 1870s, additional changes began to transform the 'look' and content of journalism: a greatly increased number of pictures and illustrations; livelier, personalized writing that emphasized human interest; and more attention paid to sports, gossip and other tangential variations of sensationalism, including an occasionally salacious report of a murder or rape. Sunday newspapers like the *News of the World* and *Lloyd's Weekly Newspaper*, which began to appear in the 1840s, were less 'respectable' than the dailies because of their overt ties to a demotic radical culture. As with daily papers, they attracted a greatly expanded readership that by the third quarter of the century had marginally more money to spend and yearned for a measure of entertainment on their day off. Although most historians do not believe that the Education Act of 1870 gave a decisive impetus to this newspaper-oriented 'explosion of literacy', it was clearly one key factor among a host of others – cultural, economic and technological – that boosted the growth of a new reading class.

New journalism

During the 1880s and 1890s, William T. Stead, Thomas P. O'Connor, Alfred Harmsworth, George Newnes, Charles A. Pearson and other proprietors and editors began to create a New Journalism in Britain, much of it influenced by American models (Wiener, 2011: 154–210). It is from this point that a mass circulation press can be said to have become a concrete reality. Many newspapers reduced their selling price to a penny or a halfpenny, while some amassed very large circulations, among them evening papers such as the London *Evening News*, which emphasized sports, crime, gossip, interviewing, pictures and headlines, in short, anything capable of attracting a large readership. Less attention was paid to parliamentary and Continental news, with leading articles diminishing considerably both in size and influence. 'Leaderettes', written in a popular, condensed style sometimes referred to as 'journalese', began to replace the weighty political analyses so central to the Victorian press. George Augustus Sala, who wrote approximately 9,000 of these 'social leaders' for the *Daily Telegraph* during a period of 33 years, stated that "the average public would much rather read an essay on the last new breach of promise case, the last new fashion, the last new folly, or song, or picture, or society lion, and especially the last new murder, than prosy deliverances on politics, native or foreign" (1891: 24). What occurred in this period was "a paradigm shift to a popular readership on a daily basis, encouraged and made possible by other trends towards the massification of culture" (Conboy, 2002: 95).

Of the progenitors of a New Journalism, Stead was the best known for a time. He drew upon prevailing genres of popular print culture (as did many of his contemporaries) but also introduced a number of innovations into the *Pall Mall Gazette*, a penny evening London paper that he edited from 1880 to 1889. Among these was the 'lightening' of typography and the use of crossheads. Likewise he printed hundreds of interviews in the paper, a relatively new journalistic technique whose popular appeal derived from its ability to personalize the news (Schults, 1972: 29–65). Both crossheads and interviewing were powerfully influenced by American journalism, which at the time was developing its own mass circulation press ('Yellow Journalism') under the aegis of Joseph Pulitzer and William Randolph Hearst. Stead also engaged in popular investigations such as the The Maiden Tribute of Modern Babylon series in 1885, which sensationally exposed the evils of child prostitution. O'Connor lacked Stead's flair for publicity and his literary brilliance, but he successfully developed a complementary version of the New Journalism in his halfpenny evening *Star*. This paper reported copiously on sports and crime, and during 1888 provided detailed coverage of the sanguinary exploits of Jack the Ripper, accompanied by ghoulish headlines. What drew Stead and O'Connor together was their joint conviction that news needed to be redefined to make it more entertaining and popular among large numbers of new readers. This culturally egalitarian conception of the role of journalism did as much as anything to divide the new age of the mass popular press from its predecessors. Stead believed that journalism needed to articulate "the aspirations, the ideas, and the prejudices of the masses of the people," and that future newspapers were likely to be "more intelligent, better printed, more copiously illustrated, less stodgy [and] more enterprising" than at present (1901: 15,

290). If anything O'Connor was more pointedly committed to a re-examination of the nature and function of news. He aimed to bring large numbers of ordinary readers into contact with a new spirit of journalism, by which he meant almost anything that appeared to interest readers: "Everything that can be talked about can also be written about" (O'Connor, 1889: 430). Harmsworth (subsequently Viscount Northcliffe), Newnes and Pearson accomplished even more than Stead and O'Connor in helping to bring about a fundamental transformation of popular journalism. All three men launched penny weekly magazines, the best known being *Tit-Bits* in 1881 (Newnes) and *Answers to Correspondents* in 1888 (Harmsworth). Their successful exploitation of 'snippets' journalism, which comprised excerpts from other publications, miscellaneous shards of useful information and well-publicized prize competitions, led the way to the creation of a full-scale popular press in the 1890s. Harmsworth's decisive contribution to this journalism was represented by the appearance of his path-breaking halfpenny morning *Daily Mail* in May 1896, with its decked headlines and photographs, coverage of sports and crime, strident imperialism, entertainment features and a brief news digest, all of which within a few years was to make it "Britain's first truly mass circulation newspaper" (Williams, 2010: 54). Pearson founded the more sensation-leaning penny *Daily Express* in 1900, the first major British newspaper to adopt the American-style method of printing news on the front page in place of advertisements. Interestingly, in contrast, the *Daily Mail* did not commence this practice until 1939. When Harmsworth re-launched the *Daily Mirror* in 1904 as the first successful tabloid-sized pictorial daily newspaper published anywhere in the world the age of mass circulation journalism can be said to have truly arrived. "Our pictures do not merely accompany the printed news. They are a valuable explanation of it" (*Daily Illustrated Mirror*, 28 January 1904).

Technology, economics and culture

There are disagreements among historians and sociologists as to the basic explanation for this profound transformation in journalism. These disagreements are broadly divisible into three areas: technology, economics and culture. Those who attribute the changes primarily to improved technology maintain that the ability to manufacture and distribute news efficiently and at greatly reduced cost provided the financial incentive to expand and meet the needs of a growing readership. Assorted milestones are generally invoked to support this interpretation: the introduction of high-speed rotary printing presses at mid-century; the effective use of stereotype plates commencing in the 1870s; cheap newsprint made from wood pulp in substitution for cotton rag paper; and breakthrough inventions such as the 'Linotype' machine from America that dramatically speeded up the casting of type by mechanizing it. By the end of the century many thousands of copies of a newspaper could be manufactured in less than an hour. It became relatively easy to break the constrictive single column rule, even when high-speed presses were employed; this in turn made possible the full use of display advertising, multiple decks and large headlines. Furthermore, by means of the halftone process, which was invented and first applied commercially in the United States in the 1880s, daily newspapers were enabled to replace wood engravings with photographs. Developments in the area of photography were soon to transform the very nature and appeal of mass journalism.

The commercialization of the press was increasingly evident by late century and a number of historians isolate this factor as decisive in the reshaping of journalism. It has been claimed that: "The transition from a public of readers to a market of readers was the single most important historical event in the history of the British press in the last two hundred years" (Chalaby, 1998: 184). Press proprietors such as Harmsworth and Pearson invested heavily in machinery and paper, and hired hundreds of reporters and editors for their professionalized staffs, including many women. As a capitalistic ethic became infused into journalism, news was effectively transformed into "a commercial product, to be shaped, packaged, and marketed with a constant eye to profit" (Baldasty, 1992: 140). After 1900 it was increasingly the practice for limited stock companies to be established within the industry as a way of attracting substantial financial involvement from groups of investors. Advertising became the chief source of income for newspapers, surpassing retail sales and political subsidies. This was especially true of pictorial display advertising, aimed at specialized groups of consumers and dependent for support primarily on large wholesale businesses and newly founded department stores. The cost of launching a daily paper now increased to several hundred thousand pounds; earlier in the century individuals or families were able to initiate such an undertaking for a fraction of this amount. Proprietors like Harmsworth and Pearson – among the first of the modern press barons – clearly were driven to capitalize journalism by the possibility of securing huge potential profits. For example, in 1905, Harmsworth's company, named the Associated Newspapers, was valued at £1.6 million. Some influential critics of popular journalism maintain that the rise of a commercialized mass press undermined a tradition of journalism constructed around a rational public sphere (Habermas, 1989). Others contend that this press became so entangled in a web of capitalism by the end of the century that almost everything, including the reading habits of millions of people and their alleged passivity in the face of an emergent culture of entertainment, can be explained in terms of the commodification of information (Postman, 1986).

Both the technological and the commercial interpretations of the popular press, while immensely suggestive, tend to downplay the cultural fundaments of change, which at least in part offer an alternative way of analyzing the events of the late nineteenth century. The cultural perspective shifts focus away from the decisions made by producers of print and instead casts light on a journalism partly shaped by the perspectives of its readers. Looked at in this way, it may be argued that journalism in Britain was democratized during the course of the nineteenth century. To be sure, democratization in this sense means that in practice a culture of entertainment and sensationalism replaced traditional forms of journalism based on pedagogical uplift and a doctrine of improvement. Yet such a celebrity-oriented press culture reflected what the majority of people seemingly wanted to read. Almost certainly, mass journalism (or 'tabloid journalism', as it is usually referred to generically) was accompanied by a decline in the quality of traditional forms of print communication. Yet, in the view of historians and sociologists who stress the importance of cultural change, the broadening of the content of journalism had the virtue of allowing millions of readers of newspapers to become partial agents of their own reading habits and not passive recipients of a capitalized news package. The redefinition of news was key to this transformation. Yet so too was the marked influence of American popular journalism, with its boisterous informality, disrespect for an established social hierarchy and seeming aversion to prescribed canons of literary quality. As Stead maintained, in proffering a vigorous claim for the validity of his journalism and that of O'Connor: "We broke the old tradition and made journalism a living thing, palpitating with actuality, in touch with life at all points" (1902: 479).

Speed

Speed was a central transformative event in popular journalism during the nineteenth century, permeating every facet of the press including technology, commercial imperatives and cultural forms. It affected how news was collected and disseminated, as well as how it was written. It informed debates about where journalism was heading and whether it was undergoing an improvement or a decline. Railways and steam ships began to undermine the cultural stability of the early Victorian decades by ushering in a coming age based on rapid communication. But the electric telegraph was the first important invention to inject speed directly into the core of popular journalism. It was used in a limited way up to the outbreak of the American Civil War and by the 1880s had become an integral part of British journalism. Dispatches began to be sent routinely by wire to London newspapers from provincial centers or from abroad by means of press agencies such as Reuters (1851), the Press Association (1868) and the Central News Association (1870). For reasons of both economy and speed, dispatches transmitted in this way had to be made succinct. As a result, the much-criticized practice of publishing stories characterized by 'small-scale' writing and snippets gathered momentum. Two further inventions that dramatically compressed time and distance and permanently changed the landscape of journalism were the telephone and the typewriter. By the 1890s reporters phoned in their breaking stories to 'rewrite men' on evening papers, who rapidly composed news accounts on Remington typewriters and sent them to compositors. In this way newspapers could publish fast-breaking news (including sports results) before being put to bed. Both Harmsworth and O'Connor required their employees to make regular use of the telephone and typewriter regardless of cost. The classic age of speed in the late nineteenth century has been conjured up in these words: "The constant patter of telegraph boys all through the night ... their showers of pink envelopes ... the busy scenes in the printing office" (Pebody, 1882: 24).

By 1900, the face of journalism had been irreversibly transformed. Reporters were regularly organized into specialized beats and competed for scoops, especially on evening papers, which were produced under conditions of intense time pressure. According to Kennedy Jones, an associate of Harmsworth, the requirements for an evening paper were "exceptional quickness – quickness of perception, quickness of decision, quickness of execution" (1919: 131). Those commuting to work provided an obvious market for such papers; presumably, the former could be won over instantly by means of a sensational crime story, a racy headline, an unexpected result from the world of football or cricket, or some bright pictures. Almost every aspect of the world of mass circulation journalism involved a competitive positioning of reporters and news editors, who were entangled in a web of daily sensationalism and excitement. Bylines became common. Columns were syndicated and widely distributed, as were political cartoons and comic strips. Interviews with celebrities and politicians jostled for space with salacious gossip about them. Above all, pictures complemented texts and soon began to supersede them. By the end of the century, technology, capitalism and a redefined news culture had merged their strengths and weaknesses into a single general-interest press product for the masses, vastly different from that of a hundred years earlier and much closer to the kind of popular, or tabloid, journalism we are familiar with today.

Further reading

D. Griffiths's (1992) *The Encyclopedia of the British Press 1422–1992* continues to be a standard reference work on modern British journalism. M. Hampton (2004) in *Visions of the Press in Britain, 1850–1950* presents a fine analysis of competing views of nineteenth-century journalism. E. Palmegiano's (2012) *Perceptions of the Press in Nineteenth-Century British Periodicals* provides a detailed summary of hundreds of articles about British journalism that appeared in 48 leading Victorian periodicals. W. Robinson's (2012) *Muckraker: The Scandalous Life and Times of W. T. Stead, Britain's First Investigative Journalist* is the most recent biography of this press pioneer.

References

Baldasty, G. (1992) *The Commercialization of News in the Nineteenth Century*. Madison, WI: University of Wisconsin Press.
Chalaby, J. (1998) *The Invention of Journalism*. London: Macmillan.
Conboy, M. (2002) *The Press and Popular Culture*. London: Sage.
Grant, J. (1871) *The Newspaper Press: Its Origin, Progress And Present Position* (volumes i–iii). London: Tinsley Brothers.
Griffiths, D. (1992) *The Encyclopedia of the British Press 1422–1992*. London: Macmillan.
Habermas, J. (1989) *The Structural Transformation of the Public Sphere: An Inquiry into a Category of Bourgeois Society* (T. Burger, Trans.). Cambridge: Polity Press.
Hampton, M. (2004) *Visions of the Press in Britain, 1850–1950*. Urbana, IL: University of Illinois Press.
Hollis, P. (1970) *The Pauper Press: A Study in Working-Class Radicalism of the 1830s*. Oxford: Oxford University Press.
Jones, K. (1919) *Fleet Street & Downing Street*. London: Hutchinson.
Lee, A. (1976) *The Origins of the Popular Press in England 1855–1914*. London: Croom Helm.
Liddle, D. (1999) "Who invented the 'leading article'? Reconstructing the history and prehistory of a Victorian newspaper genre." *Media History*, 5(1), 5–18.
O'Connor, T. (1889) "The New Journalism." *The New Review*, I, 423–434.
Palemgiano, E. (2012) *Perceptions of the Press in Nineteenth-Century British Periodicals*. London: Anthem Press.
Pebody, C. (1882) *English Journalism and the Men Who Have Made It*. London: Cassell.

Postman, N. (1986) *Amusing Ourselves to Death: Public Discourse in the Age of Show Business*. London: Heinemann.
Robinson, W. (2012) *Muckraker: The Scandalous Life and Times of W. T. Stead, Britain's First Investigative Journalist*. London: Robson Press.
Sala, G. (1891) "The world's press: What I have known of it: 1840–90." *Sell's Dictionary of the World's Press*. London: Sell.
Schults, R. (1972) *Crusader in Babylon: W. T. Stead and the Pall Mall Gazette*. Lincoln, NE: University of Nebraska Press.
Stead, W. (1901) *The Americanization of the World, or the Trend of the Twentieth Century*. New York: H. Markley.
——(1902) "Mr. T. P. O'Connor, M. P." *Review of Reviews*, XXVI, 472–79.
Steed, W. (1938) *The Press*. Harmondsworth: Penguin.
Wiener, J. (1969) *The War of the Unstamped: The Movement to Repeal the British Newspaper Tax, 1830–1836*. Ithaca, NY: Cornell University Press.
——(1988) "How new was the new journalism?" In J. Wiener (ed.) *Papers For the Millions: The New Journalism in Britain, 1850s to 1914*. New York: Greenwood Press (pp. 47–71).
——(2011) *The Americanization of the British Press, 1830s–1914: Speed in the Age of Transatlantic Journalism*. London: Palgrave Macmillan.
Williams, K. (2010) *Get Me a Murder a Day! A History of Media and Communication in Britain*. London: Bloomsbury Academic.

18
Tabloid culture
The political economy of a newspaper style

Martin Conboy

This chapter will examine the dynamic relationship between the political economy of newspapers targeted towards a mass popular market and the development of a broader mass popular culture which some have identified as tabloid culture. Viewed historically, tabloids can be understood as an extreme version of Hampton's shift from an educational to a representational ideal (2004); one which no longer views the reader as an isolated consumer but instead as part of a network of capitalized relations including other entertainment media, celebrity culture and advertising. The tabloid may have started simply as a newspaper style/format but it enters the contemporary era extended into a dominant cultural expression.

Sensation and the popular

There is nothing new about sensation. If tabloids were only about sensationalizing accounts of the news then we might be measuring their existence in centuries, ever since the development of printed newssheets in fact. Similarly, the appeal to broadly popular audiences so characteristic of twentieth-century tabloids was nothing new and nothing exclusive to the newspaper genre. Ballads, broadsides, last dying speeches and songsheets had all had regular, wide circulations for several hundred years before the advent of mass circulation newspapers. In contrast, the sensational and the popular have always provided elite journalism with a dark 'other' against which it could define itself more virtuously. Hartley (2008) identifies such a binarism when he proposes that the modernist approach to journalism has often consisted of a discourse of liberal enlightenment ranged against the distractions of popular journalism and its insistence on pandering to the tastes and passions of the crowd.

Accounts of alleged cruelty and murder in the Elizabethan quartos, the excesses of religious and political intolerance in the English Civil War and the Sunday shockers of the early Victorian era may all provide adequate testimony to the longstanding popular appeal of the sensational in printed form. However, these trends did not constitute a culture of tabloid newspapers by themselves nor did they articulate the more pervasive aspects of that culture as we have come to understand it today. It would be a more accurate assessment if we were to say that the tabloid newspaper proper drew these pre-existing characteristics of sensationalized reporting into a regular, stylized and, most importantly, commercially successful package. The tabloid delivered sensation to the masses in a particularly influential and effective form which was designed to generate the maximum amount of profit from the widest popular readership. Moreover, tabloids continue to perfect a combination of marketing, self-promotion and visual presentation enabling a commercially attractive editorial alignment with other popular media formats; a refinement of the marketing of popular taste over time.

Tabloid milestones

After this brief theorization of the components of tabloid culture, we need a chronology of the major developments in this most important of contemporary cultural forms. Changes in journalism tend to be characterized much less by startling innovation and more by the incremental incorporation and reshaping of techniques which have been tried and tested in terms of their commercial effectiveness. This chronology will demonstrate an assimilation of the tabloid impulse for profiting from the mediation of what is commercially popular, rather than a series of trigger events. Furthermore, the conversion of newspapers to the tabloid format or the development of discourses around the word 'tabloid' indicate how the tabloid itself has emerged through a process of permeation rather than being driven by sudden and definitive shifts. Our chronology will illustrate that the tabloid is characterized by a cultural encroachment which forms part of a longer process of 'popularization' familiar to students of culture in Western Europe down the centuries (Burke, 1978).

At the end of the nineteenth century, commercialization and innovation combined in the newspaper circulation wars in New York between Pulitzer's *World* and Hearst's *Journal*. The journalism which emerged during this period of intense competition was dubbed the 'yellow press' and represents the high point of the pre-tabloid era:

> Headlines were larger and bolder and scare heads attracted readers. Illustrations no longer reflected reality. They were designed to supplement the scare heads, wow readers and get them to buy newspapers …
>
> (Smythe, 2003: 210)

Some press historians have bemoaned the subsequent impact of these developments as a triumph of style over engagement. Spencer, for example, concludes his book on the yellow press thus:

> The Yellow Press in the age of Hearst and Pulitzer shaped the generation that followed with fresh concepts of marketing, reporting, layout, design and storytelling, but the modern media have relegated the concept of community to the backstage of human existence.
>
> (Spencer, 2007: 230)

We might, however, be inclined to disagree given that the essence of the tabloid is the re-creation of a new and mediated community sometimes woven within the rhetoric of the newspaper but at other times directly scoped at an institutional level or through electronic amplification of a community that had always been editorially constructed. Readers often feel that the tabloids belong to them; editors and journalists certainly write as if they do (Juergens, 1966; Conboy, 2006).

A fine illustration of the sort of engagement with community which combines editorial involvement with the rhetorical assertion of community comes in the *New York Journal*, which had been bought by Hearst in 1895. It styled itself as the purveyor of a 'journalism of action' through its public engagement during coverage of the Guldensuppe murder investigations from June 1897 onwards. On Saturday 26 June a torso was found by three boys swimming in the East River and the next day the rest of the body was found in nearby woods. The Sunday edition of the paper was headlined: "Beheaded, cast into the river." Hearst immediately assembled his designated 'Murder Squad' from among his reporters and they, in conjunction with avid readers ready to contribute to the investigations in the hope of sharing in a $1,000 reward, provided many of the preliminary clues which would lead the police to the eventual arrest of the culprits, Augusta Nack, William Guldensuppe's lover, and Martin Thorn, the actual murderer and Nack's latest lover. By 30 June the *Journal* was proclaiming on its front page: "Discovered by the *Journal*" (Spencer, 2007: 111–14). Hearst used the case to drive home claims for his style of interventionist journalism in his main headline on July 7 1897:

> **News that is news**
> The *Journal*, as usual, *acts* while the representatives of ancient journalism sit idly by and wait for something to turn up
>
> (Stevens, 1991: 93)

Pulitzer's *New York World* was just as creative in its editorial self-promotion with its own reporter Nellie Bly involved in her most famous stunt to circumnavigate the world in 80 days (1889–90) and break the record set by Jules Verne's fictional hero, Phileas Fogg. She filed lively accounts and illustrations to readers at home while the trek was used to market a wide range of clothes, games and songs. She arrived back in Jersey City on the 73rd day to triumphant headlines.

Both these New York newspapers went head to head in championing editorially coherent sections of the downtrodden in society. This strategy meshed with their editorial claims, which sought to expose corruption among the authorities to reinforce their credentials as chiming with the interests and concerns of the common man. This was by no means the first time that newspapers had successfully fostered popular sentiments but it was the first time they had exploited them so systematically and in such a fiercely competitive and profitable fashion. The forge of enterprise was well and truly ablaze.

British developments

The move towards tabloid journalism, just like the creation of mass daily newspapers, was not something predicated necessarily on a desire to extend the franchise or increase involvement in political or public life. It was driven by men who wanted to make money out of their readers and maximize the appeal of their papers to advertisers. Aware of developments in popular journalism in the United States, British entrepreneurs such as Harmsworth and Pearson sought to incorporate selected aspects into British culture. Examples of the development in Britain of the sort of periodical appeal preceding the tabloids themselves include *Tit-Bits* (1881) and *Answers to Correspondents* (1888), on the back of which Newnes and Harmsworth respectively built the capital investment which subsequently enabled the launch of successful mass newspapers.

The *Daily Mail* from 1896 was far from being a tabloid publication in style or format but it demonstrated the incrementality of popular periodical publication towards the tabloid genre. Harmsworth had consulted both Pulitzer and Moïse Millaud, proprietor of *Le Petit Journal*, before launching his halfpenny newspaper onto Britain's streets. He had adapted the morning paper to many of the features of successful French and American papers including Pulitzer's summary lead and the blending of magazine style coverage with gossip, scoops and lighter accounts of the news of the day. There was also a strong emphasis on material targeted at women. By the early years of the century it was averaging just under a million sales per day and broke the million mark for the first time in 1900. Yet the eruption of the mass press into British life in 1896 was actually a very restrained affair. Harmsworth was still cognizant of the need for his newspaper to appear respectable and commercial in its orientation to advertisers, for example, retaining adverts on its front page. In fact, it could be argued that the period between the *Pall Mall Gazette*'s fall from favor with advertisers after its provocative coverage of teenage prostitution in 1885, and the launch of the tabloid proper in the 1930s, reflects as much a shift in the taste of advertisers as that of newspaper proprietors or their readers. The layout of the *Daily Mail*'s news owed much to the experiments of Newnes and Harmsworth in the 1880s, with *Tit-Bits* and *Answers to Correspondents* respectively, in well-demarcated and regular sections to guide the eye of the 'busy reader' to the most significant categories of information: "Gossip of the day; Some interesting items; Last look round; On the seamy side; Some interesting tales."

It was the *Daily Express* from 1900 which most fully incorporated American popular influences for the first time in a British newspaper, especially in its use of news on the front page. The appointment of Blumenfeld in 1902 as editor, an American with considerable experience of popular journalism in the USA, was indicative of the identity which its owner, Pearson, wished to emulate. In terms of layout, the paper was the first to use banner headlines and several American journalists steeped in the traditions of the American popular press were employed to style the paper's content, "grafting my American branch on the British oak" (Blumenfeld, 1944: 102–12). Its coverage was marked by many of the features of the New Journalism – the use of interviews and a lively, if not sensational, writing style.

The following year, on 1 January 1901, Pulitzer and Harmsworth continued the Anglo-American experiment with popular newspaper form when they produced a one-off tabloid-sized edition of the *New York World* as a publicity stunt, claiming it was the newspaper for the new century. With hindsight, beyond its promotional chuztpah, this proved to be a remarkably prescient assertion. For one thing, they demonstrated an awareness of the commercial appeal of rapid news digests in their front-page boast: "All the news in sixty seconds."

The first British tabloid newspaper in format, if not in style, was the *Daily Mirror* from 1903, which was launched by Harmsworth, who was convinced that it would provide a successful complement to the *Daily Mail*'s appeal to women readers. It was edited by a woman and staffed entirely by women in an attempt to provide a high-class product for 'gentlewomen'. It closed within a year as a consequence of Harmsworth's lack of market research and his naïve optimism that an inexperienced editorial team could deliver his expectations with regard to circulation and appeal to advertisers. However, from the *Mirror*'s relaunch as the world's first commercially successful daily tabloid picture newspaper, it was to have a high degree of success, rivaling the *Daily Mail* in circulation until after the First World War.

America takes the initiative again

On 26 June 1919, Patterson launched in the US what we would today recognize as the first genuine tabloid newspaper, the *Illustrated Daily News*. Its success led to the rival launches of Hearst's *Daily Mirror* and Macfadden's *Daily Graphic*, both in 1924. Jazz journalism had arrived (Bessie, 1938). These papers pushed the boundaries of popular taste with their "reckless sensationalism, ruthless invasions of privacy, and picture faking" (Mott, 1961: 673). The use of photography to lead stories was a key part of the appeal of these tabloids. Philip Payne, who edited both the *Illustrated Daily News* and the *Daily Mirror*, is reported as having the goal of illustrating every story in the papers with a photograph, claiming that this was "the very essence of tabloidism" (Stevens, 1991: 119–20). The commercial success of the tabloids was recycled into the newspapers' relationship with their readers as competitions, coupons and prizes for contributions all provided the chance of financial reward for engagement with the newspaper. To cement this relationship, blue collar appeal came to be an intrinsic part of this tabloid journalism.

Perhaps the literal community which Spencer is referring to and which drove the early expansion in sales of big city newspapers before the era of the Yellow Press did become a neglected part of the mass newspapers of the late nineteenth century, but the commercial triumph of the generation of tabloid newspapers through the 1920s and 1930s in the US and later in the UK was expressed in broader mediated communities which related to advertising, lifestyle and patterns of consumption. The ways in which the tabloid begins to refine the articulation of those communities of taste and popular culture are the rhetorical keys to the success of this next wave of newspapers. Carey's interpretation of the prime function of the modern newspaper (1989, 20–21) is particularly useful in relation to the tabloids. He sees newspapers as contributing to the symbolic construction of community, expanding the rituals of conversation for the post-telegraph age. This view contrasts the more positivist view of newspapers conforming to a model of information transmission and further explains the appeal and commercial success of tabloids as links between institutions of information and their carefully constructed communities of readers.

Back in Britain

It was not until these developments in the American tabloids were picked up within the British newspaper economy, as seen in the reformulated *Daily Mirror* of the mid 1930s, that the style began to take on its identifiable modern character in Britain. From 1934, the *Daily Mirror* was relaunched as Britain's first authentic tabloid in style. Closely aligned with young, working-class and female readers, this newspaper came to be seen as the embodiment of the mass popular culture of the mid century. Its advantage over its rivals was that it was astutely targeted, on the advice of the advertising agency J. Walter Thompson, at the readers most commercially attractive to advertisers, regardless of the fact that these readers were identified as being more inclined to the left of the political spectrum (Pugh, 1998: 426). Its circulation grew after the Second World War to make it the best selling daily in the country, attaining an unsurpassed peak of 5.25 million daily sales by 1967.

Its success made it an obvious target for competitors. In 1969 the *Sun* was bought by the Australian media owner Rupert Murdoch. Dubbed the 'Dirty Digger' by the satirical magazine *Private Eye*, Murdoch already owned a television station in Adelaide – Channel 9 – and had ambitions to develop this branch of his media activity. This meant that he came to Fleet Street with a fresh view of the possibilities of using television to advertise his paper. He saw television as complementary to his newspapers not as a rival to them as many of his British-based competitors did. Murdoch took over the *Sun* primarily as he had the good business sense to see that he couldn't afford to have the presses running only one day a week for his recently acquired Sunday newspaper, the *News of the World*. He also had a wider strategic aim. He was of the view that the *Daily Mirror* had become a pale version of its glory years. Murdoch was determined to revitalize the tabloid market by recapturing what the *Daily Mirror* had encapsulated for so long; a newspaper of appeal to a younger, more affluent reader, in tune with cross-media developments in popular culture. He used Larry Lamb, himself a former *Daily Mirror* editor, to bring about this transformation. It was brash, innovative and introduced the Page 3 Girl as early as 1970 as an expression of its particular endorsement of more liberal social attitudes towards sexuality. The incorporation of the voice of the reader in letters had been a central feature of the appeal of the *Daily Mirror* especially through the war years. Amplifying this editorial expression of community to enhance its populist commercial appeal and on Lamb's insistence, the *Sun* made a point of responding to readers' letters within 48 hours. From a very different strategic direction, 'earthquake journalism' became one of the regular features of Lamb's newly launched paper, designed to draw attention to the paper's coverage of a particularly big news story. This was a guarantor of increased sales on any particular day and was copied by other tabloids as a short-term ploy to put on extra readers.

Lamb emphasized the colloquial aspect of the newspaper's style by insisting on his reporters finding what he called "talking stories" (Chippendale and Horrie, 1992: 40), that is stories which people would literally talk about after reading the paper. To extend this appeal, the use of puns by sub-editors going for maximum entertainment value was a prominent aspect of the paper as it attempted to capture the rhythms of everyday speech and the tone of popular humor. It is interesting to reflect on just how popular *Carry On* films were at this time in Britain, demonstrating that a mixture of saucy humor, innuendo and wordplay was a winning formula in the pursuit of popular taste.

Not for the first time, a tabloid newspaper was creating a successful commercial path by tuning in to broader popular tastes. Not for the first time, a tabloid newspaper was refashioning expectations of the rest of the popular newspaper market. What was different was the intensity with which the *Sun* led the march into wider areas of popular culture, embracing it and making it an intrinsic part of the tabloid staple; television, soap operas, celebrity, reality television, Royal sensation, more explicit sexual titillation all became successful elements of its tabloid populism.

One of the main processes of tabloid culture is what could be termed 'vernacularization'. This attempt to encapsulate something of the voice of the ordinary person had always been prevalent within popular print culture. In fact, Smith (1984) is of the view that popular print to a large extent allowed a popular voice to emerge. It was certainly a feature of radical print in the early nineteenth century and it became commercialized as part of a push for improved market appeal from the 1830s in the USA and became increasingly incorporated within sections of the British popular press from the 1880s. The *Daily Mirror* provided the first defining experiment of the twentieth century (Bingham and Conboy, 2009). This stylistic turning towards a vernacular approach fitted well within the process of popularizing and personalizing politics, which had been in process for most of the post-war period, the intensification of celebrity culture as a topic of conversation with readers, the domestication of the Royal family and the rise of coverage of soap operas on television. All of this meant that a general coarsening of language and an increasing proximity between reader and celebrity whether actor, politician or Royal became part of a flattened landscape of appeal to a burgeoning readership. The *Sun* was very much the standard bearer for this cultural synthesis. Celebrity sportsmen such as George Best and Brian Clough had always formed part of the *Sun*'s new-found appeal in the 70s but this was continued and refined through crossovers with pundits and ex-players who were popular on television such as Ian St John and Jimmy Greaves (1985–92).

However, beyond their stylistic innovation, the ultimate proof of the success of tabloid newspapers is long-term profitability. After its acquisition by Murdoch, the *Sun* quickly began to put on circulation, overtaking the *Mirror* and reaching 4 million daily sales for the first time in 1978. Soon afterwards, it shifted in step with political developments to offer its support to the Conservative Party. Just as the *Daily Mirror* had been able to ride the crest of a wave of popular support for the Labour Party, the *Sun* reached out to the shifting political allegiance of its core readers who also happened to be the swing demographic for the triumph of the Conservatives in 1979; the social demographic of the C2s, the skilled working classes, whose shift from Labour to Conservative was a key historical moment in British post-war politics.

Not only was the *Sun* a hugely successful commercial venture but, when combined with the equally successful *News of the World*, it enabled Murdoch to subsidize first his purchase of the upmarket *Times* and *Sunday Times* in 1981, then to see off rival tabloid ventures by undercutting their market ploys, and later to realize his ambitious BSkyB project and enable it to survive during its period of consolidation

(Taylor, 1992: 345). It is fair to say that the media market as well as the media content we have in Britain today have to a large part been shaped by Murdoch's tabloids and their enormous profits.

From the early 70s, the *Sun* had started to pay attention to the private lives of television personalities but this was to reach a new peak when the BBC soap opera, *Eastenders*, was launched in 1985 with its emphasis on the southern, young viewers and edgy storylines which the *Sun* considered very much in tune with its own identity. The paper started to concentrate on the plotlines as well as the real lives of actors with journalist Wendy Henry a central figure in the development of this sort of in-depth coverage.

The cannibalization inherent within the economy of the popular newspaper market was evident when the first direct casualty of the new tabloid circulation war, the *Daily Sketch*, closed to merge with the *Daily Mail* in its transition to a tabloid format in 1971 after the *Sun* had captured a significant share of its downmarket readership. Attracted by the *Sun's* successful trajectory, in 1978, Express Newspapers started a rival tabloid, the *Daily Star*, pushing boundaries of taste and pursuing a vibrant engagement with popular culture with a distinctly Northern identity, using a bingo game on its launch as one of its key attractions. It led to the *Sun's* first year-on-year decline since Murdoch purchased it in 1969 and buoyed by its initial success, the *Daily Star* went national from 1981. The *Sun* had however learned from its victory over the *Daily Mirror* and was not resting on its laurels. It fought back with its own bingo from 1981 but most importantly with an invigorated editorship which was to further refine the tabloid culture of Britain. Kelvin MacKenzie was appointed in 1981 to reverse this decline and press on with the tabloid revolution.

Under MacKenzie many of the prejudices and stereotypes of the paper's target audience were amplified with hostile coverage – feminists, anti-nuclear campaigners, *Guardian* readers, trade unionists, gays, anything broadly categorized as the 'looney left' (Curran, Gaber and Petley, 2005). MacKenzie emphasized the vernacular element established at the paper in an update of Larry Lamb's 'talking paper' and called it the "Hey, Doris! factor" (Chippendale and Horrie, 1992: 148–50). After the marriage of Charles and Diana in 1981 the Royal Family became open season, adding a new familiarity, even contempt, to coverage of the Royals. In 1982, the column *Bizzarre* was launched with the editor, John Blake, as a conduit to a young, music-loving readership and an increasing tendency to celebrity-style coverage. Following on the paper's extreme patriotism during the Falklands War, 'the paper that supports our boys' had reached 4,224,000 sales per day and to drive home its increasing dominance of the market in 1984 MacKenzie launched a £1 million bingo competition to rival Maxwell's version at the *Daily Mirror*.

The *Sunday Sport* from 1986 and its companion paper the *Daily Sport* from 1991 combined to add to the *Daily Star's* attempts to plumb new depths of public interest in the lives and sex lives of the rich and famous. This dynamic had led to a general shift towards what has been categorized as "bonk journalism" (Taylor, 1992). The staple intrusions into the private lives of public figures had gained a nastier, more vicious edge and were now spreading to the daily tabloids as well. The end of the 1980s and the lead-in to the Calcutt Report (1990) was a nadir for the marketability of this sort of tabloid journalism but it was not a genre which was going to be legislated out of existence.

Tabloid culture

Through the relaunch of the *Sun* in 1969, the first commercial retaliation in 1971 as the *Daily Mail* shifted to a tabloid format, the reformatting of the *News of The World* in 1984, to the tabloiding of the broadsheet trio of the *Independent*, the *Guardian* and the *Times* in 2004–5, the political economy of newspapers in the UK has been consistently bound up with the tabloid and ultimately the impact of its shape on the structure and emphasis of news content. Debates on the tabloidization or 'dumbing down' of the content of news media beyond newspapers have asserted the main impulse as being that of the tabloid newspaper proper:

> At first, the 'quality' press ignored the substantive issues of tabloid news; then decried them. These papers. ... subsequently began reporting and commenting on the behaviour of the tabloid press, which led to the vicarious reporting of the issues themselves. Finally, the broadsheet papers, too, carried the same news items.
>
> (Bromley, 1998: 31)

Anxieties surrounding the process of popularization accumulated through the launch of a lighter variety of television news from 1983 with Breakfast TV. These concerns took on nominal form when the word 'tabloidization' was coined in 1991 and this was a constant source of debate from, for example, the 1992 *News at Ten* relaunch to the very public 2002 'dumbing down' discussions at the BBC. Yet, despite critiques from within the news media and from academics wary of the popularization of information flow, many have concluded that the ability of tabloid culture to allow information to merge and interact with populist cultural forms is an interesting, even a positive move. Langer (1998) sees the process as an incorporation of other dynamics from popular culture while McNair (2003) sees it as a democratic process unfolding. Harrington (2008) believes we have reached a point where we have to reconsider the contribution tabloid news media make to our general media environment. Within the news media senior commentators such as Preston (2004) and Marr (2006) have measured praise for the impact of the more streamlined and populist approach to news which the tabloids have forced into the mainstream.

Within the dynamics of tabloidization, given the historical tendency for tabloid influences to move from west to east, there has also been an interesting counter-flow to the Americanizing spread of influence in the case of the American 'supermarket' tabloids (Sloan, 2001). The Scot Iain Calder was Generoso Pope's right-hand man in the rise of the *National Enquirer* from 1964 and the Florida-based supermarket tabloids deployed many other former Fleet Street tabloid journalists down the years, not least after Murdoch acquired a rival to the *Enquirer* in the *National Star* in 1973. It has been estimated that 80 per cent of the supermarket tabloid journalists in the mid 1970s were British. (Taylor, 1992: 91)

Golden glow or the end of an era?

Drawing upon its historical antecedents, we might assert that a tabloid 'golden age' is now emerging with the main characteristics of the genre more or less permeating all media forms of the globalized economy. As they do so, the tabloid proper is in decline. In Britain, the *Sun* has shrunk from its 4 million plus sales in the late 1980s to a little over 2 million in 2014. The Sunday tabloid the *News of the World*, ultimately one of the most profitable of tabloid institutions, closed in 2011, going out of business because its tabloid ethic had transgressed the very public it claimed to champion. Perhaps, paradoxically, the tabloid newspaper itself is becoming superfluous on account of the success of the cultural aspects of the same tabloid genre which have driven a steady rise of tabloid-style characteristics such as sensationalization and personalization across other media especially, most recently, across social media. Horrie (2003) describes the transfer of tabloid newspaper style literally into television but also perhaps prematurely asserts the death of tabloids in his book *Tabloid Nation* as tabloids continue to survive if not exactly prospering into the second decade of the twenty-first century.

Television programmes such as *Changing Rooms* (1996), *Ground Force* (1997) and *Big Brother* (2000) have been developed which draw upon and feed into audience demand for tabloid-popular media transfer and offer profitable proximity of the audience to television presenters, performers and their private lives and have continued with *X-Factor* and *Strictly Come Dancing* and their various televised spin-offs and related celebrity coverage in the popular tabloids.

Conclusion

This cross-threading of various popular cultural strands begins to mesh into a generally accessible 'common culture'. This culture goes well beyond the headlines and illustrations of a particular newspaper genre and has permeated deep within the processes and representations of everyday life. It is nowhere more true than in relation to tabloid journalism that "journalism is a part of rather than distinct from popular culture" as Dahlgren (1992) has suggested. This is because tabloid newspapers only really take off once they have developed a profitable synergy with the worlds of fashion, scandal, film and crime, and can sell this cocktail to advertisers who are happy that their commercial interests are enhanced rather than damaged by association with the content of these papers. The tabloid has moved in tune with the development of broader advertising strategies, social tolerance of scandal, the growth of a sexualized culture and increasingly graphic depictions of violence. Tabloid journalism is formed and reformed as a direct attempt to engage with mass audiences, or with more specific parts of mass audiences, starting predominantly with blue-collar readerships. As a consequence, it is driven by profit as an extreme example of the commercial imperative of journalism.

There has always been a twin drive therefore within the expansion of tabloid journalism. Both aspects of this drive have an economic focus. The first is competing against other newspapers or simply trying to stay ahead of them. The second is trying to maintain or extend the relationship with the tastes of mass readerships. Both are profit-oriented approaches to journalism. As has been observed with brutal simplicity: "Tabloid journalism is the direct application of capitalism to events and ideas. Profit, not ethics, is the prevailing motivation" (Taylor, 1992: 409).

A tabloid news culture is to a large extent the defining norm of journalism today; no longer the exiled exception but more the mainstream against which everything else needs to define itself. The BBC journalist Andrew Marr is far from negative in his assessment of the growing commonality of popular culture across all media: "The ups and downs of Kate Moss's life, golden and tormented at the same time, are of interest not to everybody, obviously, but they are to readers of *The Observer* and the *Sun*, the *Telegraph* and the *Express*" (Marr, 2006: 33).

This chimes with the view expressed by this author elsewhere that the political economy of the tabloid has generated a profitable and diverting 'common culture', with all the implications of the word 'common', from the vernacular, to the everyday, to the vulgar (Conboy, 2007a: xv). The tabloid has emerged from life as a specific and marginal media artifact to become one of the most significant structural forces of our contemporary world. It is hoped that this brief historical account of that trajectory has provided an explanation of its cultural resilience and its commercial imperatives.

Further reading

Tabloid journalism and tabloid culture more generally are lively areas of scholarship and critical thinking. Biressi and Nunn's (2008) *The Tabloid Culture Reader* is a fine survey of contributions to broader debate from a variety of media perspectives. Zelizer's (2009) *The Changing Faces of Journalism: Tabloidization, Technology and Truthiness* is a good contemporary assessment of trends in the US. Sparks and Tulloch's (2000) *Tabloid Tales: Global Debates Over Media Standards* is a panoramic view of global developments particularly in tabloid journalism per se. Johansson's (2007) *Reading Tabloids: Tabloid Newspapers and Their Readers* is a welcome ethnographic account of the appeal of the newspaper genre, while those wishing to explore the topic in another political context would do well to consult Wasserman's (2010) *Tabloid Journalism in South Africa*.

Bibliography

Bessie, S. (1938) *Jazz Journalism*. New York: Dutton.
Bingham, A. and Conboy, M. (2009) "The *Daily Mirror* and the creation of a commercial popular language: A people's war and a people's paper?" *Journalism Studies*, 10(5), 639–54.
Biressi, A. and Nunn, H. (eds.) (2008) *The Tabloid Culture Reader*. Maidenhead: Open University Press.
Blumenfeld, R. D. (1944) *The Press in My Time*. London: Rich and Cowan.
Bromley, M. (1998) "The 'tabloiding of Britain': 'Quality' newspapers in the 1990s." In H. Stephenson and M. Bromley (eds.) *Sex, Lies and Democracy*. Harlow: Longman (pp. 24–38).
Burke, P. (1978) *Popular Culture in Early Modern Europe*. London: Temple Smith.

Carey, J. (1989) *Communication as Culture: Essays on Media and Society*. Boston, MA: Hyman Publishers.

Chippendale, P. and Horrie, C. (1992) *Stick It Up Your Punter: The Rise and Fall of the* Sun. London: Mandarin.

Conboy, M. (2002) *The Press and Popular Culture*. London: Sage.

——(2006) *Tabloid Britain: Constructing a Community Through Language*. Abingdon, Oxon: Routledge.

——(2007a) "Permeation and profusion: Popular journalism in the new millennium." *Journalism Studies*, 8(1), 1–12.

——(2007b) "Foreword." In A. Biressi and H. Nunn (eds.) *The Tabloid Culture Reader*. Maidenhead: Open University Press (pp. xv–xvi).

——(2010) *The Language of Newspapers: Socio-Historical Perspectives*. London: Continuum.

Curran, J., Petley, J. and Gaber, I. (2005) *Culture Wars: The Media and the British Left*. Edinburgh: Edinburgh University Press.

Dahlgren, P. (1992) *Journalism and Popular Culture*. London: Sage.

Hampton, M. (2004) *Visions of the Press in Britain, 1850–1950*. Champaign, IL: University of Illinois Press.

Harrington, S. (2008) "Popular news in the 21st century: Time for a new critical approach." In *Journalism: Theory, Practice and Criticism*, 9(3), 266–84.

Hartley, J. (1996) *Popular Reality: Journalism, Modernity, Popular Culture*. London: Arnold.

——(2008) "The supremacy of ignorance over instruction and of numbers over knowledge." *Journalism Studies*, 9(5), 679–91.

Horrie, C. (2003) *Tabloid Nation: From the Birth of the Mirror to the Death of the Tabloid*. London: André Deutsch.

Johansson, S. (2007) *Reading Tabloids: Tabloid Newspapers and Their Readers*. Flemingsberg: Södertörns Högskola.

Juergens, G. (1966) *Joseph Pulitzer and the New York* World. Princeton, NJ: Princeton University Press.

Lamb, L. (1992) *Sunrise: The Remarkable Rise and Rise of the Best-Selling Soaraway Sun*. London: Papermac.

Langer, J. (1998) *Tabloid Television: Popular Journalism and the 'Other' News*. London: Routledge.

McLachlan, S. and Golding, P. (2000) "Tabloidization in the British press: A quantitative investigation into changes in British newspapers." In C. Sparks and J. Tulloch (eds.) *Tabloid Tales: Global Debates on Media Standards*. Oxford: Rowman and Littlefield (pp. 75–90).

McNair, B. (2003) *An Introduction to Political Communication*. London: Routledge.

Marr, A. (2006) "Brave new world." *British Journalism Review*, 17(1), 29–34.

Mott, F. L. (1961) *American Journalism: A History of Newspapers in the US Through 250 Years, 1690–1960*. Basingstoke: Macmillan.

Preston, P. (2004) "Tabloids: Only the beginning." *British Journalism Review*, 15(1), 50–55.

Pugh, M. (1998) "The *Daily Mirror* and the revival of Labour 1935–45." *Twentieth Century British History*, 9(3), 420–38.

Sloan, B. (2001) *I Watched a Wild Hog Eat My Baby*. New York: Prometheus Books.

Smith, O. (1984) *The Politics of Language, 1719–1819*. Oxford: Clarendon.

Smythe, T. C. (2003) *The Gilded Age Press 1865–1900*. Westport, CT: Praeger Publishers.

Sparks, C. (2000) "Introduction: The panic over tabloid news." In C. Sparks and J. Tulloch (eds.) *Tabloid Tales: Global Debates on Media Standards*. Oxford: Rowman and Littlefield (pp. 1–40).

Sparks, C. and Tulloch, J. (eds.) (2000) *Tabloid Tales: Global Debates over Media Standards*. Oxford: Rowman and Littlefield.

Spencer, D. R. (2007) *The Yellow Press: The Press and America's Emergence as a World Power*. Evanston, IL: Northwestern University Press.

Stevens, J. (1991) *Sensationalism and the New York Press*. New York: Columbia University Press.

Taylor, S. J. (1992) *Shock! Horror! The Tabloids in Action*. London: Black Swan.

Wasserman, H. (2010) *Tabloid Journalism in South Africa*. Champaign, IL: University of Illinois Press.

Wiener, J. H. (2011) *The Americanization of the British Press, 1830s-1914: Speed in the Age of Transatlantic Journalism*. Basingstoke: Palgrave Macmillan.

Zelizer, B. (2009) *The Changing Faces of Journalism: Tabloidization, Technology and Truthiness*. Abingdon: Routledge.

19
The regulation of the press
Tom O'Malley

This chapter discusses the history of press regulation since 1500, with particular emphasis on the nineteenth and twentieth centuries. Two established accounts of press history frame discussions of regulation. One emphasizes the significance of the lapse of pre-publication censorship after 1695 and the gradual emergence thereafter of a press free from government control. The other stresses the ways in which, although free from pre-publication controls after 1695, the press became integrated into the economic and political power structures of society and acted as an agent of social control. Discussions about regulation have focused on developments in the twentieth century, particularly after 1945, with an emphasis on whether there should be statutory or voluntary regulation of professional standards (O'Malley and Soley, 2000; Conboy, 2004; Curran and Seaton, 2010: 6–99, 334–37; Leveson, 2012: 58–61).

This chapter illustrates how the history of the press can be illuminated by surveying the nature, range and purpose of regulations since 1500. Although the purposes of specific regulations have varied, cumulatively they have been fundamental to structuring the evolving relationship between the press, the state and society. Their growing complexity since the beginning of the twentieth century reflects not just greater levels of control by the state and compliance by the industry, but also the fact that communications have become crucial to the functioning of advanced industrial societies (Thompson, 1995). Established accounts of press history have overstressed particular manifestations of regulatory change – the lapse of licensing laws in 1695 or the end of economic controls by the 1860s – at the expense of seeing regulation as the basic, if evolving, framework within which the press has operated.

This chapter starts by discussing the meanings of the 'press' and 'regulation'. It then outlines how historians have discussed the press and its relationship to the state and the market. The remaining sections deal chronologically with different types of regulation and their significance.

The press and regulation

The press can refer to many things. Here it means the broad range of printed materials which before the 1850s included newsbooks, pamphlets, broadsides, books, caricatures and ballads as well as what were, by the eighteenth century, increasingly being understood as newspapers. Over time, particularly from the mid nineteenth century to the rise in the twentieth century of newspapers with large circulations, the word 'press' tended to refer collectively to serial publications appearing at fixed daily, weekly, monthly or quarterly intervals, that is, newspapers and periodical literature.

These publications were always regulated. To "regulate" something is "to control, govern or direct ... by means of regulations or restraints" (OUP, 2013). These regulations, generally stemming from statute, have covered a wide range of activities. In 1662 a statute was enacted "for preventing the frequent Abuses in printing seditious treasonable and unlicensed Bookes and Pamphlets and for regulating of Printing and Printing presses" (Raithby, 1819: 428–35). It stipulated that all products of the printing press had to be licensed prior to publication by an officially appointed licensor and included provisions relating to the import of books, the protection of printers from those who pirated their work, restrictions on which tradesmen could sell books, the role of the Stationers' Company in registering books and printers, and the number of presses and apprentices a master printer could keep. Regulation therefore covered more than just licensing; it was also concerned with the economic well-being and organization of the printing trades (Raithby, 1819: 428–35; Siebert, 1965). The sense in which regulation refers to more than censorship or professional standards remains current: "Regulation is not just concerned with monitoring firms ... and correcting market failures. It has a positive duty to promote the public interest, that is to pursue policies which promote the welfare of UK citizens, firms and consumers" (Collins and Murroni, 1996: 162). Within this context it follows that journalism has never been free from regulations. Journalism can be understood as "the exercise by occupation of the right to free expression" which "cannot in principle be withdrawn from a few by any system of licensing or professional registration". It is however "restricted and confined by rules of law which apply to all who take or are afforded the opportunity to exercise the right by speaking or writing in public" (Robertson, 1991: 301).

Freedom and control: Approaches to press history

Traditional narratives of press history have stressed how a 'great and critical struggle' against press censorship extended across four centuries, leading ultimately to 'emancipation' from government controls (Wickwar, 1928: 14–15). Yet the lapse of the licensing laws was accidental. Politicians and government, faced with a growing demand for news and a developing printing trade, could not agree on the terms of renewal and, "in this negative and uninspiring way was the Freedom of the Press achieved: not as the result of any resounding statement of principle, but by the simple refusal of a House dominated by party politics to renew in its existing form the old Printing act" (Cranfield, 1962: 6–7).

In spite of the fact that for much of the period between 1695 and the 1860s the press was under a great number of restrictions (described below) the lapse of the licensing laws meant that "printers were able to publish newspapers and other forms of printed material with unprecedented freedom" (Barker, 2000: 1). Indeed, during the 1740s, "elements of the press ... displayed great ingenuity in circumventing the obstacles placed in their way by the law and parliamentary privilege" (Harris, 1993: 254). Independence was underpinned in the eighteenth and early nineteenth centuries by expanding advertising revenues, which helped foster a sense of independence rather than subservience amongst editors and journalists (Asquith, 1975: 720–21). Even though politicians bribed and sponsored newspapers, "without popular backing newspapers could not thrive ... Increasingly, newspapers were not dependent upon political patronage, but upon the support of their readers" (Barker, 2000: 93–94). After the lifting of economic duties, from the 1850s onwards, much of the press became linked by a combination of financial support and ideological preference to political parties. But the rise of a mass commercial press in the early twentieth century led to newspapers retreating "from those connections and, especially, from the mutual demands they entailed" (Koss, 1990: 4). Over the centuries a free press has "facilitated the progressive liberalisation of British political life" (Schweizer, 2006: 2) and made "a positive contribution to democracy" (Luckhurst, 2013: 66; Curran, 2002: 136–37).

The stress on the gradual process of emancipation from controls has been challenged robustly since the 1970s. This perspective accepts the importance of the changing legal framework since 1695, and the significance of the removal of pre-publication controls, but places more emphasis on the ways in which legal controls were replaced by market and more subtle social controls. The image of a press struggling heroically for its independence from government control was the product of the press in the nineteenth century attempting to "establish its credentials in the eyes of politicians and the public" and does not bear detailed scrutiny (Boyce, 1978: 19–20; Curran, 1978). The removal of economic controls in the nineteenth century was not about greater freedom for all papers, but was designed to help the 'respectable' press at the expense of radical and seditious publications. It made the avoidance of tax less attractive and so undermined the economic basis of the radical and working-class papers which had not previously paid it (Barker, 2000: 21; Hampton, 2004: 33).

The situation that developed after the 1850s placed control of the press firmly in the hands of respectable and politically conformist people and organizations. The costs of producing and distributing newspapers rose and this led to "a progressive transfer of ownership and control of the popular press from the working class to wealthy businessmen" (Curran and Seaton, 2010: 28–29, 35–36). The increasing dependence on advertising from the mid nineteenth century tended to favor papers which were supportive of the status quo, although overt political discrimination by advertisers diminished during the twentieth century (Curran, 1980: 109; Conboy, 2004: 108). Even if advertising did not always guide editorial policy (PEP, 1938: 22), reliance on it "encouraged a general ethos of consumerism" in society (Bingham, 2009: 22–23).

In addition, the more coercive approach of the eighteenth century, based on prosecutions and subsidies, gave way to subtler forms of control. The lobby system of giving regular un-attributable government briefings to journalists was established by 1885 and official public relations machinery grew after 1900. This was supplemented by the continued development of informal links between leading figures in the media and government ministers – in particular through joint membership of elite London social clubs such as the Carlton and the Reform (Curran, 2002: 147; Brown, 1985: 127–43). By 1906 there were 49 journalists sitting as MPs, and the Commons and Lords between them boasted 15 newspaper proprietors (Lee, 1976: 18, 78, 294–95). Thus as the nineteenth century gave way to the twentieth "the market and the state constituted a dual system of control" (Curran, 2002: 147–48).

What is missing from both of these perspectives is a fuller sense of the continuity and extent of regulation of the press across the centuries. The first tends to downplay the role of the state in regulating the press and the second places more focus on the economic and social forms of control that replaced direct state censorship and ensured the press remained a force for political stability. It is clear however that "the press was never entirely 'free'" (Bingham, 2009: 24) and that as journalism became "closer to ... centres of power and influence" there was "paradoxically a history of increasing restriction rather than liberalisation" (Conboy, 2004: 110). It is these aspects of regulation that are examined below.

1476–1695

Printing arrived in England in 1476 (Siebert, 1965: 14). The approach of governments in the two turbulent centuries which followed was detailed and complex. They combined regulation for political, religious and economic ends. Indeed politics and religion were so interconnected that making a hard and fast distinction between them in these centuries is anachronistic. In 1524 the government warned printers against printing heretical literature; in 1529 King Henry VIII (1509–47) issued a list of prohibited books. A licensing system based on royal authority was established in 1538. Royal instruments, such as proclamations, orders in Council, and decrees of the Star Chamber were used to enforce licensing and suppress seditious or heretical materials up to the outbreak of Civil War in 1641 when these controls broke down. Parliament stepped in and issued orders on printing in 1642, set up a Board of Licensers in 1643 and passed an Act for regulating printing in 1647. Further printing Acts were passed during the Commonwealth in 1649 and 1653. After the Restoration of Charles II (1660–85), a combination of orders from parliament against the publication of their proceedings, Acts for regulating printing, such as that passed in 1662 and orders from the King, were used to try and control the outpourings of the press (Siebert, 1965: 14–16). Despite the cumulative effect of these measures, by the end of the seventeenth century, the press had become an increasingly difficult medium to police. After the Restoration the licensing acts had to be renewed periodically but by 1695 no political consensus could be reached on renewal and pre-publication controls lapsed.

These controls were mixed up with economic regulation. The Crown granted monopoly rights to publish particular kinds of publication to privileged printers. In 1557 it granted a Royal Charter to the trade organization of printers and booksellers, the Stationers Company, which in return for assisting in policing the industry had its pre-eminence underpinned. As the 1662 Act illustrates, economics continued to play a key part in the regulatory framework in the form of registering publications and controlling imports and the number of printers. Regulation provoked rivalries between those printers who benefitted from the Stationers' powers and monopolies and those who did not. The Stationers defended their privileges in the discussions about the renewal of licensing in the 1690s, but were unable to secure a continuation of their commercial status in the face of political opposition (Raithby, 1819; Siebert, 1965: 260–63). Viewed overall, controls prior to 1695 were not solely focused on pre-publication censorship but were also about regulating the trade in printed materials and worked, in part, because they harnessed the economic interests of leading figures in the trade.

1695–1861

The lapse of the licensing laws led to a greater emphasis on regulation through economics, the courts and a range of laws. 1710 saw the passage of the first Copyright Act which gave authors some protection from piracy. This was followed in 1712 by the first of a series of Stamp Acts which imposed a tax on each sheet of paper and on advertisements. Further measures of this kind ensued in 1728, 1743, 1757, 1773, 1776, 1783, 1815 and 1819 (Siebert, 1965: 17; Barker, 2000: 67; PEP, 1938: 216, 219; O'Malley and Soley, 2000: 16). These had the effect of pricing stamped newspapers and pamphlets at a level which restricted their circulation. As taxation increased and newspaper circulation grew over the eighteenth century, "newspaper taxation policy seems to have been driven largely (although not wholly) by the revenue needs of the state" (Barker, 2000: 66).

After the first two decades of the nineteenth century governments saw benefits in supporting the respectable commercial press by lifting economic controls and conceding demands for relief from economically onerous libel laws. In 1836 the Provincial Newspaper Society was founded to represent the interests of these non-metropolitan owners. One of the first things it lobbied for was a reduction in stamp duty to assist those publishers who did not circumvent the stamp, and in this they succeeded. In 1836 the duty was reduced by 1d, whilst at the same time stronger penalties for evasion were introduced (O'Malley and Soley, 2000: 36; Wiener 1969: 271). The growing and vociferous Parliamentary and popular support for a press free of these taxes combined with a growing commitment to doctrines of free trade brought more regulatory benefits to publishers, although they were not always welcomed by papers which had thrived under the tax regime (Curran, 1978; Koss, 1990: 54–69). Advertisement duty was reduced in 1833 and abolished in 1853; with stamp and paper duty following suit in 1855 and 1861 respectively (Aspinall, 1950: 223; PEP, 1938: 212). Lobbying from the industry contributed to further regulatory benefits. In 1840 printers and publishers of parliamentary documents were exempted from libel actions and changes to the libel laws in 1843, 1845 and 1854 provided defences of public interest and protection from people who launched prosecutions solely to extract money from publishers (PEP, 1938: 212, 215; O'Malley and Soley, 2000: 46). The mixture of economic and political motives behind these developments was continuous with those which had operated prior to 1695.

Other measures were taken to regulate press behavior. In the eighteenth century the government used the law of seditious libel to harass, undermine and imprison opponents. This law meant that all "those involved in writing, printing, distributing and selling material could be charged when what was published was deemed likely to bring into hatred or contempt" the ruler or the government (Barker, 2000: 67–68). Governments relied on judges asserting their right to decide cases, often in the face of opposition from juries. This right was curtailed by the Libel Act of 1792. Also, for much of the eighteenth century parliament imposed controls over the publication of its proceedings (Barker, 2000: 67–68, 72–73, 78). Furthermore, governments did not hesitate to pass laws which restricted what the press could or could not do. For example, in 1797 the Mutiny Act made it a capital offense to seduce members of the armed forces away from their allegiance to the Crown. In 1819 the Criminal Libel Act allowed judges to seize seditious or blasphemous publications (PEP, 1938: 216, 219); the Treason Felony Act (1848) penalized those who advocated the abolition of the monarchy (Nicol, Millar and Sharland, 2009: 55–56); and in 1857 the Obscene Publications Act gave the police powers "to take books before local Justices to have them 'forfeited' and destroyed for obscenity" (Robertson, 1991: 180).

The years between 1695 and 1861, which saw a move away from pre-publication censorship, also saw the use of seditious libel and the development of economic regulations, their gradual removal and the passage of laws, which in different ways both controlled the press and granted concessions to a grateful industry. By 1861 regulation – for good or ill – was a reality for the press in the UK.

Regulation since 1861

In the 150 years after 1861 the regulatory framework became more complex yet more stable and, with few exceptions, was simply accepted by a press at ease with most of the regulations and capable of both challenging and using them as and when it suited. The regulatory environment included pre and post-publication censorship, collusion with state-imposed security regulations, economic regulation and measures requested by the industry to create a more liberal commercial environment.

Moral and social censorship

The desire to suppress immoral material after publication underpinned the Customs Consolidation Act (1876), which prohibited the importation of indecent or obscene works, and the Indecent Advertisements Act (1889) made it an offense to deliver obscene or indecent material on a public highway (O'Malley and Soley, 2000: 46–47). Pre-publication censorship was also imposed, but often for what were, arguably, socially desirable ends. The sensationalist and intrusive practices of the press gave rise to the Judicial Proceedings (Regulation of Reports) Act (1926) which forbade the publication of indecent medical details and full reports of divorce and matrimonial proceedings; further restrictions were imposed in 1935 and 1937. Similar restrictions on reporting cases involving juveniles were instituted in the Children and Young Person's Act of 1933. The Betting and Lotteries Act (1934) made it illegal for newspapers to give publicity to lotteries and sweepstakes in an attempt to curtail gambling (PEP, 1938: 220–21; Bingham, 2009: 140–41).

Changing social conditions led to socially acceptable forms of pre-publication censorship. In 1965 the Race Relations Act outlawed incitement to racial hatred, and in 1978 the Protection of Children Act forbade the making or distribution of indecent images of children. Tobacco advertising was banned in 2002 and in 2006 the Racial and Religious Hatred Act outlawed the expression of hatred towards people on the grounds of their religious belief whilst protecting the reporting of such speech by journalists in the course of their work (Nicol, Millar and Sharland, 2009: 126–27, 154, 226).

Political censorship

Much political censorship was justified on the grounds of state security. Freedom of expression was curtailed by the 1889 Prevention of Corruption Act, which effectively made it illegal for public servants to sell information to the press (O'Malley and Soley, 2000: 47). The Official Secrets Act of 1911 made it an offense to receive and publish any document, note or sketch without authorization (PEP, 1938: 218; Nicol, Millar and Sharland, 2009: 243). In 1912 the secret 'D' notice committee was established at which security and defense officials met with senior figures in the press "to prevent inadvertent damage to national security through the public disclosure of highly sensitive information" (Wilkinson, 2009: xi). This system continued into the twenty-first century. It testified to the ease with which the press has acquiesced in requests from the state to exercise pre-publication censorship. During the First World War (1914–18) the government gave itself extensive powers to censor the press; however, the need to use these powers was mitigated by the fact that the majority of newspapers willingly censored themselves (PEP, 1938: 211; Lovelace, 1978; Putnis, 2008).

In the tense and turbulent period after the First World War, when governments were concerned about social unrest, the Emergency Powers Act (1920) gave them power to place restrictions on public speaking and the press (PEP, 1938: 211). The Incitement to Disaffection Act (1934) made it an offense to possess or distribute leaflets which seduced members of the armed forces from their duty (Nicol, Millar and Sharland, 2009: 239; PEP, 1938: 217). During the Second World War (1939–45) the government again gave itself the power to control the press, most importantly in the form of Regulation 2D, which allowed for the banning of any publication liable to foment opposition to the successful prosecution of the war. In 1940 newsprint was rationed and government control over paper gave it the ability to influence significantly the publication of books and pamphlets (Curran and Seaton, 2010: 55, 62–63; Holman, 2005).

After the war, governments continued to impose restrictions that were, in effect, forms of political censorship. In 1984, for example, the Police and Criminal Evidence Act established a procedure which allowed police to seize the notes and photographs of journalists. The Official Secrets Act (1989) tightened up government controls over what crown servants could disclose and newspapers could publish. The decade after 2000 saw a spate of further restrictions, frequently justified as necessary to fight terrorism (as defined by the government of the day). The Regulation of Investigatory

Powers Act (2000), for example, gave governments wide discretion to intercept communications between the UK and other countries; the Terrorism Act (2000) outlawed the incitement of terrorism and placed no obligation on the prosecution to prove that the publisher intended to incite; and the Terrorism Act (2006) criminalized publications that encouraged terrorism (Nicol, Millar and Sharland, 2009: 105, 141, 243–46).

Co-operation and concessions

These constraints have gone hand in hand with legal and regulatory concessions to the industry. The industry had an interest in creating regulations that benefitted them and lobbied governments accordingly. Statutes enacted in 1889, 1888, 1952 and 1996 reformed the law of libel so as to protect publishers from vexatious and unfair litigation (O'Malley and Soley, 2000: 47, 49; PEP, 1938: 222; Nicol, Millar and Sharland, 2009: 98). The Human Rights Act (1998) gave statutory force to the right of free expression, the Public Interest Disclosure Act (1998) protected people who exposed wrongdoing in their organizations and the Freedom of Information Act (2000) opened up previously hidden areas of government to journalistic scrutiny (Nicol, Millar and Sharland, 2009: 13, 41, 110; Curran and Seaton, 2010: 391). From the mid-twentieth century laws were enacted governing media ownership, which were increasingly framed with the agreement and often at the behest of newspaper companies (Collins and Murroni, 1996; Curran and Seaton, 2010; Freedman, 2008). Regulations embedded in statute and enforced by the courts were therefore the basis on which the media operated in the UK (Petley, 1999; Carey et al., 2007).

Self-regulation

In spite of the fact that by the 1940s regulation of the press was the norm, attempts from the 1940s onwards to establish statutory regulation of press standards provoked fierce resistance from the industry. The establishment of a voluntary, industry controlled, non-statutory General Council of the Press in 1953 came after three decades of discussion about how standards in the press had declined in the era of mass circulation and was meant to circumvent the threat of legislation. Yet its failure, and that of its successors (the Press Council, 1963–91, the Press Complaints Commission, 1991–2011), to raise standards plus continued examples of intrusion into grief and privacy and sensational and inaccurate reporting led to recurrent bouts of public debate. The debates usually ended up focusing around whether standards of journalistic practice and reporting should be overseen by the industry on a voluntary basis, or be supported by a statutory framework designed to make regulation effective. At key moments in the post-1945 debates – in 1953, 1962 and 1992 – when these matters were firmly in the public eye, the proprietors managed to persuade politicians that statutory rather than voluntary regulation would either constitute pre-publication censorship or be the first steps towards it. Statutory regulation of standards did not involve pre-publication censorship, as its supporters made clear, but it was nonetheless attacked as a return to the situation prior to 1695. This was argued in spite of the fact that pre-publication censorship had never disappeared and had arguably intensified in the twentieth century, often with the willing acquiescence of the industry. These kinds of debates were rooted more in questions about what discretion proprietors should be afforded to use publications to promote their economic and political ends, rather than in any accurate estimation of the role of the law in regulating the press (O'Malley and Soley, 2000; Leveson, 2012; Shannon, 2001).

Conclusion

The press has always been regulated. These regulations have changed according to circumstances. The lapse of pre-publication censorship was an important moment in the history of regulation and so too was the removal of the stamp, paper and advertisement duties. However, after 1800 the press became part of the economic and political structures of power, a fact which obviated the need for the kind of draconian pre-publication censorship of the seventeenth century. Both of the perspectives on the history of the press outlined earlier provide indispensable ways of understanding regulation. They need to be supplemented by the perspective developed here which sees regulation as a constant, if evolving, part of the relationship between the press and the state. Regulations are the point where the relationship between the state and the press has been negotiated and refined. The challenge for historians is to investigate the circumstances surrounding the origins, nature and impact of regulations and how they have shaped both the press and the development of British society with clear consequences for the present.

Further reading

F. S. Siebert's (1965) *Freedom of the Press in England 1476–1776* is a clear guide to early regulation. Debates in the twentieth century are detailed in Tom O'Malley and Clive Soley's (2000) *Regulating The Press* and Leveson's (2012) *An Inquiry into the Culture, Practices and Ethics of the Press*. Wilkinson's (2009) *Secrecy and the Media* is a revealing account of relations between the state and the press.

References

Aspinall, A. (1950) "Statistical accounts of the London newspapers, 1800–1836." *English Historical Review*, 65(255), 222–34.
Asquith, I. (1975) "Advertising and the Press in the late eighteenth and early nineteenth centuries: James Perry and the *Morning Chronicle* 1790–1821." *Historical Journal*, 18(4), 703–24.
Barker, H. (2000) *Newspapers, Politics and English Society 1695–1855*. Harlow: Longman.
Bingham, A. (2009) *Family Newspapers? Sex, Private Life, and the British Popular Press 1918–1978*. Oxford: Clarendon Press.

Boyce, G. (1978) "The fourth estate: The reappraisal of a concept." In G. Boyce, J. Curran and P. Wingate (eds.) *Newspaper History: From the 17th Century to the Present Day*. London: Constable (pp. 19–40).

Brown, L. (1985) *Victorian News and Newspapers*. Oxford: Clarendon Press.

Carey, P., Coles, P., Armstrong, N. and Lamont, D. (2007) *Media Law* (4th ed.). London, Sweet and Maxwell Ltd.

Collins, R. and Murroni, C. (1996) *New Media, New Policies. Media and Communications Strategies for the Future*. Cambridge: Polity.

Conboy, M. (2004) *Journalism. A Critical History*. London: Sage.

Cranfield, G. A. (1962) *The Development of the Provincial Newspaper 1700–1760*. Oxford: Clarendon Press.

Curran, J. (1978) "The Press as an agency of social control: An historical perspective." In G. Boyce, J. Curran and P. Wingate (eds.) *Newspaper History: From the 17th Century to the Present Day*. London: Constable (pp. 51–75).

——(1980) "Advertising as a patronage system." In H. Christian (ed.) *The Sociology of Journalism: University of Keele Sociological Review Monograph*, 29. Staffordshire: University of Keele (pp. 71–120).

——(2002) "Media and the making of British society, c. 1700–2000." *Media History*, 8(2) 135–54.

Curran, J. and Seaton, J. (2010) *Power Without Responsibility: Press, Broadcasting and the internet in Britain* (7th ed.). London: Routledge.

Freedman, D. (2008) *The Politics of Media Policy*. Cambridge: Polity.

Hampton, M. (2004) *Visions of the Press, 1850–1950*. Urbana and Chicago, IL: University of Illinois Press.

Harris, R. (1993) *A Patriot Press: National Politics and the London Press in the 1740s*. Oxford: Clarendon Press.

Holman, V. (2005) "Carefully concealed connections. The Ministry of Information and British publishing, 1939–46." *Book History*, 8(1), 197–226.

Koss, S. (1990) *The Rise and Fall of the Political Press in Britain*. London: Fontana Press.

Lee, A. (1976) *The Origins of the Popular Press in England 1855–1914*. London: Croom Helm.

Leveson, Lord (2012) An Inquiry into the Culture, Practices and Ethics of the Press. Volume 1. London: HMSO, HC780–81.

Lovelace, C. (1978) "British press censorship during the First World War." in G. Boyce, J. Curran, and P. Wingate (eds.) *Newspaper History: From the 17th Century to the Present Day*. London: Constable (pp. 306–19).

Luckhurst, T. (2013) "'Excellent but gullible people': The press and the people's convention." *Journalism Studies*, 14(1), 62–77.

Nicol A., Millar, G. and Sharland, A. (2009) *Media Law and Human Rights* (2nd ed.). Oxford: OUP.

O'Malley, T. and Soley, C. (2000) *Regulating The Press*. London: Pluto.

OUP (2013) *Oxford English Dictionary*. Oxford, Oxford University Press. Retrieved from http://www.oed.com

PEP (1938) *Report on the British Press*. London: Political and Economic Planning.

Petley, J. (1999) "The regulation of media content." In J. Stokes and A. Reading (eds.) *The Media in Britain: Current Debates and Developments*. London: Macmillan (pp. 143–57).

Putnis, P. (2008) "Share 999. British control of Reuters during World War 1." *Media History*, 14(2), 141–65.

Raithby, J. (1819) (ed.) *Statutes of the Realm: Volume 5, 1628–80*. British History Online. Retrieved from http://www.british-history.ac.uk/report.aspx?compid=47336

Robertson, G. (1991) *Freedom, The Individual and the Law* (6th ed.). London: Penguin.

Schweizer, K. (2006) "Introduction, parliament and the press: A case for synergy." In K. Schweizer (ed.) *Parliament and the Press 1689–c.1939*. Edinburgh: Edinburgh University Press (pp. 1–9).

Shannon, R. (2001) *A Press Free and Responsible: Self-regulation and the Press Complaints Commission 1991–2001*. London: John Murray.

Siebert, F. S. (1965) *Freedom of the Press in England 1476–1776: The Rise and Decline of Government Control*. Urbana, IL: University of Illinois Press.

Thompson, J. (1995) *The Media and Modernity*. Cambridge: Polity.

Wickwar, W. (1928) *The Struggle for the Freedom of the Press 1819–1832*. London: George Allen & Unwin Ltd Brothers.

Wiener, J. H. (1969) *The War of the Unstamped. The Movement to Repeal The British Newspaper Tax, 1830–1836*. Ithaca, NY and London: Cornell University Press.

Wilkinson, N. (2009) *Secrecy and the Media: The Official History of the United Kingdom's D-Notice System*. London: Routledge.

20
The provincial press in England
An overview

Rachel Matthews

It is not just Mark Twain who has been prematurely killed off. His riposte, to his own obituary in the *New York Journal* of 2 June 1897 that "the report of my death has been greatly exaggerated," might equally be applied to the provincial press. Few industries have been subject to such dire predictions as the local and regional newspaper industry. The current climate for local papers, often dismissed as 'rags', is no different. Typical of this is the attitude of media analysts FTI Consulting whose 2013 report tells of an industry in terminal decline; yet from other perspectives the provincial press remains successful. The website for the Newspaper Society (n.d.) lists 1,100 regional and local newspapers with 1,600 associated websites. The print products boast 31 million readers a week – more than the combined readership for the national press. And as I write, the business continues to yield substantial, albeit declining, profits.

There is no doubt that the provincial newspaper industry is part way through a transformation wrought by the digital revolution. These changes have not only undermined the traditional business model for local news but also "radically altered virtually every aspect of news gathering, writing and reporting" (Franklin, 2013: 1). As the Newspaper Society indicates, websites outnumber printed products but the inability of the industry to make money from their online titles has created a complex pattern of reactions.

However, this is not the first such shift for the provincial press for whom development in the face of changing circumstances is a defining characteristic. Jeremy Black argues that the provincial press is structurally related to notions of transience because of the nature of news. This enables it to shift and react to circumstances, be they social, political, economic or, indeed, technological. In this sense, change underpins the continuity of the industry (2001: 1).

We can identify key historical moments in the development of the provincial press by charting shifts in emphasis and form between elements, including business structure, content and professional practice. Some of these shifts may have promoted rapid change while others have had a slow but equally dramatic influence. Identifying these moments enables the development of the provincial press to be theorized in six distinct stages: first, the local newspaper as opportunistic creation;

second, the characterization of the local newspaper as fourth estate; third, the impact of New Journalism; fourth, the growth of chain control; fifth, the move to computerized production and the advent of free newspapers; and sixth, the phase currently under way: the provincial press in the digital age. Nerone and Barnhurst have similarly documented the development of the US press into six phases which are not distinct but which "have nestled within each other in complicated ways" (2003: 439). However, charting this typology does enable us to distinguish the contingent from the permanent in the history of provincial newspapers.

The provincial newspaper as opportunistic creation

The first provincial newspapers in England were produced by printers seeking to profit from the emerging need for news to facilitate trade which underpinned early industrial capitalism. These newspapers were entrepreneurial products filled with 'cut and paste' content from other publications and adverts for other business interests – such as 'quack' medicines – which were produced alongside the papers. One of the early publications was the *Bristol Post Boy*, which was probably founded in 1702. Two pages long, it consisted largely of news taken from papers brought from the capital via stagecoach (Penny, 2001).

By 1723 there were 24 recorded provincial papers in Britain (Black, 2001: 9), although, of the 150 papers founded in 60 cities in England from 1701 to 1760, half are thought to have lasted fewer than five years (Wiles, 1965: 25). Exact circulations for individual titles are hard to ascertain but Ferdinand (1997: 125) concludes that in the early 1700s, a sale of 200 copies was enough to keep a paper going. By the 1760s, the most successful papers had a sale of 3,000 to 4,000. These early papers were expensive – the equivalent of £15 each in today's money – and would be exchanged and read communally; readership figures therefore outstripped individual sales. Dedicated reading rooms, where people could pay to read newspapers, were extended to the provinces and in 1839 the *Leeds Mercury* estimated each of its copies was read by between 15 and 20 people (Walker, 2006: 377).

In 1725 the *Gloucester Journal* claimed to reach from Llandaff in South Wales to Trowbridge in Wiltshire, Ludlow in Shropshire and Wantage in Oxfordshire, while other papers would signify wide coverage via titles such as Jopson's *Coventry and Northampton Mercury*. As such, the content may not have been particularly 'local'. Black (2001) contends that most readers looked to their provincial paper to provide news of the wider world, while Andrew Walker suggests that local news only gained prominence in the latter decades of the eighteenth century when there were enough competing newspapers to focus circulation on more defined areas (2006: 376). However, Wiles charts local content in the *Norwich Post* in 1708 as including news of the city itself (1965: 255).

These producers of newspapers were not 'journalists' acting according to yet to be established professional norms such as checking facts. However, these titles did become established as serial (numbered) products, which appeared at set time intervals (usually, although not exclusively, weekly) and were characterized by the inclusion of time-sensitive information. In these ways, the newspaper was establishing for itself a prominent discursive function as the purveyor of 'news' via products which were a "generic hybrid between public information source, community identity and profit, which constitutes journalism" (Conboy, 2004: 42).

The characterization of the local newspaper as fourth estate

During the nineteenth century, the provincial newspaper developed into a low-cost, mass-circulation product. The infamous 'taxes on knowledge' had meant that newspaper ownership was restricted to those who could afford to stock up on the costly sheets of pre-stamped paper. These people often invested in newspapers for their social status and used them to campaign for the values of "polite society" (Gibb and Beckwith, 1954). They were also able to specialize and concentrate on the business of newspapers alone and so form a close relationship with the communities they sought to serve, creating a "local" press (Gardner, 2008: 57). Soon after the repeal of Stamp Duty in 1855, it became economically viable to use paper supplied in bulk on a roll and to feed it into the newly developed steam presses. The removal of taxation on adverts encouraged provincial newspaper owners to further invest in mechanizing composition with the introduction of the Linotype, first used in Britain by the *Newcastle Daily Chronicle* in 1889 (Milne, 1971: 27).

The repeal of Stamp Duty was followed by a dramatic rise in the number of titles in addition to new forms of provincial newspaper – the morning and evening press. Andrew Hobbs (2009) argues the provincial press formed a comprehensive communication network, enhanced via co-operation between titles, typified by the formation of the Provincial Newspaper Society in 1836, to represent the interests of owners, and the Press Association in 1868, which saw newspaper proprietors co-operate to disseminate domestic news (Hampton, 2004: 36).

Increasingly ownership passed to 'joint-stock' companies, whose shareholders were able to raise the necessary capital to fund titles. In the 1850s it was estimated to cost £10,000–£20,000 to set up a London daily; 20 years later this was put at £100,000. In 1881, Robert Spence Watson, the Liberal political manager of Newcastle, reckoned £30,000 to establish a northern daily. Titles were expected to make a profit and would generate around 50 per cent of their income from advertising (Lee, 1976). Key political figures, such as the Liberal Andrew Carnegie, sought to establish chains of newspapers with a political stance used as a selling point in an increasingly crowded market place. Milne suggests that politics was the 'lifeblood' of these papers, which were exploited by politicians because they were "cheap, immediate and regular" (1971: 13) at a time when the nation was debating the extension of the franchise. By the 1880s, the link between the provincial press and politics weakened as titles sought to build a mass circulation by widening their appeal (Lee, 1976: 162).

Significantly, the industry legitimized its social role within the rhetoric of the 'Fourth Estate'. Hampton refines this role into the more subtle "representative ideal", according to which newspapers reflect the concerns of the reading public and communicate those concerns to those in power (2004: 9). Their content, though, suggests that these papers were heavily politicized and didactic and Hampton suggests that the irony of this construction is that it "effectively removed the 'masses' from politics by public discussion" by speaking on their behalf (ibid.).

For those who owned these titles the epoch was one in which the purpose of ownership also shifted. From being a form of public service – exemplified by Hampton's conception of the "educational ideal" (2004: 9) – proprietorship shifted to become a business and journalism became a trade or profession (Lee, 1978: 118). News gathering and newspaper production were increasingly professionalized, using the then new technologies of the telegraph and railway, although the exact nature of what it meant to be a journalist was highly contested in a debate which still continues (see, for instance, Hampton, 2005; Conboy, 2011).

The impact of New Journalism

The next stage of development marks the emergence of key professional conventions, including the Inverted Pyramid. This is a narrative structure, usually for hard news, according to which the key information is included at the top of the story, which has come to define, and normalize, the practice of the journalist. For Pöttker this presentation improved the "communicative" (2005: 63) power of news as titles sought to attract mass readerships. Matheson (2000) suggests this content formed a recognizable 'news discourse', where information was presented in the third person, as 'fact' and in a recognizable news style.

Although objectivity had been identified as a professional standard for American journalists at this time, the same was not true for the English national and provincial papers. Hampton (2008) argues extensively that the English newspaper remained partisan in stance, while valuing standards of factual accuracy and 'fair play' – resulting in a characterization of the newspaper as 'watchdog'. For the provincial press this notion was refined so that increasingly the local newspaper positioned itself as speaking for its local community (Taylor, 2006).

These shifts in content and presentation are concomitant with an increased focus on commercialization. In turn, these values informed and influenced other aspects of newspaper practice to produce the style of newspaper termed 'New Journalism'. The term here describes the increased commercialization of the content of the English newspaper, including "a lightness of tone, and emphasis on the personal and the 'sensational' and reliance on gimmicks to sell newspapers in high-stakes circulation wars" (Hampton, 2004: 37). While historians of the press debate the extent and dates of this transformation, Hampton persuasively argues that for those involved the reassessment of journalism practice was very real (ibid.: 38).

Innovations in local newspaper content included the journalistic interview and improved production in terms of design, layout and the inclusion of pictures (Conboy, 2004: 15). The changes probably followed trends established by the national newspaper industry although Walker suggests that the waning of local political power prompted the provincial newspaper to reassess its content (2006: 384). Improved transport links brought London titles to the provinces in time for breakfast and the printing of London titles in the regions meant local titles had to differentiate themselves to maintain a market share (Packer, 2006). A study of the

Midland Daily Telegraph between 1895 and 1905 shows the title developing commercially to promote itself as an advertising medium within a defined circulation area. The relevance of editorial content to the newspaper's circulation area was also emphasized by improved labeling in headlines and subdecks. This made the title appear more local, although the actual amount of space devoted to local stories remained stable (Matthews, 2014). A significant area for development was local sport, which cemented a paper's relationship with its community and offered marketing opportunities via sponsorship and sporting supplements.

The growth of chain control

The period of 1914 to 1976 may be best understood in terms of an analysis of the business structure of provincial newspapers. Commercially motivated owners consolidated their positions by buying multiple titles to create monopolistic business models within defined circulation areas. As such, the industry came to be dominated by a few, huge enterprises. Among these was Northcliffe Newspapers, part of the Daily Mail and General Trust, which in 1947 owned titles within a network of concomitant regions including the south west and Wales (Bristol, Cheltenham, Gloucester and Swansea), the Midlands (Lincoln, Leicester, Stoke-on-Trent and Derby) and Humberside (Hull and Grimsby) (Camrose, 1947: 53). Equally significant were Kemsley Newspapers Ltd, Provincial Newspapers Ltd and the Westminster Press, formed through mergers and acquisitions among a close-knit group of associates. Between 1921 and 1946 these groups increased their total holding of titles from just under 15 percent of total titles to nearly 43 percent (Royal Commission on the Press, 1947–49: Appendix IV). This consolidation of ownership was interrupted only by the restrictions imposed by the two world wars, which, while significant, are outside of the scope of this study.

Murdock and Golding (1978) cite the first quarter of the twentieth century as the period in which the national press as we understand it became established. This created a competitive backdrop for the fight for dominance between provincial newspaper titles. Best equipped were those large companies who could resource costly circulation wars, often via the evening paper – a highly refined and profitable commercial product. The result was a fall in the overall number of daily titles from 196 in 1900 to 169 in 1920 as competitors were closed. At the same time circulations – and profits – increased, making this a battle worth fighting. By 1974 the top ten newspaper groups controlled 81 percent of all provincial newspaper circulations. Increasingly these companies were structured in terms of 'publishing centers' from which multiple titles were produced in order to control costs and maximize profits (Hartley, Gudgeon and Crafts, 1977: 31).

Lee (1976) has characterized this era as one in which the philanthropic ideal underpinning the ownership of the Victorian press gives way to ownership for profit alone. This resulted in an increasing polarization between the 'millionaire owners' and the artisan workforce, which drew on the discursive construction of the press as a democratic organ to oppose consolidation. By 1931, of 9,000 journalists and photographers employed in newspapers, some 6,600 were members of the National Union of Journalists; a further 2,700 were members of the Institute of Journalists (PEP,

1938: 12–13). These two organizations epitomized competing constructions of journalism between those who saw it as an open trade and those who sought to define it as a profession, protected by Royal Charter. The print shops, employing 29,000 men, were nearly totally unionized, usually via membership of the London Society of Compositors or the National Society of Operative Printers and Assistants (Natsopa) (PEP, 1938: 15–16). These unions campaigned for improved pay and conditions and the NUJ pay structure recognized the career path of journalists who trained on local titles before progressing to national newspapers. The interests of employers were represented by the Newspaper Proprietors' Association (later to become the Newspaper Publishers Association), formed in 1908, the continuation of the Newspaper Society for provincial owners and editors, and the formation of the Joint Industrial Council to negotiate with the unions. This polarization of employee and employer was probed, somewhat inconclusively, in no fewer than three Royal Commissions into press ownership between 1947 and 1977. The first responded to the NUJ which argued that consolidation threatened the freedom of the press; the union sought to emphasize this role by co-operating with the Newspaper Society to set standards for training and conduct.

Writing of the regional press in the inter-war years, Bromley and Hayes (2002) suggest that this commercial context acted as a liberating force, creating a 'democracy of print'. Coinciding with a 'golden age' for local government, regional papers "offered *the ubiquitous civic voice*: vital yet distanced from partisanship" which scrutinized and held to account those in power (ibid.: 197). However, they suggest that this attempt to reconcile distant ownership with an editorial focus on the "parish pump" is essentially paradoxical (ibid.). Franklin and Murphy (1991) go further, reducing the ideological construction of the provincial press as a community watchdog to a functional tool which aligns the interests and definitions of that community with commercial success; as such it is open to compromise for the interests of profit.

The move to computerized production and the advent of free newspapers

Industrial relations within the provincial newspaper industry were radically restructured by the introduction of computerized production methods in the 1970s and 1980s. The innovations were made against a backdrop of rising production costs and increased competition for advertising revenue from television, radio and the then new media platforms such as Oracle and Ceefax, which prefigured the arrival of the digital newspaper. Newspapers were also increasingly the products of diversified businesses, for which publishing was just one interest among many. Reed International Ltd, for instance, produced paint, furniture and wallpaper as well as books and newspapers via subsidiaries as far afield as Australia, Canada and South Africa (Hartley, Gudgeon and Crafts, 1977: 141).

These innovations, which enabled journalists to typeset their own text, enabled titles to reduce wage costs significantly by emasculating the once dominant print unions. This was facilitated by the Conservative Thatcher administration, which sought to challenge the power of the unions in Britain. This political stance was backed by anti-union legislation – including the Employment Acts of 1980 and 1982 – which restricted the rights of unions to picket and enabled employers to take action for damages against them. This was tested by a dispute between Eddie Shah and the print unions in Warrington (Gennard, 1990: 485).

Computerization also facilitated the production of free newspaper titles, ranging from 'shopper' titles which carried adverts alone, to sophisticated newspapers indistinguishable from their paid for counterparts. Goodhart and Wintour (1986) chart the origin of the free newspaper in the UK back to Lionel Pickering, who brought the newspaper form from Australia where it was well established. He set up the *Derby Trader* in 1966 with just £4,800 in capital; by 1986 he had 10 titles turning over £10 million a year with a 10 percent profit margin (ibid.: 86). Most free titles were run on a shoestring with minimal editorial and administration costs, yet offered blanket coverage of an area to advertisers.

Such was the success of the free newspaper business model that established companies adopted it, including Reed Regional Newspapers, which by 1991 was publishing 100 free titles with an aggregate circulation of 5.8 million. Reed launched a free daily title in 1984, the Birmingham-based *Daily News*, which at its peak employed around 40 journalists. Although the number of free titles fluctuated with the economic climate, Franklin and Murphy (1991) cite a total of 1,156 titles in 1991 with a circulation of 43.5 million.

The first fully computerized newspaper in England was the *Reading Evening Post*, which was created from a pre-existing weekly title by Thomson Regional Newspapers Ltd (Royal Commission on the Press, 1977: 42). Arguments around the introduction of new technology focused on the effect on skilled labor, particularly the print workers represented by the National Graphic Association, who were effectively made redundant by the move to 'direct input' by editorial and advertising workers (Gennard, 1990). The status of editorial workers might at this point have increased because of their centrality to the production process and the NUJ was successful in implementing agreements in a substantial number of workplaces (Noon, 1991). However, the greater demands were not met by greater salaries (Franklin and Murphy, 1991: 14) because the free newspaper had effectively undermined the relationship between editorial quality and circulations. For Simpson (1981) editorial became one cost to be controlled among many and this disruption subsumed the social role of newspaper to one of profit alone. This paved the way for the 'asset-stripping' mentality of conglomerates, exemplified by Reed International which reduced two weekly papers staffed by 25 people to one free sheet with one reporter (Franklin and Murphy, 1991: 50). In this way, the promise of new technology to potentially increase the plurality of provincial newspaper titles was not realized. Instead publishers increased dominance in a local market by rationalizing products and widening the area of their monopolistic hold. This resulted in a provincial press which was increasingly homogenized and less local.

The provincial press in the digital age

The challenges faced by the provincial newspaper industry to date stem from the disruption brought by the advent of the digital age to the dual business model of selling news to readers and readers to advertisers. Local news can be accessed online for free but advertisers have not followed, reducing the revenue stream of the "print pound" to the "digital penny" (House of Commons, 2013: 3). This disruption has been exacerbated by the global recession which has affected advertising revenues. Nel (2013) charts this decline in the context of the Johnston Press. In 2007, the company owned 315 local and regional newspapers, of which 18 were daily titles; by 2012, this had fallen by 29 percent to 13 daily and 214 weekly papers and staff had nearly halved from 7,538 to 3,960. Print advertising fell sharply from £425.8 million to £181.3 million while digital revenues rose from £15.1 million to £20.6 million in the same period (ibid.: 9).

This current decline has prompted dire warnings, such as that from the analyst Enders who predicted a 50 percent fall in the number of regional newspaper titles between 2007 and 2013 (Nel, 2013: 9). The forecast is predicated largely on a continued strategy of increased integration and consolidation of titles by the major companies noted above. This operational cost cutting extended to reduction in staffing levels, the closure of local offices and centralization, for instance with the concentration of production into 'regional hubs', typified by that created by Newsquest in Newport to produce its Welsh and Gloucestershire titles (Hollander, 2013). For critics the effect of these changes is a local press which is 'local' in name only. Bob Franklin (2006) charts the increasing reliance of journalists on information subsidies, such as press releases, which inhibits their ability to scrutinize local power holders. More recently he suggests that news which is free at the point of delivery needs to be cheap to produce – so repurposed rather than original – leaving democratically significant areas such as councils and courts out as they are too costly to cover (Franklin, 2012: 601).

This has sparked concerns over the ability of local titles to serve the interests of their communities, which in turn has prompted a re-imagining of the structure and form of the provincial news industry. Innovations include changes in the form of ownership of traditional titles, exemplified by the *West Highland Free Press*, which was bought by its employees in 2009. On a larger scale is Local World Limited, a new company formed in 2012 from a partnership between Iliffe News and Media and Northcliffe Media, with Trinity Mirror holding a stake. Sir Ray Tindle, among the top ten publishers of local newspapers in Britain, has an 'ultra-local' philosophy, typified by his approach to the *Tenby Observer*, which was rescued through an insistence on content about Tenby only.

Increasing dissemination of content across digital and mobile platforms has consequences for both the content of those products and the working practices of the journalists producing them. Reporters are already expected to produce content across platforms (Skillset, 2007) and increasingly will be expected to edit and publish their own work, subverting the traditional chain of reporter–news editor–sub-editor–editor. Organizing content produced from other sources is also expected to become part of the reporter's workload. These changes, like the introduction of direct input before them, are not being made without opposition. In May 2013 the chairman of Local World, David Montgomery, caused consternation when he described journalists going out on a story as 'wasteful' and instead envisioned them as content managers and publishers (House of Commons, 2013: 4).

Research by the Media Trust (2010) suggests that the need for "local quality news and journalism" is a crucial factor in enabling people to access information about where they live and identify with those around them. Trying to meet this need has led to an explosion in hyper-local news providers. The vast majority of these operate via websites or mobile apps, which may concentrate on just one postcode area. Research suggests there were 432 active hyper-local websites in May 2012 but acknowledges that it is a 'dynamic' environment which shifts on a daily basis (Harte, 2012: 2). These news forms have attracted interest and funding from charitable and research sources because of the perceived solution they offer for the provision of local information. These sites are not necessarily staffed by professional journalists, or even by people who see themselves as journalists (Jones and Salter, 2012: 99). This signals a move to a 'mixed economy journalism' where non-professional 'citizen journalists' form networks with the professionals who collect and curate the news flow.

Conclusion

The latest challenges placed upon the provincial news industry by digital technology have far reaching implications not only for the business model of the industry, but also for those who work within it and what is expected of them. Canter suggests that the very nature of the journalist's 'top-down' approach to information dissemination is restructured by Web 2.0 technology, which has transformed readers into "prosumers, contributors and collaborators" (2013: 4). It is this networked, digital environment in which journalism has come to operate which is challenging its relationship with its audience and ultimately the role of the journalist and even those who may be defined as journalists (Franklin, 2012: 599).

Conboy (2004: 3) suggests that understanding journalism as a discursive process enables us to consider its concrete forms, including the provincial press, as social objects whose definition is a manifestation of the operation of those competing for power. This approach to the regional press enables us to examine claims which the journalism profession would have us take as constant principles, such as that of existing to promote the 'good of the town' or that of the local paper as the 'watchdog' of the local arena. This is particularly useful at times of change such as now, when these roles are being challenged and contested. Instead we can examine whose interests claims to an historic continuity serve, which in turn informs the debate about the significance of change. As Conboy (ibid.: 7) suggests, "the present forms of journalism bear all the hallmarks of these historical influences. That is why history is so important to understanding the journalism of the present day."

Further reading

Bob Franklin has written extensively on the local press. His work with David Murphy *What News? The Market, Politics and the Local Press* (1991) remains an accessible and thought-provoking assessment of the significance of local papers. His edited volume *Local Journalism and Local Media* (2006) brings together a range of scholars to explore the issues in this area. Mark Hampton's *Visions of the Press in Britain, 1850–1950* (2004) employs an historical approach to analyze our understanding of newspapers.

References

Black, J. (2001) *The English Press 1621–1821*. Stroud: Sutton Publishing.
Bromley, M. and Hayes, N. (2002) "Campaigner, watchdog or municipal lackey? Reflections on the inter-war provincial press, local identity and civic welfarism." *Media History*, 8(2), 197–212.
Camrose, Viscount (1947) *British Newspapers and their Controllers*. London: Cassell.
Canter, L. (2013) "The source, the resources and the collaborator: The role of citizen journalism in local UK newspapers." *Journalism*, 14(8), 1091–109.
Conboy, M. (2004) *Journalism: A Critical History*. London: Sage.
——(2011) *Journalism in Britain: A Historical Introduction*. London: Sage.
Ferdinand, C. Y. (1997) *Benjamin Collins and the Provincial Newspaper Trade in the Eighteenth Century*. Oxford: Clarendon Press.
Franklin, B. (2006) *Local Journalism and Local Media* (2nd ed.). London: Routledge.
——(2012) "The future of journalism." *Journalism Practice*, 6(5–6), 595–613.
——(2013) "Editorial." *Digital Journalism*, 1(1), 1–5.
Franklin, B. and Murphy, D. (1991) *What News? The Market, Politics and the Local Press*. Routledge: London.
FTI Consulting (2013) *Rags in Tatters* [white paper], 21 March.
Gardner, V. E. M. (2008) *Newspaper Proprietors and the Business of Newspaper Publishing in Provincial England, 1760–1820*. DPhil Thesis, University of Oxford.
Gennard, J. (1990) *A History of the National Graphical Association*. London: Unwin Hyman.
Gibb, M. A. and Beckwith, F. (1954) *The Yorkshire Post: Two Centuries*. Leeds: The Yorkshire Conservative Newspaper Company.
Goodhart, D. and Wintour, P. (1986) *Eddie Shah and the Newspaper Revolution*. Sevenoaks: Coronet.
Hampton, M. (2004) *Visions of the Press in Britain, 1850–1950*. Urbana and Chicago, IL: University of Illinois Press.
——(2005) "Defining journalists in late nineteenth-century Britain." *Critical Studies in Media Communication*, 22(2), 138–55.
——(2008) "The objectivity ideal and its limitations in 20th-century British journalism." *Journalism Studies*, 9(4), 477–93.
Harte, D. (2012) *Hyperlocal Publishing in the UK*. Retrieved from www.creativecitizens.co.uk
Hartley, N., Gudgeon, P. and Crafts, R. (1977) *Concentration of Ownership in the Provincial Press*. Cmnd. 6810-15. Her Majesty's Stationery Office.
Hobbs, A. (2009) "When the provincial press was the national press (c 1836–1900)." *International Journal of Regional and Local Studies*, 5(1), 16–43.
Hollander, G. (2013) "Eight sub-editor jobs at risk as Newsquest plans single Wales and Glos editing hub." Retrieved from www.pressgazette.co.uk
House of Commons Culture, Media and Sport Committee (2013) "Press Regulation." Uncorrected Transcript of Oral Evidence HC143-i.
Jones, J. and Salter, L. (2012) *Digital Journalism*. London: Sage.
Lee, A. J. (1976) *The Origins of the Popular Press in England*. London: Croom Helm Ltd.

——(1978) "The structure, ownership and control of the press." In G. Boyce, J. Curran and P. Wingate (eds.) (1978) *Newspaper History from the Seventeenth Century to the Present Day*. London: Constable (pp. 117–29).
Matheson, D. (2000) "The Birth of news discourse: Changes in new language in British newspapers, 1880–1930." *Media Culture Society*, 22(5), 557–73.
Matthews, R. (2014) "The emergence of the news paradigm in the English provincial press: A case study of the *Midland Daily Telegraph*." *Journal of Historical Pragmatics*, 15(2), 165–86
Media Trust (2010) "Meeting the news needs of local communites." Retrieved from www.mediatrust.org
Milne, M. (1971) *The Newspapers of Northumberland and Durham*. Newcastle upon Tyne: Frank Graham.
Murdock, G. and Golding, P. (1978) "The structure, ownership and control of the press, 1914–76." In G. Boyce, J. Curran and P. Wingate (eds.) *Newspaper History from the Seventeenth Century to the Present Day*. London: Constable (pp. 130–48).
Nel, F. (2013) "Pressed to change." Case study for NEMODE, an initiative under the Research Council UK Digital Economy Programme. Preston: University of Central Lancashire.
Nerone, J. and Barnhurst, K. G. (2003) "US newspaper types, the newsroom, and the division of labor, 1750–2000." *Journalism Studies*, 4(4), 435–49.
Newspaper Society (n.d.) Retrieved from http://www.newspapersoc.org.uk
Noon, M. (1991) "Strategy and circumstance: The success of the NUJ's new technology policy." *British Journal of Industrial Relations*, 29(2), 259–76.
Packer, I. (2006) "A curious exception? The *Lincolnshire Chronical* and the 'Starmer Group'." *Journalism Studies*, 7(3), 415–26.
Penny, J. (2001) *All the News That's Fit to Print. A Short History of Bristol's Newspapers Since 1702*. Bristol: Bristol Branch of the Historical Association.
Political and Economic Planning (1938) "Report on the British press." London: PEP.
Pöttker, H. (2005) "The news pyramid and its origin form the American journalism in the 19th century." In S. Høyer and H. Pöttker (eds.) *Diffusion of the News Paradigm 1850–2000*. Goteborg: Nordicom.
Royal Commission on the Press (1947–49) "Report." Her Majesty's Stationery Office.
——(1977) "Evidence submitted by Thomson Regional Newspapers Ltd, 14OE1." May 1975.
Simpson. D. H. (1981) *Commercialisation of the Regional Press: The Development of Monopoly, Profit and Control*. Aldershot: Gower Publishing Company Ltd.
Skillset (2007) "National occupational standards for journalism." Retrieved from www.creativeskillset.org
Taylor, J. (2006) "'Town' versus 'gown': The establishment of the *Cambridge Daily News* as a modern newspaper at the end of the 19th century." *Journalism Studies*, 7(3), 403.
Walker, A. (2006) "The development of the provincial press in England c. 1780–1914: An overview." *Journalism Studies*, 7(3), 373–86.
Wiles, R. M. (1965) *Freshest Advices: Early Provincial Newspapers in England*. Columbus, OH: Ohio State University Press.

21
Online and on death row
Historicizing newspapers in crisis
Tim Luckhurst

In 2003 Martin Amis published his comic novel *Yellow Dog* and, characteristically, he invented a character through whom to explore a subject dear to his heart: the cynicism of the popular newspaper press. His fictional reporter, Clint Smoker of the *Morning Lark*, writes columns excusing rapists ("the bird was wearing *a school uniform*") and is eventually sacked for celebrating the first sexual adventure of a teenage princess in a column opining "'Hi, *men!*' With these words Princess Vicky kissed goodbye to her catflap – and nun too soon says the *Lark*" (Amis, 2003: 319). The *Lark* is the worst kind of scandal sheet, a *Daily Sport*[1] spoof where journalists refer to their readers as 'wankers' and pander to their tastes no matter how depraved. In Smoker's version of a Marxist analysis "the quality broadsheets are aimed at the establishment and the intelligentsia. The upmarket tabloids are aimed at the bourgeoisie. The downmarket tabloids are aimed at the proletariat. At the *Lark* our target wanker is *unemployed*" (Amis, 2003: 71). Amis's satire pre-empts by nearly a decade the worst allegations advanced against newspapers by witnesses at the Leveson Inquiry, but it understands a core problem addressed there: popular newspapers' willingness to mould their culture in pursuit of profit. The same problem has intrigued historians of journalism for three times as long.

Radical versus liberal history

During that period, the liberal narrative that dominated British histories of journalism from the nineteenth century until the 1970s was challenged by writers of radical media theory. These scholars, inspired by Boyce's essay "The fourth estate: the reappraisal of a concept" (1978), and informed above all by the work of James Curran, base their view of journalism's recent past on the argument that mainstream journalism did not, as liberals believe, escape from official control in the mid nineteenth century. Instead, it continued to serve the interests of economic and social elites (Curran, 2009). Why freedom should inspire newspapers to promote radical causes remains a mystery to liberals, but the radicals' confidence that it should has changed discourse around the regulation of journalism in Britain. Radical media history has provided campaigners against an unregulated newspaper market with an intellectual rationale for reform: the market does not produce journalism designed for the primary purpose of informing the public sphere, they argue, it seeks profit above other goals. Therefore regulation may improve it. Professor Julian Petley (2009: 185) makes this case explicit, arguing that "the British daily and Sunday national press, far from being a watchdog over the establishment, is actually a crucial part of it." Professor Petley is Chair of the Campaign for Press and Broadcasting Freedom and a campaigner for press regulation.[2] Barnett and Gaber (2001) and Fenton (2010: 13) embrace it. Professors Barnett and Fenton are members of the Board of Directors of Hacked Off,[3] the not-for-profit company that led calls for the establishment of the Leveson Inquiry, supported its proceedings and endorsed its findings. Jewell (2013) summarizes it in his account of proposals to regulate newspapers since 1945.

Supporters of regulation underpinned by statute use this version of history to attack the three-centuries-old consensus that British newspapers should not be regulated by parliament. It helps them to overlook the distinctive nature of British democracy that makes statutory underpinning contentious here. Sir Brian Leveson (2012) reflected this transition from a liberal to a radical explanation in his report. It informed his explanation that:

> A free press contains within itself immense power to promote democratic freedoms and the public good. It also contains within itself the reverse potential, that is to say, to create undemocratic concentrations of power and undermine freedoms and the public good.
>
> (Leveson, 2012a)

The histories from which Leveson's narrative borrows have in common a view of mass-market journalism that risks underestimating its power to inform public discussion. Hampton warns that this perspective may be produced through minimal attention to empirical evidence and that it often reveals more about the author's theoretical perspective than the contents of popular newspapers (Hampton, 2009: 30).

Leveson distinguishes between free speech and the freedom to publish on the grounds that: "Freedom for commercial mass media businesses ('corporate speech') is a very different proposition from the freedom of individual self-expression ('personal speech')" (Leveson, 2012b). This reductive dichotomy reflects Curran's assertion about the emergence of popular newspapers that: "The freedom conferred by the free market was the freedom of capital to indoctrinate labour" (Curran, 1978: 60). Curran has moved beyond such caricature and acknowledges "the mind-numbing narrowness of too much media history" (2009: 20). For Leveson the caricature serves. It allows him to assert that statutory underpinning of newspaper regulation poses no threat to free speech: a view that remains anathema to some liberals, including me.

A liberal critique of Leveson

I set out my basic argument in *Responsibility without Power* (Luckhurst, 2012). A key aspect of it is that in Britain executive and legislature are not separate as they are in the United States of America and other constitutional democracies. British ministers sit in both Houses of Parliament and lead a majority in the House of Commons. This gives a British government unparalleled power to ensure its legislation is passed. To balance that power the UK has developed a system in which additional checks and balances are exercised in the public interest by the courts and the press. This reality has helped to persuade every government since 1945 not to permit statutory underpinning of press regulation. The intriguing question, which this chapter seeks to address, is why Lord Justice Leveson's findings should convince modern politicians to embrace it.

In the decade after *Yellow Dog* was published the concept of newspapers as "feral beasts" (Blair, 2007) deserving of external regulation was already established in the public sphere, but for newspaper proprietors and journalists it was just one item on a list of challenges. By 2013, crises of technology, professionalism and ethics had converged to place Britain's newspaper industry in the eye of a storm. The impact of the internet and social media saw millions of former and potential purchasers of printed newspapers opt to consume them free online or not at all. The authority and practices of professional journalism were challenged by amateur bloggers. Meanwhile, concerns generated by the hacking of the murdered schoolgirl Milly Dowler's mobile telephone by journalists at the *News of the World* spawned the fifth review of press regulation commissioned by the legislature since 1945. At its conclusion, Sir Brian Leveson recommended an ostensibly oxymoronic solution: self-regulation within a statutory framework. There should, he said, "be legislation to underpin the independent self-regulatory system and facilitate its recognition in legal processes" (Leveson, 2012c). This raised the question: would the state, this time, reverse liberal tradition and hold the fourth estate forcibly to account?

In March 2013 the three main parties in parliament agreed to use a Royal Charter to establish an independent press regulator with powers to fine newspapers and force them to publish apologies for wrongdoing. This agreement, passed by a majority of 517 in the House of Commons, was underpinned by a clause inserted into the Enterprise and Regulatory Reform Bill by the House of Lords which means that the Charter cannot be amended without the consent of a two-thirds majority in both Houses of Parliament. It is plain that there is a consensus in parliament in favour of press regulation underpinned by a statutory guarantee. Less clear is the reasoning behind this historic shift from parliament's previous view that independence from the state is essential to the well-being of a free press and Britain's representative democracy.

For Leveson, the answer is plain: his corporate speech/personal speech distinction justifies it and is justified by the radical narrative of media history. To historians, his rigid dichotomy should be at least contentious. Addressing the same distinction, Winston (2005) offers a different analysis:

> [O]f those freedoms which progressives of [Thomas] Paine's time deemed 'celestial' none is greater than the individual's freedom of expression. This is especially so when it is used to address others in the mass and therefore '[T]he liberty of the press is the palladium of all civil, political and religious rights,' (as the eighteenth-century radical who wrote under the pen-name 'Junius' put it).
> (Winston, 2005: xi)

Harcup (2013) recognises that freedom to address others in large numbers has facilitated the participation and empowerment promoted by radical and alternative journalism. Indeed, if one of mass-market journalism's failures is a tendency to privilege the opinions of the powerful, an effective antidote must involve offering alternative opinion similar access to the public sphere. Popular mass-market journalism has provided this service more often and more effectively than radical media history allows.

Bingham (2012: 312) observes that "entrenched stereotypes [have] prevented historians from properly understanding the nature of popular newspapers." He notes that such titles are "too important for their role to be assessed on the basis of assumption and stereotype" and that assumptions about "depoliticization" and "tabloidization" have been too readily used to excuse failure to consider in detail newspaper content (ibid.). Nicholson (2013: 61) reminds us that the archives of twentieth-century newspapers exist in a "remote and unvisited shadowland" because little of their content is available in digital form. This combination of failure and difficulty contributes to the view that popular newspapers exert an exclusively conservative or reactionary impact on their readers in line with the corporate capitalist interests of their proprietors. Radical scholars advance this view; Leveson embraced it. It ignores Hampton's (2009) call for empirical exploration of the press's real contribution to public debate. It overlooks existing analyses of newspaper content.

Bingham (2012: 314–15) shows that popular newspapers have rarely been as trivial or predictable as their critics suggest. They often surprise and challenge their readers. He offers in evidence coverage of 1950s and 1960s general elections in the *Daily Mail* and *Daily Express* and post-First World War encouragement of women's suffrage in the *Daily News* and *Daily Mirror*. My own scrutiny of newspaper support for dissident opinion during the Second World War (Luckhurst, 2013) reveals an editorial stance capable of contributing to the formation of informed opinion. Liberal historians cannot be complacent; Hampton (2009: 34) reminds us that "the press has better filled a liberal role in some cases than in others, and always imperfectly." Our confidence that, far from infantilizing their readers, popular newspapers facilitate public discussion of ideas is not absolute. It would be crass to suggest that popular newspapers' sole or principle purpose is to promote representative democracy. But liberal historians do not need to pretend that markets are infallible, or that a free market in journalism is perfect, to demonstrate that popular newspapers are capable of serving the greatest good of the greatest number. During the twentieth century they routinely contributed news and opinion that encouraged political debate.

Among the assumptions relied upon by those who support Leveson's recommendations is that popular newspapers in the twenty-first century are worse than they have ever been. However, while it is true that new technology has permitted new sins such as phone hacking, it would be wrong to assume that they represent an unprecedented nadir in the ethics and practices of British journalism. Bingham (2009) identifies three twentieth-century moments when demands for regulation of the press approached fever pitch and proposals for statutory regulation were debated in parliament. These occurred in the mid 1920s, when concerns arose about newspaper coverage of divorce cases, in the 1950s over treatment of sex and in the 1980s over intrusive reporting. Moral condemnation of popular journalism predates Hacked Off by more than a century; opinion formers including Queen Victoria, Keir

Hardie, Stanley Baldwin, Winston Churchill, Ernest Bevin and F. R. Leavis attacked popular newspapers for debasing cultural values or diverting the masses from their proper political concerns.

On each occasion newspapers defended themselves with arguments still familiar today. They claimed to be accountable to the tastes of their readers who would choose to buy them or not according to whether they were offended by their content. They explained that in order to inform newspapers must also entertain for if they did not, their journalism would not reach a large enough readership to fulfil its duty to the public sphere. When pressure became intense, editors articulated arguments of constitutional principle warning that regulation empowered by the state would place editorial freedom on a slippery slope down which it might slide were ministers with censorious instincts to take office. Self-interested as they may appear, these arguments repeatedly defeated the case for state regulation. Even when deliberately provoked, such as when the Labour-supporting *Daily Mirror* criticized Labour ministers in Britain's wartime coalition for behaving "like pale imitations of Tory Ministers" and condemned the coalition for leaving the people's grievances unanswered (*Daily Mirror*, 1941), a majority in parliament accepted the press's duty to hold power to account.

Use and abuse of history

Writing about the violent aftermath of the Second World War, Lowe notes that:

> Those who wish to harness hatred and resentment for their own gain always try to distort the proper balance between one version of history and another. They take events out of context; they make blame a one-sided game; and they try to convince us that historical problems are the problems of today.
> (Lowe, 2012: 377)

Media history is a relatively new branch of an established discipline. As it matures it should seek to appreciate a similar flaw in its treatment of newspaper history. Radical media historians have composed a version of the growth of popular journalism which serves the purposes of campaigners who are determined to depict the freedom of the press as liberty to exploit and mislead. Organizations including Hacked Off, The Campaign for Press and Broadcasting Freedom, and the Media Standards Trust use this description to justify state involvement in the regulation of newspapers. Throughout the era of participatory democracy, British politicians rejected such involvement. That they have chosen to embrace it in the second decade of the twenty-first century risks treating historical problems as if they are contemporary.

An unprecedented crisis

News printed on paper faces an existential crisis. Print circulation of British newspapers has declined spectacularly since 2000. Between May and October 2000 the market-leading *Sun* achieved a daily average sale of 3,624,882 copies. Its rival, the *Daily Mirror*, sold 2,217,240 copies. In the mid-market, the *Daily Mail* sold 2,337,262 copies and the *Daily Express* 994,695. Among elite titles the *Daily Telegraph* sold 977,496 copies, *The Times* 679,434 and *The Guardian* 385,702 (Audit Bureau of Circulations, n.d.). Figures published in March 2013 show that between September 2012 and February 2013: the *Sun* achieved an average sale of 2,360,915 copies; the *Daily Mirror* 1,052,474; the *Daily Mail* 1,860,653; the *Daily Express* 534,173; the *Daily Telegraph* 552,065; *The Times* 400,060; and *The Guardian* 202,272. So, the *Sun's* average sale fell by 1,263,967 copies, leaving it in 2013 with 65 percent of the circulation it had 13 years earlier, a decline of 35 percent. The *Mirror* lost 1,164,766 daily sales, leaving it with 47 percent of its previous circulation, a decline of 53 percent. The *Mail* performed relatively strongly, recording a 20 percent decline in sales over the period, a loss of 476,609 copies per day. The *Daily Express* lost 460,522 sales or 41 percent of its circulation in 2000. The *Daily Telegraph's* circulation fell by 44 percent or 425,431 copies, *The Times* by 41 percent or 279,374 copies and *The Guardian* by 48 percent or 183,430 copies. Severe circulation declines affected local and regional newspapers and advertising revenue declined precipitously.

Lee (1976: 50) tells us that, in 1863, an observer of the market for newspapers stimulated by parliament's abolition of advertising, paper and stamp duties noted: "Just as there are men who must have race-horses, or play chicken-hazard [a dice game played for small stakes], so there are others to whom newspaper enterprise is a necessity of life." The caveat is that, for an entrepreneur with a good business plan, starting a newspaper was less risky than gambling. Space in a successful title could be sold twice – once to the reader and once to advertisers – ensuring a dual income stream that would later be described as "a license to print money" (Peers, 2008).

The value of that licence has been threatened before. In the 1920s newspaper proprietors objected to competition from radio broadcasting. Nicholas (2000) shows how they obtained guarantees that the BBC would not be permitted to operate as an independent news provider, thus evading temporarily the threat that radio news might undermine newspaper sales. Radio advertising was prohibited to protect the newspapers' other income stream. However, the biggest cause of newspaper closures in the interwar years was intense competition between mass-market, national popular newspapers such as the *Daily Express*, *Daily Mail*, *Daily Mirror* and *Daily Herald*. Provincial daily titles were hardest hit. Overall, both newspaper circulation and radio listening rose during the interwar years, but BBC broadcasting changed the style and content of newspapers (Nicholas, 2000: 136–37). From the 1950s, the growth of television generated competition for viewers/readers and, following the launch of ITV in September 1955, for advertising revenue. Advertisers now had a choice of media and competition for their business helped them to keep advertising rates down. The proportion of newspaper income earned through advertising fell. To these factors were added steep increases in the wages of journalists and print workers and in the price of essential materials such as newsprint (the paper on which newspapers are printed). Price per imperial ton for newsprint rose from £11 in 1939 to £28 in 1945, to £53 in 1955 and to £250 in 1977 (Lee, 1978: 134). Newspapers increased their cover prices in response. These pressures brought about consequences newspapers had feared at the birth of radio. Aggregate circulation of national dailies declined from a peak of nearly 17 million in the 1950s to just over 14 million in the final months of 1976. Sunday circulation fell from 28.3 million in 1947 to 19.6 million (Lee, 1978: 133–34). The terms of reference issued to the 1974 Royal Commission on the Press required it to "inquire into the factors affecting the maintenance of the independence, diversity and editorial standards of newspapers" and to do so "with particular reference" to the economics of newspaper publishing and distribution (Hansard, 1974: 1322–32).

So, like the Leveson Inquiry, each previous moral crisis in the history of newspapers occurred when newspaper journalism faced a commercial challenge. In most cases this challenge was augmented by the advent of a new medium: radio in the 1920s; television in the 1950s; multichannel satellite television in the 1980s – described by Rupert Murdoch as "the most important single advance since Caxton invented the printing press (sic)" (Murdoch, 1984). But the challenge of the internet is qualitatively different. While new technologies challenged newspapers' circulation and profitability during previous periods of concern about newspaper ethics, the economic pressures on newspapers in the years immediately preceding the Leveson Inquiry were unprecedented. In the early years of the twenty-first century the licence to print money was revoked.

Three examples illustrate the scale of the financial crisis widespread in British newspapers and common throughout the developed democracies. Between 2004 and 2009, Johnston Press, owner of 13 daily newspapers, 154 paid-for weekly newspapers and 37 free weeklies in the UK and Ireland (Johnston Press, 2013) experienced the loss of 97 percent of its market value. Its peak equity value of £1.547 billion in 2004 had plummeted to just £47 million in 2009, a decline of £1.5 billion (Fenton, 2009). The Guardian Media Group, parent company to Guardian News and Media, the owner of *The Guardian*, reported operating losses of £53.9 million in 2010, £54.5 million in 2011 and £75.6 million in 2012 (Marshall, 2012). Meanwhile, Enders Analysis, a research service providing independent analyses of the media industry, foresaw continuing declines in popular and mid-market display advertising spend and considerable difficulties in the national and regional press. It concluded that "double digit declines both last year [2012] and this year [2013] are now a very real possibility" (Enders Analysis, 2013a).

The readers and advertisers who once cherished printed newspapers did not simply disappear. Today they read and advertise on newspaper websites, sometimes in very large numbers: *Mail Online*, the immensely successful internet offering from the *Daily Mail*, reached more than 100 million monthly unique users in 2012 (Reynolds, 2012). Guardian Unlimited's internet readership exceeded 50 million monthly unique users, giving it an online circulation 250 times greater than its print sales. But although the *Mail's* website was profitable and *The Guardian's* was beginning to generate revenue, each faced a problem common throughout the newspaper industry: pounds lost in the sales of printed copies and advertisements were replaced by pennies of income from the internet. Between the first half of 2011 and the first half of 2012 UK national newspaper publishers lost £6 in print advertising revenue for every £1 they recuperated in digital (Enders Analysis, 2013b). The dual income stream had become a drip, provoking several newspaper publishers including Guardian Media Group, News International and Johnston Press to increase cover prices.

Conclusion

This is the economic context into which the Leveson Inquiry was born. It provokes concerns about the future of a diverse and plural newspaper market and the survival of the edited, professional journalism upon which representative democracy has been accustomed to depend. For historians of the press, it should raise doubts about the merits of imposing on newspapers the additional costs and duties associated with regulation underpinned by statute. Cruel and criminal as it was, the hacking of telephones and harassment of individuals was not the most appalling sin journalists committed in the era of universal adult suffrage. To take just one example, active complicity between the Foreign Office news department, Downing Street, the press and the BBC in 1937 and 1938 stifled discussion of the government's policy of appeasing Nazi Germany and muffled the voices of appeasement's leading critics. Adamthwaite (1983: 283) notes that: "In effect, the government restricted public debate and limited the ventilation of alternative views." This censorship helped to persuade leading Nazis that Britain was determined not to fight. It was a shameful surrender to government and it was brought about by persuasion, not by statute or charter. McDonough (1992) shows how *The Times*, which was regarded by Berlin as the official voice of the British establishment, colluded with ministers to promote appeasement as a virtuous policy to which there was no alternative.

Since 1949, organizations seeking press reform including the National Union of Journalists, the Campaign for Press and Broadcasting Freedom, the Media Standards Trust and Hacked Off have returned repeatedly to their claim that the market does not produce journalism designed for the primary purpose of informing the public sphere and that regulation may improve it. Their case has been ably informed and supported by the radical school of media history. However, until Lord Justice Leveson reported, parliament brought each discussion of regulation to a close by concluding that state intervention in the regulation of the press would harm the public interest more than journalism's worst excesses could. Some of these excesses had profound consequences. Nevertheless, politicians of all parties represented in the House of Commons accepted the liberal view that self-regulation should continue. The sanction of public opinion had persuaded newspapers to curb misconduct in the past. It must do so again.

The extreme difficulties that have confronted newspapers in the twenty-first century might have been expected to reaffirm the virtue of the liberal position. British liberalism lacks the security offered by America's constitutional guarantee that government may make no law abridging the freedom of the press, but the existential challenges confronting newspapers invite the suggestion that this might be an excellent moment to entrench such protection in statute. Instead parliament's decision is that there must be a new, and ostensibly oxymoronic, model of self-regulation governed by charter and underpinned by statute. This novelty has been helped into existence by a campaign that deployed tactics normally associated with tabloid newspapers. Eschewing any focus on traditional radical concerns such as the distribution and concentration of ownership in the newspaper industry, it fore-grounded celebrity victims of press intrusion such as the Hacked Off campaign's poster boy, Hugh Grant. By making the political personal and sidelining political economics, this campaign achieved what better reasoned predecessors did not in periods of comparable newspaper misconduct.

The radical narrative has helped to deliver change, but historians should take heed. Leopold von Ranke, the father of evidence-based history, described our discipline as "an endless argument" (cited in Lay, 2013). Parliament's interpretation of Lord Justice Leveson's report seeks to suggest that the behaviour of a section of the British press has brought an end to part of that argument. This chapter argues that Leveson and the MPs who voted to implement his proposals have deployed one version of media history to define the future of newspaper regulation in Britain. In doing so they have sought to make actual George Orwell's prediction that 'he who controls the past controls the future'. But, in the absence of extensive analysis of twentieth-century newspaper content – a project which has barely begun – to accept the radical argument would be at best premature. The English utilitarian philosopher Jeremy Bentham observed that: "The liberty of the press has its inconveniences, but the evil which may result from it is not to be compared to the evil of censorship" (Bay, 1958: 41). Lee (1976: 23) notes that James Madison agreed: "[S]ome degree of abuse is inescapable from the proper use of everything; and in no instance is this more true than in that of the press," said America's fourth President and founding father. Leveson has not rendered such wisdom invalid; he has simply invested enormous faith in one strand of media history. It is a strand that has produced enough excellent work to deserve intense criticism and constant challenge.

Further reading

Michael Bailey's edited collection *Narrating Media History* (2009) offers a series of essays on key critical issues in media history. For a critical overview of press history in Britain, Martin Conboy's (2011) *Journalism in Britain: A Historical Introduction* addresses all of the key dynamics. Focusing on some of the pressures the press has faced, Richard Cockett's *Twilight of Truth: Chamberlain, Appeasement and the Manipulation of the Press* (1989) provides a history of the co-opting of the British press by Neville Chamberlain. Finally, Michael Schudson's (2008) *Why Democracies Need an Unlovable Press* provides a valuable introduction to the sometimes uneasy relationship between journalism and democracy.

Notes

1 The *Daily Sport* was a daily newspaper published in the United Kingdom between 1991 and 2011. It specialized in celebrity news and soft-core pornographic stories and images.
2 The Campaign for Press and Broadcasting Freedom was established in 1979 to campaign for media reform. It supports press regulation underpinned by statute (see http://www.cpbf.org.uk/body.php?doctype=join&ref=0&section=0).
3 Hacked Off was established in 2011 to campaign for change in UK press regulation policy. It participated in the Leveson Inquiry and it supports Lord Justice Leveson's recommendations (see http://hackinginquiry.org/about-2).

References

Adamthwaite, A. (1983) "The British government and the media, 1937–38." *Journal of Contemporary History*, 18(2), 281–97.

Amis, M. (2003) *Yellow Dog*. London: Jonathan Cape.

Audit Bureau of Circulations (n.d.) National newspaper circulation. [online] Retrieved from www.abc.org.uk/press

Bailey, M. (ed.) (2009) *Narrating Media History*. London and New York: Routledge.

Barnett, S. and Gaber, I. (2001) *Westminster Tales: The Twenty-First-Century Crisis in Political Journalism*. London and New York: Continuum.

Bay, C. (1958) *The Structure of Freedom*. Palo Alto, CA: Stanford University Press.

Bingham, A. (2009) "A stream of pollution through every part of the country? Morality, regulations and the modern popular press." In M. Bailey (ed.) *Narrating Media History*. London and New York: Routledge (pp. 112–24).

——(2012) "Ignoring the first draft of history?" *Media History*, 18(3–4), 311–26.

Blair, T. (2007) "On public life." Lecture delivered at Reuters, Canary Wharf, London, 12 June. Retrieved from http://news.bbc.co.uk/1/hi/uk_politics/6744581.stm

Boyce, G. (1978) "The fourth estate: The reappraisal of a concept." In G. Boyce, J. Curran and P. Wingate (eds.) *Newspaper History from the 17th Century to the Present Day*. London: Constable (pp. 19–40).

Cockett, R. (1989) *Twilight of Truth: Chamberlain, Appeasement and the Manipulation of the Press*. London: Weidenfeld and Nicolson.

Conboy, M. (2011) *Journalism in Britain: A Historical Introduction*. London: Sage.

Curran, J. (1978) "The press as an agency of social control: An historial perspective." In G. Boyce, J. Curran and P. Wingate (eds.) *Newspaper History from the 17th Century to the Present Day*. London: Constable (pp. 51–75).

——(2009) "Narratives of media history revisited." In M. Bailey (ed.) *Narrating Media History*. Oxford: Routledge (pp. 1–21).

Daily Mirror (1941) "This is a cloak for defeatism." 13 January, p. 12.

Enders Analysis (2013a) "Print media advertising update [2013–002]." Distributed to subscribers on 11 January 2013.

——2013b. "Cover prices: The old new model." Distributed to subscribers on 16 April 2013.

Fenton, B. (2009) "Lifeblood drains from local press." *Financial Times*, 31 March.

Fenton, N. (ed.) (2010) *New Media, Old News*. London: Sage.

Hampton, M. (2009) "Renewing the liberal tradition." In M. Bailey (ed.) *Narrating Media History*. Oxford: Routledge (pp. 26–35).

Hansard (1974) "Announcement by the then Prime Minister, Harold Wilson, in answer to an Oral Question in the House of Commons." HC Deb, 872, 1322–32, 2 May. Retrieved from http://hansard.millbanksystems.com/commons/1974/may/02/royal-commission-on-the-press

Harcup, T. (2013) *Alternative Journalism, Alternative Voices*. London: Routledge.

Jewell, J. (2013) "After Leveson: The 66-year press regulation journey that ends as it began." *The Guardian*, 21 February. Retrieved from http://www.guardian.co.uk/media/greenslade/2013/feb/21/leveson-report-davidcameron

Johnston Press (2013) "About us." Retrieved from http://www.johnstonpress.co.uk/about-us

Lay, P. (2013) "Digging up Richard III will not bury old arguments." *The Guardian*, 4 February. Retrieved from http://www.theguardian.com/science/2013/feb/04/digging-richard-iii-old-arguments

Lee, A. (1976) *The Origins of the Popular Press in England 1855–1914*. London: Croom Helm.

——(1978) "The structure, ownership and control of the press 1914–76." In G. Boyce, J. Curran and P. Wingate (eds.) *Newspaper History from the 17th Century to the Present Day*. London: Constable (pp. 130–48).

Leveson (2012, Nov 29) "The Leveson inquiry: The report into the culture, practices and ethics of the press." London: Her Majesty's Stationery Office.

——(2012a) "The Leveson inquiry: The report into the culture, practices and ethics of the press." Vol. 1, Part B, Chapter 2, "The freedom of the press and democracy", para. 2.19, p. 61.

——(2012b) "The Leveson inquiry: The report into the culture, practices and ethics of the press." Vol. 1, Part B, Chapter 3, "The importance of a free press: Free communication", para. 3.3, p. 62.

——(2012c) "The Leveson inquiry: The report into the culture, practices and ethics of the press." "Executive summary and recommendations", para. 70, p. 17.

Lowe, K. (2012) *Savage Continent – Europe in the Aftermath of World War II*. London: Viking.

Luckhurst, T. (2012) *Responsibility Without Power: Lord Justice Leveson's Constitutional Dilemma*. Bury St Edmunds: Abramis.

——(2013) "Excellent but gullible people: The press and the people's convention." *Journalism Studies*, 14(1), 62–77.

McDonough, F. (1992) "*The Times*, Norman Ebbut and the Nazis, 1927–37." *Journal of Contemporary History*, 27(3), 407–24.

Marshall, S. (2012) "Guardian Media Group reports pre-tax loss of £75.6m." Journalism.co.uk, 10 August. Retrieved from http://www.journalism.co.uk/news/guardian-media-group-reports-pre-tax-loss-of-75-6m/s2/a550065/

Murdoch, R. (1984) Cited by the Museum of Broadcast Communications. Retrieved from http://www.museum.tv/eotvsection.php?entrycode=britishskyb

Nicholas, S. (2000) "All the news that's fit to broadcast: The popular press versus the BBC, 1922–45." In P. Catterall, C. Seymour-Ure and A. Smith (eds.) *Northcliffe's Legacy: Aspects of the British Popular Press, 1896–1996*. Basingstoke: Macmillan Press.

Nicholson, B. (2013) "The digital turn." *Media History*, 19(1), 59–73.

Peers, M. (2008) "Slim pickings at *The Times*." *Wall Street Journal*, 11 September. Retrieved from http://online.wsj.com/article/SB122115152094823965.html

Petley, J. (2009) "What fourth estate?" In M. Bailey (ed.) *Narrating Media History*. Oxford: Routledge (pp.184–95).

Reynolds, J. (2012) "Mail Online revenue surges 74% to £28 million." Mediaweek.co.uk, 22 November. Retrieved from http://www.brandrepublic.com/news/1161068/MailOnline-revenue-surges-74-28m/?HAYILC=RELATED

Schudson, M. (2008) *Why Democracies Need an Unlovable Press*. Cambridge: Polity Press.

Winston, B. (2005) *Messages: Free Expression, Media and the West from Gutenberg to Google*. London and New York: Routledge.

Part IV
MAGAZINES

22
The role of the literary and cultural periodical

David Finkelstein

Introduction and early days

Between 1800 and 1850, the literary periodical became a dominant publishing format in British culture. Prior to the founding of the *Edinburgh Review* in 1802, there existed few substantial literary journals of note in Britain, though there were some exceptions, such as the *Critical Review*, founded in 1756 by Archibald Hamilton and Tobias Smollett, Addison and Steele's *The Spectator* (in existence from 1711–12), *The Gentlemen's Magazine* (founded in 1732), and the *Monthly Review*, begun by Ralph Griffiths in 1749. Audiences for such works were concentrated in the genteel part of Georgian society, upper-class literate elites who had the funds to purchase books, magazines and poetic publications, or those literary elites who could be found reading shared subscribed copies of newspapers and periodicals in the coffee houses that served as communication hubs in key cities such as London, Edinburgh, Oxford and Cambridge.

These titles, like their subsequent imitators, tended to be short-lived, with a bill of fare consisting mainly of literary gossip, short selections of prose and verse, and 'puff' (laudatory) summaries of new works and critical material. Such polite manners in print may have been due to an over concern with fear of critical reprisal. As the eighteenth-century contemporary commentator Ephraim Chambers summarized, the duty of a reviewer was to offer a "faithful account of the books which come into his hands"; evaluations or sharp judgements were not within a critic's province, for "when he affects the air and language of a censor or judge, he invades the undoubted right of the public, which is the only sovereign judge of the reputation of an author" (cited in Graham, 1930: 204–5). Ralph Griffiths, editor and owner of the *Monthly Review*, similarly declared that the purpose of his journal was "to enter no farther into the province of criticism, than just so far as may be indispensably necessary to give some idea of such books as come under our consideration" (Nangle, 1934: 260). Nevertheless, in order to minimize risk to critical reputations, *Monthly* reviews were anonymized, though that did not stop the *Monthly* being attacked by disgruntled recipients of critical reviews of their work. For most such productions, sales were low and often dependent on solicited private subscriptions for survival. The *English*

Review, for example, founded by the publisher John Murray in 1783, was considered a moderately successful journal yet averaged sales of just over 750 copies per month (Finkelstein, 2007: 201). Within ten years it had disappeared, absorbed into the *Analytical Review*.

The rise of the literary review

In 1802, the founding of the quarterly *Edinburgh Review* ushered in a more engaged form of critical debate in British literary culture. Four Edinburgh lawyers with literary ambitions and Whiggish temperament clubbed together to produce a quarterly journal focused on extended critical essays and reviews. Its authoritative style and the space offered for extensive critique and philosophical ponderings proved extremely popular, and the standards and parameters by which it operated became ones emulated by cultural periodical publications that followed. Its pre-eminence ensured that the critical essay was for about 20 years the dominant literary form in the reviews and magazines and the most readily marketable literary commodity. As Walter Bagehot loftily declared in 1855, review writing, contemporary professional writers and British literary reviews owed their existence to the way such opportunities had sprung from the pages of the *Edinburgh Review*. "Review writing," he noted, "is one of the features of modern literature. Many able men really give themselves up to it," though he suggested its popularity was in part due to modern reading habits, for "people take their literature in morsels the way they take their sandwiches on a journey" (Bagehot, 1884: 3). Reviewers, therefore, were crucial guides, for

> the modern man must be told what to think – shortly, no doubt – but he *must* be told it. The essay-like criticism of modern times is about the length which he likes. The *Edinburgh Review*, which began the system, may be said to be, in this country, the commencement on large topics of suitable views for sensible persons.
>
> (ibid.: 6)

The *Edinburgh Review*'s format (paper cover, article lengths and style) was quickly adopted by subsequent competitors, as was its commitment to payment for contributions, the latter an innovation the publisher Archibald Constable insisted on despite the opinion of the *Review*'s first editor (Francis Jeffrey) that contributors should be "all gentlemen and no pay" (Cockburn, 1852: 1, 145). The *Review* also adopted the pattern of contributions seen in the *Monthly Review*, where articles went unsigned, a practice that remained almost universal in British literary periodicals until the 1860s.

Monthly periodical developments

Literary journals that followed included not only John Murray's 1809 *Quarterly Review*, but also the Tory-led monthly journal *Blackwood's Edinburgh Magazine*

(1817), *The London Magazine* (1820), the *Westminster Review* (1824) and the celebrated weeklies the *Athenaeum* (1828) and *The Spectator* (1828). By the late 1820s, the literary periodical lay at the heart of British literary culture, shaping literary specialization in a manner akin to the economic and material 'division of labour' seen in the textile and manufacturing industries. Authors were commissioned to write on specific areas and topics such as economics, literature, history, politics, fiction and poetry, as per their perceived expertise. It also played a significant role in the increasing commodification of textual production as payments were measured by the sheet and copyright assignments arranged for periodical contributions. By the 1830s, further developments in the mass periodical market ensured a saturation of material across the class spectrum (Finkelstein, 2007: 209). In the 1860s, equally nimble monthly journals sprung up as a result of the repeal of the final 'taxes on knowledge', duties placed on printed material that had until then kept issue prices unaffordable for a mass public. Significant market leaders included monthlies such as *Macmillan's Magazine* (1859), the *Cornhill Magazine* (1860), the *Fortnightly Review* (1865), the *Contemporary Review* (1866) and *Longman's Magazine* (1882). Not all were profitable, but they did serve a valuable purpose for publishers keen to ensure their names and authors were present in the creative lives of targeted readers. As William Tinsley noted when told his *Tinsley's Magazine* (founded in 1867) was losing money: "What cheaper advertisement can I have for twenty-five pounds a month? It advertises my name and publications; and keeps my authors together" (Schmidt, 1984: 143).

Publishers were quick to realize there was money to be made from periodical literature if pitched at the right audience. As technology improved over the century, in the shape of efficient papermaking machines, presses and binderies, expanded steam-powered rail networks, and new outlets for retailing cultural works, printers and proprietors were able to sell and distribute more material more quickly and for less cost. Sales statistics offer insight into the exponential rise in readership of monthlies at the expense of the longer established quarterlies through to this period: *Blackwood's Magazine*, for example, saw sales rise from about 3,700 in 1820 to 5,000 in 1826, then 9,000 by 1832, before dropping down to a stable average of 6,500 in the 1860s and 1870s; its rival, the *Quarterly Review*, went from a print run of 14,000 in 1818, to 10,500 in 1829, and then an average of 9,000 by 1849; the *Edinburgh Review*, on the other hand, said to have had a circulation of around 12,000 a quarter in 1818, dropped to half that in 1828, and then to around 3,000 by 1845 onwards (Finkelstein, 2013: 81; Finkelstein, 2002: 165–66; Shattock, 1989: 97–99; Cutmore, 2013; Bennett, 1982: 236).

Late century shifts

As Graham Law and Robert L. Patten have commented, the last quarter of the nineteenth century saw a periodical boom driven by magazines aimed at mass-market sectors (Law and Patten, 2009). The shift from quarterly and monthly literary periodicals to weekly, bi-weekly and monthly miscellany magazines grew more pronounced with the entrance of new 'mass' journals funded by press magnates such as George Newnes and Alfred Harmsworth, including *Tit-Bits* (1881), which by 1886 was selling over 300,000 copies, and the *Strand Magazine* (1891), *Pearson's Magazine* (1896) and *Harmsworth Magazine* (1898), all of whom claimed a circulation of 250,000 by the turn of the century (ibid.: 167).

Between 1860 and 1896 the number of magazine titles more than quintupled, from 406 to 2097 (ibid.: 156). The major increase was in what the *Newspaper Press Directory* began defining as 'class' periodicals aimed at specific professional, social, and cultural communities. 1875 to 1900 saw significant increases in magazines and periodicals targeting scientific, trade, political and technical interests, as well as segmentation of journals focused on younger audiences, women and ethnic clusterings. 'Class' periodicals maintained critical reviewing within a mix of instalment fiction, didactic information and general interest material, in contrast to 'mass' journals whose focus was on less complex and lengthy texts. A divergence of readership was punctuated by an increasingly diverse series of reading experiences, whereby literary reviews might feature for careful perusal in weighty newspapers and monthlies, short summaries featured in inexpensive dailies for quick train reading, and occasional 'puffs' or notes featured in miscellaneous magazines aimed at publicizing particular publications of relevant news conglomerate owners.

Patrick Leary and Andrew Nash have drawn attention to the manner in which the spread of journalistic and periodical outlets during this period also sustained a professional class of critical writers, albeit ones whose existence was precarious and predicated on constant activity (Leary and Nash, 2009). By the end of the 1880s, "the favourite standby of the would-be-writer – book reviewing – had become, for many, a full-time occupation" (Cross, 1985: 210, cited in Leary and Nash, 2009: 195). Reviewing earned well if one was in demand: the critic George Saintsbury averaged £3 10s from overnight review work, while in his first year with the *Pall Mall Gazette* as a book reviewer George Bernard Shaw took home a comfortable £117 (Leary and Nash, 2009: 195; Gross, 1969: 154; Saunders, 1964: 206).

The demotic, pacy style of 'New Journalism' championed by newspaper and journal editors such as W. T. Stead and George Newnes, dismissed by Matthew Arnold in 1887 as "feather-brained", characterized the period leading up to the turn of the century (Arnold, 1887: 638–39). Newnes riposted that the appeal of miscellanies like his own *Tit-Bits* lay in being light, wholesome but also serious enough that "many of those readers may be led to take an interest in higher forms of literature" (cited in Pound, 1967: 24–25). Aspirational readers also found great pleasure in the fare offered in journals such as Newnes's *Strand Magazine* (founded in 1890), whose mix of interviews, articles, illustrations and light fiction hastened the end of the essay-based periodical, acidly characterized by Mark Pattison as "those venerable old wooden three-deckers, the *Edinburgh Review* and the *Quarterly Review* still put out to sea under the command, I believe, of the Ancient Mariner" (Pattison, 1877: 663).

Scholarly articles in monthlies paid little in contrast to work for more popular periodical outlets. So the professional male critics soon turned into "bookmen", seeking money by working across a range of genres and subject areas (Gross, 1969). George Saintsbury, Edmund Gosse, Andrew Lang and Charles Whibley were just some of many who sought a living from miscellany work. Andrew Lang's career, as Leary and Nash have noted, exemplified such a polymathic approach, with his work spanning poetry, translation, biography, history, critical reviews and general non-fiction in as many newspaper, journal and periodical outlets as would accept him. "Lang's critical voice became ubiquitous. In the words of Frank Swinnerton: 'he wrote everywhere ... upon almost every subject in the world'" (Leary and Nash, 2009: 197).

Equally significant numbers of women also developed careers in literary journalism work: in 1891, the English census listed at least 660 women who classified themselves as 'author, editor, journalist', up from 15 in 1841. Among these included Alice Meynell (a major contributor to the *Scots Observer* and the *Pall Mall Gazette*), Florence Fenwick Miller and the art critic Elizabeth Pennell (Gray, 2012: 4). The type of work they engaged in was multifarious and startling in range, as Charlotte O'Conor Eccles, writing in *Blackwood's Magazine* in 1893, noted when characterizing her standard chores for a weekly newspaper:

> A weekly newspaper offered me 30s a week for all my time from nine in the morning till six in the evening. I did a column of 'mems.' on current events; two columns of educational news; a number of sub-leaders; two Ladies' Letters; Answers to Correspondents; a 'Children's Corner,' most troublesome of all, as it involved competitions and prizes; corrected all the proofs; and had in my hands the selection of matter for the weekly, and for an educational paper. Quite enough to do I found it.
>
> (cited in Gray, 2012: 5)

Into the twentieth century

As increasing numbers of professional critics and miscellany writers were entering the marketplace at the turn of the twentieth century, venues for their outputs were changing in nature. The new century saw many established miscellanies fail, particularly those founded earlier in the nineteenth century by family firms whose house styles had not kept up with changing mores, tastes and literary developments. *Temple Bar* and *Macmillan's Magazine*, for example, ceased in 1906 and 1907; others, such as the *Cornhill* and *Blackwood's*, limped on through the century increasingly marginalized and aimed at dwindling niche audiences (the *Cornhill* closed in 1975, *Blackwood's* in 1980).

The Edwardian period witnessed changes in periodical functions and taste, and new journals started to capture those tastes. In 1902, for example, *The Times Literary Supplement* was spun off from *The Times* under the editorship of Bruce Richmond to act as cultural arbiter of new works in the field, soon taking over from the *Athenaeum* as a key space for concise yet articulate evaluations of new publications. As H. D. Traill, an early developer of the supplement's precursor *Literature* noted at the time, its ambitions were simply "to protect the reader from being overwhelmed by the continually increasing flood of books, and to that end to discriminate more carefully than is usual between books which deserve reviewing in the proper sense of the word, and those which do not" (cited in May, 2001: 8). Half the size of *The Times*, capable of being folded neatly into its sister's pages, the new review would become a key space for scholars, literary authors and men and women of letters to produce signed reviews, leaders and critical commentary. Early contributors whose names graced the pages of the weekly supplement included Desmond McCarthy, Arthur

Quiller-Couch, Edith Wharton and Virginia Woolf, and by 1914 its weekly sales stood at just under 42,000 copies (May, 2001: 95).

Other key cultural journals that followed included the *English Review*, begun in December 1908 and edited in its first year by Ford Madox Hueffer, the sixpenny Fabian society-leaning weekly *The New Statesman* (founded in 1913 by Sydney and Beatrice Webb, and featuring Desmond McCarthy as its literary editor) and the A. R. Orage-led weekly *The New Age* (1907). The latter would prove significant in advancing the careers of writers such as Wyndham Lewis, Katherine Mansfield and Ezra Pound, championing abstract art and mediating between literary experimentation, literary traditions and mass audience understanding of current fields of knowledge and trends. Its socialist leanings and political stance were joined to general surveys of critical matters, and the mix proved initially very appealing, with weekly sales and subscriptions hitting 22,000 in 1908 (Ardis, 2007: 417). Initially priced at one penny, subscription raises to threepence in 1909, then sixpence in 1913, saw circulation fading to 3,500 in November 1913, but as Ann Ardis has pointed out, this was

> nonetheless substantially larger than the circulation of the little magazines with whom the history of modernism has been most closely associated, while at the same time substantially smaller than the circulation of mainstream British quarterlies like the *Fortnightly Review*, 'smart' American magazines like the *Smart Set*, or working-class British periodicals like *T. P.'s Weekly*.
>
> (Ardis, 2007: 417)

Although read by the leading literary and political figures of the day, its readership base also encompassed socialist autodidacts, left-leaning graduates of mechanics' institutes, working men's colleges and teacher's colleges, and others characterized by Orage as "a generation rising that finds *Tit Bits* useless and *T. P.'s* [Weekly] unsatisfactory" (quoted in Ardis, 2007: 417).

The period 1914 to about 1939 has been characterized as one dominated by modernism, with consequent impact on the type of literary magazines developed during this period. Modernism has been defined as an early twentieth-century reaction to Victorian formations of art, literature and social organization, seeking to challenge prevailing orthodoxies and, in the words of Ezra Pound, loosely adapting from an ancient Confucian tale, "Make it New!" (North, 2013). Many Modernist-influenced literary magazines founded during this period aimed at experimenting with new models of literary representation, as well as struggling to find meaning and new value systems to replace those destroyed by the onslaught of war and by the ongoing political struggles, the growth of socialism, and the rise of communism and fascism that marked this turbulent era. New literary magazines emerging during this period included the *Egoist*, started in 1914 as a relaunch of the short-lived feminist journal the *New Freewoman*, a fervent promoter of imagist poetry and literary criticism and most prominent in critical terms under the editorship of T. S. Eliot from 1917 until its demise in 1919. Others that followed included the *London Mercury*, founded in 1920 and edited in its early years by J. C. Squire; the quarterly review

Criterion, launched by T. S. Eliot in 1922; *The Adelphi*, founded in 1923 by John Middleton Murry and published until 1948; and the *Scots Magazine* (1924). The 1930s saw further movement towards the political left in new literary journals such as the *Left Review* (1934–38) and, belying its small print run of between 750 and 1500 copies, one of the most influential and controversial literary periodicals of its time, *Scrutiny*, edited between 1933–53 from Cambridge by a core group of academics led by F. R. Leavis and his wife Q. D. Leavis. In its pages, Leavis and like-minded colleagues outlined the principles of New Criticism and the 'Great Tradition' of English novelists that for many decades shaped the trajectory of literary studies in Anglo-American universities.

The start of the Second World War witnessed the demise of several literary journals of the previous period, including *Criterion, the London Mercury, New Verse* and *Twentieth Century Verse*. Though wartime rationing of paper, printing facilities and manpower restricted the number of literary publications available, some did emerge during this period, the most significant being the Cyril Connolly edited monthly magazine *Horizon*, which lasted from 1940 to 1950. Connolly set high standards, published leading poets and writers of the period and featured the critical insights of individuals such as George Orwell, Arthur Koestler, Graham Greene and William Empson. Orwell would comment early on in its history that *Horizon* sought to be a "modern and democratized version" of the old highbrow literary magazine but with a circulation of between 9,000 and 10,000, it struggled to survive in the post-war years.

Post 1945

In the post-war years, new journals that were founded were grounded in less strident political and cultural movements. Among these included *The London Magazine*, founded in 1953, edited by John Lehmann and featuring key prose writers of the period. *The London Magazine* would survive through to the sixties as "bright, visual and flavoured with sexuality", but in the 1970s was, like many other literary journals of the period, financially propped up by the Arts Council for Great Britain, with publication subsidies rising exponentially from £2,000 in 1969 to £24,000 in 1979 (Thomas, 1983: 248). Founded in the same year but more successful financially was the monthly *Encounter*, dedicated to literature, the arts and politics, whose founding editor was Stephen Spender. Its pages have featured contributors of major note across social and political arenas, and its reach and significance was reflected in its circulation, which in 1964 reached a peak of 40,000 (MacNiven, 1983: 157).

The 1960s saw a shift in government realization of cultural capital in such works and subsidies channeled via the Arts Councils, such as those offered to *The London Magazine*, enabled small literary periodicals to retain a place in cultural life throughout this period. However, the late 1970s and 1980s saw a government retreat from arts funding, with the English Arts Council cutting support for several key literary periodicals (for example the *New Review* in 1978), although it continued to offer small sums to a number of small literary periodicals such as *Ambit, Agenda* and *The London Magazine*. Not until 2001 were levels of support raised to acknowledge the cultural relevance of such material to arts activity, due in part to a shift in government policies towards the arts, instigated under the Labour government in wake of its embracing of culture and the arts as a way of 'rebranding' and marketing Britain (pace the 'Cool Britannia' campaigns much in vogue during this period). In Scotland, the Scottish Arts Council, providing literary arts funding from the late 1960s onwards, created the landscape for a number of significant literary journals, such as *Akros*, *Cencrastus*, *Chapman*, *Lallans* and *Lines Review*, to flourish.

The founding in the 1970s and 1980s of both politically committed and literary adventurous periodicals such as *Spare Rib* and *Granta* saw new life injected into literary periodical formats, the latter in particular gaining much publicity and debate for its thematic issues featuring the best of Anglo-American writers. Another key player in this field was the fortnightly *London Review of Books*, started by Karl Miller, Mary Kay Wilmes and Susannah Clapp in 1979 following a year long strike at *The Times* that suspended the publication of *The Times Literary Supplement* during that period. Bucking the trend, and mirroring the example set by its transatlantic cousin the *New York Review of Books*, the *LRB* returned to the long review essay format of the *Edinburgh Review*, and over the years has succeeded in maintaining a stable circulation, which at 2012 was just over 59,000 (*London Review of Books*, n.d.).

Conclusion: The literary periodical today

The history of the literary periodical and journal in Britain over the past two centuries is bound up in cycles of development, expansion, contraction and evolution. These can be clearly seen matching similar developmental cycles in print technology. Such cultural examples moved from being high-priced miscellanies and review journals aimed at a small sector of the population to mass market publications providing material for a wide range of audiences at low cost. This was succeeded by a move to niche, focused publications. Periodical history charts a movement from productions focusing on the review essay to those incorporating illustration, fiction and personalized reportage and then back to miscellanies aimed at creating dialogue and informed debate across political, social and cultural spectrums. The advent of online resources has complicated the picture somewhat, enabling cultural critiques that once flourished in print only to be supplemented by voices in the online domain. Literary and cultural journals such as *The Times Literary Supplement*, *The New Yorker*, *The Spectator* and others have started to grasp the potential for drawing audiences to their work through online portals with added blogging features and online digital archives. The potential for literary journalism to be read is infinite in the online world, but the challenge is ensuring there is an audience willing to engage with such material in the wake of mass availability of online opinion and critical musings. We may be returning to an era where print subscriptions and purchases of literary periodicals become a privilege pursued by a small group of elites, culturally significant in small circles but dependent on subsidy or advertising revenue cross-subsidized from online versions or ventures. Moving to complete digital delivery may prove the means by which such works are sustained. It thus remains to be seen to what extent the digital form in the decades to come will supersede print as the key vehicle for delivering high quality cultural critiques.

Further reading

A strong narrative-led survey of literary periodical and journal structures and key players since 1800 can be found in John Gross's (1969) *The Rise and Fall of the Man of Letters: English Literary Life Since 1800*. A useful starting point for reviewing key trends in the Victorian era is Joanne Shattock and Michael Wolff's (1982) edited *The Victorian Periodical Press: Samplings and Soundings*. Similarly valuable in providing an overview of Modernist magazine activity spanning seven decades is Peter Brooker and Andrew Thacker's (2009) edited *The Oxford Critical and Cultural History of Modernist Magazines, Volume 1. Britain and Ireland 1880–1955*. Finally, a valuable compendium resource for individual literary magazine histories between 1698 and 1984 can be found in the four-volume series *British Literary Magazines*, edited by Alvin Sullivan (1983a, 1983b, 1984, 1986).

References

Ardis, A. (2007) "The dialogics of modernism(s) in *The New Age*." *Modernism/Modernity*, 14 (Sept), 407–34.

Arnold, M. (1887) "Up to Easter." *The Nineteenth Century*, XXI, May, 629–43.

Bagehot, W. (1884) "The first Edinburgh reviewers." In R. H. Hutton (ed.) *Literary Studies* (2 vols). London: Longmans, Green and Co.

Bennett, S. (1982) "Revolution in thought: Serial publication and the mass market for reading." In J. Shattock and M. Wolff (eds.) *The Victorian Periodical Press: Samplings and Soundings*. Leicester: Leicester University Press (pp. 225–57).

Brooker, P. and Thacker, A. (eds.) (2009) *The Oxford Critical and Cultural History of Modernist Magazines, Volume 1. Britain and Ireland 1880–1955*. Oxford: Oxford University Press.

Cockburn, H. (1852) *Life of Lord Jeffrey. With a Selection From His Correspondence* (2 vols.). Edinburgh: A & C Black.

Cross, N. (1985) *The Common Writer: Life in Nineteenth-Century Grub Street*. Cambridge: Cambridge University Press.

Cutmore, J. (2013) "Romantic circle." *Quarterly Review* archive. Retrieved from http://www.rc.umd.edu/reference/qr/index/36.html

Finkelstein, D. (2002) *The House of Blackwood: Author-Publisher Relations in the Victorian Era*. University Park, PA: Penn State Press.

——(2007) "Periodicals, encyclopaedias and nineteenth-century literary production." In I. Brown, T. Clancy, S. Manning and M. Pittock (eds.) *Edinburgh History of Scottish Literature, Vol. 2*. Edinburgh: Edinburgh University Press (pp. 198–210).

——(2013) "Selling *Blackwood's Magazine*, 1817–34." In R. Morrison and D. S. Roberts (eds.) *Romanticism and Blackwood's Magazine. 'An Unprecedented Phenomenon'*. Basingstoke: Palgrave Macmillan (pp. 69–86).

Graham, W. (1930) *English Periodicals*. New York: Nelson.

Gray, F. E. (ed.) (2012) *Women in Journalism at the Fin de Siecle: Making a Name for Herself*. Basingstoke: Palgrave Macmillan.

Gross, J. (1969) *The Rise and Fall of the Man of Letters*. London: Weidenfeld and Nicolson.

Law, G. and Patten, R. L. (2009) "The serial revolution." In D. McKitterick (ed.) *The Cambridge History of the Book in Britain, Vol. 6, 1830–1914*. Cambridge: Cambridge University Press (pp. 144–71).

Leary, P. and Nash, A. (2009) "Authorship." In D. McKitterick (ed.) *The Cambridge History of the Book in Britain, Vol. 6, 1830–1914.* Cambridge: Cambridge University Press (pp. 172–213).

London Review of Books (n.d.) "About the LRB." Retrieved from http://www.lrb.co.uk/about

MacNiven, I. S. (1983) "Encounter." In A. Sullivan (ed.) *British Literary Magazines: Volume 4, The Modern Age, 1914–1984.* Westport, CT: Greenwood Press (pp. 153–61).

May, D. (2001) *Critical Times: The History of the Times Literary Supplement.* London: HarperCollins Publishers.

Nangle, B. (1934) *The Monthly Review First Series, 1749–1789.* Oxford: Clarendon Press.

North, M. (2013) "The making of making it new." *Guernica: A Magazine of Arts and Politics,* 15 August 2013. Retrieved from http://www.guernicamag.com/features/the-making-of-making-it-new

Pattison, M. (1877) "Books and critics." *Fortnightly Review,* 22, 659–79.

Pound, R. (1967) *Mirror of the Century: The Strand Magazine, 1891–1950.* London: A. S. Barnes.

Saunders, J. W. (1964) *The Profession of English Letters.* London: Routledge and Kegan Paul.

Schmidt, B. Q. (1984) "Novelists, publishers, and fiction in middle-class magazines, 1860–80." *Victorian Periodicals Review,* 17 (Winter), 142–52.

Shattock, J. (1989) *Politics and Reviewers: The Edinburgh and Quarterly.* Leicester: Leicester University Press.

Shattock, J. and Wolff, M. (eds.) (1982) *The Victorian Periodical Press: Samplings and Soundings.* Leicester: Leicester University Press.

Sullivan, A. (ed.) (1983a) *British Literary Magazines: Volume 1, The Augustan Age and the Age of Johnson, 1698–1788.* Westport, CT: Greenwood Press.

——(ed.) (1983b) *British Literary Magazines: Volume 2, The Romantic Age, 1789–1936.* Westport, CT: Greenwood Press.

——(ed.) (1984) *British Literary Magazines: Volume 3, The Victorian and Edwardian Age, 1837–1914.* Westport, CT: Greenwood Press.

——(ed.) (1986) *British Literary Magazines: Volume 4, The Modern Age, 1914–1984.* Westport, CT: Greenwood Press.

Thomas, A. C. (1983) "The London Magazine." In A. Sullivan (ed.) *British Literary Magazines: Volume 4: The Modern Age, 1914–1984.* Westport, CT: Greenwood Press (pp. 244–50).

23
Specialist magazines as communities of taste

Tim Holmes and Jane Bentley

The first *magazine* to include that word in its title was a classic example of what Bourdieu, in *Distinction: A Social Critique Of The Judgement Of Taste* (1984 [2010]) called an "institution of legitimation". The *Gentleman's Magazine* (1731) would now be considered a newspaper more than a magazine, but everything about it from the name onwards was intended to be of assistance to, and form the habits and habitus of, a landed gentleman.

This work had been prefigured in the coffee house periodicals edited by Addison and Steele, the *Tatler* (1709) and *The Spectator* (1711), publications intended to improve the moral and intellectual life of the bourgeoisie by offering them a set of 'approved' opinions and attitudes. Scholars such as Ohmann (1996) have observed the same process of formation in trade and professional publications, aided and abetted by advertisers in whose interests it was to encourage certain markers of taste and habits of consumption.

The pioneering titles cited above clearly addressed a large but specific class of people, providing a variety of general interest content from which readers could either pick and choose their particular interests or consume the whole lot to increase their overall cultural capital. However, before any of them began to flourish a different type of journal had made its appearance – the *Ladies Mercury* (1693), which has a strong claim to be the first women's title, and therefore the first *specialist* publication, in Britain.

From their earliest days magazines have operated in two modes – the general interest publication that addresses a broad segment of the public sphere (pace Habermas, 1989) and the specialist title that focuses tightly on what Todd Gitlin (1998) characterized as a public "sphericule". The development of the magazine in a capitalist economy has seen exponential expansion of the specialist sector, with titles for every conceivable interest and sub-interest: current (2013) figures from the Professional Publishers Association show 4,765 b2b (trade) and 3,000 consumer titles in the UK (Brad, Wessenden Marketing PwC, NRS, 2013).

As a result, the magazine has become an immensely complex media artifact. Although sometimes dismissed as being too commercially focused (not a disinterested civic good) and too culturally normative (channelling identities into well-worn forms), actually trying to unravel its cultural and social meanings, or even to establish a uniformly relevant analysis of political economy with which to describe its general workings, is a far from straightforward task. In a sector that ranges from corporately owned, industrially produced fashion titles so fat with advertisements that they are literally difficult to pick up to slim artisanal independents that shun advertising altogether, it is almost impossible to talk of 'the' magazine. And that is just considering print, to which any comprehensive analysis must add websites, apps, social media components and other experimental formats. In fact, so varied are the productions of the sector, it makes more sense to use the generic plural except when describing an individual publication.

Theoretical work aiming to deconstruct, analyze or gauge the effects of magazines can take place across such a wide range of disciplines that any attempt to map the results must necessarily be multidisciplinary, if not actually fragmented. Studies have tended to occur in clustered phases, perhaps linked to wider socio-cultural movements or concerns. Feminist interpretations of magazines, particularly the women's magazine genre, form a substantial proportion of published literature and while this movement can be traced back to Betty Friedan in the USA (1963) and Cynthia White in the UK (1970) the bulk of work was undertaken in the 1980s and 1990s by scholars such as Ros Ballaster (Ballaster et al., 1991), Joan Barrell (Barrell and Braithwaite, 1979 [1988]), Margaret Beetham (1996), Brian Braithwaite (1995; Barrell and Braithwaite, 1979 [1988]), Dawn Currie (1999), Marjorie Ferguson (1983), Elizabeth Frazer (Ballaster et al., 1991), Joke Hermes (1995), Valerie Korinek (2000), Ellen McCracken (1993), Angela McRobbie (1978, 1991) and Kathryn Shevelow (1989). This was followed, in the UK at least, by a short flurry of work examining men's magazines (Berger, Wallis and Watson, 1995; Jackson, Stevenson and Brooks, 2001; Crewe, 2003) although the trend seemed to founder between the Scylla of the 'new man' being a passing cultural chimera and the Charybdis of the 'lad' reintroducing atavistic male behaviours.

Disciplines that may be brought to bear on magazines include communication theory, media history, visual design, semiotics, community, business studies, media economics, brand theory, literary criticism and fan studies. Most of these fields have supplied framing for papers delivered at Mapping The Magazine, a series of international conferences held under the auspices of the Centre for Journalism at Cardiff University (for a representative sample see Holmes, 2009).

In 1995 Professor David Abrahamson, following Wood (1956), Peterson (1964) and the Paines (1987), published *The American Magazine: Research Perspectives and Prospects*, an edited "survey of magazine research by which past and present scholarship can be understood" (Abrahamson, 1995: xvii). The title he gave his introductory chapter – Brilliant fragments: The scholarly engagement with the American magazine – reflected the perceived state of affairs; magazine studies comprised a set of works that glittered brightly as individual gems but lacked a coherent setting that could give a clear definition to the field. Seventeen years later he was engaged in a similar overview project; although the scope had expanded to a more global outlook there was still an underlying feeling that the magazine eluded simple taxonomic definition – if there were to be a field of magazine studies it would have to be a loose and probably shifting venture.

In light of this panoply of analytical options it is worth returning here to one of the basic questions, a question that has been discussed and debated in academic, industry and mixed forums – *what is a magazine?* As might be expected, there is no simple answer but it is helpful to break the elements that lead towards an answer into two categories: the physical and the philosophical. Of these, the physical must be further divided to take account of print, digital and other platforms.

Physically, a magazine is a form of *curatum* (that is to say, a body of work gathered together from disparate sources but with a specific purpose) usually, but not always, put together on page or screen with a distinct aesthethic that often incorporates a substantial element of visual appeal in the way it combines typography, photography and illustration. However, the aesthetic may also be quite austere if the specific purpose demands it; the *Economist*'s print version is a good example of this type of magazine. No-one could say it is not well designed within a distinct aesthetic but the focus is very much on words rather than pictures, leading to a dense surface appearance that reflects the concerns of the reader as a business person in search of information rather than pleasure.

This aesthetic valorization is an element of the matrix of consumption within which every curatum in every medium has a specific position. The matrix can best be considered as a coagmentation of the disparate elements that come into play during the different phases of consumption of a media product; it starts with the factors that determine the choice to consume or not; incorporates elements of appeal-to-identity (identity that can be inflected by individual or community modalities) and facilities-of-location; includes expectations formed by information needs and personal aspirations; and takes into account the increasingly disparate associations generated by divergent media platforms (print, web, app – all occupy different positions in the matrix of consumption). The multiple permutations resulting from the ways the separate components of the matrix can be combined and recombined create a profusion of opportunities that publishers can either manipulate or wrestle with, depending on the state of their understanding.

The *Economist*'s publishers, to judge by the way they use different platforms, have a more advanced understanding of this than many others which is why that publication's Tumblr feed can be somewhat more playful than the print edition: the content is different, the online medium brings different connotations of communication, and then the actual Tumblr platform encourages cultural lightheartedness. Taken together these elements position the Tumblr curatum in a different position within the matrix of consumption.

Position within the matrix is also affected by any given curatum's cultural and commercial purpose. Rob Orchard, who is the founder-editor of the indy publication *Delayed Gratification*, has posited three types of magazine – those written with the advertiser in mind; those written with the reader in mind; and those written by editors and writers who want to create something special.

Although this precept is inevitably a simplification, it can usefully be used as a filter to examine certain characteristics of the magazine form. The commercial and industrial aspects of this statement will be considered below but for the present note that the factor of having a specific audience or community 'in mind' is common to all three.

Community is a slippery word

This community-minded factor appears as a common strand in almost every discussion of what comprises a magazine, including the academic literature referred to above. In February 2013 the editor of *MacFormat*, Christopher Phin, posed the question again on the Flipping Pages blog (Phin, 2013) and came up with 17 definitions, or elements of a definition, without reaching a clear conclusion. Indeed his final words ("So what is a magazine? Fuck knows – go and make it up") throw the argument wide open again. The invitation to continue with the discussion was taken up by a number of commentators, most of whom essentially repeated the same points in slightly different formulation, especially Phin's first two, which are:

A magazine is a point of coalescence for passion

The magazines you read are always by definition about the things you're passionate about, whether that's explicit hobbies or objects, or a lifestyle you have or aspire to. And they're a reification of and focal point for that passion – something that will persist regardless of a magazine's medium. (Note, of course, that magazines don't have the monopoly on this.)

A magazine is something that makes you feel cooler/smarter/more interesting

The implicit or explicit lifestyle a magazine embodies is likely as important a factor in a purchase decision as the actual information it conveys.

(Phin, 2013)

If these widely accepted points are taken as axiomatic, one important aspect of magazines can be seen – they provide a locus around which communities can be constructed. Now, community is a slippery word that is used to indicate many different things in many different contexts but Benedict Anderson's (1983 [1991, 2006]) concept of the *Imagined Community* as a socially constructed entity, created collectively by those individuals who perceive themselves to be part of a particular group, provides a firm point of reference. Although Anderson used the concept to explain nationalism it can be applied to the communities that develop around magazines, not least because the readers of any given magazine are unlikely to know personally or encounter physically the majority of their fellow readers. The idea of a "deep, horizontal comradeship" (ibid., 2006: 7) accords exactly with the findings of academic (*operibus citati*) and commercial research (Consterdine, 2002) into the emotional bonds that bind readers to their magazines.

'Community' in this sense is well suited to the ultra-connected digital world of the web and social media but it has worked for decades in the physical world of print; indeed, as both circulation and advertising revenue of print magazines have declined, so publishers have made increasing efforts to turn imagined communities into real ones by offering readers opportunities to interact at various events. It is a newspaper that is most prominent in this field – *The Guardian*'s ever increasing range of Masterclasses can incorporate every subject that the paper covers – but magazines offer similar though more specifically focused events. Some operate at a significantly commercial level – the *Good Food* shows are held in major exhibition centres and *Top Gear* Live is performed (all over the world) in front of audiences that number in the thousands – while others are smaller and quieter; the *Little White Lies* Weekender that celebrated the film magazine's 50th issue (December 2013) was held in the rarified and tasteful surroundings of London's ICA, while writing workshops for the readers of *Psychologies* accommodate dozens rather than hundreds of participants at the Bloomsbury Institute.

Magazines as 'experience makers'

The examples above all concern magazines that have a physical, printed, existence. This is unsurprising as the overwhelming majority of magazines published anywhere in the world are still print-on-paper. There are signs that this is beginning to change, as we will see below, but for some academic commentators a magazine can *only* be print on paper. Professor Samir Husni of the University of Mississippi, as eminent a scholar of the form as one could hope to find, has written much and often about the condition of magazine publishing and in his blog post "What is a magazine, really? The debate goes on" (2010) he was moved to state categorically:

> Magazines are not just content providers, they are experience makers, printed one issue at a time. And, if it is not ink on paper, please try to find another name to define that new medium, because in my book if it is not printed it is not a magazine.
>
> (ibid.)

As indicated earlier, Professor Husni is far from the only person involved in this debate and his provocative post inspired much debate, some siding with him, some in opposition. For what it is worth, the authors of this chapter believe Professor Husni has made a category mistake (Ryle, 1949: 23), confusing physical format with cultural purpose, but his point about magazines being 'experience makers' is well made, especially when considered within a framework of communities of taste makers.

Alan Rutter, a British journalist and magazine consultant, was inspired by Christopher Phin (2013, see above) to consider the essence of a magazine on his own website (http://www.alanrutter.com). Following Husni's lead, Rutter (2013) includes the idea that a magazine is "an experience, not a commodity". Although other contributors to this transatlantic debate put forward a number of similarly abstract concepts, none goes much further or tries to elaborate a more theoretical framework that would accommodate the different characteristics encompassed by the binary dialectics print/digital; content/experience; commodity/community.

In an attempt to address this lacuna, Holmes and Nice proposed a five-point theory (2012) that separates the physical form of publication from the cultural purpose of publication and may illuminate a path leading towards the philosophical categorization of magazines. The theory hypothesizes that:

1. magazines always target a precisely defined group of readers;
2. magazines base their content on the expressed and perceived needs, desires, hopes and fears of that defined group;

3 magazines develop a bond of trust with their readerships;
4 magazines foster community-like interactions between themselves and their readers, and among readers;
5 magazines can respond quickly and flexibly to changes in readership and changes in the wider society.

(Holmes and Nice, 2012: 7)

Naturally there is scope for fuller investigation of each hypothesis but taken as a whole they offer a way out of the dead end of arguing about whether a magazine can only be authentic if it comprises, in words attributed to the maverick publisher Felix Dennis, hieroglyphics squashed onto dead trees. The inescapable fact is that magazine publishing is moving into the digital space and, in terms outlined by Boston Consulting in their famous Matrix (Boston Consulting Group, n.d.), print has become a mature proposition, unlikely to generate significant new levels of revenue. This is now so well recognized that a publisher as established as BBC Worldwide's magazine division has decided to manage print for profit and digital for growth; in other words, and to reduce a complex management proposition to a crude characterization, print magazines will be milked for their cash value while investment is directed towards developing apps (and whatever comes next) across all operating systems (Brett, 2013).

Two issues arise here – the commercial nature of magazine publishing, which may have repercussions on community and the cultivation of taste, and the opportunities offered by digital publishing to attract or construct communities.

It is a persistent criticism of magazines, and perhaps one reason why they tend to be overlooked by media academics, that they are too commercially oriented, and that concern with generating revenue both overrides consideration of their wider social responsibilities (by running bland or socially normative content) and encourages the development of very materialistic cultural capital. This argument is most frequently directed against women's magazines – a typical example could be found in *The Guardian* of 15 November 2013 when Belinda Parmar took the sector to task in a comment piece titled "Women's magazines ignore technology and demean women" (Parmar, 2013), a piece that was subsequently debated between Parmar and Lindsay Frankel, assistant editor of *Glamour* UK, on that day's Radio 4 *Today* programme. Parmar did not help her cause by appearing unable to distinguish between different magazines and their disparate communities. This kind of argument also perpetuates a fundamental misunderstanding, often found in undergraduate essays, of how magazines work in terms of addressing the tastes and interests of their readerships: they specialize.

Dedicated to taste

The mainstream magazine publishing industry works by segmenting interests and publishing content that meets those interests, restrictive though that may appear to be. Publishers can justifiably argue that they conduct extensive empirical research into discovering exactly what readers want and how they want it delivered: IPC spent £18m to launch *Look* magazine in February 2007, part of which funded members of the editorial team to spend time with their target readers to discover at first hand how they used their leisure, how they socialized and what they talked about. Whether it was sheer weight of investment or successful targeting of a community and the appeal to that community's cultural tastes, *Look* set out to sell 250,000 copies and actually achieved an audited sales figure of 318,907 – a vindication of the investment in careful targeting.

If *Look* was all about researching community, at the other end of the scale is a magazine like *Fire & Knives*, literally dedicated to taste by championing fine writing about good food. Its business model was to be supported only by subscriptions, eschewing advertising, and aimed at a niche audience the publishers (Tim Hayward and Kate Hawkings) suspected, and hoped, might exist. Gratifyingly, their suspicions proved correct and the magazine received rave reviews, but the readership was not large enough to support quarterly publication and after three years, in November 2013, Hayward and Hawkings combined *Fire & Knives* with *Gin & It* (fine writing about good drinks) into an annual hardback publication. If nothing else, their decision to remain analogue should give hope to printophiles like Professor Husni.

Fire & Knives only dipped into the outer fringes of digital publishing and there is a strong argument that this did them no favours as far as building a supportive community of readers was concerned – it is entirely possible that a blinkered dedication to print can restrict the vision of what online communities have to offer. *Riposte*, which bills itself as "A Smart Magazine for Women", launched its first print edition at the end of November 2013 after building interest and taking pre-orders through its website and Twitter feed – simultaneously creating community and generating cash. The twist was that *Riposte* re-introduced the idea of market scarcity by printing only 1,000 copies, limiting costs and boosting collectability in one fell swoop: the community is not limited to 1,000 people because of the digital components but the print community, those prepared to pay £10 plus £3 postage, is automatically restricted.

Scarcity is one of the key words in debates around journalism in the digital age, particularly news journalism. The argument is that while Gutenberg-era political economy ruled (Man, 2002), publishers could engineer scarcity not only because they owned the means of production and distribution, but because alternative producers of content had only limited access to an audience. In the post-Gutenberg era of websites, blogs, social media and readily affordable tools of production, scarcity has evaporated and community has become paramount, along with community interactions. Publishers can hide their content behind a paywall or subscription charge, but unless there is a community that particularly wants that content from that producer, the likely outcome is that most potential consumers will search for a freely available alternative.

Adam Westbrook (2013) has an interesting perspective on scarcity, paywalls and community after publishing four issues of his online magazine *Inside The Story*. In a frank assessment of his achievement, he explains the pros and cons of being a micropublisher on the macro-web. The 359 people who subscribed generated £3,500 in revenue; small numbers but enough, as Westbrook notes, to turn a profit and still have funds to try again. However, the lesson he regards as most important is that a paywall "acts more like a cage, trapping ideas inside where they can chirp, but they can't fly" (Westbrook, 2013). To put it another way, members of the community inside the paywall can communicate their taste to other members of that community but not to the much wider potential community outside – and when the subject matter is non-fiction storytelling, that is a potentially huge community with a potentially enormous range of taste.

It is not only micro or independent publishers who are experimenting with new ways of constructing and nurturing communities of taste. Team Rock was launched in June 2013 as a major media venture with a plan to serve the rock music community by combining the reach of radio with the depth of specialist magazines. The radio element was bought from GMG, has a business model that does not rely on spot advertisements, will provide "programmes and regular documentaries dedicated to specific audiences within the rock genre" and is "specifically targeted at a community we know is both passionate and valuable" (Team Rock, 2013a). The specialist music magazines, including *Metal Hammer* and *Classic Rock*, were acquired from Future Publishing and combine with the other elements to "create a worldwide platform for this large but under-served community" (Team Rock, 2013b; the company's chief executive, Billy Anderson, has also posted a video explaining Team Rock's genesis and strategy [Next Radio, 2013]).

Future Publishing may have sold some of its titles to Team Rock but the company is still focused on creating magazines that serve the needs and tastes of specific communities, although that service encompasses much more than print. The difficulty facing any publisher is how to establish a brand in a crowded market and how to ensure that brand incorporates the tastes and requirements of the community – or segment of the community – it is intended to reach. Six months before launching *Mollie Makes* in print and digital formats (May 2011), Future established a blog, a Facebook page, a YouTube channel, and – crucially – hired a Community Editor to engage with the crafting community, many of whom are very active online (perhaps as a result of digital marketplaces like etsy.com). This strategy had several positive results for Future: a social buzz developed around the title; feedback from the community helped to refine the editorial offering; individuals from the community could be identified as content generators (thus tightening the editorial–community circle even further); and when the print/digital launch arrived, *Mollie Makes* already had a following of several thousand, including 3,000 paying subcribers. An extremely important element of taste contributed to this success – as Carolyn Morgan (2012) noted, the "audience share a creative aesthetic which covers many aspects of their lives from interiors and styling to crafting and thrifting" (see also Marshall, 2013). Early engagement with the readership community allowed *Mollie Makes* to assess and understand the aesthetic (which is reflected in its layout and production values), the range of interests and the difficulty level of projects. It could be argued that in this case the Community Editor acted as a curator of taste and more generally that communities of taste become important as trusted filters in the blizzard of online content.

Virtual communities of taste

The key to this success undoubtedly lies in Future's understanding that although the craft community makes physical artifacts, a large amount of community interaction occurs via online and social channels. *Mollie Makes* proves that cultivating a virtual community of taste can pave the way to successful physical production, but also demonstrates beyond doubt that there is no necessary binary division between print and digital – in fact the forms realize their full potential when combined.

As a result, Future has formulated a digital development strategy, the most important elements of which, as regards community and taste, are:

- It's all about the community. The aim is to create content that will encourage sharing. This is a philosophical change for magazines – from 'me time' to community interaction.
- Be social all the time. This is key for marketing content and interaction with the community. Cultivate followers but be responsible and on message.
- Note the shift from editor to curator. Make your readers stars by making them contributors. Community can become a mode of distribution through sharing.
- Be useful. Create content that serves the needs of the community wherever they are and whatever they are doing.
- Communities are global. Digital content goes everywhere so be aware of cultural, economic and commercial differences.

Finally, and to return to our beginning, no consideration of communities and taste can escape the shadow of Pierre Bourdieu's (1984 [2010]) *Distinction*, but before attempting to draw parallels between the social and cultural role of magazines in constructing and defining taste, and taste-making as an outcome of the French class system, a clause in Bourdieu's preface to the English language edition of his book may help to locate the debate about commercialism. Explaining the "very French" form of his book, the author notes that "the mode of expression characteristic of a cultural production always depends on the laws of the market in which it is offered" (Bourdieu, 2010: xv).

We do not have to venture further than Bourdieu's introduction to find resonance with the idea that the community constructed around a particular magazine will codify its own cultural and aesthetic values (as shown in the example of *Mollie Makes* above), although it is necessary to substitute 'community', or even 'specialized community' for 'class' in the following abbreviated extract:

> This predisposes tastes to function as markers of 'class' … [Consumption is] a stage in a process of communication, that is, an act of deciphering, decoding, which presupposes practical or explicit mastery of a cipher or code   A work of art has meaning and interest only for someone who possesses the cultural competence, that is, the code, into which it is encoded … A beholder who lacks the specific code feels lost in a chaos of sounds and rhythms, colours and lines, without rhyme or reason.
>
> (ibid.: xxv)

Hence the bewilderment and lack of comprehension felt by a non-specialist reader of a specialist magazine; hence the lover of pure pop's dismay on first looking into *Metal Hammer*; hence Belinda Parmar's (2013) blanket dismissal of women's magazines and

Moya Sarner's (2013) effortless response: "Well, clearly, she has never read *Good Housekeeping*."

A little later Bourdieu declares:

> [N]othing is more distinctive, more distinguished, than the capacity to confer aesthetic status on objects that are banal or even 'common' (because the 'common' people make them their own, especially for aesthetic purposes), or the ability to apply the principles of a 'pure' aesthetic to the most everyday choices of everyday life, e.g. in cooking, clothing or decoration, completely reversing the popular disposition which annexes aesthetics to ethics.
>
> (2010: xxix)

From here it seems straightforward to apply the concepts of cultural capital – usually acquired "outside the educational system" (ibid.: 6); cultural appropriation – necessary for membership of the community and "giving access to its rights and duties" (ibid.: 15); or habitus – which "enables an intelligible and necessary relation to be established between practices and a situation" (ibid.: 95) – to the communities of taste that coalesce around specialist magazines. It might not even be going too far to claim that a specialist magazine provides "the structure of the symbolic space marked out by the whole set of these structured practices" (ibid.: 95).

Then again, sometimes a magazine is just a magazine.

Further reading

For additional scholarship in these and related areas, Jeremy Leslie's *The Modern Magazine: Visual Journalism In The Digital Age* (2013) looks at the early part of the twenty-first century and the rapid changes in the magazine industry during that time, as does Helen Powell's edited collection *Promotional Culture And Convergence: Markets, Methods, Media* (2013). For recent research in this area, Tanja Katarina Aitamurto's (2013) article "Balancing between open and closed: Co-creation in magazine journalism" offers insight into changes toward open or closed magazines now possible in a digital age. For a thorough and encompassing practical guide, Jenny McKay's edited volume *The Magazines Handbook* (2013) offers a key introduction to the field. Finally, for a perspective on magazines outside of Brtiain, David Sumner's *The Magazine Century: American Magazines Since 1900* (2010) looks at the rapid growth of US magazines in the twentieth century.

References

Abrahamson, D. (1995) *The American Magazine: Research Perspectives and Prospects*. Ames, IA: Iowa State University Press.

Aitamurto, T. K. (2013) "Balancing between open and closed: Co-creation in magazine journalism." In *Digital Journalism*, 1(2), 229–51.

Anderson, B. (1983 [1991, 2006]) *Imagined Communities: Reflections on the Origin and Spread of Nationalism*. London: Verso.

Ballaster, R., Beetham, M., Frazer, E. and Hebron, S. (1991) *Women's Worlds: Ideology, Femininity and the Woman's Magazine*. Basingstoke: Macmillan.
Barrell, J. and Braithwaite, B. (1979 [1988]) *The Business of Women's Magazines*. London: Kogan Page.
Beetham, M. (1996) *A Magazine of Her Own?* London: Routledge.
Berger, M., Wallis, B. and Watson, S. (eds.) (1995) *Constructing Masculinity*. New York: Routledge.
Boston Consulting Group (n.d.) "BCG history 1978: The star, the dog, the cow and the question mark." Retrieved from http://bit.ly/bostonmatrix
Bourdieu, P. (1984 [2010]) *Distinction: A Social Critique of the Judgement of Taste*. London: Routledge.
Brad, Wessenden Marketing PwC, NRS (2013) *PPA Snapshot*. Retrieved from http://www.ppa.co.uk/marketing/insightanddata/stats
Braithwaite, B. (1995) *Women's Magazines: The First 300 Years*. London: Peter Owen.
Brett, N. (2013) "Magazine publishing in the digital age." Lecture to students at the Cardiff School of Journalism, Media and Cultural Studies, 25 October.
Consterdine, G. (2002) *How Magazine Advertising Works IV*. London: PPA.
Currie, D. H. (1999) *Girl Talk: Adolescent Magazines and their Readers*. Toronto: University of Toronto Press.
Ferguson, M. (1983) *Forever Feminine: Women's Magazines and the Cult of Femininity*. London: Heinemann.
Friedan, B. (1963) *The Feminine Mystique*. New York: Dell Publishing Co.
Gitlin, T. (1998) "Public sphere or public sphericules?" In J. Curran and T. Liebes (eds.) *Media, Ritual and Identity*. London: Routledge (pp. 168–74).
Habermas, J. (1989) *The Structural Transformation of the Public Sphere: An Inquiry into a Category of Bourgeois Society*. Cambridge: Polity Press.
Hermes, J. (1995) *Reading Women's Magazines: An Analysis of Everyday Media Use*. Cambridge: Polity Press.
Holmes, T. (ed.) (2009) *Mapping The Magazine: Comparative Studies in Magazine Journalism*. London: Routledge.
Holmes, T. and Nice, L. (2012) *Magazine Journalism*. London: Sage.
Husni, S. (2010) *What is a magazine, really? The debate goes on*. Mr Magazine Blog, 11 June. Retrieved from 25/6/2010 http://bit.ly/husnimag
Jackson, P., Stevenson, N. and Brooks, K. (2001) *Making Sense of Men's Magazines*. Cambridge: Polity.
Korinek, V. J. (2000) *Roughing It in the Suburbs: Reading Chatelaine Magazine in the Fifties and Sixties*. Toronto: University of Toronto Press.
Leslie, J. (2013) *The Modern Magazine: Visual Journalism in the Digital Age*. London: Laurence King Publishing Ltd.
McCracken, E. (1993) *Decoding Women's Magazines From Mademoiselle to Ms*. Hampshire and London: The Macmillan Press Ltd.
McKay, J. (ed.) (2013) *The Magazines Handbook*. Abingdon: Routledge.
McRobbie, A. (1978) *Jackie: An Ideology of Adolescent Femininity*. Stencilled Occasional Paper, Centre for Contemporary Studies, Birmingham.
——(1991) *Feminism and Youth Culture: From "Jackie" to "Just Seventeen"*. Basingstoke: Macmillan Education.
Man, J. (2002) *The Gutenberg Revolution*. London: Review.
Marshall, S. (2013) "How Future builds an audience before launching a new title." Journalism.co.uk, 11 June. Retrieved from http://bit.ly/molliemarshall
Morgan, C. (2012) "Media pioneer: Mollie Makes." In *In Publishing Weekly*, 92, 20 April. Retrieved from http://bit.ly/molliemorgan

Next Radio (2013) "Billy Anderson: For those about to rock." [video] Next Radio, 7 November. Retrieved from http://bit.ly/andersonmag

Ohmann, R. (1996) *Selling Culture: Magazines, Markets and Class at the Turn of the Century*. London: Verso.

Paine, F. K. and Paine, N. E. (1987) *Magazines: A Bibliography for Their Analysis, with Annotations and Study Guide*. Metuchen & London: Scarecrow Press.

Parmar, B. (2013) "Women's magazines ignore technology and demean women." *The Guardian*, 15 November. Retrieved from http://bit.ly/parmarmag

Peterson, T. (1964) *Magazines in the Twentieth Century*. Urbana, IL: University of Illinois Press.

Phin, C. (2013) "What is a magazine?" Flipping Pages Blog, 4 February. Retrieved from http://bit.ly/phinmag

Powell, H. (ed.) (2013) *Promotional Culture And Convergence: Markets, Methods, Media*. Abingdon: Routledge.

Rutter, A. (2013) "What is a magazine?" Alan Rutter: My portfolio (not a blog), 11 February. Retrieved from http://www.alanrutter.com

Ryle, G. (1949) *The Concept of Mind*. Chicago, IL: University of Chicago Press.

Sarner, M. (2013) "Who said women's mags don't do tech?" *Good Housekeeping*, 15 November. Retrieved from http://bit.ly/sarnermag

Shevelow, K. (1989) *Women and Print Culture*. London: Routledge.

Sumner, D. E. (2010) *The Magazine Century: American Magazines Since 1900*. New York: Peter Lang.

Team Rock (2013a) "News Release: Team Rock to launch on National Digital One." Team Rock, 3 April. Retrieved from http://bit.ly/teamrock

Team Rock (2013b) "News Release: Team Rock acquires *Classic Rock* and *Metal Hammer* from Future Plc." Team Rock, 2 April. Retrieved from http://bit.ly/teamrock

Westbrook, A. (2013) "What I learnt by launching a web magazine." Journalism.co.uk, 28 November. Retrieved from http://bit.ly/westbrookmag

White, C. (1970) *Women's Magazines 1693–1968*. London: Michael Joseph.

Wood, J. P. (1956) *Magazines in the United States* (2nd ed.). New York: The Ronald Press Co.

24
Contexts and developments in women's magazines

Deborah Chambers

The history of women's lifestyle magazines reveals dramatic changes in representations and discourses of femininity. Within the mainstream magazine sector, a striking feature of this history is the framing of models of femininity within consumer discourses. This chapter traces the changing structures and contents of women's magazines up to the 1990s, with a focus mainly on the British context. The chapter identifies four broad phases in the history of women's magazines that correspond with the changing roles and status of women. The aim is to offer an understanding of the wider continuities and changes that have contributed to the formation of this popular cultural medium.

The chapter begins by addressing the rise of early women's magazines during the first historical phase, by focusing on the nineteenth century as a key moment when a form of women's magazines emerges which is recognizable to the contemporary reader. The second phase charts the inter-war and post-war years, featuring a class differentiation of the market to attract working, middle and upper-class women readers through romantic fiction, domestic advice and fashion, and society news. In the post-war period, magazines focused on domesticity and nuclear family values, providing guidance on thrifty household management during an austerity economy that continued to the 1960s. The 1970s to the 1980s represents a third phase of social changes in women's lives indicated by the contradictory trends of feminism and the feminine glamor expressed in magazines. A fourth phase, from the late 1980s to early 1990s, involves renewed attempts to define and target a 'new woman'.

Approaches to the study of women's magazines

Approaches to the study of women's periodicals include social histories of magazines; production-based and publishing industry studies; textual and content analyses; and studies of readerships. Initiating research, Cynthia White (1970) analyzed changes in form and content of magazines between 1693 and 1968 in relation to social trends and commercial and technological developments. Historical studies followed, demonstrating how women's magazines responded to marketing and advertising demands as well as social customs about gender roles (Ballaster et al., 1991; Beetham, 1996; Ellegard, 1984). Studies of the magazine industry and production have mainly addressed particular publishing traditions. For instance, Marjorie Ferguson (1983) provided a historical account of the publishing organizations, editors and production routines between the 1950s and 1980s in Britain. Anna Gough-Yates (2003) investigated the production, advertising and marketing of women's magazines in the late twentieth century.

Media and cultural analyses of women's magazine contents have involved textual and content analyses to uncover the editorial techniques employed in creating messages and layout. Early work of the 1960s and 1970s offered negative analyses. Women's magazines were identified as patriarchal texts that promote and validate gender inequality (Freidan, 1963; Tuchman, Kaplan Daniels and Benet, 1978). Later work, drawing on an Althusserian framework of ideology, addressed the ideological dimensions of magazines and the pleasures of reading them. In her study of the changing content of women's magazines, Janice Winship (1987) explained how women's magazines responded to the women's movement and addressed the pleasures of reading them. Textual analyses uncovered the textual strategies operating in women's magazines (Blix, 1992; Steiner, 1991). By the 1990s, studies of women's magazines focused on the possibilities of negotiated and oppositional readings (Ballaster et al., 1991; McCracken, 1993; MacDonald, 1995). A postmodern, celebratory register highlighting the pleasure, agency and critical stance of readers explained the appeal of magazines for their readers (Ballaster et al., 1991; Hermes, 1995). How readers interpret the content and imagery of magazines was also the focus of 1990s studies through ethnographic methods (Hermes, 1995). These four approaches underpin today's understandings of the key phases of the history of women's magazines.

Early women's magazines

Magazines for women emerged at a particular point in history – from the seventeenth and eighteenth centuries – when differences of gender rather than rank or wealth evolved as the main arbiter of social status for women (Beetham, 1996). Separate periodicals aimed at 'gentlewomen' emerged in this period. The first, the *Lady's Mercury*, was a weekly launched in 1693 that addressed women exclusively, claiming female authorship. Taking the form of a 'problem page', it focused on issues appropriate to the 'Fair Sex' (Ballaster et al., 1991). Defining 'proper femininity' was a central preoccupation in the shaping of early modern class and gender ideology (Ballaster et al., 1991; Beetham, 1996). 'Ladies' were defined by their marital status (wife, widow, virgin daughter), gentlemen by their class and professional status. By the late nineteenth century the target readerships extended to middle-class women with the rise of a prominent Victorian middle class. Early magazines up to the late nineteenth century advanced an ideology of the separate spheres; a separation of masculine and feminine social spaces effected through the articulation of a public sphere of politics and work against a private sphere of home and domesticity (Davidoff and Hall, 1988).

Periodicals placed an increasing emphasis on the doctrine of self-improvement, domestic thrift and hygiene (Ferguson, 1983: 16). The habitual association of domesticity with femininity exemplified by the *English Woman's Domestic Magazine* (1852) naturalized the idea of house management as women's work. The *English Woman's Domestic Magazine* also contained a monthly problem page, Cupid's Post Bag, featuring a series of anxious letters from readers whose problems focused on gentlemen callers, fiancé problems and preoccupations of etiquette. However, the magazine's triumph was its fashion coverage. By the 1860s, every edition presented a colored plate displaying models wearing the latest Parisian outfits. The magazine flattered its readers as fashion conscious while offering them a paper pattern to produce the same outfit for half the price (Hughes, 2008). Late nineteenth-century women's magazines also provided distinctive role models for the working class through expositions of domestic issues, fiction and fashion. The *English Workwoman* and the *Servant's Magazine* conveyed the idea that the domestic model (of staying at home as a full-time 'housewife') was unattainable for working-class women (Beetham and Boardman, 2001).

Magazine production in the late nineteenth century was characterized by men as *producers* and women as *consumers* of magazines (Beetham, 1996). Men had financial and discursive power in magazine production. Male editors wrote most of the magazine under a variety of female personae. For example, *Woman* was written mostly by the editor, Arnold Bennett, who adopted various pseudonyms, such as Barbara, Marjorie and Marguerite (Ballaster et al., 1991: 87). Commercial, rhetorical and structural strategies were fostered to generate a loyal reader of these serials through competitions, special offers and advertisements (Beetham and Boardman, 2001). Magazines acted as an advisor, mentor and friend. Readers were also attracted through magazine layout, serialized fiction, varied styles of writing and a mixture of novelty and familiarity (Beetham and Boardman, 2001: 4). Romantic fiction was characterized by modern fairy tales of the poor English aristocrat and American heiress or the demure governess and widowed nobleman (Ballaster et al., 1991).

From the 1880s, these periodicals relied increasingly on advertising rather than sales for their profits. With improvements in technology advertisements became more appealing and visually attractive, occupying greater proportions of magazine space. The development of the half-tone plate in the 1890s allowed sumptuous illustrations in magazines (Beetham and Boardman, 2001). By the end of the nineteenth century, lifestyle magazines formed a major platform for naturalizing advertising among women. Through periodicals, advertising was presented and offered as a *pleasure* and consumption was articulated as a *leisure activity*, as 'shopping' (Garvey, 1996). Expressed through appearance and taste, femininity was signified as style and status and yet also as something that could be bought. The transformation of periodical publishing into an industry during this period led to increasing professionalization and specialization in the genre. Advertising departments became more powerful than editorial departments. Agreements made with companies to favor their products evolved as a strategy for advertising revenue (Ferguson, 1983).

The various commercial means of producing and promoting magazines in the nineteenth century contrasted starkly with the principles and practices of the radical women's press of the period. The *English Woman's Journal* (1858–1864) was a proto-feminist magazine edited by Emily Faithfull and Louisa Hubbard (Beetham, 1996: 139). This monthly periodical campaigned for women's employment and equality and advocated the reform of laws that regulated gender discrimination. Articles written by women addressed a range of issues such as employment, education and the domestic environment. It campaigned for young women to be trained for work as engravers, commercial artists and schoolteachers. Other periodicals produced in the mid 1870s by Faithfull and Hubbard included *Women's Gazette* and *Women and Work*, which offered practical information on employment issues for lower middle-class women. Contrasting with commercial women's periodicals where femininity was equated with consumption, the objective of the proto-feminist periodicals was political campaigning for employment.

The inter-war and post-war years

The inter-war years: 1914 to 1939

The second phase of the inter-war years was characterized by a class differentiation of the market and the growing influence of advertising. This corresponded with increasing reliance on visual images from the 1930s. By now, the market was divided into three social class categories exemplified by romantic and melodramatic fiction for working-class women; home and fashion for the middle classes; and 'society' news, arts and fashion for the upper classes. Serial novels such as *Peg's Paper*, targeted at shop girls and mill workers, contained fantasy fiction dominated by intriguing cross-class romance. Modes of address conveyed the idea of the magazine as a 'friend'. *My Weekly* (1910) and *Woman's Weekly* (1911) established a personal, companionable tone which shaped magazine discourses for the future (Ferguson, 1983). Editors extended their publications appeal across the middle and working classes to boost audiences and advertisements. By transforming middle-class monthlies into weeklies and by employing 'experts' including psychologists, doctors and lawyers to respond to readers' questions, working-class women were enticed to magazine messages once reserved for their middle-class counterparts.

During the Second World War, British women's magazines took on new political directions. The part played by women in wartime and their impact on magazines has not been recognized until recently. During wartime, women's magazines became 'the voice of women'. Ferguson (1983: 18) explains that: "These journals were both a medium for, and mediators of, British wartime social policy, transmitting messages of sacrifice and hope to women busy keeping both factory wheels turning and home fires burning." In this period of austerity, women's lifestyle magazines had a particular appeal by providing advice and tips on how to cope with rations and shortages. Magazines such as *Woman* were described as 'utility journals' with a 'make do and mend' philosophy (White, 1970; Wilson, 1980).

Ferguson (1983: 19) refers to the dual wartime roles of women's journals as the "handmaidens of government and hand holders of the female population". For the duration of the war, government ministers and officials met with women's magazine editors to publicize wartime policies impacting on women. Ministry of Food directives were offered as firm guidance for housewives with an accent on feminine sacrifice. The propaganda value of specialist women's magazines was pursued by the Churchill and Attlee governments into the 1940s. The editorial authority of the commercial women's periodicals was expressed through an ethos of responsibility designed to generate trust among readers. Women's magazines contributed to a national consensus on aims, framed by shared notions of femininity (Winship, 1987). Significantly, mainstream newspapers never competed with the women's magazines. This confirmed the low priority placed on women as addressees of mainstream news. The exception was the short-lived *Daily Mirror*, a newspaper aimed at 'gentlewomen' that lasted 12 months. Like women's magazines, it encouraged women to express patriotism through sacrifice (Ferguson, 1983). Women's magazines of the early 1940s were, then, politicized to evoke notions of the dynamic and nation-wide civic engagement of women during wartime (Ferguson, 1983: 20). Women's work outside and inside the home was publicly validated as supporting the war effort.

The post-war period

In sharp contrast, post-war magazines revealed deep public anxieties about women's roles. Magazines promoted prescribed gender roles by encouraging employed women to opt out of the labor force and return to the home as full-time housewives. Journals such as *Women's Realm* (1958) consolidated a nuclear family ideology by focusing on 'home and hearth' and continued to evoke a 'mend and make do' austerity culture. Cooperation between government and magazine editors faded by the 1950s as competition between publishing houses increased. This phase is characterized by the shift from editorial definitions of 'Woman' as a fixed identity to more fluid, changeable identities (Ferguson, 1983: 22). It coincided with a trend of concentrated media ownership and the rise of more specialist markets, products and audiences. An expanding consumer economy and the rising affluence of readers generated high rewards from advertising revenue. The wartime formula of specialized audiences remained effective into the 1950s to accommodate growing class distinctions in consumer markets. For the first time, working-class women were gaining access to consumer durables. They were given chatty advice on how to purchase and use new gadgets in the home such as washing machines and steam irons. The editorial discourse conveyed a sense of homogeneity and consensus among working-class female readers.

The second half of the twentieth century

The third phase in the history of women's magazines, from the second half of the twentieth century to the 1980s, represents dramatic changes in women's lives and in magazine ownership. By now, the UK lifestyle magazine market was controlled by four publishing companies. Target marketing activated the marketing expert as a new professional whose status threatened to eclipse the authority of editors and editorial directors. During a period of conglomeration, few independent publishers of women's magazines succeeded. However, the 1970s also generated a more varied, segmented and declining female readership (Ferguson, 1983: 26).

In their attempts to understand women's changing lifestyles and tastes, publishers now approached women as a series of target groups. This targeting had begun to govern editorial policy by classifying readers along a social class scale from A to E to indicate 'lifestyle' and spending capacity. Age-class maps derived from the National Readership Survey (NRS) generated four sectors: 'younger-richer', 'younger-poorer', 'older-richer' and 'older-poorer'. Magazine categories based on such sectors generated 'general interest', 'home interest', 'young women's', 'real life story' and 'specific interests' (Ferguson, 1983: 33). Despite the advancement of second-wave feminism in the 1970s, it is striking that the most commercially lucrative women's magazines were those focusing on cookery, consumer issues and domesticity. These included *Woman and Home*, which led the market, and *Good Housekeeping*, which targeted aspiring professional women. Modern technology and the emphasis on advertising which had advanced visual images from the 1930s was consolidated by the 1970s and 80s. Through titles such as *Cosmopolitan*, visual appearance became a central preoccupation and illustrations of fashions offered 'models' for the readers. With the rise of the supermodel, visual features in magazines formed a crucial aspect of the discourse of pleasure. The extensive use of color photography distinguished magazines from newspapers and emphatically defined lifestyle magazines as 'leisure'.

Feminist analyses of women's magazines

Liberal feminist studies of the late 1960s and 1970s addressed the ways women's magazines distorted and misrepresented women. Betty Freidan (1963) and Tuchman, Kaplan Daniels and Benet (1978) claimed that these publications were harmful: they construct and justify gender inequalities. Such accounts identified women's magazines as antithetical to feminist principles and called for more positive images of women to reflect the aims of the women's movement. Rather than offering women innocent pleasures, these patriarchal texts were said to undermine women's identities. Late 1970s studies of women's magazines moved away from the theme of negative representations by drawing on more advanced theoretical frameworks such as Althusser's neo-Marxist model of ideology. Althusser's (1970) concept of interpellation explains that readers recognize themselves as subjects through ideological frameworks. Feminist media scholars argued that readers identify with and naturalize the ideological nature of magazine representations (Leman, 1980; Winship, 1987). Women's magazines were viewed as mechanisms of control that inferiorize women (Hermes, 1995; Gough-Yates, 2003).

Feminist studies of the late 1970s and 1980s combined Gramsci's concept of hegemony with a Barthesian semiotic approach and Althusserian structuralism to examine the relationship between the topics and themes of women's magazines and women's status in wider society (McRobbie, 1978; Winship, 1987). Winship (1987) showed how magazines of the late 1960s were influenced by and addressed second-wave feminism. These magazines appeared to present answers to questions about women's subordination. Yet they also articulated the theme of gender inequalities as personal and individualized problems. Winship (1987: 149) maintained that these texts promoted a 'post-feminist' woman capable of surmounting wider structural problems. She also emphasized the pleasures of reading glossy magazines. Magazines were marketed as an affordable treat for women, as a sensuous pleasure to be anticipated like a box of chocolates. However, pleasure was highly coded and structured, presenting women with few clues about ways of confronting gender oppression. Ros Ballaster et al. (1991) and Ellen McCracken (1993) analyzed the potential for negotiated and oppositional readings of magazine texts, drawing on a Gramscian perspective, and Stuart Hall's work on encoding/decoding (Hall, 1980). However, they concluded that the possibilities of counter-hegemonic readings were limited.

Cosmopolitan

Cosmopolitan (UK) (1972) exemplified the growing importance of visual images. It encapsulated the move towards multinational titles yet also a smaller, circumscribed readership through consumer lifestyle market targeting. *Cosmopolitan*'s promotion as a global brand by the Hearst Corporation is a demonstration of finely orchestrated cross-cultural diffusion. Its editorial policy was to embrace gender equality yet also celebrate conventional dimensions of femininity: love, romance and glamor. The title broke with the tradition of domesticity yet distanced itself from the women's movement (Winship, 1987: 100). As a key feature of *Cosmopolitan*, glamor was articulated through advertising rather than its fashion pages. It offered opulent consumer images associating femininity with desire, pleasure and fantasy. Winship (1987:101) explained that dream images were conveyed to promote an *aspirational femininity*. A 'single woman' tone was expressed through a celebration of a 'bohemian domesticity'. 'Rustling up' an elegant dinner was combined with strong personal styles of interior décor (Winship, 1987: 104). The editorial approach was polemical with debates about contraception, dieting, men's dominance in professions and women's levels of alcohol consumption, all expressed through individual opinions in rhetorical style. A pattern was established, of identifying and addressing personal problems such as partner infidelity and then exploring the problem by drawing on experts' opinions and personal experiences (Winship, 1987: 103).

Winship explained *Cosmopolitan*'s philosophy and editorial policy of the 1980s as an ideology of competitiveness and individual success which she described as an 'aspirational feminism' (Winship, 1987: 106). With an emphasis on the pleasures of sex, *Cosmopolitan*'s new femininity was also based on sexual self-assertiveness. Notions of liberalism were expressed through a 'playboy philosophy' based on the liberation of one's own (hetero)sexuality. This was represented by the stress on humor about men, sex and relationships in quizzes and articles. Importantly, shame and guilt was replaced by the fun of sex.

Spare Rib

In the same year as *Cosmopolitan*'s unveiling in the UK, the radical feminist magazine *Spare Rib* (1972) was launched. Following the tradition of the campaigning women's press of the nineteenth century, this monthly journal was forged by the women's movement. *Spare Rib* presented feminist debates and alternative gender roles for women. In stark contrast to glossy commercial magazines, it was a radical, anti-capitalist feminist venture, containing no corporate advertisements and run as a collective. Early issues were banned from the high street retailer WH Smith for being too radical. The October 1979 issue featured topics such as abortion, women's history and black women's lives. *Spare Rib* formed part of a group of 1970s independent radical publications which offered alternative perspectives to mass market women's magazines. Various dimensions of the movement including socialist, radical, revolutionary, feminist, lesbian, liberal and black feminist ones were debated across the pages of *Spare Rib*. The magazine folded in 1993 due to financial problems, indicating the difficulties of sustaining magazines unsupported by corporate advertising. Yet *Spare Rib*'s impact was far-reaching and in April 2013 it was announced that the magazine was to be resurrected (Dowell, 2013).

Working Woman

Among commercial women's magazines of the 1980s, the emphasis was firmly on accessing pleasures through *consumption* (Winship, 1987: 53). Feminized activities of housework, cooking, child care and personal grooming were portrayed as aesthetic pleasures. However, with women re-entering the workforce in large numbers, women's magazines had to grapple with women's demands for autonomy while delivering fashion and glamor. These contradictions were resolved by the glossies through a discourse of 'style' (Gough-Yates, 2003). Although the issue of the working woman was gaining in importance, certain ways of addressing this new woman were notable failures. The imported American title *Working Woman* (1984) only lasted for three years in the UK as a magazine targeted at the 'professional woman'. It was aimed at the affluent AB readership market and was attractive to advertisers. Yet *Working Woman* was unattractive to its target audience who viewed it as humorless and intense (Gough-Yates, 2003: 91).

Gough-Yates (2003: 93) identifies factors that doubtless contributed to the failure of *Working Woman*. First, it was 20 percent owned by Hal Publications, with the rest owned by small and private backers. As the magazine failed to attract sufficient advertising, Hal Publications withdrew in 1986, prompting overall financial collapse. In contrast, successful magazines owned by the multinational publisher IPC, such as *Options*, had fewer overheads, being buttressed by a vast infrastructure. They were better placed to attract 'lifestyle'-focused advertisers geared to young career women. A second factor was that although certain women were looking for more contemporary magazines in the 1980s, *Working Woman*'s emphasis on work at the expense of the traditional blend of 'home, leisure and pleasure' entailed too much 'realism'. Presenting excessive material on the often 'unpleasurable' theme of work in women's magazines was a risky move (Gough-Yates, 2003: 94).

New markets and the 'new woman' of the late 1980s and 1990s

Having learned their lesson from *Working Woman*, the new glossies of the 1980s avoided the precarious idea of addressing women as 'workers'. During this fourth phase, a 'new woman' was invented. Evoking the aspirational feminism led by *Cosmopolitan*, the 'new woman' was expressed within a consumer discourse through titles such as *New Woman* and titles already successful in Europe: *Marie Claire* and

Elle. Transnational brands promoted to readers and advertisers by magazines such as *Elle* (1985) and *Marie Claire* (1988) signified Europeanness, stylishness and boldness (Gough-Yates, 2003). The magazine industry needed to present itself to advertisers as being 'in tune' with potential readers in accord with contemporary femininity. Gough-Yates (2003: 117) draws on Bourdieu's (1984 [1979]) concept of 'cultural intermediaries' to explain that editors adopted the status of intermediaries between advertisers and readers. Editors presented themselves as having a 'sixth sense' to tap into the 'mood' of their readership.

However, competition from new advertising possibilities via the internet, satellite and cable TV broadcasting forced innovation. It led to the revitalization of the advertorial, tabloid-style features and weekly celebrity magazines such as *Hello!* (1988) and *OK!* (1993). Magazines extended their focus to celebrity culture. They conducted interviews and cover shoots with public figures such as film stars, singers and supermodels. Celebrities such as Angelina Jolie, Gwyneth Paltrow and Madonna featured on the covers and inside pages of the glossies. Despite their other-worldliness, such public figures were viewed as embodying the aspirations and temperaments of magazine readers (Gough-Yates, 2003: 136). The celebrity personality was presented as emblematic of individualism, success and bodily attractiveness.

The growing sexualization of images of young femininity triggered public debates and prompted reports on women's magazines which condemned their content as morally culpable (Anderson and Mosbacher, 1997). Magazine images of femininity were viewed as indicative of a moral decline in British culture. Editors defended themselves by explaining that young women bought magazines to escape from reality into fantasy. Ambiguities about the distinctions between representations and reality became a major issue in analyzing the relationship between editorial objectives and readers' pleasures. An emphasis by editors on the amusing, ironic and light-hearted tone of magazines sought to deflect accusations of negative effects on readers (Gough-Yates, 2003: 139).

How far the rhetoric of female sexual confidence expressed in magazines of the 1990s corresponded to wider social customs among young women is uncertain. Joke Hermes (1995: 146) reminded us that readers often decode women's magazines in ways that differ markedly from the preferred readings in the text. Readers may be engaging with magazines as mechanisms for imagining an ideal 'new self' which is rarely acted out in reality. However, sociological studies indicated that significant changes in representations of young people's lives were not automatically leading to equality in relationships between young men and women by the 1990s. Boys and young men continued to exercise power over young women and young women continued to negotiate their feminine identities through a male gaze (Holland et al., 1988: 10). McRobbie (1997) maintained that post-feminist images signified a further commodification of femininity.

Conclusion

The history of commercial women's magazines demonstrates the rapid domination of the industry by a small number of publishers. This history also reveals the far-reaching power of the advertising and wider marketing strategies involved in re-presenting women's social roles, identities and status. From the mid nineteenth century, women's magazines have had to sell to two sets of clients: buyers of the magazines and buyers of the magazines' advertisement pages. As Hughes (2008) observes: "Few other artefacts, after all, have to be sold twice simultaneously to be considered successful." This process demonstrates the framing of representations of femininity through consumerist discourses (Featherstone, 1991; Lury, 1999). While publishers and editors of the post-war period maintained the principles established by their eighteenth and nineteenth-century antecedents, women's magazines increasingly differentiated their target groups to adapt to women's changing aspirations. By the late twentieth century, magazines had to mediate competing commercial and feminist discourses to produce an appealing, pleasurable and glamorous model of 'woman'. This more recent phase confirms the significance for women of the pleasures of reading.

The increased focus on consumer lifestyles corresponds with the notion of the post-feminist woman (McRobbie, 1990). During the 1990s, through magazines such as *Cosmopolitan* and *New Woman*, post-feminist ideals and claims to empowerment prompted more complex narratives about 'relationships' and sexual pleasures. Through certain representational conventions, discourses of sexual assertiveness were offered to women readers as discursive strategies and ontological states in relationships with men. This indicates that the nature of the interconnections between popular representations, the enjoyment of reading and the reality of women's lives cannot be fully explained by analyzing representations alone. It highlights the need to generate methods to examine more comprehensively the relationship between representations and social reality as well as between texts and audiences.

Further reading

Margaret Beetham's (1996) *A Magazine of Her Own? Domesticity and Desire in the Woman's Magazine, 1800–1914* provides a chronological history of the ways women's magazines used images and writing to define femininity and address the desires of readers. Marjorie Ferguson (1983) in her *Forever Feminine: Women's Magazines and the Cult of Femininity* explores the ways that magazine representations of women were influenced by cultural, social and economic changes between the 1950s and 1980s, explaining how these periodicals maintained a 'cult of femininity'. Anna Gough-Yates' *Understanding Women's Magazines: Publishing, Markets and Readerships* (2003) focuses on the 1980s and 1990s. Gough-Yates explains how the production and marketing of women's magazines influenced ideas about the reader, and the emergence of images of a 'New Woman' is explained in relation to middle-class femininities. Finally, Janice Winship (1987) offers a study of 1980s women's magazines in *Inside Women's Magazines*. She examines *Women's Own*, *Cosmopolitan* and *Spare Rib* and explores the pleasures of reading and how magazines responded to the changing status of women.

References

Althusser, L. (1970) "Ideology and ideological state apparatuses." In *Lenin and Philosophy and other Essays*. London: New Left Books (pp. 170–86).

Anderson, D. and Mosbacher, M. (eds.) (1997) *The British Woman Today: A Qualitative Survey of the Images in Women's Magazines*. London: The Social Affairs Unit.

Ballaster, R., Beetham, M., Frazer, E. and Hebron, S. (1991) *Women's Worlds: Ideology, Femininity and the Women's Magazines*. Basingstoke: Macmillan.

Beetham, M. (1996) *A Magazine of Her Own? Domesticity and Desire in the Woman's Magazine, 1800–1914*. London: Routledge.

Beetham, M. and Boardman, K. (2001) *Victorian Women's Magazines*. Manchester: Manchester University Press.

Blix, J. (1992) "A place to resist: Reevaluating women's magazines." *Journal of Communication Inquiry*, 16(1), 56–71.

Bourdieu, P. (1984 [1979]) *Distinction: A Social Critique of the Judgement of Taste*. London: Routledge.

Davidoff, L. and Hall, C. (1988) *Family Fortunes: Men and Women of the English Middle Class, 1780–1850*. London: Hutchinson.

Dowell, B. (2013) "Spare Rib magazine to be relaunched by Charlotte Raven." *The Guardian*, 25 April. Retrieved from http://www.guardian.co.uk/media/2013/apr/25/sarah-raven-relaunch-spare-rib

Ellegard, A. (1984) *The Readership of the Periodical Press in Mid-Victorian Britain*. Goteborg: Goteborg University Press.

Featherstone, M. (1991) *Consumer Culture and Postmodernism*. London: Sage.

Ferguson, M. (1983) *Forever Feminine: Women's Magazines and the Cult of Femininity*. London: Heinemann.

Freidan, B. (1963) *The Feminine Mystique*. Harmondsworth: Penguin.

Garvey, E. G. (1996) *The Adman in the Parlour: Magazines and the Gendering of Consumer Culture, 1880s to 1910s*. New York: Oxford University Press.

Gough-Yates, A. (2003) *Understanding Women's Magazines: Publishing, Markets and Readerships*. London: Routledge.

Hall, S. (1980; reprinted 1992, 1996) "Encoding/decoding." In S. Hall, D. Hobson, A. Lowe and P. Willis (eds.) *Culture, Media, Language: Working Papers in Cultural Studies*. London: Routledge (pp. 128–38).

Hermes, J. (1995) *Understanding Women's Magazines*. Cambridge: Polity.

Holland, J., Ramazanoglu, C., Sharpe, S. and Thomson, R. (1988) *The Male in the Head*. London: Tufnell Press.

Hughes, K. (2008) "Zeal and Softness." *The Guardian*, 20 December. Retrieved from http://www.guardian.co.uk/books/2008/dec/20/women-pressandpublishing

Leman, J. (1980) "'The advice of a real friend': Codes of intimacy and oppression in Women's Magazines 1937–55." *Women's Studies International Quarterly*, 3(1), 63–78.

Lury, C. (1999) *Consumer Culture*. Cambridge: Polity.

McCracken, E. (1993) *Decoding Women's Magazines: From* Mademoiselle *to* Ms. New York: St. Martin's Press.

Macdonald, M. (1995) *Representing Women: Myths of Femininity in the Popular Media*. London: Arnold.

McRobbie, A. (1978) "Jackie: An Ideology of Adolescent Femininity." Occasional Paper, The Birmingham Centre for Contemporary Cultural Studies

——(1990) *Feminism and Youth Culture: From Jackie to Just Seventeen*. Basingstoke: Macmillan.

——(1997) "More! New sexualities in girls' and women's magazines." In A. McRobbie (ed.) *Back to Reality? Social Experiences and Cultural Studies*. Manchester: Manchester University Press (pp. 190–209).

Steiner, L. (1991) "Oppositional decoding as act of resistance." In R. K. Avery and D. Eason (eds.) *Critical Perspectives on Media and Society*. London: The Guilford Press (pp. 29–45).

Tuchman, G., Kaplan Daniels, A. and Benet, J. (eds.) (1978) *Hearth and Home: Images of Women in the Mass Media*. Oxford: Oxford University Press.
White, C. (1970) *Women's Magazines, 1693–1968*. London: Michael Joseph.
Wilson, E. (1980) *Only Half Way to Paradise*. London: Tavistock Publications.
Winship, J. (1987) *Inside Women's Magazines*. London: Pandora.

25
Mapping the male in magazines
Bill Osgerby

Men's magazines and masculine identities

The launch of *Arena* in 1986 heralded a seismic shift in British magazine publishing. General interest magazines targeted at women were a long-established market sector, but in Britain the idea of a popular 'lifestyle' magazine geared to men had long been thought unfeasible. *Arena*, however, defied industry skeptics. Produced by Wagadon, a small, independent publishing firm, *Arena* was an instant hit, successfully wooing male readers with a combination of features on clothes, music, movies, food, sport, travel and books. *Arena*'s achievement was subsequently emulated and exceeded by rival publishers who launched 'men's lifestyle' titles of their own. During the late 1980s and 1990s newsagents' shelves bulged with glossy general interest magazines targeted at men and by 2000 their overall monthly sales topped 2 million.

The burgeoning market for British men's magazines attracted both popular attention and academic studies. The research was constituent in a wider proliferation of scholarship – in the social sciences and humanities – that sought to interrogate the nature of masculine identities and their associated power relations across a wide variety of cultures, historical periods and institutional settings. In the fields of media and cultural studies, the analysis of masculinity was often influenced by poststructuralist theories of gender such as those developed by Judith Butler. For Butler, gender categories are multiform and historically variable rather than monolithic and timelessly fixed. Gender, Butler argues, should not be conceived as a stable identity or an "agency from which various acts follow", but instead should be recognized as "an identity tenuously constituted in time, instituted in an exterior space through a stylized repetition of acts" (Butler, 1990: 140). In these terms, gender is understood as a historically dynamic "performance" – a "corporeal style" that is fabricated and sustained through a set of performative acts and "a ritualized repetition of conventions" (Butler, 1995: 31).

Informed by such perspectives, studies of men's magazines highlighted their relationship with changing conceptualizations of 'maleness'. This work acknowledged that shifts in the market for men's magazines, together with changes in magazine content and modes of address, have been partly indebted to issues of production, marketing, advertising and editorial agenda. But research also emphasized the way changes in the character and format of men's magazines have been inextricably linked with developments in the cultural meanings of masculinity. Critical analyses of men's magazines have highlighted how their history has been entwined with broader changes in notions of masculinity; not simply as texts where wider shifts in the articulation of masculine identities are reflected, but as sites within and around which these shifts are constructed, negotiated and circulated.

The early development of men's magazines

Founded in 1731 by the British businessman Edward Cave, *The Gentleman's Magazine* is commonly regarded as the first general magazine for men. Before its launch numerous specialized journals already existed, but Cave's innovation was to create a monthly digest of news and commentary on a wide range of topics, from Latin poetry to commodity prices. Appealing to a prosperous, upper-class readership, *The Gentleman's Magazine* was edited by Cave, whose business skills brought the magazine distribution to the whole English-speaking world and, under different editors and publishers, it flourished through the eighteenth and nineteenth centuries before declining and finally folding in 1922.

While the interests of *The Gentleman's Magazine* were diverse, business news and matters of public and political life constituted much of its content. This emphasis on commercial and civic affairs substantiates notions of nineteenth-century masculine identities as being largely rooted in the realms of work and production. Historians such as John Tosh (1994), for example, highlight the codes of hard work, self-control and vigorous independence that were central to dominant codes of British masculinity during the Victorian era. In the United States, meanwhile, E. Anthony Rotundo (1993) demonstrates how models of middle-class manhood during the late nineteenth century were rooted in enterprise, productiveness and temperate respectability.

Other historians, however, have spotlighted the rise of masculine identities outside these production-oriented archetypes. In his analysis of menswear retailing in Victorian London, for example, Christopher Breward (1999) demonstrates the emergence of models of manhood rooted in fashionable display and consumer practice; and in the United States both Mark Swiencicki (1998) and Howard Chudacoff (1999) show how America's developing urban centers were, by the late nineteenth century, home to an extensive 'bachelor subculture' formed around practices of consumerism and commercial entertainments. The developing ethos of masculine consumerism also registered in the field of magazine publishing. As Tom Pendergast (2000) argues, during the late nineteenth century American general feature magazines such as *McClure's*, *Munsey's* and the *Saturday Evening Post* were initially based around masculine values of hard work, thrift and production, but gradually embraced models of manhood constructed around commodity consumption. The early twentieth century, meanwhile, saw magazines such as *Vanity Fair* (originally launched in 1892) and *New Success* (1918) offer visions of masculinity based even more explicitly around a consumerist agenda that encouraged men to think of themselves "not as objective cores of values but as ... malleable potentialities, capable of achieving multiple expressions through the goods they purchased and the way they presented themselves" (Pendergast, 2000: 140–42). For Pendergast, however, it was only with the launch of *Esquire* magazine that these fragments of masculine consumerism were pulled together into "a coherent representation of a modern masculine ideal" (Pendergast, 2000: 28).

In 1933 the height of the Great Depression saw roughly a quarter of the American workforce unemployed but that autumn the launch of *Esquire* testified to the survival of an upmarket culture of fashion and leisure. The magazine's owners, David Smart and William Weintraub, had originally produced catalogs for men's fashion stores but, as the economic downturn bit into sales, the duo had sought business alternatives and drafted in Arnold Gingrich (chief editor of their catalogs) to develop a new magazine aimed at fashion store customers. Billing itself as 'The Magazine For Men', *Esquire*'s high production values and large, colorful format ensured a hefty cover price of fifty cents. Nevertheless, industry expectations that the magazine would flounder were quickly defied. The 105,000 copies of *Esquire*'s first edition soon sold out and, though originally projected as a quarterly, the magazine went monthly with its second issue, with circulation soaring to more than 728,000 by 1938 (Merrill, 1995: 45, 51).

As Kenon Breazeale observes, *Esquire*'s grand strategy was to "organize a consuming male audience" (Breazeale, 1994: 1). From the outset Gingrich crafted the magazine into the peerless arbiter of cosmopolitan finesse. At the center of the formula was a reverence for tasteful elegance. Alongside copious advertisements for high-class menswear, *Esquire* featured its own colorful illustrations of the latest trends in male attire, complemented by coverage of fashionable nightlife, 'exotic' travelogues and features on gourmet cuisine and chic furnishings, all underlining the magazine's appeal to a readership of affluent and leisure-oriented middle-class men.

Historically, however, the realms of fashion and consumption had markedly feminine associations. This made them uncertain territory for many men anxious to avoid suggestions of effeminacy. As a consequence, *Esquire* potentially jeopardized its readership's self-image by venturing into fields closely associated with feminine social roles such as fashion, cookery and home furnishing. Indeed, this was something of which the magazine's editorial team was well aware and they worked hard to avoid effete connotations. From the outset, therefore, Gingrich went to great lengths to include elements that were, as he later euphemistically put it, "substantial enough to deodorize the lavender whiff coming from the mere presence of fashion pages" (Gingrich, 1971: 81). In line with this policy, the 1930s saw *Esquire* carefully signpost its commitment to sturdy machismo through regular coverage of sports such as baseball and boxing, together with frequent articles on daredevil pursuits such as big game hunting and bullfighting. Ruggedly masculine imagery also surfaced in many of the magazine's general articles and short stories, not least in those written by literary tough guy Ernest Hemingway, a regular *Esquire* contributor. Risqué cartoons and titillating pin-ups, moreover, underscored the magazine's claims to resolute heterosexuality. Adopting these strategies, Breazeale argues, *Esquire* worked to "displace all the woman-identified associations so firmly lodged at the center of America's commodified domestic environment" (Breazeale, 1994: 6). Using its 'macho' content to secure its masculine and heterosexual credentials, *Esquire* was free to address its readers as unabashedly style-conscious consumers, steering them 'safely' through the provinces of visual pleasure and consumer practice.

Comparable, though less successful, magazines also developed in Britain. In 1937, for example, the photojournalist Stefan Lorant launched the pocket-sized *Lilliput*. A lack of advertising meant the magazine struggled for profitability and was bought up by Hulton Press in 1938, who crafted it into a title pitched at a readership of middle-class men who aspired to racy cosmopolitanism, blending humor, short stories and general features with discreetly airbrushed nude pictorials. According to Jill Greenfield and her associates, however, it was another pocket-sized title, *Men Only*, that represented "the first British attempt at the commercial orchestration of masculinity via the medium of a men's lifestyle magazine" (Greenfield, O'Connell and Reid, 1999: 458). Launched by the publisher Pearson in 1935, *Men Only* had a format paralleling that of *Esquire*. Like *Esquire*, Greenfield et al. argue, *Men Only* combined style features with pictorials of female nudes and articles that championed 'heroic' manhood in a way that allowed the promotion of a consumption-oriented masculinity untainted by suspicions of effeminacy.

Men's magazines and the 'Playboy ethic'

The economic boom in America that followed the Second World War saw masculine excursions into the field of commodity consumption further extended. This was reflected in the world of magazine publishing by the rise of new titles pitched to readerships of style-conscious men. *Esquire* steadily carved out a new niche as a quality features magazine, but its earlier consumerist agenda was adopted by several newcomers. *True* magazine, for example, had started life as a downmarket pulp title focused on adventure stories when it was launched by Fawcett Publications in 1936, but during the mid 1940s it was reconfigured as a working-class equivalent to *Esquire*, its formula of masculine consumerism repackaged for "the hunting, beer and poker set" (Pendergast, 2000: 208). The move was a commercial masterstroke and in 1948 *True* became the first men's magazine whose circulation topped one million. Other titles also adopted *True*'s strategy. In 1951, for instance, the Publisher's Development Corporation launched *Modern Man*. With many red-blooded and traditionally 'manly' features, *Modern Man* was largely geared to the outdoors 'action man', though the magazine also tentatively embraced upscale consumption through its glossy presentation and coverage of stylish luxury goods. Above all, however, it was *Playboy* magazine that most successfully updated the *Esquire* format for a new generation of male consumers.

Launched on a shoestring budget in 1953 by its publisher and editor, Hugh Hefner, *Playboy*'s monthly circulation had skyrocketed to nearly a million a month by 1959 and soared to more than 4.5 million over the next ten years. Billing itself as 'Entertainment for Men', *Playboy*'s mix of nude pictorials and upmarket lifestyle features clearly took inspiration from *Esquire*. Indeed, since his school days, Hefner had been an avowed fan of the magazine and in 1951 had briefly worked in *Esquire*'s subscriptions department. And, amid the 1950s consumer boom, Hefner revised *Esquire*'s formula to create an editorial package that, as Carrie Pitzulo argues, went against the grain of postwar conformism and sexual conservatism by espousing a credo of "urbanity, liberal politics, style, love of leisure, and lack of familial commitment" (Pitzulo, 2011: 18).

The sexual content of *Playboy* was clearly intrinsic to its appeal, but the magazine amounted to more than slickly packaged porn. As Elizabeth Fraterrigo (2009) demonstrates, *Playboy* represented a visionary bible for the professional-managerial middle-class at a time of social and cultural flux. Responding to the explosion of consumerism after the war, Fraterrigo argues, policy makers, public intellectuals and advertisers frequently invoked a notion of 'the good life', an abstract concept that encompassed the apparent comfort, security and abundance made possible by propitious levels of economic growth. One pervasive version of this ideal was the promotion of family life and suburban domesticity; a vision that venerated traditional gender roles, conventional morality and cultural conformity. Against this, however, both Barbara Ehrenreich (1984) and Fraterrigo identify the proliferation of a 'playboy ethic' that offered "an alternative, often controversial, and highly resonant version of the good life" (Fraterrigo, 2009: 3). This was the creed proselytized by *Playboy*. Suffused with images of cosmopolitan pleasure-seeking, Fraterrigo argues, *Playboy* guided its upwardly mobile male readers through the unfolding world of commodity consumption, "offering a model for living that demystified the male consumer, showing him how to display style and taste, to assert status in the social hierarchy while sanctioning a pleasure-seeking approach to life" (Fraterrigo, 2009: 9). Indeed, this was a cultural trope that Hefner exploited to the full, his magazine's soaring circulation serving as the launchpad for an international *Playboy* business empire that embraced publishing, movie production and a chain of nightclubs, casinos and hotels.

Throughout the 1950s and 1960s *Playboy*'s success inspired a legion of imitators. *Esquire*'s publishers, for example, responded with a revamped version of *Gentlemen's Quarterly*. Originally published during the 1930s as a menswear trade journal, the magazine was relaunched in 1957 as a high-class fashion magazine for the 1950s man of style. Closer to *Playboy*'s format were a roster of other titles, all pitched to roguish men of means. For example, 1956 alone saw the launch of *Gent*, *Gay Blade*, *The Dude*, *Escapade*, *Nugget* and *Rogue*. These titles had a slick and colorful presentation and a higher quota of sexual content than *Playboy*, though their production values were poorer and their circulations were measured in hundreds of thousands rather than *Playboy*'s millions.

Compared to the United States, masculine ideals of stylish consumption reached fruition more slowly in Britain. As Frank Mort (1997) argues, the development of British consumerism was slower, partial and more uneven than the American experience. The emergence of a 'playboy ethic' in Britain, therefore, was more hesitant and less dramatic. Nevertheless, amid Britain's consumer boom of the late 1950s and early 1960s, consumerist articulations of masculinity were undoubtedly discernible. Mort's research on the Burton's fashion empire, for example, shows how this chain of men's clothes shops underwent profound change from the mid 1950s – the firm's image of formal and gentlemanly manhood being eclipsed by decor, advertising and products that foregrounded discourses of individuality, hedonism and consumer pleasure (Mort, 1996: 134–45, 1997: 19–22; Mort and Thompson, 1994).

Similar developments occurred in British magazines. *Men Only* and *Lilliput* had sold well during the war and in 1950 were joined by *Pall Mall*, its title quickly changed to *Clubman*. Mixing 'artistic' nude pictorials with film star pin-ups, humor and general features, *Clubman* declared itself "Britain's favorite entertainment magazine for discriminating men." As its title suggested, however, *Clubman* had a stuffy, parochial ambiance redolent of pipesmoke and tweed. More influential was *Man About Town*. Launched in 1951 by *The Tailor and Cutter* (a long-established menswear trade journal), *Man About Town* was originally a pocket-sized quarterly intended to provide "The What, When and How of Men's Clothes." The magazine articulated a version of masculinity that was sophisticated and urbane (exemplified by its restaurant guides, fashion advice and travel features), yet was still securely anchored in the conservative and temperate ethos of the traditional city gent. Gradually, however, the magazine's content and mode of address became more upbeat and lively. In 1961 the title was sold to Haymarket Press who abbreviated the title to *About Town* (and in 1962 simply to *Town*) and the magazine was transformed into a beacon of masculine hedonism and hectic consumption.

American titles also courted the British market. A British edition of *Esquire* was launched in 1954, but disappeared three years later. More successful was a British edition of *Playboy*. Launched in 1965, its circulation grew to 90,000 by 1972. A home-grown paean to masculine high living also appeared in 1964 with the launch of *King* magazine, though by 1967 sliding sales had forced a merger with *Mayfair* (a more explicitly pornographic title). *Club* was another British failure. Launched in 1970 by publishing giant IPC, *Club* was glossy and colorful, brimming with features on football, sex, fast cars and fashion. Overtaken by a burgeoning range of pornographic titles, however, *Club* soon faded away. *Penthouse* fared better. Consciously modeled as a British equivalent to *Playboy*, *Penthouse* was launched by the publisher Bob Guccione in 1965. Such was the magazine's success that in 1969 Guccione launched *Penthouse* in the US, though the magazine's general features were soon eclipsed by its pornographic content as *Penthouse* steadily positioned itself in the porn market.

The new man and men's lifestyle magazines

In contrast to America, Britain's more checkered history of men's magazines persuaded many in the publishing industry that general interest titles geared to men were unviable. While British men seemed happy to buy magazines focused on a specific topic or pastime, for instance cars, fishing or photography, there was skepticism about whether they would buy a title organized around a masculine identity rather than a specific hobby. During the early 1980s, however, a wave of popular style magazines such as *Blitz*, *I-D* and *The Face* suggested fresh possibilities. Produced by independent publishing companies, the new style press was staffed by writers immersed in the world of music, fashion and avant-garde culture. Launched in 1982 by Wagadon and edited by Nick Logan, *The Face* was especially successful and, while it was not explicitly a 'men's magazine', its appeal to a largely male readership suggested that a general interest title geared to men held market potential. Consequently, Wagadon launched *Arena* in 1986. Steered by Logan, *Arena* adopted the chic aesthetic flair perfected at *The Face*, integrating it with features on men's fashions and accessories, together with reviews of consumer goods and outlets (shops, restaurants, bars and clubs), all detailed in a tone that, as Ben Crewe observes, "marked out the magazine's readership as a discriminating, trendsetting, metropolitan elite" (Crewe, 2003: 34).

Arena's first audited circulation touched an impressive (for the time) 65,000 and upmarket brands were soon lining up for advertising space. *Arena* thrived throughout the following decade, its circulation edging over 93,000 in 1996. But even this was eclipsed by new rivals. Once *Arena*'s profitability was clear, the main publishers followed suit, aiming to get a share of the burgeoning men's market by creating men's 'lifestyle' titles to match their established women's magazines. In 1988, for example, the magazine publishing giant Condé Nast launched a new incarnation of *GQ* (*Gentlemen's Quarterly*), which successfully appealed to a readership which, while older and more conservative than that of *Arena*, was no less interested in the world of stylish consumerism. Exceeding 100,000 throughout the 1990s, *GQ*'s circulation was matched by a new British version of *Esquire*. The magazine's original British edition had foundered in 1957, but in 1991 *Esquire* was freshly launched onto the British market by National Magazine Company and found success by aping *GQ*'s pitch to a high-end market of style-conscious male consumers.

For many commentators the surge in British men's magazines was constituent of broader shifts in masculine identities. In journalistic accounts the success of men's 'lifestyle' titles was often related to the rise of a new masculine archetype, the 'new man', configured variously as sensitive, emotionally aware and egalitarian, or as vain and heavily invested in his physical appearance. For many academics the popularity of men's magazines was also constituent in broader cultural trends marked, as Crewe explains, by a "proliferation of imagery that represented men in ways that were more narcissistic, self-conscious, emotionally expressive, domesticated and 'feminine' than conventional iconography of patriarchal authority, action and machismo" (Crewe, 2003: 31). Theorists such as Frank Mort and Sean Nixon offered relatively positive interpretations of these new models of masculinity. Mort, for example, argued that the visual codes of the 1980s new man offered men "pleasures previously branded feminine or taboo" and worked to "rupture traditional icons of masculinity" by encouraging men "to look at themselves – and other men – as objects of consumer desire" (Mort, 1988: 194). Nixon was equally optimistic, arguing that the imagery of the new man represented a "loosening of the binary opposition between gay and straight-identified men and extended the space available within the representational regimes of popular consumption for an ambivalent masculine identity" (Nixon, 1996: 202). Others, however, were more circumspect. Critics such as Rowena Chapman (1988) and Mark Simpson (1994), for instance, argued that outside the world of advertising the cultural impact of the new man was limited, while the transgressive potential of the new man's imagery was undercut by the invariable presence of phallic symbols (in the form of champagne bottles, saxophones and so on) that expressed conventional qualities of action, power and control. Tim Edwards, moreover, highlighted the way the consumerist sensibilities associated with new man were rooted in the prevalent, conservative ideals of aspirational individualism and so should be seen "as equally personally destructive and socially divisive as they are individually expressive and democratically utopian" (Edwards, 1997: 2).

The new lad and 'lads' mags'

Despite the success of lifestyle titles such as *Arena*, men's general interest magazines were still regarded as a niche market by British publishers. However, this changed during the 1990s as a new wave of titles shifted men's magazines from the industry margins to the mainstream market. It was *Loaded* that led the way. Launched by IPC in April 1994, *Loaded* was the brainchild of an editorial team comprising Mick Bunnage, Tim Southwell and James Brown. Under their aegis the magazine consciously defined itself against the earlier lifestyle magazines. In contrast to the earnest, almost highbrow, tone adopted by the likes of *Arena* and *GQ*, *Loaded* targeted a younger, more hedonistic readership with its frenetic, irreverent style and emphasis on 'cultish' (and distinctly British) subcultures of music, fashion, sport and humor. The magazine's launch went virtually unnoticed by the publishing industry, but within nine months *Loaded* was clocking up a monthly circulation of over 100,000.

Spurred by IPC's coup, rival companies quickly launched titles that emulated the *Loaded* formula. Emap, for instance, pitched in with *FHM*. Originally owned by the independent publisher Tayvale and launched in 1985, *FHM* had started life as *For Him Magazine*, a poorly selling menswear title. Bought by Emap and relaunched in 1995, the reconfigured *FHM* was clearly influenced by *Loaded*'s recipe of humor and hedonism. Compared to its forerunner, *FHM* had fewer drink and drug references and placed more emphasis on light features and practical advice, together with a greater quota of sexualized (soft-core) representations of women. But *FHM* shared *Loaded*'s ironic humor and 'blokeish' banter. The same traits were also central to *Maxim*. Launched by the millionaire publisher Felix Dennis in April 1995, *Maxim* was targeted at a slightly older ('thirty-something') readership than its competitors, though it shared a similar editorial style, mixing features on fashion, sport and entertainment with a cheeky brashness, an assumed heterosexuality and an attitude to issues of gender, sexuality and personal relationships marked by jokey irony. The approach proved hugely popular and *Maxim*'s monthly circulation climbed to 328,000 by 2000. But even this was outstripped by *FHM*'s success. By 1996 *FHM* had become Britain's biggest selling men's magazine, and the following year had overtaken the successful women's magazine *Cosmopolitan* to become the UK's most popular lifestyle title, with a monthly circulation of over 500,000. International expansion soon followed, with *Maxim* launching a US edition in 1998 and *FHM* following suit in 1999.

Again, this shift in men's magazines was widely interpreted as being rooted in broader developments in masculine identities. Dubbed 'lads' mags' by the popular media, titles such as *Loaded*, *Maxim* and *FHM* were associated with the emergence of a new masculine archetype – the 'new lad'. As Rosalind Gill notes, while the new man was characterized as emotionally sophisticated and liberal in his attitudes to gender and sexuality, the new lad was depicted as:

> hedonistic, post-(if not anti) feminist, and pre-eminently concerned with beer, football and 'shagging' women. His outlook on life could be characterized as anti-aspirational and owes a lot to a particular classed articulation of masculinity ... A key feature of some constructions of the 'new lad' is the

emphasis on his knowing and ironic relationship to the world of serious adult concerns.

(Gill, 2003: 37)

Versions of the new lad surfaced in a range of media contexts, but it was in the 'lads' mags' that he found his clearest voice. As Nixon (1996) observes, the change had originally registered in *Arena* and *GQ* during 1991, marked by an increase in sexualized representations of women and a more "assertive articulation of post permissive heterosexual masculine scripts" (Nixon, 1996: 203). But it was *Loaded* that gave the new lad full form, its first editorial in May 1994 announcing (with a characteristically ironic inflection) that the magazine was dedicated to "life, liberty and the pursuit of sex, drink, football and less serious matters." And, as Gill argues, *FHM* and *Maxim* followed in *Loaded*'s wake, "constructing a powerful discourse of 'laddism' which kicked off against feminism, the figure of the new man and also older (unreconstructed or Neanderthal) lad identities" (Gill, 2003: 49).

For many theorists, the rise of the new lad represented a backlash against feminism. Imelda Wheelan, for example, argues that the new lad archetype marked "a nostalgic revival of old patriarchy; a direct challenge to feminism's call for social transformation, by reaffirming, albeit ironically, the unchanging nature of gender relations and sexual roles" (Wheelan, 2000: 5). Karen Ross adopts a similar perspective, contending that the 'lads' mags' were "sexist backlash masquerading as knowing parody", their ironic gloss functioning as "a cynical strategy to derail and forestall criticism, allowing magazines to peddle a discourse of self-mockery which is entirely disingenuous, allowing the expression of politically incorrect sentiment to coexist with the simultaneous claim that this is not at all what is meant" (Ross, 2010: 21). From this perspective, then, the new lad and his 'lads' mags' represented a defensive assertion of masculine power in the face of changing gender relations and the challenge of feminism.

According to Peter Jackson and his associates, however, 'lads' mags' were distinguished by a significant contradiction and ambiguity. In their research on the magazines' readers, Jackson and his colleagues found there were "many ambivalences in how the magazines were read and talked about" (Jackson, Stevenson and Brooks, 2001: 4), so that the magazines represented spaces in which "different forms of masculinity are emerging and competing for public attention" (ibid.: 145). In these terms, the magazines were indicative of the uncertainty and instability of contemporary masculine identities. But they also offered readers a sense of reassurance and "constructed certitude" amid changing notions of gender and sexuality, serving as "a kind of cultural comfort zone, giving men the discursive resources to handle their changing circumstances and experiences" (ibid.: 156). Edwards, meanwhile, sees shifts in the character of men's magazines as having "very little to do with sexual politics and a lot more to do with markets for the constant reconstruction of masculinity through consumption" (1997: 82). For Edwards, the success of the 'lads' mags' lay chiefly in their ability to sell consumer culture to men. The new lad was, Edwards argues, effectively a reconfiguration of the 'playboy ethic' – a set of cultural codes whose flippancy, robust heterosexuality and emphasis on traditionally 'male' forms of leisure (sport, drinking and generally 'larging it up') disentangled consumption from 'feminine' associations, allowing men to "use moisturizer, dress up and go shopping without appearing middle-class, effeminate or homosexual" (Edwards, 2003: 144).

Subsequent trends in British men's magazines seemed to confirm that self-conscious consumerism remained an uncertain masculine territory. In 2004 Britain's first weekly men's magazines were launched in the form of *Nuts* (published by IPC) and *Zoo Weekly* (produced by the German-based conglomerate Bauer Media Group) and, as Feona Attwood (2005) observes, both found success by intensifying trends already apparent in the monthly 'lads' mags'. Very alike in style and content, *Nuts* and *Zoo* were aimed at a market of sixteen-to thirty-year-olds and steered well clear of fashion, style and grooming. Instead, their onus was on more stereotypically masculine interests such as sport, gadgets and machines, while the knowing irony of the new lad gave way to a more 'downmarket', bawdy humor and a much greater quota of sexualized (though not explicit) depictions of women. The trend marked a 'flattening out' of distinctions between 'mainstream' men's magazines and soft-core pornography, but it also seemed to herald a resurgence of masculine archetypes rooted in machismo and chauvinism.

The future of men's magazines

During the mid 1990s the men's market was one of the magazine industry's fastest growing sectors but during the early twenty-first century it looked as though the bubble had burst. In Britain magazines were generally hard hit by the economic recession and a decline in advertising revenue, while sales of monthly men's titles slumped in the face of online competition and a new wave of free weekly titles such as *Sport* (launched in 2006) and *ShortList* (launched in 2007). Following a plunge in circulation, the closure of *Arena* in 2009 seemed to mark an end to the heyday of the aspirational men's style magazine. But the younger, more brash 'lads' mags' also fared badly, their downward sales evidenced by the fate of *Maxim*, whose monthly circulation slipped to under 46,000 in 2008, a slide that prompted the closure of its British edition the following year. In North America the situation was similar. The US edition of *Maxim* survived, though between 2010 and 2012 its circulation declined from 2.5 million to 2 million, and its 12 issues per year were cut to ten. *FHM* fared worse. The British edition endured, but in the US a dwindling circulation brought the title's closure in 2007.

Along with the magazine industry more generally, men's titles responded to changing market conditions by moving away from print editions and relying increasingly on their online incarnations. Solely web-based titles also appeared, their style and content reflecting trends already apparent in their print counterparts. In 2006, for example, Dennis Publishing launched *Monkey*, a free digital weekly that was delivered by email to its subscribers and which replicated a magazine format, though with video and audio content embedded within both editorial and advertising. Like *Nuts* and *Zoo*, *Monkey* was pitched to a young market and eschewed issues of style and grooming in favor of a formula that mixed soft-core pornography and coarse humor with features on gadgets, cars and entertainment. Initially successful, *Monkey* had spawned editions in Thailand and Scandinavia by 2009, but was closed in 2012 as its publisher focused on more specialized websites, such as *iGizmo*, *iMotor* and *Kontraband.com* (originally launched in 1999 and re-branded as *Stash* in 2013), the latter claiming to be one of the world's largest entertainment portals for eighteen-to thirty-four-year-old men.

The future of men's magazines in Britain and North American may have looked uncertain, but global markets offered some titles a new lease of life. By 2013, for example, *Maxim* boasted 15 international editions and *FHM* 18 in publishing empires that stretched from Russia and China to India and Indonesia. The international editions were tailored to their local audiences but shared the look, feel and content of the UK and US originals, whose constructions of masculinity found resonance in a growing number of international contexts. In these locales, then, magazines remained important sites for the articulation of masculine identities in a world of shifting commercial imperatives and changing notions of gender and sexuality.

Further reading

Ben Crewe (2003) in *Representing Men: Cultural Production and Producers in the Men's Magazine Market* provides an extended analysis of British men's magazines and masculinity during the 1990s. In her edited collection of essays entitled *Masculinity and Men's Lifestyle Magazines*, Bethan Benwell (2003) offers an anthology collecting a variety of analyses of the relationship between magazines and constructions of masculinity. Sean Nixon's (1996) *Hard Looks: Masculinities, Spectatorship and Contemporary Consumption* presents a detailed study of the relationship between masculinity, magazines and consumer culture in 1980s Britain. Finally, Tom Pendergast (2000) in *Creating the Modern Man: American Magazines and Consumer Culture, 1900–1950* delivers a thorough analysis of constructions of masculinity in the early US magazines.

References

Attwood, F. (2005) "'Tits and ass and porn and fighting': Male heterosexuality in magazines for men." *International Journal of Cultural Studies*, 8(1), 83–100.
Benwell, B. (ed.) (2003) *Masculinity and Men's Lifestyle Magazines*. Oxford: Blackwell.
Breazeale, K. (1994) "In spite of women: *Esquire* magazine and the construction of the male consumer." *Signs*, 20(1), 1–22.
Breward, C. (1999) *The Hidden Consumer: Masculinities, Fashion and City Life, 1860–1914*. Manchester: Manchester University Press.
Butler, J. (1990) *Gender Trouble: Feminism and the Subversion of Identity*. London: Routledge.
——(1995) "Melancholy gender/refused identification." In M. Berger, B. Wallis and S. Watson (eds.) *Constructing Masculinity*. London: Routledge (pp. 21–36).
Chapman, R. (1988) "The great pretender: Variations on the new man theme." In R. Chapman and J. Rutherford (eds.) *Male Order: Unwrapping Masculinity*. London: Lawrence & Wishart (pp. 225–48).

Chudacoff, H. (1999) *The Age of the Bachelor: Creating an American Subculture.* Princeton, NJ: Princeton University Press.

Crewe, B. (2003) *Representing Men: Cultural Production and Producers in the Men's Magazine Market.* Oxford: Berg.

Edwards, T. (1997) *Men in the Mirror: Men's Fashion, Masculinity and Consumer Society.* London: Cassell.

——(2003) "Sex, booze and fags: Masculinity, style and men's magazines." In B. Benwell (ed.) *Masculinity and Men's Lifestyle Magazines.* Oxford: Blackwell (pp. 132–46).

Ehrenreich, B. (1984) *The Hearts of Men: American Dreams and the Flight From Commitment.* London: Pluto.

Fraterrigo, E. (2009) *Playboy and the Making of the Good Life in Modern America.* Oxford: Oxford University Press.

Gill, R. (2003) "Power and the production of subjects: A genealogy of the new man and the new lad." In B. Benwell (ed.) *Masculinity and Men's Lifestyle Magazines.* Oxford: Blackwell (pp. 34–56).

Gingrich, A. (1971) *Nothing But People: The Early Days at Esquire – A Personal History, 1928–1958.* New York: Crown.

Greenfield, J., O'Connell, S. and Reid, C. (1999) "Fashioning masculinity: Men Only, consumption and the development of marketing in the 1930s." *Twentieth Century British History,* 10(4), 457–76.

Jackson, P., Stevenson, N. and Brooks, K. (2001) *Making Sense of Men's Magazines.* London: Polity.

Merrill, H. (1995) *Esky: The Early Years at Esquire.* New Brunswick, NJ: Rutgers University Press.

Mort, F. (1988) "Boys own? Masculinity, style and popular culture." In R. Chapman and J. Rutherford (eds.) *Male Order: Unwrapping Masculinity.* London: Lawrence & Wishart (pp. 193–224).

——(1996) *Cultures of Consumption: Masculinities and Social Space in Late Twentieth-Century Britain.* London: Routledge.

——(1997) "Paths to mass consumption: Britain and the USA since 1945." In M. Nava, A. Blake, I. MacRury and B. Richards (eds.) *Buy This Book: Studies in Advertising and Consumption.* London: Routledge (pp. 15–33).

Mort, F. and Thompson, P. (1994) "Retailing, commercial culture and masculinity in 1950s Britain: The case of Montague Burton, the 'tailor of taste'." *History Workshop,* 38, Autumn, 106–27.

Nixon, S. (1996) *Hard Looks: Masculinities, Spectatorship and Contemporary Consumption.* London: UCL.

Pendergast, T. (2000) *Creating the Modern Man: American Magazines and Consumer Culture, 1900–1950.* Columbia, MS: University of Missouri Press.

Pitzulo, C. (2011) *Bachelors and Bunnies: The Sexual Politics of Playboy.* Chicago, IL: Chicago University Press.

Ross, K. (2010) *Gendered Media: Women, Men and Identity Politics.* Plymouth: Rowman & Littlefield.

Rotundo, E. A. (1993) *American Manhood: Transformations in Masculinity from the Revolution to the Modern Era.* New York: Basic Books.

Simpson, M. (1994) *Male Impersonators: Men Performing Masculinity.* London: Routledge.

Swiencicki, M. A. (1998) "Consuming brotherhood: Men's culture, style and recreation as consumer culture, 1880–1930." *Social History,* 31(4), 773–808.

Tosh, J. (1994) "What should historians do with masculinity? Reflections on nineteenth century Britain." *History Workshop,* 38, Autumn, 179–202.

Wheelan, I. (2000) *Overloaded: Popular Culture and the Future of Feminism.* London: Women's Press.

26
Magazine pioneers
Form and content in 1960s and 1970s radicalism

Andrew Calcutt

> At first I couldn't even write the essay. I came back to East London and just sat around worrying over the thing. I had a lot of trouble analysing exactly what I had on my hands. By this time the *Routledge Companion* practically had a gun at my head because they had space for the essay locked into the printing presses and no essay. Finally, I told Martin Conboy, co-editor of the *Companion*, that I couldn't pull the thing together. OK, he tells me, just type out my notes and send them over and he will get somebody else to write it. So about eight o'clock that night I started typing the notes out in the form of a memorandum that began, 'Dear Martin'. About 4pm I got a call from Martin Conboy. He told me that they were striking out the 'Dear Martin' at the top of the memorandum and running the rest of it in the *Companion*. That was the essay 'Magazine Pioneers: Form and content in 1960s and 1970s radicalism'.

Writing this essay did not actually happen that way. The paragraph above is intended as an affectionate pastiche of Tom Wolfe's mid 1960s account (Wolfe, 1968: 11) of how he found the form of writing that was to become New Journalism:

> But at first I couldn't even write the story. I came back to New York and just sat around worrying over the thing. I had a lot of trouble analysing exactly what I had on my hands. By this time *Esquire* practically had a gun at my head because they had a two-page-wide colour picture for the story locked into the printing presses and no story. Finally I told Byron Dobell, the managing editor of *Esquire*, that I couldn't pull the thing together. OK, he tells me, just type out my notes and send them over and he will get someone else to write it. So about eight o'clock that night I started typing the notes out in the form of a memorandum that began 'Dear Byron'. I started typing away, starting right with the first time I saw any custom cars in California. I just started recording it all, and inside a couple of hours, typing along like a madman, I could tell that something was beginning to happen. By midnight this memorandum to Byron was twenty pages long and

> I was still typing like a maniac. About 2am, or something like that, I turned on WABC, a radio station that plays rock and roll music all night long, and got a little more manic. I wrapped up the memorandum about 6.15am, and by this time it was 49 pages long. I took it over to *Esquire* as soon as they opened up, about 9.30am. About 4pm I got a call from Byron Dobell. He told me they were striking out the 'Dear Byron' at the top of the memorandum and running the rest of it in the magazine. That was the story 'The Kandy-Kolored Tangerine-Flake Streamline Baby'.
>
> (Wolfe, 1968: 11)

Wolfe does not claim to have been the sole inventor of New Journalism, but by his account it was he who came to realize both the necessity and the full possibility of doing journalism differently. This he did first under pressure of deadlines and second in reaction to the established formats – prescribed and prescriptive – of mainstream print journalism. Dissatisfied with "somnambulistic totem newspapers" (Wolfe, 1968: 9), Wolfe took the novel-like aspects of some feature writing, especially sports features, and incorporated these into a new motto for journalism itself: write it like a novel.

Wolfe was adamant that new times – especially the emerging youth culture of the 1960s – demanded a new form of representation; hence his clarion call for the New Journalism. This essay presumes to play about with the seminal account of what made New Journalism because its author shares Wolfe's interest in new forms of publication capable of accommodating new experiences. Whereas Wolfe set himself the task of telling the story of a new generation in a characteristically new way, this essay seeks to narrate how Wolfe's British contemporaries and younger siblings followed suit. Furthermore, it will explore how some met with considerable success, while others went on to lose the plot. It would become their lot to represent the gradual demise of the political counterpart to New Journalism's formal innovation, namely, the genuinely popular form of social democracy initiated during the Second World War (1939–45) and further constructed throughout 'the Long Boom' thereafter. Accordingly, when this form of social democracy eventually lost momentum in Britain in the 1970s, its weakening was complemented by the relative decline of formal innovation in UK magazines.

In art and culture, formal development does not always correspond with progressive social content but in the pioneering magazines produced in Britain in the 1960s, these two trajectories appear well-matched. In the way the printed page was furnished, there seemed to be a new openness which was emblematic of a new configuration of power which had been opened up, at least in part, to the wider population. Conversely, in the straitened circumstances of the 1970s the wider population tended to close ranks, dividing into opposing subgroups – some radical, some radically conservative. Meanwhile, in the editorial process, the stylistic adventure of the 1960s, i.e. new styles in association with newly extended social democracy, was similarly stymied. Formal regression followed a new climate of economic restraint and increasing insularity, even among young radicals.

But this is not to suggest that relations between form and content can ever be simple and direct. Even when they happen to be in broad correspondence, as here, there are further mediating factors which qualify the relationship and complicate the picture. Accordingly, this essay starts from the premise that the pioneering work of British magazines in the 1960s and 1970s was undertaken in response to equally novel experiences. Writers, photographers, designers and editors all had to run with the pace of change. But as it turned out, some of them were well placed to keep up with the curve, while others were less well equipped to stay the course. Why? Partly as a result of different factors intrinsic to writing and design respectively, but also partly resulting from wider social factors which had a differential impact on design compared to writing.

British magazine writers could follow the lead offered by Americans such as Tom Wolfe. Moreover American-led New Journalism was still sufficiently new – it was far enough away from traditional forms of established journalism – for it to retain credibility as a radical alternative to the mainstream. Therefore, as an ostensibly new way of telling the story, this kind of journalism could run and run. So it did, and for a considerable length of time. Similarly, at the beginning of the 1960s many magazine designers took their cue from modernist design and its progressive political connotations. But by the beginning of the 1970s, the look of the modern was as discredited as the generation of post-Second World War politicians, including Labour Prime Minister Harold Wilson and Minister of Technology Anthony Wedgwood Benn, who had adopted it as their uniform.

In the early 1970s, McKie and Cook first documented the damage done to popular political aspirations during 'the decade of disillusion', i.e. the 1960s (McKie and Cook, 1972). By the early 1970s modern social policy, much of it Labour-led, had been found wanting and the UK electorate turned reluctantly towards the Conservative Party. Moreover, as the policies of social democracy fell into disrepute, so the style in which such policies had first entered the public domain, i.e. modernism, was found guilty by association. From then on, it became increasingly difficult to keep faith with modernist design. Many magazines, including those which had been confident pioneers only a few years earlier, no longer knew where to look or *how* to look.

Thus the onset of political uncertainty was most keenly felt in the art department while, in the reporters' room, the incoming form of magazine reporting – New Journalism – retained a reputation for capturing the onset of economic and social crisis.

Wartime origins of design innovation

More than 30 years earlier, in the wartime pages of the magazine *Picture Post*, three key elements had been brought closer together than ever before: (1) representation of full-scale popular participation in the historic events of the day, i.e. total war, including 'the home front'; (2) the deliberate use of modernist typefaces to encode every kind of experience, thereby emphasizing that 'we're all in this together' and confirming 'anti-fascism' as the great leveler; (3) photographs which not only depicted the details of everyday life but also endowed the everyday with historic significance.

In the configuration of these three elements, *Picture Post* declared the Second World War 'the people's war'. Conversely, 'the people's war' found popular expression in the modernism of *Picture Post*; its explicitly modern style implied recognition of people – everyday people – making history.

After the war ended in 1945, winning the peace became the order of the day and the new order was issued in much the same style. With fascism fashioned as Gothic, the design code for anti-fascism was carried over into the era of social reconstruction, carrying with it the expectation of progressive popular participation in all aspects of the public sphere, from politics and journalism to architecture and urban spaces. In typography, reconstruction was formatted in the Swiss Style of high modernism, as distilled in the typeface Helvetica, which Poynor (2007) associates with a whole set of social democratic ambitions.

Throughout the 1950s, in the continuing pursuit of these ambitions, modernity was seen as virtuous, while gerontocracy and its antiquated effects, i.e. 'the stagnant society' resulting from the rule of old men, were construed as the enemy. In the general elections of the 1960s Britain turned to a new power generation which, with their manifestos printed in appropriately modernist type, promised to modernize Britain "in the white heat of the technological revolution" (Wilson, 1963: 139). Similarly, the period before and after the 1964 general election was remarkable for the launch of a raft of magazines predicated on the *Picture Post* package of modernism and progressive popular participation. But the new magazines of the 1960s not only adopted this style as their starting point, they also sought to extend it as far as the people's eye could see.

Modernism, psychedelia and the deformation of design

In UK magazines at the beginning of the 1960s, graphic design was streets ahead of reporting. Designers such as Tom Wolsey at *Town*, Mark Boxer at *Queen* and latterly Harri Peccinotti at *Nova* all used modernist traits to capture the contemporary sense of social change. Apart from the predictable preference for *sans serif* type – always a strong indicator of modernism (Spencer, 1982) and *de rigueur* in the mid twentieth century iteration known as the Swiss Style – their magazine design is notable for being simultaneously figurative and abstract. On the printed page, human figures dissolve into abstract shapes but shapes can also resolve into the human form. The dual effect is to provide definition and suggest movement: people on the move; society in motion.

The work of these designers seems to revel in the difficult task of integrating the grain of particular experience with universal abstractions without doing either of these an injustice. This is a rare achievement, realized by unusually adventurous designers enjoying an exceptional social setting which tended to support innovation.

The influence of their magazines was far in excess of their commercial viability. Titles such as *Town* and *Queen* served mainstream periodical publishing as a *de facto* R&D department – they provided fresh blood. For example, Mark Boxer went from *Queen* to *The Sunday Times*, where in 1962 he became founding editor of the 'color supplement' (designated *The Sunday Times Magazine* in 1963). Boxer et al. took succour from the European tradition of innovative magazine graphics – as seen in pre-Second World War titles such as *Vu* and *Berliner Illustrierte Zeitung* (Taylor, 2006: 72). This tradition was imported into the UK along with refugees from fascism. *Town*'s own Tom Wolsey, for example, had been born in Aachen, moving to Britain as a schoolboy. In Wolsey's London, the European tradition converged with the influence of imaginative Americans such as George Lois (2003) who was already established as an art director at *Esquire* when Wolfe wrote his groundbreaking memorandum to Byron Dobell while Wolsey himself also built on the domestic precedent set by *Picture Post* – each issue a pictorial vindication of social democracy.

But this alignment of factors – aesthetic and economic, social and political – did not last for long. It is well nigh impossible to pinpoint exactly when the mood changed but by the beginning of the 1970s modernist magazine design already seemed tainted rather than starred. Even the social milieu which top designers moved in became something of a liability.

Town (previously entitled *Man About Town*, then *About Town*) was purchased in 1958 by Michael Heseltine's publishing company, Cornmarket (subsequently Haymarket). Heseltine, who went on to become a cabinet minister, is said to have used it as a personal status symbol. *The Queen* was subtitled 'the ladies' newspaper and court chronicle' until Jocelyn Stevens, scion of the Hulton media dynasty, bought it for himself on the occasion of his 25th birthday in 1957. Stevens shortened the title and extended its subject matter. But *Queen* continued to carry a vein of blue blood. Its resident photographer was Antony Armstrong-Jones, soon to be ennobled as Lord Snowdon, husband of Princess Margaret. Not even *Nova* – perhaps the most adventurous magazine of them all – stood entirely outside this charmed circle. Its launch editor, Dennis Hackett, had previously made his name as editor of *Queen* (Magforum, 2012).

In short, as magazine modernism became closely associated with an increasingly discredited form of social democracy, so many of the personnel associated with magazine design were too close to the British elite for the emerging counterculture to feel comfortable with them. Instead of titles to be read by the likes of John Steed and Emma Peel in *The Avengers*, this new cohort wanted a new style of publication to accompany their own appreciation of Jimi Hendrix and Pink Floyd.

On the rebound from modernism, the magazines of the late 1960s counterculture developed a new aesthetic – the psychedelic. This new aesthetic claimed to be even more progressive than its modernist predecessor and the music associated with it – no longer simply 'pop' – even dubbed itself 'progressive'. But with hindsight, psychedelia can be seen as an elaborate process of contraction. It was the stylistic complement to widespread withdrawal from the expanded horizons of post-war social democracy.

On the surface, the psychedelic style was characterized by inflation rather than contraction. In men's clothes, the smart, neat lines of 'mod' flared out – ballooned – into bell bottoms and, eventually, 'loon pants'. Meanwhile on record sleeves and magazine pages alike, inflated letters loomed out at the reader – ordinary things made extraordinary in a small-scale imitation of the effect of psychotropic drugs.

The entire look said 'mind expanding' but focusing on the *Revolution In My Head* (McDonald, 2008) could only mean withdrawing from the wider plane of political and social engagement. This revolution was mainly restricted to perception and largely confined to a minority albeit a minority which defined itself by disdain for the majority – the millions who were not hip enough to be in on it. Mind expansion, and the style concomitant with it, turned out to mean retreat not only from modernist associations but also from social democracy and its association with the majority population. Inflated type came to represent the deflation of democratic ambitions.

The regressive aspects of psychedelia were not immediately apparent. Indeed the positive side of the prospectus looms large in the London editions of *Oz*, the magazine of satirical dissent which editor Richard Neville brought with him to London after falling foul of obscenity law in Australia – though he soon found himself up against the British equivalent. For example, the 'Magic Theatre' issue of *Oz* (No 16, November 1968), put together by the Australian artist Martin Sharp and the filmmaker Philippe Mora, uses pop-art and cut-up to present an arresting panorama of the contemporary capitalist regime. The graphic juxtaposition of ordinary and extraordinary life is as intriguing and challenging as its literary counterparts, such as Hunter Thompson's *Fear and Loathing in Las Vegas* (2005). In their respective formats, they both offer apocalyptic visions of everyday life charged with political and sexual violence. On the other hand, though there is no denying its quirky intelligence, the wraparound color cover of *Oz* No 16 (Ozit, 2013) is quiescent rather than challenging, as if the cover artists who produced it had already stopped trying to grapple with contradictory reality. In a visual style which anticipates the animated sequences in *Monty Python's Flying Circus*, there is plenty of contradiction, for example in the slogan, 'this should be the end but I feel it is just the beginning'. However, contradiction appears inevitable – part of a fantastic show (the eponymous 'magic theatre') rather than something to be deliberately addressed and actively resolved. In a scene where 'all men are madmen', magic is a necessary part of the scene but the scene can only be a dream – or nightmare – beyond our ken.

In this presentation of reality in which reality cannot be rationally appropriated, type – representing in letter form the objects which go to make up our experience – is suitably large and luscious, whereas people are depicted either as cut-up clichés or as stunted little figures. Consistent with the idea of the world as a trip we cannot control, inflated type complements a deflated vision of the human subject. *Oz*'s 'magic theatre' is really a stage set for 'the minimal self' (Lasch, 1984).

While psychedelic style remained overtly expansive and superficially progressive, it proved even less sustainable than its predecessors. It was soon superseded by the minimalist modernism associated with skinheads – both relentless and resentful – and also by the anti-style of early feminism. Thus in their reaction against the erstwhile coupling of modernism and social democracy, working-class men took the former and used it to attack the open society ethos of the latter while mainly middle-class feminists developed a kind of non-style, on the basis that style itself, whether modernist or psychedelic, had previously served as packaging for patriarchal oppression.

Although they gravitated towards different ends of the political spectrum, both these developments were similarly insular. As right-wing skinheads were almost exclusive to white working-class neighborhoods, so the women's movement found itself 'in sisterhood'. In each instance, the 'hood' entailed an enclosed space and a select population. Moreover, to the extent that insiders were no longer required to engage with outsiders (except perhaps to ridicule or intimidate them), they felt less of an obligation to present themselves in ways designed to connect with the general population, i.e. the ways in which modernism and even 'mod' style had been associated with social democracy. In design terms, therefore, the skinhead's working class roots entitled him to reject fashion in favor of a supposedly classic uniform. Similarly, those rooted in sisterhood need not – indeed, they should not – be overly concerned with matters of style.

Consequently, the pioneering feminist magazine *Spare Rib* (founded in 1972) cultivated a non-style. In early issues such as No 26 (n.d.), editorial presentation is as miscellaneous as the regular feature entitled 'Info Odds and Sods' (p. 33). The writing is more essay-ish than journalistic, as in this pre-amble to an interview with the singer-songwriter Bridget St John, which appeared in issue No 28:

> The development of her music, from simply accompanying herself on guitar to her recent, more adventurous album 'Jumblequeen' released through her new record company, Chrysalis, shows growth, over which she is in control.
> (Fudger, n.d.: 43)

This was the issue (No 28) in which the editorial collective first invited readers to interview themselves, leading to a long-running series of first-person narratives, e.g. 'Trapped in Marriage' (pp. 9–10), 'Learning About Sex' (p. 11) and 'Exercise In Trust' (pp. 12–15) – all from issue No 38. These pieces point towards the subsequent rise of women's 'real life' magazines in the 1990s. However, in the latter period, 'real life' was being copy-fitted into an exact prose form which was carefully dressed down by skilled sub-editors; whereas in the *Spare Rib* originals the presentation of readers' experience really was as shapeless as a pair of (stereotypical) dungarees.

The non-style of *Spare Rib*'s pioneering days may have been partly pragmatic. At the outset, a group of women who came together partly to protest about being excluded from the professions can hardly be expected to produce the most professional looking package. But *Spare Rib*'s non-style lasted longer than it takes to learn graphic design, so the practicalities of non-professionals getting the paper out cannot fully account for it. Instead the title's non-style should be seen as a conscious form of non-assent to the magazines business and the patriarchy perceived to be inherent in it.

Meanwhile, British music journalists – most of them men – were giving birth to a new style of reporting, with King's Reach Tower, the high point of professionally produced magazine patriarchy, serving as their delivery room.

The reporter as composer: Striving for a new modernism

The music journalist Nick Kent was one of the pioneers of long form reporting in the UK. Having come up from the 'underground' magazine *Friendz*, in 1972 Kent was recruited to the *New Musical Express* by assistant editor Nick Logan (the Ilford Mod who went on to edit and publish *The Face*). Kent, alongside Charles Shaar Murray, who had graduated from the infamous *Oz Schoolkids Issue*, and Ian

MacDonald, a recent graduate of Cambridge University, was part of a radical shake-up at the paper. Instead of adult easy listening (the focus of the 1950s) or teen beat groups (1960s), in the early 1970s the NME sought to capture the new seriousness in 'progressive' music; but without being as po-faced as its rival weekly, Melody Maker.

Both titles were owned by the same publishing company, IPC. According to Kent, having "thrown its full editorial weight" (Kent, 2010: 81) behind 'progressive rock', Melody Maker's circulation had risen to 200,000, whereas the NME – with circulation figures down to 60,000 – was on notice from management that "it had only twelve issues left to turn around its dwindling demographic" (Kent, 2010: 81).

The NME's radical departure in terms of its subject-matter entailed complementary changes in presentation. Away went the bright, airy tone of news and features, the latter often consisting of 'exclusive chats' with the stars (Kent, 2007: xv). These were replaced by longer, more critical articles offering cinematic close-ups of damaged gods, in which the real-life contradiction between god-like status and damaged human beings was represented in highly modulated sentences and the kind of complex editing – cutting from past to present, jumping between fantasy and reality – which would re-appear a decade later in music videos. As a result of these changes, although it continued to appear in newsprint, the NME became much more of a magazine and far less like a traditional newspaper.

When he compiled the extended version of his 'The Last Beach Movie Revisited' in 1993, Nick Kent modified and reprised the 30,000 word text which first appeared in 1975 in three successive editions of the NME (21 June, 28 June and 12 July, 1975). It opens with a scene from 'late 74' in which Paul and Linda McCartney pay a house-call on 'reclusive mastermind' Brian Wilson of the Beach Boys:

> But Brian wasn't coming out. He stayed in there, petrified, all his guts clenched up, eyes shut tight, praying with all his might that all the tiny atoms of his body would somehow break down, so that he could simply evaporate into the thin smog-strained air surrounding him. It was all to do with something his brother Carl had told him not long before, something about Paul McCartney once claiming that Brian's song 'God Only Knows' was the greatest pop song ever written. And, in his mind, it had all become hopelessly twisted: "Like, if 'God Only Knows' is the greatest song ever written, then I'll never write anything as good again! And if I never write anything as good, then I'm finished. I'm a has-been and a wash-up, just like everyone keeps saying." ... He never came out until long after they'd all left. Someone said afterwards that you could just make out the sound of him inside that claustrophobic room, weeping softly to himself, like an unloved little boy who had recently experienced a particularly savage beating.
>
> (Kent, 2007: 3)

Kent builds his paragraph like a guitar solo, repeating key words as key notes ('all', 'something', 'never'), mounting clauses one on top of another, appearing to end the sentence before adding another lick: "And, in his mind, it had all become hopelessly twisted ... And if I never write anything as good, then I'm finished." Thus Kent's prose composition was aligned to the musical compositions favored by his readers:

his writing was very much in the moment of music-led 1970s counterculture. But in order to chime in with this moment, he drew heavily on both American New Journalism and European modernist literature.

In *Apathy For The Devil*, his 'seventies memoir', Kent acknowledges his debt to Truman Capote and Tom Wolfe (Kent, 2010: 23–24). In the Preface to *The Dark Stuff*, a retrospective collection of his music journalism, he recalls flying to Detroit in 1973 to be taken under the wing of Lester Bangs and Dave Marsh, resident writers at *Creem*, "the best rock mag in the world at the time" (Kent, 2007: xiv). "With Lester," Kent recalls, "it was all about penetration, breaking on through to the other side ... What does this music say to your soul? Do these guys even sound like they have souls to you? What's really going on here ... behind the masks?" (ibid.).

Like Tom Wolfe before him, Lester Bangs (1996) had struggled to find a form of writing that would enable reporters to get to the essence of their subject and when Kent flew back to London in the spring of 1973 he was equally determined that his writing about music would appear in a form that was true to the music itself. In rejecting the established versions of reporting, Tom Wolfe, Lester Bangs and now their British apprentice, Nick Kent, were not abandoning form *per se*. Rather, they sought to re-establish it; to find the new form that could capture more content, over and above the capacity of older formats.

For these reporters, modernist writing was not uniformly problematic. Instead they entered into a complex relationship with it, as contradictory as the modern world which modernism itself had attempted to encapsulate. On the one hand they rejected the streamlined simplification typically entailed in modern reporting formats such as the inverted pyramid (the characteristic shape of news stories in the 'totem' titles bemoaned by Wolfe) or the 'background feature'. On the other hand, Kent cites *Ulysses*, James Joyce's modernist masterpiece (1922/2010), as the biggest literary influence of his final year at school – even more so than Capote's "flawless insight" (Kent, 2010: 23) or Wolfe's "dandified upper echelon hipspeak prose style" (ibid.: 24). But he singles out Joyce for pursuing precisely what Capote and Wolfe were also aiming at: "a way to penetrate the complex innermost workings of the human imagination and evoke them sublimely in the printed word" (ibid.).

Kent also compared the role of the reporter to that of the detective – a truly modern *persona* – as in this aside on his own motivation for investigating Brian Wilson's predicament:

> It was a dirty job but someone had to do it. Looking back, I remember how the darker it got, the more my eyes lit up and the more I fantasised that I was Lou Harper, the private eye in Ross McDonald's *The Moving Target*, swimming through the murky human debris of weird-ass LA to arrive ultimately at a deeper truth.
>
> (Kent, 2007: 5)

Kent had no interest in the mainstream version of being modern as characterized in standardized journalism. For him the inverted pyramid was not modern enough; it did not do enough to embody the complexity of modern life. Meanwhile he identified with modernist writers who sought to extend the descriptive capacity of their writing, in keeping with the growing complexity of the modern world itself. Also, he kept faith with the modern idea of solving the conundrum of form and content, cracking this recurring case like a hardboiled private eye.

It is notable that the music writers who came up behind Kent et al., snapping hungrily at their heels, felt obliged to continue with this way of working rather than break away from it. Thus 'young gunslinger' Tony Parsons, writing in the *NME* about The Clash (Parsons, 1995: 6–15), is formally indistinguishable from Nick Kent on The Rolling Stones a few years earlier (Kent, 2007: 137–67). Furthermore, if you swap ostentatious wealth for histrionic poverty, and substitute one illegal drug for another, the content is not so different, either. That the next generation of reporters could not come up with anything better to do, or a better way of doing it, suggests that Kent and his contemporaries had developed a form of reporting sufficient to the demands of its time.

Conclusion: The significance of form

Does form matter? In the 1970s, activists argued that the urgency of the political situation must take precedence over stylistic considerations. In the contemporary era of immediate communication, laboring long and hard over formal composition seems almost absurd. But there is surely a relationship between the permitted formlessness of today's instant communication and the assumption that we are communicating only to people we already know. Thus instant communication defaults to interpersonal communication. It tends to confine what is being said to the interpersonal level and, insofar as it defines our existence, it persistently privatizes us – whereas in the examples above most of those who focused on form, who devoted their energies to finding new forms of composition, were intent on relaying human experience to the widest possible public. This is not to say that in today's circumstances the public could or should be reconstituted in the form of social democracy and/or modernism. Nor is it to imply that the public can be reconstituted by form alone. But it is to suggest that attention to form is not only the sign of a particular mode of address to a specific, historical cohort; it plays an important part in calling the wider public into existence.

Further reading

Kevin Jefferys' (2007) *Politics and the People: A History of British Democracy Since 1918* is a good primer on social democracy. Simon Garfield's (2010) *Just My Type: A Book About Fonts* will start you thinking about the social significance of type. I recommend the 2004 edition, with an introduction by Rick Poynor, of Herbert Spencer's *Pioneers of Modern Typography*, which illustrates the *avant garde*, largely left-wing origins of modern graphic design in Europe. *100 Years of Magazine Covers* (2006), written by Steve Taylor and designed by Neville Brody, is a panoramic collection. Nick Kent's memoir *Apathy For The Devil* (2010) complements his collected music journalism, *The Dark Stuff* (2007).

References

Bangs, L. (1996) *Psychotic Reactions and Carburetor Dung* (G. Marcus, Ed.). London: Serpent's Tail.

Fudger, M. (n.d.) "Women in music." Interview with Bridget St John, *Spare Rib* No 28, p. 43.

Garfield, S. (2010) *Just My Type: A Book About Fonts*. London: Profile.

Jefferys, K. (2007) *Politics and the People: A History of British Democracy since 1918*. London: Atlantic Books.

Joyce, J. (1922/2010) *Ulysses*. Ware: Wordsworth Classics.

Kent, N. (2007) *The Dark Stuff: Selected Writings on Rock Music*. London: Faber & Faber.

——(2010) *Apathy For The Devil: A Seventies Memoir*. London: Faber & Faber.

Lasch, C. (1984) *The Minimal Self: Psychic Survival in Troubled Times*. New York: W. W. Norton.

Lois, G. (2003) *$ellebrity: My Angling and Tangling with Famous People*. London: Phaidon.

MacDonald, I. (2008) *Revolution In The Head: The Beatles' Records and the Sixties* (2nd edition). London: Vintage.

McKie, D. and Cook, C. (1972) *The Decade of Disillusion: British Politics in the Sixties*. Basingstoke: Macmillan.

Magforum (2012) Magforum. Retrieved from www.magforum.com

Ozit (2013) *Oz Magazines: Sixties Counterculture Pop Art*, the 'Magic Theatre' issue, No 16 November 1968. Retrieved from www.ozit.co.uk

Parsons, T. (1995) *Dispatches From The Front Line Of Popular Culture*. London: Virgin Books.

Poynor, R. (2007) Interviewed in *Helvetica: A Documentary Film* (G. Hustwit, Dir.). London: Plexi Productions.

Spencer, H. (1982) *Pioneers of Modern Typography*. Aldershot: Lund Humphries.

——(2004) *Pioneers of Modern Typography* (with an introduction by Rick Poynor). Cambridge, MA: MIT Press.

Taylor, S. (2006) 100 Years of Magazine Covers. London: Black Dog Publishing.

Thompson, H. (2005) *Fear and Loathing in Las Vegas* (new edition). London: Harper Perennial.

Wilson, H. (1963) Speech to the Labour Party conference, 1 October. Recorded in Labour Party Annual Conference report.

Wolfe, T. (1968) *The Kandy-Kolored Tangerine-Flake Streamline Baby*. London: Mayflower Books (Introduction, pp. 9–14).

Part V
RADIO

27
The Reithian legacy and contemporary public service ethos

Siân Nicholas

British broadcasting has been described as "possibly the greatest single system of diverse, quality communication the world has ever seen" (Tracey, 1998: viii). Its defining public service character is exemplified above all in the British Broadcasting Corporation (BBC) and the broadcasting philosophy of its first Director General, John Reith. Yet since the launch of the BBC itself, the idea of a public service ethos in broadcasting has raised profound questions about the purpose and function of the mass media; the nature of the audience and the limits of the market; and public value, private interest and the relationship between private and public culture in society.

What do we mean by 'public service broadcasting'? On one level, it is simply a particular means of organizing a particular technology of mass communication in order to facilitate certain outcomes. However, the public service ethos is also an attitude of mind, a way of thinking about the role of broadcasting within a society. Characteristics of public service broadcasting typically cited include universality of access; diversity, distinctiveness and quality of program content; serving of minority as well as majority interests; freedom from commercial pressures through public financing and from political interference through independent oversight; public accountability; impartiality; and a commitment to innovation (Tracey, 1998: 26–32; Debrett, 2009: 808–13; Hendy, 2013: 3). Public service broadcasting is also seen as having a nationalizing function, reflecting national culture and identity and defining the boundaries of what constitutes the "national community" (Born, 2005: 512).

National media systems are social institutions, and the nature and extent of a public service ethos within a country's media system is contingent historically on the technologies it employs and the society within which it is situated. Any discussion of the history of public service broadcasting in Britain therefore has to accommodate social, political, cultural and technological change as well as changing definitions of public service, the public interest and the public good over time. It has also to recognize the extent to which public service broadcasting has always represented something beyond broadcasting itself. The public service ethos in broadcasting has been variously described as a "moral system" (Tracey, 1998: xvi), a "mission" (Hendy, 2013: 6), "a class of special pleading" (North, 2007: 34) or akin to "creationism" (Murdoch, 2009: 4). At its best, public service broadcasting has been seen as the essential expression of the democratic public sphere; at its worst, as the embodiment of an anti-market and elitist cultural hegemony. To Reith himself, broadcasting put us "in touch with the infinite" (Reith, 1924: 217). Yet the 'Reithian legacy' itself is a term often used to justify historical developments that have strayed far from Reith's original philosophy of broadcasting.

This chapter traces the origins of the idea of public service broadcasting in Britain from Reith's original vision of the role and function of broadcasting in the 1920s. It addresses how that vision evolved over succeeding decades as the political, social and media environment in which it operated changed, and considers its enduring legacy for British broadcasting in a multimedia world very different from anything Reith or his successors would have envisaged.

Public service broadcasting in Britain: The original vision

Paradoxically, public service broadcasting in Britain originated as much from specific technical, bureaucratic and commercial imperatives as from a commitment to the public good. The perceived need to control and structure the emerging technology of wireless broadcasting in Britain, prompted in part by the apparent 'chaos' of the free market in broadcasting then developing in the USA, led the General Post Office in 1922 to issue a licence to a consortium of British wireless manufacturers, operating under the name of the 'British Broadcasting Company', to produce a single national broadcasting service, funded by a licence fee paid by all households with a wireless receiver, and offering a mixed range of programing. The monopoly status of the consortium was to impose order on the airwaves and safeguard the consortium's investment. The licence fee was to obviate the need for on-air advertising and in so doing meet the concerns of advertising-dependent interests such as the newspaper Industry. The provision of programs for a wide range of audience interests was to ensure that wireless sets might be sold to the widest possible market. The BBC's public service ethos was thus initially a function of practical commercial management as much as any crusading vision of the broadcast medium's political, social or cultural function (Briggs, 1961).

However, even at this stage the language of public service dominated the British debate about broadcasting. The very first Broadcasting Committee, the Sykes Committee of 1923, specifically defined the airwaves not as a private resource but as a public utility ("a valuable form of public property") that should be regulated to protect "the public interest" (Scannell, 1990: 12). The appointment shortly after its launch of John Reith as the BBC's first General Manager proved a historic moment. Reith, a 33-year-old former engineer, war veteran and austere Scottish Presbyterian, famously claimed that prior to his appointment he "did not know what broadcasting was" (Reith, 1949: 83). Yet his grasp of the potential of this new medium was immediate and transformative. He saw broadcasting as the first mass medium of potentially universal scope and access. He brought to his role a profound sense of public duty and purpose, and a determination to use this new medium to its fullest social potential, as outlined in his manifesto, *Broadcast Over Britain* (1924). He turned the social value of broadcasting from a practical aspiration to a moral imperative.

Reith's vision of broadcasting chimed with other powerful undercurrents. Victorian ideals of service and of culture as a force for education and enlightenment, as championed by Matthew Arnold and John Ruskin, still had significant resonance in early twentieth-century Britain. Reith's own definition of the BBC's role, to bring "the best of everything into the greatest number of homes", explicitly echoed Arnold's definition of culture as "the best which has been thought and said in the world" (Reith, 1924: 147; Arnold, [1869] 2006: 5). Following the First World War, the public corporation model appeared an attractive alternative to either government control or unfettered free enterprise in the administration of public services. With universal manhood suffrage introduced only four years earlier, the idea of broadcasting as a means of democratic engagement had topical force. Reith could also call on powerful cultural allies who saw in broadcasting's educative potential a means of counteracting the malign forces of modern mass culture (LeMahieu, 1988). One of these, Lord Crawford, an influential figure in the public arts world, was appointed to chair the second Committee on Broadcasting in 1925. In 1927, following the Crawford Report's explicit endorsement of the Reithian ethos of public service broadcasting (and just a year after the establishment of another national public utility corporation, the Central Electricity Board [Hood, 1986: 55]), the British Broadcasting Company made way for the new British Broadcasting Corporation, a public corporation under the authority but not the control of the state, with the public service remit to inform, to educate and to entertain the nation.

Reith's vision was not unanimously accepted. Throughout the inter-war years the popular press, regretting their failure to grasp the potential of the rival medium, accused the BBC variously of cultural elitism, political quiescence, miserabilism (i.e. the so-called 'Reithian Sunday'), and a pervasive disdain for its audience. Listeners, they pointed out, were happier listening to the livelier commercial fare on Radio Luxembourg. Reith's emphasis on 'betterment' certainly smacked of paternalism, as did his much quoted comment that "few [listeners] know what they want, and very few what they need" (Reith, 1924: 34). His restrictive attitude to political coverage, though prudent, signaled only qualified independence. His hostility to such 'populist' initiatives as listener research was in retrospect willfully perverse. But his championing of universal access to broadcasting, marked by the BBC's investment in wireless transmitters nationwide, his philosophy of 'mixed' scheduling, with an important place for "light and 'entertaining' items" as well as more serious fare (Reith, 1924: 134), and his assertion that in broadcasting "there need be no first and third class" (ibid.: 218) were more thoroughly democratic than his critics allowed. By 1935 BBC transmitters reached 98 per cent of the British population (Briggs, 1965: 253); by 1939 three-quarters of British households, that is, nine million homes, had a radio (Scannell and Cardiff, 1991: 362).

Reith's "authoritarianism with a conscience" (see Tracey 1998: 11) made for a compelling ethos, nowhere more visible than in his radical championing of the British listening public's "communicative entitlement" to national public life (Scannell

1989: 160). His assertion that the BBC *should* broadcast news, music, theatre, sporting events, parliamentary debates, ceremonial functions, Royal occasions and other key moments of national life took on a powerful momentum to which almost every vested interest (except parliament) eventually capitulated. And from 1932, through the BBC external services, Reith created a means of exporting this ethos to the wider world.

Reith's success is marked by the speed with which public service broadcasting in Britain became seen as an embodiment of the nation itself. Outsider critiques of the BBC (especially if by American broadcasters) were regarded as attacks on British national culture (Hilmes, 2012). When Reith left the BBC in June 1938 even the popular press celebrated his immense contribution to British national life (Barrington, 1938: 10). A year later, a BBC-commissioned survey of the social impact of broadcasting appeared to vindicate Reith and his vision: "No innovation since the coming of compulsory education has affected so large a proportion of the working population as the coming of broadcasting. … Broadcasting has become an equalising and unifying factor in national life" (Jennings and Gill, 1939: 40).

The evolution of the vision: Redefinitions and challenges

Reith's particular ethos of public service broadcasting arguably did not long outlive his Director Generalship. By the time he left the BBC in 1938 the Corporation had instituted a Listener Research Department. Within a year of his departure the Reithian Sunday was being whittled away. The BBC's output during the Second World War, often considered the apotheosis of the Reithian ideal, was widely seen at the time as a betrayal of many of its key tenets. In wartime, what listeners 'wanted' and what they 'needed' became substantially the same thing. Likewise, the BBC for the first time found itself both wanting and needing to attract audiences: to make sure they were appropriately informed, to educate them about the conflict, to keep their spirits high and, incidentally, to stop them tuning to enemy radio stations. Listener research was now actively employed to understand what made programs popular and attractive as well as effective. With the wartime BBC Forces Programme the BBC effectively acknowledged that light entertainment had (at least for the duration) as much social value as high culture. BBC news gained a significance in people's lives never achieved before or arguably since and a reputation for integrity and trust that it has never lost (Nicholas, 1996). Yet many contemporary commentators, as well as BBC senior management, regarded the BBC's wartime record as a populist aberration. Under Director General William Haley the post-war BBC returned to a Reithian seriousness of intent, though through a culturally stratified system of radio networks (including the new Third Programme) which ran directly counter to the Reithian 'mixed' vision. Mixed broadcasting was relegated to the BBC's junior service, television, which now started its own national rollout. In a more expansive and questioning era, calls for a more vigorous, commercially minded post-war alternative to the BBC gathered voice (O'Malley, 2009: 22–32).

However, the introduction of commercial television in 1955, which some hoped might challenge the public service broadcasting model, in fact consolidated it.

Although financed by on-air advertising, the new ITV franchises were, like the BBC, publicly accountable, their remit, like the BBC's, to inform, educate and entertain, with specific commitments to news and current affairs coverage, regional broadcasting and children's television. British broadcasting remained defined by its public service ethos even in the mixed economy of commercial and non-commercial television (extended in turn to radio in 1973).

The duopoly proved a success: "The BBC kept ITV honest; ITV kept the BBC on its toes" (Ofcom, 2004: 2). Competition encouraged broadcasters on both sides to widen the parameters of public debate and engage more directly with social and political issues, indeed, to fulfill (perhaps for the first time) the medium's potential as "an independent public sphere" (Scannell, 1989: 145). In the 1960s, emboldened by the 1962 Pilkington Report's fulsome praise of the BBC (the "high water mark of allegiance to public service broadcasting" [Tracey, 1998: 21]), and by independent television's less deferential approach to news and current affairs, Director General Hugh Greene encouraged the BBC to challenge complacency, engage in controversy and represent the world as it was, not as it ought to be. The BBC would no longer be the guest in the sitting room, but the audience's window onto the world. This recalibration of the public service ethos, led by a Director General described as "progressive, iconoclastic, liberal and naughty" (Tracey, 1998: x) – about as far from Reith in character as could be imagined – was in keeping with the times, if not with all the BBC's audience, and prompted widespread and often heated debate about the aims and objectives of public service broadcasting into the 1970s.

The 1980s, however, demonstrated the fragility of the public service ideal when directly challenged, as attitudes to the public realm underwent a paradigm shift. With the post-war settlement under challenge from the Thatcher governments, public utilities sold off to the private sector and new broadcasting technologies promising multi-channel access via cable and satellite, previously minority critiques of public service broadcasting suddenly became mainstream (Hood, 1986: 60–65). In Professor Sir Alan Peacock, the eminent liberal economist and chair of the 1985 Broadcasting Committee, the BBC found a critic who simply did not accept the premises on which the public service ethos had conventionally been based. He viewed broadcasting as an economic commodity (and no longer a scarce one), the licence fee as a regressive tax, and broadcasting's social function as a red herring; he advocated instead a deregulated free market, with the BBC taking its chances as one among many subscription channels and public service broadcasting (defined here in the narrowest and fundamentally un-Reithian terms as minority 'quality' programing) as something to be separately funded. The BBC was unused to defending itself against those who did not accept its terms of debate. Universal provision via the licence fee was only saved by the political and technical impracticality of subscription television and the clear evidence that advertising capacity was insufficient to fund both the BBC and commercial television (McNicholas and Seaton, 2009). But Peacock's impact on the broadcasting ecology in Britain was profound. Broadcasting was now to be considered a private commodity, not a public good (Scannell, 1990: 26). The 1990 Broadcasting Act saw ITV franchises put out to tender and their public service remits diluted. Satellite and cable television development was encouraged, and the newspaper magnate Rupert Murdoch's Sky television operation launched an attempt, backed by the purchase and aggressive marketing of key sports rights, to break the public service hold on British broadcasting.

In the new highly competitive media environment of the 1990s, in which even the chairman of the new ITV franchise Carlton Communications, Michael Green, was quoted as saying that television was just "a manufacturing process" (Tracey, 1998: 12), the BBC's fight-back involved adopting the language and some of the methods of its enemies. The new BBC Director General, John Birt, pursued an internally unpopular but politically prudent strategy of wholesale administrative reform to organize program delivery within a more market-driven business model. The BBC had a long history of technological innovation, from the world's first regular high-definition television service in the 1930s to the BBC Micro home computer in the 1980s; now Birt took the initiative in preparing for the new digital television landscape, launching a 24-hour BBC news service and developing BBC Online. Backed by the BBC's internal resources and reputational value, bbc.co.uk soon became not just the most popular internet site in Britain, visited regularly by almost half of all British internet users, but the leading content site in Europe and the most used non-portal website outside the USA (Born, 2005: 9). Meanwhile, by dramatically expanding the BBC's commercial arm, BBC Worldwide, he both made the BBC more financially stable and renewed the international profile of British public service broadcasting.

Birt's successor, Greg Dyke, likewise adopted a deliberately expansive attitude and industry leadership role at a time when ITV and Channel 4's public service commitments appeared to be shrinking (Born, 2005). By backing the free-to-air Freeview digital platform when the commercial provider OnDigital failed, he reinvigorated the concept of universal provision for the digital age and in the process sidestepped the threat of subscription. His commitment to revitalizing BBC sports coverage reinforced the key Reithian idea that you cannot serve the public and at the same time justify the licence fee unless you provide it with some of everything that people want to watch or listen to. Under Dyke, BBC1 overtook ITV1 in the ratings for the first time since 1955 (Born, 2005: 473). However, his controversial departure in 2004 demonstrated that the BBC was still vulnerable to political pressure (Rogers, 2004). Ominously for the BBC, in defining public service broadcasting in terms of purposes and content outcomes rather than particular institutions the first Ofcom Public Service Broadcasting Review in 2004 deliberately left the way open for the dilution of public service remits across a multiplicity of media providers in the future (Lunt, Livingstone and Brevini, 2012: 18).

Reith's legacy: The vision today

Today, public service broadcasting as a concept and as an institutional model is widely considered to be in serious, possibly terminal, decline, superseded by a free market philosophy based on consumer choice and almost limitless supply. The surprise is that the BBC, the last public utility standing, has shown such resilience and that British broadcasting culture still holds a place for Reithian values.

Thus free universal access, though challenged in the multi-platform digital era, is still a key tenet of public service broadcasting and importance is still attached to attracting wide rather than simply large audiences. Ninety-eight percent of the public still use BBC services in any given week (Barnett and Seaton, 2010: 331). The weekly reach of BBC1 in 2013 is typically over 80 percent, compared to only around 15 percent for the highest-rated satellite station, Sky 1 (BARB, 2013). By 2007 more homes in Britain had Freeview on their main TV set than a pay satellite set-top box (Ofcom, 2007: 103); by early 2011 the BBC iPlayer was receiving over 160 million program requests per month (Hendy, 2013: 115). With the BBC, ITV and C4 all successfully exploiting cross-platform program linkages, perhaps "on-demand cross-platform access is the *new* universality" (Debrett, 2009: 810) as well as being the means by which younger users in particular continue to engage with public service media.

The public service sector is still seen as the safeguard of quality in broadcasting. The BBC's historic importance in "establishing the framework of public tastes and expectations" (Born, 2005: 492) shaped terrestrial commercial television in Britain and has influenced its digital successors. The recent shift towards the production of high-quality original programing on cable and satellite channels reflects earlier audiences' resistance to cheap and populist provision outside of sports coverage. Public service media keep commercial services honest, commercial media keep the public service broadcasters on their toes.

Despite well-known controversies throughout the history of public service broadcasting, independence from commercial and political pressures still broadly remains. The licence fee remains for the time being – if only in the absence of a more politically and technologically acceptable alternative. Editorial impartiality is still publicly supported and still protected by regulation.

Meanwhile, people's belief in their communicative entitlement remains strong, whether in broad terms (the right of access to the common public sphere provided through broadcasting) or more narrowly: the 'right' to watch certain events on television. These expectations range historically from the public service provision expected from early ITV to the 1990 Broadcasting Act's ring-fencing of a list of 'Crown Jewels' of national sporting occasions that must be broadcast free to air. While the loss of free live televised Test Match cricket, for instance, is now largely accepted (at least while free access remains on radio), no government has yet dared test the public sense of entitlement to the Olympic Games or the FIFA World Cup. Although it may well be that the degree of collective national unity fostered by television was always a comfortable cultural myth (Moran, 2013), innovations such as Twitter have tended to contribute to rather than detract from the historic notion of broadcasting as a key cultural provider of shared common experiences and a common public domain (Garnham, 1986).

Finally, the reputational value and the importance of trust in the public service sector remains as powerful as ever. In an ICM-*Guardian* poll in September 2009, 77 percent of respondents agreed that the BBC was an institution to be proud of (Barnett and Seaton, 2010: 331). When James Murdoch warned of the BBC's 'chilling' market power in his 2009 McTaggart Lecture (Murdoch 2009: 14), responses were skeptical even before the subsequent revelations of News International's phone-hacking exploits. Trust is still a defining strength of public service media and a defining problem for their competitors.

In fact, despite its much touted 'crisis of legitimacy', the momentum against public service broadcasting has arguably been weakening in recent years. Ofcom's Second Public Service Broadcasting Review (2008/9) noted a *decline* in the delivery of public value by non-BBC providers and majority support among the public for a continued central public service role for the BBC (Lunt, Livingstone and Brevini, 2012: 121–23). Its Public Service Broadcasting Annual Report for 2013 noted that audiences continue to value public service broadcasting, especially in news (85 percent), regional broadcasting (78 percent) and 'quality' programing (82 percent) (Ofcom, 2013). There remains in the UK a refusenik element that chooses not to sign up to subscription television but prefers the more self-denying choice on Freeview. Increasing public disenchantment in Britain with market orthodoxy, in particular with regard to the privatized public utilities, may suggest declining faith in the private sector's ability to provide public services (Goodwin, 2012: 75). Moreover, the Reithian brand of public service broadcasting remains strong outside the UK, with the continued success of BBC overseas. There is even an increasing interest in the 'third sector' in media in societies without previous histories of public service media such as China, Mexico, the former Yugoslavia and the Middle East (Lowe and Steemers, 2012). Above all, there have always been people who have preferred other broadcasters to the BBC – but always in the knowledge that there was a public service broadcaster to 'keep the others honest'. It is still the case that broadcasting systems are to this day typically measured above all against their public service function – and in a way that competing media, for example the press, are not. In the USA, HBO is considered a success above all because of the quality of its flagship drama series, not their ratings, which are proportionally tiny, while Fox News is deplored above all for its loose commitment to impartiality. Even the fact that the BBC is still the preferred choice of broadcaster for national and ceremonial events reflects the power of the Reithian legacy. Thus, for instance, BBC1 still attracted over half the total audience for the 2011 Royal Wedding despite coverage being available on ten separate television channels (BARB, 2011).

Conclusions

What is the future for the public service ethos in the twenty-first century? How far can it survive in an era of multi-channel, multi-platform media, of user-generated content and programs on demand, in a world in which so much media is no longer nationally bound and which sees the fracturing of the very idea of a common program and common schedule of broadcasting?

Media commentators note the need for advocates of public service media to regain the initiative, not simply preaching to the converted but deploying new arguments that re-establish the contemporary relevance of public service media (Picard, 2012: 32), engaging consumers in communication in new ways (Debrett, 2009) and demonstrating their value as a 'trusted guide' through the digital realm (Hendy, 2013: 122). They argue that a media system should treat its public "as citizens rather than consumers" (Barnett and Seaton, 2010: 327); that broadcasting still represents a public good against the privatization of information, culture and entertainment

(Scannell, 1989: 139); that not every media space can or should be an advertising medium (Barnett and Seaton, 2010: 331); and that broadcasting retains its importance in fostering the imagined national community: no longer perhaps Reith's idea of a united nation but a space in which "plurality can be performed" and diverse perspectives shared (Born, 2005: 517). They argue for the recognition that the free market cannot by its very nature guarantee to deliver trust in the way that public service media can and do. Above all, Scannell's argument is as relevant today as it was 20 years ago or, for that matter, in 1922: "equal access for all to a wide and varied range of common information, entertainment and cultural programmes carried on channels that can be received throughout the country must be thought of as an important citizenship right in mass democratic societies" (Scannell, 1990: 26).

The future is unclear. Advocates of public service values in broadcasting divide between pessimists who believe the war is already lost (Tracey, 1998) and optimists who champion a continued relevance and purpose for the public service ethos (Born, 2005; Goodwin, 2012; Hendy, 2013). Non-believers remain convinced that it is an outdated attitude of no relevance in today's world (North, 2007; Murdoch, 2009). The survival of public service broadcasting probably depends less on debates in media circles and the 'Westminster village' than on the future viewing and listening habits of the under-20s. But if, as Hendy says, the public service ethos is "to transform mere technology into a social philosophy" (Hendy, 2013: 131), the debate itself will remain a moral as much as an economic one. This very language of belief confirms that the legacy of Reith's original ethos of public service broadcasting still persists, in Britain and beyond, to this day.

Further reading

J. C. W. Reith's (1924) *Broadcast Over Britain* is the classic exposition of 'Reithian' values. Scannell's (1990) "Public service broadcasting: The history of a concept," and Debrett's (2009) "Riding the wave: Public service television in the multi-platform era" are fine outlines of, respectively, the history of the public service ethos in British broadcasting, and its contemporary challenges. For contrasting 'pessimist' and 'optimist' views of the future of public service broadcasting in Britain, see Tracey's (1988) *The Decline and Fall of Public Service Broadcasting* and Hendy's (2013) *Public Service Broadcasting*. Lowe and Steemers' (2012) edited *Regaining the Initiative for Public Service Media* contextualizes the ongoing debate with a range of European and global perspectives on the future viability of public service media.

References

Arnold, M. ([1869] 2006) *Culture and Anarchy*. Oxford: Oxford University Press.
BARB (2011) "BARB Since 1981: Top ten programmes (2011)." Retrieved from http://www.barb.co.uk/resources/tv-facts/since-1981/2011/top10
——(2013) "BARB: Total viewing summary." Retrieved from http://www.barb.co.uk/viewing/weekly-total-viewing-summary?_s=4

Barnett, S. and Seaton, J. (2010) "Why the BBC matters: Memo to the new parliament about a unique British institution." *Political Quarterly*, 81(3), 327–32.

Barrington, J. (1938) "This surprising man Reith." *Daily Express*, 15 June, p. 10.

Born, G. (2005) *Uncertain Vision: Birt, Dyke and the Reinvention of the BBC*. London: Vintage.

Briggs, A. (1961) *The History of Broadcasting in the United Kingdom: Vol I: The Birth of Broadcasting*. London: Oxford University Press.

——(1965) *The History of Broadcasting in the United Kingdom: Vol II: The Golden Age of Wireless*. London: Oxford University Press.

Debrett, M. (2009) "Riding the wave: Public service television in the multi-platform era." *Media, Culture and Society*, 31(5), 807–27.

Garnham, N. (1986) "The media and the public sphere." In P. Golding, G. Murdock and P. Schlesinger (eds.) *Communicating Politics: Mass Communications and the Political Process*. Leicester: Leicester University Press (pp. 37–53).

Goodwin, P. (2012) "High noon. The BBC meets 'the west's most daring government'." In G. F. Lowe and J. Steemers (eds.) *Regaining the Initiative for Public Service Media*. Gothenburg: Nordicom (pp. 63–78).

Hendy, D. (2013) *Public Service Broadcasting*. Basingstoke: Palgrave Macmillan.

Hilmes, M. (2012) *Network Nations: A Transnational History of British and American Broadcasting*. London: Routledge.

Hood, S. (1986) "Broadcasting and the public interest: From consensus to crisis." In P. Golding, G. Murdock and P. Schlesinger (eds.) *Communicating Politics: Mass Communications and the Political Process*. Leicester: Leicester University Press (pp. 55–66).

Jennings, H. and Gill, W. (1939) *Broadcasting in Everyday Life*. London: BBC.

LeMahieu, D. L. (1988) *A Culture for Democracy: Mass Communication and the Cultivated Mind in Britain Between the Wars*. Oxford: Clarendon Press.

Lowe, G. F. and Steemers, J. (eds.) (2012) *Regaining the Initiative for Public Service Media*. Gothenburg: Nordicom.

Lunt, P., Livingstone, S., and Brevini, B. (2012) "Changing regimes of regulation: Implications for public service broadcasting." In G. F. Lowe and J. Steemers (eds.) *Regaining the Initiative for Public Service Media*. Gothenburg: Nordicom (pp. 113–30).

McNicholas, A. and Seaton, J. (2009) "It was the BBC wot won it: Winning the Peacock Report for the corporation, or how the BBC responded to the Peacock Committee." In T. O'Malley and J. Jones (eds.) *The Peacock Committee and UK Broadcasting Policy*. Basingstoke: Palgrave (pp. 121–45).

Moran, J. (2013) *Armchair Nation: An Intimate History of Britain in Front of the TV*. London: Profile Books.

Murdoch, J. (2009) "2009 Edinburgh International Television Festival McTaggart Lecture." Retrieved from http://www.abc.net.au/mediawatch/transcripts/0937_mactaggart.pdf

Nicholas, S. (1996) *The Echo of War: Home Front Propaganda and the Wartime BBC 1939–1945*. Manchester: Manchester University Press.

North, R. D. (2007) *"Scrap the BBC!" Ten Years to Set Broadcasters Free*. London: Social Affairs Unit.

Ofcom (2004) "Ofcom review of public service television broadcasting: Phase 1." Retrieved from http://stakeholders.ofcom.org.uk/binaries/consultations/psb/summary/psb.pdf

——(2007) "Ofcom communications market report 2007: Part 2: Television." Retrieved from http://stakeholders.ofcom.org.uk/binaries/research/cmr/tv2.pdf

——(2013) "Public Service Broadcasting Annual Report 2013." Retrieved from http://stakeholders.ofcom.org.uk/broadcasting/reviews-investigations/public-service-broadcasting/annrep/psb13

O'Malley, T. (2009) "Liberalism and broadcasting policy from the 1920s to the 1960s." In T. O'Malley and J. Jones (eds.) *The Peacock Committee and UK Broadcasting Policy*. Basingstoke: Palgrave (pp. 22–44).

Picard, R. G. (2012) "The changing nature of political case-making for public service broadcasters." In G. F. Lowe and J. Steemers (eds.) *Regaining the Initiative for Public Service Media*. Gothenburg: Nordicom (pp. 27–44).

Reith, J. C. W. (1924) *Broadcast Over Britain*. London: Hodder and Stoughton.

——(1949) *Into the Wind*. London: Hodder and Stoughton.

Rogers, S. (ed.) (2004) *The Hutton Enquiry and its Impact*. London: Politicos.

Scannell, P. (1989) "Public service broadcasting and modern public life." *Media, Culture and Society*, 11(2), 135–66.

——(1990) "Public service broadcasting: The history of a concept." In A. Goodwin and G. Whannel (eds.) *Understanding Television*. London: Routledge (pp. 11–26). Also reprinted in E. Buscombe (ed.) (2000) *British Television: A Reader*. Oxford: Oxford University Press (pp. 45–62).

Scannell, P. and Cardiff, D. (1991) *A Social History of Broadcasting in Britain, Vol. I: 1922–1939: Serving the Nation*, Oxford: Blackwell.

Tracey, M. (1998) *The Decline and Fall of Public Service Broadcasting*. Oxford: Oxford University Press.

28
Pirates, popularity and the rise of the DJ

Richard Rudin

Significant moments or 'tipping points' in the development of any media are rare. Changes often occur after many years of development and can only be identified in retrospect. In the case, though, of the pirate radio phenomenon and the effect this had on the development of radio broadcasting in the UK and other European countries, not least on public service broadcasting systems, changes were identifiable at the time, most notably through government responses to them. The pirate radio stations led directly to the introduction of an all-day national pop music service on the BBC in 1967; the impetus and political pressure for legalized commercial radio, which was resolved by land-based, licensed local stations from 1973; and, to some extent, BBC local radio, which also began in 1967. It can of course never be proven that all or any of these developments would have otherwise taken place, but it can surely be no coincidence that all did so after the UK-targeted pirate services were effectively outlawed in August 1967. For the purposes of this chapter, references to pirate radio will generally mean unlicensed, commercially funded broadcasts to the UK and mainland Europe from ships and former anti-aircraft forts outside the territorial limits of countries' jurisdictions between 1958 and 1990, especially the key period 1964 to 1968.

The effect of the pirate stations was not only to force the hand of governments to provide radio services to meet an undeniable demand from the public, but also to challenge the core cultural and political philosophy that broadcasting should be a public service, paid for through a common *de facto* taxation and for the whole population, regardless of their income or propensity to change their buying habits. The switch in emphasis from the airwaves being used for an overall public good to use for private profit, with the public being regarded as consumers rather than citizens – with audiences aggregated and sold to advertisers – faced fierce political opposition. In the UK, this came from the Labour party, in government (1964–70) and opposition (1970–74); although Tony Benn, the minister responsible for broadcasting policy in a crucial period in the mid 1960s, noted in his diaries that the then Prime Minister, Harold Wilson "enjoys the pirates and has always been trying to find some way of taxing them" (Benn, 1987: 415). More rigorous objections to commercial radio came from intellectuals such as Stuart Hall and Richard Hoggart, as well as from some bishops in the established church, cultural commentators and others from what can be loosely defined as 'the Establishment' (Rudin, 2012). The 'Americanization' of British culture was fiercely resisted, and commercial radio – whether licensed or not – was associated with vulgarity and a 'lowest common denominator' approach, which was the antithesis of the philosophy of the BBC's first Director General, John Reith (Street, 2006). For decades the BBC resisted the clamor for all-day popular music services (Briggs, 1995) and for dedicated services catering to popular tastes (Curran, 2002).

The personification of the commercial radio approach, which was an essential part of the Top 40 format, developed in the USA with a high rotation of selected hit records of the day, big prize contests and a general on-air excitement (Fong-Torres 1998), was the personality disc jockey (DJ). This was someone who 'rode' the records and other programing elements, combining the roles of salesman – literally in the case of the pirate radio DJs, as they would often voice the commercial spots 'live' – and gatekeeper for editorial content. As such, the DJ can be regarded as part cultural leader, part journalist, part entertainer and part straightforward announcer (Lewis and Booth, 1989). Scannell (2007) synthesized works by Goffman (1981) and Montgomery (1986), as well as his own in-depth study of the on-air discourse of one of the best-known British DJs discussed in this chapter, Tony Blackburn, in order to evaluate the ways in which the DJ both addresses and constructs an audience through his performance and weaves the flow of talk through a live daily program. Previously, Scannell (1991) had identified five different modes of address used by Blackburn. Tolson (2006: 116) argues that the radio DJ unifies a mass but diverse audience into a unified dynamic relationship:

> Thus the old style of DJ engages listeners in an ongoing process of identification which is based around shifts of alignment ... We thereby imagine ourselves to be members of a large, diverse community, linked to each other by virtue of being listeners to his show. And it is the personality of the DJ that orchestrates this, in the live time of the 'here and now' of his show.

Given its title and its historic context, this chapter will concentrate on Tolson's 'old style of DJ' from the late 1950s to the late 1980s, before the introduction of computerized methods of voice-tracking – where DJs record all the links for a program, sometimes many days ahead of broadcast and from a location many miles from the stations' transmission areas – as well as further challenges to temporal and spatial aspects of both transmission and listenership afforded by the internet.

Challenges to the public service ethos and radio monopoly

The BBC's radio monopoly had been challenged decades before the start of the UK-targeted pirate radio stations in the mid 1960s. Entrepreneurs, who realized that there was a huge, untapped, eager market for less demanding output than the majority of what could be found on the BBC, especially on Sundays, established radio stations on continental Europe – notably in France and Luxembourg – broadcasting in English and establishing very significant audiences by the mid 1930s (Baron, 1975). The Second World War saw the end of most of these stations, aside from Radio Luxembourg, whose English-language service was revived after the war (Street, 2006). The advent of commercial or 'independent' television (ITV) and the advice from leading agencies for advertisers to switch their budgets to the new television service might have been the death knell for Radio Luxembourg had it not been for the arrival of both rock 'n' roll music and the transistor radio (Crisell, 1986).

A further and as it transpired more potent threat to public service radio monopolies in the UK and other parts of Europe came with the arrival in 1958 of the first European pirate radio station, Radio Mercur, anchored in international waters off Denmark's capital, Copenhagen (Leonard, 1996). This was followed by the Netherlands' Radio Veronica, which was to be one of the few such stations to be given a license to broadcast on land. But it was Radio Nord, which began broadcasting from the Baltic Sea near the Swedish capital, Stockholm, in March 1961 which laid the true foundations of the UK-targeted pirate radio phenomenon. The output of the station followed in almost exact detail the Top 40 US radio format of the station KLIF in Dallas. Indeed, the true founding father of European pirate radio, as well as a pioneer of the Top 40 format, could be said to be Gordon McLendon, who had built the second biggest chain of stations in the US, centred on Dallas, Texas, and then co-founded Radio Nord (Garay, 1992). By June 1961 the station had a listenership amongst 15–24-year-olds greater than the combined audience for that age group for all the Swedish radio services (Kemppainen, 2009). In July 1962, a ministerial meeting between Denmark, Finland, Norway and Sweden decided to bring their respective anti-pirate radio laws into effect at the end of that month (ibid.). Within two years European pirate radio then entered its next and best known phase, started by Irish entrepreneur Ronan O'Rahilly of Radio Caroline in March 1964.

UK pirates, US formats and techniques

Contrary to popular myth, and the depiction in the movie *The Boat That Rocked* (Curtis, 2009), Radio Caroline and the bulk of the 20 or so pirate radio stations that established themselves on ships and former anti-aircraft forts in the North and Irish seas in the mid 1960s did not have much of a rebellious, still less anarchic flavor to them. Certainly, they sounded different in many respects from the BBC's Light Programme, not least in their offering of a continuous output of popular music on record. But instances of swearing, lewd remarks and invocations to engage in wild promiscuous behavior were rare and mostly confined to what might be called the smaller, short-lived 'prank' stations, such as Radio Sutch, headed by the self-styled 'Screaming Lord Sutch' (Skues, 1994). Radio Caroline featured considerable amounts of what could be broadly described as 'light' music – orchestral tracks, standards, ballads and country music – and although the DJ chat was much more relaxed, informal, spontaneous and humorous than would be heard from most BBC presenters, it was also, for the most part, respectful and uncontroversial. The South of England-based Radio Caroline at least (stations anchored in and serving the North and South of the UK were established by July 1964) did become more of an out and out pop station with more aggressive presentation when faced with its big rival, the Texan-programed and backed Radio London, which began broadcasting from a former US minesweeper just before Christmas 1964, with a strict Top 40 format (Elliot, 1997). Chapman (1990) has detailed the different approach of these two stations in music content, DJ style and, above all, management control.

Not all the pirate stations featured pop hits as their main offering; one of the most successful was Radio 390, which broadcast so-called 'sweet' music and was a "woman's magazine of the air" (Harris, 1997). The almost revered after-midnight Perfumed Garden programs by John Peel on Radio London, which featured album tracks by US West Coast rock artists and hippy-ish poetry, happened not by design by the station's management but through Peel's willful flouting of their strictures (Peel and Ravenscroft, 2005). Furthermore, not all had aspirations to maximize audiences into a national or semi-national 'sell' to advertisers; some, such as Radio Scotland, put more emphasis on public service speech, hoping to demonstrate that a local or at least sub-regional commercial station could be both profitable and provide a genuine, valued community service (Skues, 1994).

Unlike their Scandinavian and Dutch predecessors, which had to 'create' their own DJs as their domestic stations had no music radio formats and consequently no experience on which to draw, the English language pirate stations could tap into a talent pool from North America, Australasia, South Africa and British Forces' radio. These in turn could coach the indigenous, inexperienced DJs. The stations were keen to create an on-air environment conducive to selling the products and services being advertised. As the Radio London Managing Director Philip Birch put it in 1965:

> [W]e are responsible, reliable businesspeople supplying what the public likes and wants. Offshore commercial radio has given radio a new image. For the man in the car, driving alone, and the lonely housewife, they provide constant companionship. To the teenager they mean instant 'beat' presented by a happy disc jockey with a pleasant patter which includes a package of pops and plugs.
>
> (Skues, 1994: 207–8)

Being beyond the law and regulators meant the DJs were free from the restrictions already imposed on UK commercial television (ITV) – and later to be imposed on licensed on-land stations – so that they could actively promote products, including cigarettes. Unlike the ITV and the later Independent Local Radio (ILR) stations, the DJs didn't have to have 'natural breaks' with a clear distinction between program content and advertising. They could use the guise of the 'trusted, informed friend', the one-to-one intimate relationship with listeners, to engage them in advertising promotions, such as encouragement to collect and send in tops of breakfast cereal packets, cards from tea cartons and so on (Rudin, 2007). This undoubtedly helped in persuading the national advertising agencies to switch at least part of their budgets to pirate radio (Chapman, 1992). Other significant forms of revenue came from payments to broadcast programs from US evangelists keen to reach a youth audience and who, of course, were barred from BBC airwaves (Cash, 2012). Payola – the payment for the playing of records – although not universal amongst the pirates, certainly took place (ibid.).

Whilst acknowledging these occasional lapses in integrity and obeisance to simple financial calculations, this is not to argue that there wasn't a great deal of innovation, freedom and simple joy from the pirate broadcasters that was clearly appreciated by those on board the ships and forts and which was certainly enjoyed by their very considerable audiences. According to some estimates, up to half the UK population was listening to one or more of the pirate stations at their peak and there was undoubtedly a much wider listenership to the pirates' broadcasts than the stereotypical teenager, with transistor radio clamped to the ear (Seymour-Ure, 1996: 76). Kenny Everett, inspired by Radio Luxembourg, the BBC DJ Jack Jackson and the BBC radio comedy *The Goons*, 'played' with the audio medium: dubbing and over-dubbing, splicing up and juxtaposing incongruous comedy and news clips with music, speeding up and slowing down records, singing over instrumentals and 're-versioning' tracks, phasing and adding echo/reverb (Lister, 1996). In the case of pirate radio, the obvious physical disconnection between broadcaster and listener in 'real time' (that is, other than letters and postcards sent to the UK offices and taken out to ships and forts by tender) was memorably overcome by Johnnie Walker on Radio Caroline, who would take a microphone out onto the deck of the ship and invite listeners to park their cars on the sea cliffs and then flash their headlights in a form of semaphore to reveal their names and their responses to his questions (Walker, 2008).

Aims and aspirations of pirate radio

With all the logistical and technical problems, and the limitations and expense of broadcasting in often tumultuous seas and with seasick DJs, offshore radio was clearly not a viable long-term business prospect. The backers of the pirate stations were very keen to come on shore. The ambitions for the style and content of land-based services varied from a national or semi-national continuous music station or stations (Radio London, Radio 390), to smaller, localized services (Radio 270, Radio Scotland), to a more philosophical desire for 'free radio' without legal or regulatory restrictions on speech or music content (Radio Caroline). In these various and collective aims the stations had support from significant numbers in both Houses of Parliament, business groups and the advertising industry but also considerable opposition from some politicians, the intellectual Left, many newspapers, the Musicians' Union and copyright bodies (Chapman, 1992). Both the supporting and the opposing groups contained a mixture of political, economic and cultural ideologies, and vested interests. Radio London's management were uncompromisingly campaigning for 'free enterprise radio' in the UK and they believed it was morally and economically wrong for broadcasting to be a monopoly; they found a receptive audience amongst many Conservative MPs (Rudin, 2007). Some of the pirate stations attempted to reach a deal with the music copyright bodies and strenuous efforts were made to avoid interfering with the transmissions of UK or other radio stations and ship-to-shore links with fishing, merchant or military boats and ships. Thus, the stations hoped to head off one of the most widely rehearsed complaints against pirate radio, which was that they were parasites who stole other people's artistic creations and radio frequencies (Harris, 1997).

However, another major complaint, that by literally being beyond the law through broadcasting from outside national territorial limits they were a challenge to the respect for the rule of law generally, and that there were links to criminality, seemed to be substantiated in June 1966 when a dispute between two rival pirate radio operators led to one of them being shot dead in an English country house (Johns, 2011). About three months before this tragedy the Labour Party was returned to government with a near 100 majority in the House of Commons and this, combined with the shooting, ended prevarication over dealing with the pirates. A Bill was put before the House which made it an offense for UK citizens to broadcast from, supply or advertise an unlicensed station and this came into effect at midnight on August 14 1967 (Peters, 2011). By then, all but the two Caroline stations had closed down. The DJs on the newly styled Radio Caroline International were defiant; they vowed to continue broadcasting and made implicit associations between the British government's suppression of pirate radio and the UK's defiant, lone stand against Nazi Europe (Rudin, 2007). Moreover, Walker, in particular, has been eloquent in his belief in the almost mystical importance of Radio Caroline in bringing peace and joy through music, and the freedom he and others enjoyed to say and play what they wanted. He argued that the authorities greatly feared the effects on young people of a radio station that promoted an alternative way of viewing the world and life, and that this threatened the established order and mindset; so much so that 'they' decided it had to be crushed (Walker, 2008).

In the end, starved of advertising revenue and forced to (at least officially) procure their supplies from the Netherlands, as well as base its HQ there as that country had yet to enact an anti-pirate radio law, in March 1968 both Caroline stations were simultaneously boarded, closed down and towed to shore by a company claiming unpaid tendering bills. The Radio Caroline call sign returned in a sensational and controversial style during the 1970 UK general election campaign (Butler and Pinto-Duchinsky, 1971) and it and other stations broadcast with varying degrees of success, formats and continuity in the 1970s and 80s. But there can be no doubt that the most important period in listenership and influence by offshore pirate stations on the development of European radio services peaked in the mid 1960s.

DJs, musical integrity and popularity

The Labour government's 'encouragement' for the BBC to organize a nationally broadcast replacement for the pirates in 1967 led not just to a radical shake-up of the corporation's networks and public offering, but also to a cultural and editorial change in their processes and approaches. Until it adapted and adopted important aspects of commercial pirate radio approaches, the BBC had music programs with titles that reflected the content. But from September 1967 and the launch of Radio 1, the program names gradually gave way to the names of the DJs. By 1971, nearly all the main daytime programs of Radio 1 were thus titled, although on Radio 2 the more traditional program names still predominated. So on Radio 1, the DJ *was* the program; it became centered on his (or, very occasionally, her) personality and supposedly reflected, at least in part, their musical tastes. As the BBC's 1972 handbook put it: The presenters of these 'strips', as they are called, through their friendly manner have built up a rapport with their audiences which makes them daily radio visitors to countless thousands of homes (BBC, 1972: 46).

Significantly, when DJs came on shore and joined the BBC, they also broke a hitherto strict divide in the corporation between the technical and announcing sides of the broadcasting set-up by adapting two continuity suites for self-operational mode by the DJs. This aided program spontaneity and greater unity between the DJs' speech, music and other program elements. Listeners could interact with the DJ through letters/postcards and on-air phone calls, so the DJ also became a friend and confidant. The listeners' influence on the output may still have been carefully controlled and mediated, with their contributions selected and molded to fit the predetermined output, but, through the DJ, radio can justly claim to have been the first interactive medium.

The early Radio 1 DJs were nearly all from middle-class backgrounds, privately educated and with received pronunciation. From the start of the network though it was clear that there would be a division between the popular, inoffensive, boy-next-door character – unthreatening and undemanding in the links or in the music he played – and the credible, more serious, sometimes slightly cynical character to be found in the evenings and at weekends.

Johnny Beerling was the first producer of the key Breakfast Show, hosted from its inception in September 1967 until June 1973 by Tony Blackburn, a veteran of both Radio Caroline and Radio London. Beerling greatly admired Radio London and was eager to adopt its music programing format – Top 40 – using a 'hot clock' to ensure that the biggest hits and familiar oldies predominated on a strict rotation (Beerling, 2008). Blackburn was delighted at how keen the BBC was to follow the Radio London format, at least at breakfast time, and even to buy the same US-made station identification jingles (Blackburn, 2007).

At the other end of the scale, and indeed the antithesis of this approach, was John Peel, who established himself within five years as the alternative in musical choice and presentation style, and became known for his stout refusal to join in with, or, if absolutely required to participate, studied cynicism of, the station's various on and off-air activities. Peel mused that an interest in music was regarded not as an asset but a distinct disadvantage. Station producers and managers preferred the DJs to concentrate on their public appeal as an unseen friend, even a virtual romantic interest, and be grateful for the demands for them to make highly lucrative personal appearances which all added to their huge celebrity status and their potential for TV careers (Peel and Ravenscroft, 2005).

In between the populism of Blackburn and others in the 'housewife-friendly' persona and the willfully obscure Peel sat DJs such as Johnnie Walker, who had stayed with Radio Caroline until the end in 1968 and had then been gradually eased into the Radio 1 schedules. He neither wanted to conform to the BBC's desire for him to be yet another inoffensive, mildly flirtatious but undemanding personality, playing nothing but the Top 40 hits and 'golden oldies', but nor did he want to be totally 'left-field' and on the margins of the station and popular music. When his contract came up in 1976 the station bosses were astounded that he turned down a two-year deal for programs in peak time when he was told that the album tracks had to go; from now on it would be strictly Radio 1 daytime playlist material (Walker, 2008).

Many of the former pirate DJs and management found a berth on one of the Independent Local Radio services. These were introduced from 1973 after being established by parliament, with the Bill from the Conservative government passed only after vociferous opposition by Labour. Kenny Everett and Dave Cash joined London's Capital Radio and Philip Birch took up the same position as he had had on Radio London on Greater Manchester's Piccadilly Radio (Baron, 1975). Direct US involvement in the new stations was barred and advertising was restricted to clearly delineated recorded 'spots' of no more than nine minutes an hour. Such advertising was not to be voiced by the DJ and the services were required to broadcast a wide range of programing for a 'variety of tastes and interests', with local and network news, features, documentaries, sport, even some drama, minority music and public service material of many varieties (Stoller, 2010). Commercially released music was in any case limited by a 'needletime' restriction of nine hours a day (ibid.). Despite or because of these restrictions and requirements, after a shaky start – which may have been largely due to the distinctively unpromising economic and advertising climate of the time – most of the new services established significant revenues and considerable audiences, often out-performing all the BBC network and local services available in their transmission areas (Allen, 2013). It seemed that public good and private profit could, after all, be compatible.

Conclusion

The European offshore pirate radio phenomenon of the 1960s and 70s unquestionably led to a major change in the programing choices and styles available to the public. In most cases, including the UK and Sweden, the response by governments to the unlicensed stations was to legislate to force them off the air and to instruct the existing public service broadcasters to at least partly meet the proven demand for such output through their own networks. But in most cases this only extended their respective monopolies; the demand for alternative, commercially funded and privately owned stations was hotly resisted, partly on ideological grounds. No country was prepared to welcome on shore a station such as Radio Caroline, which in any event declined to apply for licenses when commercial radio was permitted, as this would require a submission to a regulatory regime over program style, music content and speech. The sorts of freedoms enjoyed by the press, which had in the UK's case only been achieved after several centuries of conflict, were only to be realized, much later, through audio streaming on the unregulated internet. Unsurprisingly, this is where Radio Caroline re-started, after further legislation and the battering of the North Sea finally ended its ship-based broadcasts in 1990.

Running alongside these broader political, economic, cultural and ideological disputes are questions over the purpose and function of the DJ, a breed of broadcaster which, in Europe, was largely created by the pirates in the 1960s. For most listeners to music-based stations the DJs *were* the station. Their individual, carefully created and maintained on-air personalities made them almost like members of a family and undoubtedly to many became a substitute virtual friend. For listeners to 'specialist DJs' the music was more important than the presenter. However, for the bulk of the daytime DJs, who had the biggest audiences, musical credibility and personal likes and dislikes were sacrificed for mass appeal and a long career.

In the UK the uneasy and constantly contested compromise between pure commercialism and public service ideals was played out in the early days of the independent local services. From 1991, de-regulation meant there was a continuing erosion of public service requirements and the 'full service' approach. Greatly increased competition for audiences and revenues exacerbated risk-averse, carefully targeted and researched music and other program content for specific audience demographics and station brands. There was increasingly centralized control over playlists and restrictions over what the DJs could say and when they could say it. By the twenty-first century, many former pirate DJs, including Johnnie Walker and Dave Cash, rediscovered much more of the freedom of musical choice and spontaneous spirit of the pirate stations at the BBC. By then it was the commercial broadcasters who, in many cases – at least outside the breakfast time/morning drive period – were like the old-time BBC announcers, restricted to scripted announcements and required to subjugate the expression of their individual personalities to a corporate identity. Ultimately, the pirate stations hugely benefitted the BBC, which was able to combine its secure public funding to invest in content for the benefit of the listeners and the creative freedom of its DJs.

Further reading

Although neither are by established scholars, both *When Pirates Ruled the Waves* (Harris, 1997) and *Pop Went the Pirates* (Skues, 1994) contain a wealth of primary sources, including original interviews, on the formation and development of the pirate stations, their personnel both on and off-air, and their battles with government and other agencies. *Selling the Sixties* (Chapman, 1992) is a lively and well-researched work from an established academic on the adaptation of US-originated commercial styles of broadcasting to British sensibilities. *Death Of a Pirate* (Johns, 2011) is an intriguing mixture of a dramatic narrative of one of the most notorious episodes in UK pirate history (the fatal shooting of one pirate radio operator by a rival) and a more traditional academic style in the author's argument of how British culture was influenced by the impact of these stations. *Sounds of Your Life* (Stoller, 2010), written by an industry insider, provides a thorough and well-informed guide to the development of authorized, land-based commercial radio services in the UK. For analysis of how DJs and other types of broadcasters both construct their discourse and interact with their audiences, *Broadcast Talk* (Scannell, 1991) provides one of the most detailed and perceptive works in the field, drawing on and developing from previous studies.

References

Allen, D. (2013) "Independent local radio in the West Midlands: BRMB and Beacon Radio in the 1970s." *Media History*, 19(4), 496–513.
Baron, M. (1975) *Independent Radio: The Story of Commercial Radio in the United Kingdom*. Lavenham: Terence Dalton Limited.
BBC (1972) *BBC Handbook 1972*. London: BBC.
Benn, T. (1987) *Out of the Wilderness: Diaries 1963–67*. London: Arrow Books.
Beerling, J. (2008) *Radio 1: The Inside Scene*. Bloomington, IN: Trafford.
Blackburn, T. (2007) *Poptastic: My Life In Radio*. London: Cassell.
Briggs, A. (1995) *The History of Broadcasting in the United Kingdom: Competition 1955–1974. Vol. V*. Oxford: Oxford University Press.
Butler, D. and Pinto-Duchinsky, M. (1971) *The British General Election of 1970*. London: Macmillan.
Cash, D. (2012) *He Sounds Much Taller: Memoirs of a Radio Pirate*. Kindle edition.
Chapman, R. (1990) "The 1960s: A comparative study of Radio London and Radio Caroline." *Popular Music*, 9(2), 165–78.
——(1992) *Selling the Sixties: The Pirates and Popular Music Radio*. London: Routledge.
Crisell, A. (1986) *Understanding Radio*. London: Routledge.
Curran, J. (2002) "Media history and the making of British society, c. 1700–2000." *Media History*, 8(2), 135–54.
Curtis, R. (2009) [film] *The Boat That Rocked*.
Elliot, C. (1997) *The Wonderful Radio London Story, 1964–67: The Life and Times of Big L*. Frinton-on-Sea: East Anglian Productions.
Fong-Torres, B. (1998) *The Hits Just Keep On Coming: The History of Top 40 Radio*. San Francisco, CA: Miller Freeman.
Garay, R. (1992) *Gordon McLendon: The Maverick of Radio*. New York: Greenwood Press.
Goffman, E. (1981) *Forms of Talk*. Philadelphia, PA: University of Pennsylvania Press.
Harris, P. (1997) *When Pirates Ruled the Waves* (6th ed.). Glasgow: Leonard and Boyd.
Johns, A. (2011) *Death of a Pirate: British Radio and the Making of the Information Age*. New York: W.W. Norton.
Kemppainen, P. (2009) "Pirates and the new public service radio paradigm." *The Radio Journal: International Studies in Broadcast and Audio Media*, 7(2), 123–33.
Leonard, M. (1996) *From International Waters: 60 Years of Offshore Broadcasting*. Heswall: Forest.
Lewis, P. and Booth, J. (1989) *The Invisible Medium: Public, Commercial and Community Radio*. Basingstoke: Macmillan.
Lister, D. (1996) *In the Best Possible Taste: The Crazy Life of Kenny Everett*. London: Bloomsbury.
Montgomery, M. (1986) "DJ talk." *Media, Culture and Society*, 8(4), 421–40.
Peel, J. and Ravenscroft, R. (2005) *Margrave of the Marshes*. London: Bantam.
Peters, K. (2011) "Sinking the radio 'pirates': Exploring British strategies of governance in the North Sea, 1964–91." *Area*, 43(3), 281–87.
Rudin, R. (2007) "The politics of the introduction of commercial radio in the UK: A clash of ideologies produces a troublesome birth." *Southern Review*, 39(3), 93–108.
——(2012) "Not over here! How British elites used national newspapers to engage in debates of licensed commercial radio stations." In M. Mollgaard (ed.) *Radio and Society: New Thinking for an Old Medium*. Newcastle upon Tyne: Cambridge Scholars Publishing (pp. 30–50).
Scannell, P. (ed.) (1991) *Broadcast Talk*. London: Sage.
——(2007) *Media and Communication*. London: Sage.
Seymour-Ure, C. (1996) *The British Press and Broadcasting since 1945*. Oxford: Blackwell.

Skues, K. (1994) *Pop Went the Pirates*. Sheffield: Lambs' Meadow Publications.

Stoller, T. (2010) *Sounds of Your Life: The History of Independent Radio*. New Barnet: John Libbey.

Street, S. (2006) *Crossing the Ether: British Public Service Radio and Commercial Competition 1922–1945*. Eastleigh: John Libbey.

Tolson, A. (2006) *Media Talk: Spoken Discourse on TV and Radio*. Edinburgh: Edinburgh University Press.

Walker, J. (2008) *Johnnie Walker: The Autobiography*. London: Michael Joseph.

29
Breaking the sound barrier
Histories and practices of women's radio

Caroline Mitchell

Introduction

According to Kate Lacey, "Radio is one of the sites where gender is produced, reproduced and transformed" (1996: 244). The first collection of research about women and radio (Mitchell, 2000a) recognized that women's cultural relationship to radio, whilst largely overlooked by media academics, had undergone great changes. It uncovered and recovered 'hidden' histories about women working in radio and explored the development of programing and programs by and for women within different sectors of radio. It reflected the emerging but fragmented theory and research in this area including gendered radio, the nature of female audiences and perspectives about women working in the industry and how women's radio stations in the community sector enable women to get on air and define media space themselves.

Over the last two decades the study of women and radio has gained momentum and has been enriched by researchers coming from a wide range of disciplines including history (see below), development and participatory communication studies (e.g. Jallov, 2007), sociolinguistics (Gill, 1993) and feminist cultural and media studies. Feminist media historians have filled in some of the huge gaps left by mainstream media histories (Skoog, 2011). Studies of the media industries and gender at international, national and local level have provided qualitative and quantitative evidence of discrimination and under-representation (Simms, 1985; Gallagher, 1995; Michaels and Mitchell, 2000; Creative Skillset, 2011; Franks, 2011).

In this chapter I am concerned with histories of women's participation and production, particularly at grass roots level. I explore the pathway that women's community radio, a sector that is neither state/publicly owned nor commercial but nonprofit oriented and accessible to people in both structure and programs (Lewis and Booth, 1990), has provided for women to different parts of the radio industry.

Radio has been a site of much feminist media critique, activity and activism and both established programs like the BBC's Woman's Hour and newer women's stations and programs within community radio have created spaces for feminist/women's organizations and acted as "connectors" (Thompson, Anfossi Gómez and Suárez Toro, 2005) between social and political movements, including women's movements and the audience. Feminist Media Studies "has always combined a critical edge with a creative disposition and a political motivation" (Gallagher, 2001: 11). Increasingly women who have worked in different parts of media industries have been able to use their first-hand experience of employment and production practices relating to female presenters and producers to explore and expand the debate about diversity and women's access to the airwaves (see also Ross and Byerly, 2006).

Feminist radio histories and studies have contributed to our understanding of organizational and media cultures that enable women to fully engage with radio and participate actively and meaningfully as audiences and producers. I will use a case study of the history of *Fem FM*, the first women's radio station in the UK, established 20 years ago (Mitchell, 2000b), to explore their experiences as producers of radio with particular reference to developments in the radio industry between the broadcasts and the present day.

Historical perspectives on the position of women and radio in media history

> History has many themes. One of them is that women should be quiet.
> (Ehrick, quoting Hall Jamieson, 2009: 69)

Michele Hilmes argues that "it is history writing that has consigned women to the sidelines, not historical events themselves (1997: 132). Feminist media history has been a minority area within media and cultural studies but feminist historians and researchers are reinstating it as one important narrative in a number of competing narratives (Curran, 2009). Increasingly we find historical accounts of women's radio work as presenters, producers and managers and about the cultures of the institutions and organizations they work in, as Skoog states, writing women back into history (2011). There has been a significant increase in the number of studies of individual female broadcasters that shed light on the issues and adversities they faced and whether they were able to overcome them. The wealth and availability of BBC archival materials has lead to themed historical analytical overviews and case studies such as Andrews' study of the domestication of broadcasting (2012), Baade's discussion about women listeners to the BBC in the Second World War (2007) and Hilmes' (2007) study of how women's culture was represented in BBC wartime dramas through the interplay between producers, writers and notions of what audiences want.

Historical studies of the relationship between women and radio on different continents are emerging and the overwhelming 'picture' is that historically wherever women's voices were heard they were "muted, private and largely outside what R Murray Shafer calls 'signal' sound listened to consciously and that often carry messages and or authority" (Ehrick, 2009: 72). Studies of early radio in Britain (Karpf, 1980; Nye, Godwin, and Hollows, 1994), Germany (Lacey, 1996) and the United States (Halper, 2001; Ganzert, 2003; Mazzarella, Hains and Thiel-Stern, 2013) found that whilst women *were* on the radio they largely remained in acceptable roles and arenas so that the "patriarchal soundscape" (Ehrick, 2009) remained intact. Between 1924 and 1940 the BBC manager Hilda Matheson was able to create a newsroom culture where women's authority was respected (Carney, 1999; Hunter, 2000). The BBC, however, has a history of under-representation of female radio journalists (Luscombe, 2013) and over many decades there has been management intransigence to appoint and promote women in key production and management roles and evidence that newsrooms and studios were dominated by men, "where power is experienced, wielded and often homosocially shared" (Ross and Carter, 2011: 214).

Although broadcast since 1946, the BBC's flagship program Woman's Hour has relatively few studies about it despite former editor Sally Feldman keeping it on the research map (Feldman, 2000, 2007). Skoog (2009, 2013) demonstrates how the program both enabled a range of women to be heard and represented the wider important function of enabling the BBC to know more about its female audience in the post-war years:

> it saw the potential of radio as a bridge between the public and the private. Such complexity thus helped broadcasters in the British context further advance programming style, and the significance of the female audience or women's programming should therefore not be underestimated.
> (Skoog, 2009: 11)

Kate Murphy, another long-time BBC Woman's Hour producer turned academic, shed light on a key period of the BBC's early history using archives and interviews to discuss the influence of prominent female managers and to explore the range of jobs held by women, the 'marriage bar' and how this affected women's progression in the BBC (2011).

Minic's research, based on contemporary interviews with program producers, discusses how Woman's Hour successfully addresses its audience by combining "identity, diversity, equality, and transformative politics" but she questions whether the program can be truly diverse as it is "to a certain extent limited by the demographics of its audience, its time slot, and mainstream character, which create the program's own majorities and minorities among women" (2008: 313).

Studies of women's radio in action

Carter notes that "with the 'mainstreaming' of feminism, one enduring assumption has been that women's success is to be measured by virtue of the extent to which we have been able to overcome exclusion from spaces associated with masculine dominance" (2004: 235). Alternative feminist media, which aims to "express and celebrate viewpoints of specific groups of women" (Steiner, 1992: 123) has been one way that this has been achieved.

There are now several documented models and definitions of women's and feminist radio and case studies of the desirable conditions for sustainable stations at a time when radio is constantly adapting to new financial, technological and political challenges (Mitchell, 2004; McGann, 2007). In her study of European women's radio, Jallov identified where women's radio takes place:

> in an all women's station, in an autonomous collective in a mixed station, in a women's group who are not totally autonomous in a mixed station … an

> individual making a woman's show, an individual woman working in a mainstream setting with a gender conscious perspective.
>
> (1996: 16)

Carter defines three models of access: "the liberal feminist path, where women replace men in already established broadcast positions; alternative or public radio stations, which dedicate a portion of broadcast time to women-centered programming; and where entire stations have women's programming" (2004: 169).

Women's radio stations have existed since the early 1950s. In the United States WHER-FM was an all-women's commercial radio station that broadcast in Memphis in 1955. It promoted itself as "a thousand beautiful watts" and all the station's presenters were women. It was owned and managed by three businessmen and it gave female broadcasters 'visibility' until it closed once the novelty of hearing women had worn off (Ganzert, 2009). Another commercial women's station, Viva Radio, opened in London in the mid 1990s. The station's launch marketing was aimed at "the professional woman of today juggling her family, her social life and her career" (Mitchell, 2000b: 106). However, competing and conflicting discourses of feminism and femininity surrounded the station's marketing and program policies and it was sold as a middle of the road music station a year after opening (Mitchell, 2000b).

Most women's radio stations and programs exist within grass roots, non commercial community stations and have proved to be sustainable only if formalized, structural ways are found for women to secure their representation, airtime and resources (Mitchell, 2004). Radiorakel was the first feminist community station and was set up in 1982 in Oslo, Norway. It still broadcasts and has a strong presence on the web, labeling itself as an alternative, women run station (Radiorakel, n.d.). Although men participate and listen to the station, it has a policy of having a female manager and more women than men in every area. It has journalism training for participants and has educated around 1,500 people in the various disciplines within radio broadcasting, with many going on to become well-known personalities within Norwegian broadcast media.

Transnational women's radio organizations such as Women's International Newsgathering Service (WINGS) and Feminist International Radio Endeavor (FIRE), which have for many years been part of broadcasting and networking feminist news, features and events (Mitchell, 2004; Lacey, 2004; Thompson, Anfossi Gómez and Suárez Toro, 2005), have now harnessed the internet and social media to widen their dissemination and make more links with feminist campaigns and other connected social movements. Women's community radio stations have been a key development tool for tackling social and economic equality for women in African countries, improving the status of women inside and outside the home and providing opportunity to voice women's issues and concerns (Jallov, 2009).

As a networking and communications tool the internet is a virtual extension of women's radio space (Mitchell, 2004), connecting feminisms in local and global spheres and contributing to women's technological citizenship. Online stations and digital archives of women's radio are further indications of the value placed on women's radio history and their ability to document and provide access to accounts of feminist activity and to communicate the women's movement within and beyond country borders. New forms of individual and collective audio expression have been enabled by new technologies via internet stations, podcasting, online work and innovative sound projects led by women. For instance, Astute Radio uses social media, podcasting, a website and workshops to promote positive change between men and women and "give women a voice – to express their views and share their expertise about life in business, the workplace and at home" (Astute Radio, n.d.). Digitalization has contributed to open access, online and collaborative archives, for example, the recent funding of the "American women making history and culture, 1963–1982" archive of holdings from the Pacifica network of community stations, which will:

> document the emergence and evolution of the Women's movement in cities across the United States over the included timespan, as well as the unique role Pacifica Radio played by providing a place for women to create and air programming that communicated the movement.
>
> (Pacifica Radio Archives, n.d.)

Fem FM: Voice and the authentic representation of women's lives

> Your mother, your daughter, your sister, your lover, we're your friend. Fem FM. We're everywoman, Fem FM.
>
> (*Fem FM* jingle)

On 8 March 1992 a small piece of media history was made in the city of Bristol, England. Over 200 women, including the author of this chapter, set up the first women's radio station in Britain. The project lasted a year, culminating in an eight-day broadcast using a short-term license from the then UK Radio Authority. After Fem FM, several other women's community stations aired enabling a discursive space to be opened up about representation, equal access and the nature of 'women's radio' (Mitchell, 2000b). An evaluation was made after the station finished (Mitchell and Caverly, 1993) and in 2013 follow-up interviews were carried out by the author of this chapter with people who had been closely involved in Fem FM as part of research relating to the launch of the Fem FM Archive (Bristol City Council, 2014), which is being published for the first time as part of this chapter. Extracts from these interviews will be used to focus on some of the continuities and changes for these women as listeners to and producers of radio with a focus on the ways that they were able to have an on-air 'voice' through a women's station.

The women who volunteered for the station had different motivations for getting involved. They were mystified as to why program controllers and station managers claimed that women 'just didn't apply' for on-air jobs and angered by claims that they didn't have the 'right voice' for radio. There was also a desire to hear more about 'ordinary' women and for issues relating to women's lives to have more airtime than the single hour a day afforded by the BBC's Woman's Hour. Some saw the station as a stepping stone to working in radio; others already working in the industry whilst offering themselves as role models or mentors also wanted support to further their careers in radio.

The common excuses that women's voices are unsuitable for radio because audiences don't like listening to women or because women don't have the right tone of voice have been used time and time again in public discourses since the early days of radio to justify the exclusion of women from radio (Cramer, 1993; Karpf, 2007). In 2013 the Chair of the UK radio industry pressure group Sound Women said these attitudes still existed but she couldn't find out where this kind of audience research came from. "It's a complete myth ... a whole industry spent decades reporting this as if it was the god's own truth and it makes me exhausted and exasperated that it's still being bandied around" (Williams, 2013). This was reflected in the Fem FM responses:

> Everyone who was on the air in Britain seemed to be blokes ... there were all these men's voices. It was the first time that I had been aware of the research that women's voices were irritating on air – they were too high pitched and yet I was surrounded by all these mellifluously spoken women thinking 'I don't agree!'
>
> (presenter)

Gill (1993) revealed how broadcasters and radio station managers accounted for the lack of women presenters at the radio stations where they worked. Using critical discourse analysis she interrogated statements that had been used to exclude women broadcasting on an equal footing with men: "even as broadcasters declared their desire to see more women DJs, they produced discourse which was ideological – because the accounts they produced served to justify and perpetuate inequality within radio" (Gill, 1993: 93).

Successive quantitative data analyzed by the UK industry training body Creative Skillset (2011, 2013) found that on UK radio women are woefully underrepresented in almost every category of presenter role and there are still what Gill names "stark and continuing inequalities and exclusions that relate to race and ethnicity, class, age, sexuality and disability as well as gender in the mainstream radio industries" (2007: 255).

One experienced presenter who had trained and mentored women at Fem FM described her experiences working in the BBC in the eighties and nineties:

> We had a program organizer who didn't believe in women presenting. He thought we were OK to read the news and do reports and a little bit of presenting but it really (he thought) wasn't fair on the listeners to inflict a female voice on them for any length of time. Because of course (puts on high voice) we are really squeaky and laugh a lot and say inappropriate things. Luckily for me he left but you can't get more sexist than that.
>
> (volunteer)

The primary reason for women to get involved in community stations such as Fem Fm was to gain on-air experience as presenters and to get support from others in a similar position:

It was about feeling strong in the presence of women and giving each other strength and confidence. Have you ever heard of a male DJ lending his top record to another? No. We shared and encouraged each other. I feel a better person as a result. Thanks Fem.

(volunteer feedback sheet, 1992)

Interviewees who had first-hand experience of presenting on Fem FM had conflicting accounts of the status of female DJs in 2013. One presenter who now manages an internet radio station described how music presenting had been previously perceived as an amateur activity or hobby but had changed in status:

Nowadays the men seem to be more accepting of the women around them playing music than they did before. In the past it was a novelty thing if women were involved; now … it's serious to those women who are playing Bass music, R and B, Reggae, whatever, they are looking to make a career out of it, to be known out of it.

(presenter)

Another woman who combined her club and broadcast DJ work with other arts activities indicated that acceptance by male presenters was only one influential factor:

You still don't see many female DJs in clubs. If you want to be a female DJ and up there on that top ten *MixMag* list or something, you've got to be blond, get your tits out, ra ra. Annie Mac is the big female DJ now and she works really hard and is brilliant and plays diverse music. She's pregnant now so it will be interesting to see what happens when she is juggling families and careers. That's why they give up.

(presenter)

Her final point about women experiencing gender inequality when they have children is reflected in Creative Skillset's research findings (2011) that many women have been leaving the industry before or during middle age.

For women on Fem Fm, hearing themselves 'authentically' on the air (Loviglio, 2007) was extremely important. One station that met with approval from several interviewees in 2013 was BBC 6 music:

They are real, they talk about real things, they have kids, they are professional but you know they are not wearing black suits and stilettos – you know they are earthy and grounded as well and that's part of their success.

(volunteer)

The range of opportunities available to women to break into radio and expand the narratives available to them and people listening has been extended through new sectors of community-based stations committed to representing social change and promoting cultural macro narratives of cooperation rather than competitiveness and horizontality in contrast to hierarchy (Couldry, 2010).

Conclusions

The Fem FM case study supports the notion that a greater critical mass of women within a production team or station contributes to a better working culture for women and their perception that they have a public voice. They valued the nature of a 'female friendly' radio station, collaborative working styles, 'being in it together', integrated training, confidence building and availability of role models. These were in stark contrast to negativity, barriers and the sexism women had experienced in mainstream BBC or commercial settings.

This chapter has discussed a range of historical and feminist cultural studies of radio which demonstrate that mainstream radio station employment practices and programing content in the main continue to reflect the sexist patterns of the media industries and society in general (Loviglio, 2007; European Institute for Gender Equality, 2013). Historical studies of media organizations, people and practices have traditionally focused on activities and achievements within mainstream organizations at the expense of smaller scale and alternative community based work. Despite being a minority area within media and cultural studies, a history of women and radio has been carved out and the nature of programing by and for women, including feminist discourses of radio, has been explored. Studies of women and radio have uncovered many historical and contemporaneous examples of women being both *excluded* from full involvement in radio and *actively challenging* mainstream media representations to interact with radio and perform gender (Butler, 1990) in new ways, and women's community radio stations are a site for this.

As research about women and radio develops in the international environment we see new initiatives and methodologies bringing together feminist historical, radio, media and cultural studies research about practice and work in the arena of women and radio. Women's Radio in Europe Network (WREN, n.d.) connects academics across the sector and their recent call for contributions sums up the importance of research about women and radio in the first half of the twenty-first century:

> As new questions of technological citizenship, media literacy, and transnational circulation arise in media studies and media history, we believe that women's radio can once more offer important new insights.
> (Skoog and Badenoch, 2012)

Acknowledgments

I would like to thank the following for their help, support and advice: The Centre for Research into Media and Cultural Studies at the University of Sunderland; Sunderland colleagues Richard Berry, Andy Cartwright, Elaine Drainville and Martin Shingler; all the Fem FM interviewees; Caitlin Hobbs; my radio 'sister' Trish Caverly; my newfound collaborators in WREN (Women's Radio in Europe Network), particularly Alec Badenoch, Nazin Hayradi and Kristin Skoog; and finally Tony O'Shea for his incisive mind and technical support.

Further reading

The collection *Women and Radio: Airing Differences* (Mitchell, 2000a) is a good starting point, introducing a wide range of perspectives about women's relationship with radio and providing ethnographic, historical and vocational approaches to women's radio studies. Thompson, Anfossi Gómez and Suárez Toro's (2005) "Women's alternative internet radio and feminist interactive communications" is about how new technologies and platforms can be harnessed for feminist global communications and is an excellent case study to introduce this area. Quantitative research about women's status in the UK broadcasting industry and case studies and podcasts about women working in radio/audio can be found at the Sound Women (n.d) website, a network of over 1,000 women working in audio committed to raising the profile of women who work in the radio and audio industry, developing talent and celebrating achievement. "Women at the BBC" (BBC, n.d.) is a webpage written by a producer/academic and is an illustrated account of roles women have played in the BBC since its inception. Its largely uncritical narrative can be complemented by reading Andrews' (2012) *Domesticating the Airwaves: Broadcasting, Domesticity and Femininity*, which addresses how radio both entered and constructed the gendered domestic space of the home.

References

Andrews, M. (2012) *Domesticating the Airwaves: Broadcasting, Domesticity and Femininity*. London: Bloomsbury Academic.
Astute Radio (n.d.) Astute Radio. Retrieved from www.astute-radio.com
Baade, C. (2007) "BBC between factory and home. Music while you work and women listeners at the wartime BBC." *Feminist Media Studies*, 7(3), 34–338.
BBC (n.d.) History of the BBC: Women at the BBC. Retrieved from http://www.bbc.co.uk/historyofthebbc/resources/in-depth/women_at_bbc.shtml
Bristol City Council (2014) Fem FM Archive. Retrieved from http://www.bristol.gov.uk/page/leisure-and-culture/fem-fm-archive
Butler, J. (1990) *Gender Trouble: Feminism and the Subversion of Identity*. London: Routledge.
Carney, M. (1999) *Stoker (The life of Hilda Matheson)*. Llangynog: Privately published.
Carter, S. (2004) "A Mic of her own: Stations, collectives and women's access to radio." *Journal of Radio Studies*, 11(2), 168–183.
Couldry, N. (2010) *Why Voice Matters: Culture and Politics After Neoliberalism*. London: Sage.
Cramer, J. A. (1993) "A woman's place is on the air." In P. Creedon (ed.) *Women in Mass Communications* (2nd Edition). London: Sage (pp. 154–66).
Creative Skillset (2011) "Tuning out: Women in the UK radio industry: A Skillset report for Sound Women." Retrieved from http://www.soundwomen.co.uk/research/
——(2013) "Sound Women on air." Retrieved from http://www.soundwomen.co.uk/research/
Curran, J. (2009) "Narratives of media history revisited." In M. Bailey (ed.) *Narrating Media History*. London: Routledge (pp. 1–21).
Ehrick, C. (2009) "Savage dissonance: Gender, voice and women's radio speech." In D. Suisman and S. Strasser (eds.) *Sound in the Age of Mechanical Reproduction*. Philadelphia, PA: University of Pennsylvania Press (pp. 69–94).

European Institute for Gender Equality (2013) "Review of the implementation of the Beijing Platform for Action in the EU Member States: Women and the media: Advancing gender-equality in decision-making in media organizations." Lithuania: EIGE.

Feldman, S. (2000) "Twin peaks: The staying power of BBC Radio 4's Woman's Hour." In C. Mitchell (ed.) *Women and Radio: Airing Differences*. London: Routledge (pp. 64–72).

——(2007) *Desperate Housewives: 60 years of BBC Radio's Woman's Hour*. London: Westminster University.

Franks, S. (2011) "Attitudes to women in the BBC in the 1970s: Not so much a glass ceiling as one of reinforced concrete." *Westminster Papers*, 8(3), 123–142.

Gallagher, M. (2001) "The push and pull of action and research in feminist media studies." *Feminist Media Studies*, 1(1), 11–15.

——(1995) *An Unfinished Story. Gender Patterns in Media Employment*. Paris: UNESCO.

Ganzert, C. F. (2003) "All-women's radio: WHER-AM in Memphis." *Journal of Radio Studies*, 10(1), 80–92.

Gill, R. (1993) "Justifying injustice: Broadcasters' accounts of inequality in radio." In E. Burman and I. Parker (eds.) *Discourse Analytic Research*. London: Routledge (pp. 75–93).

——(2007) *Gender and the Media*. Cambridge: Polity Press.

Halper, D. L. (2001) *Invisible Stars: A Social History of Women in American Broadcasting*. New York: M. W. Sharpe.

Hilmes, M. (1997) *Radio Voices: American Broadcasting, 1922–1952*. Minneapolis, MN: University of Minnesota Press.

——(2007) "Front line family: 'Women's culture' comes to the BBC." *Media Culture Society*, 29(5), 5–29.

Hunter, F. (2000) "Hilda Matheson and the BBC, 1926–40." In C. Mitchell (ed.) *Women and Radio: Airing Differences*. London: Routledge (pp. 41–7).

Jallov, B. (1996) *Women's Voices Crossing Frontiers: European Directory of Women's Community Radio Stations and Women's Radio Production Collectives*. Sheffield: AMARC Europe.

——(2007) *Community Radio in East Africa: An Impact and Sustainability Assessment of Three Community Radios within the EACMP*. Commissioned by SIDA Department for Democracy and Social Development.

——(2009) "Stories of community radio in East Africa: Powerful change." MAZI 18 newsletter Communication for Social Change Consortium. Retrieved from http://www.communicationforsocialchange.org/photogallery.php?id=395

Karpf, A. (1980) "Women and radio." In Baehr, H. (ed.) *Women and Media*. London: Pergamon Press (pp. 41–54).

——(2007) *The Human Voice: The Story of a Remarkable Talent*. London: Bloomsbury Publishing.

Lacey, K. (1996) *Feminine Frequencies: Gender, German Radio, and the Public Sphere, 1923–1945*. Ann Arbor, MI: University of Michigan Press.

——(2004) "Continuities and change in women's radio." In A. Crisell (ed.) *More than a Music Box: Radio Cultures and Communities in a Multi-Media World*. New York, Oxford: Berghahn Books (pp. 145–64).

Lewis, P. M. and Booth, J. (1990) *The Invisible Medium: Public, Commercial and Community Radio*. Basingstoke: Palgrave Macmillan.

Loviglio, J. (2007) "Sound effects: Gender, voice and the cultural work of NPR." *The Radio Journal: International Studies in Broadcast and Audio Media*, 5(2&3), 67–81.

Luscombe, A. (2013) *Forty Years of Radio News*. Frankfurt am Main: Peter Lang.

Mazzarella, S. M., Hains, R. C. and Thiel-Stern, S. (2013) "Girlhoods in the golden age of U.S. radio: Music, shared popular culture, and memory." *Journal of Radio and Audio Media*, 20(1), 117–33.

McGann, N. (2007) "Women in Irish community radio." In R. Day (ed.) *Bicycle Highway: Celebrating Community Radio in Ireland*. Dublin: The Liffey Press (pp. 89–104).

Michaels, K. and Mitchell, C. (2000) "The last Bastion: How women become music presenters in UK radio." In C. Mitchell (ed.) *Women and Radio: Airing Differences*. London: Routledge (pp. 238–249).

Minic, D. (2008) "What makes an issue a woman's hour issue?," *Feminist Media Studies*, 8(3), 301–15.

Mitchell, C. (ed.) (2000a) *Women and Radio: Airing Differences*. London: Routledge.

——(2000b) "Sisters are doing it ... From Fem FM to Viva! A history of contemporary women's radio stations in the UK." In C. Mitchell (ed.) *Women and Radio: Airing Differences*. London: Routledge (pp. 94–110).

——(2004) "Dangerously feminine? Theory and praxis of women's alternative radio." In K. Ross and C. Brierley (eds.) *Women and Media: International perspectives*. Oxford: Blackwell Publishing (pp. 157–84).

Mitchell, C. and Caverly, T. (1993) "Fem FM evaluation report." Available from C. Mitchell, University of Sunderland.

Murphy, C. (2011) "On an equal footing with men? Women and work at the BBC 1923–39." Doctoral thesis, Goldsmiths College, University of London. Goldsmiths Research Online.

Nye, S., Godwin, N. and Hollows, B. (1994) "Twisting the dials: Lesbians on British radio." In L. Gibbs (ed.) *Daring to Dissent: Lesbian Culture from Margin to Mainstream*. London: Cassell (pp. 147–67).

Pacifica Radio Archives (n.d.) Pacifica Radio Archives: A Living History. Retrieved from www.pacificaradioarchives.org

Radiorakel (n.d.) Radiorakel. Retrieved from http://radiorakel.no

Ross, K. and Byerly, C. (2006) *Women and Media: A Critical Introduction*. Oxford: Blackwell Publishing.

Ross, K. and Carter, C. (2011) "Women and news: A long and winding road." *Media Culture Society* 33(8), 1148–65.

Simms, M. (1985) *Women in BBC Management*. London: BBC.

Skoog, K. (2009) "Focus on the housewife: The BBC and the post-war woman, 1945–55." *University of Westminster Networking Knowledge: Journal of the MeCCSA Postgraduate Network*, 2(1), 1–12.

——(2011) "An interview with Maria Di Cenzo." *Westminster Papers*. Retrieved from http://www.westminster.ac.uk/__data/assets/pdf_file/0004/124879/003An-interview-with-Maria-Dicenzo-Kristin-Skoog.pdf

——(2013) "Striving for editorial autonomy and internal recognition: The setting up of BBC's Woman's Hour 1946–55." In M. Andrews and S. McNamara (eds.) *Women and the Media: Feminism and Femininity in Britain, 1900 to the Present*. London: Routledge (pp. 99–112).

Skoog, K. and Badenoch, A. (2012) Call for papers, "Women's radio in Europe: Sounding out the boundaries." November. Copenhagen.

Sound Women (n.d.) Sound Women. Retrieved from http://www.soundwomen.co.uk

Steiner, L. (1992) "The history and structure of woman's alternative media." In L. F. Rakow (ed.) *Women Making Meaning: New Feminist Directions in Communication*. London: Routledge (pp. 121–43).

Thompson, M. E., Anfossi Gómez, K. and Suárez Toro, M. (2005) "Women's alternative internet radio and feminist interactive communications." *Feminist Media Studies*, 5(2), 215–36.

Williams, M. (2013) Interviewed for Sound Women podcast. Retrieved from https://soundcloud.com/soundwomen/swp4

WREN (n.d.) Women's radio in Europe network: Sounding out the boundaries. Retrieved from http://womensradioineurope.org

30
Radio drama

Hugh Chignell

A media historian interested in British radio drama might be surprised by the absence of any published history of the subject or the lack of relevant articles in academic journals. In his survey of British radio drama, Priessnitz (1981) laments the paucity of reviews in the press (compared to theatre reviews) and the poor quality of radio criticism, which is often merely "personal preference". Asa Briggs, in volume five of his history of British broadcasting (1995), covering 1955–74, a volume of over 1,100 pages, barely mentions radio drama at all. He does mention the great radio dramatist Giles Cooper, but for his television not his radio writing. There is no mention at all of Val Gielgud (Head of Drama at the BBC from 1934 to 1963) or Samuel Beckett. We should not be tempted by this omission to think that there is nothing of interest for the media historian in radio drama; far from it – from its invention early in the twentieth century drama has been used in a variety of ways on radio and the story of its development is instructive for students of both radio and drama.

The historical study of radio drama presents a problem of classification. Some drama heard on radio is an adaptation of a stage play or a book or even a film. This may differ from the drama written especially for radio and the latter often makes fuller use of radio's unique qualities. There is also the 'radio feature', which combined documentary with creative and dramatic elements and was a very important part of BBC radio output in the last century. It will be examined here. Then there are long-running radio serials (most notably *The Archers* since 1951) not to mention various types of radio comedy. For the purposes of this chapter I will not discuss radio comedy in any depth and I will confine my remarks to the twentieth century. In effect this is a schematic account of radio drama in the analogue, as opposed to the digital, era, a theme I will return to in the conclusion. This is also, for reasons of space, only a history of BBC radio drama; a fuller account would have to acknowledge, for example, drama broadcast by Radio Luxembourg in the 1950s and during the era of Independent Local Radio from 1973 to 1990.

The early years

Following radio drama experiments of different kinds before the arrival of the BBC in 1922 (see in particular the account by Alan Beck, n.d.), it did find a place alongside talks, music and religion in the early days of BBC radio. It is generally accepted that Richard Hughes' experimental *A Comedy of Danger* (15 January 1924) was the first play written for BBC radio. The fact that this was set in a coal mine in the dark suggests the early caution and uncertainty attached to radio drama – if the listeners cannot see anything then perhaps there should be literally nothing to see! Early BBC output also included extracts from stage plays (only extracts were allowed by West End theatres and even these were denied after April 1923) so on 16 February 1923 there were scenes from Shakespeare's *Julius Caesar*, *Henry VIII* and *Much Ado About Nothing*. Early plays written for radio took different forms and some were characterized by a particularly fast-paced delivery with rapid scene changes. This was true of the work of Cecil A. Lewis, the titles of whose plays suggest their action-packed nature: *Pursuit*, *The Night Fighters* and *Montezuma* (all from 1928). Similarly, L. du Garde Peach's often historically based plays exploited radio's ability to shift scenes in the blink of an eye. A rather more serious contribution to early radio drama was to be heard in the work of Lance Sieveking, described in glowing terms by David Hendy as a modernist whose experimental *The Kaleidoscope* (1928) pushed at the boundaries of drama production (Hendy, 2013: 170). Here radio drama was richly symbolic and expressed not only Sieveking's wartime experience but also his artistic connections. This is what the unsuspecting listener might have heard:

> Fragments of dialogue, poetry, and music, clapping melting into the sound of the sea, the passionate avowals of a lover melting into the sweet singing of a choir, dance tunes melting into the symphonic grandeur of Beethoven. Vignette after vignette drifted out of the loudspeakers, interspersed seamlessly with the impressionistic sounds of cafes or countryside or battlefield.
> (Hendy, 2013: 170)

The well known theatre producer Tyrone Guthrie was another important radio playwright and in his *Squirrel's Cage* (1929) and *The Flowers Are Not For You To Pick* (1930) he developed his non-realist approach to radio drama. As Ian Rodger put it, "Guthrie's radio plays do not pretend we are listening to an actual event in real life. The characters are social archetypes and they are brought to the ear so their social and political dilemmas may be discussed" (Rodger, 1982: 16).

As the BBC became more established after its incorporation in 1927 (as the British Broadcasting Corporation) and then its move to the magnificence of Broadcasting House in 1932, the Drama Department settled into better equipped studios and acquired a culturally conservative head of department, Val Gielgud. The technology of radio drama production and reception at this time was in rapid development. The physical conditions of both were developing as the listener had access to improved radio sets and greatly improved reception with the installation of the Daventry long wave transmitter in the early 1930s. Patchy local radio services were replaced by regional medium wave transmission at the same time, all of which conspired to improve the experience and quality of radio listening, an essential component of effective radio drama. Meanwhile, in Broadcasting House drama producers could use the ultra modern Dramatic Control Panel which enabled production using a number of studios (all live) including actors, music and effects.

Typical radio drama of the pre-war period included the stage classics, especially Shakespeare, and also historically based dramas. In his account of the BBC and the British Empire at this time, Thomas Hajkowski describes the eight-part adaptation of A. E. W. Mason's *The Four Feathers* (BBC Home Service, 13 December 1939) which "dramatized the life of the imperial hero" (Hajkowski, 2010: 19). In a similar vein *Gordon of Khartoum* (1935) was a ninety-minute dramatization of Gordon's last stand and other dramas were made about Lord Kitchener and the explorer David Livingstone.

A picture emerges, therefore, by the beginning of the war of a rather safe and ideologically conservative sphere of production and artistic output, but that is really only part of the story. Enter the Features Department. In 1936 a features department was created in the BBC to produce this now largely defunct, factually based genre of radio. The (near) impossibility of recording on location produced a hybrid programme which attempted to be partly documentary but was scripted and acted in the studio often with musical accompaniment. Features producers, many of whom were politically radical (including Archie Harding, D. G. Bridson and Francis Dillon), developed an interest in the working class and political subjects. D. G. Bridson's *The March of the '45* (1936) was a groundbreaking feature which described the march of the Scottish army in 1745 but set against the social and political landscape of the thirties. Some of the most important musicians and poets of the time were drawn to the work of Features including Benjamin Britten and William Walton (the former's first commission was for Bridson's *King Arthur* in 1937) and then one of the most influential figures in the history of the BBC, the poet and classicist Louis MacNeice.

The war and post-war

Even in this brief survey of the history of radio drama it is worth pausing to consider the influence and output of Louis MacNeice who began work at the BBC in 1941. His work was mainly produced in the Features Department and its importance is hard to overstate. His first major production for Features was *Alexander Nevsky* (broadcast two days after Pearl Harbour) based on the Eisenstein film and featuring the BBC chorus and the actor Robert Donat. It was followed in October 1942 by *Christopher Columbus* which celebrated the 450th anniversary of Columbus's 'discovery' of America. Written as a verse play, *Columbus* had two main influences – Bridson's *The March of the '45* and the American poet Archibald MacLeish's *The Fall of the City* (1937) which had established, at least in America, the potential of verse drama. *Columbus* was an epic production, starring Laurence Olivier, with music by William Walton and performed by the BBC Symphony Orchestra and a Chorus conducted by Sir Adrian Boult. According to Briggs it "created a sensation in artistic circles on both sides of the Atlantic" (1970: 585). It is a sign of the fluidity of the BBC at that time and the generic uncertainty attached to drama that MacNeice made his most celebrated radio drama not for his friends in Features but for Val Gielgud in the Drama department. Widely seen as a triumph and a defining moment in BBC history, MacNeice's *The Dark Tower* (1946) was a verse drama, a poetic parable in which Roland is a 'quest-hero' (Coulton, 1980: 80) destined to fight the nameless evil. The music was composed by Benjamin Britten (Cyril Cusack was Roland) and the result not only confirmed MacNeice's place in the BBC but also inspired the next generation of radio dramatists.

A fellow poet who MacNeice knew well, both for his poetry and for his radio acting, was Dylan Thomas. In his account of Thomas's career in the BBC, Ralph Maud estimates that between 1943 and his early death in 1953, he was a radio actor or performer on 145 separate occasions including in eight dramatic roles for MacNeice (Maud, 1991: xii). Maud suggests that although they were close, Thomas was at times envious of the critically acclaimed and probably much more financially secure MacNeice. And yet it was Dylan Thomas, not his distinguished and lauded contemporary, who wrote the most famous British radio drama of the twentieth century. *Under Milk Wood* (25 January 1954, BBC Third Programme) is "easily the most celebrated full-length play for radio" (Lewis, 1981: 72) also referred to as "quite simply the best radio play ever written" (Walford Davies in Lewis, 1981: 72). The play was produced by Douglas Cleverdon, one of the stars of the Features Department, and describes a day in the dreams and lives of the characters of the little Welsh town Llareggub (famously 'bugger all' backwards). Although the original stage version featured Thomas himself as the First Voice he was replaced for the broadcast by Richard Burton. If the curse of radio drama is its evanescence, its 'here today but gone tomorrow' impermanence, then *Under Milk Wood* emphatically overcame this by its repeated broadcasts (repeated three times in three months on the Third Programme and then on the Home Service and six times on the General Overseas Service). This is not to mention its publication as a book, its release in 1954 on record, various stage performances, endless repeats and reworking on radio and even a film.

The war had a powerful impact on radio; both news and talks were radically transformed, as I have argued elsewhere (Chignell, 2011), and while MacNeice and others were making epic 'drama features' a much more populist form of drama was emerging, also the result of American influence. Radio 'soaps' were a staple of American radio and they filled the daytime schedule. The radio drama serial had no place in Reith's BBC but the need to persuade Americans of all classes to support Britain and back American entry into the war overcame these scruples. The North American Service had been set up in 1941 as a means of talking to America and drawing the US into the war. *Frontline Family* was first broadcast to America in March 1941 and depicted the life of an ordinary British family in the Blitz. The daily 15-minute episodes were very popular (Hilmes, 2012: 148) but their broadcast to a domestic audience was, unsurprisingly, strongly resisted by Gielgud. *Frontline Family* was subsequently broadcast on the General Overseas Service and so became a hit in Australia and parts of Africa but was unheard in the country whose life and tribulations it represented. Despite internal BBC resistance the serial did have its admirers and after the war morphed into *The Robinson Family* on the newly launched Light Programme. The Drama Department succumbed to the inevitable and established a serials section which then produced the action serial *Dick Barton* from 1946 and the replacement for *The Robinson Family*, the resolutely suburban *Mrs Dale's Diary*. Then from 1950, *The Archers*, 'an every day story of country folk' (as it was originally billed) began its extraordinary journey; it remains hugely popular to this day.

A Golden Age?

The crucial post-war development for radio drama was the launch of the uncompromisingly cultural Third Programme in 1946. In her influential account of the network, Kate Whitehead wrote:

> Virtually every creative writer in Britain during the period 1946 to 1970 had some contact with the Third Programme, whether as a contributor of material or as part of the audience influenced by its frequently avant-garde broadcasts.
>
> (1989: 16)

In the first week of the Third Programme there were broadcasts of Shaw's *Man and Superman* (three and a half hours uncut) and an unabridged version of Sartre's *Huis Clos*. The 'Third' became the home of 'difficult' dramatic works including classical Greek drama and foreign plays (Brecht, Camus and Ionesco). The more adventurous approach to radio drama was encouraged by the appointment of Donald McWhinnie as Gielgud's assistant in 1953; this was generally seen as a turning point in the development of BBC radio drama and an encouragement for avant-garde work (Whitehead, 1989: 139). Perhaps this was the golden age of radio drama as listeners were exposed to work influenced by the Theater of the Absurd at the end of the 1950s (the term itself was coined by Martin Esslin, Gielgud's successor as Head of Drama from 1963). Writers such as Harold Pinter (*A Slight Ache*, 1959; *The Caretaker*, 1962) and Samuel Beckett (*All That Fall*, 1957; *Embers*, 1959) pioneered this approach. Although Beckett wrote mainly for the stage, as well as various novels, his few radio plays and those adapted from the stage were well suited to the 'blind' medium of radio. As Sean Street has written, Beckett was "a dramatist for whom radio and poetry come together potently in his finest writing" (2012: 20). Beckett's spare, non-visual and word-driven drama was somehow 'radiogenic' and was also a cultural highpoint in the post-war BBC. For Katharine Worth, Beckett's "rare and curious" plays "had an impact out of all proportion to what might have been expected" (1981: 192). One consequence of his work was the need for complex and sophisticated sound effects, requirements that eventually led to the creation of the Radiophonic Workshop which was to become a powerful aid for imaginative and experimental radio drama (Wade, 1981: 241).

Beckett was certainly not the most important radio dramatist of the 1950s and 1960s. Even more important was the work of a dramatist for whom radio was the primary medium, probably the greatest of all radio dramatists, Giles Cooper, who wrote 31 original radio plays, nine of them for the Third Programme. Cooper was another writer influenced by Absurdism and he exploited radio's apparent weakness – the lack of pictures. The listener could not be sure what was real and what was fantasy. Cooper explored the world between the everyday and absurd, dream-like fantasy. In *Under the Loofah Tree* (1958) we encounter a man in his bath dreaming of winning the Victoria Cross then trying to drown himself before returning to his banal existence. In *Mathry Beacon* (1956), described by Frances Gray as his 'masterpiece' (1981a: 64), a group of soldiers guard a secret weapon and at the same time create a perfect community. Ignorant of the end of the war they carry on in a polygamous fantasy before eventually succumbing to materialism. Cooper often dealt with ordinary people trapped in unremarkable domestic locations. This bland statement of the human condition is strangely reminiscent of the comic radio and television situation comedy *Hancock's Half Hour* in which Hancock plays an endlessly frustrated and trapped suburbanite.

Decline and fall?

There can be little doubt that by the mid 1960s radio drama had proved the case for its existence as a substantial cultural force. But this was also a difficult decade for admirers of the form. MacNeice died in 1963 as a result of pneumonia and pleurisy contracted while recording underground for his last radio play, the autobiographical *Persons from Porlock*. Soon after that the Features Department itself was closed and its sixteen producers were sent off to work in Drama or Talks. Giles Cooper died as a result of falling from a train in Surbiton in 1966. But the greatest challenge to radio drama was undoubtedly the success of television. Television drama had obvious advantages over the radio equivalent and there were some brilliant examples on both the BBC and ITV – from policy changing realism (*Cathy Come Home*, BBC, 1966) to iconic fantasy dramas (*The Prisoner*, ATV, 1967–68) or popular long-running series such as *The Avengers* (ABC TV, 1961–69) and of course the 26-part sensation on BBC 2 in 1967, *The Forsyte Saga*, to mention a very few indeed. The radio critic David Wade suggested that after a golden age of radio drama in the 1950s and early 60s, a decline set in (1981: 225). As someone whose job it was to listen extensively to radio drama it is hard to ignore his remark about the "wretched state of mind I found reflected in the drama of the late sixties and early seventies" (ibid.: 227). Wade put this decline down partly to the loss of listening ability in the audience who no longer had the ear for serious and sustained listening. In addition he blamed the failures of dramatists themselves, no doubt lured by the temptations of television. The BBC's response to the declining radio audience in the 1960s was to publish the highly influential policy document "Broadcasting in the seventies", which took further the reorganization of radio networks into Radios One, Two, Three and Four by producing a more specialized or 'format' style on each. So Radio Four became the home of drama (and other forms of speech-based output) while Radio Three turned its attention to classical music. Wade pointed out that the result of this was to create a more predictable and organized drama schedule with long-running 'slots' including 'Drama Now', 'The Monday Play', 'Thirty Minute Theatre' and 'Saturday Night Theatre'. Although Wade believed that the standard of plays on Radio Four had improved, the result was still what he called "plays for clearing up the lunch to" (1981: 222). He saved his greatest disapproval for the output of Radio Three which in the 1970s produced about two plays a week. He felt that some of these plays "combined in equal measure negligibility and pretentiousness" (ibid.: 240), deciding later in his article to stop pulling his punches and just call it "junk". His final judgment was: "I consider that what ought to be a beautiful and exciting garden at best maintains a tolerable show, at worst looks faded and run-down" (ibid.).

The case for the decline of radio drama is clearly a strong one but there is also evidence that despite the inadequacies of the listener and the rivalry of television, radio drama did adapt and survive in the final decades of the last century. Gray (1981b) provides an in-depth critical analysis of two remarkable historical dramas of the 1970s – David Rudkin's *Cries from Casement As His Bones Are Brought to Dublin* (1973) and John Arden's *Pearl* (1978). In Rudkin's play the audience is taken from Casement's grave in Pentonville Prison to his heroic reburial in Dublin and along the way we hear the voice of the murderer Dr Crippen. The ambition of the play is striking, "an exploration of what it means to be an Ulsterman and of how people define their social, political and sexual selves" (Gray, 1981b: 71). Possibly yet more complex and ambitious was Arden's *Pearl* which speculated about an unlikely alliance between English Puritans and Irish Catholics against the crown in the 1640s. Arden exploited radio's ambiguity as the listener was invited to see a stage play written and performed within the drama from a variety of points of view. The play featured complex changes of point of view and time as it morphed from fiction to fact. Both of these radio plays exploited to the full the potential of radio to create a life-world in the mind of the listener. Both required considerable acts of imagination and neither was for the uncommitted listener or the culturally faint-hearted.

David Hendy's definitive account of the history of Radio Four (2007), arguably the single most important work of British radio history, deals with radio drama in a fairly cursory manner. It probably says something about the unremarkable nature of many radio plays that Hendy found little reason to discuss them. His main argument is to identify something of a crisis in the 1970s. Following the brilliance of radio drama in the 1950s and 60s, few playwrights were attracted to radio drama in the 1970s, discouraged by the bad pay (roughly one quarter of the rate paid for television drama) and also the lack of radio reviews in the press. There was, however, a possible solution in the creation of a more cinematic approach to radio drama (Hendy, 2007: 195). Hendy contrasts the safe 'middle ground' of radio drama, full of adaptations of well-loved classics (P. G. Wodehouse, *Just William*, Dickens and so on) with a growing body of work based on a fascination with stereophonic or hi-fi radio. One of the most interesting and celebrated dramatic productions on Radio Four was not produced by the drama department but by Light Entertainment. This was the comic science fiction serial *The Hitchhiker's Guide to the Galaxy* (1978) by Douglas Adams and featuring 'The Book' played memorably by Peter Jones. The production made use of the Radiophonic Workshop and extensive post-production to create a "richly textured comic-book style of production" (Hendy, 2007: 194). Its success with a younger audience helped to change commonly held views of Radio Four and attract younger listeners. The combination of comedy and science produced a drama serial which was both 'low brow' and 'high brow' (ibid.). Other examples of large-scale even epic radio drama include the work of the eminent features and drama producer Michael Mason (*The Marriage of Freedom and Fate*, 1974; *The British Seafarer*, 1980). Similarly, the epic 26-part serialization of Tolkien's *The Lord of the Rings* (a total of 13 hours) starred Ian Holm and Michael Hordern and, reminiscent of the golden age of radio drama, featured some notable original music. The work has had a long life in cassette and CD form as well as rebroadcasts in other parts of the world.

Conclusion

It is instructive to look at the history of analogue broadcast radio drama from the perspective of our contemporary digital culture. Digital technology has enormously increased the range of media available to us all and perhaps an archaic form like radio drama should not survive the icy winds of interactivity and social media. The irony is, however, that digital audio makes possible not only the niche broadcasting of Digital Audio Broadcasting (BBC 4 Extra) but also the experimental and culturally rich world of podcasting. To take a contemporary example of this renaissance in radio drama the BBC production of Neil Gaiman's *Neverwhere* (2013) is strongly reminiscent of radio drama in its golden age with its extraordinarily stellar cast of actors. The drama was produced by Dirk Maggs whose commitment to cinematic audio, inspired by *Hitchhiker's,* placed *Neverwhere* in that tradition of epic radio. The availability of drama online and its promotion on websites such as Radio Drama Revival gives audio drama a new lease of life and extra promotion to a global audience. So digital media has undoubtedly been good for 'audio drama' as listeners can access a huge variety of contemporary and classic drama on mobile devices but, as in *Neverwhere*, it was the legacy of twentieth-century drama which inspired and made possible today's success. There are two further reasons for the survival of the form. Even though the stage or film might be the preferred platform for some dramatists' work, radio (or audio) seems to remain attractive as part of a palette of opportunities. So, for example, despite the great stage successes of writers such as John Mortimer, Alan Plater, Tom Stoppard and David Edgar, they all also wrote for BBC Radio Four's 'The Monday Play' in the 1980s. Perhaps the speech-centric nature of radio drama allowed them to work in a slightly different way and try out new approaches. It is interesting to track the life of some of these plays as they appeared in some cases on radio and the stage at different moments in their lives. So David Hare's *Knuckle* (Monday Play, 1981) was originally written for the stage whereas John Mortimer's *Edwin* (Monday Play, 1982) transferred to the stage after its radio performance. A similar argument is suggested by the veteran radio critic Gillian Reynolds, who claims that great actors are attracted to work in radio (alongside stage, television and film careers) by the freedom it gives them and because there are more opportunities and more scope (*Daily Telegraph*, 26 March 2013).

For the media historian, radio drama lacks the wider political significance of radio news and current affairs or the social and cultural impact of, for example, television documentary. Having said that, radio's invisibility has allowed the production of plays and adaptations which were culturally significant and at times compellingly adventurous. Radio drama also provides yet another way of understanding how the BBC, arguably the world's most famous cultural institution, interprets its public service role. Early in its development, before the Second World War, radio drama was an opportunity to give a relatively uneducated population access to plays for the first time. After the war, the BBC's place as a site of cultural innovation and the home of the avant-garde took priority. Radio drama's 'decline' after that can be seen as the result of seeing radio drama primarily as a form of entertainment. And so in radio drama's analogue history it served to express the full variety of public service functions. Contemporary digital audio drama has the potential to educate, inform and entertain but it does so drawing on a twentieth-century legacy.

Further reading

Three books published in a very short space of time are essential reading for the student of radio drama: Ian Rodger's (1982) *Radio Drama* is an inspiring and perceptive introduction and the two edited collections *British Radio Drama* (Drakakis, 1981) and *Radio Drama* (Lewis, 1982) are both full of historical detail. Although highly eclectic and perhaps over-ambitious, Tim Crook's (1999) *Radio Drama: Theory and Practice* contains some provocative historical observations. The recent flowering of radio history has produced some focused writing on moments in radio drama history including *Network Nations: A Transnational History of British and American Broadcasting* (Hilmes, 2012) on early BBC radio serials and Hendy's (2013) article on Lance Sieveking, "Painting with sound: The kaleidoscopic world of Lance Sieveking, a British radio modernist."

References

Beck, A. (n.d.) "'The invisible play': BBC radio drama 1922–28." Retrieved from http://www.savoyhill.co.uk/invisibleplay/index.html
Briggs, A. (1970) *A History of British Broadcasting in the United Kingdom, Vol. III: The War of Words*. Oxford: Oxford University Press.
——(1995) *A History of British Broadcasting in the United Kingdom, Vol. V: Competition*. Oxford: Oxford University Press.
Chignell, H. (2011) *Public Issue Radio: Talks, News and Current Affairs in the Twentieth Century*. Basingstoke: Palgrave.
Coulton, B. (1980) *Louis MacNeice in the BBC*. London, Boston, MA: Faber and Faber.
Crook, T. (1999) *Radio Drama: Theory and Practice*. London: Routledge.
Drakakis, J. (ed.) *British Radio Drama*. Cambridge: Cambridge University Press.
Gray, F. (1981a) "The nature of radio drama." In P. Lewis (ed.) *Radio Drama*. London and New York: Longman (pp. 48–77).
——(1981b) "Giles Cooper: The medium as moralist." In J. Drakakis (ed.) *British Radio Drama*. Cambridge: Cambridge University Press (pp. 139–57).
Hajkowski, T. (2010) *The BBC and National Identity in Britain, 1922–53*. Manchester: Manchester University Press.
Hendy, D. (2007) *Life on Air: A History of Radio Four*. Oxford: Oxford University Press.
——(2013) "Painting with sound: The kaleidoscopic world of Lance Sieveking, a British radio modernist." *Twentieth Century British History*, 24(2), 169–200.
Hilmes, M. (2012) *Network Nations: A Transnational History of British and American Broadcasting*. New York and Abingdon: Routledge.
Lewis, P. (1981) "The radio road to Llaraggub." In J. Drakakis (ed.) *British Radio Drama*. Cambridge: Cambridge University Press (pp. 72–110).
——(1982) *Radio Drama*. Harlow: Longman.
Maud, R. (ed.) (1991) *Dylan Thomas: The Broadcasts*. London: J. M. Dent.

Priessnitz, H. (1981) "British radio drama: A survey." In P. Lewis (ed.) *Radio Drama*. Harlow: Longman (pp. 28–47).
Rodger, I. (1982) *Radio Drama*. London: Macmillan.
Street, S. (2012) *The Poetry of Radio: The Colour of Sound*. London and New York: Routledge.
Wade, D. (1981) "British radio drama since 1960." In J. Drakakis (ed.) *British Radio Drama*. Cambridge: Cambridge University Press (pp. 218–44).
Whitehead, K. (1989) *The Third Programme: A Literary History*. Oxford: Clarendon Press.
Worth, K. (1981) "Beckett and the radio medium." In J. Drakakis (ed.) *British Radio Drama*. Cambridge: Cambridge University Press (pp. 191–217).

31
Radio sports news
The longevity and influence of 'Sports Report'

Richard Haynes

"It's five o'clock and time for today's *Sports Report* ... "

Sport has been an important feature in the history of British radio broadcasting (Booth, 2008). Sport can draw large audiences, and in contemporary radio commands a significant amount of airtime and resource from both public service and commercial radio stations. The BBC's sport and news channel Radio 5 Live consistently reaches over 6 million listeners a week (Rajar, 2013), its major rival Talk-Sport scheduled 130 live football commentaries in 2013 and both stations share the rights to coverage of the 2014 World Cup from Brazil (Reynolds, 2013). The coverage of sport on radio has been developed in two main formats: live running commentaries from outside broadcasts and news reporting on sport. One might also add more general sports features, documentaries, talks, quizzes, phone-ins and even comedy hybrids, but in terms of the mainstay of sports coverage live running commentaries and news bulletins are the most readily recognized forms of radio sport.

In spite of being one of the most popular genres of radio, either on UK-wide networks including BBC Radio Five Live and TalkSport or nationally on BBC or commercial stations in Scotland, Northern Ireland and Wales or regionally in England, sport has been noticeably neglected in mainstream broadcasting histories. Although more popular histories of running radio commentary have been published (Booth, 2008), there is an impoverished literature on the subject of radio sports journalism and news. Most references to sport in histories of radio refer to the lineage and style of ball-by-ball or play-by-play commentaries on live sport (Briggs, 1965; Crisell, 1994), but rarely do they provide sufficient detail of sports journalism on radio as a specific aspect of news activity. Work on radio news and journalism also has a tendency to set the world of sports journalism aside (Starkey and Crisell, 2009). There are exceptions, particularly research which has focused on either contemporary issues in sports journalism (Boyle, 2006) or textbooks which provide guides to the practice of sports broadcast journalism (Steen, 2007). However, such texts do not provide detailed histories of British sports journalism and its development in radio broadcasting. Where histories of sports broadcasting do exist in the UK and the US, in both radio and television, research tends to gravitate to an analysis of live broadcasts from sport, and the institutional relations of broadcasters and sports rights holders (Oriard, 2001; Williams, 2011). So while we know a lot about the development of running commentary at the BBC (Huggins, 2007) and the interwar practice of using plans or grids published in the *Radio Times* (Haynes, 2009), we know far less about radio journalism practice in the coverage of sport in news bulletins and dedicated sports news programing.

One reason for the oversight is the greater notoriety and fame of some of the great exponents of commentary on radio, which in British broadcasting included Howard Marshall, Wynford Vaughan-Thomas, Raymond Glendenning, John Arlott and Brian Johnston among others. Many, if not all of these broadcasters were also journalists in their own right, but they are rarely celebrated for being so. Rather, it was their artistry and ability to convey a scene as it happened that captured the imagination of audiences and ensured their celebrated place in British broadcasting history, which has been the focus of numerous popular books on British sports broadcasting (Martin-Jenkins, 1990; Hudson, 1993; Johnston, 2000; Sellens, 2005; Booth 2008). Outside broadcast commentaries are also more likely to be replayed in radio documentaries and talks on major sporting events and achievements, and therefore retain greater potency in popular collective memories of radio's past.

These observations open up questions concerning how to redress this imbalance and recognize a specific form of radio journalism that demands a more nuanced consideration. There are several good reasons for doing so. First, contemporary radio fills many hours with sport-related news. Traditionally in most radio cultures sports news sits in between the main bulletin and the weather report. However, sport figures in its own right as stand-alone news, results and features programs, attracting their own distinct audiences who listen in for comment and analysis. For example, the BBC's daily broadcasts of the London 2012 Olympics attracted over 8 million listeners, with presenters Peter Allen and Colin Murray winning the Radio Academy Award for Best Sports Program in 2013 (The Radio Academy, 2013). How sports news programs became established in British broadcasting and what their unique contribution has been to that history is therefore worthy of exploration. Second, radio sports journalism, specifically as practiced at the BBC since the late 1940s, has contributed to the establishment of particular conventions in the coverage of sport that not only spread to other radio stations, at home and abroad, but also influenced the coverage of sport on television in important ways. How and why were these conventions developed? Who were the key people involved in shaping them, and how were these adopted across different media technologies? Herein lies the third reason for investigating the history of sports radio news: understanding this past can tell us much about how the sports media of the future might be shaped, not least in terms of the interconnectedness between sport, media technologies and their audiences. Are there formal codes and styles of sports journalism that permeate all forms of sports news and how it is produced, distributed and consumed?

One way to use evidence from the media's past is to focus on a specific program format that has endured over time because it has gradually changed in response to changes in sport, media technologies and audience desires. In the British context, the radio sports program that has managed to achieve this feat of endurance is Sports Report. For more than half a century, Sports Report has blended sports journalism with expert analysis on the events of British sport on a Saturday from precisely 5pm in the late afternoon on BBC Radio 5 Live. It has become 'cult radio', from the bouncing rhythm of the brass band playing its signature tune 'Out of the Blue', originally composed by Hubert Bath, through to the ritualistic sombre reading of the day's football results, it is a genuine broadcasting institution, much like the Today program, Woman's Hour or Desert Island Discs. So beloved is the 'Out of the Blue' theme tune that in January 2013 the BBC received a barrage of complaints for replacing it with a new introductory music (Metro, 2013). Created by the Scottish radio producer Angus Mackay, Sports Report arguably transformed the nature of the BBC's approach to sports news in the latter half of the twentieth Century and went on to influence other sports news programing in both public and commercial radio, the evolution of television sports formats and, in a contemporary context, the era of 24-hour rolling sports news channels such as Sky Sports News.

What follows is a brief cultural history of a very simple radio program which has managed to survive the onset of television, but not only that, it has influenced the dominant medium of television in character and form. This cultural history is premised on the value of combining multiple methods of historical media research (O'Malley, 2002) including: an institutional history of post-war BBC Radio based on the BBC Written Archives; autobiographical accounts from sports journalists who worked on the program and interviews with leading sports broadcasters who at one time or another passed through the environs of Sports Report; and textual histories of BBC recordings, some collated by the BBC in commercialized recordings of their output, others based on clips used in BBC radio documentaries about sports broadcasting.

The chapter ultimately traces the genesis of this particular genre of radio news journalism as it developed in the UK. Sports Report was largely driven by topical news values as distinct from the immediacy effect of running commentaries provided by the BBC's outside broadcast department, which was led by its pioneering head Seymour Joly de Lotbiniére (Haynes, 2009). Nevertheless, Sports Report's 'liveness' and ability to entertain was, and remains, a signature feature of the program and its style of broadcast journalism. The chapter therefore analyzes competing tensions between journalistic ideologies of news reporting, such as reporting on the economics and politics of sport, and a desire to maintain a lighter, topical focus on sport, driven by core values of entertainment and the celebration of sporting celebrity (Rowe, 2007). It also analyzes the response of radio sports news to the development of televised sport, which provided both competition and a counterpoint to the form and style of reporting that emerged on radio during the 1950s and on through to the end of the century.

Finally, the chapter will reflect on the influence of broadcasting institutions on the shape and scope of radio sports news programing, which helps us to understand the influence of organizational dynamics and management of broadcast talent on the development of program formats.

Sports news and the influence of Angus Mackay

Born in Glasgow, producer Angus Mackay joined the BBC as a trainee news editor in 1938. He was formerly the journalist and sports editor of the *Scotsman* and like many BBC producers of the post-war era he had a military background, which molded a meticulous approach to radio production in terms of program planning and timing. His no-nonsense approach gained him a reputation for being domineering, ferocious, austere, fearsome and a hard taskmaster. But such epithets have also contributed to the construction of a legendary status among many who worked with him.

Mackay's own ideas on radio journalism reflected the emergent professional ideology of BBC journalism more broadly – precise, impartial, accountable, high standards of working practice and adherence to hierarchical editorial control. But he also introduced his own ways of working that reflected his personal style and single-minded approach to reporting on sport in which he held strong convictions about what the radio listener wanted to know and hear.

Mackay did not like other departments interfering in his productions or dictating the terms and conditions of access to sport because of particular rights deals or contractual arrangements with commentators or summarizers. This particular aversion to others meddling in his business was often targeted at BBC colleagues in radio outside broadcasting who operated in their own department, separate from sports news. The Outside Broadcasting Department handled the live coverage of sport and negotiated access to the rights to broadcast from sport for the BBC. The News Department had to arrange access to sports stadia much like any other news outlet would but did not pay for the privilege. Although most post-war radio commentators were employees of the BBC, including Brian Johnston, Rex Alston and Robert Hudson, many, including the pre-eminent horse racing, football and boxing commentator Raymond Glendenning, were employed on a freelance basis, which meant they could work across outside broadcasts and news output, creating a potential conflict in availability between the two areas of the BBC. The occupational tensions of those who worked in sports news and live sports broadcasts would provide an important institutional context in the evolution of radio sports journalism at the BBC. Although many personnel moved back and forth between radio sports news and radio commentaries, there was no mistaking the different function both forms of sports broadcasting had in terms of editorial control and relations with sport itself: outside broadcasts from sport tried to give the listener a front-row seat from live sporting action, whereas sports news was interested in providing a results service with post-event reaction and analysis.

The distinction between news and outside broadcasts had been institutionally cast in the first decade of the BBC. Prior to the Second World War the BBC's sports news output had been constrained under more general agreements with national and local presses and the major news agencies. Sports bulletins were brief and mainly restricted to scores provided via the press agencies, yet BBC audience research in 1938 revealed the popularity of 'sports news' as 58 percent of the listeners surveyed tuned in regularly to the five-minute bulletins (Huggins, 2007: 500). In 1927 the BBC was only permitted to broadcast news after 6.30pm and was restricted to 400 eye-witness accounts per year (Schlesinger, 1978: 21). Although such agreements kept newspaper proprietors in abeyance they had a serious affect on the availability and timing of sports news, which in 1939 was still being broadcast after 6.15pm so as not to spoil sales of the evening editions (Mackay, 1955: 10). Such constraints were lifted during the Second World War and remained so afterward. In October 1947 the lifting of constraints on reporting from sport events led the Assistant Controller of the Light Programme, John M'Millan, to ask Mackay if he would like "to try your hand at putting together a sports programme out on the air at 5.30pm in the Light Programme?" (Mackay, 1955: 10). The request, recalled Mackay, was "something of a thunderbolt" (ibid.) and had a massive impact on his own personal vision for sports news.

Sports Report, devised by Mackay, was launched on 3 January 1948 on the newly formed Light Programme. Its signature theme tune, 'Out of the Blue', had been discovered literally at the last minute among the BBC's record library but it has become an iconic piece of music associated with BBC radio sports broadcasting. The format was pretty straightforward: a 30-minute results program which linked to BBC studios across the UK to receive brief football match reports from regional broadcast journalists. During its formative history, regional football reporters would make their way to the local studio, compose themselves, and their match report, and deliver what Mackay called "an accurate, informative picture of a game in something like a minute and a quarter" (Mackay, 1955: 16). The program would also include interviews, topical discussion and comment on relevant sports news, with invited guests in the studio talking with the main presenter of the program (a role Mackay referred to as 'The Narrator'). This format is now so familiar as to seem mundane and banal, but in 1948 it represented something of a significant departure in broadcast sports journalism.

At the head of it all was the role of presenter, which in the formative years was taken up by sports commentator Raymond Glendenning. Glendenning later commented that handling the studio end of the rapid-fire tour of the British Isles and the various inputs frequently "left him limp" (Glendenning, 1953: 85), an indication of the energy needed to keep track of the multiple conversations, flow of information and analysis. Unfortunately, Glendenning's mellifluous style was hampered by the need to read the meticulous scripts written by Mackay and his delivery often appeared slow and cumbersome. Other presenters came and went including Stewart MacPherson, Howard Marshall, Cliff Michelmore and the BBC's first ever football commentator George Allison, who upon leaving Broadcasting House after a single appearance on Sports Report in 1949 was so stressed by the exacting pressure of the program and numerous technical hiccups that he turned to Mackay and said, "Never again, Angus, never again" (Mackay, 1955: 10). In 1950 Mackay eventually met the man who would elevate the presentation of the program to new heights and set the benchmark for radio sports broadcasting in the UK. Eamonn Andrews was an Irish freelance journalist and boxing commentator who joined the BBC in 1950 to present the new light entertainment program Ignorance Is Bliss. Mackay had heard Andrews and liked his easy style, crisp delivery and ability to manage various contributions from studio panellists (Mackay, 1955: 20).

The importance of Mackay's role as an impresario come producer cannot be overstated. Although straightforward in concept, the program's goal was to pull together eye-witness reports, interviews and comment from the regional studios of England and the home nations in Cardiff, Belfast and Glasgow. It also used roving reporters at stadiums up and down the country, fighting against the weather, limited technology and ill-prepared sportsmen and women who were fronted up to the microphone. The technique was aided by a new piece of technology, the Commentator Operated Outside Broadcast Equipment, or COOBE for short, which could be plugged in to a Post Office line that linked directly to Broadcasting House and produced clear, high-quality broadcast feeds from stadium to studio. The technology, neatly stored in a briefcase, prevented the need to supply sound engineers at all outside broadcast venues and provided a user-friendly system that reporters could readily use without too much training. To audiences, this quick-fire romp across the nation's sporting venues was a revelation and provided news and reports they wouldn't otherwise have had access to until the arrival of the following day's newspapers.

It is worthwhile pondering on the notion of professionalism in radio broadcasting in this context, as it is an attribute often associated with many of the presenters of Sports Report over the years. Professionalism in news journalism often refers to an ability to apply particular norms and values of journalism in a skilled and articulate way. The craft of gathering and reporting the news is particularly celebrated in this respect (Soloski, 1989). Decisions on the hierarchy of news are also a key feature of this process (Harcup and O'Neill, 2001) and in this respect Sports Report presented the broadcasters with the acute challenge of gathering the day's sports news and rapidly analyzing this information in a cogent and coherent narrative for the listener. The tensions between the bureaucratic structure of the BBC and the need for fleet-of-foot instinctive journalism was therefore ever present in the production of Sports Report which struggled against both time and logistical constraints to deliver a program which seemed controlled and seamless.

Immediacy and regional mobility

An important characteristic of twenty-first-century media, particularly that of modern journalism, is mobility, in terms of the ability to produce media content in any place or time, in a variety of formats. Contemporary sports reporting, by and large, is increasingly beholden to the dominant force of a global, highly commodified, sports industry (Rowe, 2007). This means sports journalists wait upon sports organizations and their major stars to dictate the terms of communication and engagement through press conferences, pre-arranged interviews and orchestrated strategic public communications (Boyle and Haynes, 2011). Sport in the mid twentieth century was different, but no less institutionalized and conservative in its very nature. But one way around this was the mobility of the roving sports journalist with a microphone. The flexibility to investigate whatever seemed right at the time and the technical ability to do so made Sports Report essential listening for its audiences, who were taken on a journey around Britain to hear from sportsmen and women up and down the country in their moments of success and failure, glory and condemnation.

Sports Report always began with the day's classified football scores, working its way through the hierarchy of football leagues in England, Scotland and more recently Wales, a tradition that continues to this day. For more than 20 years the results were read by John Webster from the BBC's Presentation Department. The role was later adopted by James Alexander Gordon, whose intonation as he read the names of the teams was suggestive of the result, and who held the role for more than 40 years until his retirement in 2013.

Although the results service is the bedrock of the program, its core values and dynamic stem from the link between the program's producer and presenter. Conventional communication between the producer in the gallery and the radio presenter in the studio would usually rely on some form of 'talkback' technology, which enabled the producer to communicate with a presenter or commentator through an earpiece. Sports presenters and commentators alike became adept at listening to instruction while continuing to speak and deliver their lines to the audience. For those working on Sports Report Mackay's method of direction was slightly more esoteric, with him often sitting next to the presenter, feeding information and news stories directly in to their ear while they tried in vain to repeat word for word Mackay's 'off the cuff' copy. "It was most disconcerting to have Angus' lips in contact with your earhole," wrote Desmond Lynam, "and if you didn't react immediately to his instruction, for the very valid reason that you couldn't actually hear it, he would become apoplectic with rage" (Lynam, 2005: 32). It was a technique Mackay used to great effect and it maintained the sense of immediacy and the impression of seamless, well-oiled continuity, or 'slickness', that became synonymous with the program. It was an editorial practice that served the program well for nearly a quarter of a century before Mackay eventually retired from broadcasting in 1972.

Sports news, outside broadcasting and relations with sport

When the BBC first covered sport on radio in 1927 it adamantly stuck to the view that it was no different to the press who received complimentary collective access to sports stadia and covered sport for free (Haynes, 1999). Newspapers, and therefore broadcasting, gave sport exposure and widened its audience and popularity. However, the governing authorities of sport, and the proprietors of sports venues, soon began to view this differently; broadcasting was a threat to attendance of sport, particularly when there was live commentary, and those with a vested interest in sport wanted some kind of compensation for potential lost gate receipts. The BBC Outside Broadcast department, under the stewardship of Seymour Joly de Lotbinière, spent much of the 1930s in negotiations with the likes of the Football Association, the MCC (Marylebone Cricket Club), and horse racing, boxing and other promoters for access to sport through payment of what was termed a 'facilities fee'. Although such fees were incredibly modest by contemporary standards, they nevertheless required subtle management of relations with sport, and a clear view of how best to spend the BBC's finite, publicly funded resources. From the perspective of sports administrators and sports promoters the BBC was a single monolithic organisation. The terms and conditions of the BBC's access to sport were consistent with the view that such contracts applied to all departments of the BBC. This posed a problem for BBC news reporting on sport which perceived itself to be much like any other form of news outlet – there to report on the action and results after the event, and therefore not bound by rights agreements.

Mackay fiercely defended his right to control sports news output rather than cede control to the Outside Broadcasting Department. For him, OBs were entertainment-driven and distinct from the news values of the broadcast sports journalism he was intent on developing. For those working in OB, Mackay was truculent and highly defensive of his own domain in the bureaucratic structure of the BBC.

Internal episodes of strife between MacKay and the outside broadcasting departments of both radio and television became a feature of the BBC's coverage of sport throughout the first three decades of Sports Report, leading to what the racing commentator Peter Bromley termed a "Chinese wall" emerging between the two departments (Bromley, 1988: 32). Early signs of discord had surfaced as early as 1938, during the visit of the Australian cricket team, which included the legendary Don Bradman. Mackay sent a news reporter to Lords to interview the Australian players while they were practicing for the first Test against England. The Australians had agreed to a ban on any interviews prior to the match, which had been written in to a rights contract between the MCC and the BBC's outside broadcast department, and Mackay's actions inadvertently upset the MCC and his colleagues in the fledgling BBC Television service (Haynes, 2009).

On occasion the two sides clashed over the BBC's external relations with sport. This was most evident in the BBC's handling of boxing, which throughout the 1940s to the early 1960s was dominated by two competing agents cum impresarios, Jack Solomons and Harry Levene. Solomons was a fishmonger turned boxing promoter who challenged American dominance in the control of world title fights and blazed a trail in adding glitz and glamor to the world of British boxing. For much of the first decade of Sports Report he was the guest of choice when a representative from the sport was needed and he regularly appeared on the program to promote the latest young talented boxer or major title fight on his books. Early on in the program's history, presenter Stewart MacPherson had been reprimanded by the then Director General, Sir William Haley, for proactively plugging one of Solomons' promotions. Mackay was berated for allowing such a blatant error of judgment and asked to provide future 'safeguards' against such commercialized broadcasts.[1] In his own words, he was "the cigar-and-carnation guy you see doing the old gracious and spacious act at the ringside", which would include "hob-nobbing with the high-brows, the low-brows and the no-brows, exchanging a kind word or two with peers, politicians, film stars and jockeys" (Solomons, 1955: 98). His flamboyant style and hegemonic position in British professional boxing clearly appealed to Mackay's desire to have guests at the forefront of their sports with something to say and entertain the listeners.

However, Solomons' arch rival Levene had cultivated a stronger relationship with the BBC's outside broadcasting departments, in both sound and television. From 1956 Levene had been key to the BBC securing World Heavyweight title fights on television, in contrast to Solomons who had struck a number of deals with the BBC's commercial rival ITV. Throughout the 1950s Solomons had frustrated the outside broadcasting department regarding broadcast rights to major championship fights, playing off the BBC's interests with those of ITV. His repeated appearance on Sports Report seemed at odds with his intransigent approach to rights negotiations. At the same time, Levene rarely made an appearance on the program, which threatened to undermine the strong relationship he had developed with managers in outside broadcasting. The spat between boxing promoters reflected broader tensions across the BBC in the scope and territorial reach of BBC departments in the coverage of sport; in the 1950s and 60s there were genuine 'turf wars' in the BBC over access to sports administrators and sporting guests (Hudson, 1993).

Another dynamic element of the program was the use in the studio of Fleet Street sports journalists who were ready to debate and discuss the issues of the day. Regular slots were kept for the journalists Peter Wilson (*Daily Mirror*), Bill Hicks (*News Chronicle*) and sports columnist Jim Manning. The professional status of such journalists gave the program kudos and distinguished it as having its roots in news as opposed to outside broadcasting. Sports journalists and sporting guests were requested to be controversial wherever possible and if guests showed reticence in answering a difficult line of questions, the program's presenter would be prompted to push for an answer. Where outside broadcasts tried to paint the picture of being at a live event, often drawing back from controversy, Sports Report strove to open up debate and discussion in sport between journalists, sports stars and administrators. Until 1970, when outside broadcasting and sports news were unified by Robert Hudson, the then Head of Radio Sport, the BBC's sports journalism suffered from internal battles for resources and personality clashes.

The expansion of sports news and the challenge of television

In 1955 Mackay won a concession to extend the program from 30 minutes to an hour. This enabled more in-depth post-match analysis and discussion among studio guests. It was also radio's response to the relatively emergent new medium of television, particularly following the introduction of the live Saturday sports magazine program Grandstand, launched in 1958. Grandstand itself had been a response to direct competition from ITV for sports coverage and was an important vehicle for various live and recorded sports events to coalesce. Moreover, Grandstand took a cue from Sports Report in the live broadcasting of results as they came in to the studio. As the boxing commentator Harry Carpenter, who was a contributor to both Sports Report and Grandstand, later recalled, television owed a strong debt to its radio pioneer:

> This is one of the things about Sports Report, it pioneered so much in our business. Now when Sports Report started in January 1948, the sorts of things we now take for granted, not only in radio but in television, were unheard of. This programme has done an awful lot in making these sorts of things possible. I'm thinking in particular of the sort of techniques that he used here that are quite by the way now, of calling out reporters from all over the country at various football grounds. This had never been done before.
> (BBC, 1995)

David Coleman, now emerging as British television's pre-eminent sports presenter and commentator, excelled at interpreting the wider meaning of the football results as they emerged on the 'teleprinter', a visual mechanism for displaying football scores as they came in on the wires. In a similar vein to Andrews' unflappable style on

Sports Report, Coleman held court in the center of people's television sets with a flurry of analysis and commentary on the ups and downs of league tables, record-scoring runs or the end of a string of defeats.

The desire for football fans to have up-to-the-minute information on the weekend's matches has driven the concept of rolling sports news to new heights, with the development of 24-hour sports news channels such as Sky Sports News in the UK. Of particular note is BSkyB's weekend program Gillette Soccer Saturday, a marathon of a program that lasts between five to six hours. Originating at the birth of the English Premier League in 1992, and presented by Jeff Stelling, the program provides a quick-fire results service from across the country with reporters – many of whom are former professional players – placed at stadia across the nation. In the studio, Stelling as compare and analyst of scores, scorers, league tables and statistical minutia, is joined by a panel of former players such as Charlie Nicholas, Phil Thompson, Paul Merson and Matthew Le Tissier who watch matches live on monitors and update the audience on events. The studio presentation is overlaid with the customary graphical interface of 24-hour rolling news, with a constantly evolving banner of scores set on the right hand side of the screen and a bright red rolling ticker tape results update running across the bottom of the screen. Although the technology, intensity and statistical profundity of the program has proved an innovative advance in live match-day reporting, which rivals anything produced on radio, it does, however, include the core features originally developed by Sports Report of a live results service, with nationwide eye-witness accounts blended with comment and analysis in the studio.

With the rise of multi-channel pay-television, and the evolution of niche sports channels, radio broadcasting of sport unexpectedly gained new momentum. The renaissance in British radio sport was due to a number of developments in both service and programing which drew on innovations in other nations and other media, including the fan phone-in. The commercial station Radio Clyde in Scotland was one of the first stations to introduce a football phone-in when producer Richard Park launched Saturday Superscoreboard in 1978. Although phone-ins had existed in British radio since the late 1960s, a sports-focused phone-in for fans to air their passions and grievances about the day's sport had not been introduced until Clyde's innovation. Park had listened to American sports phone-ins and thought it was a format that could be imported to British audiences (Haynes and Boyle, 2008). Sports phone-ins and other forms of interactivity and user-generated media became a commonplace feature of the British broadcasting environment. Although the BBC's Sports Report includes fan comment via the BBC website, mobile texts, Twitter and emails, it does not include phone-calls, which are channeled instead through a dedicated program, 606, which it launched in 1991. Originally hosted by the former music journalist Danny Baker, the program took its name from the time slot it received following Sports Report and the 6 O'clock news bulletin, although it has developed into its own brand and is a genuine pan-media fan forum which can appear throughout the week depending on sporting events. The show was partly inspired by the successful local BBC Radio Sheffield program Praise or Grumble, but it also caught the zeitgeist of British football culture of the time which had seen an explosion of fan-based media such as fanzines (Haynes, 1995) and fan biographies such as Nick Hornby's *Fever Pitch: A Fan's Life*, published in 1992.

The second reason for the renaissance in radio sport came from the direct challenge from pay-television and the exclusion of large numbers of sports fans who were unable or unwilling to subscribe to Sky Sports to watch their favorite stars and teams in action. BBC Radio 5, which had been launched as a sports, children's and educational channel in 1990, and was later reformulated and branded Radio 5 Live to encompass news and live sports, gave radio sports commentaries and sports news a dedicated broadcasting home for the first time. With the launch of the English Premier League in 1992, and the increased commodification and gentrification of the sport, the BBC targeted its programing at a predominantly 20–50-year-old male audience and among media commentators commonly became known as 'Radio Bloke'. The rolling news service remains heavily inflected with sports news and with the move of the station to Media City in Salford it gained a strong identity and steadily grew its ratings across the BBC's Medium Wave, digital, mobile and iPlayer platforms.

Conclusion

Radio sports journalism in the UK is synonymous with the format and style of programing innovated by Angus Mackay and his editorial control of Sports Report from 1948 to his retirement in 1972. Attested as the launch pad for a career in sports broadcasting by many who worked on the program, and admired by millions of listeners who over seven decades tuned in to hear the 'Out of the Blue' theme tune followed by the day's results, Sports Report has a very particular place in the annals of British radio broadcasting. The program introduced innovative formats and technologies of sports reporting, many of which have stood the test of time and have been adopted and refined beyond the BBC and into the realm of television. Indeed, the format was so successful that it outlived its creator and continues to form the linchpin of BBC radio's analysis of the British sporting weekend.

In July 2013, following the retirement of the results announcer James Alexander Gordon, the BBC revealed that the new voice of the service would be the former Radio Four news reader Charlotte Green, the first woman to hold a regular featured role on the program. The public announcement of Green's appointment emphasized the absence of women from many of the key roles in the BBC's sports output, particularly programs which primarily focused their attention on male-dominated sports such as football. Interviewed about her new role Green was phlegmatic about the fact that a woman was reading the football results:

> Looking at it now, I suppose it partly reflects the nation's obsession with football. And the fact is there was going to be change after 40 years. Plus the fact it was a woman taking over. Though I really don't know why that should be so amazing. We've had a female prime minister, for goodness sake. I don't think gender is significant. What matters is doing a professional job.
> (White, 2013)

Convention in radio sports broadcasting has dictated that women be excluded from prominent roles in this field of journalism, something Mackay and subsequent producers of the program failed to address. The sound of a woman reading the scores on Sports Report may begin to buck that historical exceptionalism. But Green's quote is also suggestive of the enduring influence of a professional ideology in BBC news journalism: that the core skills and craft of journalism are what matter within any form of factual broadcasting, including sport. What Angus Mackay achieved with the innovation of sports news in Sports Report was a set of standards which continue to inform and reverberate through all that the BBC does around sport on radio. He identified the core needs of the audience for immediacy of information about the day's results, combined with concise and authoritative analysis of sport by journalists up and down the country. In their social history of broadcasting Scannell and Cardiff (1991) note that broadcasting from major sporting events such as Test Cricket, the FA Cup Final, the Boat Race and the Derby was an important device for national cohesion and helped create a sense of a national sporting calendar. In its own banal way, Sports Report created a weekly call to sports lovers across the country to tune in and share the ups and downs, and ins and outs of the national passion for football, cricket, horse racing and boxing among other sports. This desire for immediate news and analysis from sport continues today across radio, television and the internet, and Sports Report continues to have its place in the panoply of sports news media. The program's endurance is a legacy of Mackay's stubbornness to stick to what was then a set of emergent principles of BBC news journalism that displayed a commitment to accuracy, impartiality and diversity of opinion. Sports Report continues to provide all three in a 30-minute bundle every Saturday evening.

Further reading

In *The History of Broadcasting in the United Kingdom* Asa Briggs (1961, 1965, 1970, 1978, 1995) offers a comprehensive account of the history of broadcasting in the United Kingdom in five volumes. Dick Booth (2008) provides a history of sports broadcasting since the 1920s in *Talking of Sport: The Story of Radio Commentary*. In *Cricket and Broadcasting* (2011) Jack Williams offers a stimulating account of the ways in which radio and television broadcasting have impacted on cricket since 1945. Nicollas Sellens' book *Commentating Greats* (2005) has warmly acknowledged the contribution of some of Britain's most celebrated and influential sports commentators and broadcasters. Finally, Guy Starkey and Andrew Crisell (2009) provide a historical and contemporary analysis of radio broadcasting in *Radio Journalism*.

Note

1 BBC WAC, William Haley to Angus MacKay, "Sports Report", 8 May 1949, R30/3,152/1.

References

BBC (1995) *I'll Eat My Hat*. BBC Radio 5 Live, 29 December.
Booth, D. (2008) *Talking of Sport: The Story of Radio Commentary*. Cheltenham: Sport Books.

Boyle, R. (2006) *Sports Journalism: Contexts and Issues*. London: Sage.
Boyle, R. and Haynes, R. (2011) "Sport, the media and strategic communications management." In L. Trenberth and D. Hassan (eds.) *Managing Sport Business: An Introduction*. London: Routledge (pp. 318–38).
Briggs, A. (1961) *The History of Broadcasting in the United Kingdom, Vol I: The Birth of Broadcasting*. Oxford: OUP.
——(1965) *The History of Broadcasting in the United Kingdom, Vol. 2: The Golden Age of Wireless*. Oxford: OUP.
——(1970) *The History of Broadcasting in the United Kingdom, Vol. III: The War of Words*. Oxford: OUP.
——(1978) *The History of Broadcasting in the United Kingdom, Vol. IV: Sound and Vision*. Oxford: OUP.
——(1995) *The History of Broadcasting in the United Kingdom, Vol. V: Competition*. Oxford: OUP.
Bromley, P. (1988) *My Most Memorable Races*. London: Stanley Paul.
Crisell, A. (1994) *Understanding Radio*. London: Routledge.
Glendenning, R. (1953) *Just a Word in Your Ear*. London: S. Paul.
Harcup, T. and O'Neill, D. (2001) "What is news? Galtung and Ruge revisited." *Journalism Studies*, 2(1), 261–80.
Haynes, R. (1995) *The Football Imagination: The Rise of Football Fanzine Culture*. Aldershot: Arena.
——(1999) "'There's many a slip 'twixt the eye and the lip': An exploratory history of football broadcasts and running commentaries on BBC radio, 1927–39." *International Review for the Sociology of Sport*, 34(2), 143–56.
——(2009) "'Lobby' and the formative years of radio sports commentary, 1932–52." *Sport in History*, 29(1), 25–48.
Haynes, R. and Boyle, R. (2008) "Media sport." In N. Blain and D. Hutchison (eds.) *The Media in Scotland*. Edinburgh: Edinburgh University Press (pp. 253–70).
Hornby, N. (1992) *Fever Pitch: A Fan's Life*. London: Victor Gollancz Ltd.
Hudson, R. (1993) *Inside Outside Broadcasting*. Newmarket: R & W Publications.
Huggins, M. (2007) "BBC radio and sport 1922–39." *Contemporary British History*, 21(4), 491–515.
Johnston, B. (2000) *A Delicious Slice of Johnners*. London: Virgin Books.
Lynam, D. (2005) *I Should Have Been At Work!* Edinburgh: Harper Collins.
Mackay, A. (1955) "How it all began." In A. Mackay and E. Andrews (eds.) *Sports Report*. London: Sportsmans Book Club (pp. 7–21).
Martin-Jenkins, C. (1990) *Ball By Ball: The Inside Story of Cricket Broadcasting*. London: Grafton.
Metro (2013) "Listeners stunned as famous Sports Report music is 'replaced'." *Metro*, 7 January. Retrieved from http://metro.co.uk/2013/01/07/listeners-stunned-as-famous-sports-report-music-is-replaced-3342097/
O'Malley, T. (2002) "Media history and media studies: Aspects of the development of the study of media history in the UK 1945–2000." *Media History*, 8(2), 155–73.
Oriard, M. (2001) *King Football: Sport and Spectacle in the Golden Age of Radio and Newsreels, Movies and Magazines, the Weekly and the Daily Press*. Pembroke, NC: UNCP.
The Radio Academy (2013) The Radio Academy Awards 2013: Best Sports Programme. Retrieved from http://www.radioacademyawards.org/winners/index.cfm?winners_year=2013&winners_award_group_id=1&winners_award_category_id=1
Rajar (2013) Quarterly listening. September 2013. Retrieved from http://www.rajar.co.uk/listening/quarterly_listening.php
Reynolds, J. (2013) "World Cup 2014 radio rights to go to TalkSport." *The Guardian*, 15 November. Retrievd from http://www.theguardian.com/media/2013/nov/15/world-cup-2014-radio-rights-talksport-brazil

Rowe, D. (2007) "Sports journalism: Still the 'toy department' of the news media?" *Journalism*, 8(4), 385–405.

Scannell, P. and Cardiff, A. (1991) *A Social History of British Broadcasting, 1922–1939: Serving the Nation, Volume 1*. London: Wiley Blackwell.

Schlesinger, P. (1978) *Putting 'Reality' Together: BBC News*. London: Routledge.

Sellens, N. (2005) *Commentating Greats*. London: West Ridge Books.

Solomons, J. (1955) "Big-time promoter." In E. Andrews (ed.) *Sports Report*. London: Sportsmans Book Club (p.98).

Soloski, J. (1989) "News reporting and professionalism: Some constraints on the reporting of the news." *Media, Culture & Society*, 11(2), 207–28.

Starkey, G. and Crisell, A. (2009) *Radio Journalism*. London: Sage.

Steen, R. (2007) *Sports Journalism: A Multimedia Primer*. London: Routledge.

White, J. (2013) "Charlotte Green living childhood dream reading classified football results." *Daily Telegraph*, 20 December. Retrieved from http://www.telegraph.co.uk/sport/football/10531248/Charlotte-Green-living-childhood-dream-reading-classified-football-results.html

Williams, J. (2011) *Cricket and Broadcasting*. Manchester: MUP.

32
Radio's audiences

Guy Starkey

Not least because the medium of radio has already passed its centenary, there has long been a tendency among scholars of communication, media and cultural studies to characterize it as one of the 'old' media. This is often meant pejoratively, as if the radio has already become irrelevant and may soon die out altogether. In reality, though, over much of that time radio has been evolving and considerably so since the development of digital production and distribution technology began to gather pace in the 1980s and 1990s. In its earliest forms, the popular term for radio was 'the wireless', a term which became so old-fashioned that until very recently it became a signifier of old age in the person using it. Now the word 'wireless' has once again become established in the lexicon of the most technologically aware and radio remains a major feature on the increasingly digitized media landscape around which today's audiences have to navigate. Radio's audiences have been evolving, too, in terms of how and why they access radio broadcasts, as have the various ways in which radio broadcasters engage with their listeners. It should no longer be surprising that today radio stations seek to exploit the additional opportunities to recruit and retain listeners afforded them by the internet and by mobile communication devices. That the levels of interactivity between broadcaster and listener which exist today should not be confined to the 'developed' world was less predictable and we often find that in parts of Africa, for example, audiences exist which benefit from the unique characteristics of radio as a medium in ways that are more critical to their survival than to our own.

Radio has not always served merely to inform, to educate and to entertain in the manner characterized by the first Director General of the BBC, John Reith, as being central to the role of providing a public service (Hendy, 2013: 21–25). Its role has often been to persuade, to motivate, to evangelize or to propagandize in various ways. For example, advertising is an overt attempt to persuade listeners to buy a product or service (Starkey, 2013: 143–46), audiences are sometimes encouraged to change behavior through public information announcements, some stations have sold airtime to evangelistic churches and radio was used extensively in the Second World War and the Cold War to promote competing ideologies across the English Channel and the Iron Curtain (Starkey, 2007: 26, 119–20). Different audiences have responded in different ways to such attempts to affect their behavior. Even the ways in which radio's audiences are measured have evolved. Electronic audience metering technology appeared at first to offer new certainties around who is listening and how large an audience they might constitute. Such certainties have since been recognized as elusive.

This chapter will examine radio's audiences as they have evolved over the past century, from the perspectives of both broadcasters and scholars. It will examine such trends as have emerged in the development of radio as a public service and as a way of delivering audiences to advertisers. Most significantly, the recording and theorizing of radio's history will be examined in relation to radio's audiences and our various understandings of them, in ways which recognize the essential characteristics of a medium which may well be relatively old but which remains important in the lives of many who choose to listen to it.

'Listening in', together

At first, radio's audiences wouldn't even have recognized the term 'radio'. When this, the first electronic medium of *simultaneous* mass communication, was first popularized it became almost instantly known as 'the wireless' (Crisell, 1994: 17). There is of course a certain irony in this, because 'wireless' has relatively recently become a term which can signify a lifeline, or at least a means of connecting with the internet, and so, 'virtually', persons and entities beyond our immediate physical reach. Similarly, the original wireless was, some 90 years ago, widely perceived to be groundbreaking in technological terms and subsequently turned out to be significant in sociological terms as a catalyst for change. The first radio audiences were themselves pioneers, or what we today might call 'early adopters', of the new communication technology that had suddenly become publicly available to those who could afford it. In the way we now sometimes label younger generations 'digital natives' – or people who are naturally accustomed to a world of digital communication – these pioneering audiences quickly became, without knowing it, something we might retrospectively term 'analogue natives', in that analogue radio broadcasting swiftly became ubiquitous in their lives, so that soon they came to depend upon it.

However, 'listening in' to the wireless, to use the phraseology of the era, was not a trivial matter. The receiving equipment was large and cumbersome (Chignell, 2009: 97) and dependent on electrical circuitry that incorporated 'valves' (Street, 2002: 16) which were both vulnerable to accidental damage, being largely made of glass, and initially useless until they had 'warmed up' after electrical current had passed through them for a few minutes. The batteries needed to power this circuitry were also large and cumbersome by today's standards and they were often loaned from a high street electrical store which would have already become established as an important link in the chain between broadcaster and listener because of its ability to charge up batteries for its customers and hire them out against a deposit and for a fee. To add to the complication and the expense of listening to the wireless, in many countries, including Britain, sound broadcasting quickly became funded through the mechanism of a license fee, in the same way that a television receiving licence is still required here today (Crisell, 1994: 18–19).

So in essence, and despite the significant personal commitment needed to actually tune in to these early wireless broadcasts, such pioneering radio audiences as existed early in the last century were engaging with a new phenomenon that promised to broaden their horizons and to bring into their homes experiences which until then had had to be physically sought, rather than merely happened upon by chance. Many of those experiences were familiar ones, but ones that could not have been experienced aurally except outside the home. It was not long before elements of music hall, the most popular collective mass entertainment of the period, albeit one to which audiences had had to travel, began appearing in regular radio programing. Many of the sub-genres of early radio light entertainment borrowed styles, content and modes of address from the music hall (Starkey, 2013: 165, 166), becoming adapted for radio in order to compensate for two apparent disadvantages of this new medium of mass communication: the physical absence in literal terms of the audience from the events they were witnessing through sound and listeners' inability to literally see for themselves who was talking or singing and what they were doing. Despite these limitations to broadcast sound, music hall soon went into decline as the growing popularity of the wireless – as well as the cinema – gathered pace. Now audiences could experience for themselves words, music and other sounds from outside the home, accessing information, entertainment and, yes, some content that was 'educational', if not necessarily organized into formal courses of learning, in the manner of early broadcasts 'for schools'. These audiences could see in their own minds, without leaving home, the imagined world that words, music and sounds can create (Crisell, 1994: 42–63), which contrasted with the text and still-image-bound printed press and the cinema, with the given moving images that filled its screens, but which remained, by contrast, mostly asynchronous with any original action.

The wireless broadcast by the Canadian inventor Reginald Fessenden on 24 December 1906 is commonly recognized in the west as the first ever radio program of speech and music (Starkey, 2007: 159). By then the technology, of course, was not particularly new. The pioneers of early radio broadcasting had already demonstrated the science behind it in the previous century, notably when the Italian Guglielmo Marconi showed how signals transmitted 'without wires' could be sent to someone else with a working receiver over initially modest and then ever greater distances. The broadcasting historian Andrew Crisell notes (1994: 17) that initially, at least, the perceived uses of radio were limited to point-to-point communication and so of greater interest to shipping and the military than the general public as a means of communicating distress messages or sensitive information to members of the war effort, wherever they might be. In this way, the first wireless transmissions were not intended as a broadcast, or 'scattering' of content to whomsoever might be in range of the transmitter, but more as a direct, sender–receiver transaction that nonetheless could be eavesdropped upon by any number of suitably equipped third parties. Such 'eavesdroppers' as might have existed then included short-wave radio enthusiasts with two-way radios, each with their own identifier, or 'call sign', who continued to use the technology for long-distance communication. This use of the technology was briefly popularized on a more local scale in the 1970s with the growth of citizens band radio (Starkey, 2011: 161–62).

Unlike Fessenden, who after his first broadcast in 1906 went on to explore the commercial potential of other inventions, Marconi and others subsequently perceived somewhat belatedly that using electro-magnetic radio waves to randomly 'scatter' programing content that might prove attractive over wide areas to emerging mass audiences could encourage sales of radio receiving equipment to mass markets and so produce a significant income from the technology. By the early 1920s experimental radio broadcasting was being replaced by the introduction of regular services from many of the European capitals, among them London, from where a station with the call-sign 2LO began broadcasting on 14 November 1922 (Street, 2002: 11–26). The Marconi Company soon merged with others to form the British Broadcasting Company, which was renamed the British Broadcasting Corporation in 1927, when it was re-established as a result of government intervention as a publicly owned body with the public service obligation that was defined in practice by Reith. A detailed chronology of the BBC is to be found in Briggs (1961) and his subsequent volumes, while other broadcasting historians such as Crisell (1997), Hendy (2007) and Street (2002) have produced more selective histories. Around the world, and with varying degrees of agility, regular 'wireless' broadcasting began in other cities, often adopting other styles, genres and funding models, until radio's reach became almost worldwide. In 2012, the BBC began celebrating on air the 90 years since the birth of regular broadcasting in the United Kingdom, with programs of commentary mixed with archive recordings designed to mark the importance of the anniversary.

At first, the 'blindness' of radio, or at least the blindness of the *experience* of listening to radio (Starkey, 2013: 25–26), troubled neither the medium nor its audiences to any great extent. The absence of given pictures, which could anyway be seen later on in various genres of other media, for example in print or in newsreels at the cinema, was not initially considered a problem by radio's newfound audiences. The ability of the mind to create images for the individual is a powerful one, drawing upon information provided by spoken monologue or dialogue, or even deriving meaning from an infinite range of sonic triggers, such as ambient sounds, music or added sound 'effects'. Such triggers to the imagination are themselves often used in combination, perhaps with acted, monologic or dialogic speech, to add additional layers of meaning, and quickly became commonly molded through conventional use to develop aural codes that are quickly understood or 'decoded' by audiences in ways potentially akin to the intentions of the producers (Chignell, 2009: 71–74).

The experience was new and exciting, and far from being one which was confined to the early adopters. The simultaneity of transmission which afforded early radio an immediacy that could be replicated by no other medium meant 'listening in' to a broadcast became a popular activity (Crisell, 1994: 19). In climates which discouraged going out on cold, wintry evenings, the wireless was a welcome and easily accessible source of entertainment that could be enjoyed in the home with a minimum of discomfort, unlike going out to a public venue. 'Liveness' is in itself compelling in many ways (Crisell, 2012) and once radio established itself as a source of fresher news than could be accessed from a printed newspaper or a cinema newsreel, immediacy, particularly during wartime, made the ownership of a wireless receiver very desirable. As production equipment became more portable and later tape recorders were developed and became increasingly available to radio producers and reporters (Chignell, 2009: 44–47), radio content was able to shed its original studio-bound nature and figuratively 'take' listeners to distant locations and witness events they simply could not experience directly for themselves (Fleming, 2002: 12).

Typically, the wireless set occupied a privileged place in the domestic sitting room, parlor or family lounge, depending on the social status of the family unit and the particular term they would use to describe the one room of the house that was dedicated to collective relaxation. The listening experience of those early audiences was often a collective one, with the bulky radio set, soon probably powered by more reliable mains electricity, providing the new focal point of the room, a spot perhaps previously occupied in wealthier households by a piano. The ritual family after-dinner sing-along had, in many homes, been replaced by an act of tuning in to a regional or national wireless broadcast or even one from a neighboring country, such as Ireland or Luxembourg. Of course, the early radio stations' schedules often featured popular programing or conveyed news of events too recent to be reported in the evening newspaper and which, uniquely, could be the subject of wider discussion at work or in town the next day. Because this first electronic medium was now able to draw together large audiences listening simultaneously, the shared experience of hearing the same content as neighbors, colleagues and others, and *being able to react to it*, gave radio a distinct cultural significance that neither newspapers nor public venues could achieve. Even listening *at* work became common and became seen as beneficial for productivity in some of the large factories geared up for mass production during the Second World War. In 1940 the BBC introduced *Music While You Work* to stimulate workers engaged in otherwise repetitive manual tasks that required little higher-level cognitive activity. Because 24-hour broadcasting did not arrive until 1973, a whole factory radio station, the United Biscuits Network, was created for closed-circuit distribution and playback of music and chat through loudspeakers, with overnight shift workers particularly in mind. For the medium of radio, though, it was not long before that domestic centrality in the shared experience of the family and of wider British society, as elsewhere in the developed world, was displaced in the rudimentary sense of the position it occupied in the home and in audiences' evening routines by the arrival of a new electronic medium, television (Starkey and Crisell, 2009: 7–8).

Portable radio, solitary listening

It is worth noting here that the actual *transmission* of television uses the very same technology as radio, albeit on different frequencies and requiring more bandwidth because of the additional data required to transmit given pictures to accompany the sound. A significant difference is that the frequencies allocated to television broadcasting require stronger signals to achieve adequate reception, normally requiring greater proximity of the viewer to the transmitter than those frequencies originally used by radio. They also require more elaborate aerials which are highly directional in nature and usually situated atop a roof or some other high vantage point. However, such inconveniences did little to deter widespread early adoption of this technological enhancement of the practice of broadcasting and in the development of television as a mass medium the critical moment in the United Kingdom is widely considered to have been the coronation of Queen Elisabeth II in 1953 (Crisell, 1994: 26). In many neighborhoods, the few owners of a television set found themselves hosting viewing 'parties' of people who came to gather in their living rooms in order to witness not just the sounds and verbal commentaries describing the ceremony, but to *see* the events taking place in London in an ocular and not merely cognitive way. Of course, a further irony is that the early television pictures lacked most of the clarity and certainly the color of today's high-definition television, but the occasion provided the newer medium with the early recognition and popular appeal it needed to become firmly established as the new focal point of the living room – largely at the expense of radio.

Audiences for radio quickly went into decline as over the 1950s and the 1960s the after work collective family evening audience turned its attention to the television, abandoning radio. Television even borrowed from radio some of its more successful program genres and stars in a mostly one-way transaction that was especially evident with the arrival of intentionally popular commercial television in 1955. Commercial competition for BBC radio had arrived unofficially in the late 1920s and the 1930s with the launch of popular radio stations broadcasting from the continent (Crisell, 1994: 22). Among them were Poste Parisien, Radio Normandy and most significantly Radio Luxembourg, which was reported in the 1930s to have attracted larger UK audiences on Sundays than the BBC because those audiences preferred the commercial stations' light entertainment programing to the comparatively dull output of the BBC under the stewardship of the reputedly rather dour John Reith (Hendy, 2007: 2–3). His ideas around strict religious observance of Scottish Presbyterian approaches to the Sabbath meant there was little entertainment broadcast by the BBC on Sundays (Crisell, 1994: 22). After the 1939–45 war, only Luxembourg had recommenced English-language broadcasting to the UK, and it was programs such as *Double Your Money* that were transferred to the new Independent Television (ITV) to satisfy audience demand for light-hearted, undemanding entertainment (Stoller, 2010: 17).

Yet radio has, on more than one occasion, defied widespread predictions of its early demise and shown that it is a resilient medium. Some commentators offered dire warnings in the 1950s, suggesting that radio was already an 'old' medium which could not withstand the increased competition from a newer medium that more recent advances in technology had brought. What confounded such predictions then was the development of an electrical component called the transistor which meant that much smaller, portable radio sets could be developed relatively cheaply for mass markets without needing the valve technology that kept television receivers bulky, dependent on mains power and mostly living room-bound until and beyond the 1980s (Fleming, 2002: 25). Radio manufacturers quickly seized on the ready markets for not just small, portable 'transistors' or 'trannies' as they were popularly called, which could be carried around and even taken into the garden or to the beach, but also car radios. Because radio can be consumed, and even enjoyed, passively, while listeners pursue some other repetitive activity, such as cooking, washing up, ironing, decorating and, most importantly in terms of sheer amount of listening, driving, audiences and their ways of accessing radio *content* quickly evolved in line with the technology (Crisell, 1994: 12–14). The development of FM (frequency modulation) broadcasting, using radio frequencies on what was initially called the VHF (very high frequency) band, brought better quality sound than the original transmissions using AM (amplitude modulation). So, as domestic hi-fi audio equipment became popular, sitting room accessories in the 1970s – 'tuners' – were typically incorporated within them. Audiences were largely just as happy, though, with the quality of the radio broadcasts they could access through their small, often multiple, portable transistor radios. Of course, this change in the availability of radio content meant that the evolution of radio listening included a trend towards solitary rather than collective listening.

With that trend came distinct changes in audiences' daily patterns of listening. The peak hours of the day for radio became the breakfast slot, as radio's easy availability in the bedroom, kitchen and even the bathroom meant it could provide an entertaining and often informative accompaniment to the early-morning routine. Listening at home was now followed by listening in the car, on the school run or on the way to work. Industry audience surveys began to show that from the breakfast-time peak, radio audiences typically went into decline through mid morning, perhaps recovering a little at lunchtime, then declining further in the early afternoon and probably staging a modest recovery as the evening drive home began, before plummeting into early evening and the now well-established switch to television (Barnard, 2000: 101). Of course, differences exist between listening patterns to different radio stations, and in different cultures, which means some Spanish stations' audiences recover significantly mid afternoon in the summer because listening increases during siesta time. In Britain, because the arrival of the socio-cultural teen revolution of the mid 1950s and early 1960s produced a new market segment that was keen on discovering new music, young people became a discrete target audience for radio stations in the evenings, and bedroom listening while doing homework, as well as under-the-bedclothes listening after 'lights-out' became common (Chignell, 2009: 67). This maverick listening hastened the end of full-service broadcasting, aimed at scattered programing to please the whole family, while providing a lifeline to the continuing English-language service of Radio Luxembourg, the geographical reach of which was by then dictated by the hours of darkness since AM transmissions traveled further across the British Isles from the Grand Duchy of Luxembourg after dusk. Thus, a whole generation of British teenagers grew up listening to the brashly presented sequences of virtually non-stop American and British top 40 music broadcast by 'Fabulous 208', a name which became an essential part of the station's branding, being based on the wavelength of the medium wave transmitter it now occupied.

In the early 1960s British radio audiences were not offered much modern 'pop' music by the BBC, whose post-war realignment of its domestic services had left it broadcasting the Home Service and the Light and Third Programs of broadly talk and drama, middle-of-the-road music and cultural output respectively. It took a further challenge to the BBC's monopoly, that of the offshore pirate stations, with Radio Caroline leading the attack in 1964, to demonstrate to the BBC and to government that there was now a large, underserved audience for all-day pop music (Stoller, 2010: 20). Although within three years the British government had enacted legislation to close down the offshore pirates, they were a catalyst for the introduction of not only a new national BBC radio network to a reorganized bouquet of Radios One, Two, Three and Four, but also BBC local radio and then an initially modest network of privately owned and commercially funded Independent Local Radio stations (Baron, 1975). The detailed history of the accelerating fragmentation of the radio industry which ensued and which continues today is well documented by Stoller (2010) and Starkey (2011) among others, but in essence it has meant a parallel fragmentation of audiences as stations have increasingly dropped any original full-service commitment to scattering programing which might please certain audiences some of the time in favor of razor-sharp targeting of often very narrowly defined audiences made up largely of solitary listeners, many of them in their cars. Their musical preferences can provide the focus of industry research to determine which songs should be playlisted in order to attract and retain them as often and for as long as possible.

Radio's audiences today: Interactivity and passivity

It is worth noting here that both industry and academics have developed various ways to 'know', or at least to measure, radio's audiences. One of the particular problems for the industry has been the invisibility of audiences, which cannot be measured either by counting sales, as the Audit Bureau of Circulation (ABC) does for the newspaper industry, or by connecting measuring devices to receivers, in the way that currently the Broadcasters' Audience Research Board (BARB) and its predecessors, JICTAR (the Joint Industry Committee for Television Audience Research) and TARAC (Television Audience Research Advisory Council), have done for television. Radio's portability is, in this respect, a disadvantage, because attaching measuring devices like BARB's set-top box to every radio in the house and the car would be impractical. How would incidental listening at work, in shops, gyms or hairdressers' be identified? Much of what we 'know' about the size of early radio audiences can be attributed to commissioned opinion polling by market research companies and then street interviews by the BBC Listener Research Department. Later, stratified random panel surveys began (Starkey, 2004), with respondents asked to keep a diary of their radio listening by the Joint Industry Committee for Radio Audience Research (JICRAR) (1974–92) and subsequently by Radio Joint Audience Research (RAJAR). The robustness of the data collected in this manner has more recently been questioned, especially since the development of *portable* electronic listening meters, worn like a wristwatch or a now old-fashioned 'pager' (Starkey, 2003). Meanwhile, academic research often concentrates on small groups of listeners, through focus groups and questionnaires, sometimes producing interesting results robust enough to generalize to wider populations. This is not unlike the market testing of songs carried out by some music stations to determine which should be added to the playlist and which should be discarded.

Today, even in the UK, one of the most advanced countries in the world in introducing digital radio *transmission* (O'Neill, 2010), broadcast distribution remains overwhelmingly analogue with only very tentative talk of a digital switchover as has already occurred in television. Yet the medium of radio is proving once again to be resilient in ways which could not have been predicted even a short time ago. Today in Britain, radio listening is at record levels (RAJAR, 2013), partly due to its relatively recent emergence on a wide variety of new and established platforms, such as live streaming, podcasting, the UK Radio Player, the BBC iPlayer Radio, social networking sites, mobile phones, tablets, the internet and television EPGs, some of which also provide opportunities for audience measurement. Despite being told once again that radio would succumb to the threat from newer media to steal its audiences, radio would appear to be as resilient now as it has ever been. As stations put complementary text, images and archived and extended or 'best of' audio content on their websites, new forms of user-generated content have appeared in traditional radio genres. And at the same time as the available choice of stations continues to grow and further *fragment* audiences, à la carte and diasporic listening bring remote and specialized radio stations to international audiences where once only medium and short wave transmissions significantly disrupted geographical, political and socio-economic boundaries to the dissemination of news and information and human cultural interaction. This is not confined to the developed world, as, for example, Damome's study of radio station websites in Togo illustrates (2011).

Paradoxically, as radio's present and seemingly its future seem increasingly characterized by its potential for audience interaction, it may simply be the way in which radio can be enjoyed passively that guarantees its survival (Starkey, 2011: 183–85). Just as the development of the transistor radio in the 1950s lent the medium a new portability and its audiences new ways of listening in while performing other more mundane tasks, now radio remains uniquely available both inside and outside the home for secondary consumption. As competing demands for audiences' attention multiply, radio may well remain a firm favorite for years to come.

Further reading

There are several works which delve into the history of radio and audiences. Asa Briggs' *The History of Broadcasting in the United Kingdom: Volume I: The Birth of Broadcasting* (1961) offers the first in a series of detailed volumes chronicling the 'official' history of the BBC. Andrew Crisell's *An Introductory History of British Broadcasting* (1997) is one of a number of more concise histories, which includes the development of the commercial sector.

Richard Rudin's *Broadcasting in the 21st Century* (2011) considers some of the recent developments in broadcasting, exploring how new media forms are changing audiences' pleasures, expectations and demands. Finally, Martin Shingler and Cindy Wieringa, in *On Air: Methods and Meanings of Radio* (1998), provide an important early contribution to the development of a body of literature within the then emerging discipline of radio studies.

References

Barnard, S. (2000) *Studying Radio*. London: Arnold.
Baron, M. (1975) *Independent Radio*. Lavenham: The Lavenham Press.
Briggs, A. (1961) *The History of Broadcasting in the United Kingdom: Volume I: The Birth of Broadcasting*. Oxford: Oxford University Press.

Chignell, H. (2009) *Key Concepts in Radio Studies*. London: Sage.
Crisell, A. (1994) *Understanding Radio* (2nd edition). London: Routledge.
——(1997) *An Introductory History of British Broadcasting*. London: Routledge.
——(2012) *Liveness and Recording in the Media*. Basingstoke: Palgrave Macmillan.
Damome, E. (2011) "The community of radio listeners in the era of the internet in Africa: New forms and new radio content, the Fan Club Zephyr Lome (Togo) as a basis for analysis." In A. Gazi, G. Starkey and S. Jedrzejewski (eds.) *Radio Content in the Digital Age: The Evolution of a Sound Medium*. Bristol: Intellect Books (pp. 235–46).
Fleming, C. (2002) *The Radio Handbook*. London: Routledge.
Hendy, D. (2007) *Life on Air: A History of Radio Four*. Oxford: Oxford University Press.
——(2013) *Public Service Broadcasting*. Basingstoke: Palgrave Macmillan.
O'Neill, B. (ed.) (2010) *Digital Radio in Europe: Technologies, Industries and Cultures*. Bristol: Intellect Books.
RAJAR (2013) "RAJAR data release – quarter 1, 2013." London: Radio Joint Audience Research.
Rudin, R. (2011) *Broadcasting in the 21st Century*. Basingstoke: Palgrave Macmillan.
Shingler, M. and Wieringa, C. (1998) *On Air: Methods and Meanings of Radio*. London: Hodder Arnold.
Starkey, G. (2003) "Radio audience research: Challenging the gold standard." *Cultural Trends*, 12(45), 43–79.
——(2004) "Estimating audiences: Sampling in television and radio audience research." *Cultural Trends*, 13(1), 3–25.
——(2007) *Balance and Bias in Journalism: Representation, Regulation and Democracy*. Basingstoke: Palgrave Macmillan.
——(2011) *Local Radio, Going Global*. Basingstoke: Palgrave Macmillan.
——(2013) *Radio in Context* (2nd edition). Basingstoke: Palgrave Macmillan.
Starkey, G. and Crisell, A. (2009) *Radio Journalism*. London: Sage.
Stoller, T. (2010) *Sounds of your Life: A History of Independent Radio in the UK*. New Barnet: John Libbey.
Street, S. (2002) *A Concise History of British Radio*. Tiverton: Kelly Publications.

Part VI
FILM

33
The British cinema
Eras of film
Tom Ryall

The British film has a lengthy history which can be traced back to the pioneer stage of the medium in the late nineteenth century when Britain, along with the United States, Germany, France and other nations, staked claims to the invention of cinema. Dividing the hundred years plus of that history into 'eras', segments of historical time possessing a degree of internal coherence, has been done in a range of ways utilizing a medley of criteria.

Many factors influence the construction of historical periods relating to cinema. From general film history comes the broad division common to all national cinemas between silent and sound cinema with the latter divisible further into the classical sound era (1930s–1950s), based on big studio production, and the post studio period (1960s to the present) with its more fragmented structures. Such periods also relate to the significance of cinema-going as a largely urban leisure activity which peaked in the 1940s, declined significantly in the post-war years, then began a kind of recovery in the 1980s in the context of a burgeoning and varied audio-visual environment. Laid upon those divisions are the momentous events of history – the First World War, the Great Depression of the 1930s, the Second World War and the Cold War – which had profound effects on the course of international cinema. Laid upon those factors is the history of one national cinema – that of America – which above all others has shaped and determined the course of many national cinemas through its economic, artistic and general cultural influence. The British cinema has been especially susceptible to American influence and one way of writing its history is in terms of the industry's resistance to Hollywood domination both at the level of political and industrial impact and at the level of cultural influence.

From the point of view of aesthetics and film form, film scholars have also developed numerous conceptual schemes for the analysis of the British film. 'Realism', despite the somewhat elusive nature of the term, has been particularly important as a central concern for accounts of the national cinema. The cinematic lineage from the 1930s documentarists, led by John Grierson, through the wartime realism of films such as *In Which We Serve* (1942) and *Millions Like Us* (1943), to the British 'new wave' of working-class orientated films in the early 1960s such as *Saturday Night and Sunday Morning* (1960), and to recent film-makers such as Ken Loach, embodies a traditional view of the development of the British film though one based on a strong set of assumptions about the role of the cinema as social agent. Such assumptions have been challenged by recent writing on the British film and, as Alan Lovell has suggested, the "strongest positive thrust from the new scholarship has been an attempt to validate 'anti-realist' film-making" (2009: 7). Raymond Durgnat (1970) and Charles Barr (1977, 1986) have developed a critical strand which interrogated the enshrined status of the 'realist' documentary-influenced film. Conceptual couplets such as realism/fantasy, prestige film/genre cinema, documentary/fiction, popular cinema/art film, exterior/interior cinema and other variants enabled British film history to find places for the eccentric vision of Powell and Pressburger, for the Gainsborough costume melodrama, for the crime film, for popular comedies, for the Hammer horror film, and for a strong vigorous popular cinema neglected by orthodox critical opinion and counterposed to the restrained aesthetics of the 'realist' film.

This chapter divides the history of British cinema into 'eras' that can be organized according to some of the institutional and artistic factors, political history, global film history, film form and aesthetics mentioned previously. At various times in its history, the British film industry has been affected by other national industries, especially though not exclusively the American film industry, by domestic government legislation and by artistic currents of influence from popular Hollywood films and from European art cinemas. Like the British body politic, the British film is lodged between America and Europe with the industries of each offering different templates – popular cinema, the art film – for the development of a national cinema with a distinctive identity. In the 1940s, Lindsay Anderson suggested that "the British cinema seems to hover between the opposite poles of France and Hollywood" (1949: 113), while in the 1990s, Christopher Williams suggested that "British film-making is caught between Hollywood and Europe, unconfident of its own identity, unable to commit or develop strongly in either direction" (1996: 193). This chapter will trace the history of British cinema through various phases in which the numerous pressures, strains and influences on the cinematic institution acquire a specific form marking them as distinctive 'eras'.

The silent British film

The first phase in the history of British cinema is marked by two contrasting periods: the first decade of cinema when British films were in the forefront of the shift from the single-shot "cinema of attractions" (Gunning, 1991: 41) to the multi-shot narrative film; and the mid 1920s when, in the words of a later policy think tank report, "the British film industry was well on the way to extinction" (PEP, 1952: 41). A period of early promise with pioneering breakthroughs in film form was followed by a decline mitigated somewhat by the appearance of some notable film-makers in the 1920s. British film-makers were actively and significantly involved in the development of the medium from its earliest days in the 1890s, working to perfect the technologies that enabled 'moving pictures'. William Friese-Greene, R. W. Paul, Birt Acres and Louis Le Prince (a Frenchman working in England) are significant figures in the early history of film technology working "more or less in parallel with the Lumières" (Barr, 2009: 145), the French pioneers often regarded as the inventors of the medium. Early British film-makers were also closely involved in the development of various film genres including actualities (documentary), comic and trick films. However, the most significant development was probably the 'chase' film in which a series of narrative events was presented through a number of integrated shots, a crucial move in the development of what became the dominant form of cinema throughout the world, the narrative film. As the film historian Tom Gunning has noted, the "earliest chase films were made in England, with Williamson's *Stop Thief* (1900), Mottershaw's *A Daring Daylight Burglary* (1903) and Haggar's *Desperate Poaching Affray* (1903) providing prototypes" (1991: 66). In addition, the British pioneer G. A. Smith was closely involved in the development of one of the earliest color techniques, Kinemacolor, "the first successful photographic color-motion-picture process" (Kindem, 1982: 136). This early vibrant strand of film-making based in various locations in Britain (London, Brighton and Hove, Sheffield, Leeds, Wales) had a wide impact during a period when films were traded internationally with a degree of ease. Indeed, many British companies had well-established international links with various overseas markets including the American market through their involvement in the photographic and lantern trade which had developed in the nineteenth century.

Despite such a promising beginning, the silent era in British cinema is often regarded as a critical failure and by 1927 its lowly status with the intellectual critical community was signaled by a suggestion in the high-brow magazine *Close Up* that "an announcement 'British Film' outside a movie theatre will chill the hardiest away from its door" (quoted in Low, 1971: 298). The First World War had disrupted the development of film production in Europe while the American industry, with a massive domestic market providing a stable financial base, had moved into a powerful global position and, by the early 1920s, American rather than British films formed the staple cinema-going experience for the British audience. British production declined during the 1920s and it has been estimated that at one stage around 95 percent of the films appearing on British screens were foreign, mainly American (PEP, 1952: 41). Even so, several hundred films were made in Britain during the decade though most were dismissed by critics as too hidebound by traditional literary and theatrical sources (adaptations of Shakespeare and Dickens), as socially and politically irrelevant, as stylistically inferior to American films (slow-paced rather than dynamic), and, with some notable exceptions, as unresponsive to the modernist experiments in the emerging 'art' cinemas of Germany, France and the Soviet Union. In contrast to the revolutionary qualities of the early British short films, the 1920s British feature film has been characterized as conservative, insular and lacking in popular appeal. Historians such as Rachael Low have seen the 1920s as a period of transition, "when the old guard of producers were weeded out and the ground cleared for more highly capitalized companies with modern business methods and a modern style of production" (1971: 156). Producers such as Michael Balcon and Herbert Wilcox replaced the more established and conservative companies (Stoll, Ideal, Hepworth) and new young directors such as Alfred Hitchcock with *The Lodger* (1926) and Anthony Asquith with *Underground* (1928) made films which were more in keeping with the directions being taken by the American cinema and the new European 'art' films, especially those from Germany. More recent scholarship, however, has looked more closely at the body of films consigned to critical oblivion and presented a more complex account of the period. Andrew Higson (1995: 51–58) has suggested that a conservative film-maker like Hepworth worked within an aesthetic rooted in a 'pictorialist' approach to image composition while Christine Gledhill has presented a positive image of a cinema maturing on the basis of a "reinvention, within the stabilizing practices of a new international medium, of inherited pictorial, theatrical and storytelling traditions" (2009: 163). The traditional British films made by the well-established studios and directors may not have slotted into either the popular or the Modernist contours of the international cinema but in drawing on indigenous artistic conventions from photography and the theater, it has been suggested, an alternative to the American mainstream and the European avant-garde was constructed.

The interwar years and the 'golden age'

British cinema underwent several changes in the early sound period. The advent of the sound film rendered the silent picture obsolete; the precarious state of the production industry in the mid 1920s prompted the government to intervene with legislation; and there was a restructuring of the industry into two major combines (Gaumont British, Associated British Picture Corporation) with interests in production, distribution and exhibition, together with the emergence of new ambitious companies such as Alexander Korda's London Films. The decade also saw a program of ambitious studio building with Pinewood and Denham opening in the mid 1930s. The Cinematograph Films Act of 1928 required distributors (including the powerful Hollywood firms) and exhibitors to incorporate quotas of domestically produced films in their offerings, providing a degree of market protection for the indigenous industry and, along with the new vertically integrated companies and the new studios, promising to provide a secure infrastructure for the British cinema. However, the decade is usually characterized in terms of artistic failure. The Hollywood majors commissioned inexpensive films – 'quota quickies' – to meet their quota obligations and despite Korda's ambitious big budget films such as *The Private Life of Henry VIII* (1933) and the famous Hitchcock thrillers such as *The 39 Steps* (1935), it was the infamous quota quickie which often defined the status of the British cinema of the time. As with the silent period, critical opinion was harsh on the films produced, quickies and prestige films alike, especially in respect of their failure to confront social and political themes, their failure to reflect "the agony of those times", to quote the producer Michael Balcon (1969: 99). Critics compared the fiction films of the period unfavorably with the emergent documentary cinema which flourished on the basis of sponsorship by both the state (the Empire Marketing Board, the Post Office) and private industry (Shell) under the general guidance of John Grierson. However, the dismissal of the 1930s entertainment film ignores the vigor and vitality of the genre cinema of the time which drew upon the popular culture of the music hall and the crime novel (George Formby, Gracie Fields, the

Hitchcock thrillers). And as with the critical 'rehabilitation' of the silent British film, recent scholars have found merit even in the cheaply produced quota quickie genre films of the time (Napper, 2009).

The paradigmatic 'era' in British film history is the 1940s, a decade with a widely perceived coherence deriving from the historical event of the Second World War and its aftermath, together with a high degree of critical enthusiasm for the films of the period among both contemporary critics and subsequent commentators. Charles Drazin, for example, opens his study of the leading figures of the period with the claim that the "1940s were the finest years in the history of British cinema" (1998: 1) and for many the decade constitutes the 'golden age' of the British film. Yet, in a sense, the 1930s was a necessary prelude to the 'golden age' and, as Linda Wood has suggested, by "1939 Britain possessed the necessary facilities and personnel with the relevant expertise to produce the kind of quality films which could not have been made in this country previously and on a sustained basis" (1986: 6). A number of factors converged in the 1940s to realize the potential of the British cinema. There was effective though informal government supervision of production in the conditions of war which engendered a common ideological focus on war propaganda by film-makers. Documentary film-makers drew close to their fiction counterparts, producing a fresh aesthetic based on the fusion of dramatic narrative and the documentary realism of the 1930s and differentiating the British film from its Hollywood counterpart. Some of the key titles of 'the golden age' were made by film-makers or playwrights with established careers, such as Asquith or Noël Coward. Many, however, were made by directors and directing teams embarking on their first features in the war period after 'apprenticeships' in the industry during the 1930s as scriptwriters or editors, actors or quota picture directors. They included the Powell and Pressburger team, the Launder and Gilliat team, David Lean, Laurence Olivier and Carol Reed. There was also the emergence of a new and powerful production company, the Rank Organization, which absorbed much of the existing industry (production companies, studios), forming a conglomerate comparable to a Hollywood major.

The Second World War, of course, provided dramatic and urgent subject matter including the intense drama of the home front (civilian life during the Blitz, for example) as well as the exciting events of military engagement on land, sea and air. Although only about a third of the total number of films produced during the war had wartime subject matter, titles such as *In Which We Serve* (1942), *The Way Ahead* (1943), *The Way to the Stars* (1945), *Fires Were Started* (1943) and *Millions Like Us* (1943) form a powerful image of a national cinema. Such films addressed the social and political upheaval of the war and displayed the combination of fictional narrative and documentary which established itself as a distinctively British approach to dramatic cinema. The 'golden age' extended beyond 1945 and the war titles along with later films such as *Brief Encounter* (1945), *Henry V* (1945), *Odd Man Out* (1946) and *The Red Shoes* (1947) were seen as constituting a cinema of 'quality', to use the term coined by contemporary critics. Such films, characterized by 'realism', 'naturalism' and 'restraint', offered hopes of a genuinely national cinema which, it was felt, had failed to materialize in previous eras (Ellis, 1996: 66–67). British films also won prizes at significant international festivals with both *Brief Encounter* (1945) and

The Third Man (1949) winning the critics' prize at Cannes in their respective years and *Hamlet* (1948) winning the International Grand Prize at the Venice Film Festival. The three films also figured in Hollywood's Academy Awards with David Lean and Carol Reed nominated in the Best Director category and *Hamlet* winning the Best Picture award for 1948. The 'quality' film sat somewhere between the sophisticated European cinema and the energetically exciting/emotionally involving Hollywood film, not in the sense of the hesitant identity noted by writers such as Anderson (1949) and Williams (1996) but rather in a more confident vein. Critical opinion in the 1940s was enthusiastic, asserting that "British films suddenly seemed to have acquired a positive cultural identity of their own. No longer were they patently inferior to Hollywood" (Ellis, 1996: 66). Subsequent commentary endorsed this with the distinguished and influential French critic André Bazin noting "the appearance of a British cinema that was original and free from the influences of Hollywood" (1968: 33).

As an 'era', the 1940s was marked by very specific circumstances: a momentous historical event which impacted on all aspects of life, generating a sense of common purpose among the artistic community; an effective level of state control during the war period; a clear ideological focus matched by an innovative realist aesthetic; a new and powerful industrial configuration; and a tranche of skilled film-makers. Sustaining the high levels of achievement, however, proved difficult and the next era of British film was marked by declining audiences and competition from a new medium of visual entertainment, the television.

Post-war decline: The television era

Like its predecessors in the 1920s and 1930s, the 1950s British film has often been judged negatively. As a recent study suggests, "it is widely perceived as being a dull period – an interregnum sandwiched between the inventive 1940s and the exciting 1960s" (Harper and Porter, 2003: 1). The 'golden age' of the 1940s had ended with a severe crisis in the film industry – the collapse of the Korda group and drastic retrenchment in the Rank Organization. Government action at the end of the 1940s had renewed the quota arrangements for the British film and established new sources of finance for the industry. It had also concluded an Anglo-American agreement which required the Hollywood majors to invest some of their British distribution earnings in domestic production. In contrast with the 1930s, however, American companies including MGM and Warner Bros financed large budget pictures rather than the quota quickies which had blighted the reputation of the British film previously. Films such as *Treasure Island* (1950), *The African Queen* (1952), *Captain Horatio Hornblower R. N.* (1952), *Ivanhoe* (1952), *Knights of the Round Table* (1953) and *The Bridge on the River Kwai* (1957) featured top Hollywood stars including Humphrey Bogart, Katharine Hepburn, Gregory Peck, Robert Taylor and William Holden, along with top directors such as John Huston and Raoul Walsh. Many were major box-office successes both in Britain and in the US. Despite the significant American involvement, however, many of the films were grounded in British sources both historical and literary. The films also used British actors such as Robert Newton,

Alec Guinness, Jack Hawkins and Stanley Baker, and top British technical staff including the cinematographers Freddie Young and Jack Cardiff.

The framework for the development of the British cinema in the 1950s, however, was also formed by an enlarged and flexible quota, fixed according to domestic production capacity; by new sources of production finance and subsidy such as the National Film Finance Corporation, effectively a state financed film bank; and by the established commercial companies such as Rank, the Associated British Picture Company and Ealing. US finance became increasingly important as the decade progressed but there was still a significant amount of indigenously financed cinema. Annual production figures doubled compared with the wartime years and, as Robert Murphy has suggested, "in the fifties film production enjoyed greater health and stability than might have been expected given the competition from television" (1989: 230). Many of the US-financed films were large budget historical spectaculars while the dominant domestic genres during the period were comedies such as the high-profile Ealing titles and a number of combat films set in the Second World War. Though Ealing comedies such as *The Man in the White Suit* (1951) and *The Ladykillers* (1955) have commanded subsequent critical attention, Rank Organization titles such as *Genevieve* (1953) and the *Doctor* films beginning with *Doctor in the House* (1954), the comedian Norman Wisdom's films starting with *Trouble in Store* (1954), and the early *Carry On* films were more successful at the box office. Ealing and Rank also made a number of war films including *The Cruel Sea* (1953) and *The Dam Busters* (1954) both of which were major box-office successes. Ealing films apart, such titles have not attracted a great deal of subsequent critical attention and, as one commentary has it, the period "is commonly characterized as the era in which the national cinema retreated into quaintly comic evocations of community or into nostalgic recollections of the war" (MacKillop and Sinyard, 2003: 2). Yet such sentiments were to the public taste and films such as *Doctor in the House*, *The Dam Busters*, *Reach for the Sky* (1956) and *Carry On Nurse* (1959) were number one in the trade paper *Kinematograph Weekly*'s popularity polls for their release years, proving to be more popular than the Hollywood films which dominated British picture houses (Harper and Porter, 2003: 249).

Despite this, the significance of the cinema as a leisure activity was changing with the spread of television ownership often cited as a key though not sole factor in the process. Though British films were produced in reasonable numbers and were doing well at the box office, audience figures were in decline, indeed had been in decline since the 1940s. The record wartime attendances which peaked in 1946 at over 1,600 million were followed by a decline through the 1950s, particularly from the middle of the decade onwards when commercial television companies began broadcasting alongside the BBC. By 1960 admissions were 500 million, less than one third of the wartime figure, and it was a trend that was to continue until the 1980s as the audience declined to 54 million in 1984 (see Figure 1.2 in BFI, 2012: 11). Yet during this lengthy era of audience decline, many notable films were made. These include the critically esteemed 'new wave' realist films (*Saturday Night and Sunday Morning* [1960], *A Kind of Loving* [1962]), iconic British cinema of a different kind including 'Hammer horror' and the *Carry On* … cycle, the eccentric stylized visions of Nicolas Roeg and Ken Russell, the films of Ken Loach and Mike Leigh and their distinctive 'realisms', bold innovatory films such as *The Draughtsman's Contract* (1982) and *My Beautiful Laundrette* (1985) from television's Channel Four, iconic genre films such as *Get Carter* (1971) and *The Long Good Friday* (1981) and, with *Chariots of Fire* (1981) and *A Room with a View* (1985), even the stirrings of the 'heritage' film which was to assume an important place in the British cinema of the 1990s.

Revival: 1980s to the present

The era of decline culminates in the mid 1980s. Audiences had deserted the cinema and, in the words of one study, "it looked as if cinema exhibition had dropped below the threshold for survival" (Docherty, Morrison and Tracey, 1987: 2). The 1984 admissions total was 54 million yet by the end of the decade – by 1990 – the audience admissions figure had almost doubled to over 97 million. Locating the beginning of an 'era change' in the mid 1980s, from decline to the contemporary success story, is appropriate for two reasons. First, the audience decline was arrested, reversed, and was to continue to rise steadily to the present day with the most recent annual admissions figure at 171 million, almost a return to the situation of the early 1970s (BFI, 2012: 11). Second, the exhibition sector altered dramatically, taking a new direction in the middle of the decade. Although many cinemas were closed during the 1960s, some had adjusted to the declining audiences by converting their large auditoriums, built for the era of the mass audience, to create twin or triple-screen venues out of the traditional stalls plus balcony structures. However, as Hanson suggests, this move was not always successful:

> There were significant drawbacks to many conversions. Poor sight lines in the lower auditoria were caused by the necessity of off-centering the screen to make way for an emergency exit and aligning them with a shared projection box located at the corner. The low ceilings and narrow halls also meant much reduced screen sizes.
>
> (Hanson, 2007: 121)

Though the multi-screen move was right, simply tinkering with the old venues was not the answer; a fresh start was required. The key development was the advent of the multiplex, a purpose-built cinema with a large number of screens (the first in Britain had ten), usually located on the edges of towns, often in shopping malls. Although some traditional cinemas did remain, the numbers of multi-screen cinemas increased dramatically with the most recent figures indicating that three quarters of the cinema screens in Britain are in multiplexes (BFI, 2012: 96).

The 'decline and regeneration' pattern was also evident in film production. Production volume in the 1950s and early 1960s remained steady with an annual figure of over a hundred films although the figures began to dip in the mid 1960s and there was a significant decline through the 1980s. In 1989, the figure of 30 films produced was an eerie echo of the desperate state of the British production industry in the mid 1920s (BFI, 2002: 34) and for many the British cinema again seemed on the brink of 'extinction'. The dire 1989 statistic was in the wake of deregulation by the Conservative government of the day which, as Toby Miller suggests, "unraveled a gradually accreted system of subvention which had protected and stimulated the British film industry since the 1927 Cinematograph Films Act" (2000: 37). However, despite the removal of quotas and the dissolution of the National Film Finance Corporation and other forms of support, British cinema underwent something of a renaissance in the 1990s, "a return from near-paralysis of its film industry," as the American showbiz magazine *Variety* noted (1997: 1). Production levels climbed gradually from the 30 films of 1989 to nearer the figures from the 1950s and 1960s (100 plus annually) by the end of the decade. The principal commercial producer of the 1990s was the European-based PolyGram Filmed Entertainment and many of the most successful titles came from its British subsidiary, Working Title. Films such as *Four Weddings and a Funeral* (1994), *Bean* (1997), *Elizabeth* (1998) and *Notting Hill* (1999) placed Britain on the international film map. Smaller production concerns including television companies (Channel Four, the BBC) also contributed to the revival often in co-production arrangements. Indeed, Channel Four was involved with *Four Weddings and a Funeral* and *Elizabeth* as well as with smaller off-beat successes such as *Trainspotting* (1996). It was also involved, in conjunction with the American Twentieth Century Fox, in one of the major successes of the decade, *The Full Monty* (1997), described by *Variety* as "a global cultural phenomenon and one of the defining British movies of its era" (2001: 7).

A new source of finance became available in the mid 1990s with the government decision to allocate money from the recently established National Lottery to the film industry. A key element in this move was the decision to allocate funding to a small number of franchised consortia of experienced producers on an extended basis, enabling them to build up production portfolios in the manner of the traditional film studio with the aim of bringing stability to the industry. 'Sustainability' was the buzzword and, in a complementary move, the government created a new organization – the Film Council (later renamed the UK Film Council). It began operations in 2000, drawing together a variety of existing institutions including the Arts Council's Lottery Film Department and the British Film Institute to create what was conceived of as a rational structure to underpin a sustainable film industry and to promote 'film culture' through support for film education in schools and universities. Despite the critical and/or commercial success of titles such as *Wilde* (1997), *Ratcatcher* (1999), *Topsy-Turvy* (2000), *Billy Elliot* (2000), *Gosford Park* (2001) and *Bend it Like Beckham* (2002), many Lottery supported titles failed on both counts. Lottery funded films *per se* acquired a reputation for poor quality from a hostile press though the hostility often seemed directed at the 'public subsidy' element in their production as much as at the intrinsic qualities of the individual titles (Petley, 2002).

Nevertheless British films in the first decade of the new century continued on an upward trajectory with "a gradual increase in the number of UK feature films made, from an average each year of 40 in the 1980s to 80 in the 1990s and to 130 a year since 2000" (Perkins, 2012: 314). There were continuities with British films of the previous decade with production supported through the UK Film Council until its abolition in 2010, with various forms of tax breaks designed to attract private investment and with a continued involvement by television companies especially in the low budget sector. As ever, the American presence is still of major significance to the British film with the figures above including Anglo-US co-productions such as the Harry Potter series and the James Bond films. Though such films have been largely financed by the major American studios, they were partly made in British Studios with British production personnel and drawing upon British cultural content thus qualifying as 'British' in legal terms for taxation and other purposes.

Endthought: The British film now

The period of revival, in film production, in cinema audiences, which began in the mid 1980s was also a period in which the broad audio-visual and communications landscape began to change dramatically, multiplying the ways in which films were viewed. The cinema audience attending the multiplex still exists but the major source of film viewing is television supplemented by DVD and video on demand, together with online viewing on computers and mobile phones (BFI, 2012: 135). In the traditional eras of cinema, films came and went with a limited public life before disappearing altogether or being lodged in archives for future screenings at film festivals and in specialized cinemas. The contemporary era 'preserves' films, prolonging their public lives through the electronic media, and it may be the case that the proliferation of viewing opportunities means that a new 'era' of British cinema is beginning. Films are now watched in a variety of ways though it is worth emphasizing that the continuities with the traditional elements of the experience – cinemas, the picture show – remain "as the crucial first step in the life cycle of a film" (Perkins, 2012: 310).

Further reading

Two edited collections, Ashby and Higson's *British Cinema, Past and Present* (2000) and Curran and Porter's *British Cinema History* (1983) provide effective overviews of the course of British cinema through a combination of general reflective pieces on the notion of British cinema together with detailed studies of topics such as censorship, Hammer horror cinema, the British New Wave, middlebrow cinema and the heritage film. Two historical surveys offer distinctive and detailed overviews of the sweep and scope of the British film in its social, cultural and institutional contexts: Street's (1997) *British National Cinema* charts the development of the British film with a strong focus on studios and genres and Sargeant's (2005) *British Cinema: A Critical History* devotes more attention to individual films including a number of titles often neglected by writers on the history of British film.

References

Anderson, L. (1949) "Alfred Hitchcock." *Sequence*, 9(Autumn), 113–24.
Ashby, J. and Higson, A. (eds.) (2000) *British Cinema, Past and Present*. Abingdon: Routledge.
Balcon, M. (1969) *Michael Balcon Presents ... A Lifetime of Films*. London: Hutchison.
Barr, C. (1977) *Ealing Studios*. London/Newton Abbot, Devon: Cameron & Tayleur/David & Charles.

——(1986) *All Our Yesterdays*. London: BFI Publishing.
——(2009) "Before *Blackmail*: Silent British cinema." In R. Murphy (ed.) *The British Cinema Book*. London: BFI/Palgrave Macmillan (pp. 145–54).
Bazin, A. (1968) "The evolution of film language." In P. Graham (ed.) *The New Wave*. London: Secker & Warburg/BFI (pp. 25–51).
BFI (2002) *BFI Film and Television Handbook 2003*. London: British Film Institute.
——(2012) BFI Statistical Yearbook 2012. Retrieved from http://www.bfi.org.uk/sites/bfi.org.uk/files/downloads/bfi-statistical-yearbook-2012.pdf
Curran, J. and Porter, V. (eds.) (1983) *British Cinema History*. London: Weidenfeld & Nicolson.
Docherty, D., Morrison, D. and Tracey, M. (1987) *The Last Picture Show? Britain's Changing Film Audiences*. London: British Film Institute.
Drazin, C. (1998) *The Finest Years: British Cinema of the 1940s*. London: André Deutsch.
Durgnat, R. (1970) *A Mirror for England*. London: Faber & Faber.
Ellis, J. (1996) "The quality film adventure: British critics and the cinema 1942–48." In A. Higson (ed.) *Dissolving Views: Key Writings on British Cinema*. London: Cassell (pp. 66–93).
Gledhill, C. (2009) "Late silent Britain." In R. Murphy (ed.) *The British Cinema Book*. London: BFI (pp. 163–76).
Gunning, T. (1991) *D. W. Griffith and the Origins of American Narrative Film*. Urbana and Chicago, IL: University of Illinois Press.
Hanson, S. (2007) *From Silent Screen to Multi-Screen*. Manchester: Manchester University Press.
Harper, S. and Porter, V. (2003) *British Cinema of the 1950s*. Oxford: Oxford University Press.
Higson, A. (1995) *Waving the Flag: Constructing a National Cinema in Britain*. Oxford: Clarendon Press.
Kindem, G. (1982) "The demise of Kinemacolor." In G. Kindem (ed.) *The American Movie Industry*. Carbondale and Edwardsville, IL: Southern Illinois University Press (pp. 136–45).
Lovell, A. (2009) "The British cinema: The known cinema?" In R. Murphy (ed.) *The British Cinema Book*. London: BFI (pp. 5–12).
Low, R. (1971) *The History of the British Film 1918–1929*. London: George Allen & Unwin Ltd.
MacKillop, I. and Sinyard, N. (2003) *British Cinema of the 1950s: A Celebration*. Manchester: Manchester University Press.
Miller, T. (2000) "The film industry and the government: 'Endless Mr Beans and Mr Bonds'?" In R. Murphy (ed.) *British Cinema of the 90s*. London: BFI Publishing (pp. 37–47).
Murphy, R. (1989) *Realism and Tinsel: Cinema and Society in Britain 1939–1949*. London: Routledge.
Napper, L. (2009) "A despicable tradition? Quota quickies in the 1930s." In R. Murphy (ed.) *The British Cinema Book*. London: BFI (pp. 192–201).
PEP (1952) *The British Film Industry*. London: PEP (Political and Economic Planning).
Perkins, S. (2012) "Film in the UK, 2001–10: A statistical overview." *Journal of British Cinema and Television*, 9(3), 310–32.
Petley, J. (2002) "From Brit-flicks to shit-flicks: The cost of public subsidy." *Journal of Popular British Cinema*, 5(1), 37–52.
Sargeant, A. (2005) *British Cinema: A Critical History*. London: BFI Publishing.
Street, S. (1997) *British National Cinema*. Abingdon: Routledge.
Variety (1997) 15–21 December, p. 1.
  (2001) 2 8 April, p. 7.
Williams, C. (1996) "The social art of cinema: A moment in the history of British film and television culture." In C. Williams (ed.) *Cinema: The Beginnings and the Future*. London: University of Westminster Press (pp. 190–200).
Wood, L. (1986) *British Films 1927–1939*. London: British Film Institute Library Services.

34
British cinema and history
James Chapman

Ever since the nineteenth century there has been a distinction between academic history and popular history: while the former concerns itself with meticulously documented scholarship, the latter is essentially about telling stories. The most powerful medium of popular history in the twentieth century was the cinema. Leslie Halliwell, the doyen of popular film historians, remarked in his memoir *Seats in All Parts* that cinema "gave me an idea of what happened in history, admittedly a hazy one since Disraeli and Voltaire and Richelieu and Rothschild all seemed to look like George Arliss" (Halliwell, 1985: 10). The fact that cinematic history has often had a somewhat loose relationship with recorded history has been a significant obstacle to the acceptance of film by historians. In the 1930s, for example, the Historical Association was "gravely concerned at the effect on children and adults of film purporting to represent historical personages which are being shown in the picture palaces, and considers that steps should be taken to assist teachers and others to estimate the accuracy of such films" (Harper, 1994: 66). As a consequence, the response to historical films by professional historians has generally not looked far beyond the question of their authenticity; complaints that the king wears his spurs on the wrong side of his shoes (*The Private Life of Henry VIII*) or that the South Wales Borderers were not formed until after the Battle of Rorke's Drift (*Zulu*) exemplify the level at which many historians have engaged with historical film. In the absence of more meaningful engagement with the subject from historians, therefore, it is to film and cultural studies that we must turn. It was once said that the genre of British historical film "can safely be ignored as being of little intrinsic interest" (Lovell, 1972: 6). This is no longer the case. Indeed recent scholarly studies have put historical film at the centre of critical and aesthetic discourses around British cinema. Historical film features in discussions over the economic and cultural viability of British national cinema; it has been understood as a vehicle for the projection of national identity and the dissemination of dominant ideologies; it has figured prominently in debates around quality and aesthetics; and it has been the subject of a fierce debate over the politics of so-called 'heritage cinema'. These critical issues have, to a large extent, displaced the now rather sterile debate over the authenticity of historical film, though this occasionally resurfaces in the critical reception of major films such as *Elizabeth* (1998).

Historical film and national cinema

Historical film has been central to the project of establishing a British national cinema as an alternative to the economic and cultural hegemony of Hollywood. This project has been both an industrial one (British producers seeking to make films that are distinctively British in content and themes) and a critical one (the analysis of British films as cultural and aesthetic artefacts that have something to say about British national identity). It was a historical film, Alexander Korda's *The Private Life of Henry VIII* (1933), that really put British cinema on the international map. Some of the most successful British films have had historical subjects, including Academy Award winners *Lawrence of Arabia* (1962), *Chariots of Fire* (1981), *Gandhi* (1982) and *The King's Speech* (2011). And historical film has been central to the strategies of ambitious producers – including Alexander Korda in the 1930s, the Rank Organization in the 1940s and Goldcrest in the 1980s – who have sought to break into the world market on the back of expensively produced historical films.

A national cinema is understood foremost in terms of the themes and subject matter of its films (Richards, 1997). And there is no better genre for the representation of nationally specific subject matter than historical film: every nation has a history that is unique. British producers have naturally been inclined towards making films on British subjects and themes. The royal biopic has been a particular favourite, with films based on the lives of Henry VIII (*The Private Life of Henry VIII*, *Henry VIII and His Six Wives*), Lady Jane Grey (*Tudor Rose*, *Lady Jane*), Elizabeth I (*Young Bess*, *Elizabeth*, *Elizabeth: The Golden Age*) and Queen Victoria (*Victoria the Great*, *Sixty Glorious Years*, *Mrs Brown*, *The Young Victoria*). Other historical subjects have included statesmen (*The Iron Duke*, *The Prime Minister*, *The Young Mr Pitt*, *Young Winston*), military leaders (*Nelson*, *Lawrence of Arabia*, *Khartoum*), explorers (*Drake of England*, *Rhodes of Africa*, *Scott of the Antarctic*), writers and artists (*The Trials of Oscar Wilde*, *Shakespeare in Love*, *Becoming Jane*) and scandalous society figures (*Nell Gwyn*, *Beau Brummell*, *Scandal*). Another recurring motif has been the dramatization of famous historical events such as the defeat of the Spanish Armada (*Fire Over England*) or the sinking of the *Titanic* (*A Night to Remember*), while other films celebrate notable British achievements in fields such as aviation (*They Flew Alone*) and sport (*Chariots of Fire*). The favourite periods for producers of historical films are those which give rise to narratives of national greatness – the Tudors, the building of the British Empire, the Second World War – whereas there have been fewer films about the Dark Ages (*Alfred the Great*) or periods of internal conflict such as the English Civil War (*Cromwell*, *To Kill A King*).

As well as the content of its films, however, a national cinema can also be understood in terms of its institutions and critical practices (Higson, 1995). There have been numerous examples of how both industry and official bodies have sought to promote historical film as a vehicle for the projection of Britain. The film critic F. D. Klingender, writing in 1937, argued that historical films served different ideological functions: "They may be straight propaganda for specific social aims, they may be more subtle attempts in which a particular situation of the past is held up as a mirror to the present, or they may be pure means of escape into the realms of fancy clothed in the settings of a former age" (Klingender, 1937: 8–9). The idea that Britain should take responsibility for the screen representation of its own past had been an argument advanced in favour of the introduction of protective legislation for the film industry in 1927 in the form of a quota of British films for distributors and exhibitors (Dickinson and Street, 1985). And there is evidence, too, that the British Board of Film Censors sought to use its control of content to mandate a particular type of history. In 1947, for example, it rejected a proposal from Columbia Pictures to produce a film of Comyns Beaumont's notorious book *The Private Life of the Virgin Queen*: "It is known that some American films have twisted and adapted OUR history to suit THEIR needs, but it would be reprehensible if a British producer followed suit by basing a film on this travesty of history" (Chapman, 2005: 6).

However, the 'Britishness' of British cinema has been called into question by the changing cultural and political economies of the film industry. Even in the 1930s it had been claimed that the influx of foreign émigré artistes into the film industry was diluting the indigenous talent pool. One critic later suggested that *The Private Life of Henry VIII* "had little British about it except its subject, its stars, and that it was made near London. Its story, direction, photography, settings and music were all by Continentals" (Rotha, 1949: 546). The technicians involved in making *The Private Life of Henry VIII* included a Hungarian director (Alexander Korda), writer (Lajos Biro) and art director (Vincent Korda), a German composer (Kurt Schroeder) and a French cinematographer (Georges Périnal). Korda, however, gave short shrift to the idea that this made the film any less British: "An outsider often makes the best job of a national film. He is not cumbered [sic] with excessively detailed knowledge and associations ... I know there are people who think it odd that a Hungarian should direct an English historical film, but I can't see their argument" (Anon, 1933: 14–15).

Since the 1950s, moreover, it has increasingly been the case that British cinema has been backed by Hollywood dollars. MGM led the way with a triptych of medieval chivalric epics – *Ivanhoe* (1952), *Knights of the Round Table* (1953) and *The Adventures of Quentin Durward* (1955) – while other American producers to have dabbled in British history include Joseph E. Levine with *Zulu* (1964) and Hal B. Wallis with *Anne of the Thousand Days* (1969) and *Mary, Queen of Scots* (1971). American investment became a necessity for the British film industry following the decline of cinema-going since the 1950s: historical film was always one of the more expensive genres and the economics of the marketplace meant that the declining British audience was simply not large enough to recoup the costs of production. For US producers, British historical film offered 'prestige' subject matter that was qualitatively different from Hollywood – as evidenced by the Academy Awards showered upon Fred Zinnemann's film of Robert Bolt's play *A Man for All Seasons* (1966) – while investment was encouraged by tax incentives and production subsidies. In the sense that they are a combination of US economic and British cultural capital, films such as *Zulu*, *Lawrence of Arabia* and *Gandhi* are perhaps best understood as Anglo-American productions.

History and ideology

The ideological project of British historical film during the heyday of cinema-going as a social practice – roughly between the 1930s and the 1950s – was the projection of a national identity that subsumed class and regional differences into a broad national consensus. This is a strategy of royal films such as Korda's *The Private Life of Henry VIII* and Herbert Wilcox's *Victoria the Great* (1937) which emphasize the loyalty of subjects towards their monarch but also the monarch's sense of duty towards his or her subjects. In other films there is evidence that producers employed the past as a commentary on the present. Victor Saville's *The Iron Duke* (1934) for the Gaumont-British Picture Corporation reflected the pro-appeasement politics of the time in its representation of the Duke of Wellington as a conciliatory figure seeking to protect the future peace of Europe by resisting demands from other powers for a punitive settlement on the defeated France at the Congress of Vienna. There were clear echoes here of the harsh treatment of Germany in the Treaty of Versailles. A few years later, as the threat of Nazi Germany became more apparent and policy shifted gradually away from appeasement, films such as Korda's *Fire Over England* (1937) and Wilcox's *Sixty Glorious Years* (1938) were strident calls for national preparedness in response to foreign aggression.

It was during the Second World War that British cinema was most closely aligned with an official view of history. The Ministry of Information promoted a historical narrative that presented Britain as a bulwark of liberal values and as a champion of progressive social reform. There was a cycle of films dramatizing national resistance to foreign tyranny, such as *This England* (1941), *The Prime Minister* (1941) and *The Young Mr Pitt* (1942) (Aldgate and Richards, 1986: 138–67). To this list we may also add *Lady Hamilton* (1941), produced by Alexander Korda in Hollywood (Glancy, 1999: 105–11). The culmination of this cycle was Laurence Olivier's film of *Henry V* (1944), a patriotic epic that adapted Shakespeare's text to the ideological demands of wartime Britain. *Henry V* paraded its propagandist credentials openly: it was dedicated "to the Commandos and Airborne Troops of Great Britain – the spirit of whose ancestors it has humbly been attempted to recapture in some ensuing scenes." The parallels between past and present are nothing if not explicit: France/Germany, Henry/ Churchill, Agincourt/D-Day. Rarely, for a Shakespearean adaptation, *Henry V* was a popular as well as a critical success: its marketing as a 'prestige' attraction in the United States after the war is a reminder that even a film conceived within the ideological context of British war propaganda was also an economic and cultural commodity (Street, 2002: 96–106).

However, the projection of Britain was not only a requirement of wartime conditions. With the need for narratives of resistance to Fascism having passed, producers of historical films now had to negotiate Britain's declining world power status. One way of doing this was through films dramatizing British pluck and fortitude in times of adversity. Examples of this strategy included Ealing Studios' *Scott of the Antarctic* (1948), Rank's *A Night to Remember* (1958) and *Zulu* (1964), which in the hands of producer-star Stanley Baker became a tribute to the courage of Welsh troops without recourse to the jingoism of previous British Empire epics. The 1950s cycle of Second World War films, including *The Dam Busters* (1955), *The Battle of the River Plate* (1956) and *Dunkirk* (1958), were understood by critics at the time as a last hurrah for Britain as a great power (Chapman, 1998). Following the cultural changes of the 1960s, which saw the fragmentation of the cinema-going audience and the emergence of assertive new youth cultures, it was no longer possible for the film industry to cling to old-fashioned values such as duty and heroism. Hence the cynical, anti-establishment politics of films such as Tony Richardson's *The Charge of the Light Brigade* (1968) and the distinctly unheroic tone of war epics such as *Battle of Britain* (1969).

Questions of quality and taste

Historical film has been a site for contesting taste. There has often been a disjuncture between the views of (mostly middle-brow) film critics on the one hand and the popular preferences of cinema audiences on the other. Critics have generally favoured films that treat the past authentically and with due reverence. The sober documentary-influenced realism of films such as *Scott of the Antarctic* and *A Night to Remember* recommended them to critics who saw their unsensational narratives as a distinctly British style that was qualitatively different from Hollywood (Ellis, 1996). However, this critical discourse has no place for films that do not conform to its strict parameters of sober realism and emotional restraint. Hence sensational costume melodramas such as those produced by Gainsborough Pictures in the 1940s or the historical spoofs of the 'Carry On ... ' series have been disparaged or even ignored in the critical orthodoxy. A critical project of recent British film studies has been the reclamation of what Julian Petley has aptly termed "the lost continent" of British cinema (Petley, 1986).

The Gainsborough melodramas of the mid 1940s – films such as *The Man in Grey* (1943), *Fanny by Gaslight* (1944), *The Wicked Lady* (1945) and *Jassy* (1947) – exemplify this lost continent. These films represented everything that the 'quality' critics despised: they were characterized by sensational narratives, melodramatic excess and a flamboyant visual style. The *Manchester Guardian* famously dismissed *The Wicked Lady* as "an odd mixture of hot passion and cold suet pudding" (*The Manchester Guardian*, 1946). However, these films were enormously popular with cinema audiences, especially women, who responded to their emotionality and female-centred narratives. Sue Harper has argued that these films "should be given major currency in debates about the cultural resources of the wartime and postwar period" (Harper, 1994: 123). The Gainsborough films were freed from the discourse of historical authenticity: hence they mobilize the past in a symbolic and ritualistic way that "provided a site for a carefully costed expressionism whose practitioners had been unhappy working in the theater or other studios because of the dominance of a realist orthodoxy" (Harper, 1994: 119). A feature of the work of revisionist critics such as Harper and Pam Cook (1997) is that it extends the boundaries of genre to include not just 'historical film' (usually understood as films based, however loosely, on real events and people) but also 'costume' or 'period' film (films set in the past that may not be based on actual events or people, such as literary adaptations). Most historians, in contrast, would not consider fictional stories such as *The Wicked Lady* as historical subjects.

Even within historical film, more narrowly defined, however, questions of quality and taste sometimes arise. Two examples, some 65 years apart, must suffice to illustrate this. The popular success of *The Private Life of Henry VIII* was due in large measure to its irreverent attitude towards history and Charles Laughton's boisterous performance as a bluff King Hal. For C. A. Lejeune of *The Observer*, *The Private Life of Henry VIII* "is the British prestige picture that we have been demanding for ten years back, not pedantic, not jingoistic, but as broadly and staunchly English as a baron of beef and a tankard of the best homebrew" (Lejeune, 1991: 89–90). However, these qualities did not please some commentators. The Earl of Cottenham was moved to protest that "a great king should be portrayed to the world as a vulgar buffoon … Henry VIII is held up to the world at large as a strutting mountebank, petulant, shallow, discourteous and of revolting habits" (*The Daily Telegraph*, 1933). Hence the film threw into sharp relief differences between popular history (Henry VIII as a glutton and a tyrant) and academic history (Henry as a refined and learned king). In 1998, *Elizabeth* also provoked controversy for its suggestion that the 'virgin queen' was in fact nothing of the sort and had enjoyed a passionate affair with Robert Dudley. This prompted an indignant editorial in the *Daily Telegraph*: "To question Elizabeth's virtue some 400 years after her death is not just a blackguardly slur upon a good, Christian woman, but an insult to our fathers who fought for her. It should rouse England to chivalrous anger" (*The Daily Telegraph*, 1998). It will be clear that what was at stake here was not so much the film's historical authenticity – whether Elizabeth and Dudley were lovers is impossible to say with any certainty – but rather that its challenge to the conventional historical view of Elizabeth as the 'virgin queen' was seen as overly sensational and in poor taste.

Critics and the politics of heritage cinema

In the 1980s and 1990s historical film discourses took a more politically charged turn with the emergence of a debate over what came to be called 'heritage' cinema. The original focus of this debate were the films of the director Ismail Merchant and the producer James Ivory, especially their cycle of adaptations of E. M. Forster – *A Room With A View* (1986), *Maurice* (1987) and *Howards End* (1992) – though the term has been extended to include adaptations by other film-makers, such as David Lean's *A Passage to India* (1984), and historical films based on original screenplays, such as *Chariots of Fire* (1981). The terms 'heritage film' and 'heritage cinema' are critical labels that do not have any currency in the film industry itself. They are used to describe films set in either a historical or a fictional past that are generally characterized by their literate scripts, slow pacing and highly pictorialist cinematography. Most of the films in the heritage cycle are set in the Victorian, Edwardian or inter-war periods, many of them are literary adaptations (especially of E. M. Forster) and in all instances the focus of interest is with the upper classes. In fact slow-paced, pictorialist costume films have long been a feature of British cinema – examples prior to the heritage cycle include *Far from the Madding Crowd* (1967), *The Go-Between* (1971) and *Barry Lyndon* (1975) – but the heritage label acquired a certain intellectual currency in the 1980s due to the foundation of English Heritage in 1983 and the emergence of the so-called 'heritage industry'.

Partly because it is a critical term rather than an industry category, heritage cinema has been fiercely contested. On one level, the heritage debate is an argument over 'good' and 'bad' cinema. Andy Medhurst, for example, describes *A Room With A View* as "a film-for-people-who-hate-cinema" (Medhurst, 1995: 17) and argues that "the careful period authenticity, sugary tourist-board visuals and just-right outfits act as guarantees of quality, material substance designed to hide the slightness of the narrative" (Medhurst, 1996: 29). Andrew Higson similarly felt that what he called the "museum aesthetic" of heritage cinema had the effect of detaching films from the social and political intentions of the source texts and therefore denied a more critical examination of the past: "The films, however, construct such a delightfully glossy visual surface that the ironic perspective and the narrative of social criticism diminish in their appeal for the spectator" (Higson, 1993: 120).

Against the argument that heritage cinema is aesthetically and culturally conservative, however, can be set the view of other critics who do see the films as offering a degree of social criticism. Sarah Street suggests that "much of the social critique to be found in Forster's novels *does* surface in the films" (Street, 1997: 104) and cites the plight of outsiders including homosexual men (*Maurice*) and those denied social mobility (*Howards End*). And in *The Remains of the Day* (1993), based on the novel by Kazuo Ishiguro, the butler Stevens' unquestioning loyalty to Lord Darlington is linked with aristocratic support for Fascism in the 1930s. Jeffrey Richards is even more stridently of the view that, far from being conservative, heritage films are "profoundly subversive" as they "provide a continuing and comprehensive critique of the ethic of restraint, repression and the stiff upper lip, of the surrender of personal happiness to higher notions of duty and self-sacrifice" (Richards, 1997: 169).

Ultimately the heritage film debate can become overly reductive: these films cannot be reduced to a simplistic conservative/subversive dichotomy. Like most film cycles there are examples that fit more readily into one category than another, while other films are open to readings as both conservative and progressive texts. *Chariots of Fire*, for example, has been understood as both a pro-Thatcherite and an anti-Thatcherite film. On the one hand, for the Right, *Chariots of Fire* is a celebration of national greatness expressed through the metaphor of sporting achievement, while on the other hand, for the Left, it is a narrative of struggle against social injustice, focusing on outsiders (a Presbyterian Scot and a Jew) who defy the establishment. *Chariots of Fire* also demonstrates how contextual factors may influence the political meaning of a film. Both the director (Hugh Hudson) and the writer (Colin Welland) were supporters of the Labour Party, but this did not prevent it from being subsumed within the patriotic rhetoric of the Falklands War in 1982 following Welland's declaration (upon accepting his Academy Award in Hollywood) that "the British are coming" (Chapman, 2005: 286–87).

Alternative and marginalized histories

A charge sometimes levelled against British historical film is that it focuses on dominant groups (the English, men, the upper classes) at the expense of marginalized groups. While there have been films dramatizing the historical experiences of, say, seventeenth-century radicals (*Winstanley*, 1975) or working-class Liverpudlians in the

Spanish Civil War (*Land and Freedom*, 1995), these remain rare examples in a genre more heavily populated by Tudor monarchs and Victorian statesmen. The autobiographical films of directors such as Bill Douglas (*My Ain Folk*, 1973) and Terence Davies (*Distant Voices, Still Lives*, 1988) can be seen as an attempt to represent history from the 'bottom up' rather than the 'top down'; their slow narration and modernist devices associate these films with the tradition of art cinema.

The US academic Robert Rosenstone has argued for an alternative form of historical representation on film that offers a more searching interrogation of the past. He advocates a style of film that "finds the space to *contest* history, to interrogate either the metanarratives that structure historical knowledge, or smaller historical truths, received notions, conventional images" (Rosenstone, 1995: 8). There are very few examples of British historical film that work in this way. Peter Watkins' television drama-documentary *Culloden* (1964), shot using non-professional actors and non-naturalistic devices such as interviews to camera by participants, exemplifies Rosenstone's model, in that it "provides a series of challenges to written history – it tests the boundaries of what we can say about the past and how we can say it, points to the limitations of conventional historical form, suggests new ways to envision the past, and alters our sense of what it is" (Rosenstone, 1995: 12). Perhaps the fullest example of an alternative form of historical film-making in Britain is *Winstanley* (1975). Directed by Kevin Brownlow and Andrew Mollo, *Winstanley* uses non-professional actors and adopts unconventional devices such as non-linear narrative that distance it from the more familiar type of historical film. This refreshingly original treatment met with approval from historian Christopher Hill, who felt it was authentic to the subject:

> Good historical films are sufficiently rare for it to be worth drawing attention to *Winstanley* ... Although made on a shoe-string budget, the film's detail is meticulously accurate, down to the shoes which the Diggers wear, the agricultural implements they use, the breed of animals they farm ... But more important than this convincing background is the imaginative reconstruction of the world in which the Diggers lived – still torn by social conflict, but one in which fundamental reform still seemed possible. This film can tell us more about ordinary people in seventeenth-century England than a score of textbooks.
>
> (Hill, 1975: 132)

It is rare for a professional historian to offer such a glowing testimonial to a historical film. Yet Hill also recognized that "*Winstanley* is never likely to be a commercial success" (ibid.). It remains the case that the most commercially successful historical films tend to be those that conform to an accepted popular narrative of British history that privileges well-known periods and people; obscure seventeenth-century radicals have rather less star appeal than Elizabeth I or Winston Churchill. This returns us to the point made at the beginning that historical film is essentially a vehicle of popular history rather than academic history. To this extent, historical film may be said to be locked in a self-perpetuating cycle with its source material. It draws upon popular history for its subject matter and in so doing perpetuates that same history.

Further reading

Jeffrey Richards' (1997) *Films and British National Identity: From Dickens to Dad's Army* is a wide-ranging, at times quite polemical, discussion of the representation of national identity including both historical and non-historical films. Sue Harper's (1994) *Picturing the Past: The Rise and Fall of the British Costume Film* is an exemplary historical study of genre focusing on the 1930s and 1940s and is particularly strong at mapping production cycles and analyzing the visual codes of films. James Chapman's (2005) *Past and Present: National Identity and the British Historical Film* is a series of case studies of historical films from the 1930s (*The Private Life of Henry VIII*) to the 1990s (*Elizabeth*). The heritage film cycle and associated critical debates are explored by Higson (2003) in *English Heritage, English Cinema: Costume Drama Since 1980*, which includes case studies of *Howards End* and *Elizabeth*. Finally Monk and Sargeant's (2002) edited collection *British Historical Cinema* is a wide-ranging collection of essays, including a good survey of the heritage film debate.

References

Aldgate, A. and Richards, J. (1986) *Britain Can Take It: British Cinema in the Second World War*. Oxford: Blackwell.
Anon (1933) "Alexander Korda and the international film." *Cinema Quarterly*, 2(1), 13–15.
Chapman, J. (1998) "Our finest hour revisited: The Second World War in British feature films since 1945." *Journal of Popular British Cinema*, 10(1), 63–75.
——(2005) *Past and Present: National Identity and the British Historical Film*. London: I. B. Tauris.
Cook, P. (1997) *Fashioning the Nation: Costume and Identity in British Cinema*. London: British Film Institute.
The Daily Telegraph (1933) "Henry VIII on the film: Vulgar buffoon or great king." *The Daily Telegraph*, 3 November, p. 12.
The Daily Telegraph (1998) "Elizabeth intacta." *The Daily Telegraph*, 9 March, p. 21.
Dickinson, M. and Street, S. (1985) *Cinema and State: The Film Industry and the British Government, 1927–84*. London: British Film Institute.
Ellis, J. (1996) "The quality film adventure: British critics and the cinema, 1942–48." In A. Higson (ed.) *Dissolving Views: Key Writings on British Cinema*. London: Cassell (pp. 66–93).
Glancy, H. M. (1999) *When Hollywood Loved Britain: The Hollywood 'British' Film, 1939–45*. Manchester: Manchester University Press.
Halliwell, L. (1985) *Seats in All Parts: Half a Lifetime at the Movies*. London: Granada.
Harper, S. (1994) *Picturing the Past: The Rise and Fall of the British Costume Film*. London: British Film Institute.
Higson, A. (1993) "Re-presenting the national past: Nostalgia and pastiche in the heritage film." In L. Friedman (ed.) *British Cinema and Thatcherism: Fires Were Started*. London: UCL Press (pp. 109–29).
——(1995) *Waving the Flag: Constructing a National Cinema in Britain*. Oxford: Clarendon Press.
——(2003) *English Heritage, English Cinema: Costume Drama Since 1980*. Oxford: Oxford University Press.
Hill, C. (1975) "Notes and Comments." *Past and Present*, 69(1), 132.
Klingender, F. D. (1937) "From Sarah Bernhardt to Flora Robson: The cinema pageant of history." *World Film News*, 1(12), 8–11.

Lejeune, A. (ed.) (1991) *The C. A. Lejeune Film Reader*. Manchester: Carcanet.
Lovell, A. (1972) "The unknown cinema of Britain." *Cinema Journal*, 9(2), 1–8.
The Manchester Guardian (1946) "Picture theatres." *The Manchester Guardian*, 1 January, p. 3.
Medhurst, A. (1995) "Inside the British wardrobe." *Sight and Sound, New Series*, 5(3), 16–17.
——(1996) "Dressing the part." *Sight and Sound, New Series*, 6(6), 28–30.
Monk, C. and Sargeant, A. (eds.) (2002) *British Historical Cinema*. London: Routledge.
Petley, J. (1986) "The lost continent." In C. Barr (ed.) *All Our Yesterdays: 90 Years of British Cinema*. London: British Film Institute (pp. 98–119).
Richards, J. (1997) *Films and British National Identity: From Dickens to Dad's Army*. Manchester: Manchester University Press.
Rosenstone, R. (1995) "Introduction." In R. A. Rosenstone (ed.) *Revisioning History: Film and the Construction of a New Past*. Princeton: Princeton University Press (pp. 3–14).
Rotha, P. and Griffith, R. (1949) *The Film Till Now: A Survey of World Cinema*. London: Spring Books.
Street, S. (1997) *British National Cinema*. London: Routledge.
——(2002) *Transatlantic Crossings: British Feature Films in the USA*. London: Continuum.

35
'The Horror!'
Matt Hills

Writing about horror films in the context of British media history brings with it a number of perils. First, there is the question of how national identity can relate to genre fiction.

What counts as Brit horror?

Is 'British' horror that which is produced in Britain? Could the term also refer to texts linked to British auteurs but funded with Hollywood money or made outside the UK? Might it also refer to British cultural contexts within which foreign horror is consumed? Perhaps 'British horror' is all of these things: production-oriented; authorship-oriented and culture/context-oriented. As Peter Hutchings has remarked:

> films thought of as ... unproblematically American can be shown to have had a significant British input in terms of the creative personnel who fashioned them ... [e.g.] the 1935 Universal horror film *The Bride of Frankenstein*. While an important component of a British national cinema must be its propensity to address specifically national issues and concerns, account also needs to be taken of films like *The Haunting* ... which testify to the importance of American-financed production in Britain throughout the 1960s.
> (Hutchings, 1993:15)

Even as the referent 'British horror' threatens to multiply, however, so too might 'Britishness' itself fragment into English, Scottish, Welsh and Irish identities, remaining far from unified. Although there have been influential studies of British horror: *Hammer and Beyond: The British Horror Film* (Hutchings, 1993), *Beyond Hammer: British Horror Cinema Since 1970* (Rose, 2009) and *British Horror Cinema* (Chibnall and Petley, 2002), other authors have focused on 'English Gothic Cinema' (Pirie, 2008) and *English Gothic* (Rigby, 2000). Meanwhile, 'Celtic' horror has been explored (Jones, 2002; Blandford, 2007), along with distinctively Scottish versions of the genre (Martin-Jones, 2010).

And there is also a further issue: that of historical narrative. How can 'British horror' be narrated across a number of historical phases?

What is the story of British horror?

Mark Jancovich has noted this particular difficulty:

> One of the main problems with most histories of horror is ... that they are 'narrative histories', and narratives need not only an end but also a central protagonist. In other words, narratives usually end either in a sense of perfect fulfillment ... or in destruction and failure.
>
> (Jancovich, 2002: 9)

Perhaps the most common narrative of British horror involves focusing on the success of Hammer Productions in the 1950s and 1960s (Hutchings, 1993), marking out these decades as a golden age before viewing the 1970s as a tragic decline into 'failure', with British productions eventually being eclipsed by the US slasher movie. The rise of multiplex-friendly horror franchises displaced British horror, since British efforts, usually lower-budget titles rather than commercially viable franchises, were unable to compete with Hollywood's newfound dominance of horror from the 1970s onwards, other than in isolated cases, for example the successes of *Hellraiser*, *28 Days Later* and *Shaun of the Dead* (Rose, 2009). As Jancovich observes:

> the focus on ... classic films tends to repress the diversity within periods, and it is for this reason that most histories tend to focus on one particular national context. They simply cannot create a clear narrative line [otherwise].
>
> (Jancovich, 2002: 9)

Hammer's decline and the rarer emergence of post-70s British horror 'classics' certainly sustains a 'narrative line', but other meaning-making strategies have also significantly shaped histories of British horror. Rather than positioning the 50s and 60s as a peak of industrial invention via the likes of Hammer and Amicus, followed by a creative trough, alternative accounts have stressed cultural contexts more than film productions, resulting in an altered but no less clear 'narrative line'. The 'Video Nasties' debacle of the 1980s tends to dominate context-oriented accounts, whilst auteur-fixated stories of British horror have clustered around key creatives, whether working in Hollywood or not, such as James Whale, Alfred Hitchcock, Terence Fisher, Stanley Kubrick, Ridley Scott, Clive Barker, Neil Jordan, Julian Richards, Danny Boyle and Neil Marshall. In this chapter I will utilize narrative history while also being mindful of Jancovich's (2002) concerns about narrative histories leading to overly simplistic and limited accounts of 'British' horror where following such a 'clear narrative line' may suppress diversity and complexity.

What is the affect of British horror?

It is often assumed that the primary *raison d'etre* of horror is quite simply to scare spectators. And yet the horror genre typically generates a far wider range of affects, including a sense of belonging to dedicated (fan) audience communities. As such, connections between horror and nationhood may run deeper than "national issues and concerns" (Hutchings, 1993: 15), with both horror and nationhood being characterized by versions of "imagined community" (Anderson, 2006: 35). In *Film/Genre*, Rick Altman terms genre-based groupings "*constellated communities*"; like Benedict Anderson's imagined communities occurring at a national level, they too "cohere only through repeated acts of imagination" (Altman, 1999: 161). Where the nation is (re)composed out of "mass ceremony: the almost precisely simultaneous consumption" of mass-mediated news (Anderson, 2006: 35), with individual newspaper readers imagining a mass of others reading the news at the same time as them, horror's constellated community also imagines fellow consumers engaging with texts at the same time (in the cinema or across a window of release) in a kind of niche ceremony. And just as the nation's imagined community is "visibly rooted in everyday life" (ibid.: 35–36) thanks to mass availability of the same newspaper, so too are constellated communities visibly rooted in horror's paratexts such as promotion, publicity, commercially available magazines, genre-focused news websites etc. On some occasions, British horror fans no longer need to imagine their fellows, since they can gather together at festivals such as London's FrightFest and Aberystwyth's Abertoir (Hills, 2010) or they can share their genre interests online (Cherry, 2010). However, British horror's audience community is typically imagined on the basis of fan materials and industry paratexts.

This makes fandom an affective microcosm, in a sense, of Anderson's national 'imagined community', though the two modes of community also diverge in important ways. National identities are enforced as well as imagined: they are subject to legal definitions of citizenship and governmentality, whereas horror's 'constellated community' is an elective affinity, less prone to practices of policing (though it can certainly be marked by fan constructions of authenticity). And whereas the national imagined community tends to be extensive, with its "banal nationalism" flagged in almost all areas of (popular) culture and everyday life (Billig, 1995), horror's constellated community remains subculturally contained in niche spaces and times of media consumption – though, again, it may be lived extensively by fans for whom a commitment to the genre results in everyday engagement.

Comparing horror's constellated community and Britain's imagined community also emphasizes the extent to which "[o]ld notions about identities ... self-evidently belonging to particular (national) cultures and societies seem to be repudiated by vast, expanding cultural networks" (Edensor, 2002: 27) such as online fandom. British horror fans can, for example, access movies which have been censored in the UK, denied a classification, or not given a commercial release, by knowing where to look online. When *The Human Centipede 2* was effectively banned (i.e. not given a classification) by the British Board of Film Classification (BBFC, 2011), fans were able to watch the film uncut, if they so wished, via online streaming. What Ramon Lobato terms "informal economies" of cinema proffer "circulatory networks [that] are largely subterranean, meaning that texts move through space and time with a lower level of interference from ... state censorship" (2012: 43). This circumvention of national state powers – a kind of piracy as 'resistance' and 'access' (Lobato, 2012: 80, 82) – may appear to suggest "that national identity is a waning force" (Edensor, 2002: 28) and that fandom's constellated community can, under certain circumstances, come into tension with, and even supplant, the affects of nationality's imagined community.

Posing the two as a binary is a simplification, however. As Tim Edensor comments in *National Identity, Popular Culture and Everyday Life*, "the apparent fluidity of identity and the lack of spatial and cultural fixity can provide a discursive and affective focus for reclaiming a sense of situatedness" (2002: 28). British horror audiences can simultaneously negotiate (or evade) the structural impositions of national censorship and commerce – consuming horror transnationally – as well as drawing on notions of Britishness which ground "identity in shared, unreflexive feelings" (Edensor, 2002: 28), perhaps even patriotically celebrating the cultural relevance of British horror. Constellated community is hence not only a microcosm of imagined community; the two can also intertwine through the reflexive disruption of national identities as well as the (un)reflexive celebration of national cinema as a kind of 'underdog' compared to Hollywood's bigger-budget franchises. What Elke Weissmann posits in a different but related context (the TV drama industry) is thus seemingly just as accurate for British horror today: audiences interact with "the fantasy of a national system … in an industrial context which has become distinctly transnational" (2012: 185) as a result of the cultural mobility of creatives, the flow of global capital (often prompted by specific tax breaks for film production) and the interconnectedness of cultural contexts and anxieties via 24/7 news media. Although Peter Hutchings argues that British horror may refract "national issues and concerns" (1993: 15), key strata of cultural contexts are arguably now meaningfully transnational rather than national *per se*. Contemporary economic recession is not a characteristically 'British' (or Scottish, Welsh, Irish, English) issue, even if the precise economics of this have played out somewhat differently in different national frames. Equally, fears surrounding post-9/11 terrorism or Islamic religious fundamentalism (which have been allegorically tackled in horror texts) are not restricted to national levels of meaning.

But if 'British' horror is now a questionable category, due both to globalizing tendencies and to the rise of devolution and alternative national identities within the UK (Blandford, 2007), the same may not have been true for horror's emergence as a genre in the eighteenth century (Carroll, 1990). As Darryl Jones has suggested:

> Modern Britain was conceived in horror. The development of the Gothic novel, and thus of modern horror fiction, in English, in the second half of the eighteenth century, coincides with (is both a component and a by-product of) the period of the formation of a British national identity.
> (Jones, 2002: 8)

Jones strongly distinguishes between contemporary and historical constructions of 'Britishness'. In the latter case, he argues that literary gothic horror was historically articulated with a dominant Protestantism and set against the "Celtic gothic" of otherness and counter-Enlightenment (Jones, 2002: 18). Whilst discussing 'British horror' therefore makes sense, for Jones, in relation to eighteenth-century literature such as Matthew Lewis's *The Monk* (1796), it has an uneasy place in contemporary analysis:

> I have … serious problems with any notion of a contemporary 'British' identity, as I take it as an imperializing synonym for 'Englishness', and as

expressive of an imposed unity which no longer obtains and has become damaging. However, as the ... historian Linda Colley has argued, it is entirely proper to describe the process of forming a national identity across the eighteenth century as 'British': "we can plausibly regard Great Britain as an invented nation superimposed, if only for a while, onto much older alignments and loyalties".

(Jones, 2002: 47 n. 1)

Indeed, it can be argued that scholarship has accorded with Jones's concern and there has been a shift away from analyzing 'British horror' (Hutchings, 1993) to instead thinking about English traditions as well as explicitly nominating Scottish, Welsh and Irish contributions.

English horror and the golden age of Hammer

An awkward slippage between 'British' and 'English' sometimes remains present in horror scholarship. For example, the updated edition of David Pirie's (2008) *A New Heritage of Horror: The English Gothic Cinema* comes emblazoned with a quote from Martin Scorsese, applauding this book as "The best study of British horror movies". The book's back cover blurb continues to paratextually veer between "British horror" and "UK culture", despite Pirie's impressive focus on English horror. In fact, Pirie's work offers a clear narrative history of English traditions, even positing a filmic point of origin:

> Between 1942 and 1945 the British Board of Film Censors [as it was then known] and the COI (Central Office of Information) actually banned the import into Britain of all 'H' certificate films (as horror films were then designated). Eventually, in 1945, the ban was lifted and that year saw the making of Ealing Studios' *Dead of Night*, which deserves its reputation as the most important English supernatural thriller prior to the late 1950s.

(Pirie, 2008: 16)

Jonathan Rigby's (2000) *English Gothic* also accords a key place to *Dead of Night*, but places it amongst a far wider range of films, including James Whale's *The Old Dark House* from 1932, all characterized as "British Horror in Embryo" (ibid.: 8–35). It may seem surprising today that horrifying films were given their own censorship category ('H') prior to the 1950s and furthermore that it was only in the mid 40s that a now-celebrated English horror film lineage began to emerge. *Dead of Night* was a portmanteau film, made up of a series of different segments rather than a single storyline; this structure enabled it to build to multiple narrative payoffs, as well as offering a cleverly self-referential conclusion. Portmanteau horror has been a recurrent device of English horror, used by Amicus Productions in the 1960s and 70s in films such as *Dr Terror's House of Horrors* (1964), *Torture Garden* (1967), *The House That Dripped Blood* (1970), *Asylum* (1972), *Tales from the Crypt* (1972), *From Beyond the Grave* (1973), *Tales that Witness Madness* (1973) and *Vault of Horror* (1973). This "recognizable type" of national horror (Hutchings, 1993: 132) has also been nostalgically recreated in *The League of Gentlemen*'s (2000) Christmas Special (Hunt, 2008: 76–77) and Mark Gatiss's TV horror *Crooked House* from Christmas 2008 (Jowett and Abbott, 2013: 43).

David Pirie's narrative history of English horror moves from beginning to middle to end, and the middle phase is dominated by Hammer Films. Likewise, Rigby demarcates 1954 as the beginning of the 'First Flood' in *English Gothic*, with both critics stressing the place of Hammer's breakthrough monster film, *The Quatermass Xperiment*, which went into production in 1954 and was released the following year. Similarly contributing to this consensus in British media history, Peter Hutchings' first 'timeline' chapter in *Hammer and Beyond* ranges between "1945–55: from *Dead of Night* to *The Quatermass Experiment*" (1993: 24–53).

The 'H' certificate was replaced in 1951 by the infamous X-rating and Hammer altered the titular spelling of *Experiment* to *Xperiment* in order to highlight that the film was an 'X' title. *The Quatermass Xperiment* also benefitted from the fact that it was an adaptation of the hugely popular Quatermass TV serials, and the combination of alluring, edgy content and a pre-sold property produced a sudden, massively popular hit for the company. 'British horror' was revolutionized by Hammer's emergence as a cultural and economic force (it even received the Queen's Award to Industry in 1968), and Hammer's place in media history books was cemented by *The Curse of Frankenstein* in 1957 and *Dracula* in 1958, both directed by Terence Fisher and both beginning long engagements with these pop-cultural, gothic figures.

The Curse of Frankenstein also marked Hammer's move into color horror movies (Hammer would eventually become famed for the 'Kensington gore' shade of its theatrical blood). The film outraged a number of press reviewers at the time; one suggested that "a new certificate 'SO' – Sadists Only" was called for (Pirie, 2008: 35; Hutchings, 1993: 6). Hammer's breakthrough films offered an unusual combination of X-rated, critically disreputable status along with historical period-drama settings and the use of familiar literary-gothic figures. Despite the fulminating of certain reviewers, there was perhaps a curious air of respectability to the transgressions of Frankenstein and Dracula. David Pirie argues that it was "the eruption of the English horror movie into the middle-class cinema of the ... 1950s [that] was so ... disturbing" (2008: 224), and Hammer's 'heritage' trappings can certainly be read as a relatively safe cultural container for representations of violence and sexuality. Indeed, it was when Hammer began focusing centrally on contemporary settings – and competing with the more graphic imagery of 1970s American horror – that it began to lose a sense of its own established brand and identity.

Narrative histories of horror typically align Hammer with a golden age of commercially successful, vibrant British film production, discussing the company's 'Final Days' and the search for a 'New Horror Mythology' (Pirie, 2008: 185, 192) in its wake. Rigby's *English Gothic* ends its Part Five with Hammer's final horror film, *To The Devil A Daughter* (1975), before entitling Part Six 'British Horror in Retreat' (2000: 226–28). The later 1970s and 1980s tend, therefore, to be interpreted in the shadow of Hammer's rise and fall, with this event acting as the major narrative pivot. The focus on Hammer, while commemorating a great 'British' triumph of the 50s and 60s, tends to edge out scholarly appreciation of more diverse strains of 'British' horror. For example, the British production *Night of the Demon* was released in 1957, between *The Curse of Frankenstein* and *Dracula*, drawing on the writings of M. R. James and representing a different English tradition, the chilling ghost story, when compared to Hammer's output (Rigby, 2011: 92). Likewise, although Peter Hutchings sets out some useful analysis of Amicus Productions, "Britain's number two horror production company" of the 1960s and 70s (1993: 132), this is again very much defined against Hammer. Ironically, it is Hammer itself which now exists in its own historical shadow. The company was brought back to life in 2008 via the MySpace-partnered web serial *Beyond the Rave*, directed by Matthias Hoene, who would later go on to direct horror-comedy *Cockneys vs Zombies* (2012). 'New' Hammer's most commercially successful title to date has been *The Woman in Black* (2012), starring Daniel Radcliffe and adapting Susan Hill's 1983 novel, but the resurrected company operates in a very different media context to its predecessor. Blogging, tweeting, publishing Hammer novels and releasing Hammer audio 'chillers' as well as making films, this incarnation confronts "convergence culture" where branded content can move across platforms and circulate as "transmedia storytelling" (Jenkins, 2006). Hammer was once an important film producer, but it is now called upon to act primarily as a brand, leveraging its back catalog for nostalgic fans through blu-ray/digital restorations whilst seeking to reach new youth audiences via experiments such as the web serial.

Exploring Welsh, Scottish and Irish horror

If Hammer has hogged the narrative limelight of British horror history, then conflating 'English' and 'British' horror has also tended to marginalize Welsh, Scottish and Irish identities, again creating a clear narrative line by repressing diversity. Some scholars have begun to address this difficulty. Darryl Jones (2002) considers how films as different as *The Old Dark House* (1932) and *The Wicker Man* (1973) represent distorted, fantastical geographies – crossing from England into Wales and traveling from the mainland to Lord Summerisle's island "off the west coast of Scotland", respectively, both lead to diegetic spaces of otherness. As Jones puts it: "their location doesn't exist at all in any normal cartographic sense" (2002: 28), but each case aligns not with a distant, exoticized foreign land such as *Dracula*'s Transylvania, but rather with a 'Celtic gothic' defining England ('Shrewsbury' in particular in *The Old Dark House*) as a site of dull normality.

This concept of the rural, uncivilized, even pagan periphery set against England-as-norm has been reiterated across the history of 'British' horror, almost acting as an analogue to US traditions of 'redneck' or 'hillbilly horror'. For instance, soon after its 2008 resurrection Hammer worked on *Wake Wood* (2011), an Anglo-Irish production partnered with Fantastic Films, set in a small (fictional) Irish town lending the film its title. *Wake Wood* was intertextually indebted to *The Wicker Man*, riffing on the concept of pagan rites used by the town's community and shielded from outsiders. The same production company, Fantastic Films, also worked on the Anglo-Irish horror film *Outcast* (2010) which featured Irish characters living on an Edinburgh housing estate and combined social realism with lycanthropic horror in a metaphorical examination of what it can mean to be an 'outcast' (Rigby, 2011: 288–89).

This blend of social realism and horror has often been a feature of micro-budget Celtic gothic, as for example in *Urban Ghost Story* (1998). Similarly observing a collision between realism and monstrosity in an overview article tackling 'Irish Horror Cinema', the noted genre film critic Kim Newman champions writer-director Billy O'Brien's *Isolation* (2006) for addressing "the economic plight of traditional farm folk left behind by the 'Celtic Tiger' boom" (Newman, 2006). At the same time, *Isolation*'s finale is marked by a "high quality monster runabout":

> In grimly realistic, Irish rural mode, farmer Dan (John Lynch) is clearly close to cracking up and troubled by the difficulty his pregnant cows are having in coming to term … The film offers a long, atmospheric build-up, full of pregnant pauses, withheld explanations and desperate characters who never quite explain their awful situations … O'Brien follows examples like … *Wild Country* (2005), telling a familiar story in an unusual manner.
> (Newman, 2006)

The other film name-checked here by Newman, *Wild Country*, has also been subjected to detailed analysis, this time in David Martin-Jones' (2010) *Scotland: Global Cinema*. Although horror using Celtic settings such as a County Wicklow farm in Ireland or the Scottish Highlands can be made on a low budget (there's less need to build expensive sets), aestheticized images of rugged landscapes and peripheral, rural environments can also travel through the globalized marketplace as markers of difference, and as somewhat exoticized locales. Accordingly, Martin-Jones ponders whether twenty-first-century Scottish horror movies such as *Dog Soldiers* (2002) and *Wild Country* represent a kind of "Tartanry", with a touristic image of Scotland represented via the Highlands (Martin-Jones, 2010: 116). Contrasting this style of civilized meaning-making ('Dr. Jekyll') which caters for "an English-led Britain" with the monstrous, repressed energies of an autonomous and primal Scotland ('Mr Hyde'), Martin-Jones argues that Celtic horror might oscillate between these two poles (ibid.: 115). This possibility – with liberated Scottish national energies being figured via the werewolves of *Dog Soldiers* and *Wild Country*, suggests that the "horror film … is a very capable medium for allegorically engaging with the resurgence of national independence in the Celtic peripheries around the time of devolution" (ibid.: 128). Indeed, Welsh nationalism has also been fantastically coded in Julian Richards' (1997) *Darklands* (Blandford, 2007: 95–96). Although it may be tempting, in terms of British media history, to read such nineties and noughties horror films as the 'return of the (nationally) repressed', speaking back to England-as-Britain, such a narrative line is overly 'clear' and tidy. British horror is often far more multivalent: Martin-Jones' (2010) playful notion of Jekyll-and-Hyde doppelgangers may be closer to the genre's ideological ambivalence.

The unifying force of a moral panic?

However, at certain moments in its history, British horror has thoroughly deserved the label 'British' and has been powerfully unified in its cultural meanings. One such occasion was the Video Nasties moral panic of the 1980s, which led to a change in UK law (1984's Video Recordings Act or VRA) and the popular categorization of highly disparate horror titles, released on videocassette, as 'nasties'. As Kate Egan has noted:

> video nasties is not a universally or internationally recognized film term – it is used, primarily in Britain, to refer to a set of British cultural circumstances, and, in the sense that Hollywood studios and film-makers never consciously made video nasties, the category isn't an industrial term that informs ... film production.
>
> (2012: 3)

Instead, the so-called 'nasties' were nominated and identified via cultural sites such as Britain's tabloid press, especially the *Daily Mail*, which ran a moralizing campaign to "ban the sadist videos" (Egan, 2012: 80), and legal-governmental agencies such as the Department of Public Prosecution (DPP), which compiled a shifting list of video titles felt to be prosecutable under the 1959 Obscene Publications Act. The video nasties were paradigmatically British as a result of the legal, state and discursive powers which defined them in the UK context. The films themselves were a curious mixture, including *Cannibal Holocaust* (1980), *Driller Killer* (1979), *Tenebrae* (1982) and *Zombie Flesh Eaters* (1979) among many others: these weren't British films, but they were made meaningful within British culture, especially by press and state intervention.

As a new medium in the UK, video was unregulated in the early 1980s and the conservative Thatcherite government of the day was very much dedicated to voluntary industry codes of conduct and the free run of the market. Into this context stepped a potent combination of moral campaigners such as Mary Whitehouse along with the *Daily Mail*'s crusading journalists. Films such as *The Evil Dead* (1981) were drawn into the video nasties controversy despite efforts to market Sam Raimi's work in relation to "the art of special effects, and the film's dark humor", thereby attempting to reassure concerned parties that the film was a fantasy rather than anything more sinister (Egan, 2011: 26). Media and cultural studies scholars such as Martin Barker and Julian Petley sought to challenge the illogicality of the 'nasties' campaign, in particular its crude investment in 'media effects' – ostensibly aimed at protecting vulnerable child audiences – and the sometimes almost absurd lack of knowledge among campaigners regarding the film texts being demonized (Barker and Petley, 2001). But perhaps the greatest irony of the 'nasties' moral panic was that it unfolded as a newspaper 'horror story', constructing unquestionable evil (the nasties) along with innocent victims who had to be morally protected (Egan, 2012: 95).

After press coverage, police seizures of suspect videos and multiple prosecutions, the government eventually felt that it had to respond with a new regulatory framework, and the Video Recordings Act 1984 was the outcome. This gave the BBFC new powers to classify film titles specifically for home video release and resulted in a British situation where celebrated horror films such as the oeuvre of Italian auteur Dario Argento were unavailable or restricted to cut editions. Describing the VRA as a "draconian censorship regime", Peter Hutchings points out that it has given many horror films a cult cachet, with collectors in the pre-internet era acquiring "samizdat third- or fourth-generation copies" from fellow fans (2003: 130–31). There is thus a further irony in the media history of British horror. By seeking to strictly censor and regulate the genre, UK authorities have given horror's constelled community a rallying point for their own oppositional identity, and hence an energizing support for the cult status of 'underground' fandom (Hills, 2005: 98–106).

The media history of British horror is a vast topic, and one that I've barely scratched here. I have, though, followed Jancovich (2002) by suggesting that it is important to be wary of narrative histories of horror, given that they often suppress complexity in favor of shaping clear narrative lines (of triumph and decline; of 'classic' texts and controversies). And I have argued for the need to think carefully about the cultural politics of British identity. 'British' horror has often seemed to mean 'English' horror, and it is only by paying closer attention to 'Celtic gothic' that we can discern other modes of horror, as well as a history which perhaps allegorically codes developments surrounding devolution. Above all, though, horror is marked by its own constelled communities of genre fandom, akin to the imagined community of the nation itself. It isn't just that some horror is felt to be British (by production, auteur or cultural context): horror inspires affective attachments and 'banal' belongings (Billig, 1995) that are intriguingly similar to, and different from, those of national identity.

Further reading

Noel Carroll's (1990) *The Philosophy of Horror* still gives one of the clearest introductions to how the horror genre in general might be defined and theorized, whilst Steve Chibnall and Julian Petley's (2002) edited collection *British Horror Cinema* zeroes in on the relevant national context. Given the prominence of Hammer in histories of Brit horror, Peter Hutchings' (1993) *Hammer and Beyond: The British Horror Film* is also indispensable. Both David Pirie (2008) in *A New Heritage of Horror* and Jonathan Rigby (2000) in *English Gothic* specifically focus on English horror, illustrating how Scottish, Welsh and Irish components also need to be considered.

References

Altman, R. (1999) *Film/Genre*. London: BFI.
Anderson, B. (2006) *Imagined Communities* (revised edition). London and New York: Verso.
Barker, M. and Petley, J. (eds.) (2001) *Ill Effects: The Media/Violence Debate* (Second Edition). London and New York: Routledge.
BBFC (2011) *The Human Centipede 2 (Full Sequence)*. Retrieved from http://www.bbfc.co.uk/releases/human-centipede-2-full-sequence
Billig, M. (1995) *Banal Nationalism*. London: Sage.
Blandford, S. (2007) *Film, Drama and the Break-Up of Britain*. Bristol: Intellect Books.
Carroll, N. (1990) *The Philosophy of Horror*. New York and London: Routledge.
Cherry, B. (2010) "Stalking the web: Celebration, chat and horror film marketing on the internet." In I. Conrich (ed.) *Horror Zone*. London and New York: I. B. Tauris (pp. 67–85).

Chibnall, S. and Petley, J. (eds.) (2002) *British Horror Cinema*. London and New York: Routledge.

Edensor, T. (2002) *National Identity, Popular Culture and Everyday Life*. Oxford and New York: Berg.

Egan, K. (2011) *Cultographies: The Evil Dead*. New York and London: Wallflower Press/Columbia University Press.

——(2012) *Trash or Treasure? Censorship and the Changing Meanings of the Video Nasties*. Manchester: Manchester University Press.

Hills, M. (2005) *The Pleasures of Horror*. London and New York: Continuum.

——(2010) "Attending horror film festivals and conventions: Liveness, subcultural capital and 'flesh-and-blood genre communities'." In I. Conrich (ed.) *Horror Zone*. London and New York: I. B. Tauris (pp. 87–101).

Hunt, L. (2008) *BFI TV Classics: The League of Gentlemen*. London: BFI Publishing.

Hutchings, P. (1993) *Hammer and Beyond: The British Horror Film*. Manchester and New York: Manchester University Press.

——(2003) "The Argento effect." In M. Jancovich, A. Lazaro Reboll, J. Stringer and A. Willis (eds.) *Defining Cult Movies*. Manchester and New York: Manchester University Press (pp. 127–41).

Jancovich, M. (2002) "General Introduction." In M. Jancovich (ed.) *Horror, The Film Reader*. London and New York: Routledge (pp. 1–19).

Jenkins, H. (2006) *Convergence Culture: Where Old and New Media Collide*. New York and London: New York University Press.

Jones, D. (2002) *Horror: A Thematic History in Fiction and Film*. London: Arnold.

Jowett, L. and Abbott, S. (2013) *TV Horror*. London and New York: I.B. Tauris.

Lobato, R. (2012) *Shadow Economies of Cinema*. London: BFI/Palgrave Macmillan.

Martin-Jones, D. (2010) *Scotland: Global Cinema – Genres, Modes and Identities*. Edinburgh: Edinburgh University Press.

Newman, K. (2006) "Irish horror cinema." *The Irish Journal of Gothic and Horror Studies*, 1. Retrieved from http://irishgothichorrorjournal.homestead.com/kim.html

Pirie, D. (2008) *A New Heritage of Horror: The English Gothic Cinema*. London and New York: I. B. Tauris.

Rigby, J. (2000) *English Gothic: A Century of Horror Cinema*. London: Reynolds and Hearn.

——(2011) *Studies in Terror: Landmarks of Horror Cinema*. London: Signum Books.

Rose, J. (2009) *Beyond Hammer: British Horror Cinema Since 1970*. Leighton: Auteur Press.

Weissmann, E. (2012) *Transnational Television Drama*. Basingstoke: Palgrave Macmillan.

36
The documentary tradition
Peter Lee-Wright

'Documentary' is a term used prolifically without much agreement on its meaning. The film historian Bill Nichols called it "a fuzzy concept" (Nichols, 2010: 21). It means different things to different people, fulfilling different functions at different times. The English filmmaker John Grierson coined the term in a review of the Canadian Robert Flaherty's film about the natives of Samoa, *Moana* (1926), and went on to define it as the "creative treatment of actuality" in an article in *Cinema Quarterly* (Grierson, 1933: 8). The definition remains unimproved upon, though the debate continues on how much license should be extended to the 'creative' aspect, and what constitutes 'actuality'. Significantly, Flaherty directed his subjects, for example the Inuit in *Nanook of the North* (1922) and Irish fishermen in *Man of Aran* (1934), to do things for the camera that they would not do in everyday life. Nanook was forced to hunt with the harpoon he had long since replaced with a rifle; the fishermen were made to put to sea in the face of a coming storm they would never have braved had Flaherty not insisted. In *Moana* he made the Samoan women wear grass skirts.

Yet the British Association of Film and Television Arts (BAFTA) Best Documentary award from 1959 to 79 was called the Robert Flaherty Award, during a period in which the increasingly purist ideas of *cinéma vérité* (literally 'film truth') came to hold sway. Some documentarists argued that it was now possible to film situations without impacting upon them. In the 1920s Flaherty had had to build a giant, open-sided igloo to admit his cumbersome 35mm cameras and the lights he needed to film. The uptake of lighter, 16mm cameras and faster film stock during the 1960s made it progressively possible to film in most situations without the need to rearrange reality. This led to an explosion of observational filmmaking, from the 70 ethnographic films made in Africa by the legendary French documentarist Jean Rouch, to so-called Direct Cinema in the United States, with films such as Robert Drew's seminal *Primary* (1960), a documentary on the American presidential primary, and his follow-up *Crisis: Behind a Presidential Commitment* (1963). Among Drew's crew were Albert Maysles and D. A. Pennebaker, who went on to define the rock documentary, Maysles (with his brother David) making *What's Happening! The Beatles In The U.S.A.* (1963) and the Rolling Stones tour film *Gimme Shelter* (1970), and Pennebaker with his Bob Dylan film *Don't Look Back* (1967) and *Monterey Pop* (1968). Meanwhile, Frederick Wiseman was commencing his monumental series of films about American institutions with his harrowing record of a hospital for the criminally insane in *Titicut Follies* (1967), shot on black-and-white film and using only the actuality of diegetic sound.

In that one decade, the role of documentary film had grown to become an inevitable accompaniment to public life, whether in politics or popular entertainment. Where the Hollywood feature had traditionally offered audiences a mode of escape, with reality only intruding in the accompanying newsreels, documentary features melded the two genres to give people insights into their society and its organization, as well as a privileged seat at the events they missed, such as *Woodstock* (1970). It was as if reality had become provisional unless endorsed by the filmic record. The equally rapidly developing school of media studies seized upon this perceptual transformation. In Canada, Marshall McLuhan wrote presciently of "the global village" and coined his famous aphorism "the medium is the message" (McLuhan, 1964: 8). In France, Guy-Ernest Debord wrote *La Sociéte du Spectacle/The Society of the Spectacle* (1967), appropriating the title from the work of his contemporary, Roland Barthes, and decrying the corrupting effect of "a social relation between people that is mediated by images ... Everything that was directly lived has moved away into a representation" (Debord, 1967: 1). Debord co-founded the Situationist International, influential in the Sorbonne-led Paris Uprising of 1968, which helped precipitate an international student revolt against the increasing commodification of Western society and its uncritical promotion through the media.

Those 'soixante-huitards' ('68ers) were much exercised by the notion of destroying the dehumanizing spectacle, throwing a brick through the metaphorical screen. In an ironic appropriation of that image, Ridley Scott's Superbowl ad for the 1984 launch of Apple's Mac computer pictured an Orwellian dictatorship where Big Brother's screened speech is interrupted by a dissident blonde athlete lobbing a hammer through the screen. Apple saw itself as David talking on the Goliath of IBM. Such is the self-cannibalizing nature of the screen industry, with images constantly purloined and perverted to other purposes. The opening sequence of *Don't Look Back* (1967), with Dylan casually discarding the lyric cue cards over *Subterranean Homesick Blues*, is credited with being a prototype of the music video. Music now cannot be sold without the endorsing power of the video. The medium remains the message; we are now surrounded by screen images, but documentary remains a plastic term.

Documentary 'truth'

Since its inception, documentary has had a contested relationship with the truth, as well as predating fictional features. The first film made for public projection was a 46-second documentary short, the Lumière Brothers' *La Sortie des usines Lumière à Lyon/Workers Leaving the Lumière Factory* (1895). Their subsequent 50-second *L'arrivée d'un train en gare de La Ciotat /The Arrival of a Train at La Ciotat Station* (1895) reputedly had audiences panicked at the sight of the oncoming train. This is probably an urban myth but it dramatizes film's visceral effect. In post-revolutionary Russia, Lenin immediately saw its potential for giving the peasants' struggle epic scale and purpose. Dziga Vertov's seminal newsreel series *Kino-Pravda/Cine-Truth*

(1922) may have intended, in his words, to "catch life unawares" (Vertov, quoted in Michelson and O'Brien, 1984: 69) but his inventive use of editing and montage was unashamedly subjective: "I'm an eye. A mechanical eye. I, the machine, show you a world the way only I can see it" (ibid.). In 2009 the Canadian filmmaker Rob Spence realized that metaphorical concept. He had lost an eye in a shotgun accident and had it replaced with a wireless video camera (see eyeborg.com). His documentary truth remains subjective, dependent upon when Rob opens his eye and what he chooses to focus on.

These remain the central challenges for documentary filmmakers: what to focus on, with what objective purpose. Whatever the *ciné véritistes* say, the moment the camera finds a subject, focuses and films, it is making a judgment about verity and value. From the start, propagandists saw the benefit of documentary celebrating and promoting social movements. Mexico's 1911 uprising produced the first Latin American revolutionary cinema. Soviet film charted the great engineering efforts that dragged Russia out of its feudal past, such as Victor Turin's epic film about the building of the railway line between Siberia and Turkestan *Turksib* (1929). Leni Riefenstahl's Goebbels-financed *Triumph des Willens/Triumph of the Will* (1934) and her subsequent films on the 1936 Berlin Olympics were the ultimate statement of the grand triumphalist aesthetic of the Third Reich, a documentary match for Hollywood epics such as D. W. Griffiths' *The Birth of a Nation* (1915) and *Intolerance* (1916), with their equally disturbing endorsement of racial superiority.

The political purposing of documentary remains as pertinent today. Emad Burnat is a Palestinian farmer and self-taught cameraman whose Sundance award-winning *5 Broken Cameras* (2011) records resistance to Israeli bulldozing of his village's land to build a wall and the repression which destroys both people and his five cameras. Jafar Panahi is an Iranian filmmaker, who was banned for 20 years from making films or leaving his country for producing "propaganda against the regime". *This is Not a Film* (2011) is a documentary self-portrait of Jafar's effective imprisonment in his own apartment, largely shot on an iPhone, with his imagining the film he might have made cleverly subverting the filmmaking ban. Such films are not just powerful testimonials but central to a documentary tradition that not only reveals human life but also its often painful context. The truths so revealed, welcome in the West, are clearly not approved of in Israel and Iran.

In America, an essentially commercial and politically supine television culture has aided the revival of the cinema documentary as an argumentative vehicle. Thirty years ago, a cinema opening for a documentary was a rarity. Today there are several a week. One of the filmmakers responsible is Errol Morris. His *The Thin Blue Line* (1988) told the story of Randall Dale Adams, a man wrongly convicted of murdering a police officer, using a then novel, now much copied, approach of reconstructing the story from several points of view. Morris called it "the first non-fiction *film noir*" on PBS TV in September 1988 but, more importantly, it was billed on release as "the first movie mystery to actually solve a murder" because its inescapable conclusion led to Adams' release from death row. Few films are so politically effective as well as being so stylistically influential.

Michael Moore first brought his more prosaic – what one could call his 'shambling Everyman exposing corporate malfeasance' – character to the screen with *Roger and Me* (1989), his pursuit of the General Motors boss Roger Smith for the loss of 30,000 jobs in his hometown of Flint, Michigan. Moore's satirical investigative approach was initially more appreciated in the UK which enabled him to make the series *TV Nation* (1994–95) for the BBC, and *Michael Moore Live* (1999) and *The Awful Truth* (1999–2000) for Channel 4. Moore's subsequent feature films articulated arguments largely avoided by the broadcast media: *Bowling for Columbine* (2002) pursued America's lethal love of firearms; *Fahrenheit 9/11* (2004) attacked Bush for exploiting 9/11 to prosecute war and *Sicko* (2007) compared the corporate greed of American healthcare to Britain's NHS at the time and the health systems in Canada and Cuba. They are among the ten top-grossing documentaries of all time. Winning the Oscar for *Columbine*, Moore used his acceptance speech to attack Bush's war-mongering, thereby becoming a hate figure for the American Right and exposing the political fault-line in American culture.

The British documentary tradition was initially less political. John Grierson's own *Drifters* (1929), about the North Sea herring fishing industry, set a template for documentary that lasted throughout the twentieth century. Its framing and montage is more about capturing the rhythm of life than the politics of the people or the economics of their industry. Industry itself sponsored many of the observational films made during the 1920s and 1930s, with both Shell and the General Post Office having their own film units, the latter responsible for Harry Watt's acclaimed *Night Mail* (1936), with its poetic narrative by W. H. Auden and music by Benjamin Britten. Only Arthur Elton and Edgar Anstey's *Housing Problems* (1935), with its then unusual use of working-class voices describing those problems, prefigures later 'social message' documentary and even that has been dismissed as Gas Board propaganda (Winston, 2008: 88). But, with the coming of the Second World War and the co-opting of filmmaking to the state imperatives of the Ministry of Information, documentary films did develop a political bent, as expressed in the title of *London Can Take It!* (1940), Harry Watt and Humphrey Jennings' riposte to the Blitz. Jennings, whom film director Lindsay Anderson called "the only real poet the British cinema has yet produced" (Anderson, 1954: 181), went on to make other stirring hymns to the Home Front, such as *Listen to Britain* (1941) and *Fires Were Started* (1943). Propagandist though Jennings' films were, his humanity and his artistry elevate them above that mechanical mode and have secured him a permanent post in the pantheon of documentary greats.

Documentary theses

British propaganda has always been more subtle than most, relying on selective and nuanced truths more than bombastic lies. British broadcasting, licensed and regulated by government, is obliged by those licences to be 'objective and impartial'. This used to mean, particularly at the BBC, a slavish balancing of any original political position expressed by its equal and opposite. This reductive two-dimensionalism has been progressively relaxed in favor of plurality of view over time. Only at election time does the Representation of the People Act (2000) enforce a proportionately numerical division of airtime between competing candidates. For the last 40 years, there has been a growth in documentaries adopting a particular viewpoint or interest. The Community Program Unit was set up in 1972 to offer a screen platform to individuals, communities, ideas and interests that were under-represented elsewhere on television. Although still bound by BBC guidelines, editorial control of *Open Door* (1972–82) and *Open Space* (1983–95) was effectively ceded to the groups which had been granted programs. Despite political parties being excluded, this meant that unorthodox philosophical positions and unsung social concerns were frequently featured unchallenged. Elsewhere, documentaries became freer to take partial positions, trusting increasingly sophisticated audiences to make up their own minds.

A sea change in British television was signaled by the arrival of Channel 4 in 1982, the first channel whose programs were made exclusively by independent production companies and whose initial remit was to be creative and different. Its founding chief executive was Jeremy Isaacs, the award-winning executive producer of, among much else, *The World at War* (1973) and *Ireland: A Television History* (1981). He was determined to take the fight to the existing duopoly of the BBC and ITV with challenging programing, not least through provocative documentaries, including the specialist areas of science and history. One of Channel 4's longest-running series, *Secret History* (1991–2004), took a spikily revisionist approach, contradicting received views about everything from the Romans to the Nazis. Channel 4 became the natural home for dedicated controversialists. The right-wing Scottish historian Niall Ferguson presented a revisionist history of the British *Empire* (2003) which sought, in the sub-title of the accompanying book, to show *How Britain Made the Modern World*. Then there is the anti-environmentalist Martin Durkin, whose documentaries inevitably cause complaints. His 1997 series *Against Nature* and his 2007 film *The Great Global Warming Swindle* were both censured by the respective regulators (ITC and OFCOM) for deliberately misleading his scientific contributors but Durkin revels in his notoriety and it is evidently good for business. Commenting on another of Durkin's programs, the environmentalist George Monbiot wrote: "Science on Channel 4 has been reduced to a crude manifesto for corporate libertarianism" (Monbiot, 2000), but that reflects a wider cultural shift. A rapidly expanding multi-channel television environment, and a contracting advertising budget, were changing the economics of UK television, not least in documentary. At the high end, long single documentaries, as featured in the BBC's *Storyville* and Channel 4's *True Stories*, are generally only made with international co-production funding. At the other end, the commercial interests of sponsorship deals discourage anything too problematic.

In the USA, cinema documentaries continued to carry the arguments that mattered. Morgan Spurlock's *Super Size Me* (2004) charted the physical and psychological damage of spending a month eating exclusively at McDonald's, revealing the corporate cynicism largely responsible for America's obesity epidemic. In Britain, this film helped prepare the ground for TV cook Jamie Oliver's campaigning television series *Jamie's School Dinners* (2005) to have a positive impact on government policy, improving school food. In 2006, the former American Vice-President Al Gore was filmed giving his impassioned slide show about the threat of global warming and, against all the odds, an old-fashioned lantern slide lecture competing against original films, *An Inconvenient Truth* not only won two Oscars but joined Michael Moore in the top ten most successful documentaries ever made. *An Inconvenient*

Truth was shown in 2006 to the then UK Labour Cabinet environment committee, just before a meeting to decide new targets for carbon reduction. So impressed were they, the ministers initially voted to increase those targets to double what the Chancellor, Gordon Brown, had up to then argued was all the government could afford. The Downing Street Chief of Staff at the time, Jonathan Powell, admits that such well-made, interesting and engaging documentaries have the power to influence policy, as long as they are backed by a public campaign.

Alex Gibney's *Enron: The Smartest Guys in the Room* (2005) should also have been shown to politicians, for it charted the exposure by the young journalist Bethany McLean of the biggest fraud in American history, leading to the collapse in 2001 of the Enron Corporation. Despite investment from the (eight) leading US banks, no one had previously been inclined to investigate the verity of Enron's claims of astronomic profit figures. Had lessons been learned from Enron, the worst excess of the 2008 banking collapse may have been avoided, but the soul of documentary has become more relativist in recent years. A case in point is *Restrepo* (2010), Sebastian Junger and the late Tim Hetherington's account of 15 months embedded with US paratroopers in the Korengal Valley in northeast Afghanistan, claimed in the film at that time to be "the deadliest place on Earth". *Restrepo* is agnostic on the causes and questionable values of war. It is about the humans caught up in it. Given a free hand to report America's disastrously costly war in Vietnam (1959–75), reporters and filmmakers were eventually credited with undermining its popular support at home. Now they are perceived as enemies rather than neutral in most war zones and most footage is acquired through safely embedding with units, inevitably providing a partial, limited focus. There are still honorable exceptions, such as Olly Lambert's *Syria Behind the Lines* (2013), where he spent five weeks filming with both government and rebel forces. But this remains a human document, not an overtly political film, and it is not just in war that television has seen the triumph of the personal over the political.

Television documentary

With the technical limits of broadcast spectrum, competition was limited in television for its first few decades, whether with the three commercial networks in the USA (ABC, CBS, NBC) or state-regulated public broadcasting services in Europe, such as the BBC and ZDF in Germany. Producers were given considerable license to come up with the programs they wanted to and documentary departments, particularly in Britain, enjoyed great prestige along with that freedom. The traditional organizing principle which emerged during the 1960s and 1970s was program strands, established weekly slots that nurtured a stable of talent, turning out individual documentaries that merely shared an editorial sensibility, not a stylistic straitjacket. These ranged from documentary strands concentrating on current affairs such as BBC1's *Panorama* (1953–present), Granada TV's *World in Action* (ITV 1963–98) and Channel 4's *Dispatches* (1987–present), to more general subject matter, for example *The Tuesday Documentary* (BBC1 1968–94), *Forty Minutes* (BBC2 1981–94) and *Cutting Edge* (Channel 4 1994–present).

With the arrival of multi-channel television in the 1990s, and the subsequent plethora of catch-up services and online options, commissioners found program strands predicated on the assumption of a loyal following returning weekly with an 'appointment to view' no longer secured audiences. Substantially fewer single documentaries are now made, except in current affairs, and, with the additional exception of international co-production/acquisition strands *Storyville* (BBC4) and *True Stories* (Channel 4), the growing demand has been for serial narratives that do ensure a returning audience. The so-called 'docu-soap' adopted the established dramatic devices of the soap opera – a returning cast of familiar human archetypes, ongoing conflict with regular events and cliffhanger endings – to hook viewers. The seminal series was the BBC's *Driving School* (BBC1, 1997) which featured learner drivers attempting to pass their test, making a star of a fearsomely batty Welsh cleaner called Maureen Rees whose persistent failure was the series' leitmotif. Many other such series exploited this approach, including a behind-the-scenes documentary at Heathrow, which became the long-running series *Airport* (BBC, 1996–2005) and its ITV imitator, *Airline* (1998–2006). It was this rather desperate herd behavior, as more and more similar series were commissioned, that over-exploited the docu-soap phenomenon and hastened its demise.

Ironically, it was one of the late lamented strands mentioned above, *World in Action*, that had unwittingly invented what eventually became the next big thing: the factual format. In 1964, a young documentary researcher called Michael Apted came up with the original idea of testing on children of the time the Jesuit co-founder Francis Xavier's maxim: "Give me a child until he is seven and I will give you the man". His documentary about 14 seven-year-olds from a wide range of social backgrounds was so successful that Apted has returned to film the group every seven years since, most recently as *56 Up* (2012). The British Film Institute, in its list compiled in 2000 of 'The Hundred Greatest Television Programmers', only cited one single documentary, *28 Up* (1985), though even this, as we have seen, was one of an occasional series. Despite being about ordinary Brits going about everyday lives, it enjoys great status in the United States. The late American film critic Roger Ebert said: "It is an inspired, almost noble use of film. It helps us understand what it is to be alive" (Ebert, 2005).

That definition – understanding what it is to be alive – could be applied to much modern documentary, maintaining the mission of many documentarists in previous generations who have also presumed an analytical purpose. Whereas *Open Space* (see above) programs were selected mainly for the importance of their ideas, the same department's groundbreaking *Video Diaries* (BBC2, 1990–99) focused on individual experience, captured through the then novel idea of filming solo in reflective mode. It was a transformative moment both technically and editorially. It foresaw the democratization of filmmaking that home video and digital technology had promoted and which today allows anyone to make movies on their mobile phone. Less well remarked is the way that it captured the individualist zeitgeist, introducing a new era of reflexivity where the first person dominates. It is no coincidence that *Video Diaries* debuted at the end of the Thatcher era, which was marked by her infamous dictum that: "There is no such thing as society ... There are individual men and women" (Thatcher, 1987). In the past, only the leaders in their respective fields could address the camera with authority, for example top journalists like the Dimblebys in current affairs, leading professors in landmark series such as *Civilisation: A Personal View by Kenneth Clark* (BBC2, 1969) and Jacob Bronowski in *The Ascent of Man* (BBC2, 1973). Documentaries routinely eschewed the interpolation of personality between the subject and the lens, unless it was straight reportage. In the twenty-first century, the dominant mode is the personal and the hunt has been for the factual format that best marries individual aspiration to an engaging enterprise.

One initially successful format was *Faking It* (Channel 4, 2000–2004), made by the UK company, RDF Media. This took someone from an ordinary job and spent a month training them to do something entirely different; for instance, one naval petty officer became a drag queen. Their experience was shot in conventional documentary style but the formatted denouement was when they faced a panel of experts alongside some real practitioners of the respective art and had to con them that they were not the 'faker'. It made for the classic dramatic ending, 'will they, won't they succeed?', but the fatal flaw was that the audience didn't like it when they failed. The next, much more successful documentary format, also by RDF Media, was *Wife Swap* (Channel 4, 2003–9). This never failed the viewer because every week it did the obvious thing, swapping a pair of wives by inserting them into each others' predictably incompatible homes and watching the sparks fly. Black v. white, vegan v. carnivore, even gay v. straight, the format could be relied upon to deliver some vicarious conflict. It still plays on ABC in the United States and in many other countries around the world. The third winning format, again from RDF Media, was *Secret Millionaire* (Channel 4, 2006–12). This parachuted a wealthy person into a poor community as some kind of volunteer, watched them evolve empathy and understanding with this new community, then had them reveal their wealth and hand over a cheque before disappearing back to their real life. This also plays in other countries where the reassertion of patronizing Victorian philanthropy in place of systemic improvement must be equally acceptable to audiences.

Many of the makers of such programs come from traditional documentary backgrounds. They argue that these devices bring a much larger audience to the experience of real life than would conventional documentary on social issues.

Whilst the former BBC4 channel controller Richard Klein approvingly calls such formats 'constructed documentary', the question remains: how real is the life or the experience if transformed by the artificial conceit and constraints of the program format? Not many of us would consider our best likeness to be the picture of us taken at the moment of impact in a car crash. Yet this tendency, lumped together under the oxymoronic category 'reality television', has become an unstoppable leviathan in the business of modern television.

A more recent iteration combines the car-crash constructions of formats with the docu-soap, employing attractive young people to perform their social lives in front of the cameras. The concept originated in the USA with the California-based *The Hills* (MTV, 2006–10) and New Jersey's *Jersey Shore* (2009–12). The UK joined in with *The Only Way Is Essex* (ITV2, 2010–present; usually called *TOWIE*), described by *The Guardian* newspaper as "real people in modified situations, saying unscripted lines but in a structured way" (Dent, 2010). It is a particular kind of 'real', since the characters are distinguished by their fake tans, dyed hair, false nails and other bodily modifications.

The production teams' job is to construct filmic situations and wind up emotional tensions between the participants so that the audience may vicariously enjoy their trysts and tantrums. Both participants and audiences share a knowing pleasure in the falsity of the form, apparently viewing the screen performers as avatars for the situations in which they may find themselves in real life, playing out stratagems as in a video game. It is a long way from traditional documentary though it uses documentary techniques and crews and shelters under the 'reality television' umbrella, spawning imitators. *Made in Chelsea* (E4, 2011–present) does for London's Hooray Henries what *TOWIE* has done for Essex girls. The UK version of *Jersey Shore*, *Geordie Shore* (MTV, 2011–present) has evolved the format by taking its native Newcastle cast abroad for series in Mexico and Australia, bringing it closer to the dream fulfillment that the talent show competitions (which are also dubbed 'reality television') promise.

One other recent television development is truer to the veracity of traditional documentary although it still excites fevered debate. The veteran documentarist Paul Watson loathes being called 'the father of reality television' but his series *The Family* (BBC2, 1974), charting the everyday life of the Wilkins family in a Reading flat and transmitting during filming, was enormously influential in both the unmediated nature of its 'warts and all' picture and the reflexivity of a family responding to their instant notoriety. In 2008 Channel 4 decided to revive the idea (without Watson's consent as there is no copyright in program titles) deploying the use of a fixed rig of cameras and microphones within the Hughes family's house. This was done remotely, recording their life for four months, and condensed into eight episodes of *The Family* (2008). Two more series, with the Indian Grewal family (2009) and the Nigerian Adesina family (2010) followed. However, their impact was not in the subject matter but in the technique. The use of a fixed rig had been developed for the Big Brother house in the series *Big Brother* (Channel 4, 2000–2010; Channel 5, 2011–present), an immersive game show where contestants misbehave under 24-hour surveillance until they are ejected by popular vote. Although the nature and content of *Big Brother* was constructed even more than *TOWIE*, the notion that such surveillance could also capture unmediated reality gained traction.

In 2010, Channel 4 rigged the maternity ward at Southampton Hospital with 40 cameras to produce *One Born Every Minute* (2010–present), a series that simply shares the intimate pleasures and pains of childbirth with a succession of mothers and couples facing this extraordinary event in their lives. One might have thought the predictable repetition this promises would suffer from the law of diminishing returning audiences, but not so. The first series won the 2010 British Film and Television Academy (BAFTA) award for Best Factual Series and continues to attract a large audience. In an atomized society, there is little shared knowledge about such common experiences as birth and death and this documentary series performs an invaluable service in making good that lack. As *The Telegraph* critic wrote, "the greatest drama remains real life. The task of television is to reveal it without getting in the way" (Wilson, 2010). Not only are there no camera operators or directors in the way, the edited films go out without intrusive narration. *24 Hours in A&E* (2011–present) follows a similar aesthetic, now deploying 90 cameras in the Accident and Emergency department of King's College Hospital, London to record life and death as it happens. Insofar as many are in no condition to grant permission on arrival, this is sought after the event and back stories are filmed in traditional documentary interview mode. Unlike many of the bloodthirsty ambulance-chasing documentary series made, *24 Hours in A&E* manages to be both unflinchingly graphic and sensitively human at the same time. As the lead film editor, Rupert Houseman, says: "The multi-camera selection enables us to go slowly, sharing the human moments, in a way that single-camera shooting would find much harder to sustain" (Houseman, 2013). Many documentarists might disagree but this won the Best Documentary Series of 2012 in the UK Royal Television Society Awards.

Documentary technology

The continuously evolving technology of recording, editing and distribution has transformed the production landscape. As the media commentator Clay Shirky has observed, the gateway to production formerly held by the commissioner is now in the hands of the producer but the filter of reception is firmly in the hands of the consumer (Shirky, 2008). Virtually anybody now has the means to make a documentary, and an encouraging number express the wish so to do, but their likeliest distribution platform is online sites such as YouTube or Vimeo. Consumption is in the unreliable hands of Facebook friends' 'likes' and word of virtual mouth. The vagaries of viral transmission can make for extraordinary impact. The American action group Invisible Children Inc's 30-minute video *Kony 2012* (2012) about the campaign to capture a Ugandan warlord garnered 100 million hits worldwide, leveraging a US Senate resolution and an African Union decision to send in troops. The filmmaker Jason Russell had a nervous breakdown as a result of the unexpected pressure. Yet in stark contrast the Korean singer Psy's *Gangnam Style* (2012) music video got over 1.5 billion hits in its first six months, making it the most watched video ever, and his career goes from strength to strength.

Documentary has become a fact of life, rather than the record of the facts of life. Where once Dziga Vertov's "I am a camera" was revolutionary, we are now all cameras and, while most of those are confined to posting party pictures on Facebook, it makes our reading of the documentary spectacles presented to us compromised by skepticism. Recent events have fuelled this. Revelations of mendacious justifications of war, abuse of political expenses, bankrupt banks being bailed out by the public purse and a popular press having lost its moral compass, have all led to a public loss of trust in what it is told. Television chasing the elusive bottom line has not helped, yet issues of ethics still exercise the public mind, not just over issues of truthful representation, but also about individual dealings with the public. As the documentary theorist Bill Nichols writes:

> These questions boil down to questions of trust – a quality that cannot be legislated, proposed or promised in the abstract so much as demonstrated, earned and granted in negotiated, contingent, concrete relationships in the here and now.
>
> (Nichols, 2006: 181)

The documentary tradition can only ever be rooted in the here and now. Even when it attempts to interpret the historical past or the scientific future, it does so through the eyes and technology of the present. It is a referential sounding board for our views and values. As is said of journalism, it is the first draft of history, but its truths are necessarily provisional.

Further reading

Bill Nichols is the foremost film theoretician writing on documentary film, who defined its 'six modes', and the second edition of his *Introduction to Documentary* (2010) is a good introduction. Stella Bruzzi offers a more modernist approach with interests in gender and identity in the second edition of her *New Documentary* (2006). The filmmaker Kevin MacDonald and Mark Cousins' *Imagining Reality: the Faber Book of Documentary* (2006) is a wide-ranging anthology of writings on the form, about and by its makers, from Vertov to Kieslowski. Peter Lee-Wright's *The Documentary Handbook* (2010) expands this essay's thesis of documentary having developed and fragmented into multiple forms and sub-genres. The most recent collection of writings on the history, theory and issues of documentary is *The Documentary Film Book*, edited by Brian Winston (2013).

References

Anderson, L. (1954) "Only connect: Some aspects of the work of Humphrey Jennings." *Sight and Sound*, 23(4), 181–186.

Bruzzi, S. (2006) *New Documentary*. Abingdon: Routledge.

Debord, G. (1967) *La Société du spectacle* (*The Society of the Spectacle*) (1970). St Petersburgh, FL: Red & Black Publishers.

Dent, G. (2010) "Grace Dent's TV OD." *The Guardian*, 23 October. Retrieved from http://www.theguardian.com/tv-and-radio/2010/oct/23/tv-od-the-only-way-is-essex

Ebert, R. (2005) Speaking on *Fifty Greatest Documentaries*. Channel 4, 9 October.

Grierson, J. (1933) "The documentary producer." *Cinema Quarterly*, 2(1), 7–9.

Houseman, R. (2013) Speaking to film students at Goldsmiths College, University of London, March 2013.

Lee-Wright, P. (2010) *The Documentary Handbook*. Abingdon: Routledge.

MacDonald, K. and Cousins, M. (2006) *Imagining Reality: the Faber Book of Documentary*. London: Faber and Faber.

McLuhan, M. (1964) *Understanding Media: The Extensions of Man*. New York: McGraw-Hill.

Michelson, A. and O'Brien, K. (1984) *Kino-Eye: The Writings of Dziga Vertov*. Berkeley, CA: University of California Press.

Monbiot, G. (2000) "Getting your science from charlatans." *The Guardian*, 16 March. Retrieved from http://www.theguardian.com/comment/story/0,3604,181798,00.html

Nichols, B. (2006) "What to do about documentary distortion? Toward a code of ethics." Documentary.org, March/April. Retrieved from http://www.documentary.org/content/what-do-about-documentary-distortion-toward-code-ethics-0

——(2010) *Introduction to Documentary* (2nd ed.). Bloomington, IN: Indiana University Press.

Shirky, C. (2008) *Here Comes Everybody*. New York: Penguin Books.

Thatcher, M. (1987) Interview by Douglas Keay. *Woman's Own*, 23 September. Reproduced in full on Thatcher Foundation website. Retrieved from http://www.margaretthatcher.org/document/106689

Wilson, B. (2010) "One Born Every Minute, Channel 4, review." *Daily Telegraph*, 9 February. Retrieved from http://www.telegraph.co.uk/culture/tvandradio/7198234/One-Born-Every-Minute-Channel-4-review.html

Winston, B. (2008) *Claiming the Real: Documentary: Grierson and Beyond* (2nd ed.). London: British Film Institute.

——(ed.) (2013) *The Documentary Film Book*. London: British Film Institute.

37
The censors' tools
Julian Petley

A tool much relied upon by UK censors of one kind or another in the pre-digital age was a sharp blade – used, for example, by the British Board of Film Censors to excise celluloid images of which it disapproved, and, in the first half of the 1930s, by British distributors of foreign magazines to snip out stories about the affair between the Prince of Wales and Wallis Simpson, stories which they feared might invite legal action if published in the UK. Indeed, the issue of *Time* magazine which reported in October 1936 that Mrs Simpson had filed for divorce appeared on British newsstands with four whole pages cut out. Another tool whose name at one time was almost synonymous with censorship in the UK was the 'blue pencil', the means favored by the Lord Chamberlain for removing offending lines, or indeed entire scenes, from the plays which he was responsible for examining.

These, however, are fairly crude and obvious tools. Rather more subtle are various forms of media licensing which, at their most effective, discourage or indeed prevent censorable material from coming into being in the first place.

During and after the Leveson Inquiry into the culture, practice and ethics of the press there was a great deal of alarmist talk in the papers about the possibility of a new system of press licensing being introduced. Much of this was nothing more than opportunist scaremongering and what it pointedly ignored was that the original licensing system was operated not by the state alone but by the state acting in concert with powerful publishing interests.

Licensing the press

The licensing system was operated in the sixteenth and seventeenth centuries partly via the Stationers' Company. Founded in 1403 and granted a Royal Charter in 1557, this was essentially a guild or trade organisation. Its Charter enabled it to establish a publishing monopoly, since anyone wishing to publish had to be a member. The Stationers were also granted considerable powers of censorship by the state, being legally empowered to seek out and destroy works emanating from unlicensed publishers and anything that the authorities deemed subversive or seditious. Its powers were enshrined in measures such as the Decree for Order in Printing, which was issued in 1586 by the much feared Court of the Star Chamber, and the Licencing

Order of 1643, leading Milton to write his famous defence of freedom of expression, the *Areopagitica*. The restoration of the monarchy in 1660 resulted in the Licensing Act 1662, whose full title is revealing: 'An Act for preventing the frequent Abuses in printing seditious treasonable and unlicensed Books and Pamphlets and for regulating of Printing and printing Presses'. Under the Act, printing presses could not be set up without permission from the Stationers' Company; 'Messengers to the Press' were empowered by warrant of the king or a secretary of state to search for and enter the premises of unlicensed printers; the number of London printers was reduced to 20; only four foundries were licensed to cast type; all master printers had to post a £300 surety against possible future transgressions; and every book had to include a facsimile of its license and the name and address of its printer. Punishments for infringing the rules were severe. A Surveyor of the Press was created in 1663, who both exercised a monopoly on news publications and acted as censor of all other printed matter. Its first incumbent was Sir Roger L'Estrange, whose two journals, the *Intelligencer* and the *Newes*, were published 'With Privilege', thus becoming the monopoly press. As he put it in a later publication, the *Observator*: "It is the *Press* that has made 'um *Mad*, and the *Press* must set 'um *Right* again" (quoted in Winston, 2005: 53) which clearly demonstrates that the government's intention was not merely the suppression of works of which it disapproved but also the production of news which adhered to what today would be called the official line. His main target as censor was works which made "the multitude too familiar with the actions and counsels of their superiors, too pragmatical, too censorious" (ibid.) and "the great masters of the popular style" who "speak plain and strike home to the capacity and humours of the multitude" (quoted in Hill, 1985: 51).

In 1695, the Licensing Act was allowed to lapse. There were several reasons for this. First, the Stationers' Company had blatantly abused its monopoly over patents and copyrights and had brought the whole system into disrepute. Second, with printing becoming ever easier and cheaper, the licensing system was increasingly difficult to police. Third, licensing was coming to be seen as an unwarranted interference in what had become a profitable business. Fourth, it was seen to be incompatible with the freedoms established by the Declaration of Rights in 1689. And finally, the authorities had already begun to find new means of discouraging freedom of expression, in the form of prosecutions for blasphemy, sedition and criminal libel, as well as what came to be known as the 'taxes on knowledge'.

However, far from being consigned to history in 1695, licensing was to re-occur in the twentieth century, albeit in different forms and in new media.

Licensing the cinema

The first time that it re-appeared was when the Cinematograph Act 1909 gave local authorities the power to license film exhibition. This was in order to protect the public against cinema fires (quite common in the early days of flammable film), but councils soon began to abuse their licensing powers by withholding licenses from cinemas which showed films which they deemed unsuitable. And so, in 1912, the Cinematograph Exhibitors' Association, faced with a bewildering array of varying local censorship practices and standards, formed the British Board of Film Censors (BBFC). Gradually, the majority of local authorities came to have faith in the BBFC's judgements, and in 1924 it received judicial recognition when the Divisional Court upheld the validity of a condition that "no cinematograph film ... which has not been passed for ... exhibition by the BBFC shall be exhibited without the express consent of the council" (quoted in Robertson and Nicol, 2008: 820). This effectively meant that as long as a local council reserved the right to overrule BBFC decisions, it was entitled to make it a condition of granting a license to a cinema that the cinema screened only BBFC-classified films. And in 1952, the Cinematograph Act imposed a duty on licensing authorities to restrict the admission of children to cinemas that showed works "designated by the licensing authority or such other body as may be specified in the license, as works unsuitable for children"; this reference to "such other body" was the first parliamentary acknowledgement of the BBFC.

Local authorities' licensing provisions were re-enacted in 1982 and consolidated in the 1985 Cinemas Act. Most local authorities now adopt 'model licensing conditions' drafted by the Home Office, which include the stipulations that:

(a) No film, other than a current newsreel, shall be exhibited unless it has received a certificate of the British Board of Film Classification or is the subject of the licensing authority's permission;
(b) No young people shall be admitted to any exhibition of a film classified by the Board as unsuitable for them, unless with the local authority's permission;
(c) no film shall be exhibited if the licensing authority gives notice in writing prohibiting its exhibition on the ground that it 'would offend against good taste or decency or would be likely to encourage or incite to crime or to lead to disorder or to be offensive to public feeling'.

(Quoted in Robertson and Nicol, 2008)

And so, since, in the last analysis, the BBFC has to take into account when classifying a film the sensibilities of local fire brigade or watch committees, this means, as Geoffrey Robertson states, that in Britain: "The cinema, alone of art forms, is subject to moral judgement by local councils" (1993: 263). Films banned by local authorities include *Ulysses* (1967), *The Devils* (1971), *Straw Dogs* (1971), *Last Tango in Paris* (1972), *The Life of Brian* (1979) and *Crash* (1996).

State video censorship

It might be supposed that when films could eventually be viewed in the home, they would finally escape any form of licensing. However, quite the opposite was to be the case, as I have explained in detail elsewhere (Petley, 2011).

The arrival of home video in 1979 posed a considerable problem for the authorities as it unleashed a torrent of material which the BBFC had either cut or banned outright when submitted to them for cinema exhibition, or which most certainly would have been cut or banned had it been submitted. Inevitably, such material provoked a storm of protest from moral campaigners such as Mary Whitehouse, who found ready allies in illiberal newspapers such as the *Daily Mail* and the *Sun*, and it was not long before the cries of 'Something Must be Done!' reached the ears of the police, the Director of Public Prosecutions and MPs. That 'something' turned out to be prosecuting a number of what had come to be known (courtesy of Peter Chippindale in *The Sunday Times*, 23 May 1982) as 'video nasties' under the Obscene Publications Act, and drawing up a list of titles which were liable to prosecution (a modern form of the *Index Librorum Prohibitorum*), but this was not sufficient for those campaigning for the censorship of the new medium, who finally achieved their objective in the Video Recordings Act 1984. This required that before any feature film could be distributed on video in Britain, it had to be classified and, if necessary cut, by the BBFC, which could also ban any video outright. This means that BBFC video classification certificates, unlike classification certificates awarded to cinema releases, have statutory force. These can quite properly be regarded as a form of license.

The Act requires the BBFC to have "special regard to the likelihood" of videos which it classifies as "being viewed in the home". This clause relates not only to the possible presence of children, but also to the fact that the video viewer, unlike the cinema spectator, has the power to replay scenes, or play them in slow motion, or freeze an individual image, a prospect clearly viewed with alarm by the architects of this legislation. This means that films on video are even more strictly regulated than films in the cinema.

In the four years after the passing of the Act, the BBFC was required to classify every feature film on video that was currently on the market, as well as to classify all new releases. The former in itself produced a form of censorship, as many of the smaller distributors either would not or could not pay the considerable classification fees and so simply withdrew their videos from distribution. This impacted particularly hard on independent and minority-taste films. By 1988, 30 videos rated as U (1.1 percent of the total submitted), 130 as PG (5.1 percent), 188 as 15 (6.7 percent), 725 as 18 (28.9 percent) and 56 (30.4 percent) as R18 (the category which could be sold only in licensed sex shops) had been cut and 25 were rejected outright (BBFC, 1989: 10). Bizarrely, then, it was films in the adult categories which were, and have remained, overwhelmingly the main victims of the new censorship system. Equally bizarrely, it was precisely at this moment that the BBFC changed its name to the British Board of Film Classification, even though it was actually carrying out more censorship than ever before! So although the Video Recordings Act was represented by its creators and a complicit press as simply a means of ridding the country of the 'video nasties', what it in fact created was a massive and draconian apparatus of state video censorship uncomfortably reminiscent of the 'licensers of the press' discussed above.

The beauty of the Act, from the authorities' point of view, is of course its sheer simplicity: from 1984 onwards it has simply been illegal to supply a feature film on video without a BBFC certificate. However, the Act was tightened even further in 1994 by amendments made in the wake of the murder of James Bulger by two other children. Prompted by the ill-judged and uncalled for remark by the trial judge that "I suspect that exposure to violent films may be in part an explanation" for the murder, the press pack once again re-ignited the 'video nasty' panic, at one point pinning the entire blame, absurdly, for this tragic incident on the horror film *Child's Play 3* (1991). The amendment required the BBFC, when classifying a video, to

> have special regard (among the other relevant factors) to any harm that may be caused to potential viewers or, through their behaviour, to society by the manner in which the work deals with (a) criminal behaviour; (b) illegal drugs; (c) violent behaviour or incidents; (d) horrific behaviour or incidents; or (e) human sexual activity.

Unsurprisingly, video censorship is stricter in the UK than in any other European country, except the Republic of Ireland.

The BBC: 'Liberty on parole'

Licensing also features in broadcasting, albeit in different forms. Thus the BBC's operations are sanctioned by two documents. The Charter, which is usually renewed every ten years, is the BBC's constitutional basis and sets out its public purposes, as well as outlining the duties of the BBC Trust (formerly the Governors). Meanwhile the Agreement, which is with the Secretary of State for Culture, Media and Sport, lays down the terms and conditions under which the BBC is permitted to broadcast, including its funding arrangements and regulatory duties.

The BBC has consistently argued that these documents guarantee its independence from government, but, without taking the crass Murdoch line that the BBC is simply a state broadcaster and whilst thoroughly endorsing the commitments to the principles and values of public service broadcasting (PSB) enshrined in the documents, it could equally be argued that the Charter and Agreement actually constitute a form of government-granted license to broadcast. Add to this the fact that members of the BBC Trust (which replaced the Governors in 2007) are nominally appointed by the monarch acting on the advice of the Prime Minister, but effectively by the government of the day, and one can see that the BBC's independence from the state is not as watertight as both parties are wont to claim. Certainly both Harold Wilson and Margaret Thatcher imposed Governors whom they hoped would 'tame' the BBC. Thus, as Tom Burns put it in 1977, from the General Strike of 1926 onwards

> the BBC fell an easy victim to ... the calculated imprecision of its relationship with the State ... an imprecision which the BBC has been lulled, or gulled, into believing allows it all the liberty, independence, autonomy that can be hoped for, but which has proved, time and again, to be liberty on parole – the terms of which can be altered, without notice, by the Government.
> (Burns, 1977: 20–21)

Such a situation is bound to make it difficult for the BBC to deal with politically contentious issues and positively invites self-censorship of one kind or another, especially when the BBC feels itself to be out of favor with government.

As far as the Agreement is concerned, there are two particular areas of concern relating to the BBC's independence and thus its ability to express itself freely. The first concerns the government's involvement in determining the level of the license fee, which from time to time needs raising because of increased production costs. This became a matter of considerable contention in the 1980s, as the Thatcher government was deeply hostile to the BBC, as was the Tory press. Thatcher herself wanted the licence fee to be replaced by revenue from advertising while the Murdoch-led multi-channel television environment which the Tory 'deregulation' of broadcasting had deliberately brought into being was presented by many influential voices, not least those belonging to the BBC's commercial rivals, as spelling the license fee's obsolescence. Indeed, it is no exaggeration to state that in the 1980s the BBC's very existence hung in the balance. Thanks largely to 'reforming' itself along the lines demanded by the Tories, the BBC survived, but its political problems were to continue, since 'New Labour' was eventually to prove itself quite as committed to broadcasting 'deregulation' and quite as friendly to Murdoch and hostile to the BBC as the Tories under Thatcher.

The effect of government hostility towards the BBC has been undoubtedly to make it extremely cautious when dealing with matters which could prove contentious and which thus might have an impact on future license fee negotiations, and this inevitably has encouraged various forms of self-censorship. Steven Barnett and Ivor Gaber describe its situation in the 1980s:

> It would have been impossible under such pressurized circumstances for the BBC's political journalism to have remained untainted by government influence. The process was never anything as overt as crude censorship, but every programme-maker and journalist was aware that senior government figures were scrutinizing BBC output for the slightest sign of what they might interpret as 'bias' and that complaints would be swift, robust and directed at senior management. One producer on the BBC's flagship current affairs programme *Panorama* said of the programme: "There was an enormous sensitivity about what *Panorama* was up to: are we going to offend the government, are we going to cause a great deal of fuss? So that meant if you had a sensitive programme ... you had people crawling all over it."
> (Barnett and Gaber, 2001: 74)

Or as the former BBC Head of Programmes, Michael Grade, put it in 1992:

> BBC staff used to say that ITV might be rich, but the BBC were bold. But in recent years that boldness has been replaced by an enervating caution which starts at the top and quickly becomes the culture of the whole organisation. There's talk inside of the 'pre-emptive cringe'.
> (Grade, 2005: 163)

Direct and indirect censorship at the BBC

The second aspect of the Agreement which opens the door to both externally imposed censorship and self-censorship concerns Section 81(4) which states that "the Secretary of State may give the BBC a direction in writing that the BBC must not broadcast or otherwise distribute any matter, or class of matter, specified in the direction, whether at a time or times so specified or at any time". However, it should be noted that other broadcasters have always been subject to the same restriction by successive Television and Broadcasting Acts, and currently are restricted by Section 336(5) of the Communications Act 2003, which gives the Secretary of State the power to require Ofcom (the Office of Communications), which licenses all broadcasters in the UK other than the BBC, to direct them "to refrain from including in their licensed services any matter, or description of matter, specified by the Secretary of State". So it was that, after years of complaints by both Labour and Tory governments that broadcasters were 'biased' towards the Republican cause in their coverage of Northern Ireland (for an annotated list of programs that provoked rows see Curtis, 1998: 279–99) the Thatcher government was able to make it illegal to broadcast words spoken by representatives of 11 Irish organizations and indeed words spoken in support of these organizations. This resulted in a very significant diminution in the number of Republican voices on the UK airwaves and the measure was not rescinded until September 1994 as part of the Northern Ireland peace process (for an account of the casualties of the broadcasting ban see Curtis and Jempson, 2003). Direct political censorship was also employed when, on 31 January 1987, Special Branch officers raided the offices of BBC Scotland and seized all six films in the *Secret Society* series. Their warrant, under the Official Secrets Act, had been authorized by the Lord Advocate, the Scottish equivalent of the Attorney General, and, like him, a member of the government. The films were eventually returned and all but one were transmitted. What they revealed was certainly politically embarrassing but in no conceivable way breached the Act. However, the Stasi-like behavior of the government and Special Branch wrought incalculable damage worldwide to the BBC's reputation as an independent broadcaster.

Most government attempts to censor the BBC have been rather more indirect, however. One method has been to let the BBC know privately that the government would prefer a particular program not to be shown, in the hope that the Corporation will itself ban it. This is exactly what happened in the case of the 1965 nuclear war film *The War Game* (Tracey, 1982). Alternatively, the pressure can be applied very publicly, as happened in 1985 in the case of *Real Lives: Edge of the Union*, in which the government was greatly aided in its task by a Board of Governors swayed by its Thatcher-appointed Vice Chairman, William Rees-Mogg (Barnett, 2011: 91–102; Leapman, 1997: 294–331). A more common tactic, however, has been for the government to complain vociferously about programs of which it disapproves in the hope that the BBC can thus be scared out of making similar programs in future, a process in which significant sections of the press routinely take the government's side. Apart from Northern Ireland, as mentioned above, the all-too-numerous subjects which have attracted significant amounts of government and press flak have included the Suez crisis (Barnett, 2011: 40; Negrine, 1994: 108–10), the Falklands War (Harris, 1983; Glasgow University Media Group, 1985; Morrison and Tumber, 1988; Boyce, 2005: 148–70), the British role in the American bombing of Libya in April 1986 (Leapman, 1997: 343–45; O'Malley, 1994: 58–60) and the justification for the Iraq War, controversy over the BBC reporting of which led to the Hutton Inquiry and the consequent resignation of both the Corporation's Director General, Greg Dyke, and its chairman, Gavyn Davies (Tumber and Palmer, 2004: 139–72; Kampfner, 2004: 338–77).

The ITV franchise system

The licensing system as far as ITV is concerned is rather different, in that ITV companies are franchised (that is, licensed) not by the government but, as noted earlier, by Ofcom. Previously this role was played by the Independent Television Authority (ITA, 1954–72), the Independent Broadcasting Authority (IBA, 1972–90) and the Independent Television Commission (ITC, 1991–2003). Like the BBC Governors, the members of the ITA, IBA and ITC were appointed by the government of the day from amongst the ranks of the 'great and the good' and the same is true for Ofcom.

Although it should be stressed from the outset that both the ITA and the IBA constantly sought to ensure that ITV franchisees adhered to PSB standards, this did include, on occasion, cutting or even banning programs that they regarded as failing to do so. Particular problems were caused by programs which Authorities believed to infringe the impartiality requirements enshrined in successive Television and Broadcasting Acts (for accounts of rows see Sendall, 1983: 294–307; Potter, 1989: 103–23), frequently causing program-makers to complain that these were being interpreted in a very conservative fashion, one which privileged mainstream, 'consensual' political thinking whilst making it difficult for dissenting voices to be heard. The hard-hitting Granada current affairs series *World in Action* (1963–98) ran into repeated difficulties (Goddard, Corner and Richardson, 2007: 185–214) as did Thames Television's *This Week* (1956–92) and, as with the BBC, programs about Northern Ireland proved particularly contentious (Curtis, 1998: 279–99; Potter, 1990: 199–213; Holland, 2006: 111–67).

On the other hand, however, there were occasions on which the IBA passed programs which the government made abundantly clear it should have banned, and in these cases, there are distinct parallels with the situation of the BBC outlined above. The two most high-profile rows involved the Thames Television dramatized documentary *Death of a Princess* (1980), which the government and its press allies accused of endangering Britain's relationship with Saudi Arabia (Petley, 1984), and, above all, the *This Week* episode *Death on the Rock* (1988) which, for questioning the official version of the killing of three members of the Provisional IRA in Gibraltar, provoked a veritable firestorm of government and press flak (Bolton, 1990: 189–306; Holland, 2006: 197–205). Indeed, not long after the latter controversy, the IBA was abolished and Thames lost its franchise.

The market as censor

There are those who see this as a government-administered punishment for *Death on the Rock*. This is undoubtedly too crude, but what is undeniable is that by the end of the 1980s the IBA and the ITV companies had precious few friends in government (by now it had become *de rigueur* in government circles to refer to the BBC and ITV as the 'cosy duopoly') and that, whether by accident or design, the changes wrought to ITV by the Broadcasting Act 1990 meant that regular serious current affairs programing quite simply disappeared from the network in the ensuing decade. This can certainly be seen as a form of censorship, albeit one performed indirectly by market forces rather than directly by the mandarins of the ITA/IBA. In brief, Channel 4 became an independent company competing with ITV for advertising revenue; the ITV licensees were no longer chosen on the basis of the strength of their PSB commitments but were forced to bid huge sums of money in a competitive auction for their licenses, subject only to a rather nebulous 'quality threshold'; and the IBA was replaced by the 'light touch' Independent Television Commission. Unlike its predecessors, this did not have the power to censor programs prior to broadcast, but, equally, its ability to impose PSB requirements on franchise holders was far weaker; franchises were no longer awarded for fixed periods, after which they had to be re-applied for; licensees now effectively ticked their own PSB boxes and the regulator's role was reduced to monitoring their performance retrospectively and delivering mild rebukes to those who failed to live up to even their limited PSB obligations. In the newly competitive, ratings-hungry broadcasting environment, serious current affairs programs came rapidly to be seen as commercially unviable on ITV and consequently ceased to exist in any meaningful quantity (Fitzwalter, 2008). Paradoxically, then, the market eliminated what the previous regulators, for all their forays into censorship, had actually encouraged and protected.

But a further paradox lies in the fact that the commercialization of ITV served actually to increase, not lessen, the dependence of its broadcasters on government. Thus Greg Dyke, formerly the Group Chief Executive of London Weekend Television, warned prophetically in 1994 of the growth of a 'dependence culture':

> In ITV some of us naively believed that once the franchises had been awarded in 1991 the old pass-the-parcel rules would reappear and we would be free from the need to lobby and 'stay close' to government, as the PR men would put it, for a decent period. Of course, nothing has been further from the truth. For a range of reasons – a combination, I suspect, of the inadequacies of the Broadcasting Act, the business ambitions of some of the ITV companies and the changing face of competition partly due to the changing face of television technology – the larger ITV companies now always want something more out of government. This, I would suggest, is a potential threat to a politically free broadcasting system and potentially gives enormous power to the government of the day.
>
> (Dyke, 2005: 174–75)

Such a situation – the combination of the economic imperative to maximize ratings and the political imperative at least not to offend government and thus provoke it into enacting policies which might be economically disadvantageous to the ITV companies – can only encourage the kind of over-caution which all too easily shades off into self-censorship.

Conclusion: Censorship and self-censorship

In this chapter, I have suggested that if we are to understand how censorship has traditionally operated in the UK then we need to look beyond the obvious means employed to cut or ban already published works and to understand the various systemic factors which have led the media to censor themselves (and, in the case of the press, to call for the censorship of other media). At the start, I explained how foreign press reports of the affair between the Prince of Wales and Mrs Simpson had been crudely censored in the UK, but rather more significant are the processes whereby the British press kept their readers entirely in the dark about this matter (which was common knowledge in the US and continental Europe) until just a week before the abdication of the man who by then had become Edward VIII. As Richard Cockett points out, this silence was "preserved exclusively by a clandestine series of 'gentleman's agreements'. It was a quintessential example of that amorphous British entity 'the Establishment' at work" (1989: 14). These agreements were between the King himself and Esmond Harmsworth, son of the *Daily Mail* owner Lord Rothermere, plus the *Daily Express* owner Lord Beaverbrook, who also enlisted the help of Sir Walter Layton of the *News Chronicle*; similar agreements existed between the Cabinet and Geoffrey Dawson, the editor of *The Times*, and Lord Kemsley, who owned *The Telegraph*. Comparable arrangements between the Cabinet and much of the press ensured that, during the 1930s, the full horror of events taking place in Nazi Germany was never reported, and that most papers unwaveringly backed the policy of appeasement pursued by the British government. Events such as these should prompt us to think long and hard about the media's own role in and complicity with the censorship process, as well as to ponder on which topics today are subject to self-censorship via similar forms of collusion between the media and other parts of the Establishment.

Further reading

Georgina Born's 2004 work, *Uncertain Vision: Birt, Dyke and the Reinvention of the BBC*, offers a remarkably detailed account of life inside the BBC in the 1990s, one which is crucial to understanding the internal processes and external pressures which tended to lead to the kinds of self-censorship outlined in this chapter. James Curran and Jean Seaton's *Power without Responsibility: Press, Broadcasting and the Internet in Britain* (2010) provides a classic account of the British media with a critical overview of the context in which censorship of the press and broadcasting takes place in Britain. For reading on censorship Julian Petley's *Censorship: A Beginner's Guide* (2009) is a useful primer to the various tools used by censors of one kind or another, and contains a chapter on the British Board of Film Classification. Further, Guy Phelps' work *Film Censorship* (1975) is an authoritative account of the history of the British Board of Film Censors and of its working methods in the 1970s. Finally, John Trevelyan's *What the Censor Saw* (1973) provides an insider's view of the workings of film censorship in Britain up until the early 1970s.

References

Barnett, S. (2011) *The Rise and Fall of Television Journalism: Just Wires and Lights in a Box?* London: Bloomsbury Academic.

Barnett, S. and Gaber, I. (2001) *Westminster Tales: The Twenty-first-century Crisis in Political Journalism*. London: Continuum.

Bolton, R. (1990) *Death on the Rock and Other Stories*. London: WH Allen/Optomen.

Born, G. (2004) *Uncertain Vision: Birt, Dyke and the Reinvention of the BBC*. London: Secker & Warburg.

Boyce, D. G. (2005) *The Falklands War*. Basingstoke: Palgrave.

BBFC (British Board of Film Classification) (1989) *BBFC Annual Report for 1988*. London: British Board of Film Classification.

Burns, T. (1977) *The BBC: Public Institution and Private World*. London: The Macmillan Press Ltd.

Cockett, R. (1989) *Twilight of Truth: Chamberlain, Appeasement and the Manipulation of the Press*. London: Weidenfeld and Nicolson.

Curran, J. and Seaton, J. (2010) *Power without Responsibility: Press, Broadcasting and the Internet in Britain*. Abingdon: Routledge.

Curtis, L. (1998) *Ireland: The Propaganda War*. Belfast: Sásta.

Curtis, L. and Jempson, M. (2003) *Interference on the Airwaves: Ireland, the Media and the Broadcasting Ban*. London: Campaign for Press and Broadcasting Freedom.

Dyke, G. (2005) "A culture of dependency: Power, politics and broadcasters." In B. Franklin (ed.) *Television Policy: the MacTaggart Lectures*. Edinburgh: Edinburgh University Press (pp. 173–81).

Fitzwalter, R. (2008) *The Dream That Died: The Rise and Fall of ITV*. Leicester: Matador.

Glasgow University Media Group (1985) *War and Peace News*. Milton Keynes: Open University Press.

Goddard, P., Corner, J. and Richardson, K. (2007) *Public Issue Television: World in Action, 1963–98*. Manchester: Manchester University Press.

Grade, M. (2005) "The future of the BBC." In B. Franklin (ed.) *Television Policy: The MacTaggart Lectures*. Edinburgh: Edinburgh University Press (pp. 157–64).

Harris, R. (1983) *Gotcha! The Media, the Government and the Falklands Crisis*. London: Faber and Faber.

Hill, C. (1985) *The Collected Essays of Christopher Hill. Volume 1: Writing and Revolution in 17th Century England*. Brighton: The Harvester Press.

Holland, P. (2006) *The Angry Buzz: This Week and Current Affairs Television*. London: I. B. Tauris.

Kampfner, J. (2004) *Blair's Wars*. London: Simon & Schuster.

Leapman, M. (1997) *The Last Days of the Beeb*. London: Coronet.

Morrison, D. and Tumber, H. (1988) *Journalists at War: The Dynamics of News Reporting During the Falklands Conflict*. London: Sage.

Negrine, R. (1994) *Politics and the Mass Media in Britain*. London: Routledge.

O'Malley, T. (1994) *Closedown? The BBC and Government Broadcasting Policy, 1979–92*. London: Pluto.

Petley, J. (1984) "Parliament, the press and the *Death of a Princess*." In A. Goodwin, P. Kerr and I. Macdonald (eds.), *BFI Dossier 19: Drama-Documentary*. London: BFI (pp. 89–105).

——(2009) *Censorship: A Beginner's Guide*. Oxford: Oneworld.

——(2011) *Film and Video Censorship in Modern Britain*. Edinburgh: Edinburgh University Press.

Phelps, G. (1975) *Film Censorship*. London: Victor Gollancz.

Potter, J. (1989) *Independent Television in Britain. Volume 3: Politics and Control, 1968–80*. London: Macmillan.
——(1990) *Independent Television in Britain. Volume 4: Companies and Programmes, 1968–80*. London: Macmillan.
Robertson, G. (1993) *Freedom, the Individual and the Law*. Harmondsworth: Penguin.
Robertson, G. and Nicol, A. (2008) *Media Law*. London: Penguin.
Sendall, B. (1983) *Independent Television in Britain. Volume 2: Expansion and Change, 1958–68*. London: Macmillan.
Tracey, M. (1982) "Censored: *The War Game* story." In C. Aubrey (ed.) *Nukespeak: The Media and the Bomb*. London: Comedia (pp. 38–54).
Trevelyan, J. (1973) *What the Censor Saw*. London: Michael Joseph.
Tumber, H. and Palmer, J. (2004) *Media at War: The Iraq Crisis*. London: Sage.
Winston, B. (2005) *Messages: Free Expression, Media and the West from Gutenberg to Google*. Abingdon: Routledge.

Part VII
TELEVISION

38
The television sitcom
Brett Mills

As is common for all genres, precisely defining sitcom is a problematic task. Analyses of the genre usually take a textual approach, attempting to delineate those characteristics which recur across those programs assumed to belong to that category. This is primarily to try and distinguish it from other, related genres: "On the genre dial it [sitcom] sits somewhere between 'sketch comedy' and 'situation drama'" (Hartley, 2008: 78). Yet it is hard to precisely delineate the boundaries between these forms and it is possible to see a program such as *The League of Gentlemen* (BBC2, 1999–2002) as both a sketch show and a sitcom, as it contains both episodic and series-long narratives, yet individual scenes function equally well as stand-alone sketches. A starting definition of the sitcom might be "a short narrative-series comedy, generally between twenty-four and thirty minutes long, with regular characters and setting" (Neale and Krutnik, 1990: 233). The serial nature of the genre responds to the specifics of television broadcasting, according to which audiences return to situations and characters they know week after week, meaning that the pleasures of sitcom (like much television) can respond to the knowledge audiences have from previous episodes. Series such as *Linda Green* (BBC1, 2001–2) and *Gavin & Stacey* (BBC3/1, 2007–10) would fit the definitions outlined above but might also be categorized as 'comedy drama'. Therefore there remains "much disagreement over exactly which programmes are sitcoms and which aren't" (Mills, 2005: 25), and more recent genre analysis has instead been more interested in how genres function and how the situation in which "we all agree upon a basic understanding of what a sitcom is" (Mittell, 2004: 1) comes into being. It is precisely the assumed obviousness of sitcom as a genre, aligned with the perceived naturalness of the humor they contain, that means they are a ripe site for unpicking highly constructed social norms because it is often wrongly assumed that such straightforward entertainment "*doesn't* require us to think" (Mills, 2009: 5).

This means that exploring sitcom can be a fruitful task as it is assumed that humor, which is itself culturally and historically specific, is "rooted in social processes" (Billig, 2005: 32). National broadcasting systems usually exist within regulations that proscribe television's particular social functions, such as the BBC's remit to "create content ... for all ages and communities" (BBC, 2013: 26). This means that the kinds of comedy transmitted via those systems point towards some kind of intended collective consciousness. Furthermore, this suggests that as societies change, so does the kind of comedy seen on television. Sociological analyses of comedy can therefore be used in exploring the sitcom and the debate recurs about whether comedy arises from a "defiant tradition" (Jenkins, 1994: 2) or upholds social inequalities as it is "ill-natured, scornful, and full of contempt" (Wickberg, 1998: 54). Comedy can be seen as "a prime testing ground for ideas about belonging and exclusion" (Medhurst, 2007: 39) because it invites audiences to laugh at those who are different, thus reasserting hegemonic norms. Yet it might also be a space within which atypical, progressive behavior is celebrated and accepted via laughter and, according to Freud (1997/1905), is a necessary process for cultures and individuals to vent the repressions societies place upon them. This is explored in more detail in the section on 'representation' below.

Sitcom's history is traced back to forms of comedy that preceded television and its roots lie in the movement of comedians from theatre and stand-up to radio and then into television (Murray, 2005: 1–39). Prior to broadcasting, comedians in music halls in Britain and vaudeville in the United States were able to tour a single routine for many years, safe in the knowledge that having performed their jokes to a local audience in a theatre in one town did not prevent them from doing the same in another town to a different audience. When broadcasting began, radio (and, later, television) looked to the music hall and vaudeville for ready-made comedy stars whose performances could be transported wholesale to the new medium, and whose skill and success were already apparent (Neale and Krutnik, 1990: 212). Such a shift, though, caused two problems. First, this meant a single performer could no longer maintain a career with only one routine, as once a nationwide audience had encountered it via broadcasting it could not be reused. Second, the serial nature of broadcasting required a significantly larger amount of material, over a longer period of time, than music hall and vaudeville performers were used to generating. In order to accommodate these challenges, programers quickly developed situations and regular characters from which stories could be generated, moving away from the individual performer in the process and developing the "structuring principles of *situation* comedy" (Neale and Krutnik, 1990: 215) which persist today.

The mutable nature of genre is evident in the difficulty in identifying the 'first' sitcom. In America radio programs featuring Jack Benny – including *The Canada Dry Program* (NBC/CBS, 1932–33) and *The Jell-O Program Starring Jack Benny* (NBC, 1934–42) – are seen as significant steps in the genre's evolution, while in the UK *Mr Muddlecombe, JP* (BBC, 1937) has a claim as "the first sit-com [that] appeared on British radio" (Neale and Krutnik, 1990: 221) and *Pinwright's Progress* (BBC, 1946–47) has been seen as "British television's first authentic half-hour situation comedy series" (Lewisohn, 2003: 626). Key in the genre's television development was the inauguration of a particular shooting style which remains core to sitcom's aesthetic: the 'three-headed monster'. This was a "three-camera set-up with studio audience format that freed television situation comedy from its stiff stage restraints" (Putterman, 1995: 15), which was developed for *I Love Lucy* (CBS, 1951–57). Rather than performing outwards to the studio audience, the three-headed monster instead captured a wide shot of two characters talking and then trained a close-up on each of those performers. By cutting to a close-up of a character as they say something funny and then cutting to a close-up of the other character as they respond, programs are able to get two laughs from one joke and the reaction shot thereby becomes central to the comic moment in the sitcom. As will be shown below, there are many sitcoms that now no longer use this shooting style but it is still the case that the most popular recent British sitcoms such as *My Family* (BBC1, 2000–2011), *Miranda* (BBC2/1, 2009–present) and *Mrs Brown's Boys* (RTÉ1/BBC1, 2011–present) continue to employ a sitcom aesthetic developed over five decades ago. While the sitcom can be defined by its comic content and its serial narrative structure, its visual style and aesthetic are also defining components.

The Britcom

The British sitcom, then, can be seen to have its origins in American broadcasting. In the early years of British television, many American series, such as *The Burns and Allen Show* (CBS, 1950–58) and *I Love Lucy*, were imported and broadcast to mass audiences. Yet it is *Hancock's Half-Hour* (BBC, 1956–60) which "is the yardstick against which all subsequent British sitcoms have been measured" (Lewisohn, 2003: 342) and which is typically seen as being the first example of the genre which managed to take the form of the sitcom and use it in a manner which responded to the British national character. In its working-class setting the series can be seen to respond to wider forms of representation within British culture at the time, in which a social realist depiction of 'ordinary' lives filtered into theatre, literature, cinema and photography. While not all American sitcoms are aspirational and about the wealthy, the "suburban middle-class family sitcom" (Haralovich, 2003: 69) recurs within such broadcasting. British television, on the other hand, has always had "a concern, variously expressed, to represent working class life" (Wagg, 1998: 9) and *Hancock's Half-Hour* can be seen as an early successful example of the sitcom genre's ability to interlace comedy and entertainment with a depiction of contemporary society infused with "a naturalism of language, characterization and location allowing for almost-believable story lines and audience identification" (Goddard, 1991: 78).

Congruent with this social depiction is the program's portrayal of its eponymous character. Hancock is, on the whole, a miserable character who responds to his lack of fortune with a recurring cry of "Stone me!", and who is self-centered, rude and pompous. Perhaps most importantly, he is a character riddled with personal and social faults, yet, on the whole, remains oblivious to these and instead is repeatedly astonished at the reactions of others to his behavior. He is, in essence, a character lacking self-awareness and in this key aspect he defines a dominant trend in British sitcom characters which is largely absent in the genre's American counterpart. Indeed, the majority of the 'great' British sitcom characters conform to this characteristic, which can be seen in Harold Steptoe in *Steptoe and Son* (BBC, 1962–74), Basil Fawlty in *Fawlty Towers* (BBC2, 1975–79), Del Boy in *Only Fools and Horse* (BBC1, 1981–2002), both Gary and Tony in *Men Behaving Badly* (ITV/BBC1, 1992–98) and David Brent in *The Office* (BBC2/1, 2001–3). This difference between British and American sitcom has been seen as evidence of the specifics of the origins of humor in the two countries, in which American comedy's Jewish origins (Brook, 2003) are largely absent in Britain. Such Jewish comedy has a heritage of producing wise-cracking, self-aware characters who often control situations through humor. British characters, on the other hand, tend to be relatively powerless and we are invited as an audience to find them funny.

In its depiction of comedically powerful characters American sitcom often portrays a relatively stable and homogenous society. By contrast, "Class, of course, is a recurring social and cultural theme throughout the history of English (and British) situation comedy" (Medhurst, 2007: 145). While the class structure is a stable one, it is often depicted in sitcom as stifling and imprisoning, rather than evidence of a homogenous society. Series such as *Dad's Army* (BBC1, 1968–77), *Rising Damp* (ITV, 1974–78) and *Keeping Up Appearances* (BBC1, 1990–95) all depict characters with pretensions to move up the social ladder and the comedy that ensues results from their failure to do so. In this sense, the British sitcom can be seen to be a conservative form, which invites audiences to find individuals' desire to 'better' themselves funny and whose circular, serial narratives doom such characters to forever remain where they are (Grote, 1983).

Debates about representation

Perhaps the most prevalent approach used to explore sitcom has been the exploration of representation. To be sure, concerns over the representations television offers, and the assumed consequences these have for those groups being represented, recur in both the academic and the popular debates that circle the medium in general. Yet an extra inflection is given to debates about representation in terms of the sitcom because of the specifics of the comedic aspect of the genre. That is, there has been much discussion as to whether the fact that audiences are positioned to find the occurrences and characters in a sitcom funny alters at all their understandings of the representations on offer. Perhaps the most obvious example of this are the debates concerning the "right-wing ... prudish, monarchist bigot" (Lewisohn, 2003: 767) Alf Garnett, who appeared in the series *Till Death Us Do Part* (BBC1, 1965–75) and *In Sickness and In Health* (BBC1, 1985–92) amongst others and who berated the changes going on in the world around him using racist and sexist language. The program's narratives repeatedly paint Garnett as a fool for the views he holds and the boorish manner in which he treats others and indeed the production team intended the program as a critique of such views. Yet some audiences were found to sympathize with Garnett and he became a mouthpiece for those views he was intended to mock (Husband, 1988). What this does highlight are the various ways in which audiences are capable of reading programs, and the difficulty in arguing that a particular representation is 'acceptable' or not. Considering that comedic genres such as the sitcom are typically categorized as 'entertainment' and that entertainment is often understood as "fluff" (Gray, 2008: 7) separate from the 'serious' world of politics and society, there can be a response to debates about sitcom representation that insists it is 'just a joke' and comedy has no consequences other than laughter. Yet long-fought battles over sitcom representation suggest otherwise.

For British comedy this is arguably most apparent in the 'Alternative Comedy' movement of the 1980s. This was a term used to categorize a number of comedy writers and performers who emerged via the stand-up comedy club circuit in Britain in the 1980s and whose performance style and content has been seen to challenge the "bland prolefeed of the situation comedies which formed[ed] the staple diet of television entertainment" (Wilmut and Rosengard, 1989: xiii) at the time. Its most obvious tenet was a desire to present material that was "anti-sexist, anti-racist" (Littlewood and Pickering, 1998: 296), for it presumed that the majority of comedic material prior to that date was ideologically problematic in terms of race and gender. In exploring the ways in which comedy portrayed minorities and less powerful groups, it both assumed that broadcast humor had potentially significant social consequences and used comedy to critique cultural norms. While the movement began in comedy clubs, many of the performers quickly moved to television and the resulting sitcom *The Young Ones* (BBC2, 1982–84) "reflected the free-basing, high-octane, in-your-face" (Lewisohn, 2003: 846) nature of this comedy in its tales of four students sharing a flat. The fact that "the 'establishment', at first, was horrified and reviled in equal measure" (Lewisohn, 2003: 846) by the program was a result of the brash, loud performance style but also because the series critiqued the comedy that had preceded it.

Yet the assumed progressive nature of this comedy has also been called into question, not least because Alternative Comedy can be seen as both a liberating and a conservative movement, as its non-sexist, non-racist ideology limits the possibilities of humor. So while humor that upsets the Establishment could be seen as progressive, the sitcom's status as mass culture broadcast to millions on television means, some have argued, that there is no attempt to "alter the relationship between dominant teller and the 'other-who-is-told'" (Littlewood and Pickering, 1998: 302). What this highlights is that thinking about the relationships between representation and the sitcom can focus on a number of factors and while progressive content may be introduced, it remains the case that only certain kinds of people get to appear on television comedy and the medium does not function as a comedic "public sphere" (Habermas, 1989/1962) as it might – that is, a 'public sphere', as envisioned by Habermas, in which a wide "range of 'voices' ... are allowed, or invited, to participate" (Mills and Barlow, 2012: 296) in debates on topics that affect us all. Considering that humor's social role is seen as vital to its power (especially in Britain/England, where an idea of identity is related to the 'national sense of humor' [Fox, 2005: 61; Medhurst, 2007]), there are questions to explore concerning what comedy is and is not allowed for broadcast, and which comic voices get to communicate to the mass audiences television can reach.

That said, it remains the case that key debates about sitcom representation center on particular groups and how they are formulated in the genre. In the United States, such research has often focused on race, with explorations of series such as *The Cosby Show* (NBC, 1984–92) examining audience responses to the series (Jhally and Lewis, 1992; Fuller, 1992). Such debates have been much more marginal in British sitcom, not least because the genre remains resolutely white in the UK, despite series such as *The Fosters* (ITV, 1976–77), *The Kumars at No. 42* (BBC2/1, 2001–6) and *The Crouches* (BBC1, 2003–5). Instead, gender has played a much more central role in such representational debates. The "recurrence of a particular and narrow range of female comic stereotypes" (Porter, 1998: 65) has been seen to exemplify the representation of women in sitcom, with male characters more often being given the powerful role of joke-teller in such series. This means that those programs which are seen as offering alternative, more progressive, feminist representations are commonly lauded and are presented as evidence of other ways that comedy can work. The writer Carla Lane has created many sitcoms intended to explore a range of specifically female experiences, such as *The Liver Birds* (BBC1, 1969–78, 1996), *Solo* (BBC, 1981–82) and *The Mistress* (BBC2, 1985–87). In its tales of a woman unhappy with her domestic housewife role, Lane's series *Butterflies* (BBC2, 1978–83) has been assessed as "creating a cultural space for women where they could prioritize their issues and concerns" (Andrews, 1998: 59) akin to consciousness-raising activities of the radical feminist movement.

Later programs such as *Absolutely Fabulous* (BBC1, 1992–96, 2001–4, 2011–12) have been seen to depict the "unruly woman" (Rowe, 1995) who refuses to appear and behave in manners acceptable to patriarchal norms that limit and disempower women. *Absolutely Fabulous*'s employment of physical humor is seen as a powerful depiction of the female body which has traditionally been required to be as unnoticeable as possible (Feuer, 2008). Similar physical humor can be seen in programs with lead female characters such as *Miranda* and *Some Girls* (BBC3, 2012–present). The unruly nature of comedy means that humor and the sitcom might be a more powerful site for the critique of patriarchal norms than other genres.

Technology and the multi-channel environment

As noted above, the sitcom, like many genres, encompasses many styles and formats which makes defining it difficult. The 'traditional' sitcom is understood as one employing the 'three-headed monster', yet there are also many more recent series that are not shot in front of a studio audience and are filmed using a single camera. These often, though not always, take the form of mock-documentaries (Roscoe and Hight, 2001), as evidenced by series such as *Operation Good Guys* (BBC2, 1997–2000), *Marion & Geoff* (BBC2, 2000–2003), *The Office*, and *Twenty Twelve* (BBC4/2, 2011–12). A number of these series have been referred to as "comedy vérité" (Mills, 2004), for their humor explores the "relationship between television, factual representation, and audiences" (Mills, 2008: 90) through the representation of the effects a camera crew can have on those being filmed and the performances individuals carry out in order to appear as 'interesting' television. While such programs appear, on the surface, to be markedly different from the sitcom that preceded them, their shooting style continues to foreground the reaction shot as a key marker of comic intent and they are set within particular settings with recurring characters, just as sitcoms have always been. Newer forms of sitcom, then, must negotiate their innovations and the generic markers which are necessary for programs to be understood as sitcom at all.

The sitcom has also responded to more fundamental changes in broadcasting, in particular the movement in Britain in the 1990s away from terrestrial television and its five channels to a satellite, cable and digital broadcasting structure in which audiences commonly have access to hundreds of different channels. As a national, publicly funded broadcaster, the BBC continues to attempt to produce programs on its BBC1 channel intended for large, wide, family audiences, and insists that, "Good comedy continues to resonate with audiences, particularly when it reflects the texture of British life" (BBC, 2012: 18). Yet it also produces sitcom for other, niche audiences, and has a remit to develop new comedy writers. Its youth-orientated BBC3 channel "celebrates new British talent" (ibid.: 4) and gives space to comedy writers new to the medium. This has produced series such as *Two Pints of Lager and a Packet of Crisps* (BBC2/Choice/3, 2001–11), *Bad Education* (BBC3, 2012–present) and *Pramface* (BBC3, 2012–present).

Indeed, it has been the case that channels have often used sitcom in an attempt to define themselves. For example, the history of Channel 4 can be traced via its comedic output from its early Alternative Comedy programing in the *Comic Strip Presents ...* (C4, 1982–present), to *Desmond's* (C4, 1989–94) – which "finally established the black British sitcom" (Lewisohn, 2003: 219) – to the topical, satirical *Drop the Dead Donkey* (C4, 1990–98), the popular-culture-infused *Spaced* (C4, 1999–2001) and the attempt to revive the traditional sitcom in *Father Ted* (C4, 1995–98) and *The IT Crowd* (C4, 2006–10, 2013). Its sister channel, E4, aiming for a younger audience, found the school setting of *The Inbetweeners* (E4, 2008–10) to be representative of the target viewership.

Other channels have similarly drawn on sitcom and comedy in order to market themselves, often reviving older series. To this end, the comedy and entertainment channel Gold broadcast the most recent output from the *Comic Strip Presents ...* , and brought back *Red Dwarf* in 2009 and 2012, even though the program had originally run on BBC2 from 1998 to 1999, and Steve Coogan's Alan Partridge character, who had been seen on the BBC radio and television series *The Day Today* (BBC2, 1994), *Knowing Me, Knowing You ... with Alan Partridge* (BBC, Radio 4 1992–93, BBC2 1994–95) and *I'm Alan Partridge* (BBC2, 1997–2002), returned in 2012 in *Mid Morning Matters With Alan Partridge* on Sky Atlantic and that series was itself a reworked version of an internet-only series distributed via YouTube and the website of the lager company Foster's. These activities point towards the more diverse routes that now exist for writers and performers to distribute their comedy and suggest that the traditional course from theatre to television via radio is now supplemented by online routes. Furthermore, the non-terrestrial broadcaster Sky appointed its first Head of Comedy in 2010, moving into a genre that had previously been the territory primarily of the older, terrestrial broadcasters. Sky's output has included programs such as *Spy* (Sky1, 2011–12), *Moone Boy* (Sky1, 2012–present) and *Hunderby* (Sky Atlantic, 2012).

According to these accounts the sitcom remains a genre central to television broadcasting and its iterations across particular broadcasters, for particular audiences, and its employment of a wide range of styles and content all demonstrate the flexibility the sitcom can encompass.

Further reading

Medhurst's *A National Joke: Popular Comedy and English Cultural Identities* (2007) gives an overview of English comedy and comedians related to ideas of national identity. Mills's *Television Sitcom* (2005) and *The Sitcom* (2009) explores genre, industry, programs and audiences. Neale and Krutnik's *Popular Film and Television Comedy* (1990) offers an overview of analytical approaches to comedy, with a section on sitcom.

References

Andrews, M. (1998) "Butterflies and caustic asides: Housewives, comedy and the feminist movement." In S. Wagg (ed.) *Because I Tell a Joke or Two: Comedy, Politics and Social Difference*. London and New York: Routledge (pp. 50–64).

BBC (2012) BBC Annual Report and Accounts 2011/12, Part 2: The BBC Executive's Review and Assessment. London: BBC.

——(2013) BBC Annual Report and Accounts 2012/13, Part 1: The BBC Trust's Review and Assessment. London: BBC.

Billig, M. (2005) *Laughter and Ridicule: Towards a Social Critique of Humor*. London: Sage.

Brook, V. (2003) *Something Ain't Kosher Here: The Rise of the 'Jewish' Sitcom*. New Brunswick and London: Rutgers University Press.

Feuer, J. (2008) "The unruly woman sitcom (*I Love Lucy, Roseanne, Absolutely Fabulous*)." In G. Creeber (ed.) *The Television Genre Book* (2nd edition). London: British Film Institute (pp. 68–9).

Fox, K. (2005) *Watching the English: The Hidden Rules of English Behaviour*. London: Hodder and Stoughton.

Freud, S. (1997/1905) *Jokes and Their Relation to the Unconscious*. London: Penguin.

Fuller, L. K. (1992) *The Cosby Show: Audiences, Impact and Implications*. Westport, CT: Greenwood Press.

Goddard, P. (1991) "*Hancock's Half-Hour*: A watershed in British television comedy." In J. Corner (ed.) *Popular Television in Britain: Studies in Cultural History*. London: British Film Institute (pp. 75–89).

Gray, J. (2008) *Television Entertainment*. New York and London: Routledge.

Grote, D. (1983) *The End of Comedy: The Sit-Com and the Comedic Tradition*. Hamden: Archon.

Habermas, J. (1989/1962) *The Structural Transformation of the Public Sphere: An Inquiry into a Category of Bourgeois Society*. Cambridge: Polity Press.

Haralovich, M. B. (2003) "Sitcoms and suburbs: Positioning the 1950s homemaker." In J. Morreale (ed.) *Critiquing the Sitcom: A Reader*. New York: Syracuse University Press (pp. 69–85).

Hartley, J. (2008) "Situation comedy: Part 1." In G. Creeber (ed.) *The Television Genre Book* (2nd edition). London: British Film Institute (pp. 78–81).

Husband, C. (1988) "Racist humor and racist ideology in British television, or, I laughed till you cried." In C. Powell and E. C. Paton (eds.) *Humor in Society: Resistance and Control*. Basingstoke: Macmillan (pp. 149–78).

Jenkins, R. (1994) *Subversive Laughter: The Liberating Power of Comedy*. New York: Free Press.

Jhally, S. and Lewis, J. (1992) *Enlightened Racism: The Cosby Show, Audiences, and the Myth of the American Dream*. Boulder: Westview Press.

Lewisohn, M. (2003) *Radio Times Guide to TV Comedy* (2nd edition). London: BBC Worldwide.

Littlewood, J. and Pickering, M. (1998) "Heard the one about the white middle-class heterosexual father-in-law? Gender, ethnicity and political correctness in comedy." In S. Wagg (ed.) *Because I Tell a Joke or Two: Comedy, Politics and Social Difference*. London and New York: Routledge (pp. 289–310).

Medhurst, A. (2007) *A National Joke: Popular Comedy and English Cultural Identities*. London and New York: Routledge.

Mills, B. (2004) "Comedy vérité: Contemporary sitcom form." *Screen*, 45(1), 63–78.
——(2005) *Television Sitcom*. London: British Film Institute.
——(2008) "The Office." In G. Creeber (ed.) *The Television Genre Book* (2nd edition). London: British Film Institute.
——(2009) *The Sitcom*. Edinburgh: Edinburgh University Press.
Mills, B. and Barlow, D. (2012) *Reading Media Theory: Thinkers, Approaches and Contexts*. Harlow: Pearson.
Mittell, J. (2004) *Genre and Television: From Cop Shows to Cartoons in American Culture*. New York and London: Routledge.
Murray, S. (2005) *Hitch Your Antenna to the Stars: Early Television and Broadcast Stardom*. New York and London: Routledge.
Neale, S. and Krutnik, F. (1990) *Popular Film and Television Comedy*. London and New York: Routledge.
Porter, L. (1998) "Tarts, tampons and tyrants: Women and representation in British comedy." In S. Wagg (ed.) *Because I Tell a Joke or Two: Comedy, Politics and Social Difference*. London and New York: Routledge (pp. 65–92).
Putterman, B. (1995) *On Television and Comedy: Essays on Style, Theme, Performer, and Writer*. Jefferson: McFarland.
Roscoe, J. and Hight, C. (2001) *Faking It: Mock-Documentary and the Subversion of Factuality*. Manchester: Manchester University Press.
Rowe, K. (1995) *The Unruly Woman: Gender and the Genres of Laughter*. Austin, TX: University of Texas Press.
Wagg, S. (1998) "'At ease, corporal': Social class and the situation comedy in British television, from the 1950s to the 1990s." In S. Wagg (ed.) *Because I Tell a Joke or Two: Comedy, Politics and Social Difference*. London and New York: Routledge (pp. 1–31).
Wickberg, D. (1998) *The Sense of Humor: Self and Laughter in Modern America*. Ithaca and London: Cornell University Press.
Wilmut, R. and Rosengard, P. (1989) *Didn't You Kill My Mother-in-Law? The Story of Alternative Comedy in Britain from The Comedy Store to Saturday Live*. London: Methuen.

39
Drama on the box
Lez Cooke

Since 2000 there has been a significant historical turn in television drama studies. Previously, books on British television drama were either edited collections about writers, such as George Brandt's *British Television Drama* (1981) and Frank Pike's *Ah! Mischief: The Writer and Television* (1982); books by people who had worked in the industry, such as Irene Shubik's *Play for Today: The Evolution of Television Drama* (1975) and Shaun Sutton's *The Largest Theatre in the World: Thirty Years of Television Drama* (1982); or academic volumes such as John Tulloch's *Television Drama: Agency, Audiences and Myth* (1990) and Robin Nelson's *TV Drama in Transition: Forms, Values and Cultural Change* (1997).

In 2000, however, several books were published which collectively marked an important development in television drama studies. Jason Jacobs' *The Intimate Screen: Early British Television Drama* (2000) was the first full-length study of what might be described as the 'first age' of British television drama, the period of the BBC's monopoly from 1936–55. John Caughie's *Television Drama: Realism, Modernism and British Culture* (2000) was a rigorous analysis of significant moments in British television drama from the 1930s to the 1990s and the collection edited by Jonathan Bignell, Stephen Lacey and Madeleine MacMurraugh-Kavanagh, *British Television Drama: Past, Present and Future* (2000), brought together academics and practitioners who had contributed to a ground-breaking conference, '"On the Boundary": Turning Points in Television Drama, 1965–2000', at the University of Reading in 1998.

Other books published in 2001–3, such as Giddings and Selby (2001), Cardwell (2002), Chapman (2002), Sydney-Smith (2002), Cooke (2003) and Finch, Cox and Giles (2003) confirmed the renewed interest in television historiography, 20 years after the publication of Brandt's (1981) foundational work. Since 2003 there have been several AHRC-funded research projects and conferences on British television drama history which have resulted in further publications, including Bignell and Lacey (2005), Wheatley (2007) and Cooke (2012). This process of the historiographical reassessment of British television drama shows no sign of abating, with the University of Westminster undertaking a three-year research project from 2012 to 2015 on 'Screen Plays: Theatre Plays on British Television', which includes the production of a database of all theater plays produced on British television since 1936, and Royal Holloway University of London also undertaking a three-year project from 2013 to 2016 on 'The History of Forgotten Television Drama in the UK'.

Much of this recent research on the history of British television drama has focused on the early, largely lost, history of British television, from its official beginnings in 1936 to the arrival of Independent Television (ITV) in 1955, and on what is often described as the 'golden age' of British television, from the late 1950s to the early 1980s. With hindsight, however, it now seems possible to identify three distinct 'ages' of British television. The first age is the period of the BBC's monopoly, from 1936 to 1955, when nearly all television was transmitted live and very little was recorded for posterity. The second age begins with the arrival in 1955 of a commercial competitor for the BBC and ends with the 1990 Broadcasting Act, a piece of legislation which did much to usher in a new deregulated era of multiple channels and new working practices, a 'third age' of British television which continues to the present.

This tripartite periodization is unique to British television. Other writers have produced different periodizations of television history. In his book, *Seeing Things: Television in the Age of Uncertainty* (2000), John Ellis identifies three eras, beginning with an "era of scarcity, which lasted for most countries until the late 1970s or early 1980s", followed by "an era of availability, where several channels broadcasting continuously jostled for attention, often with more competition in the shape of cable or satellite services" and a third "era of plenty ... in which television programmes (or, as they will be known, 'content' or 'product') will be accessible through a variety of technologies" (Ellis, 2000: 39). In America, the terms TVI, TVII and TVIII have been used to describe, respectively, the network era of US television (roughly 1948–75), the post-network era (roughly 1975–95) and the post-1995, digital-global era (see Nelson, 2007: 7).

While there is some logic, especially in the American context, to periodizations such as TVI, II and III, which overlap to some extent with Ellis's eras of 'scarcity, availability and plenty', in the British context there seems a greater logic in identifying 1936–55 as the 'first age' of British television, when television was not only scarce but remains largely invisible to us today as a consequence of the almost complete absence of recorded programs. While television was more 'available' in Britain from 1955 to 1990, despite there being only two channels until 1964, when BBC2 was introduced, and only three until 1982, when Channel Four began broadcasting, the logic behind identifying this as a 'second age' of British television resides in it being a period governed by the principles of 'public service' broadcasting, which began to be eroded when satellite TV arrived in 1989, signaling a shift to a deregulated, multi-channel age which the 1990 Broadcasting Act (introduced by a Conservative government advocating 'free-market' principles) did much to encourage. The 'third age' of British television, therefore, really begins in 1990 and is marked by similar attributes to those of TV III and Ellis's 'era of plenty', with particular consequences for the concept of public service broadcasting and the production of television drama, consequences which are still transforming British television today.

The first age of British television drama: 1936–55

When the BBC began a regular television service in September 1936 it was restricted to a small audience within range of the transmitter at Alexandra Palace in north

London. It was also restricted to a few hours of broadcasting in the afternoon and evening each day and, in terms of drama, was dependent to a large extent on material adapted from the stage. The personnel involved in early television drama came mostly from radio and the theater, bringing with them the dramatic forms prevalent in those media. Consequently, pre-war television drama consisted of extracts from stage plays transmitted under program titles such as *Play Parade* and *Theatre Parade*, full-length stage adaptations, such as Jan Bussell's production of George Bernard Shaw's *How He Lied to Her Husband* (tx. 7 July 1937) and outside broadcasts of plays from West End theaters, such as J. B. Priestley's *When We Are Married*, transmitted live from St. Martin's Theatre in London on 16 November 1938.

Original drama for television was rare before the war. The first such production was probably *Felicity's First Season* (tx. 13 September 1938), written by Charles Terrot and produced by George More O'Ferrall, and there was an innovative original drama by R. E. J. Brooke called *Condemned to be Shot* (tx. 4 March 1939), produced by Jan Bussell, which was shown entirely from the point of view of the central character who, at the end of the 20-minute drama, was shot by a firing squad.

Plays, and extracts from plays, were predominant before the war, but there was one early example of a television serial, a form destined to become one of the staples of television drama. *Ann and Harold* (tx. July–August 1938), written by Louis Goodrich and produced by Lanham Titchener, was a five-part serial (each episode was 15–20 minutes long) about the romance of a London society couple, featuring Ann Todd and William Hutchison in the title roles. Unlike most pre-war drama, which was adapted from the stage, *Ann and Harold* was first produced for radio, in 1932.

When television resumed after the Second World War, on 7 June 1946, the prewar policy of adapting stage plays continued but there was increasing recognition of the need for new material written especially for television if television drama was to develop as anything other than an imitation of the theater. One of the first post-war plays to be written for television was J. B. Priestley's *The Rose and Crown* (tx. 27 August 1946) which departed from the ubiquitous middle-class drawing room by setting the action in the bar of a public house in north-east London.

Television's relationship with theater grew more antagonistic after the war, with West End theaters refusing to allow the live transmission of plays because of concerns about the effect upon theater attendance. As a consequence, the Outside Broadcast Department, which was responsible for these live transmissions, was forced to turn to repertory theatres instead (see Harris, 2008: 156). But the decline of this form of drama was ultimately beneficial as it forced television drama to develop its own aesthetic rather than relying on the live transmission of 'photographed stage plays' (Jacobs, 2000: 2–3, 77).

One way in which television drama began to move away from its dependency on stage adaptations was by producing series and serials rather than single plays. These were either literary adaptations, shown in six episodes, such as *Little Women* (tx. December 1950–January 1951), from the novel by Louisa May Alcott, and Jane Austen's *Pride and Prejudice*, which was first serialized on television in February–March 1952, or they were original serials such as Francis Durbridge's *The Broken Horseshoe* (tx. March–April 1952). But the real breakthrough in original television drama came with Nigel Kneale's *The Quatermass Experiment*, produced by Rudolph Cartier, shown in six parts from July to August 1953. *The Quatermass Experiment* tapped into the concerns of the contemporary audience, reflecting anxieties about the atomic bomb and the possibility of invasion and 'infection' by unknown forces, with its story of an astronaut who returns to Earth carrying an alien infection. The audience was gripped by the serial and it was followed by two sequels in 1955 and 1958–59, as well as another Kneale/Cartier collaboration, the *Sunday Night Theatre* adaptation of George Orwell's dystopian novel *Nineteen Eighty-Four* (tx. 12 and 16 December 1954).

Nineteen Eighty-Four was a landmark in 1950s television drama, partly because of its departure from the genre of middle-class drawing-room drama to show a bleak, futuristic Britain under totalitarian rule, but also because of its technological innovations, using film inserts to an unprecedented extent in order to open out the drama, expanding its scope and ambition beyond anything that had preceded it. While the hallmarks of early television drama were 'intimacy', as a result of bringing drama into the home, and 'immediacy', as a result of it being broadcast live, Rudolph Cartier's achievement with *Nineteen Eighty-Four* was to combine these attributes with an expanded vision of the potential of television drama to embrace larger issues of contemporary concern.

It was a sign of television drama's increasing maturity and variety that serials such as *Quatermass* and plays such as *Nineteen Eighty-Four* were being produced at the same time that drama series and long-running serials were being developed. *The Grove Family*, a weekly series about a lower-middle-class suburban family living in the London suburbs, began on 9 April 1954 and continued through to 1957, by which time its cozy depiction of suburban life was being challenged by more exciting forms of drama on the new commercial network, ITV.

1954 also saw the arrival of the police detective series *Fabian of the Yard* (1954–56) which was shot entirely on film, marking a departure from the live television drama that had prevailed up to then. Shooting on film enabled a new kind of aesthetic to be developed, closer to that of the cinema, whose audiences were beginning to be eroded by the new medium. It also enabled television programs to be sold abroad, introducing a commercial incentive for the BBC, even before ITV arrived on the scene. *Fabian* was the first of what would prove to be one of television's most popular and enduring genres and it was followed by the long-running *Dixon of Dock Green* (1955–76) which started in July 1955, just two months before the first ITV companies began broadcasting in the London region.

The second age of British television drama: 1955–90

The ITV network was introduced gradually between 1955 and 1962, struggling initially to attract advertising revenue because of its limited audience reach. But by the end of August 1957, when ITV began broadcasting in Scotland, the Head of Scottish TV, Roy Thompson, was able to claim that owning an ITV franchise was "like having a licence to print money" (cf. Johnson and Turnock, 2005: 21). By 1958 ITV had captured three-quarters of the television audience that had access to both channels with its populist programing of quizzes, game shows, variety programs and imported American drama.

ITV was viewed with suspicion by some as a brash, American-style network, far removed from the high-minded principles established by John Reith at the BBC, but the protracted discussions which led to the 1954 Television Act ensured that ITV should contain an element of public service broadcasting alongside its more populist programing. Consequently news, current affairs and 'serious' drama were present in the ITV schedules from the very beginning. While the ITV companies did produce popular drama series such as *The Adventures of Robin Hood* (ABC, 1955–59), *Emergency – Ward 10* (ATV, 1957–67) and *Shadow Squad* (Granada, 1957–59), single play anthology series such as *Play of the Week*, *Television Playhouse* and *Armchair Theatre* were an important part of ITV's drama programing. Plays often attracted large audiences and there was an eclectic mix of adaptations from novels and the stage as well as original drama, with the latter featuring prominently on *Armchair Theatre* following the appointment at ABC TV of the Canadian producer Sydney Newman as Head of Drama in 1958. When Harold Pinter's original television play *A Night Out* was transmitted on *Armchair Theatre* in April 1960 over six million viewers were watching and the play topped the ratings for that week.

Granada Television, under the leadership of Sidney Bernstein, also offered an impressive range of 'serious' plays and popular drama series but its big success was *Coronation Street* (1960–present). Conceived as a twice-weekly serial about the inhabitants of a fictional northern street, it proved popular with audiences all over the country and was topping the ratings within a year. Granada's anthology drama series, such as *The Younger Generation* (1961), *Saki* (1962), *The Victorians* (1963) and *The Liars* (1966), were original and innovative and the company's drama output set a challenge for the BBC which lost a number of personnel to the ITV companies in the late 1950s and early 1960s.

However, with a new Director General, Hugh Carleton Greene, and a new Head of Drama, Sydney Newman, poached from ITV in 1963, the BBC began to fight back with new programs such as *Z Cars* (1962–78), *Doctor Who* (1963–present) and *The Wednesday Play* (1964–70), the latter establishing a reputation for innovation and controversy which was maintained by *Play for Today* (1970–84) in the 1970s. Series such as *Z Cars* and anthology play series such as *The Wednesday Play* were notable for dealing with contemporary issues, tapping into the 1960s zeitgeist with plays such as *Up the Junction* (1965) and *Cathy Come Home* (1966). Meanwhile ITV countered with a distinctive brand of 'telefantasies', such as *The Avengers* (ABC, 1961–69) and *The Prisoner* (ATV, 1967–68) which were enhanced by the transition to color television in 1969 (both were being made in color from 1967 but the switchover from monochrome to color TV did not take place until November 1969 on the main channels, BBC2 having switched to color in December 1967).

The transition to color television was followed by an increase in costume dramas in the 1970s, following the huge success of *The Forsyte Saga* on BBC2 in 1967. *Upstairs Downstairs* (LWT, 1971–75) was ITV's response and it proved immensely popular, lasting for 68 episodes spanning the period from 1903 to 1930. *The Duchess of Duke Street* (BBC1, 1976–77) and *When the Boat Comes In* (BBC1, 1976–81) were also set in the early decades of the 20th century, as was Jim Allen's *Days of Hope*

(BBC1, 1975), a radical four-part drama directed by Ken Loach and produced by Tony Garnett, a partnership which was responsible for a number of politically progressive dramas on the BBC from the mid 1960s to the mid 1970s.

The single play continued to be popular in the 1970s, especially on the BBC, where *Play for Today* (1970–84) provided an outlet for writers such as Trevor Griffiths, David Hare, Alan Plater, Dennis Potter and Jack Rosenthal, but ITV gradually phased out production of the single play in the 1970s in favor of series and serials which were more cost-effective than the single play. In addition to long-running historical series such as *Upstairs Downstairs*, ITV produced multi-part literary adaptations such as the 26-episode *Clayhanger* (ATV, 1976), from Arnold Bennett's Potteries trilogy, and contemporary police series such as *Special Branch* (Thames, 1969–74), *New Scotland Yard* (LWT, 1972–74) and *The Sweeney* (Thames, 1975–78). There was also a shift towards filmed dramas in the 1970s, both within *Play for Today* and in contemporary drama series such as *The Sweeney*, *The Professionals* (LWT, 1977–83), *Law and Order* (BBC2, 1978) and *Out* (Thames, 1978).

There was still space for original authored drama in the 1970s, despite the increase in long-running drama series on both the main channels. Dennis Potter had established a reputation for innovative, original drama in the 1960s and the six-part *Pennies from Heaven* (BBC1, 1978) extended that reputation by including fantasy musical sequences in a narrative set during the 1930s Depression. Howard Schuman wrote several innovative video dramas in the 1970s, exploiting the creative possibilities of new video technology, including the entirely studio-based *Rock Follies* (Thames, 1976) and *Rock Follies of 77* (Thames, 1977), about an all-woman rock group, which included stylized musical sequences that, like *Pennies from Heaven*, went against the grain of the trend in the 1970s towards more realistic, location-based drama.

The decline of the single play continued in the 1980s as dramas were increasingly shot on film, resembling films made for television rather than plays recorded in the studio. *Play for Today* ended in 1984, to be replaced by *Screen Two* in 1985 and *Screen One* in 1989, filmed drama series modeled on *Film on Four*, which had been introduced by the new Channel Four in 1982. Channel Four was the first significant change in British television since the arrival of ITV in the mid 1950s and it ended the BBC/ITV duopoly which had endured throughout the 'golden age' of television drama from the late 1950s to the early 1980s. Established as a 'publisher' rather than a producer of its own programs, Channel Four depended on a network of independent production companies for its material which included the twice-weekly Liverpool soap opera *Brookside* (1982–2003), produced by Mersey Television, which was radically different in both its production methods and in dealing with issues rarely dealt with on the existing soaps. The channel also featured dramas by writers such as Alan Bleasdale, John McGrath and Willy Russell which were set outside of London and the south, continuing a tradition which the Senior Commissioning Editor for Fiction at Channel Four, David Rose, had established in the 1970s when he was Head of BBC English Regions' Drama in Birmingham (see Cooke, 2012).

The 1980s saw a number of television writers responding to the divisive effects of Thatcherism on British society, not least Alan Bleasdale's scintillating *Boys from the Blackstuff* (BBC2, 1982), a five-part series (produced by BBC English Regions' Drama) that dramatized the effects of government policy on the working-class in Liverpool so successfully that it was given an unprecedented repeat on BBC1 two months after the series ended on BBC2. Troy Kennedy Martin's *Edge of Darkness* (BBC1, 1985) also received a swift repeat on BBC1 after its transmission on BBC2 in late 1985. An engrossing six-part nuclear thriller, *Edge of Darkness* speculated on the development of a secret state which allowed private companies to pursue profit-making ventures, regardless of their impact on the environment. Even popular drama series such as *Casualty* (BBC1, 1986–present) were critical of the effects of government policy on the National Health Service, while the four-part Channel Four drama *The Nation's Health* (C4, 1983), written by G. F. Newman, provided a devastating critique of the state of the health service.

It could be argued that the introduction of a fourth television channel, breaking the BBC/ITV duopoly, marked the beginning of a new era in British television but in retrospect Channel Four, in the 1980s, represented the final flourish of a 'golden age' of public service broadcasting before the advent of a far more competitive era in the 1990s. There is no doubt that Thatcher's Conservative government had not expected the kind of radical, progressive programing that Channel Four commissioned from the new independent production companies and steps were taken in the late 1980s to introduce legislation that would transform the broadcasting landscape in Britain, bringing to an end a prolonged period of creativity in which writers, directors and producers enjoyed the freedom to produce a wide range of radical, innovative, quality drama. In the third age of British television such opportunities were to be severely diminished.

The third age of British television drama: 1990–present

The late 1980s saw the beginnings of significant change in the landscape of British television. Satellite television arrived in February 1989 when Rupert Murdoch's Sky TV began broadcasting, followed by British Satellite Broadcasting in March 1990, but there was not yet a market for two satellite companies and in November 1990, with both companies suffering massive financial losses, they merged to form British Satellite Broadcasting (BSkyB).

Meanwhile the 1990 Broadcasting Act introduced a number of measures designed to increase competition in broadcasting. A major change was the introduction of a new procedure for issuing ITV contracts, by inviting companies to bid for a franchise, with the new contracts being awarded to the highest bidder, subject to passing a 'quality threshold'. Channel Four, which had previously received advertising revenue from the ITV companies, was required to sell its own advertising from 1993, a change which many believed would lead to the channel becoming more 'populist' in its programing. The Act also required the BBC and ITV to take at least 25 per cent of their programing from independent production companies.

These changes saw a move towards a more deregulated broadcasting system where competition for audiences in an increasingly multi-channel environment began to erode the concept of public service television that had prevailed since the 1950s. The BBC, under its new Director General, John Birt, introduced a system of Producer Choice which was designed to make the BBC more competitive but at the cost, many of its critics argued, of squeezing out creativity. Consequently many of the most creative writers, producers and directors from the 'golden age' of television drama found it much more difficult to get innovative, 'quality' drama commissioned, partly because innovative, quality drama was both risky and expensive and the new cost-conscious management at the BBC was less inclined to take risks with drama unless it was virtually guaranteed to attract audiences.

The third age of British television drama was therefore marked by a shift from producer-led drama to consumer-led drama with an increase in focus groups and market research in order to establish what the audience wanted, rather than presenting viewers with new forms of experimental, innovative or radical drama that they might not like. This led to an increase in tried and tested genres such as hospital drama and police series, with fewer opportunities for the more unusual or 'challenging' forms of drama that had been produced in previous decades.

While ratings had always been a concern among the ITV companies, this now became important across the spectrum of television scheduling, with the BBC far more concerned about ratings than it previously had been. As competition increased, with a fifth terrestrial channel starting in 1997, Sky introducing an ever-increasing number of satellite channels and all of the existing companies introducing digital channels in the 2000s, the audience fragmented into niche markets, with different channels targeting different audience segments, differentiated by age, gender, class or education.

Regional identity continued to be important to some extent, with different regional companies catering for regional and national audiences with dramas such as *Coronation Street*, *Emmerdale* (formerly *Emmerdale Farm*, 1972–present), *Heartbeat* (1992–2010) and *Taggart* (1983–present) but with the regional ITV companies embarking on a series of mergers and takeovers, finally forming one large consolidated company, ITV plc, in 2003, the concept of regional drama was gradually eroded. ITV's justification for this was that it needed to be bigger to compete with other large companies in the global marketplace, such as Sky, the BBC and the American networks.

Consequently the emphasis shifted towards the production of dramas that could be exported to global markets, such as *Agatha Christie's Poirot* (1989–2013), *Hornblower* (1998–2003) and *Midsomer Murders* (1997–present) (see Steemers, 2004). The BBC also focused more on dramas that might be sold abroad and a new cycle of costume dramas emerged in the mid 1990s including *Martin Chuzzlewit* (1994), *Middlemarch* (1994) and *Pride and Prejudice* (1995). Co-productions with foreign companies, especially American and Australian companies, became increasingly important in this new global marketplace and in 2005 the BBC entered into a multi-million pound partnership with the American company HBO to produce *Rome* (2005 and 2007), a historical drama filmed in co-production with the Italian company RAI.

In contrast to this move towards big-budget co-productions, a new wave of innovative, low-budget dramas appeared on the BBC and Channel Four, including *This Life* (BBC2, 1996–97), *Queer as Folk* (C4, 1999–2000), *Clocking Off* (BBC1, 2000–2003) and *As If* (C4, 2001–4), targeting younger viewers with a colorful, energetic style, up-tempo music and fast-moving narratives. With the advent of youth-oriented digital channels such as E4 and BBC3 in the 2000s, further new drama series were introduced, including *Torchwood* (BBC, 2006–11), a spin-off from the revived *Doctor Who* (BBC1, 2005–present), which graduated in successive series from BBC3 to BBC2 and then BBC1, *Skins* (E4, 2007–13) and *Misfits* (E4, 2009–13).

With the growth of the internet and concerns that the younger audience was being lost to it, television companies also started diversifying to produce internet dramas, available in short 'webisodes'. As television started to become available on a proliferating number of platforms, such as computers, laptops, tablets and mobile phones, the established television companies, working with a variety of new independent production companies, began seeking new ways to market new forms of television drama alongside the existing tried and tested popular series and big-budget prestige productions.

In the twenty-first century television drama has diversified to such an extent that, while some dramas, such as Stephen Poliakoff's slow-paced *Perfect Strangers* (BBC2, 2001) and the BSkyB series *Theatre Live!* (Sky Arts 1, 2009) may hark back to the theatrical origins of television drama, there is now a sufficiently wide variety of drama available on the terrestrial and satellite channels and the internet to suggest that British television drama may be enjoying a new 'golden age' to rival that of the 1950s–80s.

Further reading

Lez Cooke's (2003) *British Television Drama: A History* is the only book to provide a complete history of British television drama. Jason Jacobs' (2000) *The Intimate Screen: Early British Television Drama* is the best book on the first age of British television drama. John Caughie's (2000) *Television Drama: Realism, Modernism and British Culture* provides a rigorous theoretical analysis of significant moments in the history of British television drama. Lez Cooke's (2013) *Style in British Television Drama* analyzes changes in television drama style over a 50-year period. Jonathan Bignell and Stephen Lacey's (2014) edited collection *British Television Drama: Past, Present and Future* includes contributions from academics and practitioners and is revised and updated.

References

Bignell, J. and Lacey, S. (eds.) (2005) *Popular Television Drama: Critical Perspectives*. Manchester: Manchester University Press.
——(eds.) (2014) *British Television Drama: Past, Present and Future* (2nd edition). Basingstoke: Palgrave Macmillan.
Bignell, J., Lacey, S. and MacMurraugh-Kavanagh, M. (eds.) (2000) *British Television Drama: Past, Present and Future*. Basingstoke: Palgrave.
Brandt, G. (ed.) (1981) *British Television Drama*. Cambridge: Cambridge University Press.
Cardwell, S. (2002) *Adaptation Revisited: Television and the Classic Novel*. Manchester: Manchester University Press.
Caughie, J. (2000) *Television Drama: Realism, Modernism and British Culture*. Oxford: Oxford University Press.
Chapman, J. (2002) *Saints and Avengers: British Adventure Series of the 1960s*. London: I. B. Tauris.

Cooke, L. (2003) *British Television Drama: A History*. London: British Film Institute.
——(2012) *A Sense of Place: Regional British Television Drama, 1956–82*. Manchester: Manchester University Press.
——(2013) *Style in British Television Drama*. Basingstoke: Palgrave Macmillan.
Ellis, J. (2000) *Seeing Things: Television in the Age of Uncertainty*. London: I. B. Tauris.
Finch, J., with Cox, M. and Giles, M. (eds.) (2003) *Granada Television: The First Generation*. Manchester: Manchester University Press.
Giddings, R. and Selby, K. (2001) *The Classic Serial on Television and Radio*. Basingstoke: Palgrave.
Harris, K. (2008) "Evolutionary stages: Theatre and television, 1946–56." In D. Shellard (ed.) *The Golden Generation: New Light on Post-War British Theatre*. London: British Library (pp. 152–79).
Jacobs, J. (2000) *The Intimate Screen: Early British Television Drama*. Oxford: Oxford University Press.
Johnson, C. and Turnock, R. (eds.) (2005) *ITV Cultures: Independent Television Over Fifty Years*. Maidenhead: Open University Press.
Nelson, R. (1997) *TV Drama in Transition: Forms, Values and Cultural Change*. Basingstoke: Macmillan.
——(2007) *State of Play: Contemporary "High-End" TV Drama*. Manchester: Manchester University Press.
Pike, F. (ed.) (1982) *Ah! Mischief: The Writer and Television*. London: Faber & Faber.
Shubik, I. (1975) *Play for Today: The Evolution of Television Drama*. London: David-Poynter; rev. ed. Manchester University Press, 2000.
Steemers, J. (2004) *Selling Television: British Television in the Global Marketplace*. London: British Film Institute.
Sutton, S. (1982) *The Largest Theatre in the World: Thirty Years of Television Drama*. London: BBC.
Sydney-Smith, S. (2002) *Beyond Dixon of Dock Green: Early British Police Series*. London: I. B. Tauris.
Tulloch, J. (1990) *Television Drama: Agency, Audiences and Myth*. London: Routledge.
Wheatley, H. (ed.) (2007) *Re-viewing Television History: Critical Issues in Television Historiography*. London: I. B. Tauris.

40
The origins and practice of science on British television

Timothy Boon and Jean-Baptiste Gouyon

Both science and television have been extraordinarily powerful forces for economic, social and cultural change in the period since 1945. It follows that the television representation of scientific and technological subjects should be an exceptionally potent subject for revealing core elements of our culture. And yet science television has until recently been the province of a very small coterie of scholars. As a result, what we know about the story of the history of science on television is uneven. However, especially in a volume of this breadth, where it is possible to draw comparison with other fields, it is important to ask what it has meant, over the substantive period of British television history, to present science, specifically on television. But we must work with what we have, and this essay follows the weight of the literature in covering the period before 1980 in significantly more depth than the last few decades.

What has it meant to viewers to experience science television programs?

The fundamental point about the history, institutions and influence of television is that it was the growth of viewers that drove its development. Television license holders increased 300-fold in the key years of expansion between 1947 and 1955, by which date 4.5 million homes had sets; there were 13 million by 1964 when BBC2 started; in 2009–10, 25 million licenses were in force. All the same, it is difficult to make direct links between these bald figures and the experience of viewers of science television programs. One approach is to look at the intended, or 'inscribed', audience by studying the programatic statements made by producers about the viewers they expected and the mode in which they expected the programs in question to be viewed. Gordon Rattray Taylor, editor of *Horizon* between 1964 and 1966, for example, was keen that the program should provoke "the sort of conversation which springs up when a scientist and a non-scientific friend get talking over a beer, a coffee or a glass of after dinner brandy" (Taylor, 1964). Aubrey Singer, the Head of Department, similarly asserted that in science broadcasting "the level of communication is between equals in intelligence: to an audience that is well disposed toward, but with no special knowledge of, the subject matter" (Singer, 1966: 13). In the foundation of *Horizon*, the producers also bandied about, at the level of metaphor, different magazine titles in seeking to establish the appeal of the program – was it more like *Scientific American*, *New Scientist* or *Encounter*? And, over its first five years, it oscillated between these different modes (Boon, 2014).

Natural history television, for its part, was thought of along the lines of what we would call now a top-down model of science communication. This is suggested by the words of Desmond Hawkins, the head of West Region programs, who founded the BBC Natural History Unit (NHU) in 1957. With its natural history programing, he said, BBC television "has brought [into British homes] a reliable flow of expert comment and factual report [...] films of bird-life and animal behaviour which equip us with a range of knowledge that a Bewick or a Gilbert White might envy" (Hawkins, 1957: 7). And although in 1962 Hawkins put out, as a warning to "idealist enterprises" (Hawkins, 1962: 2), the dictum that "the first aim of a prestige program should be to win an audience" (ibid.), it is notable that one early participant in natural history television, James Fisher, recalled in 1959 in relation to the program *Look*, that:

> None of the distinguished naturalists and cinematographers whom Peter Scott has introduced talk down to their public. Indeed, they talk not to their public so much as to each other in the relaxed yet lucid voices that they would use in any normal discussion of their profession amongst themselves. The fact that by so doing they capture and please their audience is itself proof that natural history needs no aid to acceptance ...
>
> (Fisher, 1959: 9)

Audiences for natural history television were thus imagined as passive witnesses to a learned discussion rather than as active interlocutors in this discussion.

In conjunction with imagining their potential audience by comparison with print journalism, producers and managers also considered audience questions by debating issues of the comprehensibility of programs. It is clear that the intrinsic difficulty of science was an issue in programing, but not necessarily in a negative sense; it is as though they saw a kind of 'aesthetic of difficulty' in which the abstruseness of science could be part of its appeal. This had been seen in 1949 when a special enquiry was commissioned into the comprehensibility of a radio broadcast, where one of the striking findings was that "interest was not confined to any one group but was found in all and was, in fact, most strong where the content of the broadcast was only partly understood" (Boon, 2008: 189; Jones, 2013a). Difficulty was also an issue when the long-running series *Eye on Research* was canceled in 1962. Richard Hoggart has argued that notions of elevated quality in television have often been aligned with perceived levels of 'difficulty' (Hoggart, 2004: 116). Science television has often occupied this niche of perceived quality linked to abstruseness of subject matter.

More directly, it is true that the BBC did undertake a significant amount of viewer research, and so the archives do often hold audience response reports for many of the programs and series that were broadcast. These reports, typically around two pages in length, show the responses of a panel of viewers to the program in question. They are headed by the 'reaction' or 'appreciation index', effectively a percentage quality rating by viewers, followed by selected comments. For example, the report on the episode 'Patterns of Heredity' in the series *Eye on Research* (24 May 1961) had a 'reaction index' of 75; one of the recorded comments reads:

> "All in favour of programs of this type. The general public are, for the most part, unaware of research activity in this field. Television is the answer to this lack of knowledge": thus did a Docker sum up his appreciation for this program.
>
> (Anonymous, 1961)

It is, however, important to grasp that these reports were not so much designed to shed light on the subjectivity of the science program viewer as to audit the effectiveness of the production process. It would, all the same, certainly be possible to conduct an extensive analysis of these reports and to gain a greater insight into the reaction of selected viewers over time to science as to other television programs.

There is no evidence, either, that the scientists involved in science broadcasting gave much consideration to the audience; they too were much more concerned with the ways in which science should be propagated than with what kinds of programs the viewers might prefer to watch, understand or enjoy.

What have science television programs meant to scientists?

If the historical study of audiences for science television gives few leads, then more is known about the other participants in science television: the scientists themselves and television producers. The post-war period saw a distinct increase in scientists' interest in moving image media (Boon, 2008). Compared to the pre-war period, when only a small number of scientists became actively involved in documentary filmmaking, from the 1950s scientific élites actively sought out a presence on television. In this Cold War world, where the atomic bomb, new biological science and automation seemed in different ways to threaten the stability of society and culture, there was a job to be done as never before in conveying the positive role and contributions of scientific research to the public. Even before television began to reach substantial British audiences from the time of the Coronation in 1953, science was one of the agenda items for the newly reformed BBC General Advisory Council, seven of whose 49 members were scientists. Discussions which initially focused on radio were soon extended to include, then to be dominated by, the new medium. In 1949 the nuclear physicist Marcus Oliphant, one of the Council's scientist members, set in train a sequence of interactions between élite science and the BBC. He initiated a debate on the broadcast representation of science by calling for the BBC to appoint an advisory committee on scientific broadcasting and to employ more scientists as producers. After careful internal discussion there resulted an unhappy two-year period in which the senior biomedical scientist Henry Dale was employed as scientific advisor to the BBC. This only seems to have demonstrated the intrinsic problems of the advisor model, where such an individual is expected to compel respect but is not part of the normal management hierarchies of the broadcaster. It also revealed the main and continuing problem in discussions between these two professional groups: that for scientists and broadcasters to argue about the representation of science in broadcasts tends to lead to contests of professional expertise (Jones, 2013b; Boon, 2008). Individual scientists appeared in television programs, where relations with individual producers were often cordial. But this did not prevent institution-level relationships from being quite troubled; repeatedly, in 1958, 1961 and from 1985, organized élite scientists sent delegations to, or otherwise directly communicated by other means with, the most senior staff of the Corporation to complain that there was too little coverage of science, or that it was done ineffectively, or without sufficient control from the scientists themselves. The Corporation was always careful to manage its responses to ensure that control over the medium was never ceded to their petitioners. The scientists, who stressed their cognitive expertise, would have preferred to have charge of how science was shown on television thereby expressing a wish to control the public relations of science. To achieve this aim they very often favored series of something closely akin to broadcast courses of lectures in basic science. There is also some evidence that the different interest groups within science and engineering were also fighting battles between disciplines (Boon, 2008: 221).

The BBC Natural History Unit, on the other hand, had been careful to maintain strong links with scientists. One of the dreams of Desmond Hawkins throughout the sixties was that it would become a kind of hybrid institution where scientists would do research and television producers would make programs about their work. This never materialized but in 1962 Hawkins could report that scientists actively sought the participation of the Unit in their activities, through invitations to either participate in congresses, or to contribute papers to scientific journals. And "in one notable case (the return of the Osprey as a breeding species)", revealed Hawkins, "our programme research was more comprehensive than the entire literature" (Hawkins, 1962: 3). This suggests that to the scientists interested in animal behavior, the BBC NHU was seen as a participant in the knowledge-producing activity rather than simply a mediator between them and non-specialist audiences.

What has it meant to broadcasters to make science television programs?

For the senior staff of the BBC, science was among the interests they needed to address, as the Director General, Sir Ian Jacob, wrote in 1956: "Our national position depends a great deal upon our standing with that part of the nation which is responsible for and actively concerned with political, economic and scientific matters (Jacob, 1956). In their responses to the approaches of scientists, program producers for their part tended to stress that the use of television as a medium was their professional expertise and property (Jones, 2013b). For example, in response to a 1958 Royal Society-British Association delegation to the Director General, the leading producers of science television in the Talks and Outside Broadcast Departments, James McCloy and Aubrey Singer respectively, prepared statements about their production processes. Both producers emphasized the importance of their access to senior scientists and how the views of scientists at the Royal Society, for example, led them to interesting work to report. McCloy expressed his respectfulness towards science directly, whilst asserting the importance of interesting the viewer: "Whatever the showmanship involved in presentation, the program aims at being entirely responsible in its treatment of science. It must be responsible not only in question of fact but also in selection and emphasis, and earn the good will of the scientific profession" (McCloy, 1958). In choosing stories to cover, Singer stressed suitability for the medium and McCloy favored the importance of choosing only subjects that were comprehensible to the audience (Boon, 2008: 222).

In discussions with scientists like these, the producers hammered out the BBC's policy, and this was expressed in a public lecture in February 1966 by Aubrey Singer:

> Those of us engaged in broadcasting science to a general audience are forced to frame our attitudes in the light of this world we see around us. […] We place ourselves so that the inbuilt vested interests can be viewed as objectively as our own unconscious leanings of background and upbringing will allow. To this end, as a foundation to our policy, we have firmly decided *that the broadcasting of science shall be in the hands of broadcasters.*
> (Singer, 1966: 8, original emphasis)

Here he voiced with particular directness the view of the producers: that "the aim of scientific programming […] is not necessarily the propagation of science, rather its aim is common with all broadcasting, an enrichment of the audience experience" (ibid.: 9). For him, "the televising of science is a *process of television*, subject to the principles of programme structure, and the demands of dramatic form. Therefore, in taking programme decisions, priority must be given to the medium rather than scientific pedantry" (ibid.: 13, original emphasis). 1966 also saw the foundation of the BBC's Science Consultative Committee, a concession to the scientists who had lobbied for more influence over science broadcasting in the context of the Pilkington Committee into the Future of Broadcasting. Broadly speaking and as far as the detailed research conducted so far allows us to see, the effect of this six-monthly meeting was to neutralize the tension between élite science and the BBC by providing a forum in which the scientists felt that they were listened to. Meanwhile, relations between individual scientists and journalist-producers tended to be businesslike, even cordial, and the coverage of science was generally positive, and certainly very rarely critical.

In Bristol, Desmond Hawkins defined how the Unit should relate to scientists in a way that would encourage collaboration on an equal footing, but at the same time establish a strict boundary between the process of television-making and science and, at the same time, a clear division of labor between television producers and scientists. To the former program-making, to the latter the production of the raw material from which programs are made:

> In handling this subject we expose ourselves to the critical scrutiny of scientists, and their approval is an important endorsement. Moreover, it is their

work that throws up the ideas and instances and controversies from which programmes are made. We look to them as contributors, as source material, as consultants and as elite opinion on our efforts. In short we need their goodwill.

(Hawkins, 1962: 7)

The televising of natural history was thus defined as a way of knowing and of producing knowledge rather than as a matter of translating the knowledge produced by scientists.

Who were the producers?

At the BBC, science and technology programs were produced by several different departments, mainly settling down as the responsibility of Science and Features in the 1960s. Responsibility for natural history, by contrast, was separately located in a specialist department established in Bristol at a distance from London, the main production centre. The conventions that grew up in natural history television were also different in mode, as its proponents made claims that it not merely *represented*, but actually *did* natural history by making television programs.

The televising of natural history on the BBC was started in the 1950s by naturalists who saw in the medium a means of bringing natural history to a larger audience than their network of public lectures had previously been able to achieve. They were primarily naturalists making films. And they left a mark, although in later years they were marginalized because the production of natural history television programs became a profession. The first professional producers of natural history programs, foremost amongst whom was Christopher Parsons (1932–2002), learned their trade from their interactions with these naturalists and were in this way acculturated to natural history. Second, from the start, the Bristol unit was always part of networks of natural history and participated in a vivid local tradition of natural history (Davies, 1998). As Hawkins noted in 1962, "the [West] Region itself is generally regarded as a 'naturalists' paradise': it offers […] a vigorous tradition of field-work by local naturalists" (Hawkins, 1962: 1). It thus appears that doing natural history television was, and remains, a specialism.

By contrast, across most of our period, television producers saw the making of science television as like making any television program. This is visible from the time of the 12-part series *The World is Ours* (1954–56), five of whose episodes were on broadly medical or scientific themes. These were produced by the generalist Norman Swallow, with the first generation documentarist Paul Rotha in the background as Head of the Documentary Department (Boon, 2008: 204–7). In the 1950s, it is true, alongside these generalists there were a few individuals, notably James McCloy, who specialized in science programs, in McCloy's case, *Inventor's Club* (1948–56), *Frontiers of Science* (from 1956) and *Science is News* (from 1958). But Aubrey Singer, who became the key figure in the development of science television, took a distinctive approach. What he did was to alight on science as a subject that wasn't being terribly energetically pursued elsewhere and – despite having no qualifications or background in science – built his career on science by creating new televisual forms around it. As a producer within and ultimately the Head of the Outside Broadcast Department, Singer pioneered a type of live television science program, a 'built OB program' created to be transmitted from particular locations, unlike conventional OBs that televised existing events such as state occasions. First he produced the 1957 spectacular live special broadcast on the eve of the International Geophysical Year, *The Restless Sphere*, a program that included narration from the Duke of Edinburgh and Richard Dimbleby and several live OB feeds from different parts of the world. Other specials followed, but the breakthrough series for regular science broadcasting was *Eye on Research*, which took live OB cameras to dozens of scientists' laboratories across the country, over seven series between 1957 and 1961. The team that Singer assembled for this program, including his loyal deputy Phil Daly and the science writers Gerald Leach and Gordon Rattray Taylor, went on to be the core of the team responsible for the launch of *Horizon* in May 1964 (Boon, 2014). It is striking that of the ensuing generations of producers who started on *Horizon* – including the first, the documentary film director Ramsay Short – the majority of them passed through science programing into more general television production (Boon, 2013). Within what became the Science and Features Department, many careers began with what were effectively apprenticeships in television technique, starting with stints producing short items on *Tomorrow's World* (1965–2003) and then production of 50-minute films for *Horizon*, moving afterwards into general production duties treating subjects that had little connection with science or technology. In other words, Singer's assertion (Singer, 1966: 9) that "the aim of scientific programming is common with all broadcasting, an enrichment of the audience experience" has also worked the other way; that production skills developed in science could be employed across television.

How have different scientific subjects been treated by television?

In television, as in culture more generally, 'science' means many different things – although problems of definition need not delay the historian as it makes sense simply to use the categories used by the people we study. There have been many influential and long-running series in the last 60 plus years covering every aspect of science, technology and medicine. These have included *Tomorrow's World* (1965–2003), *Equinox* (1986–2001), *QED* (1982–99), *Crucible* (1982–83) (see Young, 1995) and many others. Landmark series such as Jacob Bronowski's *The Ascent of Man* (1973) have also established science's standing as a subject for television. Medicine and public health have often enjoyed their own specialist strands in addition to featuring within mainstream science broadcasting. In the early 1950s, documentary drama was most often the preferred medium, with programs such as *Family Doctor* (3 September 1952) and *Medical Officer of Health* (21 September 1954). Medicine was also the focus of OB treatment, with the first series of *Your Life in Their Hands* in 1958 (Boon, 2011). Many series have ensued, including prominent mega-series such as Jonathan Miller's *The Body in Question* (1978–81).

Horizon

Perhaps the dominant feature of science on BBC television in this period has been *Horizon*, with a 50-year life and more than 1,100 programs broadcast. Against this background, after a period of uncertain format and tone in its first few years, *Horizon* became the major fixture of BBC's science coverage. The first *Horizon* program, *The World of Buckminster Fuller*, was broadcast on 2 May 1964. From the outset, the editorial independence that Singer, as Head of Department, provided enabled producers to range across science and its implications, ever in search of the good story. As the media scholar Roger Silverstone noted, each episode of *Horizon* is the outcome of a unique process of construction which is at the same time contingent and creative (Silverstone, 1985: 162). Any attempt at producing statements about *Horizon* in general for a given period of time is therefore doomed to be contradicted by individual examples. Yet the 1994 *Horizon* episode *The Far Side*, which David Malone was invited to produce to mark the thirtieth anniversary of the program, suggests some trends in its coverage of science and technology. Overall, *Horizon* producers have always been concerned with reporting on science and technology. The values and beliefs informing their work are those of investigative journalism.

In an initial period, covering the half decade from 1964, the program tended to support the view that science and technology would eventually bring progress and prosperity to the world at large. This trend is exemplified in the 1964 program *The Knowledge Explosion*, featuring a sequence with science fiction author Arthur C. Clark promising that the future will be 'absolutely fantastic'. Another example is the 1966 *Man in Space*, drawing an uninterrupted path of progress from the first steps of the US space exploration program to Apollo and the projected moon landing. This trend can be seen culminating, yet with an overtly racialized tone, in 1968 with *Black Man – White Science*, in which the domination of the world by the West is ascribed to the unique features of western culture which gave rise to modern science and technology. Similarly the program *Bread* (1969) can be interpreted as a continuation of this celebratory trend. Here, western food research is praised for its efforts to 'feed the world', efforts which are only hampered, it is suggested, by 'backward looking' Third World populations. But 1969 audiences also saw programs such as *After Apollo*, questioning the military consequences of the US space program; *For the Safety of Mankind*, telling of a group of people who thought it their duty to pass nuclear secrets between the western and the eastern block in order to stop the arm race; and *Machines and People*, featuring the then Science and Technology Secretary Tony Benn, inviting audiences to reflect on the social cost of scientific and technological innovation.

Towards the beginning of the seventies, *Horizon* was taking a more critical turn that would be confirmed throughout the decade. It was thus falling in line with the critical approach to science and technology observed in other mass media for the period (Bauer and Gregory, 2007). This is exemplified in programs such as *Man Made Lakes of Africa* (1972), which was concerned with how the Volta and Aswan dams affected the environment, or *Who Needs Skills* (1974), which questioned the impact of 'progress' on social relationships in the work place.

The eighties and early nineties can be characterized as the synthesis moment of what appears a dialectical relationship between *Horizon* and the sciences. One of the main features of the period was the explosion of information and communication technologies. A string of programs including *Spies in the Wire* (1984), *In the Light of New Information* (1987), *Colonizing Cyberspace* (1991) and *The Electronic Frontier* (1993), continued questioning the social consequences and the politics of scientific and technological innovation. These programs all tended to emphasize the primacy of politics over science and technology. At the same time as these programs pointed at the dangers of unchecked science and technology, they hinted at the notion that properly controlled, science and technology could be efficient means of bettering the human condition. Thus *Horizon* seems to accompany the rise of the movement for public engagement and democratic accountability for science and scientists that took place in Britain and elsewhere in the 1990s (eg. Callon, Lascoumes and Barthe, 2009).

Natural history television

In May 1953, television set owners were invited to watch an outside broadcast live from the Wildfowl Trust at Slimbridge, an ornithological research station and the home of the amateur naturalist Peter Scott (1909–89). As the first program of its kind to come out of the BBC West Region studio in Bristol, this broadcast marks the beginnings of natural history television in Britain. It was also the opening salvo that led to *Look* (1955–68), the long-running series which, for more than a decade, embodied wildlife for British TV audiences. So much so that Desmond Hawkins could boast that:

> Programmes like ... *Look* have shown that they can hold the attention of an audience of several millions. Such broadcasters as Peter Scott ... enjoy a measure of popularity that would certainly not be scorned by the more orchidaceous and spectacular stars of the entertainment world.
> (Hawkins, 1957: 7)

As if the series had been shaped by the inaugural live broadcast from Scott's residence, each episode took place in a studio setting reproducing Scott's study. The first programs involved Scott showing his own films of birds and wildlife. Then, having run out of material, he invited his naturalist friends to show their footage (Davies, 2000). The conversations taking place in the studio revolved around two topics: animal behavior in the wild as revealed by the observation relayed through the film, and technical issues related to filming. Natural history television started in Britain at a time when the study and observation of live animals in the field was still a fringe practice, not yet considered to be proper science but very much the province of amateur natural historians. *Look* both installed audiences as witnesses to knowledge production and established the television studio as a place where natural historical knowledge could be gathered and discussed, under the reassuring oversight of the trusted figure of Peter Scott (Gouyon, 2011).

The NHU's next flagship program, *Life* (1965–68), was dedicated to examining all aspects of animal behavior and operated along the same lines as its predecessor. Hosted by the curator of mammals at the London Zoo, Dr Desmond Morris, it staged studio encounters between biologists so as to debate, often in a heated manner, issues related to the study of animal behavior. Audiences were thus again invited to witness the making of science, performed this time by scientists discussing their trade in a TV studio and arguing over theoretical points under the supervision of a trusted figure. But *Life* also introduced a new dimension to natural history television. The film sequences illustrating the conversations between scientists were all shot by cameramen from the BBC NHU, whose expertise lay in the mastery of film technology rather than in natural history. In other words, *Life* introduced the notion that the NHU could valuably participate, with their footage, in the scientific debate (Gouyon, 2011). We might, using Thomas Gieryn's coinage, say that the structure of the program made the television studio into a 'truth-spot', a place lending credibility to knowledge claims (Gieryn, 2006).

In 1960, ITV, the rival network, started broadcasting the series *Survival* which was produced by Anglia TV and which proved immensely successful. Whilst *Look* primarily catered for middle-class audiences, *Survival* was self-consciously pitched to attract "the great mass of viewers [...] available in the industrial areas of the Midlands and the north" (Willock, 1978: 28). With the aim of pleasing working-class audiences, the series producers, Colin Willock and Aubrey Buxton, chose to dispense with the studio-based style the BBC privileged and instead produced a film-based series.

Assessing the competitive strength of the BBC NHU in 1962, Desmond Hawkins stated that "Anglia, though a later arrival and professionally less competent, is potentially more dangerous" (Hawkins, 1962: 4). The BBC reply to *Survival* eventually came in 1967, in the shape of *The World About Us (TWAU)*, a new series similarly made exclusively on film. In its rivalry with ITV, though, the BBC in 1967 had an advantage: color. David Attenborough, who as BBC2 Controller oversaw the start of color transmissions, stated at a press conference that color television was "natural television" (Raynor, 1969). This formula, successful with critics, could imply that the BBC's representations of nature were more valuable than those found on ITV. Indeed, since the early fifties, television had been shaped as a technology of direct witnessing through such programs as *Look*. Attenborough's statement encapsulates the notion that color television is the quintessence of observational realism, in other words that the medium is true to nature. In the case of natural history programs, this statement suggested that color representations of wildlife, as seen on BBC2, had more knowledge value than those in black and white, shown on ITV.

The launch of *TWAU* in the context of the beginning of color transmission entailed a departure from the studio-centered strategy of foregrounding a trusted personality (Peter Scott, Desmond Morris) overseeing a learned conversation between experts. In its place developed an approach based on advertising the filmmaking process as a way of producing knowledge. From this point onward, questions of technical expertise in relation to the handling of the camera, the editing process and post-production in general became central to asserting the cognitive legitimacy of natural history television. Such a shift should not solely be ascribed to the transition from a studio-centred culture of television broadcasting to a film-based one. It should also be understood as an expression of the BBC NHU's newly gained self-confidence in its technical ability, and a sign that the Unit had, a decade after its foundation, reached maturity.

This is evidenced, for example, in internal discussions during the negotiations that took place with Alan Root in the late sixties to secure his contribution to *TWAU*. Advising on the arguments Bristol should use, David Attenborough suggested as "a bargaining point" the "BBC expertise inextricably involved in the film in the shape of editing, dubbing and recording" (Attenborough, 1966). This self-confidence shaped the relationship between natural history film-makers and life scientists in a way that maintained the latter at the periphery of the film-making process, at best as advisors, or as providers of raw data on which film-makers could exert their expertise. A strict boundary was delineated, patrolled by technical experts – the natural history film-makers. This was the time, at the end of the sixties, when Robert Reid, the Head of Science and Features, could write in the high-profile science journal *Nature* that if a scientist takes over the responsibility for producing television science programs, then they have to "acquire the professional skill and experience of a producer, and devote a producer's time and energy to his program. He will cease to be a scientist. To that extent […] broadcasting is back in the hands of the broadcasters" (Reid, 1969: 458). According to Reid, one could not be at the same time a scientist and a science or natural history broadcaster.

Conversely, in the seventies, natural history television was increasingly presented as a means of producing knowledge and of revealing aspects of the natural world that had escaped scientists' attention. This is notable, for instance, in an interview David Attenborough gave following the release of his masterpiece, *Life on Earth* (1979):

> We were able, for instance, to put together views of living amphibians which no one had been able to see in that range of time ever. No zoo could show you that amount. The visual effect was devastating. It had the same effect on me [Attenborough] as it did on everyone else. I remember the first time I saw the amphibian program. I was speechless. My jaw was sagging with wonder.
>
> (Wapshott, 1980)

The series presented natural history television as a means of turning each viewer's living room into a naturalist's study. A program is like a drawer in such a study that contains a collection of specimens. Watching the television program enables spectators "to roam freely across the universe" (Outram, 1996: 261), just like naturalists in their study. In the same interview about *Life on Earth*, Attenborough hammered it home, quoting a letter from a member of the audience who congratulated him "for reminding me why it was that I became a zoologist 50 years ago" (Wapshott, 1980). Following the 1979 release of *Life on Earth*, natural history television was in this sense claimed as the genuine heir of the original spirit of scientific enquiry. This somewhat conservative assertion was reiterated in a 1984 article about *The Living Planet*, Attenborough's second series, constructed on the model of *Life on Earth*: "The attempt to see things as a whole has largely been abandoned by laymen and specialists alike, but Attenborough mediates between the two" (Appleyard, 1984). Following *Life on Earth*, natural history television was endowed with the capacity to convey genuine generalist knowledge of the natural world, allowing the audience to embrace it in its totality. And the logic of this mode of knowing rests on the notion that sight – observation – is the alpha and omega of the production of knowledge about nature.

The increasing emphasis on natural historical knowledge production in television from the 1970s marginalized scientists. This can also be seen in more recent natural history television, especially in the emergence of the genre of 'making-of documentaries' (MODs). In these MODs, such as for example *Making Waves*, attached to *The Blue Planet* (BBC, 2000), film-makers often appear interacting with scientist advisers in the field. From these sequences emerges the notion that the participants in the film-making process – natural history film-makers and field biologists – produce the knowledge they need, and that the two kinds of knowledge are complementary to each other, rather than concurrent.

Conclusions

In this essay we have sought to give the broadest account possible of science on British television, given the rather rudimentary state of the scholarship. It is evidently the case that more intensive historical study, especially of more recent decades, may well lead to substantial revisions of the picture presented here. And this will not simply be a matter of 'big data', but of complex cultural artefacts in their thousands that have made professional careers and developed televisual technique at the same time that, on occasion, they have also contributed to scientific knowledge whilst entertaining millions of viewers. If, as seems to be a sound judgment, Singer was correct that "the televising of science is a process of television" (Singer, 1966: 9), then the destiny of science broadcasting as a television subculture has also been bound up with the fortunes of television in general. Its producers have been obliged to follow fashions in the medium, as for example when *Horizon* producers, in common with most BBC documentary makers, were expected to adopt Robert McKee's storytelling techniques so that they could apply his principles of storytelling as conflict resolution to making science palatable to television audiences (Lees, 2010: 130). Furthermore, in a multi-channel television environment, science television must increasingly become more like other kinds of television programing as producers seek the elusive viewer who will stay with a program for more than one 15-minute segment. What hope for 'difficult' television then?

Further reading

Bousé's (2000) *Wildlife films* provides some more elements about the history of the presentation of wildlife on British and American TV. Burgess and Unwin's (1984) essay "Exploring the living planet with David Attenborough" is a good insider's account of the process of producing natural history TV. Tim Boon's *Films of Fact* (2008) gives a longer historical background to the themes discussed here.

References

In what follows, archival papers that can be accessed at the BBC Written Archives Centre in Caversham are referenced using the acronym BBC WAC, followed by a folder reference number.

Anonymous (1961) Audience Research Report. BBC WAC R9/7/52.
Appleyard, B. (1984) "Attenborough goes back to nature." *The Times*, 19 January, p. 10.
Attenborough, D. (1966) Controller-BBC2 to Editor Natural History Unit, 17 June, BBC WAC WE/21/57/1 – Root, Alan.
Bauer, M. and Gregory, J. (2007) "From Journalism to corporate communication in post-war Britain." In M. Bauer and M. Bucchi (eds.) *Journalism, Science and Society*. London: Routledge (pp. 33–51).
Boon, T. (2008) *Films of Facts: A History of Science in Documentary Films and Television*. London and New York: Wallflower Press.
——(2011) "On the varieties of medical filmmaking: An alternative path to the cultures of biomedicine." In M. Jackson (ed.) *Oxford Handbook of the History of Medicine*. Oxford: Oxford University Press (pp. 617–34).
——(2013) "British science documentaries: Transitions from film to television." *Journal of British Cinema and Television*, 10(3), 475–97.
——(2014) "The televising of science is a process of television: Establishing *Horizon*, 1962–67." *British Journal for the History of Science*, in press.
Bousé, D. (2000) *Wildlife films*. Philadelphia, PA: University of Pennsylvania Press.
Burgess, J. and Unwin, D. (1984) "Exploring the living planet with David Attenborough." *Journal of Geography in Higher Education*, 8(2), 93–113.
Callon, M., Lascoumes, P. and Barthe, Y. (2009) *Acting in an Uncertain World. An Essay on Technical Democracy*. Cambridge, MA and London: MIT Press.
Davies, G. (1998) "Networks of nature: Stories of natural history film-making from the BBC." Unpublished PhD Dissertation, University College London.
——(2000) "Science, observation and entertainment: Competing visions of post-war British natural history television, 1946–67." *Ecumene*, 7(4), 432–59.
Fisher, J. (1959) "Foreword." In H. Sielmann, *My Year With the Woodpeckers*. London: Barrie and Rockliff (pp. 9–11).
Gieryn, T. F. (2006) "City as truth-spot: Laboratories and field-sites in urban studies." *Social Studies of Science*, 36(1), 5–38.
Gouyon, J.-B. (2011) "The BBC Natural History Unit: Instituting natural history film-making in Britain." *History of Science*, 49(4), 425–51.
Hawkins, D. (1957) *The BBC Naturalist*. London: Rathbone Books.
——(1962) BBC Natural History Unit. Report by Head of West Regional Programs. BBC WAC WE 17/2/1.
Hoggart, R. (2004) *Mass Media in a Mass Society: Myth and Reality*. London: Continuum.
Jacob, I. (1956) Memo to Gerald Beadle, 20 July 1956, BBC WAC T16/61/2.
Jones, A. (2013a) "Clogging the machinery: The BBC's experiment in science coordination, 1949–53." *Media History*, 19(4), 436–49.
——(2013b) "Elite science and the BBC: A 1950s contest of ownership." *British Journal for the History of Science*, published online 7 November. Retrieved from http://dx.doi.org/10.1017/S0007087413000927
Lees, N. (2010) *Greenlit: Developing Factual TV Ideas from Concept to Pitch: The Professional Guide to Pitching Factual Shows*. London: A&C Black.
McCloy, J. (1958) Presentation of Science by Television. Memo to Mary Adam, 7 October, BBC WAC T16/623.

Outram, D. (1996) "New spaces in natural history." In N. Jardine, J. A. Secord and E. C. Spary (eds.) *Cultures of Natural History*. Cambridge: Cambridge University Press (pp. 249–65).
Raynor, H. (1969) "Reality through the spectrum." *The Times*, 15 November, Colour Television Supplement, p. 2.
Reid, R. W. (1969) "Television producer and scientist." *Nature, 223*(5205), 455–58.
Silverstone, R. (1985) *Framing Science: The Making of a BBC Documentary*. London: BFI.
Singer, A. (1966) "Science broadcasting." In *BBC Lunch-Time Lectures: Series 4*. London: British Broadcasting Corporation.
Taylor, G. R. (1964) Science for All, 17 November, BBC WAC T14/3, 316/1
Wapshott, N. (1980) "The perfect teacher back with animals." *The Times*, 1 March, p. 14.
Willock, C. (1978) *The World of Survival*. London: André Deutsch.
Young, R. M. (1995) "What I learned at summer camp: Experiences in television." Retrieved from http://human-nature.com/rmyoung/papers/paper29h.html

41
History on television
Ann Gray

In the late twentieth century the small world of television professionals and pundits was driven to comment on a surprise phenomenon witnessed in British television. In October 2001 John Willis, the former Director of Programmes for Channel 4 and the Director of Factual and Learning at the BBC, declared that "History programing is one of the few thriving sectors of the electronic media ... Given lift-off by the helium of David Starkey and Simon Schama. TV history is hot" (Willis, 2001). History television was compared to the spate of gardening programs that at the time dominated the schedules and referred to as 'the new gardening' or in fashion jargon, 'the new black'. The new millennium seemed to be an apposite time to herald this fascination with the past, but the seeds of the television history boom had, in fact, been sown several years earlier. A notable year was 1995, which saw the launch of the History Channel and in the UK the foundation of the BBC's dedicated History Unit. A portent of things to come was the transmission that year on Channel 4 of *Landscapes* (1995) presented by the author of the book of the same name, a then unknown and rather awkward presenter, the historian Simon Schama who was later to become one of the stars in the TV history galaxy. Two years later in 1997 Channel 4 split the History Department from the more general Documentary Unit rendering it more independent in commissioning and thereby acknowledging the increasing significance of history programing to the Channel. These changes in satellite and terrestrial television were also reflected in the independent production sector where new companies were being established, a number of which specialized in history programing.

This chapter, drawing on research carried out for the AHRC-funded Televising History 1995–2010 project, interrogates this so-called 'history boom' in and on television in the UK, other parts of Europe and the US. By 'history on television' I refer to television programing about the past that grounds its claims to authenticity through recourse to documentary and/or experiential constructions of events and life in past times. The project examined such programing within the specified period in terms of its contents, genres, modes of address and narration as well as its contexts, inter-texts and processes of production and distribution. It is worth noting, however, that representations of the past can also be seen on British television across popular genres such as costume drama and literary adaptation, causing a number of critics to draw attention to this seeming obsession with and nostalgia for the past at the expense of more contemporary material. This criticism apart, the seeming appetite of both producers and audiences for the past has been a distinct feature of television output in the first two decades of the twenty-first century. Thus, even excluding historical fictions, television programs about the past are proliferating in both number and variety. At the same time television, combining elements of the global and the local, is itself becoming increasingly diverse and multifaceted: international co-productions sit alongside expansion in modes of program delivery and development of adjacent platforms such as program-specific internet sites and the fostering of various forms of interactivity between programs and audiences/users. This diversity in the broadcasting landscape coincides with the reassessment of the meaning of identity, belonging and community, and hence of history itself (Nora, 2002; Huyssen, 2003).

Significance of 'history' to public service broadcasting

The BBC as the leading national broadcaster of radio and later of television was keen from its commencement to position itself within the national psyche and in particular to play a leading role in constructing a sense of that identity for the nation. Clearly the representation of the nation's past was a significant part of its output. Since one of its earliest outside broadcasts, the Coronation of Queen Elizabeth II on 2 June 1953, the BBC has sought to knit the nation together in its sense of past and present. Thus the nation's events, for example, state funerals, Royal occasions, national sporting events, etc. are a crucial part of their output and reinforce their commitment and role as the national public service broadcaster (Dayan and Katz 1992). In this sense the BBC records the nation's history and has become the prime producer and holder of the nation's 'memory bank' (Bourdon, 2003).

In addition to the recording of these national events, the broadcast media have been key sites for the narration of histories, and the past has long been a favored location for both dramatic and factual television programs. The BBC and, in its earliest manifestation, ITV, chose history programing as flagship indicators of their public service output. Serious and sober presentations about events in the past were the main fare but notable larger scale and more ambitious programs were the BBC's commemoration of the outbreak of the First Word War with its series *The Great War* (1964) and Thames Television's *The World at War* (1973/74). Both series ran to 26 episodes and employed a potent mix of archive and interviews with high production values, for example, in the use of classical music and dramatic narration by well-known and respected stage actors. They established an important form of history programing which was authoritative, entertaining and popular, and which fulfilled the broadcasters' statutory brief for the provision of quality programing. This contribution of historical documentary was especially important for ITV in demonstrating its commitment to more serious fare but also for the BBC at different points in its history, providing persuasive evidence of public service contribution when the license fee was due for renewal.

Developments in history programing were not confined to the UK. For example, in the US, where public history is a much more established mode of communicating information about the past than in the UK, Ken Burns, a self-defined popular historian, and owner of his own production company Florentine Films, was commissioned by PBS to make a number of history documentaries. The topics included *The Statue of Liberty* (PBS, 1985) and *The Congress* (PBS, 1989). However, the best-known example of his output is the 11-hour series *The Civil War* which was transmitted in 1990 across five nights in September of that year to great acclaim, attracting an average of 12 million viewers across the transmission period (Edgerton and Rollins, 2001: 170). Burns took an avowedly populist stand and drew criticism from professional historians who objected to his romantic view of the past and his tendency to fashion self-serving myths and in particular those which justified the moral right of the US military. If *The Civil War* was not considered to be 'good history' by some, it was certainly considered to be 'good television' by producers and commissioners on both sides of the Atlantic. Thus, confidence began to grow in the power of the past to provide rich content, endless stories and engaging narratives and, importantly, to bring in the audiences. UK producers and commissioning editors were therefore keen to develop more popular forms of history programing for domestic and eventually international audiences.

Returning to the UK, and considering a specific institutional setting, in the 1990s a cohort of media professionals were working on factual programing at the BBC and a number of them were specifically drawn to historical subjects. The institutional context is, of course, critical for any creative and professional development and, in the case of the BBC, the period when Michael Jackson was heading up the Arts Programming Unit for BBC2 provided opportunities for a number of researchers and producers to work on the channel's arts and culture program, *The Late Show* (BBC2 1989–95). For example, Martin Davidson, now History Commissioning Editor at the BBC, moved from publishing to work on *The Late Show* in the late eighties because, as he described it to me in an interview, "there was a kind of window for people who could work across cultural politics in television where consumerism, culture and politics were coalescing in an interesting way and advertising and the media were a particularly potent intersection" – not, he added, in history, which, in his words "then was as dull as ditchwater" (Gray, 2010: 63). Janice Hadlow, Controller of BBC2 from 2008 to March 2014, had also moved from radio into television to produce *The Late Show*. Hadlow was referred to by everyone I spoke to during my research period as the most influential individual who had shaped history programing in the last decade in the UK and she has clearly encouraged and inspired a number of highly creative individuals who are now in key positions as broadcasters and as independents. In 1995 the BBC established its History Unit and Hadlow started work on the series *A History of Britain*, persuading Simon Schama to author and present. Since that time, and before moving back to the BBC in 2008, she has been Head of History, Art and Religion and Head of Specialist Factual at Channel 4 (where she commissioned, amongst other programs, Niall Ferguson's *Empire* and David Starkey's *Six Wives of Henry VIII*) and Controller of BBC4. Although she now has a wider remit, as she did at BBC4, Hadlow's commitment to history programing and what she calls 'serious' programing in general is clear.

Laurence Rees, head of the History Unit, was also a major figure in making and promoting high quality, serious, largely military history programs and, working with the historian Professor Ian Kershaw, made the first of the three series *Nazis: A Warning from History* (BBC2, 1997), *Horror in the East* (BBC, 2001) and *Auschwitz, the Nazis and 'the Final Solution'* (BBC2, 2005). But it was, perhaps, Hadlow's confidence in the return of presenter-led, authored history which triggered an interesting period in the development of history as commodity and in particular the branding of presenters and their outputs. Thus Simon Schama, David Starkey and, to a lesser extent, Niall Ferguson became household names and were certainly considered as 'safe bets' by commissioners for forthcoming history series (Bell and Gray, 2007; Beck, 2012). All their television series were accompanied by the publication of their authored books and most have now transferred to DVD with the prolonged shelf life that the printed and digital formats imply. These male historians, along with the already established Michael Wood, who had been presenting a popular but serious style of history programing since the 1980s, became highly visible and, for some, highly paid television 'personalities'. Their academic credentials provided weight and legitimacy to their scripts and presentational styles nurtured by the television professionals persuasively delivered knowledge about the past. It was to be much later in the period under consideration that female historians were to gain visibility and I have written elsewhere about the gendering of television history programing (Gray and Bell, 2013).

'New' genres, formats and 'new' audiences

At the turn of the century the key competitors for audiences and advertisers in the UK were the terrestrial channels and their policies and strategies with regard to history programing were framed, to a great extent, by this 'internal' market. ITV, whilst continuing to commission some history content, had been relieved of much of its public service obligation and therefore did not attempt to compete with the BBC in this area of programing. However, Channel 4, founded in 1982 with its remit to provide innovative, experimental and distinctive programing, has positioned itself as competition for the BBC, especially BBC2 and latterly BBC4.

Given its remit Channel 4's approach to history was, from its inception, rather different from the BBC with a perhaps predictably subversive and investigative style. The channel established an early strand, *Today's History* (1982–84), which was a response to the BBC's established *Timewatch* series but which included titles such as *Invisible History, Why War?* (1982) and *Women and Society* (1983), indicative of its more critical address. The series was not re-commissioned after 1984 and it wasn't until 1991 when John Willis launched *Secret History* and later *Secret Lives* (1995–97) that history content once again had a regular presence in the schedules. However, with the arrival of Michael Jackson from the BBC (1998) who brought with him Tim Gardam, the first editor of *Timewatch,* and Janice Hadlow, history began to flourish on Channel 4. This movement of creative talent between the BBC and Channel 4 created a vibrant environment in which developments within history programing thrived. In addition, this was a period when the independent sector was growing in the UK (Potter, 2008). It was during this time that independents such as Lion TV, Blakeway Productions, Flashback and Wall to Wall were established and set about creating new ways of doing history on television. As one of the CEOs told me, "there was a particular concentration of talent at that time who were all looking to reinvent history television" and they were working within a production business environment competing with each other for history commissions, the subject area within 'factual' which witnessed the fiercest competition (Gray, 2010).

One of the most remarkable of these was to lay the foundation for the first 'history format', that of 'the House'. Wall to Wall had been commissioned by a science commissioner to make a series about the history of science and technology. They, and the producer at Channel 4, came up with the 1900s House idea in which a family traveled back in time, living as, in the first instance, their Victorian ancestors might have done, without advanced household technology. Enabled by increasingly mobile and discreet camera technology, this hybrid genre drew on distinctive modes of television. First, it involved 'ordinary' people 're-enacting' domestic and family life, each episode featuring an emotional narrative arc in which 'characters' were challenged by both their environment and personal relationships. These were familiar tropes of popular television which invited empathy and a sense of 'being there' for the viewer. Peter Grimsdale, then (1999) Commissioning Editor of Channel 4, noted that "*1900 House* made people think 'wow', putting ordinary people, from today, into historical situations in the past and see how they get on, what a great idea, let's do some more of that" (Sills-Jones, 2009: 327). Indeed, the success of *1900 House* (1999), which averaged 3.5 million viewers – high for history programing on Channel 4 – led to the commissioning of *1940s House* (2001) and *Edwardian Country House* (2002). This format extended the audiences for television history, then predominantly middle-class males, and in particular interested younger people and female viewers.

Another remarkable and enduring format came from Wall to Wall which also drew on television logics as it tapped into the existing and developing interest in genealogy and family history. The idea for *Who Do You Think You Are?* (BBC2, 2004–5; BBC1, 2006–present) was initially pitched by Alex Graham, the CEO of Wall to Wall, a decade earlier and his persistence proved fruitful for his own company and the BBC. The format, where a 'celebrity', usually drawn from television, sets out on a journey to discover aspects of their own family history, combines the apparent requirement of broadcasters to present a familiar face for their audiences with 'first-person television' (Dovey, 2000) and the strong narrative pull of the journey. The earlier series, done in collaboration with the Open University, provided detail of how to research family history and every episode contextualized the individual journey within a broader history through the use of archives and voice-over. Much of the contextual history covers topics and regions which would otherwise remain absent from the schedules in that commissioning editors would be unlikely to invest in what would be considered low interest or contentious material. This is, perhaps, 'history by stealth' in that the historical narrative is softened, domesticated and personalized via familiar celebrities (Holdsworth, 2010) but that does not reduce its value as a form of knowledge about the past. At the time of writing *Who Do You Think You Are?* is still being commissioned for the BBC's most popular channel and continues to draw audiences who perhaps would not consider watching a more traditional type of history program.

Co-productions and international programing

Thus far the programs under discussion have been financed in the main by terrestrial channels. Increasingly, funding from a number of production sources has become a significant factor in high-end genres of television (Christophers, 2009). This applies to fictional genres but also to documentaries. This is necessary because of mounting production costs but also the increasingly intense competition for international markets in the digital age of television. Natural history programs have notably drawn on co-production finance and have, for the BBC, been a lucrative export (Cottle, 2004). History programs have also drawn on co-funding and sought to provide material for international markets. Unlike natural history genres, however, cultural, political and historical differences are salient in relation to the subject area and modes of presentation that are subject to 'reversioning' to suit specific cultural and geo-political markets. In 1994 the UK government published the White Paper *The Future of the BBC* in which the BBC was encouraged to become a more national and multi-media enterprise which should be "building on its present commercial services for audiences in this country and overseas" (quoted in Steemers, 2004: 84). In 1995 BBC Worldwide was formed and was encouraged to develop and enter international markets. Key to their activities in the US was their partnership with the Discovery Channel, formed in 1998. In factual genres, general history programing and the history strand *Timewatch* are included in their co-productions and have provided valuable and marketable content for Discovery and BBC investment. History as content has been important in this relationship and especially in large productions conforming to what Mjøs in his study of cross-national partnerships refers to as the "blockbuster logic within factual television" (Mjøs, 2011: 186). The first of these 'super event history' television programs was the *Building the Great Pyramid* (2002), a co-production between BBC, Discovery and NDR. Large-scale productions followed such as *Pompeii: The Last Day* (2002), *Pyramid* (2002) and *Colosseum: Rome's Arena of Death* (2003). All employed CGI special effects and techniques more associated with cinematic forms than television and were screened in the US, the UK and other parts of the world. Following these productions, commemorative 'historical event' programing provided the BBC with a national and international platform. For example, the 2004 *D-Day 6.6.1944*, a co-production with Discovery Channel, ProSieben (Germany), France Deux and TelFrance to commemorate the 60th anniversary of the D-Day landings, had a distinctly cinematic and popular feel, combining dramatization and documentary elements which included eye-witness accounts from veterans and the use of archive material (Chapman, 2007). This emphasis on the popular is important in order to attract the largest possible audiences and the respective national bases of the co-funders was also reflected in the content, casting and locations of the filming. This was critical in this case as the narrative was not cast from one nation's perspective but encompassed the Allied Forces of Britain, Germany, France and the USA.

Conclusion

This necessarily brief and schematic account of the 'history boom' on television has sought to indicate how history as a topic and subject area has provided valuable content throughout the history of broadcasting. Furthermore, the content itself is malleable and has served the different demands of television within different contexts and in periods of enormous economic, technological and social change. This resilience can be seen as we trace its importance for the demonstration of a responsible approach to public service, to the need to engage with wider and new audiences, to the requirement, especially in the case of the BBC, to internationalize and attract funding for programs bearing high production values and, finally, entering the digital era history as a resource. The already mentioned *D-Day 6.6.1944* was a so-called 360 production with delivery across different platforms accessed through ITV. This included *The Peoples' War* website which is of direct relevance to the suite of programs in the commemorative season. This invited viewers to put their experiences on the site, exhorting that "Your memories are part of our history", and included specific applications linked to *D-Day* providing, for example, the contextualization of the events of D-Day in 'real time' and the 'back story' of the characters appearing in the program itself. Here history lends itself to interactivity, bringing the audience in via the website and encouraging them to be part of the creation of memories, national and otherwise (Bennett, 2008).

It is the case that after leaving school most people get their knowledge of the past from television. This is of profound importance and especially so as we move into what Graham Turner has referred to as the "age of entertainment" (Turner, 2010) where the necessity to attract audiences within the context of literally hundreds of channels, let alone other enticing distractions from the internet, is paramount for broadcasters. Whilst there are good examples of these pressures producing excellent television history, some of which have been noted above, there are others where the desire for novelty, spectacle and international reach can seriously compromise veracity and integrity. This raises questions about what kind of history these changing contexts demand, who selects the topics for treatment and most significantly perhaps, what subject areas are excluded – what and whose history is not part of this public circulation of the past. Whether television remains the dominant form of communication and for how long is a subject for debate but, although its death has been pronounced on more than one occasion, it remains for the immediate future at least the most powerful form of communication which, in its domestic platform, effortlessly insinuates itself into our everyday lives and sense-making processes. My argument is that as the broadcasters and producers obviously do not have a pre-designed curriculum for history programing, the content and style of such outputs are shaped by the vicissitudes of television itself as it battles the waves of the swelling oceans of entertainment and information in order to stay afloat.

Further reading

For further resources on the topics discussed in this chapter, Ann Gray and Erin Bell's *History on Television* (2013) considers recent changes in the media landscape which have affected to a great degree how history in general, and whose history in particular, appears onscreen. Amongst a range of sources it draws on interviews with television professionals and academic historians. Bell and Gray's edited collection,

Televising History: Mediating the Past in Postwar Europe (2010) is comprised of essays which examine the representation of history on television in the context of the immense economic and political changes experienced in Europe in the post-war era, and particularly in the past three decades. Further comparative work can be found in Gary R. Edgerton and Peter C. Rollins' *Television Histories: Shaping Collective Memory in the Media Age* (2001), which analyzes factual and fictional output from the United States. A recent publication by Peter Beck, *Presenting History Past & Present* (2012) focuses directly on the role and function of presenters in representing the past, not only on television but also in other popular forms.

References

Beck, P. J. (2012) *Presenting History Past & Present*. London: Palgrave Macmillan.
Bell, E. and Gray, A. (2007) "History on television: Charisma, narrative and knowledge." *European Journal of Cultural Studies*, 10(1), 113–33.
——(eds.) (2010) *Televising History: Mediating the Past in Postwar Europe*. London: Palgrave Macmillan (pp. 59–76).
Bennett, J. (2008) "Interfacing the nation: Remediating public service broadcasting in the digital television age." *Convergence*, 14(3), 277–94.
Bourdon, J. (2003) "Some sense of time: Remembering television." *History & Memory*, 15(2), 5–35.
Chapman, J. (2007) "Re-presenting war. British television drama-documentary and the Second World War." *European Journal of Cultural Studies*, 10(1), 13–33.
Christophers, B. (2009) *Envisioning Media Power. On Capital and Geographies of Television*. Lanham, MD: Lexington Books.
Cottle, S. (2004) "Producing nature(s): On the changing production ecology of natural history TV." *Media, Culture & Society*, 26(1), 81–101.
Dayan, D. and Katz, E. (1992) *Media Events and the Live Broadcasting of History*. Cambridge, MA: Harvard University Press.
Dovey, J. (2000) *Freakshow: First Person Media and Factual Television*. London: Pluto Press.
Edgerton, G. R. and Rollins, P. C. (2001) *Television Histories: Shaping Collective Memory in the Media Age*. Lexington, KY: The University Press of Kentucky.
Gray, A. (2010) "Contexts of production: Commissioning history." In E. Bell and A. Gray (eds.) *Televising History: Mediating the Past in Postwar Europe*. London: Palgrave Macmillan (pp. 59–76).
Gray, A. and Bell, E. (2013) *History on Television*. Abingdon: Routledge.
Holdsworth, A. (2010) "*Who do you think you are?* Family history and memory on British television." In E. Bell and A. Gray (eds.) *Televising History: Mediating the Past in Postwar Europe*. London: Palgrave Macmillan (pp. 234–47).
Huyssen, A. (2003) *Present Pasts: Urban Palimpsests and the Politics of Memory*. Palo Alto, CA: Stanford University Press.
Mjøs, O. J. (2011) "Marriage of convenience? Public service broadcasters' cross-national partnerships in factual television." *International Communication Gazette*, 73(3), 181–97.
Nora, P. (2002) "Reasons for the current upsurge in memory." Eurozine. Retrieved from http://www.eurozine.com/articles/2002-04-19-nora-en.html
Potter, I. (2008) *The Rise and Rise of the Independents: A Television History*. London: Guerilla Books.
Sills-Jones, D. (2009) *History Documentary on UK Terrestrial Television, 1982–2002*. Unpublished PhD thesis, University of Aberystwyth.

Steemers, J. (2004) *Selling Television: British Television in the Global Marketplace*. London: BFI.
Turner, G. (2010) *Ordinary People and the Media: The Demotic Turn*. London and Thousand Oaks, CA: Sage.
Willis, J. (2001) "The past is perfect." *The Guardian*, 29 October. Retrieved from http://www.theguardian.com/media/2001/oct/29/mondaymediasection.humanities

42
'Reality TV'
Su Holmes

Misha Kavka and Amy West have argued that:

> Dates are anathema to Reality TV. As markers of historical time, dates have an objectifying, distancing effect. Instead of dates and years, Reality TV counts hours, minutes and seconds, setting participants against deadlines, insisting on time in its smallest parameters. To locate oneself in the time of history goes against the power of reality programing – and of the televisual medium itself – to create intimacy and immediacy.
>
> (2004: 136)

Given that this volume seeks to explore media *history*, this seems to be an intriguing way to begin a chapter on the subject of Reality TV. This quote speaks more generally to the idea that television, with its claim to liveness and 'presentism', has rarely been seen as an appropriate medium for the representation of history (Kavka and West, 2004: 136). It also reflects prevalent ideas about Reality TV's relationship with the public sphere; that it has instigated an (often apparently regrettable) popularization of factual programing in its presentation of only 'television time', as played out in spaces created only for *television* consumption.

Whilst this primarily refers to particular aesthetic strategies of Reality TV, it is undoubtedly the case that Reality TV *does* have a history. Indeed, in teaching undergraduate students who are now largely too young to have engaged with the first UK *Big Brother* (2000), I am often suddenly reminded of how long even this recent history is. Despite oft-cited pronouncements of a demise (especially around 2007–8), Reality TV has continued to enjoy a high level of visibility in global television schedules, cultural debates and academic scholarship. As Kavka notes in her recent book on the subject:

> one cannot overestimate the impact of reality TV. In just two decades, it has transformed programming schedules, branded satellite and digital channels, created a celebrity industry in its own right and turned viewers into savvy readers of ... the mechanics of program production.
>
> (Kavka, 2012: 2)

Factual programing is arguably the area of television culture which has seen the most significant changes in recent years. The emergence of terms such as 'popular factual programing', 'docusoap', 'Reality TV' and newer variants such as 'scripted' or 'structured' reality indicates this shift, which has attracted much comment from cultural critics, academics, broadcasters and viewers. With newer forms of programing jostling for space within the category of factual programing (a category which once meant television news, current affairs or documentary) not everyone has seen this as a welcome shift in television culture. But although such debates and discourses are important in understanding the circulation of Reality TV as a cultural form, as well as its relationship with the contemporary television landscape, its persistence, and continued popularity, demands that we judge it on its *own* terms – as a form of generically hybrid programing which seeks to attract and appeal to audiences in new ways. With this in mind, this chapter will explore Reality TV as a historical, scholarly and cultural terrain, with a primary focus on the British context.

Approaches to defining Reality TV

From the perspective of television, media and communication studies, Reality TV has represented a highly visible site for exploring and debating many aspects of contemporary television, ranging across questions of history, genre, the politics of representation (gender, class, ethnicity and sexuality), the mediation of neo-liberal models of selfhood, the cultural and economic construction of contemporary celebrity, the fluid articulation of global and 'local' in format trade, the rise of television interactivity and multi-platform television, to questions of reception and fandom.

A chapter on Reality TV would seem to immediately demand a clear and succinct definition of the form, but this is actually neither possible nor productive here. Despite the wide (and often 'common sense') use of the term Reality TV across television listings, reviews, social media, scholarly work and student essays, what actually *groups* the programs referred to as such is often unclear. If working from a textual level, it seems difficult to isolate any definitive aesthetic, formal or thematic attributes which would represent a common ground. Some programs referred to as Reality TV occupy self-enclosed episodes, while others adopt an ongoing serial structure or a series form. Not all adopt a similar low-grade 'reality' aesthetic or are low-budget programs, and some make greater use than others of the hand-held camera, montage sequences and musical cues. Not all shows pivot on the spectacle of placing the self under pressure in a television-created environment, and not all involve a relationship between interactivity and eviction, fostering a combination of co-operation and competition between contestants and handing part of the narrative control to the audience. Furthermore, given the rise of celebrity-based formats, not all shows are based around the claim to display the experiences of 'ordinary' people.

Although this problem of definition may be particularly acute with regard to Reality TV, as the term is used in a particularly wide-ranging manner, and the programing itself is seen to be a self-conscious combination of existing genres such as documentary, soap opera, game show and talk show, this example may simply point to the limitations of textual approaches to genre. Recent work on television genre has emphasized how generic categories need to be understood as fundamentally intertextual, operating at the level of relations *between* texts, as well as in the material which circulates *around* them. For scholars such as Mittell (2004), such discourses do not simply offer 'extra' contextualizing material; they are constitutive of the generic category itself. Some scholars have indeed suggested that a discursive approach to genre is most fitting in discussing Reality TV. So James Friedman has argued that "what separates the spate of contemporary reality-based television … [is] the open and explicit sale of television programing as a representation of reality" (2002: 7) which refers us more to marketing than the program texts themselves.

This kind of approach, which focuses more on examining the use of generic labels *around* the text rather than trying to extract a 'proper' or 'correct' definition of a genre, enables us to consider how the term 'Reality TV' is used in highly opportunistic ways, depending on the context in hand. As I have argued elsewhere (Holmes, 2008b), a key issue here is how such labels are used to express the *cultural value* of factual programing. For example, *Wife Swap*, which began in the UK in 2003 on Channel 4 (and in which two women swap homes and families for two weeks), has variously been described as "serious factual programing that examines social issues", "'Reality' – salacious tabloid crap", as well as one of "the most important documentary series of the decade" (Robinson, 2004: 18). It is not the program itself which alters across these definitions but rather the perspective and investment of the observer. So this chapter focuses on programing which has been popularly associated with the 'reality' label, whilst acknowledging that this is always contested and complex.

Because the generic status and cultural value of Reality TV are contested sites, so is its history (Kavka, 2012: 2). For example, whilst British journalists have positioned the British observational documentary filmmaker Paul Watson as 'the Godfather' of Reality (Hoggart, 2006) due to his role in making the pioneering programs *The Family* (1974) and *Sylvania Waters* (1994), both of which aimed to record 'real' family life in unprecedented ways, this is a label he fiercely rejects, in large part because he sees Reality TV as a debasement of documentary fare. Equally, given the range of programing associated with the 'reality' label, the generic and program history here would differ across case studies. It makes sense, for example, to think about the history of the game show or the talent show for programs with a competition element, but not for others. In this context, the discussion of a history for the 'Reality TV' label very much illustrates the idea of history as less a pile of objective 'facts' than a form of subjective interpretation which has multiple strands, explanations and voices.

Histories of Reality TV

In terms of mapping potential histories of Reality TV, whole genres have been invoked, such as the evidential claims of documentary, the multiple narrative strands of soap opera, the confessional mode of the talk show, or the referent of the quiz or game show, which has historically placed 'ordinary' people in competitive and unscripted situations. Equally, scholars have emphasized particular key examples or flashpoints, both within these genres and more widely, and these are taken from a range of historical periods, ranging across the 1950s, the 1970s and the 1980s. For example, as indicated above, an important referent in the British context is seen to be Paul Watson's 12-part documentary serial, *The Family* (BBC1, 1974), which focused on the working-class Wilkins family from Reading and is widely regarded as the British counterpart to *An American Family* (PBS, 1973). A British documentary on the history of 'ordinary' people on television claims that in *The Family*, viewers "watched real life as it happened … The Wilkins family became our first Reality TV stars."[1] There is little doubt that *The Family* was seen at the time as a landmark program, as is suggested by press headlines and the critical reception of the serial (Holmes, 2008a).

The BBC foregrounded its aesthetic innovation. Its press release, entitled "New Real-Life Documentary Serial for BBC", drew attention to how *The Family* exploited "new microphone techniques" as well as new lightweight cameras which allowed "interior filming without artificial lights."[2] Critics also expressed surprise at the fact that a "BBC serial [will] star … real people", suggesting that this was something *new*. Beyond this *The Family* also provoked debate over questions of privacy, and television's role in mediating and often re-shaping the boundary between public/ private (something which has historically been divided *by* the family). From the initial descriptions of the program as a "much heralded peepshow", to the clear distaste expressed for the "doubtful privilege of displaying [one's] sordid life to the public gaze" (Afton, 1974), the program, as with the subsequent advent of Reality TV, was clearly seen as offending bourgeois sensibilities. This was also in part instigated by the program's focus on a working-class family whose social mores and sexual morals elicited much distaste. In comparison, Watson's discourse about the program took a broadly Marxist stance to questions of class, social access and representation, foregrounding the importance of giving 'ordinary' people a voice. Here we clearly see evidence of the much larger cultural construction in British culture (also in evidence with the advent of Reality TV) which has historically aligned notions of the 'real' or 'authentic' with the British working class. (Reference points here would also be the British documentary movement of the 1930s, or the 'British New Wave' in cinema, television and theater in the 1960s.)

Whereas *The Family* claimed to film 'real life' as it happened, despite the fact that the serial ended up demonstrating the considerable celebrity of the family as the program unfolded, another widely cited reference point is *Candid Camera*, which began on American television in the late 1940s (a version was previously on radio), which consisted of preconceived scenarios set up in a public place to "lure unwitting participants, whose reactions are secretly filmed" (Kavka, 2012: 17). The inventor, Allen Funt, wanted to see how people reacted when they were "unposed, unrehearsed and completely off-guard" (cited in Kavka, 2012: 16). The UK version wasn't developed until the late 1960s. As elaborated below, here we see the idea, later fully embraced by Reality TV, that the 'real' on television is to be found at the level of the self, with people offering 'authentic' and 'unstaged' reactions to artificial circumstances.

Other suggested antecedents have been sourced in 'real crime' television, such as *Crimewatch* in the UK (1984–present), and *Unsolved Mysteries* (1987) and *America's*

Most Wanted (1988–present) in the US. Although their ostensible purpose was solving crime – and in the UK *Crimewatch* is very much presented as part of the BBC's public service ethos – they also offered an exciting appeal to the 'real' in the use of re-enactments and CCTV footage. Yet these examples exist very proximately to what for some scholars is the emergence of popular factual programing *proper*: the early 1990s saw a number of what became known as 'flashing blue light' programs, focusing on the work of the police and the emergency services, which offered a low-grade camcorder aesthetic and fast-moving action sequences (see Dovey, 2000).

The second half of the 1990s saw the rapid development of what journalists came to call the 'docusoap' due to its self-conscious hybridization of factual and fictional styles, principally the observational documentary and the soap opera. With the pressure to drive costs down in an increasingly competitive multi-channel landscape (and at a time when certain traditional genres, such as documentary and sitcom, were struggling in the schedules), the docusoap's ability to offer high ratings at relatively low cost was very appealing to broadcasters. Unlike the international context for 'real crime' programing, the docusoap was a home-grown phenomenon (Kavka, 2012: 61), marking the clear arrival of what John Corner would later term the 'documentary as diversion' (Corner, 2006). Although programs such as *Airport* (BBC, 1996), *The Cruise* (BBC, 1997), *Vets in Practice* (BBC, 1997–2002) and *Airline* (ITV, 1998–2010) borrowed the emphasis on institutions and workplaces which had been crucial to the focus of observational documentary, they largely focused on interpersonal conflict and the individual narratives of 'star' performers, as articulated through the multiple narrative structure of the soap opera. Indeed, although taking into account previous examples such as *The Family*, the docusoap marks the advent of the relationship between celebrity and popular factual programing, with several of the key 'characters' enjoying varying degrees of visibility in the wider media. Early examples of these were Jane McDonald, a cruise-ship singer from *The Cruise*, as well as Jeremy Spake, a Ground Services Manager from *Airport*. Both of these early docusoap stars went on to present television programs.

Journalistic (see Coles, 2000) and to some degree academic discourse (see Izod, Kilborn and Hibberd, 2000; Dovey, 2000) expressed concern at the apparent 'dumbing down' of factual programing and it is certainly the case that much of the early academic work in this field focused on the relationship between popular factual programing and documentary, with the former cast usually cast in an unfavorable light. Jon Dovey, for example, bemoaned how trying to analyse the docusoap through the critical and theoretical methodologies emerging from documentary studies was like trying to use "surgical instruments to eat birthday cake" (2000: 136). One of the reasons Reality TV has generated such heated debate about the current state and future of television is that documentary has traditionally been positioned as a 'serious' genre and in the European context a key form of public service broadcasting. Even though fiction has in fact historically examined many serious social, political and cultural issues and even though documentary very much borrows from the narrative strategies of fiction (in terms of editing and characterization, for example), we tend to associate fiction with 'entertainment' and the factual moving image with something more instructive. The rise of popular factual programing or Reality TV has challenged these assumptions, to controversial effect. This was made abundantly clear with the subsequent advent of what became variously known as the 'formatted reality' or the 'gamedoc' phase, in which factual programing increasingly incorporated elements of the game or talent show, with examples such as *Big Brother* (UK, 2000–present), *Survivor* (UK, 2001–2), *The Amazing Race* (2001–present), *Popstars* (UK, 2001), *Pop Idol* (UK, 2001–3) and *I'm a Celebrity ... Get Me Out of Here!* (UK, 2002–present). It was certainly in the period 1999–2001 when, led by *Big Brother*, the term 'Reality TV' gained a wider currency in the press, television viewing guides and everyday conversation. This is also very much the period of the global Reality format, with successful program formats being licensed to multiple countries simultaneously.

While the docusoap aimed to take the viewer to real social situations which pre-dated the recording of the program, the later formats unfolded within arenas constructed solely *for* television, taking an acute interest in the performance of personal identity. While *Big Brother*, for example, was constructed as an opportunity for observation, it was also clearly understood by program-makers, contestants and viewers as a performative opportunity in its own right. Indeed, from a scholarly point of view, it seemed increasingly problematic to criticize such shows for failing to live up to a documentary remit when they were not in any sense claiming or aiming to *be* 'documentaries'. In this respect, and as noted at the start of this chapter, it became increasingly crucial to judge Reality TV as a textual and cultural form in its own right.

The emphasis on Reality TV as somehow being more contrived and constructed than traditional factual programing tends to imply that documentaries once simply observed and recorded life 'as it happened'. This is clearly not the case, and there is a rich heritage of debate which has interrogated documentary's claim to reflect reality (see Winston, 2000). From this point of view, it might be suggested that the highly performative context of Reality TV has at least drawn attention to the constructed nature of the real, offering a "refreshing change from the more conventional kind of play-acting, that of pretending that the camera is not there and that the space of action is purely naturalistic" (Corner, 2006: 95).

Understanding reality ...

The early formatted reality programs were explicit about their staging of reality. They incarcerated diverse participants – either 'ordinary' people or celebrities – in a house or dropped them in a jungle, with the clear intention to create conflict and tension. But as the term 'Reality TV' evidently suggests, this does not indicate that such programing has abandoned a claim to the real. On the contrary it actually intensifies it, shifting the locus of the real onto the self. This, however, is a site of contest within the programs which needs to be constantly debated, negotiated and restated. For example, the primary topic of conversation across the history of the UK *Big Brother* is *selfhood* – 'who is performing for the camera?', 'who is being real?' – and the biggest insult that can be levied at a contestant is that they are being 'fake'.

Given that much television, in the form of news, documentary or drama, has historically made a claim to the real, the question has been raised as to why we suddenly needed to label a category of programing 'Reality TV' at this time. In this regard,

Reality TV has been linked to postmodern debates about the 'death of the real' (Dovey, 2000). From this perspective, so much of our everyday lives is now mediated and mediatized that it is difficult to clearly distinguish between 'the real' and its 'representation' (Baudrillard, 1994). As a result, and as Reality TV suggests, we paradoxically look to *produce* the real (which again creates a context in which the image precedes the real, so arguably the cycle starts again).

But as the discussion above and of course the very title of Reality TV suggests, such programing remains deeply invested in the idea of capturing the real (self). The programs acknowledge that the environment is constructed and that the characters are 'cast', but they fundamentally promote the idea that human reality *can* unfold in a space made for television consumption. As Annette Hill's audience research on Reality TV has explained, Reality TV engages a

> particular viewing practice: audiences look for the moment of authenticity when real people are 'really' themselves in an unreal environment ... [Capitalizing] on the tension between performance and authenticity, [the programs] ask contestants and viewers to look for the 'moment of truth' in a highly constructed and controlled television environment.
> (Hill, 2002: 324)

As this suggests, whilst normalizing the idea of surveillance and turning it into play, Reality TV can be seen as combining a postmodern skepticism towards the real with a more modernist investment in the real as identifiable and desirable. In fact, across formats, the contestant most likely to win a Reality show is often the one who is seen as most having been 'themselves' on screen and never the contestant who has been seen to 'play a good game'.

This period also saw the emergence of audience interactivity in the form of voting and the exploration of a multiplatform address which combined both 'new' and 'old' media technologies. This very much pivots on the passing of audience judgement, assessing the often moral 'value' of Reality participants as they are framed by the show (Wood and Skeggs, 2011), even when the ostensible purpose may simply be to launch a popstar or to give an 'ordinary' person a shot at media visibility. But this discourse of judgement is germane to other forms of Reality programing which do not always invite explicit audience intervention.

Kavka observes how, whilst the earlier formats continued to flourish, during the period 2001–5 "dating, marriage, child-rearing and self-presentation all became viable topics for reality TV" (2012: 111). Here, the "driving force was broadened from competition to challenge" and Reality TV adopted a pedagogic function, "teaching viewers how to behave while entertaining them with and through play" (Kavka, 2012: 111). Although the idea of locating moments of 'authentic' selfhood remained crucial to the appeal to the 'real', the question in these types of programing is less who is being 'real' than "what does reality TV *do*?" (Kavka, 2012: 112).

Much of what some scholars call lifestyle programing has often been discussed under the 'reality' label, whether television is seeking to transform the self, the image, the house, the business, the child, the family or the community. From *What Not to Wear* (2001–7), *Ladette to Lady* (2005–8) and *Wife Swap* (2003–8) to *Jamie's*

School Dinners (2005), *Supernanny* (2005–present), *How Clean is Your House?* (2003–9), *Brat Camp* (2005–7) and *Mary Queen of Shops* (2008–9), such programing is offering the possibility of "life interventions" (Kavka, 2012: 142) that will ostensibly result in better selves whilst teaching "self-governance" (ibid.: 138). It is certainly crucial to pay attention to the textual 'rules' of the format and the ideological constraints through which these are played out. (This will vary from format to format, but in the makeover structures, for example, women who do not fit what are ostensibly middle-class and heterosexual versions of femininity will find themselves 're-shaped'.) But that is not the same as saying that such 'life intervention' programs offer simplistic or homogenous ideological 'messages' about how to live in contemporary society. For example, although this is a much wider issue that cannot be explored here, it might be suggested that a popular format such as *Wife Swap* actually raises *questions* about the domestic organization of the family and domestic citizenship that would lack a similar power in documentary or fiction (Holmes and Jermyn, 2008).

Scripting reality

This is of course just one way of grouping such texts, and this chapter has aimed to make clear how there are multiple ways of thinking about the definition, development and categorization of reality programing. Any such boundaries are of course also always "in process" (Neale, 1990). For example, 2010 onwards saw what might be termed a further development in British reality programing, significant less in terms of the number of texts which demonstrated this shift than for the implications it had for Reality TV's claim to the 'real'. *The Only Way is Essex* (*TOWIE*) (2010–present) and *Made in Chelsea* (2011–present) were influenced by the models of MTV's *Laguna Beach* and *The Hills* (Woods, 2012: 1). Variously referred to as 'structured reality', 'scripted reality' or 'dramality', this form to some degree looks back toward the docusoap phenomenon, in so far as it seeks to offer insight into the comings and goings in a particular, pre-existing milieu (the highly classed cultures of young people living in Essex and Chelsea). But as the production company of *TOWIE*, Lime Pictures, explains, it is distinguished from 'fly on the wall' Reality TV, as "producers set up dramatic scenarios which are then filmed" (cited in Woods, 2012: 2). In shifting closer to conventional understandings of scripting and casting from fictional television, the sense of a documentary aesthetic is also eschewed for higher production values (and thus a dramatic look). But returning us to the complexity of generic hybridity discussed at the start of this chapter, these are texts that truly hover on a fascinating boundary: they are not smooth and professional enough to be read as fiction, whilst awkward pauses and evident staging disrupts the sense of an unseen, observational eye (ibid.: 5). Woods argues that this can actually be seen in a positive light, in so far as their "performative play" suggests the "impossibility of the docusoap's 'authenticity' … while recognising the innate artificiality and construction of Reality TV, highlighting the complex audience engagement offered by the form" (ibid.: 15).

Although *TOWIE* and *Made in Chelsea* can certainly be seen as 'glocalized' versions of the American shows cited above (ibid.: 1), they are not formats as such. In this regard, Reality TV has done much to foreground the contemporary significance of format adaptation in contemporary television. Although the trading of formats between different countries has occurred since the earliest days of television (and radio), the importance of the format has undoubtedly increased, not least because broadcasters are more likely to be risk-adverse in the multi-channel environment and therefore keen to capitalize on and repeat successes which have been 'proven' elsewhere. But rather than simply exploring evidence of global homogenization, scholars have also explored how the adaptation of Reality formats plays out the process of cultural translation (Moran, 1998: 165). Formats are attractive to broadcasters precisely because they offer an idea that has been 'tried and tested' elsewhere, with the possibility for 'local' inflection and adaptation.

There is not space to explore particular examples of individual formats here (see Waisbord, 2004), but on a much wider level, and in terms of the British context, it is worth noting that what runs right through many of the programs discussed in this chapter, from *The Family* to *Big Brother*, *Wife Swap* and *TOWIE*, is a concern with class. As explored earlier, the notion of accessing 'real' or 'ordinary' people in British popular culture has historically been enmeshed with discursive constructions of the British working-class. In terms of Reality TV, much of the distaste about 'awful' ordinary people appearing on television was couched in terms of class (the most high-profile example of this in the UK would be the late Jade Goody, who originally emerged from *Big Brother* in 2003) and its construction of celebrity also reflects on this framework (see Biressi and Nunn, 2005). Formats from *Big Brother* and *Britain's Got Talent* (2007–present) to *X Factor* (2004–present) often play out narratives (and promises) of class mobility. This is not new in the context of celebrity construction, but with Reality TV the spotlight appeared to be shining on representatives of the 'audience'. Biressi and Nunn observe, for example, how in many British formats there appeared to be a "submerged narrative about escape across class boundaries" (2005: 151). It would now be difficult to argue, at least when looking at formats such as *X Factor*, that such a narrative is even 'submerged'. Although there are clear precedents for this, such as the bin man Andy Abraham in the 2005 series, or Tesco-worker Mary Byrne in 2010, telling runner-up Jahmene Douglas that he definitely wasn't "going *back* to Asda" seemed to become something of an obsession for judge Louis Walsh in *X Factor* 2012. The *X Factor* is a highly visible example of a chronic anxiety about remaining in the 'ordinary', i.e. *unmediated*, world (see Couldry, 2000) while of course the successful contestants must appear to stay connected to their 'ordinary' lives if they are to be received as 'real' and 'authentic'. But in the British context, this 'ordinary' world is invariably imagined in class terms. In this respect, whilst Reality TV may offer 'escape' and mobility to the 'lucky' few, we are reminded how celebrity is fundamentally hierarchical and exclusive, no matter how much it appears to proliferate (Turner, 2004).

Further reading

For additional scholarship in this area, Anita Biressi and Heather Nunn's *Reality TV: Realism and Revelation* (2005) provides a discussion of class as a recurrent theme in the reception of Reality TV participants. Misha Kavka provides a useful introduction to the field, with a particular focus on historical precedents, in *Reality TV* (2012). Finally, Jason Mittell's *Genre and Television: From Cop Shows to Cartoons* (2004) is a useful exploration of the complexity of television genres and television genre theory, with discussion of Reality TV.

Notes

1 *I'll Do Anything to Get on TV* (Channel 4, 10 April 2005).
2 BBC Press Release, 11 March, 1974. In file T66/55, BBC Written Archive Centre.

References

Afton, R. (1974) "The Family." *The Evening News*, 4 July [BBC Press cuttings on *The Family*. Page numbers are not included in the archive].
Baudrillard, J. (1994) *Simulacra and Simulation*. Ann Arbor, MI: University of Michigan Press.
Biressi, A. and Nunn, H. (2005) *Reality TV: Realism and Revelation*. London: Wallflower.
Coles, G. (2000) "Docusoap: Actuality and the serial format." In B. Carson and M. Llewellyn-Smith (eds.) *Frames and Fictions on Television: The Politics of Identity Within Drama*. Chicago, IL: University of Chicago Press (pp. 27–30).
Corner, J. (2006) "A fiction (un)like any other?" *Critical Studies in Television*, 1(1), 89–96.
Couldry, N. (2000) *Inside Culture: Re-imagining the Method of Cultural Studies*. London: Sage.
Dovey, J. (2000) *Freakshow: First Person Media and Factual Television*. London: Pluto.
Friedman, J. (2002) *Reality Squared: Televisual Discourse on the Real*. New Brunswick: Rutgers University Press.
Hill, A. (2002) "Big Brother: The real audience." *Television and New Media*, 3(3), 323–41.
Hoggart, P. (2006) "Through a glass, darkly." *The Times*, 18 November. Retrieved from http://entertainment.timesonline.co.uk/tol/arts_and_entertainment/tv_and_radio/article632954.ece
Holmes, S. (2008a) "'Real and riveting: A family in the raw': Revisiting *The Family* (1974) after reality TV." *International Journal of Cultural Studies*, 11(2), 193–210.
——(2008b) "'A term rather too general to be helpful': Struggling with genre in reality TV." In L. Geraghty and M. Jancovich (eds.) *The Shifting Definitions of Genre*. Jefferson, NC: McFarlane (pp. 159–80).
Holmes, S. and Jermyn, D. (2008) "'Ask the fastidious woman from Surbiton to hand-wash the underpants of the aging Oldham Skinhead … ': Why not *Wife Swap*?" In T. Austin and W. de Jong (eds.) *Rethinking Documentary: A Documentary Reader*. Berkshire: Open University Press (pp. 232–45).
Izod, J., Kilborn, R. and Hibberd, M. (2000) (eds.) *From Grierson to the Docusoap: Breaking the Boundaries*. Luton: University of Luton Press.
Kavka, M. (2012) *Reality TV*. Edinburgh: Edinburgh University Press.
Kavka, M. and West, A. (2004) "Temporalities of the real." In S. Holmes and D. Jermyn (eds.) *Understanding Reality Television*. London: Routledge (pp. 136–49).
Mittell, J. (2004) *Genre and Television: From Cop Shows to Cartoons*. London and New York: Routledge.
Moran, A. (1998) *Copycat TV: Globalisation, Programme Formats and Cultural Identity*. Luton: Luton University Press.
Neale, S. (1990) "Questions of genre." *Screen*, 31(1), 45–66.

Robinson, J. (2004) "Pap – or 'porn with a purpose'?" *The Observer*, 18 July, p.18.

Turner, G. (2004) *Understanding Celebrity*. London: Sage.

Waisbord, S. (2004) "McTV: Understanding the global popularity of television formats." *Television and New Media*, 5(4), 359–83.

Winston, B. (2000) *Lies, Damn Lies and Documentary*. London, BFI.

Woods, F. (2012) "Classed femininity, performativity and camp in British structured reality programming." *Television and New Media*. Retrieved from http://tvn.sagepub.com/content/early/2012/11/04/1527476412462246.full.pdf

Wood, H. and Skeggs, B. (2011) "Reacting to reality TV: The affective economy of an 'extended social/public realm'." In M. Kraidy and K. Sender (eds.) *The Politics of Reality Television: Global Perspectives*. London and New York: Routledge (pp. 93–105).

43
Journalism and current affairs
Stephen Cushion

More than a decade into the 21st century television news remains by some distance the primary source of information for most people in the UK (Ofcom, 2011). Although online media have rapidly expanded over the last decade or so, with increasing mobile news consumption – on phones, tablets, laptops, workstations and other emerging platforms – television continues to be the most influential medium. Needless to say, television programs today rarely attract the tens of millions they once did. However, far from television being in terminal decline – as many new media enthusiasts had predicted – overall viewing is rising in the multi-channel, online era (Plunkett, 2010). Nevertheless, like in other news media television news audiences have declined since the 1990s and into the new millennium. But despite the ascendancy of multi-channel television the average size of evening television bulletins has remained roughly the same (Ofcom, 2010).

Television journalism, of course, cannot be defined by fixed-time news bulletins alone. In recent years it could include afternoon chat shows such as *Loose Women* and the *Daily Politics*, or comedy news including *The Daily Show* in the US and the UK's *10 O'clock Live*. Television journalism, in other words, is an increasingly hybrid genre (Cushion, 2012a). However, this chapter will primarily focus on the development of television news bulletins and current affairs programing in the UK. After all, these represent the earliest formats of television journalism and continue to act as flagship news programs for broadcasters. The chapter will historically contextualize the shifting broadcast, regulatory and journalism cultures that shaped news over time and which help explain the nature of contemporary television journalism, including the rise of 24-hour news channels in the 1980s and 1990s. In particular the UK's public service broadcasting infrastructure will be discussed along with the impact commercial news has had in the enhancement or deterioration of standards in television journalism.

Public service framework and values: The birth and development of television news

The origins of television news in the UK lie with the BBC, a public service broadcaster launched in the 1920s. The BBC was conceived as a medium that would pursue, as a committee reviewing how it should be funded put it, "a high standard of broadcast programmes" (Sykes Committee, 1923). Whereas broadcasting in the US was being pioneered by commercial interests and funded by advertisers, this approach was roundly rejected, since it posed "a risk of lowering the standard of broadcasting" (ibid.). To this day the BBC has been funded by a licence fee to carry out its public service obligations in the UK (although the BBC's worldwide programing generates commercial revenue via advertising).

News was central to the BBC's then Director General Lord Reith's understanding of public service broadcasting. News, after all, had the power to 'inform, educate and entertain' viewers, Reith's shorthand philosophy of BBC programing. While remaining impartial was enshrined in the BBC's licence fee arrangements to prevent any outright bias or partisanship, the broadcaster's ability to remain independent of the government was undermined somewhat by its coverage of the 1926 General Strike. By the late 1930s BBC independence had been restored somewhat, with radio news bulletins becoming a much listened to fixture of its programing.

For well over a decade before the arrival of television, the BBC had mastered the art of news on radio, not least during the Second World War, when millions of people relied on its supply of information. A few years after the war had ended, the development of television was reinvigorated but the genre of news took some time to fully gravitate to the small screen. An early news format appeared as a television newsreel in 1948, familiar to cinema audiences of this generation. Meanwhile the BBC's reporting of the Queen's coronation in 1953 was watched by 20 million viewers, an event historians believe triggered the purchase of millions more TV sets (Williams, 1998: 156–57). In the same year the first *Panorama* was broadcast, an extended current affairs program dealing with a small number of stories. It was not until July 1954 that a first news bulletin was aired, but it did not resemble today's format. Rather than utilizing the visual potential of television, for much of the program a still image was used with an unseen presenter narrating the news. The early years of television news, in other words, were shaped by the form and style of radio journalism. While the BBC soon responded to its critics with on-screen presenters, it was arguably the arrival of Independent Television (or ITV as it was renamed) in 1955, a commercial channel, which prompted the public broadcaster to get to grips with the medium of television.

The launch of ITV generated considerable concerns about an Americanization of British television, since for many the incursion of commercial values driven by advertising represented the US system of broadcasting. As Lord Reith put it colorfully in a debate about the possible introduction of ITV at the House of Lords in 1952, "somebody introduced smallpox, bubonic plague and the Black Death Somebody is minded now to introduce sponsored broadcasting into this country" (Reith, 1952). But it is important to remember that ITV was introduced as – and remains today – a *commercial* public service broadcaster, with a licence agreement that obliges the channel to schedule certain types of programing, including the regular supply of impartial television news. As news was so critical to the channel's ethos and identity, a separate organization – Independent Television News (ITN) – was established to oversee a national journalism service, since ITV was – and continues to be – made up of regional companies.

ITN's influence on television journalism was immediate and laid the generic foundations for familiar conventions widely used in news bulletins today. First and foremost, television news had faces presenting the news, with journalists authoritatively projecting their own voices and personalities in programing (Conboy, 2004). Whereas the BBC was accused of being somewhat elitist and deferential in its journalistic approach, ITN embraced the voices of 'the people' via the use of 'vox pops' and a more adversarial style of quizzing politicians. As the BBC began to respond to ITV's journalism and, moreover, became a less paternalistic broadcaster, it triggered a more competitive era of television news making, captured in the BBC's 2011 fictional drama, *The Hour*. The mostly young and idealistic cast are routinely seen challenging the upper echelons of power and attempting to out 'scoop' ITV's more populist drive for ratings. The drama represents the BBC at a critical time, a departure from its Reithian conservatism to a more daring treatment of politics, not least in the 1960s political satire *That Was The Week That Was*. By this time television had become the public's primary source of news, outflanking the priority once afforded to newspapers and radio (Crisell, 1997: 100).

However, television's new-found popularity had raised political anxieties. A 1962 Pilkington committee report into television standards criticized ITV and its then regulator the Independent Broadcasting Authority (IBA) for not honoring its public service obligations. Post-Pilkington, UK television journalism witnessed a more heavyweight schedule of current affairs programing, such as ITV's *World in Action* (see Goddard, Corner and Richardson, 2007). Meanwhile its news bulletins were strengthened and earned critical appraisal (Curran and Seaton, 2010: 173). Likewise, the BBC launched half hourly evening bulletins in the late 1960s and early 1970s, with more continuous pictures shaping coverage due to technological advances. Within this short post-war history, a period of relative maturity can be observed, with new programing pioneered and television news conventions introduced, many of which remain recognizable norms and routines in contemporary journalism.

While some of the values underpinning public service broadcasting were tested in the post-war years, television news remained a closely regulated and impartial service delivering peak-time programing. Unlike in the US, the state had prevented excessive commercial influence on broadcasting. However, the institutions and structures that television news had grown up within were about to be subject to considerable changes in a new era of deregulation and multi-channel television.

The changing nature of television news programing: The weakening of public service broadcasting in a multi-channel environment

The 1980s and 1990s shook the foundations of television's infrastructure. While Channel 4 had become the UK's third terrestrial broadcaster in 1982 – once again with public service obligations included in the provision of news which ITN produced – by the end of the decade multi-channel television had arrived. Up until this point the UK – and much of Europe – had been reluctant to deregulate broadcasting from the state. But under a free market Thatcher Government, new satellite technology brought the promise of competition and choice to a new and potentially lucrative globalized market. BSB (now known as BSkyB) began broadcasting in 1989 without the obligation to deliver public service programing. Four channels were launched, including a dedicated news channel – Sky News – the first in Europe. Likewise, in the US enhanced deregulation brought an explosion of channels in the 1980s and 1990s including CNN, the world's first rolling news channel (Cushion, 2010b). The impact of CNN and 24-hour news television more generally is explored later.

In a more deregulatory climate, the UK's broadcast ecology began to be redefined. While the BBC had escaped being dismantled by a 1986 Peacock Committee review, the 1990 Broadcasting Act lightened the public service obligations commercial broadcasters had previously had with a less robust regulator policing content (Cushion, 2012a: 50–51). ITN, for example, was no longer a not-for-profit organization and, according to observers, began reorienting its news agenda to appeal to a wider constituency of viewers (Crisell, 1997; Williams, 1998). Channel Five, a commercial channel launched in 1997, today offers perhaps the most unashamedly tabloid coverage among UK broadcasters, reassembling the style and format of US television news.

Systematic longitudinal studies of television bulletins confirmed the changing agendas of terrestrial commercial news since the 1990s. So, for example, Harrison's (2000: 207) study found that "ITN's Channel 3 news programs, GMTV News, Channel 4's Big Breakfast News and Yorkshire Tyne-Tees Television's Calendar News programs all show a strong commitment to a high percentage of human interest coverage." "The current trend," she concluded, was "towards the maintenance of mainstream mass audiences through introducing a faster tempo to the news programs and providing interesting and entertaining news stories" (ibid.: 207). Meanwhile, Barnett, Seymour and Gaber's (2000: 12) study of television news bulletins between 1975 and 1999 identified that "there has undoubtedly been a shift in most news bulletins towards a more tabloid domestic agenda … This shift has been particularly apparent over the last 10 years in the two ITN bulletins." Nonetheless, they added, UK television journalism offers a more balanced diet of stories, mix of international news and serious mode of address than the wholesale US commercial channels. Indeed, it has been argued that television in the US hypercommercialized over this period of time (McChesney, 2000). Without any meaningful public service obligations, the intense competition between channels delivered a more populist and sensationalist approach to television journalism (Caldwell, 1995).

The battle for news ratings was more subtly waged in the UK, with channels attempting to break free of long-standing public service commitments. So, for example, while both the BBC and ITV are legally required to air television news in peak time, at the turn of century both bulletins were re-scheduled to later night slots. This began in 1999 when ITV moved its late night bulletin from 10pm to 11pm because it wanted to run uninterrupted entertainment programing prior to the news broadcast. But as viewing figures soon dropped, the then regulator – the Independent Television Commission (ITC) – returned ITV's bulletin to its 10pm slot. In the meantime, the BBC had moved its bulletin from 9pm – where it had been scheduled for the past 30 years – to 10pm to schedule more drama and entertainment programing in peak time. Both channels currently run a late night bulletin at 10pm, but ITV has recently explored the possibility – primarily to save costs in local newsgathering – of halving its early evening national and regional coverage to make way for a quiz show (Brown, 2011). In other words, to remain competitive in a more crowded marketplace commercial broadcasters have increasingly been arguing – in the provision of news and other costly programing – that they do not have the necessary resources to fulfil the public service obligations they once delivered. A 20-year study of current affairs programing from 1978 to 1998, for example, discovered that on commercial television – notably ITV – there had not only been a decline in the proportion of air time in the 1990s but topics had become softer with political, economic and international issues downsized (Barnett and Seymour, 1999). Current affairs programing, it was concluded, was reliant to a large extent on the BBC, where "output continued to rise in recognition of its public service obligations" (Barnett, 2012: 160).

Into the 2000s, New Labour replaced the ITC with a new, even 'lighter' regulator – the Office of Communications (Ofcom) – which policed all commercial media and telecommunications content. In the words of a 2002 Communications Bill, Ofcom's remit should "not involve the imposition or maintenance of unnecessary burdens" (cited in Cave, 2004: 65). By contrast, the BBC Trust – the BBC's regulator, which replaced the board of governors in 2007 – has a more interventionist mandate to protect public service values. In doing so, the BBC Trust routinely carries out reviews of BBC content and expects any of its public service obligations not being fulfilled to be corrected and enhanced, such as its reporting of the nations and devolved politics (Cushion, 2013). A 2007 review of BBC national television news reporting found that the nations beyond England were marginalized in coverage and, at times, English policies were assumed to be relevant UK-wide (Cushion, Lewis and Groves, 2009). After a set of evidence-based recommendations, a 2010 follow-up review observed several improvements in the BBC's impartial reporting of the nations and accuracy in political coverage (Cushion, Lewis and Ramsay, 2010). Commercial television news, however, was found lacking in both reviews, notably on Sky News, the channel with the least public service responsibilities (Cushion, Lewis and Ramsay, 2012). However, the erosion of local and regional news can also be observed on ITV, despite this content once being central to its public service ethos and the channel's identity. Whereas the BBC had 18 regional bulletins in its 6.30pm slot in 2009, ITV reduced its allocations from 17 to nine.

Well into a decade of the twenty-first century, the public service obligations of television, which had grown up in the so-called 'golden era' of broadcast journalism, had been significantly downsized. A more crowded, multi-channel television environment with competition rife online as well as in print had exerted considerable pressure on resources for the delivery of news, never the most profitable nor ratings-friendly genre at the best of times. The model of public service broadcasting had thus been weakened and some of its values were to be undermined further with the rise and influence of 24-hour television news.

Live, rolling news values and conventions: The influence of 24-hour television and commercial competition

So far television news has been discussed in the context of the supply of current affairs programing or fixed-time bulletins. But since CNN launched a 24-hour news channel more than 30 years ago, television journalism has offered a continuous, always-on, rolling news service. As multi-channel television cultures have become more widespread around the world, there has been a rise in 24-hour news television channels (Cushion and Lewis, 2010). The BBC launched its national rolling news channel in the UK in 1997, seven years after Sky News. Since then, both channels have competed fiercely to become "Britain's Most Watched News Channel" – an on-screen slogan the BBC regularly uses to punctuate its news updates since winning the ratings war (Cushion, 2010a). Indeed, this competitive thirst aptly captures the journalistic development of rolling news channels. For whereas television news in the UK grew up exposed to public service obligations and influences, CNN – a commercial international news channel – defined many of its norms and routines almost two decades before the BBC had even launched its own service.

However, CNN's journalistic credentials were questioned when the channel first launched. With minimal resources to fill a 24-hour cycle of news, it lacked the resources the big three American network channels had established over previous decades (Cushion, 2010a). Compared to the network's polished news packages, rolling news production appeared a semiotically disorganized medium. But this raw approach to journalism – with its on-screen reporters without a script to hand or prolonged instances of live footage – fast became a familiar part of CNN's editorial distinctiveness. The rolling news channel could thus claim to be first with news stories, be first on location when a news story broke, and, unlike television news's initial reluctance in the 1950s, be first to provide a visual window on what was happening in the world. CNN's exclusive live pictures of the 1991 war in Iraq brought the channel to the attention on the world stage, celebrated in the 2002 Hollywood movie *Live from Baghdad*.

CNN's generic conventions have since become a familiar part of rolling, 24-hour news coverage around the world (Cushion, 2010a). Indeed, a longitudinal study of both Sky News and the BBC News channel – the UK's two main domestic news channels – confirmed both had enhanced their proportion of live, breaking news stories between 2004 and 2007 (Lewis and Cushion, 2009). But rather than reflecting a more newsworthy agenda, a close comparison of Sky and BBC coverage in 2007 revealed just one in four stories were labeled 'breaking news' by *both* channels. In other words, breaking news appeared more of a branding exercise with channels aggressively competing to 'break news' first as opposed to a reflection of news values or editorial merit. But, as Lewis (2010) has argued, the urgency 24-hour news channels afford to broadcasting live, breaking pictures represents a missed opportunity for better informing viewers about the world. After all, without the constraints of half-hour bulletins, rolling news has the time to explore stories in more depth, to unpack their significance and thus provide the context and background critics have suggested television news can sometimes overlook (Philo and Berry, 2004). While the resources needed to fund a 24-hour cycle tend to conspire against a routine agenda of investigative journalism, there remains a potential for rolling news channels to be shaped by public service values of the Reithian kind. And yet, ever since CNN began broadcasting, the emphasis has been on delivering news live, as it happens and these values have become deeply ingrained in the editorial mindsets of many 24-hour news channels around the world (Cushion and Lewis, 2010).

Of course, the influence of 24-hour news channels should not be overblown. Unless a major news story is breaking, such as the terrorist atrocities of 9/11 or 7/7, rolling news viewers ordinarily represent a miniscule share of the audience. Nevertheless, the rhythms and routines shaping 24-hour news channels are arguably beginning to influence the broader culture of television journalism. So, for example, a detailed study in 2012 of three UK evening television news bulletins – on the BBC, ITV and Channel 5 – showed their editorial conventions and practices resembled the format of rolling news channels (Cushion and Thomas, 2013). While pre-packaged news was the format most used, every bulletin in various ways carried live news conventions. This editorial priority towards 'liveness' was reflected in its prominence in news agendas, with close to half of Channel Five's headline stories, for example, using live two-ways, where an anchor interviews a reporter outside well-known locations such as 10 Downing Street.

Indeed, political news, above all, stood out as the most reported live news topic, with political editors in particular routinely delivering their on-screen judgments. Channel Five's political editor, Andy Bell, for example, accounted for over 40 percent of *all* live news examined in the three-week sample. When live political news was compared to non-live stories on all three channels, edited packages contained four sources per item, whereas for two ways the ratio was below one. The editorial decision to employ more live conventions in fixed bulletins, such as two ways, therefore appears likely to lead to more interpretative and less source-driven journalism.

Comparing UK, US and Norwegian evening bulletins, a study found that the degree in which television news bulletins resembled the format and style of rolling news varied according to how far ingrained the journalistic culture of 24-hour news was in each country (Cushion, Aalberg and Thomas, 2014). While Norway's first domestic rolling news channel was not launched until 2007, 24-hour news channels in the US and UK have – as this chapter has explored – been operating for decades. As a consequence, it was in these two countries where bulletins displayed live, interpretative and on-location reporting most prominently. In other words, the values of 24-hour news channels appeared to be having a systemic editorial impact on television news bulletins in the US and UK (see also Cushion, Roger and Lewis, 2014).

How might television news bulletins evolve in the immediate future? As viewers increasingly have access to a range of instant news – not just on dedicated channels, but on tablets, phones and work computers – it could result in television news bulletins abandoning their once traditional role in conveying what happened over the course of the day. Caught up in the immediacy of contemporary news culture, live action and interpretative reporters could play an increasingly prominent part in television news bulletins.

The future of television journalism: Commercial impact but public service safeguards

Since television in the UK began broadcasting news over 60 years ago, its journalism and current affairs programing have undergone some profound changes.

While the conventions of radio news defined the early years of television journalism, the visual nature of the medium soon began to influence the selection and editorial output of news. This was amplified by the arrival of 24-hour news channels in the 1980s and developments in satellite technology. Into the new millennium, many news channels have increasingly relied upon live pictures to fill air time. Indeed, the emphasis on live, breaking stories on rolling news channels has even begun to shape fixed-time bulletins, with conventions such as the live two way today playing a prominent role in routine coverage.

But while the character of television news has changed over successive decades, it remains important to understand how the changing ecology of broadcasting has impacted on the quality of news alongside technological advancements and evolving newsroom practices. As the US political economist Bob McChesney (2002) has put it, "media systems are not 'natural', but ... are the direct result of explicit public policies." Whereas the US system of broadcasting developed a free-market model in the 1920s with minimal regulatory obligations, the UK developed a media system shaped by public service values. As this chapter has explored, studies have shown that while UK television news has maintained a relatively highbrow and impartial news agenda of politics and social policy stories, US coverage has become more tabloid, sensationalist and politically bias (Cushion, 2012b), for the US withdrew the legal requirement for broadcasters to be impartial in 1987, thus allowing news channels such as Fox News and MSNBC to be openly partisan. Successive UK governments, by contrast, have withstood lobbying pressure to relax impartiality guidelines arguably due to the long-lasting influence of the public service broadcasting ethos and its statutory underpinning.

Of course, commercial competition has entered the UK marketplace in recent decades and pressure to deregulate commercial broadcast media has resulted in television channels operating with less imposed public service responsibilities. This has implications for the quality of television news, as recent evidence suggests that the level of regulatory obligations for each broadcaster shapes the type of news agenda pursued (Cushion, 2012b). A longitudinal study of television news bulletins from 1975 to 2009, for example, demonstrated that commercial public service broadcasters – including ITV, but most strikingly Channel Five – had enhanced their tabloid agenda in a more deregulated environment whereas the BBC had remained relatively upmarket (Barnett, Ramsay and Gaber, 2012).

Nevertheless, the three terrestrial channels – ITV, Channel 4 and Channel 5 – continue to operate as commercial public service broadcasters with a legal commitment to air news programing and remain impartial. This arguably explains why television news ranks as the most trusted source of information whereas in the US, where there are no robust requirements to remain impartial, cable and network viewers hold far less confidence in the accuracy of coverage (Cushion, 2012a). This would suggest that television journalism in the UK can maintain its status as the most popular and trusted source of information for most people in the country if the structures and values that first shaped its development can be protected from government interference and market pressure.

Further reading

Steven Barnett (2012) in *The Rise and Fall of Television Journalism: Just Wires and Lights in a Box?* provides a review of the history of UK television news. Stephen

Cushion (2012a) offers a comparative review of US and UK television news in *Television Journalism*. Richard Sambrook (2012) in his report "Delivering trust: Impartiality and objectivity in the digital age" discusses the past and future regulation of broadcast news in the twenty-first century. Finally, Stephen Cushion (2012b) in *The Democratic Value of News: Why Public Service Media Matters* offers a comparative assessment of public and commercial television news internationally.

References

Barnett, S. (2012) *The Rise and Fall of Television Journalism: Just Wires and Lights in a Box?* London: Bloomsbury Academic.

Barnett, S. and Seymour, E. (1999) 'A Shrinking Iceberg Travelling South … ': Changing Trends in British Television: A Case Study of Drama and Current Affairs. London: University of Westminster Publication.

Barnett, S., Ramsay, G. N. and Gaber, I. (2012) *From Callaghan to Credit Crunch: Changing Trends in British Television News 1975–2009*. London: University of Westminster publication.

Barnett, S., Seymour, E. and Gaber, I. (2000) *From Callaghan to Kosovo: Changing Trends in British Television News*. London: University of Westminster publication.

Brown, M. (2011) "ITV considered replacing half of evening news with gameshow." *Media Guardian*, 18 January. Retrieved from http://www.guardian.co.uk/media/2011/jan/18/itv-early-evening-news

Caldwell, J. T. (1995) *Televisuality: Style, Crisis, and Authority in American Television*. New York: Rutgers University Press.

Cave, M. (2004) "Ofcom and light touch regulation." In C. Robinson (ed.) *Successes and Failures in Regulating and Deregulating Utilities*. Cheltenham: Edward Elgar Publishing.

Conboy, M. (2004) *Journalism: A Critical History*. London: Sage.

Crisell, A. (1997) *An Introductory History of British Broadcasting*. London: Routledge.

Curran, J. and Seaton, J. (2010) *Navigating the Rocks: Power Without Responsibility: The Press, Broadcasting and New Media in Britain* (7th edition). London: Routledge.

Cushion, S. (2010a) "Rolling service, market logic: The race to be 'Britain's most watched news channel'." In S. Cushion and J. Lewis (eds.) *The Rise of 24-Hour News Television: Global Perspectives*. New York: Peter Lang.

——(2010b) "Three phases of the 24-hour television news genre." In S. Cushion and J. Lewis (eds.) *The Rise of 24-Hour News Television: Global Perspectives*. New York: Peter Lang.

——(2012a) *Television Journalism*. London: Sage.

——(2012b) *The Democratic Value of News: Why Public Service Media Matters*. Basingstoke: Palgrave.

——(2013) "Assessing, measuring and applying 'public value tests' beyond new media: Interpreting impartiality and plurality in debates about journalism standards." In L. Barkho (ed.) *From Theory to Practice: How to Assess and Apply Impartiality in News and Current Affairs*. Chicago, IL: Chicago University Press.

Cushion, S. and Lewis, J. (2010) (eds.) *The Rise of 24-Hour News Television: Global Perspectives*. New York: Peter Lang.

Cushion, S. and Thomas, R. (2013) "The mediatization of politics: Interpreting the value of live versus edited journalistic interventions in UK television news bulletins." *International Journal of Press/Politics*, 18(3), 360–80.

Cushion, S., Aalberg, T. and Thomas, R. (2014) "The mediatization of news and journalistic interventions: A comparative analysis of television news in the US, UK and Norway." *European Journal of Communication*, 29(1), 100–109.

Cushion, S., Lewis, J. and Groves, C. (2009) "Reflecting the four nations? An analysis of reporting devolution on UK network news media." *Journalism Studies*, 10(5), 655–71.

Cushion, S., Lewis, J. and Ramsay, G. (2010) *Four Nations Impartiality Review Follow-Up: An Analysis of Reporting Devolution*. London: BBC Trust Publication.

Cushion, S., Lewis, J. and Ramsay, G. (2012) "The impact of interventionist regulation in reshaping news agendas: A comparative analysis of public and commercially funded television journalism." *Journalism: Theory, Practice and Criticism*, 13(7), 831–49.

Cushion, S., Roger, H. and Lewis, R. (2014) "Comparing levels of mediatization in television journalism: An analysis of political reporting on US and UK evening news bulletins." *International Communication Gazette*, 76(6).

Goddard, P., Corner, J. and Richardson, K. (2007) *Public Issue Television: World in Action 1963–98*. Manchester: Manchester University Press.

Harrison, J. (2000) *Terrestrial TV News in Britain: The Culture of Production*. Manchester: Manchester University Press.

Lewis, J. (2010) "Democratic or disposable? 24-hour news, consumer culture, and built-on obsolescence." In S. Cushion and J. Lewis (eds.) *The Rise of 24 Hour News Television: Global Perspectives*. New York: Peter Lang.

Lewis, J. and Cushion, S. (2009) "The thirst to be first: An analysis of breaking news stories and their impact on the quality of 24-hour news coverage in the UK." *Journalism Practice*, 3(3), 304–18.

McChesney, R. (2000) *Rich Media, Poor Democracy: Communication Politics in Dubious Times*. Urbana and Chicago, IL: University of Illinois Press.

——(2002) "It's a wrap? Why media matters to democracy." Open Democracy, 8 May. Retrieved from http://www.opendemocracy.net/democracy-globalmediaownership/article_61.jsp

Ofcom (2010) "Halt in decline of flagship TV news programmes." June 30. Retrievd from http://media.ofcom.org.uk/2010/06/30/halt-in-decline-of-flagship-tv-news-programmes

——(2011) "UK audience attitudes to the broadcast media." London: Ofcom publication.

Philo, G. and Berry, M. (2004) *Bad News From Israel*. London: Pluto Press.

Plunkett, J. (2010) "Television viewing increases despite rise of internet and social media." *The Guardian*, 19 August 19. Retrieved from http://www.guardian.co.uk/uk/2010/aug/19/television-viewing-increases-internet

Reith, J. (1952) Speech at the House of Lords, 22 May. Hansard col 1297.

Sambrook, R. (2012) *Delivering Trust: Impartiality and Objectivity in the Digital Age*. Oxford: Reuters Institute for the Study of Journalism, Oxford University.

Sykes Committee (1923) "Report on the Broadcasting Committee."

Williams, K. (1998) *Get Me a Murder a Day! A History of Mass Communication in Britain*. London: Bloomsbury Academic.

Part VIII
DIGITAL MEDIA

44
Technology's false dawns: The past of media futures
Lily Canter

The future of newspapers is once more under scrutiny. Throughout history each step forward in communication technology, whether it be the invention of the telegraph, the radio or the television, has brought with it fatalistic cries predicting the demise of the printed press. Further reinforcements have joined this tradition in the past two decades with the unprecedented expansion of the internet appearing to signal that the end of paper and ink is nigh. But the pessimistic media soothsayers seem to have rather missed the point. Instead of speculating about whether the printed newspaper will exist in 10, 20 or 50 years' time, the more pertinent question is what form will this news medium take? History tells us that newspaper is a versatile form of communication which has always adapted to changing circumstances and the emergence of competing media. Indeed this 'editorial Darwinism' (Franklin, 2008: 307) is the key to its 400-year survival. All too often scholars and journalists alike separate the printed press from its online counterparts despite the continual convergence of newsrooms and practitioners' roles. In the twenty-first century, a newspaper journalist is now a multimedia, digital journalist who writes copy for the paper, the website, the mobile website, social media channels and increasingly for tablet applications as well. This convergent journalism is both journalistic and economic and sees the coming together of different news platforms in terms of both production and ownership. Print media companies have once more adapted to market conditions and now hope to "find salvation by embracing innovation and integrating digital media" (Paulussen, 2011: 59). The newspaper may have had a long and illustrious narrative as a printed product but its future survival may now lie in multiple digital reincarnations.

Same media, different technology

The introduction of digital news content, via newspaper websites, social media platforms, and mobile and tablet apps, has been developed by publishing companies in Britain, and worldwide, during the past decade with billions of pounds being poured into new media technology. This technological drive has arisen in response to a growing consumer appetite for internet usage in the home and on the move. In Britain 80 percent of households have access to the internet – a total of 21 million households – and a further 51 percent of internet users use a mobile phone to connect to the internet (Office for National Statistics, 2012). These customers are still consuming the same news medium – the written word – but it is being delivered by a different technology. As the American media scholar Henry Jenkins sets out in his book *Convergence Culture*, "history teaches us that old media never die and they don't even necessarily fade away. What dies are simply the tools we use to access media content" (2008: 13). The delivery technologies, the tools which are used to communicate the information, may become obsolete and get replaced over time, but the media evolve. In the example of news media, the written word is one type of news medium. It exists within a set of social and cultural practices and journalistic norms and routines which have evolved from the printed press. However, the delivery technologies used to communicate the written word are numerous and include – although not exclusively – newspapers, magazines, internet enabled computers, mobile phones and tablets. Each of these delivery systems may be more or less popular in time and their audiences may change from elite to mass, and back again, depending on the historical context, but the integral medium of the written word remains the same. It is therefore important to explore the historical context of this particular medium in order to better understand new technology systems and how to incorporate them into our media futures. This chapter focuses on the historic similarities between the evolution of newspapers in Britain and the emergence of digital, internet-enabled technologies in the late twentieth century. The primary focal points are news consumption, economy and audience.

A desire for local news

It is without question that the advancement of technology has changed the scale and scope of news accessible on a daily basis to people in western society. In the twenty-first century news is global, fragmented and mobile. There is more news, "across an unprecedented range of media, than at any time since the birth of the free press in the eighteenth century" (Hargreaves, 2005: 1). Yet the existence of almost instantaneous 24-hour worldwide news is less than a generation old. In its modest beginnings news was spread by word of mouth or handwritten letters and was therefore limited by geography and how fast a man could ride a horse. But as transport and communication technology developed so did the spread of news. The seventeenth century printed press allowed newspapers to be distributed across an entire city before the arrival of the steam engine and electric telegraph in the nineteenth century enabled news to be transported across the country and later between continents. By the twentieth century mass audiences could be reached via radio and later television with news from around the globe. The worldwide web made this news accessible any time of day, anywhere in the world, at the touch of a button. Yet despite its global capacity audiences still consume local and national news in the highest proportions. Geographic relevance remains one of the most important news values

(Harcup and O'Neill, 2001) to consumers and "there is continuity in life still being predominantly local for most people; readers still want local news and advertising" (Hobbs, 2011: 12). Even in the post-digital era local relevance is a common factor in newspaper coverage (Brighton and Foy, 2007) due to its heightened relevance to the reader.

For the majority of people the desire for local news is driven by practical and material concerns such as the quality of schools and hospitals, and issues of crime, employment and houses prices (Aldridge, 2007). The technology may allow audiences in Bournemouth to read news about elections in Botswana but they are far more likely to want to know if Bournemouth Borough Council is increasing their council tax bill or changing their kerbside recycling collection. The desire for local and highly relevant news dates back to the early days of the eighteenth century provincial newspapers. The first local newspapers began to emerge in 1701 and by 1760 there were 130 newspapers printed outside the capital (Cranfield, 1962). Initially these provincial newspapers selected and filtered the best information from the numerous London papers and as consequence the content was predominantly national and foreign news (ibid.). However, by the end of the eighteenth century competition was increasing as provincial newspapers began operating closer to one another, reducing the territory and allowing for more local news and advertisements (Walker, 2006). From the 1780s onwards local news was the key to success and many newspapers beat off competitors if their rivals neglected the importance of local news. Over the next 100 years the number of provincial titles increased to 938 by 1877, with each newspaper covering a specific geographic area in terms of its circulation and content. And although circulation figures were low at around 10,000, the readership was far higher at 150,000 per newspaper on account of the fact that an average of 15 to 25 people read just one copy of a newspaper (ibid.). Provincial newspapers continued to flourish well into the nineteenth century as the arrival of the telegraph enabled them to take on the London press. Local newspaper offices were able to receive national and international news within minutes, publish it locally and then distribute it to the local community far quicker than newspapers carrying the same information could arrive by train from London. This new electronic telegraph era led to the creation of the Press Association in 1868, a co-operative national and international newsgathering service made up of a string of northern newspapers (ibid.). Today the Press Association remains a vital component of regional newspapers and consumption of local news remains similarly healthy. Each week more than 31 million people in Britain pick up a local newspaper – almost 50 per cent of the population. A further 62 million web users log onto local news websites each month – a figure which has doubled in less than three years. According to the Newspaper Society (2013) there remain 1,100 core newspapers and 1,600 websites in the British local media, a sign that the industry, in statistical terms at least, is most definitely not in decline. If the figures are to be believed local media in Britain are reaching more people than ever before and the consumption of local news is as vibrant as it was in its nineteenth-century heyday. History tells us that local news is fundamentally important to our everyday lives even when it competes in a global marketplace but the present day shows us that local news delivery systems are shifting. Research on local British newspaper websites reveals that 50 percent of readers have swapped their daily newspaper buying habits for daily news viewing online (Canter, 2012a) and an increasing number are accessing local news websites via mobile phones and tablets. Circulation figures across regional newspapers reflect the growing online trend with many newspapers attracting a higher daily readership online than offline. For example, the Newsquest publication the Bournemouth *Daily Echo* has a daily circulation of 24,000 – a decline of more than six per cent year on year – but a rapidly increasing online presence with 31,000 daily visitors to dailyecho.co.uk – a rise of 22 per cent year on year (Hold the Front Page, 2013). In many respects the uptake of online news today mirrors the growth of newspaper consumption in the seventeenth and eighteenth centuries – albeit at a much steadier rate. As seen with the growth of provincial newspapers, when more products come into the marketplace, competition increases and demand soars, leading to a fragmentation of audiences.

Despite this strong market presence local newspaper groups are struggling to compete with the growth of the internet and the subsequent drop in advertising revenues (Singer et al., 2011). A paradox exists where the consumption of online news is increasing substantially yet publishers are unable to transform this increased demand into profits. As Briggs (2012: 14) reasons, "it's not a readership problem; it's a revenue problem" and the web has in reality helped newspapers to evolve from a print product to a digital product which still meets local news consumption demands. This digital technology also enables local news organizations to tell stories through multiple means, on multiple platforms. A story is no longer stationary text, it can also be told via live blogs, photographic slideshows, animated graphics, audio clips, online videos and hyperlinks. These can be accessed not only on a newspaper website but also via associated social media platforms including Facebook, Twitter, Flickr and Tumblr, and through mobile phone and tablet apps. This transmedia storytelling (Jenkins, 2008) offers multiple points of entry and a variety of media, thus enabling news organizations to seize upon fragmented audiences. But the content and sentiment are essentially the same. In 2012 the *Southern Daily Echo* released a special edition iPad app commemorating the 100th anniversary of the sinking of the Titanic and the impact it had on the ship's home port of Southampton. Using archives from the newspaper, 'Titanic: The Southampton Story' contained interactive text, videos, photos and maps to "bring to life the human stories behind one of history's most enduring tragedies" (Daily Echo, 2012). But the newspaper also took a more traditional approach and printed a supplement containing stories and photos from its archive, telling the dramatic story in an alternative format. Whatever the delivery system – a printed supplement or an electronic app – the core concept remains the same: to tell human interest stories within their historical context.

Economy of scale

The production and subsequent consumption of news may be shifting onto digital, internet-enabled devices but the capitalist business model remains the status quo, as it has done for two hundred years. Indeed the political economy of newspapers is leading the adaptation of delivery systems as publishers desperately try to compete within the fragmented online marketplace. Despite the normative claim of the British press to being the historic watchdog of the state's activities, no such legal societal obligations exist. Some editors may proclaim the role of the media as a facilitator of the public sphere (Rusbridger, 2010), whilst various scholars hold journalism responsible for giving people independent information to enable them to govern themselves (Kovach and Rosenstiel, 2007), yet throughout its history journalism has existed as an uneasy relationship between democracy and commercialism – much like the internet. Indeed, the evolution of British journalism is arguably indebted to the growth of both democracy and a free market economy. Whilst the histories of journalism and democracy are closely linked (McNair, 2008), the local press as it is recognized today peaked in the late nineteenth century in direct correlation to the growth of capitalism and with it advertising (Franklin and Murphy, 1991). Although advertising was not a major source of profit in the early years of provincial newspapers, as they were funded by sales, political parties and philanthropists (Hobbs, 2011), it became increasingly important as production costs rose and the market economy expanded into the nineteenth century. The rise in costs coupled with the reduction in retail prices brought about by tax abolition meant newspapers were sold at a loss and began to rely heavily on advertising for profit. By the early years of the twentieth century provincial newspaper proprietors pursued their newspaper interests "as commercial enterprises rather than as political projects" (Walker, 2006: 374) and provincial newspapers were viewed as potentially highly profitable commercial ventures. Furthermore, the political agenda was starting to fade in the late nineteenth century in part due to increasing political centralization which meant local government had less power and therefore was less newsworthy in terms of political stories to fill local newspapers (ibid.). As far back as the turn of the twentieth century local newspapers were turning to more sport, crime and human interest stories in order to compete with the rising popular national tabloid press. This move towards more popular content and the pursuit of commercial interests over public affairs accelerated in the twenty-first century. Globalization in the second half of the twentieth century saw small family newspaper businesses swallowed up by multi-national conglomerates via widespread acquisitions and mergers. In particular the relaxation of ownership rules in the Broadcasting Act of 1996 and the 2003 Communications Act led to an even greater consolidation of the newspaper industry. Consequently local newspapers have been left in the hands of a few major-profit driven corporations, some with American parent companies, and the monopolies seen today have emerged.

The free market economy has been crucial to the survival of newspapers and has enabled a once elite product to be rolled out to the masses. And like the provincial newspapers of the industrial revolution, the consumption of online and digital news is currently in an evolving process from the elite to the middle class to the mass market. During the seventeenth century the printing trade was greatly restricted by the 1663 Printing Act which not only acted as a censor but also only licensed printers in London and the two university towns of Cambridge and Oxford. This meant that in the provinces only the rich could afford to subscribe to the London newspapers or hand-written newsletters (Cranfield, 1962). However, once the act lapsed in 1696, the restrictions ceased and the newly found freedom of the press encouraged an abundance of new titles to spring up in London. The market quickly became saturated and printers started to look further afield, setting up printing houses in provinces such as Bristol, Shrewsbury and Norwich in the 1690s. By 1701 local newspapers had begun to arrive, 80 years after the first recorded London newspaper, the *London Gazette*. These country newspapers were cheaper than London papers as they were printed weekly and there was no postal cost, therefore they appealed to the property-owning middle class of shopkeepers, farmers and merchants (Harris, 1996). Newspapers were no longer the sole domain of the upper class as the market made them affordable to a wider readership. However, the biggest impact on provincial newspapers was arguably the abolition of taxes on knowledge – Advertisement Duty was abolished in 1853, Stamp Duty was abolished in 1855 and Paper Duty was abolished in 1861 – following a campaign for a free market press by the reconstituted Peoples' Charter Union in 1848 (Curran, 1978). This dramatic change gave newspapers freedom from state economic control and opened up the market to a mass audience as the price of newspapers dropped. The move from elite to mass readership took almost 200 years, during a period of huge social, political and technological development. And arguably the same is happening today in the online news marketplace, within a much tighter timescale.

The 2001 Living in Britain report (Walker et al., 2001) was the first time the government officially measured household internet access. At this time a third of all households in Britain had dial-up internet access. Professional and managerial households were most likely to have access (68 percent and 61 percent respectively) compared with 26 percent of semi-skilled and 15 percent of unskilled manual workers. These figures appeared to support the scholarly argument that newspaper websites strengthened the social divide as they were dominated by educated elites (Sparks, 2003). But a decade later the online social landscape represents a wider public sphere with spaces opening up for a variety of demographics. Online news websites attract digital natives and migrants and almost half of British adults now access their news online (Office for National Statistics, 2012), revealing a shift from the elite to the middle classes. Furthermore, the number of households with internet access has shot up to 80 percent, with 93 percent of these using broadband. Internet usage is a daily habit with 33 million adults logging on every day, double the figure recorded in 2006. The speed of this widespread access is further accelerated by the take up of smart phones, with a third of the population already accessing the internet using a mobile phone every day (ibid.). With this ease of internet access consumers are increasingly swapping their daily newspaper buying habits for daily news viewing online (Canter, 2012a) and in respect of local newspaper websites there is evidence to suggest that these readers are now broadly representative of the population as a whole. As the technology becomes cheaper and more widely available, like the spread of provincial newspapers in the eighteenth century, news websites seem destined to become the sphere of the masses.

The public as participant

'Citizen journalism', 'reader participation' and 'audience collaboration' have been the buzz words of the twenty-first century among scholars (Hermida et al., 2011;

Gillmor, 2006) and editors (Maguire, 2011; Rusbridger, 2010) alike, heralding a new dawn of active audiences rising up from their passive positions on the sofa to take to the streets armed with their mobile phones and a keen eye for recording action. Every major news event covered by the mainstream media, and increasingly minor ones as well, is accompanied by a barrage of eyewitness accounts, photographs, comments, tweets and YouTube videos from the public, giving their insight from the ground and reaction to the news. Research indicates that comments on mainstream newspaper websites are the most popular form of participatory journalism both in the UK and internationally (Canter, 2012b; Örnebring, 2008) and it has rapidly risen since the introduction of Web 2.0. But the act of participation in the news is not a contemporary concept as it arguably dates back to the origin of newspapers. Rusbridger (2010) maintains that audience participation is a tradition started by newspapers in Britain which has allowed people to express themselves freely for centuries. Furthermore, Web 2.0 is simply expanding this trend, for the greater good of journalism. And concrete evidence of reader participation in journalism can be seen as early as the eighteenth century, with British newspapers such as *The Evening General Post* leaving space at the end of the third page for reader comments which were then posted on to friends or relatives attached to the paper (Wiles, 1965).

The concept of audience inclusion in the news process, whether it be in the recording, production, response to or dissemination of news, has been a recurring theme throughout the history of Western newspapers. The alternative participatory movement in Britain that emerged in the 1960s was a direct resistance to the commercialization of the local press. Whilst mainstream local newspapers were relying on stories from official sources – police, courts, councils, health authorities, MPs, companies and charities – the alternative press, such as the *Liverpool Free Press* and the *Leeds Other Paper*, turned to the public, including activists, the unemployed and those living on housing estates (Harcup, 1998).

Although by the 1990s the alternative local press had been wiped out by the power of the market and the domineering mainstream press, its legacy remains today. The established press was forced to take note of ordinary citizens and community groups, and the public began to speak for themselves through fanzines, lobbying groups and ultimately the web (Harcup, 1998). Across the Atlantic in the United States a related movement known as public or civic journalism developed during the late 1980s. This grassroots reform movement grew in response to a widening gap between citizens and government with the final straw being the "dismal press coverage" (Glasser and Craft, 1998: 205) of the 1988 US presidential campaign, which focused on strategy over political substance. The public journalism campaign held as its main premise the assumption that democracy was in decay and that the role of the press was to promote and improve public life rather than merely report on it. Like the alternative press movement in Britain, public journalism had limited influence but has arguably been revitalized today by the internet and independent news websites such as Indy Media.

Move forward two decades and we find that mainstream media organizations are embracing audience participation online and opening up channels of communications to facilitate previously unheard voices (Canter, 2013; Rusbridger, 2010). Yet there is a deep skepticism that this push towards participation is being driven by capitalism. A constant friction exists between the social goals of journalists and the commercial pressure to make and maintain profit. This has been heightened in the Web 2.0 era as newspaper profits decline and companies seek ways to cut costs by gaining content from readers for free (Örnebring, 2008). Indeed McChesney and Nichols argue that the current industry crisis was created by "media owners who made the commercial and entertainment values on the market dramatically higher priorities than the civic and democratic values that are essential to good journalism" (2010: 3). Furthermore, journalists acknowledge that the drive towards greater audience participation is motivated by economic factors (Canter, 2013) to increase profits via the building of brand loyalty and the boosting of website traffic to remain competitive (Vujnovic, 2011). Thus online participatory spaces on newspaper websites have become an ambiguous playground where they have the capacity to enable greater democracy whilst simultaneously being driven by economic imperatives – as they have done for the majority of their history.

Conclusion

History tells us that newspapers have evolved and thrived within the liberal free market and in truth it has been the specifics of this political economy which have determined the survival and adaption of this communication medium from a physical to a virtual media product. Journalists have always had to finely balance economic and civic obligations and audience participation has consistently been one method to fulfill both these demands. British newspapers operate within a commercial model, as they have done for several centuries, and therefore it should be expected that economic goals will drive the practice. Yet as Vujnovic (2011) reasons, although money is needed to underwrite the social goal of journalism, the augmentation of media revenue should not be the goal in itself. But with their exceedingly high profit margins it appears that news publishers have tipped the balance too far in favor of commercial goals. Current profit margins are likely to be unsustainable (Fowler, 2011) which may force such companies to redress the balance between economic and civic obligations.

The survival of newspapers may therefore lie in an alternative business model that goes further back in history to the roots of the family-run news organization. The provincial papers of the seventeenth and eighteenth centuries were run for a profit but on a far more modest scale than the ever increasing profit margins expected by global news conglomerates today. The independent local newspaper industry in Britain, which is based on a variety of business models, is faring much better in the current economic climate. These companies have much lower profit margins and lower debt levels, and many are family-owned. They are also developing new methods of online and digital delivery. Former regional newspaper editor Neil Fowler (2011: 24) argues that these small business models "could be the foundation for the future" because the current economies of scale model is failing both the market and the public. Furthermore, Fowler argues that the big four UK regional press publishers – Johnston Press, Trinity Mirror, Northcliffe Media and Newsquest – should return their hundreds of newspaper titles to local ownership. The same argument is being made in America, where small companies are beginning to find successful online business models. As the business commentator Mark Briggs (2012: xv) convincingly argues, the building of the future of news "is more likely to happen in new entrepreneurial ventures than through continuing to try to right the unwieldy old ships of media." New media technologies, in particular Web 2.0, are not the guarantors of a new dawn of profitable, participatory journalism, but they provide tools with great democratic potential when placed in the correct hands, under the right economic, social and cultural conditions. And journalists have always strived to tell the truth and provide a mouthpiece for the public whatever the tools of their trade. Furthermore, the desire for news remains the same whether it is noisily pressed into a vast metal sheet or silently transmitted onto a touch-screen phone.

Further reading

Mark Briggs' *Entrepreneurial Journalism: How to Build What's Next for News* (2012) provides an optimistic and fascinating look at successful online journalism ventures including a wealth of case studies. David Croteau and William Hoynes' *The Business of Media* (2001) is a comprehensive book outlining the commercial backdrop of the British media. Natalie Fenton's 2010 work *New Media, Old News: Journalism and Democracy in the Digital Age* offers a collection of chapters discussing the nature and challenges of emerging digital news platforms. Finally, Henry Jenkins' *Convergence Culture: Where Old and New Media Collide* (2008) provides a detailed examination of media in its cultural and historical context.

References

Aldridge, M. (2007) *Understanding the Local Media*. Maidenhead: Open University Press.
Briggs, M. (2012) *Entrepreneurial Journalism: How to Build What's Next for News*. London: Sage.
Brighton, P. and Foy, D. (2007) *News Values*. London: Sage.
Canter, L. (2012a) "Web 2.0 and the changing relationship between newspaper journalists and their audiences." White Rose eTheses Online. Retrieved from: http://etheses.whiterose.ac.uk
——(2012b) "The misconception of online comment threads: Content and control on local newspaper websites." *Journalism Practice*. iFirst Article, 1–16. Retrieved from: http://www.tandfonline.com/doi/abs/10.1080/17512786.2012.740172
——(2013) "The source, the resource and the collaborator: The role of citizen journalism in local UK newspapers." *Journalism: Theory, Practice and Criticism*. iFirst Article, 1–19. Retrieved from: http://jou.sagepub.com/content/early/2013/02/19/1464884912474203
Cranfield, G. (1962) *The Development of the Provincial Newspaper 1700–1760*. Oxford: Clarendon Press.
Croteau, D. and Hoynes, W. (2001) *The Business of Media*. Thousand Oaks, CA: Pine Forge Press.
Curran, J. (1978) "The press as an agency of social control: An historical perspective." In G. Boyce, G., Curran, J. and Wingate, P. (eds.) *Newspaper History from the Seventeenth Century to the Present Day*. London: Constable (pp. 51–75).
Daily Echo (2012) Titanic iPad App. *Southern Daily Echo*. Retrieved from: http://www.dailyecho.co.uk/heritage/titanic/app

Fenton, N. (2010) *New Media, Old News: Journalism and Democracy in the Digital Age*. London: Sage.
Fowler, N. (2011) "Time for a radical change in who owns the regions." *Press Gazette*, 12, 22–24.
Franklin, B. (2008) "The future of newspapers?" *Journalism Practice*, 2(3), 306–17.
Franklin, B. and Murphy, D. (1991) *What News? The Market, Politics and the Local Press*. London: Routledge.
Gillmor, D. (2006) *We the Media: Grassroots Journalism by the People for the People*. Farnham: O'Reilly.
Glasser, T. L. and Craft, S. (1998) "Public journalism and the search for democratic ideals." In T. Liebes and J. Curran (eds.) *Media, Ritual and Identity*. New York: Routledge (pp. 203–18).
Harcup, T. (1998) "There is no alternative: The demise of the local alternative newspaper." In B. Franklin and D. Murphy (eds.) *Making the Local News: Local Journalism in Context*. London: Routledge (pp. 105–16).
Harcup, T. and O'Neill, D. (2001) "What is news? Galtung and Ruge Revisited." *Journalism Studies*, 2(2), 261–80.
Hargreaves, I. (2005) *Journalism: A Very Short Introduction*. New York: Oxford University Press.
Harris, R. (1996) *Politics and the Rise of the Press 1620–1800*. London: Routledge.
Hermida, A., Fletcher, F., Korrell, D. and Logan, D. (2011) "Your friend as editor: The shift to the personalized social news stream." Proceedings of the 2011 Future of Journalism conference held at Cardiff University. Cardiff: Cardiff University.
Hobbs, A. (2011) "Lessons from history: Why readers preferred the local paper in the second half of the nineteenth century." Proceedings of the 2011 Future of Journalism conference held at Cardiff University. Cardiff: Cardiff University.
Hold the Front Page (2013) "ABC figures: How all the regional dailies performed." *Hold the Front Page*. Retrieved from: http://www.holdthefrontpage.co.uk/2013/news/abc-figures-how-all-the-regional-dailies-performed
Jenkins, H. (2008) *Convergence Culture: Where Old and New Media Collide*. New York: New York University Press.
Kovach, B. and Rosenstiel, T. (2007) *The Elements of Journalism*. New York: Three Rivers Press.
McChesney, R, and Nichols, J. (2010) *The Death and Life of American Journalism: The Media Revolution That Will Begin the World Again*. New York: Nation Books.
McNair, B. (2008) "Journalism and democracy." In K. Wahl-Jorgensen and T. Hanitzsch (eds.) *The Handbook of Journalism Studies*. London: Routledge (pp. 237–49).
Maguire, C. (2011) "Social media and the regional press." Proceedings of the 2011 NCTJ Digital Journalism Seminar held at the Press Association. London: Press Association.
Newspaper Society (2013) Welcome to the NS. Retrieved from: http://www.newspapersoc.org.uk
Office for National Statistics (2012) "Internet access – Households and individuals." Retrieved from: http://www.ons.gov.uk/ons/rel/rdit2/internet-access—households-and-individuals/2012/stb-internet-access–households-and-individuals–2012.html
Örnebring, H. (2008) "The consumer as producer – of what?" *Journalism Studies*, (9)5, 771–85.
Paulussen, S. (2011) "Inside the newsroom: Journalists' motivations and organizational structures." In J. B. Singer, D. Domingo, A. Heinonen, A. Hermida, S. Paulussen, T. Quandt, Z. Reich and M. Vujnovic, *Participatory Journalism: Guarding Gates at Online Newspapers*. Chichester: Wiley-Blackwell (pp. 59–75).
Rusbridger, A. (2010) "The Hugh Cudlipp lecture: Does journalism exist?" *The Guardian*, 25 January. Retrieved from http://www.theguardian.com/media/2010/jan/25/cudlipp-lecture-alan-rusbridger
Singer, J. B., Domingo, D., Heinonen, A., Hermida, A., Paulussen, S., Quandt, T., Reich, Z. and Vujnovic, M. (2011) *Participatory Journalism: Guarding Open Gates at Online Newspapers*. Chichester: Wiley-Blackwell.

Sparks, C. (2003) "The contribution of online newspapers to the public sphere: A United Kingdom case study. *Trends in Communication*, 11(2), 111–26.

Vujnovic, M. (2011) "Participatory journalism in the marketplace: Economic motivations behind the practices." In J. B. Singer, D. Domingo, A. Heinonen, A. Hermida, S. Paulussen, T. Quandt, Z. Reich and M. Vujnovic, *Participatory Journalism: Guarding Open Gates at Online Newspapers*. Chichester: Wiley-Blackwell (pp. 139–54).

Walker, A. (2006) "The development of the provincial press in England c.1780–1914: An overview." *Journalism Studies*, 7(3), 373–86.

Walker, A., Maher, J., Coulthard, M., Goddard, E. and Thomas, M. (2001) National Statistics: Living in Britain: Results from the 2000/01 General Household Survey. London: The Stationery Office.

Wiles, R. (1965) *Freshest Advices: Early Provincial Newspapers in England*. Columbus, OH: State University Press.

45
Change and continuity
Historicizing the emergence of online media
Scott Eldridge II

The emergence of online media is often framed in ahistorical terms. Observers have described online and digital 'revolutions' (BBC, 2010; Kaufman, 2012), some going so far as to suggest that the internet heralds change so radical that journalism may not survive (Hirst, 2011). Such reactions frame the internet and online media as either providing wholly new and exciting possibilities, or as unique challenges and even threats to established media. In these instances, accounts of online media and change favor the hyperbolic over the historic. When set in the context of media history, the adoption of online media begins to reflect something familiar, resonant with both the enthusiasm and the trepidation that has accompanied past technological changes. This chapter will look at key moments of media and technological emergence throughout British media history to contextualize the dynamics seen within online media.

To situate the adoption of internet technologies in this broader view, this chapter explores media–technology relationships during the introduction of the steam press, the telegraph and early broadcast. These three techno-media junctures may well be able to ground our understandings of a fourth, the emergence of online media. Through looking at British news media's adoption of technologies, the 'radical change' associated with the internet can be placed in historical perspective. This chapter focuses on selected points of technological emergence and identifies key dynamics through an exploration of how news media embraced technological opportunities for boosting commercial strength and elevating societal roles, and where in moments of change the roles of news media have adjusted. Whether focusing on a rise in the primacy of news in the era of the steam press, expanded and speedier coverage with the telegraph or new forms of news media with broadcasting, looking at news media's history of engagement with technology shows that change seems constant. Within such flux, however, some attributes of the relationship between technology and media persist, even in the most radical of contemporary developments online.

Technology and media

Whether speaking of an established format, such as print, or more recent innovations, as with the internet, media are reliant on communicative technology to reach their audiences. This reliance can result in media change being viewed as *caused* by technological progress, or articulated in the lexicon of *revolution* where one change upends the other. "Media need technology," writes Alan Bell, "and technology needs technicians" (Bell, 1991: 12). Bell's observation highlights a sometimes awkward reality for media: it is reliant on technology for content to reach audiences, yet not fully in control of that relationship. With each of the technologies explored here, this has been the case to greater and lesser degrees. However, the technology–media relationship is more complex and, within Britain's media history, changes made around technology have reflected a combination of economic, cultural and political factors, on top of the technological (Briggs and Burke, 2009: 19; Conboy, 2004: 187, 2011). As Briggs and Burke write in reference to the rise of industrial printing:

> To speak of print as the agent of change is surely to place too much emphasis on the medium of communication at the expense of the writers, printers and readers who used the new technology for their own different purposes.
> (Briggs and Burke, 2009: 19)

So while technology has a role to play, it is not singular in causing change. The steam press allowed newspapers in Britain to increase their volume but it was not until duties on paper and advertising were cut that they began to fully realize their commercial potential (Curran, 2010). Factors beyond technology affected the adoption of the telegraph and while wires criss-crossed major American cities, Britain saw a slower adoption of the new technology with greater emphasis placed on gathering news from abroad (Wiener, 2011). While not 'agents of change', these technologies of the nineteenth century were a boon for news media and offered the opportunity for news media owners to increase their commercial heft and secure a more prominent role in British society.

In the twentieth century, the media–technology relationship shifted once more. The emergence of broadcast technology did not empower existing news media so much as it ushered in new formats. Broadcast was perceived from the beginning as a threat to the existing order, and its emergence was restrained and its initial impact limited (Crissell, 2012). Yet factors beyond technology contributed to an eventual strengthening of broadcast and the BBC came into its own as a news medium when national crisis loomed and again when war broke out (Scannell and Cardiff, 1991). With the internet, technology has provoked change yet again and while news media have used internet technologies for decades, the emergence of online media has presented a unique set of challenges outside technology. To be certain, while the technologies of the internet have allowed news media to communicate through genre-bending means, the tenor of that change remains tied to previous techno-media junctures. Through that historical view, online media's emergence can be grounded not as surprisingly new, but rather as reflective of the media and technological changes that came before it.

The *Times* and the steam press

The introduction of the Köenig Bauer rotary steam press by the *Times* in 1814 signaled the start of an industrial age of printing. When, on November 29, the *Times* announced its latest edition was the result of this new press, the dynamics of change were framed as an opportunity for the new technology, the paper, and its readers:

> The reader of this paragraph now holds in his hand one of the many thousand impressions of the *Times* newspaper, which were taken off last night by a mechanical apparatus. A system of machinery almost organic has been devised and arranged, which, while it relieves the human frame of its most laborious efforts in printing, far exceeds all human powers in rapidity and despatch.
> (quoted in Andrews, 1859: 80)

The *Times* described the new printing press as a radical shift, "the practical result of the greatest improvement connected with printing since the discovery of the art itself" (ibid.). With this announcement, the enthusiasm around technological change is reflected through the relationship not only with the audience, but also with stakeholders in the *Times*' new venture (Briggs and Burke, 2009). Holding in their hands something new, rapidly printed and unmatched by human endeavor alone, the adoption of the steam press brought printing to an industrial scale. While in the eighteenth century newspapers were already contributing to a more literate and civic-minded public (Conboy, 2004: 60), the industrial scale of printing acted to amplify this (Temple, 1996: 22).

It was not technology alone that allowed newspapers to reach greater audiences or strengthen commercially. Instead, a complement of social and political decisions contributed key elements to the media changes seen during this period. Among these was the lifting of the 'taxes on knowledge' (ibid.: 18), including advertising duties. These were reduced in 1833 and cut again in 1853. In the years that followed this second reduction, advertising in the British popular press grew by 50 percent. By the turn of the century, £20 million was being spent on advertising (Curran, 2010: 29). Alongside the boost in advertising revenues, a reduction in stamp duties and a drop in the sales price of newsprint allowed newspapers to recoup more of their printing costs and in order to broaden their readership still further owners dropped their cover prices. In the early 1900s, newspapers with "bigger papers, more staff and the introduction of sale-or-return arrangements with distributors ... helped to underwrite a further halving of the price of most popular papers to 1/2d [half a penny]" (ibid.).

Amid these commercial, political and technological factors, editorial changes were also taking place. The *Times*' decision to adopt a rotary steam press was quickly followed by editorial interventions by Thomas Barnes, who envisaged a newspaper that would act as a thought leader, drawing on public opinion and a network of correspondents (Conboy, 2004: 114–15). As the tenor of coverage shifted towards news events and fact-based content, newspapers sought to establish themselves within civic and political discourses (Wiener, 2011: 81). While the *Times* notably heralded its patriotic enlightenment, the move towards professionalization was not due to technology alone, but rather a response to intense competition, an effort to bolster the credibility of its journalism separate from its business activities and its history of receiving annual government subsidies in return for a favorable political stance (Conboy, 2004: 114). In the end, as with the decision to embrace the steam press, making these changes sated its middle-class readership's desire for independent journalism and "the desire of advertisers to be associated with a newspaper with the ear of such an affluent and influential clientele" (ibid.).

The telegraph: Extending reach, enriching content

What the steam press made possible, the telegraph enhanced. Invented in 1844, it emerged as a point-to-point tool for transmitting business and commercial information, became a fixture of news reporting out of the Crimea in the 1850s (Wiener, 2011: 81) and by the 1870s the telegraph was regularly used to transfer news digests (Chapman, 2005: 59–60; Potter, 2007). The adoption of the telegraph by British news media enhanced the primacy of news events in newspapers with an emphasis on reporting the latest information from abroad in London's newspapers, at speed. As Andrew Marr puts it, with the telegraph, "the era of sail and horses was elbowed aside" (2005: 331), though to suggest that the telegraph changed everything radically or immediately would miss some key elements of change.

For British journalism, the use of the telegraph to report from abroad allowed newspapers to report news from the Crimea with immediacy and specifically saw the *Times* stake a claim as an "enlightened patriotic opinion" leader, with news that outpaced the government's (Conboy, 2004: 118). Implanting the importance of reporting news speedily from abroad in newspapers such as the *Times*, the use of such technology was further enhanced as overland and undersea cables connected the UK (via Ireland) to the US in 1858, enabling quick coverage of the US Civil War, with further connections to Asia in 1872 and South America in 1874 (Temple, 1996: 24).

While on the surface the telegraph and its broad connections seem to signal a globalized style of news reporting, there were uniquely British attributes to its adoption. In contrast to their American colleagues, British journalists primarily sent information to the UK from abroad, rather than across Britain. Wiener sees this as the result of the country's main newspapers being concentrated on Fleet Street, whereas in the US news and politics extended across major metropolitan areas (Wiener, 2011: 67). In London, the *Times* and the *Daily News* enjoyed a comfortable hold on the print market and were unfazed by the regional press, which was outside the 'press and politics' axis of London. These newspapers continued to rely on the rail networks up until the Franco-Prussian war in 1870, when the telegraph was nationalized and Britain was more fully 'wired' (ibid.).

Change was not just the result of technology, but rather "the combination of news agencies and the invention of the telegraph [which] brought a much more reliable and economical supply of steady information" (Conboy, 2004: 125). With the arrival of the Reuters news agency in 1851, "authoritative and up-to-date foreign and national news was now readily available, and essential to a newspaper's credibility and commercial success" (Temple, 1996: 24). Originally founded to convey financial information out of London, "Reuters developed a reputation for probity, reliability and, with the introduction of transatlantic cables, speed" (ibid.) that extended beyond the British capital. In the years and decades following, Reuters was able to break transatlantic news in the UK, such as the assassination of the US president

Abraham Lincoln in 1865, and the role of wire services as quick arbiters of information became established as invaluable to communication processes.

By 1870, US journalists working out of London were using telegraphy extensively to cover the Franco-Prussian war (Marr, 2005: 331). This technique was picked up by the *Daily News* and *Tribune*, which saw the speed of their reporting outpace that of the *Times* (ibid.). To many, including Marr (2005), the incorporation of the telegraph in news content also signaled a shift in writing style, as the expense of technology forced reporters to focus their prose and develop a more direct writing style to convey news, rather than commentary (ibid.: 331). This has led to some mythologizing about the telegraph as the 'cause' of increased objectivity and of the adoption of the inverted pyramid in reporting (Pöttker, 2003), something Maras (2013) sees as overly deterministic. For Wiener (2011: 70), the alignment of the telegraph and objectivity is a development tied to Reuters, which adopted objectivity in its reporting, favoring speed and tight language to maximize the commercial appeal of its content on both ends of the transatlantic cable.

Resonant fears: The emergence of broadcast

While newspapers' adoption of the steam press has been correlated to a rise in the importance of news and the societal role of newspapers, and while the telegraph enhanced that primacy and an increased emphasis on speed, broadcast news media expand both aspects. However, the differences accompanying the technological change within broadcasting are stark and its emergence was met with far more trepidation than enthusiasm. Broadcast's eventual adoption as a medium for news conversely benefited from that early resistance and it provides a unique case that has shaped the adoption of public service broadcasting in Britain which continues to resonate with online media.

As broadcast technology emerged in the twentieth century, it gave rise to a new medium, radio:

> It was to add a completely new reach and status to journalism's repertoire and it was to do this, in the first instance in Britain at least, protected from the economic pressures for profitability that defined the activities of most other areas of journalism.
>
> (Conboy, 2004: 188)

Conboy (2004; 2011) points to the technologies of broadcast radio and later television as embedded within the media–technology junctures of the nineteenth and early twentieth centuries. In the early regulatory frameworks around radio, this is direct. As radio emerged first as a technology for wireless telegraphy, it fell under the Telegraphy Acts of 1869 and 1904. As its more familiar spoken format developed, this too grew within the same regulatory frameworks. Early broadcast technologies of radio came under the control of the Post Office (Conboy, 2004: 188) and radio was secured as a public corporation in 1925, and by royal charter in 1927. This becomes a key characteristic of its emergence as a news medium, as this regulatory history is compounded by the trepidation of both government and newspapers.

Already government-regulated, the emerging medium of radio was immediately perceived as a threat to the newspapers' hold on news reportage and newspaper proprietors successfully lobbied to restrict broadcast of news to 30 minutes daily. Its emergence was further minimized by newspapers not covering broadcast schedules, so that the BBC and the emergence of broadcasting for news media was slowed, but not halted (Williams, 2010: 12, 2006). Two key events in the BBC's early years saw it establish a place for itself in the news media landscape. First, in 1926, the BBC came into its own as a news medium when, during the general strike that halted newspaper presses, broadcasting was able to maintain coverage of the strike and to relay government information as part of its public mandate. This proved to be the first turning point in its staggered emergence. With the newspapers unable to do the same, or to resist its status as a news medium, the BBC broadcast five bulletins a day. As Conboy relays, the national emergency around the general strike allowed the then BBC general manager John Reith to further establish the broadcaster as he envisioned: an independent communicator of news, around which a British nation could cohere, "thus playing a part in the construction of a reinvigorated sense of mediated national community" (Conboy, 2004: 190). This, says Briggs (1995: 7), allowed Reith to develop the BBC as a national conscience and moral voice.

The second key point of change came during the Second World War, when the BBC was able to define its role as an independent news source, supplanting the newspapers whose capabilities were again limited, though this time by rationing and depleted advertising revenue (Conboy, 2004: 194). The Second World War saw the BBC demonstrating both its strength in relaying news and the viability of broadcast as news media but also its ability to weather the challenges that wartime can bring to other means of mass communication (Crissell, 2012). As points through which the BBC could define its public service mandate, these two moments in the early twentieth century also allowed broadcast to define its autonomy in relation to its regulatory framework. The BBC has largely continued to balance its independence in reporting from the constraints of profit-making and this cultural identity has continued to resonate as online technologies have emerged.

As Scannell and Cardiff (1991) point out, the emergence of the BBC and of broadcast in Britain around the BBC is less a story of technology than one of the founding of the idea of public service broadcasting. Where the steam press allowed newspapers to empower their commercial ambitions, and the telegraph contributed further to that, broadcasting led to the emergence of a publicly regulated, but simultaneously independent, BBC. Ironically, the establishment of the BBC as a public service broadcaster and the reactions by commercial newspapers to its arrival linger in the way news media in Britain have moved online, a transition where the BBC has played an outsized role.

The internet: Breaking boundaries, diffusing genres

This final section will compare the rise of online media and the embrace of internet technologies against the three previous techno-media junctures. This highlights moments of continuity amid change; the eager embrace of online media to enhance content and to broaden reach. In addition, it points to moments of trepidation in the perceived threat of a diffuse media landscape and the real threat of a fractured commercial model.

As much as this chapter advocates a long view of media and technology, it would be naïve to say there has not been tremendous change in the most recent of technological shifts. Online technology and online media have been unique in terms of scale and speed but also in their upending of the commercial model of newspapers, especially removing the ability to profit from advertising (Siles and Boczkowski, 2012). Media have encountered changes to how audiences access their content and how media access audiences in ways that reflect history but remain uniquely contemporary. Nationally, media are multi-modal and global and boundaries have diffused so to now speak of British news media without recognizing a global audience would be myopic. Still, there are uniquely British attributes that have shaped the rise of online media, the result of past interactions between media and technology within the UK, particularly with regard to the BBC. Whether change has been resisted or embraced, these add understanding to the technological opportunities faced presently.

Online news media

The internet, as a technology, emerged out of a 1969 US military project, ARPANET (Advanced Research Project Agency Network), which connected the computer systems first of US military bases and then of corporations and universities (Curran, 2012). By the late 1980s it had spread across the US and by 1993, a more full-bodied internet capable of transmitting both text and images had reached Europe and the UK (Deuze, 1999). As user-friendly software wrapped the online infrastructure in GUIs (Graphical User Interfaces), the internet as a network grew to offer a new means, online, for print and broadcast media to engage with new means of content distribution.

In terms of news media, the internet's infrastructure and technologies provided alternative and flexible means of reaching audiences (Curran, 2002: 135). These were seized upon enthusiastically at first, and in the mid 1990s and early 2000s, newspapers in the US and UK were beginning to experiment with putting their content online (Allan, 2006; Boczkowski, 2004: 33). The dynamism of online media technologies offered the chance for print media to publish their content beyond the page, and for broadcasters to extend beyond set audio-visual delivery and broadcast schedules (Deuze, 1999). However, the change would prove to be more than just expansive and within the dynamics of change there has been a diffusion of both genres and of profit-making capabilities. In exploring this diffusion, the BBC's online presence offers a clear demonstration of one way of embracing these challenges.

While a textually dominant online news media environment in those early years ostensibly favored the press over audio-visual broadcasting, online media has seen such distinctions dissolve (Livingstone, 2004). The BBC has been online since 1994, with the advent of the BBC networking club. However, it was the introduction of its news site in 1997, and its reconfigurations in 1999 and the early 2000s, that allowed it to develop a more distinctive presence. In its shift from broadcast only to online also, the BBC made use of teletext technology that ferried texts prepared from broadcast reports directly to the website (Deuze, 1999: 375). As the infrastructure of the internet at the time lacked robust capabilities for video, sound and images, the BBC's use of such software allowed it to develop a textual form online outside its familiar broadcast structures from an early point and accelerated its move from a distinctly broadcast character to an identifiably multimedia environment.

Rapidly becoming a multi-modal media entity with stakes in broadcast and online, the BBC's web presence benefited from the recognition its offline media garnered globally, with nearly two-thirds of its traffic from outside the UK (Alexa, 2013a). But the BBC has also forced the issue of the cost and access to news content online, which has continued to shape the way media go online, and its early online positioning has allowed it to dominate in that environment. As its online content became more focused following the 2004 Graf Report, the BBC has played a role in how other British news media have contended with change online (BBC, 2004). Tied to its public service mandate, the BBC's online news has always been free and accessible to all. Put simply, within Britain this means there will always be a source of UK news for anyone online, so audiences need not pay to access news content (Siles and Boczkowski, 2012; Thorsen, 2001: 224). For many news media in Britain, and specifically print news media, the presence of a free BBC news site renders the idea of subscription plans and paywalls redundant (Herbert and Thurman, 2007: 213), confounding efforts to develop and maintain sustainable business models online (Myllylahti, 2013). While this struggle for commercial stability has seen nearly all British news media struggle, it has also spurred media to seek broader audiences online and outside the UK.

New opportunities: Beyond boundaries

During the height of media adoption of the telegraph, newspapers broadened their international content and coverage, and embraced industrial and early electronic advancements, all the while remaining largely national in terms of distribution and audience. Similarly, with the exception of its World Service, the BBC's broadcast reach was limited by transmission power, public mandates and national regulations. Online, these boundaries have become permeable and it is impossible to speak of British media without acknowledging their global reach. To illustrate this point, the *Daily Mail* boasts the most visited English language newspaper site globally (Durrani, 2013) and the *Guardian* has not only moved online, but also established unique US and Australian operations and, as of December 2013, can claim the overwhelming majority of its web traffic from overseas visitors (Alexa, 2013b; Sawers, 2013).

Furthermore, news media are extending their content beyond familiar formats and while bereft of historical context, new developments ranging from Twitter to blogs to mobile news apps have offered new discourses of revolutionary change (Kahn and Kellner, 2004; Vis, 2013). Traditional forms have also seen new life online. Longform journalism, building on traditions of magazine and literary reporting styles and genres of the 1900s, has also seen a reinvigorated presence online (Campbell, 2013).

In the early twenty-first century there has also been a rise in in-depth reporting, benefited by online content and data journalism (Marshall, 2011), while "contextual journalism has emerged as a powerful and prevalent companion to conventional reporting" (Fink and Schudson, 2013: 16). To claim any of these as trends rather than merely data points, however, would be historically naïve, even as they reflect the elements of change and continuity across media history. Furthermore, even as the online and traditional media relationship sometimes appears harmonious, the trepidation that met broadcast can still be found as new entities that purport to adopt journalistic roles are met with hesitance or are explicitly rebuffed (Eldridge, 2013).

Conclusion

With online media, change has seemed radical and in some ways it has been. News media have seen a fracturing of previously distinct genres, of established models of commercialization and profitability, and in how audiences are approached. Yet this chapter has shown how news media's history of technological change is reflected in the online environment. It has suggested that we may be better advised to compare the seemingly unparalleled contemporary changes with the older enthusiasms and commercial empowerment which greeted the steam press and telegraph, while at the same time contrasting this with the more cautious reaction to broadcasting. When set against this history, online media present both enthusiasm and trepidation, and have allowed media empowerment, alongside the diffusion of influence.

Emerging out of traditional media structures, expanding audiences and distribution models have allowed online media to be increasingly treated as borderless products. As internet technologies reach audiences in a dramatically faster manner, these shifts amplify the expansive and networked space within which online media can engage. Yet the changes associated with online media reflect the bevy of factors that have textured the media–technology relationship through the past centuries. Whether it was the cost of paper and the politics of taxes alongside the steam press (Curran, 2010), or the commercial factors compounding the expanse of the telegraph (Wiener, 2011: 70), or the trepidation that greeted broadcast established under a public service mandate (Conboy, 2004: 191), media and technological change is influenced by an array of factors that color the specific ways in which news media have embraced technology. These same factors have set the stage for how British media have adopted online media and continue to shape their engagement with the internet.

Further reading

This chapter has benefited tremendously from Martin Conboy's *Journalism: A Critical History* (2004) and *Journalism in Britain: A Historical Introduction* (2011). Joel Wiener's (2011) *The Americanization of the British Press, 1830s–1914* provides a further exploration of the comparative differences in how news media have embraced technology. Focusing on the online era, Pablo Boczkowski's (2004) *Digitizing the News: Innovation in Online Newspapers* and the historical overviews provided by James

Curran in his, Natalie Fenton's and Des Freedman's (2012) *Misunderstanding the Internet* provide useful context to the changes news media have encountered online.

References

Alexa (2013a) BBC.co.uk site information. Retrieved from http://www.alexa.com/siteinfo/bbc.co.uk
——(2013b) Guardian.co.uk site information. Retrieved from http://www.alexa.com/siteinfo/guardian.co.uk
Allan, S. (2006) *Online News: Journalism And The Internet*. Maidenhead: McGraw Hill.
Andrews, A. (1859) *The History of British Journalism from the Foundation of the Newspaper Press in England to the Repeal of the Stamp Act in 1855*. London: Richard Bentley.
BBC (2004) "At a glance: The Graf Report." Retrieved from http://news.bbc.co.uk/1/hi/entertainment/3866355.stm
——(2010) "The virtual revolution." Retrieved from http://www.bbc.co.uk/programmes/b00n4j0r
Bell, A. (1991) *The Language of News Media*. Oxford: Blackwell.
Boczkowski, P. J. (2004) *Digitizing the News: Innovation in Online Newspapers*. Cambridge, MA: MIT Press.
Briggs, A. (1995) *A History of Broadcasting in the United Kingdom, Volumes I–V*. Oxford: Oxford University Press.
Briggs, A. and Burke, P. (2009) *Social History of the Media: From Gutenberg to the Internet*. Cambridge: Polity.
Campbell, D. (2013) *Visual Storytelling in the Age of Post-Industrialist Journalism*. World Press Photo Academy. Retrieved from http://www.worldpressphoto.org/multimedia-research
Chapman, J. (2005) *Comparative Media History*. Cambridge: Polity.
Conboy, M. (2004) *Journalism: A Critical History*. London: Sage.
——(2011) *Journalism in Britain: A Historical Introduction*. London: Sage.
Crissell, A. (2012) *Understanding Radio*. Abingdon: Routledge.
Curran, J. (2002) "Media and the making of British society, c.1700–2000. *Media History*, 8(2), 135–54.
——(2010) "The industrialization of the press." In J. Curran and J. Seaton (eds.) *Power Without Responsibility: Press, Broadcasting and the Internet in Britain*. Abingdon: Routledge (pp. 23–36).
——(2012) "Rethinking internet history." In J. Curran, N. Fenton and D. Freedman (eds.) *Misunderstanding the Internet*. Abingdon: Routledge (pp. 34–65).
Curran, J. Fenton, N. and Freedman, D. (eds.) (2012) *Misunderstanding the Internet*. Abingdon: Routledge.
Deuze, M. (1999) "Journalism and the web: An analysis of skills and standards in an online environment." *International Communication Gazette*, 61(5), 373–90.
Durrani, A. (2013) "Mail Online and Guardian lead record highs for newspaper sites in January." *Media Week*, 22 February. Retrieved from http://www.mediaweek.co.uk/news/1171927
Eldridge, S. A. II (2013) "Boundary maintenance and interloper media reaction." *Journalism Studies*, 15(1), 1–16.
Fink, K. and Schudson, M. (2013) "The rise of contextual journalism, 1950s–2000s." *Journalism*, 15(1), 3–20.
Herbert, J. and Thurman, N. (2007) "Paid content strategies for news websites." *Journalism Practice*, 1(2), 208–26.
Hirst, M. (2011) *News 2.0 – Can Journalism Survive the Internet?* Crows Nest, Australia: Allen and Unwin.

Kahn, R. and Kellner, D. (2004) "New media and internet activism: From the 'Battle of Seattle' to blogging." *New Media & Society*, 6(1), 87–95.

Kaufman, M. (2012) "The internet revolution is the new industrial revolution." Forbes Entrepreneur Blog. Retrieved from http://www.forbes.com/sites/michakaufman/2012/10/05/the-internet-revolution-is-the-new-industrial-revolution

Livingstone, S. (2004) "Media literacy and the challenge of new information and communication technologies." *Communication Review*, 7(1), 3–14.

Maras, S. (2013) *Objectivity in Journalism*. Cambridge: Polity.

Marr, A. (2005) *My Trade*. London: Pan Macmillan.

Marshall, J. (2011) *Watergate's Legacy and the Press: The Investigative Impulse*. Evanston, IL: Northwestern University Press.

Myllylahti, M. (2013) "Newspaper paywalls – the hype and the reality." *Digital Journalism*, 2(2), 1–16.

Potter, S. J. (2007) "Webs, networks, and systems: Globalization and the mass media in the nineteenth- and twentieth-century British Empire." *Journal of British Studies*, 46(3), 621–46.

Pöttker, H. (2003) "News and its communicative quality: The inverted pyramid –when and why did it appear? *Journalism Studies*, 4(4), 501–11.

Sawers, P. (2013) "Going global: The Guardian newspaper announces a new '.com' domain for its UK, US and Australian websites." The Next Web. Retrieved from http://thenextweb.com/media/2013/05/24/the-guardian-newspaper-announces-a-new-com-global-identity-for-its-uk-us-and-australian-websites

Scannell and Cardiff (1991) *A Social History of British Broadcasting: 1922–1939*. Oxford: Wiley-Blackwell.

Siles, I. and Boczkowski, P. J. (2012) "Making sense of the newspaper crisis: A critical assessment of existing research and an agenda for future work." *New Media & Society*, 14, 1375–94.

Temple, M. (1996) *The British Press*. Maidenhead: McGraw Hill.

Thorsen, E. (2001) "BBC news online: A brief history of past and present." In N. Brugger (ed.) *Web History*. New York: Peter Lang (pp. 213–32).

Vis, F. (2013) "Twitter as a reporting tool for breaking news." *Digital Journalism*, 1(1), 27–47.

Wiener, J. (2011) *The Americanization of the British Press, 1830s–1914*. Basingstoke: Palgrave.

Williams, K. (2006) "Competing models of journalism? Anglo-American and European reporting in the information age." *Journalistica*, 2, 43–65.

——(2010) *Read All About It! A History of the British Newspaper*. Abingdon: Routledge.

46
Personal listening pleasures
Tim Wall and Nick Webber

Music consumption in the early twenty-first century has increasingly been mediated through distinctive technologies of listening such as headphones, car radios or the iPod. Each of these devices has a surprisingly long history and they were developed and then taken up for use in a variety of institutional and cultural contexts. Listening to music using these technologies is often associated with the idea of the personalization of listening and individual control over the sonic world in which we immerse ourselves. It is easy to see this as an example of the increasing privatization of cultural experiences. However, cultural practices are rich and diverse and, while there were clearly significant shifts in the sonic world during the twentieth century, our experience of music has always been an interesting balance of the private and the public, the individual and the collective, the personal and the communal. In fact, it is in the distinctions between these ideas that we can begin to understand the diverse ways in which we realize the pleasures of listening and make music meaningful.

The history of personal listening, then, is not as clear as it first seems. This is in part because the very concepts we use blur into one another. An opposition between private and public listening seems to suggest that we are talking about types of control over access, the binary of personal and collective seems to allude to issues of ownership, and the poles of individual and communal are suggestive of the different experiential nature of the types of listening available. Nevertheless, the fact that the words used in these binary oppositions are often employed as synonyms indicates that ideas of control, ownership and experience are intertwined in the history of music media.

In this chapter, we explore the relationship between technologies of listening and the cultural experience of music and other sonic forms. We aim to go beyond some of the common stories of technological development and social use, which are built around grand narratives in which the reproduction of sound is perfected and the listening experience is privatized. This enables us to avoid the conclusion that personal listening has become either an example of increasing individual control or, conversely, of damaging and alienating isolation from others. We consider the development of these technologies as responses to cultural imperatives within developed societies and the way they are linked to ideas of entertainment, portability and private experience. In addition, we examine the institutionalization of access to music through recordings and radio and how new forms of music media are ordered by the major organizations which came to dominate their economic control. To explore these ideas, we consider how we listen, where we listen, when we listen and, ultimately, what listening means.

How we listen

Personal listening seems to be symbolized by the act of wearing headphones; cutting us off from the outside world and restricting the sonic world we enjoy to an exclusive domain. Likewise, the mobility of modern listening seems intimately linked to our ability to take a source of audio content with us wherever we go. In narrating the recent history of music listening through the iPod, Michael Bull (2007) has focused on this audio playout device, along with headphones, as seminal, transformative technologies, which have created not only new sonic landscapes but also new forms of personal cultural practice. In doing so, Bull has followed a wider thread of explanation in which media technologies are seen as the primary agents in processes of change. Brian Winston has provided a useful summary of the extent of this tendency towards technological determinism amongst media academics and offers a counter argument that new technologies are accommodated within, rather than transformative of, existing social practices (1998: 2).

There is substantial evidence that Winston's thesis grapples more effectively with the personalization of listening than Bull's does. Both the qualities of personal and mobile listening associated with the iPod have much longer histories than may be at first imagined and even discovering the precise moment in which the technologies were born can be difficult. The invention of headphones is variously claimed to date to 1910,[1] 1937[2] and 1958.[3] The social context of these technologies is equally telling. In 1910, Nathaniel Baldwin aimed his invention at a military market; in the 1930s, Beyerdynamic targeted the media industry; and in the 1950s, Koss brought stereo headphones into the home. While the rhetoric of the various manufacturers of these devices proposes that they revolutionized personal listening, we can find much earlier attempts to realize the cultural imperative of the privatized sonic space. Telephones, famously patented in 1876 by Alexander Graham Bell, employed an earpiece, and early telephone operators employed headsets combining earpiece and mouthpiece in the 1880s (see Schubin, 2011). Stankievech has argued that "the site where cultural techniques of listening were both developed and reified" is to be found in the early nineteenth century development of the stethoscope, when we began to realize that the sound field was "virtually located within the head" (2007: 56).

Likewise, a simple chronology of mobile listening is usually recounted through the primacy of the transistor radio in cars and pocket radios, mass-produced from the 1950s; the Walkman, launched in 1979 by the Japanese electronics company Sony; and the iPod (totemic of all portable digital music players), which saw the realization of mobile listening on a mass scale. Yet once again, none of these innovations in personal and mobile listening in themselves established new cultural practices. Portable radios had existed both in cars and outside them before the transistor was invented (Wall and Webber, 2014); the concept of using a portable tape recorder with headphones was not new in 1979, as a 1974 photograph in which two headphone-clad

Japanese girls demonstrate a radio-cassette player makes clear (see Society for the Nationaal Archief, 2014). The iPod followed in the footsteps of a number of less successful mp3 players, including the Diamond Rio and the MPMan, which was produced by a company of the same name, the self-styled "inventor of the mp3 player" (Mpman Europe, 2014).

We should rather see the popular incarnations of these devices as highly specialized forms of pre-existing technologies, adapted to particular kinds of functionality appropriate to personal listening; the Walkman enhancing personalization by losing its recording and speaker features and the transistor radio enhancing mobility through lightweight components. These technological innovations are just one part of a complex picture of personal listening, not in themselves a response to technology but instead realizations of cultural imperatives. The way that human agents acted within underlying social structures is as important as the way that technology was deployed in specific historical moments. How we listen, then, is in an important sense just part of who is listening, where and when. As a consequence we might propose that personal listening pleasures can be best understood as cultural phenomena that remake listening space and time along with listener identity. In the sections that follow, we take each of these in turn.

Where we listen

Listening was perhaps made more symbolically private when it was first realized in the domestic space. The telephone, and the electrophone developed from it, allowed audio to be relocated from public settings to the homes of the wealthy at the turn of the twentieth century. Feeds from churches and operas were delivered through headsets (Crook, 1999: 17), with those listening potentially sitting in the same room and sharing a musical experience, but accessing that experience privately, as pictures from the time demonstrate (Freshwater, 2012). Radio, the first institutionalization of wireless communication, was in the early decades of the twentieth century converted (counter-intuitively) from a military technology valued for its mobility to a domestic technology embodied in a piece of home furniture (VanCour, 2008: 168–85). Domestic access to the supposedly public performance of music was a central part of the cultural uplift missions of broadcasters in North America and Europe (Briggs, 1961; Hilmes, 1997; Doerksen, 1999). The corresponding association of music listening and domestic space became naturalized, a 'common-sense' conception reinforced in the academic literature by the notion of inhabitation of space, leading Bull, following Baudrillard, to suggest that we might conceive of personal stereos as "mobile homes" (Bull, 2001: 239).

Of course, radio was subsequently displaced from the living rooms of an increasing number of middle-class homes by television, relocating (in the US) to the car (Gomery, 2008: 144), to elsewhere in the household and, as the introduction of the transistor facilitated the production of smaller radios, into the pocket (Schiffer, 1993). While mobile listening pre-dated the invention of the transistor, the wider opportunity to enjoy "music on the move" was a significant cultural change within the USA of the late 1950s. Eulogies to the new American pop culture of the late

1950s and early 1960s gave a central place to the car, and to pop music in cars. In addition, there was a new sense of space wrought by radio during this period, reflecting what Jody Berland (1993) has called 'radio space'; the different senses of space created by the programing and listener experience of radio, bounded at the most basic level by the broadcast footprint of a single radio station but also the creation of the programing of radio itself. The portability of receivers, first in the car and ultimately in the shirt pocket, intersected with the signal of the radio stations they received and the music programing that these stations broadcast.

In 1946 nearly 40 percent of the nine million cars in the US had radios, growing by 1963 to 60 percent of the then 50 million cars (Douglas, 1999: 226). The car, radio and rock 'n' roll are intimately linked in US film depictions of the period, such as *American Graffiti* (Lucas, 1973), which opens with a radio being tuned to a soundtrack of the DJ Wolfman Jack and early 1960s pop. In Europe, conversely, the portability of radio receivers was more important than music mobility and was often deployed to separate the young listener from the family orientation of earlier radio listening (Barnard, 1989). Cultural patterns of consumption were matched by fundamental changes in radio ownership and production in the US between 1945 and 1965. The networks of affiliated radio stations sharing mixed programing were eclipsed for a time by the independent Top 40 local music stations, which came to the fore driven in part by commuting, and domestic and leisure-time youth listening (Rothenbuhler and McCourt, 2002). The publicly funded national radio services which dominated in Western European countries resisted both the programing formats and commercial imperatives for a few decades longer (Barnard, 1989).

A wider cultural imperative of portability and mobility in the 1960s created new senses of space associated with the car and 'listening on the go' pocket radios, together with a move to more localized senses of radio space. The mobile music it ushered in was the product of changing demographics, media ownership arrangements and programing; and these imperatives continued to drive innovation. Improvements in headphone technology and the widespread use of the compact cassette in the 1970s resulted in hi-fidelity portable recorded music players such as the Walkman and headphone listening became increasingly popular in public spaces from the 1980s onwards.

Both Walkman and iPod are presented in the academic literature as strategies to govern the user's relationship with urban space: interventions in the acoustic design of the city (Hosokawa, 1984: 175), strategies of control used to transform urban streets into "privatized pleasure palaces" (Bull, 2005: 347). Through the experience of personal listening, mediated through headphones, users are able to ignore the space through which they pass, to detach themselves from it and view it as a film (Bull, 2005: 350). Elsewhere, scholars explore the use of headphones in the workspace, both as a control strategy and for the effects of this practice on productivity (for instance, Oldham et al., 1995), and in more diverse places – the prison, for example (Bonini and Perrotta, 2007).

In many ways, the history of music listening is built around distinctions between public and private spaces. However, there is no consistency amongst cultural and media historians about what this means. For instance, Du Gay et al., (1997: 113–14) see headphone listening as transferring a domestic practice into public space while

Uimonen (2004: 58–59) has suggested that public use of a cell phone constitutes a privatization of public space, through an expansion of acoustic territory. From a different perspective, personal listening is seen to isolate the listener from the space in which they find themselves, creating privacy in any context (Bull, 2001; Bonini and Perrotta, 2007: 184, 188). The car is often constructed as a possibly even more private extension of the domestic environment (Bull, 2001: 186), and there is a naturalness in conceiving of headphones as providing "unusual intimacy", as many users do (Schönhammer, 1989). These notions are reinforced through other channels too. For example, in a 2003 advertisement for the iTunes online music store, we see a young woman enjoying what is very clearly "her *private* experience, her *private* music" (Rodman and Vanderdonckt, 2006: 252).

However, people's actual practices and experiences seem to undermine these naturalistic assumptions, making the idea of privacy problematic both as something domestic and as something represented by personal listening. The home has continued to be a venue for individual listening, as a variety of studies indicate (see, for instance, DeNora, 2000; Livingstone, 2002), and while we might follow the line that, as domestic activity, all personal listening is private, there is a sense that some instances of domestic listening are more private than others. People clearly often use music and volume itself, rather than headphones, to create personal spaces (DeNora, 2000: 56). Portable music devices such as transistor radios and portable cassette players automatically afford an element of public access to music (Chow, cited in Du Gay et al., 1997: 139), although the dominant listening experience may be strictly personal in its design and focus. In addition, once music achieves a certain volume, any idea of privacy breaks down and previously personal listening acquires a public context. Passers by experience the booming of bass from car speakers, fellow commuters the hiss of high frequencies on another's headphones; as Schönhammer remarked, "one hears only the 'garbage' of someone else's private acoustic world" (1989: 135).

It would seem, then, that while an illusion of privacy is presented to the user, we cannot see personal listening as truly, individually private. Perhaps the closest approach to auditory privacy is the example of the electrophone above, in which each person, wearing a headset to consume the music, is private to the others. Yet there is a collective experience even here, both of sharing the music and of sharing a space. Bull (2007: 61) records a modern example; the family in the car, each with their own personal listening devices to allow them to consume their own choice of music, via headphones. The history of private listening, then, has always been informed by two dimensions, the perceived privacy of the user's experience and the situation of that experience in space, reinforcing the importance of where personal listening takes place. The capacity for privacy is a reciprocal arrangement, a form of social contract, and personal listening offers a form of "communal privacy"; it becomes private when everyone else is doing it too.

When we listen

As we noted above, a connection is often made between personal listening and mobile listening, and this with good reason since a significant site for the consumption of music through personal listening is the journey to or from work. This association has a long history too. Perhaps the most indicative example of the relationship between time and personal listening is that of radio. The night has long been associated with personal music listening and radio has been a central enabler of this. Hobbyist 'listeners-in' and the popularity of jazz are strongly linked to the early days of American radio in the 1920s (Douglas, 1999: 83–100) and extra-territorial broadcasts at night shaped the timing of British popular music listening of the 1960s (Chapman, 1992).

Berland notes the way that, from the 1970s onwards, radio broadcasts became organized into a series of conventional 'day parts', built upon the routines of a standard industrial day: breakfast, driving to work, morning and afternoon and finally the return drive home (Berland, 1993). Radio time has always built upon the binary opposition between work and leisure, and although radio from the Second World War onwards featured "music while you work" (Baade, 2012: 60–82), the earliest radio programing was most often considered to be a leisure activity. The shift to the mobile car radio in the mid 1950s established a new set of dominant radio programing structures and the idea of distracted listeners using radio as a secondary medium, one that involves them while they do something else. Radio time was then built around an 'imagined listener' of three kinds: the industrial worker, primarily as commuter, who determines the breakfast and drive times; the middle-class housewife, seeking entertainment to underwrite her domestic chores, perhaps supplemented by those workers who were allowed radios in the paid workplace; and the youthful listener, who determined evening broadcasts and sought a distinct cultural experience, away from parents engaged with the television. For the cultural critic Theodor Adorno (1945), radio in 1940s America acted as social cement, binding people into forms of social conformity which regulated both work and leisure time for the benefit of capitalism.

This emphasis on industrial time and secondary listening was adapted and consolidated into the 1960s but pop radio and FM/freeform radio altered radio's relationship to time significantly, with the programing, consumption and technology of radio producing in combination new senses of time. Again mainly US phenomena of the late 1950s and early 1960s, they became the foundation for public service broadcasting developments around specialist music in the UK in the 1970s (Wall and Dubber, 2009).

Radio's role has decreased, partly due to the widespread consumption of personal recorded music technologies such as the Walkman and, subsequently, the iPod. Yet personal listening and people's experience of the day remain intimately related, in defining their relationship with time. Where the radio does not 'announce' the time through the deployment of particular music, users instead choose music appropriate, for them, to a particular time; "angry, loud music at night," for example (Bull, 2005: 349). In terms of time, arguments about personal listening as a facet of control are persuasive; users listen to music that they choose in order to reclaim time as leisure or pleasure from the daily routine, the commute or the rhythm and noise of the workplace (Bull, 2005: 347; 2007: 108–20). The recreational imperative has thus been increasingly supported by mobile personal listening technologies, providing experiences which allow consumers to integrate leisure activities into their day in a manner which changes their relationship to particular periods of time, such that it has become possible to say, "I treasure my commuting time as a much-needed private space" (Bull, 2005: 353).

What listening means

Personal listening reflects not only listeners' relationships with time and space, but also their relationships with one another and with those around them. This is not only a history of spatial and temporal mobility but also one of social mobility. The electrophone was the technology of "well-off people" (Crook, 1999: 17), and it was radio which brought personal listening to a broader demographic. As radio use grew, broadcasters engaged with their audience's sense of themselves in two primary ways: by responding to their conception of group identity and by addressing them directly. Group identity became the basis for organizing programs and then whole stations around niche audiences, addressed mainly through DJs and the music they played. Commuters, domestic housewives, urban African Americans and, later, young people emerged as the most significant of such audiences. By the late 1930s sponsored serial dramas – the soap operas – made up over half of daytime airtime on the networks while the magazine format program established a new way to speak to women and their concerns (Hilmes, 1997: 264–70, 277–87). With origins rooted in African American jive talk, the disc jockey appeared initially in programing targeted at communities of African American listeners and by 1946 there were 400 stations throughout the US aimed at this market (Barlow, 1999).

The talk of the DJs produced a more personal relationship with the listener and rhythm and blues records became key elements of an urban black identity for African Americans through the 1950s (George, 1988). R&B crossed over to the mainstream pop market in a new form of bi-racial pop on Top 40 radio (Ward, 1998). Listening to a particular station had become both a choice and a statement, in effect an expression of identity. In Europe, fueled by concerns about Americanization, the cultural domination of nation-state broadcasters such as the BBC allowed only a few spaces for youthful popular culture. It is no surprise, then, that the entrepreneurs behind the sea-based, unlicensed broadcasters started in the hip clubs of 1960s London and drew on models of US pop radio's direct musical and personal address to drive their programing (Chapman, 1992).

From the 1970s on, this model of identity was nuanced by the enabling implications of a new range of technologies. Listening to audio compact cassettes, or any of the variety of formats which came afterwards, emphasized new forms of allegiance. Whether this involved choices of tape or mixtape, of CD, or of mp3 playlist, identity could be performed more directly by the listener, through direct choice; the personalization of personal listening, a cultural practice exploited by Sony in its 'lifestyling' of the Walkman for different demographics and locales (Du Gay et al., 1997: 62–74). That fashion of this kind communicates and identifies is best indicated by a well-known modern icon – the white earbuds sold with Apple iPods. Furthermore, sound leakage or speaker use made these public performances; a practice even more widely dispersed by the use of cell phone ringtones (Uimonen, 2004).

Such attributes and behavior have often met with a hostile reception, manifest in the 1960s insults of "transistor addict" and "bleatnick" (Douglas, 1999: 226), or directed at the "earphone being" of the Walkman age (Schönhammer, 1989: 128–29). Du Gay et al., (1997: 115–18, 141–43), following Chambers, conceived of the Walkman as something "out of place", transferring a private activity to a public space and creating a form of "moral panic". And headphone use continues this apparent breaking of rules in the interpersonal space. Schönhammer remarks that "people with earphones seem to violate an unwritten law of interpersonal reciprocity; the certainty of common sensual presence in shared situations", creating a sense of separateness and isolation which irritates more than the optic isolation of one who reads the newspaper in the subway (1989: 130, 133). In attempting to understand this push towards isolation through listening, Bull deploys the term "accompanied solitude", drawing on Adorno's concept of we-ness (Bull, 2007: 5–6).

To emphasize the technological mediation here may be to set aside the importance of the cultural activity inherent in this process. Experimentation with personal listening in cars has suggested that the emphasis is on "accompanied" rather than "solitude" (Östergren and Juhlin, 2006: 188); driving is a social practice. Indeed, reflecting on the identity implications of personal listening, we could conclude that being in accompanied solitude does not require the music to be false company but only to provide common currency with others. Hosokawa (1984: 177–79) conceived of Walkman users as sharing a secret; in consuming music by personal listening, we know that others, elsewhere, are consuming similar music – perhaps even by the same artist, perhaps even the same song – and in that musical appreciation we are part of a community. Thus the music does not replace company, but situates the listener within company, not necessarily co-present but as much of an "imagined community" as that of Benedict Anderson's newspaper readers (Anderson, 1983).

Conclusions

A rich understanding of the relationship between technology and cultural practices in the unfolding history of mediated listening demands that we examine the ideas of the private and public spheres, the differences between personal and collective ownership, and the poles of individualism and communality. In this history we do not find any simple shift towards greater privatization of listening, and there has been no obvious drive of technology to make us act in particular ways. Different technologies enable different ways to listen, but music playback machines, broadcasting and internet distribution systems, as well as loudspeakers and headphones, were developed to meet existing cultural goals.

Early radio, the Walkman and the iPod are perhaps the most studied milestones, but others, like the HiFi headphones and mixtape cassette cultures of the 1960s to 1980s, are ripe for further investigation.

In all such studies we must remember that the notion that personal listening is simply private listening is difficult to sustain. The consumption of music is just as much part of identity performance as the consumption of fashion or fashionable technology, and while personal listening may be aimed at separation from the immediate social world, people always hear as part of a community.

Further reading

For insightful examinations of personal listening technologies, see: Susan Douglas's (1999) *Listening In: Radio and the American Imagination: From Amos 'n' Andy and Edward R. Murrow to Wolfman Jack and Howard Stern*; Paul Du Gay et al.'s (1997) *Doing Cultural Studies: The Story of the Sony Walkman*; and Michael Bull's (2007) *Sound Moves: iPod Culture and Urban Experience*. Brian Winston (1998), in his *Media Technology and Society: A History: From the Telegraph to the Internet*, is informative on the relationship between technology and culture. Finally, Sumanth Gopinath and Jason Stanyek's (2014) edited *Oxford Handbook of Mobile Music* offers a substantial and varied contribution to this field.

Notes

1 Nathaniel Baldwin's 'Baldy Phones' (Singer, 1979: 48, 50).
2 Beyerdynamic's first dynamic headphones (see Beyerdynamic, 2014).
3 Koss 'stereophones' (see Koss, 2014).

References

Adorno, T. W. (1945) "A social critique of radio music." *Kenyon Review*, 7(2), 208–17.
Anderson, B. R. O. G. (1983) *Imagined Communities: Reflections on the Origin and Spread of Nationalism*. London: Verso.
Baade, C. L. (2012) *Victory Through Harmony: The BBC and Popular Music in World War II*. Oxford: Oxford University Press.
Barlow, W. (1999) *Voice Over: The Making of Black Radio*. Philadelphia, PA: Temple University Press.
Barnard, S. (1989) *On the Radio: Music Radio in Britain*. Milton Keynes: Open University Press.
Berland, J. (1993) "Radio space and industrial time: The case of music formats." In T. Bennett, S. Frith, L. Grossberg, J. Shepherd and G. Turner (eds.) *Rock and Popular Music: Politics, Policies, Institutions*. London: Routledge (pp. 104–18).
Beyerdynamic (2014) "Beyerdynamic – once and today." Retrieved from http://europe.beyer dynamic.com/company/once-today.html
Bonini, T. and Perrotta, M. (2007) "On and off the air. Radio-listening experiences in the San Vittore prison." *Media, Culture and Society*, 29(2), 179–93.
Briggs, A. (1961) *The Birth of Brodcasting*. Oxford: Oxford University Press.
Bull, M. (2001) "Soundscapes of the car: A critical ethnography of automobile habitation." In D. Miller (ed.) *Car Cultures*. Oxford: Berg (pp. 185–202).
——(2005) "No dead air! The iPod and the culture of mobile listening." *Leisure Studies*, 24(4), 343–55.
——(2007) *Sound Moves: iPod Culture and Urban Experience*. London: Routledge.
Chapman, R. (1992) *Selling the Sixties: The Pirates and Pop Music Radio*, London: Routledge.
Crook, T. (1999) *Radio drama*. London: Routledge.

DeNora, T. (2000) *Music in Everyday Life*. Cambridge: Cambridge University Press.
Doerksen, C. J. (1999) "'Serving the masses, not the classes': Station WHN, pioneer of commercial broadcasting of the 1920s." *Journal of Radio Studies*, 6(1), 81–100.
Douglas, S. J. (1999) *Listening In: Radio and the American Imagination: From Amos 'n' Andy and Edward R. Murrow to Wolfman Jack and Howard Stern*. New York: Times Books.
Du Gay, P., Hall, S., Janes, L., Mackay, H. and Negus, K. (1997) *Doing Cultural Studies: The Story of the Sony Walkman*. London: Sage.
Freshwater, R. (2012) "Electrophone system." The Telephone File. Retrieved from http://www.britishtelephones.com/electrophone.htm
George, N. (1988) *The Death of Rhythm & Blues*. London: Omnibus.
Gomery, D. (2008) *A History of Broadcasting in the United States*. Malden, MA: Blackwell.
Gopinath, S. and Stanyek, J. (2014) *Oxford Handbook of Mobile Music*. New York: Oxford University Press.
Hilmes, M. (1997) *Radio Voices: American Broadcasting, 1922–1952*. Minneapolis, MN: University of Minnesota Press.
Hosokawa, S. (1984) "The Walkman effect." *Popular Music*, 4(4), 165–80.
Koss (2014) "Koss history." Retrieved from http://www.koss.com/en/about/history
Livingstone, S. M. (2002) *Young People and New Media*. London: SAGE.
Lucas, G. (1973) *American Graffiti*. US: 110 mins.
Mpman Europe (2014) "MPMAN, inventor of the mp3 player." Retrieved from http://www.mpmaneurope.com/en
Oldham, G. R., Cummings, A., Mischel, L. J., Schmidtke, J. M. and Zhou, J. (1995) "Listen while you work? Quasi-experimental relations between personal-stereo headset use and employee work responses." *Journal of Applied Psychology*, 80(5), 547–64.
Östergren, M. and Juhlin, O. (2006) "Car drivers using sound pryer – joint music listening in traffic encounters." In K. O'Hara and B. Brown (eds.) *Consuming Music Together: Social and Collaborative Aspects of Music Consumption Technologies*. Dordrecht: Springer (pp. 173–90).
Rodman, G. B. and Vanderdonckt, C. (2006) "Music for nothing or, i want my mp3." *Cultural Studies*, 20(2), 245–61.
Rothenbuhler, E. and McCourt, T. (2002) "Radio redefines itself, 1947–62." In M. Hilmes and J. Loviglio (eds.) *Radio Reader: Essays in the Cultural History of Radio*. New York: Routledge.
Schiffer, M. B. (1993) "Cultural imperatives and product development: The case of the shirt-pocket radio." *Technology and Culture*, 34(1), 98–113.
Schönhammer, R. (1989) "The Walkman and the primary world of the senses." *Phenomenology and Pedagogy*, 7, 127–44.
Schubin, M. (2011) "Headphones, history, & hysteria." Schubin Café. Retrieved from http://www.schubincafe.com/2011/02/11/headphones-history-hysteria
Singer, M. (1979) "Nathaniel Baldwin, Utah inventor and patron of the fundamentalist movement." *Utah Historical Quarterly*, 47(1), 42–53.
Society for the Nationaal Archief (2014) "Japanse meisjes tonen radio-cassettercorders." Gahetna. Retrieved from http://www.gahetna.nl/en/collectie/afbeeldingen/fotocollectie/zoeken/weergave/detail/q/id/ac53e71a-d0b4-102d-bcf8-003048976d84
Stankievech, C. (2007) "From stethoscopes to headphones: An acoustic spatialization of subjectivity." *Leonardo Music Journal*, 17, 55–59.
Uimonen, H. (2004) "'Sorry, can't hear you! I'm on a train!' Ringing tones, meanings and the Finnish soundscape." *Popular Music*, 23(1), 51–62.
VanCour, S. (2008) *The Sounds of 'Radio': Aesthetic Formations of 1920s American Broadcasting*. PhD Thesis, University of Wisconsin-Madison.
Wall, T. and Dubber, A. (2009) "Specialist music, public service and the BBC in the internet age." *The Radio Journal*, 7(1), 27–48.

Wall, T. and Webber, N. (2014) "Changing cultural co-ordinates: The transistor radio and space/time/identity." In S. Gopinath and J. Stanyek (eds.) *Oxford Handbook of Mobile Music*. New York: Oxford University Press (pp. 118–30).

Ward, B. (1998) *Just My Soul Responding: Rhythm and Blues, Black Consciousness and Race Relations*. London: UCL Press.

Winston, B. (1998) *Media Technology and Society: A History: From the Telegraph to the Internet*. London: Routledge.

47
Futures of television
John Corner

As many writers have noted, what is indicated by 'television' can vary according to context. 'Television' is a specific technology of production and transmission, for many years having its most widespread and routine physical manifestation in the 'television set'. It is also a major part of the information, entertainment and leisure industry internationally, involving large and complex institutions working within various kinds of business model. For many people, however, the meaning of television (perhaps in its casual, taken-for-granted designation as 'TV') is much more to do with kinds of initially domestic but now increasingly mobile *experience* which, with variations, have been shared worldwide. This is an experience of watching and listening, learning and enjoying, being gripped by depicted events and also being relaxed, of being recreated. All these dimensions are active in the idea that television is a 'medium', a distinctive set of opportunities, a distinctive *means*, for creativity and communication which can be usefully compared and contrasted with cinema and radio as well as the varieties of photographic and printed material. In his classic book, *Television: Technology and Cultural Form*, Raymond Williams (1974) showed his awareness of the multi-faceted character of television and tried to trace some of the lines by which it had developed into such a significant phenomenon. His account drew on his sense of the way in which television's domestic presence, its collapsing of times and spaces and the generic range of its portrayals combined to make it a socially shaping technology of an unparalleled kind.

Across all these dimensions, it has been clear for some time that 'television' is changing, and questions about how fast, in what direction and with what consequences have been regularly discussed both inside and outside the academy. Clearly, the dynamics of 'convergence' with digital applications, including the web, have been a primary point of reference, connecting with other shifts in production, distribution and consumption. As I shall discuss later, some commentators have worked with the idea of 'post-television' to indicate the predicted scale of the displacement they envisage, whereas others have been more cautious (see for instance Spigel and Olsson, 2004 and Turner and Tay, 2009).

I want to explore ideas about where television is headed, about the key factors undergoing transition and about the sometimes surprising capacity of 'established' forms of television to continue to thrive, despite their being located in a very different media landscape from the one in which they developed.

The issue of how television is now accessed and how it fits into daily routines and times is perhaps a good place to start. I will then look at the profile of television in Britain, set within its distinctive contexts of change – economic, technological and cultural. Closing to a tighter focus, I will raise questions about how television journalism is positioned within emerging patterns of provision and use. In a concluding section, I consider some further aspects of the lively academic debate about television's future, finally presenting a summary agenda.

Spaces and times

It is clear that, gradually but with increasing pace over the last decade or so, television has been 'freed' from the limitations that have previously framed access to it and regulated the temporal regimes within which it could be watched. Culturally, the decisive move to forms of home recording (first tape and DVD and then hard drive) broke the relationship to a broadcast schedule which had previously been a key element of television's cultural profile, at the same time as it allowed an increasingly rich and varied range of options from non-broadcast sources. The separation of viewing time from transmission time was, as many commentators have pointed out, a major shift in the kinds of choices viewers were able to make, in both what they watched and when they chose to watch it. The implications of time-shifting for the commercial logics of television production are still being worked through and this will continue as a mix of predictable and unpredictable developments occur in the next few years. The model of the broadcast audience 'bound' to the times of television, and with limited channel options, has often generated a positive (and now nostalgic) sense of national, communal engagement, of collective experience, and this affirming sense is still detectable in the televising of major 'live' events, including sporting events. Other commentators have seen the earlier 'national community' situation more negatively, as variously constraining of television's potential as a medium around which a wide range of 'individual' choices could and should be exercised. Whatever the position taken here, the combination of increasing channel choice with 'time-shift' options, 'catch up' services and the range of other audio-visual materials that can be enjoyed through television equipment (including via 'on demand' provision) has quickly broken down the older model. Even the 'live' viewing of broadcast material as it is transmitted (material which in many cases will be recorded), while it is still a significant part of television use, involves rather different relationships when it occurs as a consumer choice across an extensive array of broadcast and non-broadcast options for watching. Television's relations with its viewer-consumers have therefore been transformed, requiring alternative and innovative approaches to attracting, engaging and keeping an audience. All program forms have been affected in this transformation, in which the once dominant idea of television as a 'flow' of meanings coming through into the home from a limited number of institutional sources, powerfully signifying television as *reception*, is being exchanged for an emerging sense of television *as a kind of content* which is *sought out* (the idea of 'flow' is developed in Williams, 1974; see Corner, 1999 for a discussion). Watching television has become a more individualizing and less collectivizing experience and television's dispersal across so many outlets of 'choice' has had implications for its social and political identity, which has become less defined across the new diversities.

Most recently, the ways in which television is accessed have also become an important factor in its profile as both an informational and a recreational medium. The use of a rapidly developing technology of mobile devices has not only helped change the 'time' framing of television use but also the spaces within which a television experience can be had. In the home, the enjoying of television gradually spread out from the late 1970s to include other rooms in addition to the living room, as lower prices allowed multi-set ownership (children's bedrooms figured prominently in the emerging picture here). This served to weaken 'family viewing' demographics and encouraged a range of more narrowly targeted programing. Something of a 'return' to the main living areas, if not to a 'common experience', appears to have followed the wider availability of smaller devices, varying in screen size from tablet computers to phones, that can be attended to in shared space (including by earphone use) and whose capacity to receive television has begun to displace the need for additional sets (see Telescope, 2013; Ofcom, 2013). Across all the available evidence, there is no doubt that the parallel and convergent use of computers and mobile devices alongside both conventional sets and the 'smart' sets which allow direct access to online material is continuing to reconfigure the types of television being watched as well as the ways of watching it. Outside the home, of course, television is accessible in any number of locations, including forms of transport and the wide variety of kinds of 'waiting' that everyday life involves. It has ceased to be something only attended to in stretches of 'leisure time' and has made itself available for insertion into the 'gaps', often quite short, in stretches of time defined primarily in other ways.

Among other things, the visual and aural modes of television have adapted to these changes in spatial and temporal co-ordinates, quite apart from the expansion of generic possibilities which has been introduced. At one pole, television has become, with varying levels of sophistication, 'home cinema', its large screens delivering qualities of image and sound that allow for an ambitious, engaging aesthetics much closer to that of cinema production than has previously been possible. At the other pole, it has become data and entertainment on the move, with an audio-visual organisation, influenced by the web, friendly to the sometimes tiny screens on which it is accessed and the busy settings in which this might occur.

Institution and economy

Whatever the future holds for television, it is clear already that the institutional forms through which it is produced and distributed have already changed and will be required to change further. The 'institutionality' of television has sometimes been a little overlooked in discussion of it within academic television research. In earlier writing on the medium, I noted the way in which

> an analytic way of seeing television institutionally, rather than simply pointing to the fact of corporations, companies, production houses, etc. is

to focus on the way in which institutional forms act as a matrix for, and a nexus between, the various constituents of television. Institutions give the processes of television (including viewing experience) their specificity, a specificity with a historical, national character which is the product of given political, social and cultural factors interacting with available technology.

(Corner, 1999: 12)

The kinds of 'specificity' which television in Britain had for many years will be modified as its institutional profile is revised and the kinds of 'matrix' and 'nexus' involved are revised too. One of the main reasons for institutional revision is undoubtedly economic – the ways in which television is paid for are shifting and the sheer range of distributive 'channels' through which even 'broadcast' television reaches its viewers is one key part of this. The guiding idea of 'public service broadcasting' which has shaped the character of British television for so long still survives, although increasingly the formulation of its principles and the policies developed as a consequence have been subject to reformulation (see Donders, 2011 for a Europe-wide survey). This process has taken account of the more intensively commercial and competitive setting within which television operates and the limitations on the use of public funding, so essential to the sustaining of PSB policies, which have been introduced. British PSB, although the concept has extended beyond the activities of the BBC, has had the BBC as a pivotal institution in determining values and practices and therefore an 'adequate' grant of public money (related to revenue from the licence fee paid by viewers) has been necessary for its continuation. As the value of the funds made available to the BBC by governments has declined (there was a 20 percent reduction in the value of the allocation in 2010), the BBC has had to reposition itself more firmly as a 'commercially viable' as well as a 'publicly funded' operation. Sometimes, this shift has been justified by governments as a move made necessary by shortage of public funds (particularly during the current [2014] period of national deficit) but within Conservative circles the idea of 'scaling down' the activities of the BBC as a 'national' broadcaster by cutting its budget and forcing it into more commercial strategies against competition has been an attractive one for some time. It stems from a political desire to reduce the impact of what are seen as the 'Left-leaning' inclinations of the BBC as well as enthusiasm for a more market-oriented media system. Nevertheless, despite these challenges, and others, the BBC has managed to sustain a dominating presence in the British television landscape which can seem surprising when viewed against the more dire prophecies of collapse under a combination of political and market pressures and the new conditions of digital culture. Many of its strategies for survival in these conditions, including for the maintenance of its international quality 'brand', have clearly worked well. As a major *producer* of television across all the genres it has also made itself distinctive when assessed alongside those companies which rely extensively on buying their programs from external sources.

Perhaps the biggest factor affecting the shape of terrestrial 'independent' (commercial) television in Britain has been the proliferation of 'choice' beyond the broadcast model. This has reduced audience share, causing a subsequent reduction of advertising revenue. Advertising revenue has also declined through a combination of other factors, most notably the shift towards web advertising and those moves towards the 'time shifting' of programs which have led to spot advertising not receiving the attention it did when the established mode for watching television was broadcast transmission. With this 'problem' in mind, the ITV iplayer service for catch-up viewing has currently made the avoidance of advertising breaks, or even the fast-forward viewing of them, impossible – so one potential escape route from attention to advertising content has been cut off, but a number of others remain. It is significant that web advertising expenditure exceeded that for television from 2009 and there is no chance of this gap closing in the future (Sweney, 2009). Making money from television has therefore had to include sponsorship but also an increasing number of subscription channels. Yet as more television content is found 'free' on the web, the attraction of subscription channels, even for movies and specialist interest programing, is at risk of diminishing, a tendency likely to be increased by any downturn in households' disposable income.

In predicting the future, it is interesting to look at the pattern of channel use in Britain at the moment. Here, as in other areas of broadcasting policy, Sylvia Harvey has produced a series of detailed commentaries, often as documents intended as responses to policy proposals and as contributions to public debate. A recent paper (Harvey, 2011) brings out some surprising facts about British television within the current or near-recent situation of multi-channel viewing. She notes that

> the five channels designated as 'public service' (PSBs) and required by the 2003 Communication Act to meet cultural and citizenship objectives have demonstrated themselves to be, together, the most popular and successful in the market. In 2009 – and in the context of a wider market of 490 licensed TV channels in the UK – these providers retained a majority share of 58% of total audience, with individual channel shares as below: BBC1 (20.9%), BBC2 (7.5%), ITV1 (17.8%), Channel 4 (6.8%) and Channel 5 (4.9%) (Ofcom, Communication Market Report 2010: 164).
>
> (Harvey, 2011)

Harvey goes on to comment that "some figures indicate that with 'portfolio' channels included (e.g. ITV2, BBC3) the total market share of the 5 PSB channels is around 71%" and contrasts this with the total market share of BSkyB across all its channels of 7.4 percent (ibid.). When it comes to spending on original, first run productions, she cites a figure of 90 percent of investment coming from the 5 PSB channels and notes how investment has dropped during the period 2003 to 2009.

The pattern indicated by these figures is perhaps more surprising still when it is placed against the indications (from Ofcom Communications Market Reports) that subscription provides the largest revenue flow for the British television economy followed by advertising and then forms of public funding. So the publicly funded television of the BBC is still a strongly preferred option even in multi-channel homes despite the stronger revenue streams available to other providers.

As I write this chapter, more recent research from 2012 on total viewing time, conducted by Telescope (2013), indicated an average viewing of 4 hours and 2 minutes a day, which was *up* from the average of 3 hours and 36 minutes recorded in

2006. This survey noted a reduction in the amount of TV sets in the home, related to the increase, noted above, in the domestic use of other devices on which television content could be viewed. It concluded that the present situation, notwithstanding rapid change, is still one in which new technology is 'complementing' rather than 'replacing' traditional forms of viewing, although it recognized that *what* is viewed now extends across a far wider range of options.

How to make television profitable will undoubtedly pose a challenge in the next decade, especially since, quite apart from the shifts in advertising spend noted above, there are indications that the take up of subscription services has faltered. The level of support given to the BBC, which could either be further constrained or strengthened within a wider framework of Public Service Media, will be a vital element in the overall picture and one highly dependent on the broader governmental agenda concerning the informational and cultural economies and the role of the market in their development.

Television journalism: Cause for concern?

Whatever the future holds for television as a medium of entertainment across the vast generic range of drama, comedy, sport, special-interest programing, reality shows, talk shows, history and travel series etc., its identity as a platform for forms of journalism will certainly be subject to change, perhaps of a quite radical kind. News is mostly watched 'live' if watched at all and the wide array of options which people now have for updating themselves on global, national and regional events has changed the temporal framework in which television news works. Within television itself, the arrival of dedicated news channels (on this, see Cushion and Lewis, 2010) has made it possible to switch to television news at any time of the day within the terms of conventional domestic viewing, quite apart from the options for quick updates on a variety of devices when out of the home. The use of web sources for news, including newspaper sites, has added to this range. One effect has been on the status of the conventional flagship news programs in early and late evening. The identity of these programs as 'ritual viewing', offering a comprehensive update on events (one traditionally preceded by the revelatory 'drama' of their headlines), has started to become weakened by the very way in which the news-world is becoming perceived as, as it were, 'ongoing' rather than 'periodic'. Added to these technologically induced shifts, there has been in the United Kingdom the threat of a further loosening of those Public Service protocols, noted above, which, among other things, sought to sustain the seriousness and integrity of television news provision, as a 'public good' necessary to the health of democracy. They did this by stipulating requirements that protected it from the possibility of its being compromised by too directly commercial an influence on its content and character.

In the increasingly competitive and 'de-regulated' circumstances emerging, the way in which television conceives of its journalism, both what it offers within its news packages and how it offers it, has clearly needed regular attention and will continue to need it as the entire profile for the mediation of 'news' sees further shifts.

A recent and finally pessimistic account of where television news is headed is provided by Steven Barnett (2011). In the preface to a book considering its topic within a broad historical survey, he baldly states the predicament in which he sees television journalism now placed:

> [G]reat television journalism is under threat. It has already virtually disappeared in the United States, where the legacy of Edward R. Murrow and other revered journalistic voices from the past were long ago overwhelmed by an unregulated market that cared little for the democratic role of journalism. And now it is under threat not just in the United Kingdom but in many other developed and developing countries whose politicians are being seduced into believing that the marketplace is the universal panacea.
> (Barnett, 2011: xi)

In looking at the emerging, technologically enabled possibilities which have been viewed positively by some commentators, Barnett regards 'citizen journalism' as no replacement for the role played by good, professional reporting, however well it may work both as a new route for accessing diverse sources and as a vigorous 'ground level' complement to mainstream accounts. He regards the way in which 'citizen journalism' has sometimes been celebrated as a democratization of news production, its potential to displace professional accounts regarded as a wholly positive tendency, as mistaken in its assumptions about how news values relate to political values and to political structures.

From the perspective of 2013, it seems unlikely that significant 'protective' measures will be taken to insulate television news from marketplace dynamics. Meanwhile, the shift towards an increased variety in the sources from which people get their news accounts is likely to continue. In order to make itself attractive to viewers, who are using it now within a variety of settings, news programing will almost certainly confirm at least some of Barnett's fears and become more inclined, outside of narrowly targeted programing, to run with 'human interest' stories and stories relating to show business and sport. It will be more wary, outside of specialist upmarket slots, of extensive treatment of international affairs beyond those related to conflicts in which the UK is directly involved. This is so, whatever achievements of professional reporting are still to come. It is possible to overstate the scale and speed at which such a process will occur (premature predictions of disaster are a feature of academic writing about television news as well as of television itself!) but strong countervailing factors are hard to discern. The tone, too, of television news is likely to continue to be modified – shifting further towards the informal if not the chatty in ways which, while they increase the sense of sociability which news material can generate, also work to constrain the discursive range within which the serious and the complex can receive an adequate exposition to popular audiences.

This situation significantly compounds the longstanding challenge of adequately making 'serious' content 'popular', a challenge which television journalists have variously grappled with across the years using a number of imaginative approaches as well as, occasionally, resorting to compromise and to cliché. What can be a distorting obsession with 'liveness' and the 'breaking' story (often involving long periods of empty speculation) and with 'immediacy' (often involving the delivering of reports from settings associated with the news item even when this setting merely provides a connotative backdrop) are tendencies likely to be further encouraged.

Forecasting futures

In this final section I want to look at some aspects of the broader debate about what is happening to television, including accounts which reference the international contexts within which any consideration of the British situation clearly has to be set. This will allow me to develop a summarizing agenda about the possible futures of television, giving emphasis and development to a selection of the points made earlier.

I suggested that a tendency to regard the process of transformation in too accelerated and wholesale a fashion had taken hold in a number of books and journal articles. Sometimes, in a variation of this, the term 'TV' indicates the older broadcast model being left behind while 'television' is the strongly continuing multiplatform present and future (see Spigel and Olsson, 2004). The reasons for exaggerated claims about the scale of change lie partly in the broader difficulties and uncertainties of coming to terms with an emerging digital economy and culture, challenges which governments as well as academic fields of study variously face. It has been too easy to see television and television culture as part of 'legacy media' against an emerging, dominant order centered on new media use. The suggestion that we are moving into, or are actually already in, a 'post-television' era carries with it a satisfying sense of drama. It also has a polemical and self-congratulatory edge, suggesting that too much emphasis is still being placed on outmoded systems and cultural forms in a way which needs the clean sweep of a brave new perspective (as embraced by the writer). An even stronger version of the 'post' idea is the direct declaration that television is dead. The media scholar Toby Miller recently made some sharply critical remarks about this kind of proposition:

> Every year, every season, every week, pundits celebrate or lament what they divine as the passing of the mass audience. The mysterious disappearance of this group is understood as the demise of terrestrial, broadcast TV. It's La fin de la télévision [The End of Television] (Missika, 2006) or La televisión ha muerto [Television is dead] (De Silva, 2000). But here's the secret: the problems for traditional broadcast networks today are satellite, cable, and genre-dedicated channels; the recession; and piracy – not the loss of an audience for television per se.
>
> (Miller, 2011)

So recognizable elements of the older 'television' (perhaps even of the older 'TV' if that distinction is made) remain, its dominance over the media landscape as a source both of entertainment and of information continuing, if in revised forms. Part of this resilience derives from television's sheer flexibility, its capacity to re-invent its profile in relation to changing economic, technological and cultural conditions. Even the 'television set', far from becoming obsolete, has been subject to massive upgrades in size and audio-visual quality. Streams of television still pour into many British homes, even if what is watched is no longer schedule-bound and even if television operates in an expanding range of settings beyond the domestic.

Writing about television change, the Norwegian scholar Jostein Gripsrud suggests that the use of television as a marker of everyday times is likely to survive:

> One of broadcast media's basic functions has been, and will almost certainly continue to be, that of marking the rhythms of time during the day, the week, and throughout the year. This concerns a fundamental social-psychological need.
>
> (Gripsrud, 2004: 217)

Clearly, national patterns will vary considerably here, as will the rate at which 'time-marking' increasingly emerges from *within* the pattern of home choices rather than being imposed *upon* home life by television schedules. Through what avenues might further significant change come about within a British television system that has been steadily under transformation for many years? Here, I think we can identify four lines of shift:

a *Technology*. Technological development will continue to produce new media options other than television but also new ways of attending to television content as well as producing it. Facebook, Twitter, YouTube and streaming services like Netflix will all be part of the picture here, alongside other entrepreneurial initiatives. However, digital technology should be recognized in its functions as an 'enhancer' of the television experience, quite often supportive of it rather than displacing it.

b *Economics*. A further intensification of the market context for British television is likely to occur, with a continuing weakening of Public Service policy. Television's institutions will see related shifts in priorities of investment and some forms of journalism, current affairs and documentary will be particularly exposed. Channel identity, based on generic emphases and demographically informed strategies of theme, address to the viewer and type of multiplatform presence will become ever more important in the increased competition to win attention within viewers' daily and weekly routines.

c *Cultures of viewing*. There is strong generational change coming through in attitudes to television content – what to watch, when and how – but the use of television as a central medium of home entertainment across a variety of options and genres supported by multiplatform activity looks set to continue for some while. Forms of drama and of sporting coverage will be a key part of this centrality. Mobile viewing on personal devices will become ever more established for certain kinds of content, some of it specially designed for this kind of access.

d *Patterns of content and form*. There will be a search both for new kinds of content and for innovation around core generic forms and beyond, in part relating to what is happening elsewhere in audio-visual culture. There will be an increasing use of digital archive material, both as a directly accessed source of entertainment and knowledge for viewers and as the basis for forms of compilation programing and 'themed' scheduling. Television involving forms of viewer interaction and participation will become more widespread as the new digital contexts allow this, and the successful models to emerge will establish themselves as part of everyday television culture. The expanding aesthetic range made available, both through technological affordance and the increased market possibilities for niche and short-form content, will slowly modify the 'grammar' of the medium.

Of course, many factors and forces could come into play to complicate or contradict these predictions. The study of television will need to be alert to these at the same time as it continues to adjust to what is already happening. Here, perspectives on the past, perhaps paradoxically, have an important role. The history of television has always been important in trying to understand the uncertainties of its present and future. Historical as well as contemporary data will continue to require critical attention in assessing what lies ahead and in debating its possible consequences.

Further reading

Two collections, Spigel and Olsson's (2004) *Television After TV: Essays on a Medium In Transition* and Turner and Tay's (2009) *Television Studies After Television: Understanding Television in the Post-Broadcast Era*, provide excellent and still relevant reading on the fundamental issues regarding television's future. They contain a good mixture of research evidence and debate. In the UK, trade journals such as *Broadcast* and the surveys and reports of Ofcom (ofcom.org.uk) are an invaluable source of information on recent and imminent tendencies.

References

Barnett, S. (2011) *The Rise and Fall of Television Journalism*. London: Bloomsbury.
Corner, J. (1999) *Critical Ideas in Television Studies*. Oxford: Oxford University Press.
Cushion, S. and Lewis, P. (2010) *The Arrival of 24-Hour News Television*. Oxford, Bern, New York: Peter Lang.
De Silva, J. P. (2000) *La Television ha Muerto*. Barcelona: Gedeista Editorial SA.
Donders, K. (2011) *Public Service Media and Policy in Europe*. Basingstoke: Palgrave Macmillan.
Gripsrud, J. (2004) "Broadcast television: The chances of its survival in a digital age." In L. Spigel and J. Olssen (eds.) *Television After TV: Essays on a Medium in Transition*. Durham: Duke University Press (pp. 210–23).
Harvey, S. (2011) "Submission to the Department of Culture, Media and Sport in response to Secretary of State Jeremy Hunt's open letter, 'A Communications Review for the Digital Age'." Retrieved from http://www.docstoc.com/docs/143434304/Sylvia-Harvey–Department-for-Culture-Media-and-Sport
Miller, T. (2011) "TV is dead." *Critical Studies in Television*. Retrieved from http://cstonline.tv/tv-is-dead
Missika, J.-L. (2006) *La Fin de la Television*. Paris: Seuil.
Ofcom (2013) "The communications market report 2013." Retrieved from ofcom.org.uk
Spigel, L. and Olsson, J. (eds.) (2004) *Television After TV: Essays on a Medium in Transition*. Durham: Duke University Press.
Sweney, M. (2009) "Internet overtakes television to become biggest advertising sector in the UK." Retrieved from http://www.guardian.co.uk/media/2009/sep/30/internet-biggest-uk-advertising-sector

Telescope (2013) "Telescope: A look at the nation's changing viewing habits from TV Licensing." Retrieved from http://www.tvlicensing.co.uk/cs/media-centre/news/view.app?id=1362435475983

Turner, G. and Tay, J. (2009) *Television Studies After Television: Understanding Television in the Post-Broadcast Era*. Abingdon: Routledge.

Williams, R. (1974) *Television: Technology and Cultural Form*. London: Fontana.

48

Video games and gaming
The audience fights back

Tristan Donovan

Introduction

The March 2012 release of *Mass Effect 3* marked the conclusion of a trilogy of games that, in game player circles at least, had come to be regarded as a science-fiction work comparable in importance to *Star Wars* and *Star Trek* (Munkittrick, 2012; Sterling, 2012). A significant part of the trilogy's appeal was the promise that the choices made by players over the course of all three games would alter the experience in such a way as to personalize the story to them. In the first game, for example, players face a choice between executing or freeing the last surviving queen of the Rachni aliens, which is a decision that alters events in the subsequent two games (BioWare, 2007). Similarly, while all players controlled a character called Commander Shepard, they could select the gender of their character, a choice that closes off or opens up different possibilities for romantic and sexual encounters. These examples are just two of many story influencing choices available to players over the course of the trilogy.

Given this high degree of player influence, the ending of *Mass Effect 3* marked the resolution of a story personalized to the player that had been told over a four-and-a-half-year period and involved in excess of 100 hours of play to fully experience. But instead of personalized conclusions, the several endings were mostly identical, sparking criticism from players who felt their choices had been ignored (Crosscade, 2012; Lincoln, 2012).

Usually this would be the end of the matter. Players would voice their disappointment but the ending created by BioWare, the Canadian game development studio that made the series, would stand. But rather than accept the situation, players campaigned for a new ending. A campaign group called Retake Mass Effect 3 attracted tens of thousands of 'likes' on Facebook while a poll of more than 16,000 people on BioWare's own internet forum found that 87 percent wanted the ending to be changed (Langshaw, 2012). In response BioWare created a free update to the game to download that revised the endings so that they were more reflective of the choices players had made (Yin-Poole, 2012a). As Morisset (2013) notes, the decision to replace an existing ending is a novel event in any media. As such the incident represents something of a watershed in the relationship between players and game developers, and challenges the traditional notion that creators create and audiences consume.

The incident also presents a challenge to the emerging field of video game studies, which, as Mäyrä, Van Loo and Quandt (2013) found, is still drawing on many different and divergent academic traditions. Konzack (2007) divides studies of digital games into eight groups, of which the often opposing aesthetic perspectives of narratology and ludology have been particularly influential in how games are analyzed within academia. Narratology sees games as a narrative media and draws on film and literary theory while ludologists take the stance that it is the rule structures of games that matters. While the narratology and ludology may provide (competing) explanations of why *Mass Effect 3* caused a backlash from players, neither seeks to explain why players felt, quite correctly as it turned out, that they were in a position to successfully demand that the game's endings be revised.

It is my contention that the player–developer conflict over *Mass Effect 3* is a notable illustration of longer-term trends within the video game medium that have served to break down the boundaries between developers and players, and are driven as much by the games industry as the audience. These trends are the result of several interrelated but distinct developments in the history of video games, each of which I will cover here in turn.

The nature of the video game medium

As a medium, video games have several distinct qualities that serve to blur the usual boundary between creator and audience. The first of these qualities is the significant influence earlier game forms such as board games, card games and sports have had on video games. These games have a long history of flexible and evolving rules as the myriad games based on traditional playing cards demonstrates. Role-playing games, themselves a drastic evolution of tabletop war games, have been especially influential on video games and while these games are usually accompanied by extensive rules there is significant scope for player interpretation and reinvention of these rules. As such games, in the broadest sense, have always been a malleable medium where participants are potentially free to alter the rules that govern the experience.

Another important quality of video games is that, with the exception of many games of the 1970s such as *PONG* (Atari Inc., 1972) and the games of the Magnavox Odyssey console which were built from fixed electronic circuits (Donovan, 2010), they exist as software. While software can be highly complicated, it is malleable. With the right tools and knowledge software can be changed and, increasingly, software is more an ongoing than a discrete creation. This is very much true of video games and today it is largely standard practice in the games industry that developers will create extra content or updates that fix errors or tweak how the game functions for already published games. For example, the iPhone/iPad version of *Angry Birds* had five updates in 2012 alone including some that added new levels to the game (iTunes, 2013). This situation reinforces how games are fluid in nature and can be altered, subtly or significantly, even after they are released to the public in 'completed' form. The final important quality is that video games are experienced as something analogous to a conversation between the player and the software. As Fernández-Vara (2009) says, game players in effect double as spectators and performers: "The player is an active performer because she is also an interactor; but she is also the audience of the performance, since she is the one who makes sense of the system and interacts accordingly." It is, therefore, assumed by both the player and the developer that there will be some degree of audience agency in the experience. Players expect to have some control over a game and for the developers the question is how much control to give players rather than whether to give them control. These three qualities suggest that video games are viewed by both their makers and their players as malleable works where the audience is a participant in the experience rather than a spectator.

The influence of hacker culture

The culture of hacking is another important factor that has served to erode the player–developer boundary throughout the history of video games. Hacking is often used in reference to computer-based crime but it is the original meaning that matters here. Levy (2010) defines hacking as "a project undertaken or a product built not solely to fulfill some constructive goal, but with some wild pleasure taken in mere involvement." In other words, hacking is undertaken by people who enjoy tinkering with technology. Levy sets out several qualities of the 'hacker ethic' that are relevant here, namely, that there should not be boundaries to accessing information, equipment or knowledge; that information should be free to use; and that decentralized systems are better than centralized bureaucracy.

This ethic played a central role in the birth of video games. During late 1961 and early 1962 a group of Massachusetts Institute of Technology students created *Spacewar!*, the first video game made purely for entertainment that did not simply replicate an existing game in software (Donovan, 2010). Its creation was a hack, an unsanctioned piece of work on a computer reserved for serious academic activities, and in line with the 'hacker ethic' it was given away to other computer users without charge. *Spacewar!* went on to directly inspire the first two coin-operated video games that marked the start of the game industry (ibid.). During the early to mid 1970s, when computers were largely restricted to institutional use, hacker culture was very much embedded in game-making circles. Programmers would create games covertly, as computer administrators would delete them if spotted, and share them freely with each other. While the era's arcade video game industry was more commercially orientated, those it employed to build their games were also part of this culture.

The hacker ethic moved out of the institutional computer lab and into the home with the arrival of personal computers in the late 1970s. The initial years of personal computers were marked by a shortage of games and other software to buy so computer use at this time tended to focus on tinkering with the technology to see what could be done. In the UK this way of using computers continued well into the first half of the 1980s and is best reflected in how the games and computer magazines of the time published listings of computer code for games for readers to type in (Kirkpatrick, 2012). As such, computer users were expected to have some working knowledge of programing, something reflected in the inclusion of the code for a game called

Chomp in Amis' (1982) *Invasion of the Space Invaders*. *Chomp* was written in the programing language BASIC for the Sharp MZ-80K but Amis advises readers that it can "easily be adapted for other home sets" with the clear expectation that readers will have the know-how necessary to do this.

The necessity of having some programing knowledge to use a computer meant that the barrier between a game maker and a player was highly porous. Illustrative of this is how the UK games industry began with people selling games they had made at home via mail-order advertisements in the computing press. Noteworthy British game companies such as the games publisher Codemasters and Rockstar North, developers of the *Grand Theft Auto* series, both originated in this era of "bedroom programers" (Dailly, 2004; Donovan, 2010). Even when companies with other interests moved into the games business they relied on the audience to double as the source of their games as illustrated by Richard Branson's company Virgin Games, which ran adverts in the popular computing press asking for readers to send in games for possible publication (*Your Computer*, 1983).

Players not only used this knowledge to make the jump from amateur to professional game developer, they also used it to alter commercially released games with the aid of devices such as Action Replay. Launched in 1983 by the UK firm Datel, Action Replay allowed players to pause games and then use their knowledge of programing to examine and alter the game (Allen, n.d.). This was primarily done using the PEEK and POKE commands of BASIC. PEEK allowed users to see what was stored in a specific location within the computer's memory while POKE allowed users to change the information that was stored. Using these commands it was possible for players to see how a game worked and change it, most often to make the game easier. These devices became a part of British game culture during the 1980s with magazines publishing POKE commands for commercially released games with little sign of objection from the UK games industry.

Although hacking games in this way was mainstream within Britain's computer-dominated gaming culture, this was not the case in the USA where the Nintendo Entertainment System (NES) console dominated the market during the late 1980s. This difference is illustrated not only by the lack of POKEs published in American computer games magazines that served a similar market to the UK publications that did include these codes, but also by Nintendo's unsuccessful legal action against Lewis Galoob Toys after it launched the Game Genie, an Action Replay type device for the NES that was developed by Codemasters (Kent, 2001). Nintendo objected to the way the device allowed players to alter NES games and argued that it would make games too easy or detrimentally alter how they functioned or looked.

But while the lack of POKEs in American computer magazines suggests there were some cultural differences between the UK and the USA, Nintendo's actions are primarily reflective of the protectionist nature of the console business. Console manufacturers make their money by controlling what is released on their systems and taking a share of the income. The Game Genie was not approved by Nintendo and so it was entering a market the company wanted to keep under its control. Furthermore, there are examples of American players hacking commercial computer games, including *Castle Smurfenstein*, a hack of Muse Software's *Castle Wolfenstein*, which has been credited as the first hacked game (James Au, 2002).

From this we can see that hacking became part of player and developer culture during the 1980s and, in the UK at least, was not regarded as a threat by the games industry.

Customization

If hacking represented a bottom-up force for a less discrete boundary between players and developers, there was a corresponding top-down effort by developers to give players more influence over what they played. This can broadly be summed up as 'customization' – developers including tools or options in their games that enable players to personalize the experience in some way. In its most simplistic form this could be the ability to input your own name into *Football Manager* or to select the gender of the player character in *Ant Attack*, neither of which have any bearing on the game itself (Toms, 1982; White and Sutherland, 1983). But even in the early 1980s more elaborate customization options were on offer, most notably in the form of editing tools that players could use to create new levels or scenarios for games.

These edits and options have become widespread and, over time, have given players more and more freedom to adjust the experience to suit their own desires, whether that is to make a game easier or harder, change the clothes of player characters, alter the direction of the story or, as is possible in *World of Warcraft*, redesign the user interface. In some cases, such as *The Sims* and *Minecraft*, the ability of players to customize the experience is the game. As Jones (2008) notes, these options "are places where the roles of designer and user, creator and player, converge." As such game developers have been giving players greater and greater ability to mold games as they wish, fostering an expectation among players that, at least in some genres of game, they can expect to be able to put their own stamp on the game.

'Modding'

The bottom-up push of hacking by players and the top-down push of customization options came together in the 1990s in the form of 'modding', a practice that overturned the greater divide between players and developers that started to open up in the late 1980s as the industry developed beyond a cottage industry and the technology became more complex.

Modding, a term derived from the word modification, refers to player-made games that piggyback on the software of commercial games and are built using tools provided by the developer. It differs from hacking in that the practice is encouraged and facilitated to some degree by developers. It is also different from customization since customization occurs within the framework of the game rather than enabling the game to be transformed into something unrelated to the original product.

The rise of 'mods', as these player creations are known, is largely due to the first-person shooters *Wolfenstein 3D* and *Doom*, both made by the Texan development studio id Software. *Wolfenstein 3D* became popular with hackers, who figured out how to use the game's software to create new levels, which they then shared with each other. Rather than ignoring or opposing these hacks, id Software gave purchasers of its next game, *Doom*, all the tools they need to make mods. These mods could then be played by anyone who owned a copy of the game. The decision offered benefits to both the audience and id Software. It became easier for players to use *Doom*'s software for their own ends and in turn other players could use the mods others created to experience the game in new and different ways. For id Software mods improved the appeal of their game. As id Software's Jay Wilbur suggested: "[A] game that might exhaust its time in the marketplace in six to 12 months might get an additional 12 or 18 months or more depending on how popular it is because users are creating more content" (quoted in Donovan, 2010: 261).

Other developers followed suit and by the late 1990s modding tools were commonplace in first-person shooters released on PCs and were spreading into other game genres. Developers also began importing ideas from mods into commercial games. One prominent example is the *Threewave CTF* mod for *Quake*, an adaption of the outdoor team game 'capture the flag' (Dante, 1999). The popularity of the mod led to professional developers adding a capture the flag mode to their games. Today it is a staple multiplayer option in first-person shooter games. Several popular player-made mods have been turned into standalone commercial games including the 1999 mod *CounterStrike* and, more recently, *DayZ* – a mod that turns the military simulation *ARMA II* into a zombie horror game (Yin-Poole, 2012b).

Modding is not without its risks to the games industry. Rockstar North, the developers of *Grand Theft Auto: San Andreas*, faced a political backlash due to the *Hot Coffee* mod, which gave players access to an otherwise inaccessible sex game that had been abandoned during development but left hidden within the code due to the difficulty of removing it. The mod resulted in major American retailers removing the game from its shelves, class action lawsuits and a Federal Trade Commission investigation (Parkin, 2012). More recently *School Shooter: North American Tour 2012*, a mod for *Half-Life 2*, sparked outrage, some of which was aimed at the developers of the original game (Stratford, 2011; Tito, 2011). Such risks, coupled with the legal concerns about maintaining ownership, have led to differing attitudes within the games industry towards modding (Vanderhoef, 2009) but, at this time, the practice is established enough that it seems unlikely that this means of dissolving the barrier between player and developer will disappear.

Internet communities

As well as providing a means to distribute mods, the internet encouraged the growth of online multiplayer games, including multiplayer role-playing games that bring together thousands of players in persistent virtual worlds. The origins of these games pre-date the internet and most can trace their lineage back to a 1979 game called *MUD*. Developed by two students at the University of Essex, *MUD* used the computer networks of the day to allow players to play together in a fantasy world described in text. The game became something of an unplanned social experiment that saw the emergence of a virtual culture among players with its own slang and social norms which defined the game as much as the decisions of its creators

(Donovan, 2010). This player-generated culture continues in present-day virtual worlds and sometimes leads to tension between the players who populate these worlds and their creators. One demonstration of this is the 'Warrior Protest' of January 2005 in *World of Warcraft*, where players who objected to changes to the game organized a protest within the game prompting threats of bans from its developer (Taylor, 2006). Less overtly confrontational challenges also emerge in such games, including the need to manage virtual economies to prevent inflationary or deflationary spirals that could ruin the enjoyment of players. The need for the developers of these games to manage the players day to day requires developers to think of their games as ongoing, evolving services rather than one-off products, which reinforces the idea that games are works in progress rather than products that are ever truly finished.

The internet has also allowed like-minded players to congregate online, for example on social media websites or internet forums, and this has led to the games industry paying more attention to how it manages and interacts with the player community. This is a marked shift from the earlier years of the industry, when game publishers would have little direct contact with their audience since it usually needed to go through retailers or the media to reach them. This change is most clearly illustrated by the growing importance of community managers within the industry, whose role is summarized by Samantha Russell, the director of community relations at Codemasters, as "being the voice of the players within the company and being the voice of the company to the players" (personal communication, 16 May 2013).

As well as carrying out promotional work to keep players excited about their company's products, both Russell and Hollie Bennett (personal communication, 21 May 2013), the UK digital and community manager at Sony Computer Entertainment Europe, say the feedback they get from players feeds into the game development process. "Being able to talk directly to the players has completely altered how we approach game development," says Russell. "If we want input from players on a proposed direction in which we are going or thinking about going we can, within half an hour, have actual usable data" (personal communication, 16 May 2013).

Another way that players are having an increased input into game development is through crowdfunding, where the audiences donate money towards the cost of making a game. This method of funding game development has encouraged some developers to make games in genres that would be regarded as too niche to make financial sense to large game publishers, such as Double Fine Productions' adventure game *Broken Age* which raised more than $3.3m from more than 87,000 backers (Dutton, 2012). Double Fine's Tim Schafer said: "We could not have gone to a publisher and said we wanted to make a graphic adventure – at all. Maybe if we were only asking for $100,000 or something" (quoted in Klepek, 2012).

Even bolder is *Project CARS*, a racing simulation that at the time of writing is being developed by the London-based developer Slightly Mad Studios. The company asked players to fund the game and offered a cut of the profits and the chance to have a direct input into the game's development in return. While its profit-sharing model has faced difficulties due to rules surrounding investment schemes, the initiative has allowed players to get highly involved in the day to day of game development from testing the latest version of the game to choosing what features should or should not be included in the game (Donovan, 2013).

Closer links between players and developers are, however, not always harmonious and both Bennett and Russell have received death threats from angry fans. "I've had plenty of death threats," says Bennett:

> [The fighting game] *Tekken* was a big one for death threats but it does depend on your community ... the first-person shooter people are probably a lot more demanding than the Japanese role-playing game community because they are so used to not getting what they want that when they do it's much more of a treat for them.
> (personal communication, 21 May 2013)

According to Russell, this abuse reflects how involved game players are with the medium:

> [The community] can be very demanding but that's just a manifestation of their passion for gaming ... It does take a specific sort of person to deal with that. We get abuse almost daily, whether via emails or on the internet. We've even had death threats threatening that they will come to the gates and wait for us to leave and then get us ... The really great community manager will be able to see through the baiting, trolling and sniping and sift out what the crux of the problem is and deal with it in a professional way.
> (personal communication, 21 May 2013)

As the above shows the internet has brought the games industry into closer contact with its audience and, while this sometimes causes conflict, it makes it more likely that players' opinions will influence how games are made and run. In the case of crowdfunding, the relationship is even deeper with the audience doubling as consumer and paymaster.

From these trends it is clear that the audience-driven change to the end of *Mass Effect 3* is less strange that it may at first seem, even if it remains unusual. As software-based products video games are an inherently flexible medium and the actions of both players and the games industry over time have served to reinforce the idea that games are and should be malleable. The games industry's closer ties with players through community managers have also made the industry more aware of and reactive to player reactions and opinions.

Conclusion

Since its inception the games industry has been moving towards a collaborative relationship with its audience, despite the death threats and controversial mods that come with that closer relationship. As a result the video game audience is increasingly having an influence on how and what games are made that goes significantly beyond the choice of buying or playing a game, and given that there is little sense of either the audience or the industry wanting to reverse this trend, this blurring of the audience–creator boundary seems likely to increase further in the future.

Further reading

Lev Manovich's (2009) paper "The practice of everyday (media) life: From mass consumption to mass cultural production?" looks at the changing relationship between player and creator in a wider context. Lars Konzack's (2007) "Rhetorics of computer and video game research" is a useful introduction to the field of game studies as are the essays collected in Katie Salen and Eric Zimmerman's *The Game Design Reader* (2006). My own book, *Replay: The History of Video Games* (2010), covers many of the historical developments mentioned above in more detail. Finally, the player-created levels of *LittleBigPlanet 2* (2011) are a good example of user-generated content in video games.

References

Allen, R. (n.d.) "What is Action Replay?" eHow. Retrieved from http://www.ehow.co.uk/info_8720519_action-replay.html

Amis, M. (1982) *Invasion of the Space Invaders*. London: Hutchinson.

Atari Inc. (1972) *PONG* [computer program] USA: Atari Inc.

BioWare (2007) *Mass Effect* [computer program] Canada: Microsoft Game Studios.

Crosscade (2012) Mass Effect 3 – Ending movie comparison – All the colors. [online video] Retrieved from http://www.youtube.com/watch?v=rPelM2hwhJA&feature=player_embedded

Dailly, M. (2004) "The complete history of DMA design." Retrieved from http://www.dmadesign.org

Dante (1999) "A look at CTF, *Planet Quake*." Retrieved from http://planetquake.gamespy.com/View.php?view=MOTW.Detail&id=61

Donovan, T. (2010) *Replay: The History of Video Games*. Lewes: Yellow Ant.

——(2013) "Driving ambition: pCARS, crowdfunding and the FSA." Eurogamer.net. Retrieved from http://www.eurogamer.net/articles/2013-04-18-driving-ambition-pcars-crowdfunding-and-the-fsa

Dutton, F. (2012) "Double Fine adventure Kickstarter total tops $3.3m." Eurogamer.net. Retrieved from http://www.eurogamer.net/articles/2012-03-13-double-fine-adventure-kickstarter-total-tops-USD3-2m

Fernández-Vara, C. (2009) "Play's the thing: A framework to study videogames as performance." Proceedings of the Digital Games Research Association. Retrieved from http://www.academia.edu/233644/Plays_the_Things_A_Framework_to_Study_Videogames_as_Performance

iTunes (2013) "Angry Birds version history." Retrieved from https://itunes.apple.com/gb/app/angry-birds/id343200656?mt=8

James Au, W. (2002) "Triumph of the mod." Salon. Retrieved from http://www.salon.com/2002/04/16/modding

Jones, S. E. (2008) *The Meaning of Video Games: Gaming and Textual Strategies*. New York: Routledge (p. 168).

Kent, S. L. (2001) *The Ultimate History of Video Games*. New York: Three Rivers Press.

Kirkpatrick, G. (2012) "Constitutive tensions of gaming's field: UK gaming magazines and the formation of gaming culture 1981–95." Game Studies. Retrieved from http://gamestudies.org/1201/articles/kirkpatrick

Klepek, P. (2012) "$1.6 million and counting." Giant Bomb. Retrieved from http://www.giantbomb.com/articles/16-million-and-counting/1100-3981

Konzack, L. (2007) "Rhetorics of computer and video game research." In J. P. Williams and J. H. Smith (eds.) *The Players' Realm: Studies on the Culture of Video Games and Gaming*. Jefferson, NC: McFarland & Company.

Langshaw, M. (2012) "*Mass Effect 3* fans campaign to change ending." Digital Spy. Retrieved from http://www.digitalspy.co.uk/gaming/news/a370523/mass-effect-3-fans-campaign-to-change-ending.html

Levy, S. (2010) *Hackers: Heroes of the Computer Revolution*. Sebastopol, CA: O'Reilly. Kindle ebook edition.

Lincoln, R. (2012) "*Mass Effect 3* ending-hatred: 5 reasons the fans are right." Game Front. Retrieved from http://www.gamefront.com/mass-effect-3-ending-hatred-5-reasons-the-fans-are-right

Manovich, L. (2009) "The practice of everyday (media) life: From mass consumption to mass cultural production?" *Critical Inquiry*, 35(2), 319–31.

Mäyrä, F., Van Loo, J. and Quandt, T. (2013) "Disciplinary identity of game scholars: An outline." Proceedings of DiGRA 2013: DeFragging Game Studies. Retrieved from http://people.uta.fi/~tlilma/disciplinary_identity.pdf

Morisset, T. (2013) "The end of the end as we know it: A philosophical look at the narration in *Mass Effect*." Inter-Disciplinary.net. Retrieved from http://www.inter-disciplinary.net/critical-issues/wp-content/uploads/2013/05/morissetvideopaper.pdf

Munkittrick, K. (2012) "Why *Mass Effect* is the most important science fiction universe of our generation." io9. Retrieved from http://io9.com/5886178/why-mass-effect-is-the-most-important-science-fiction-universe-of-our-generation

Parkin, S. (2012) "Who spilled Hot Coffee?" Eurogamer.net. Retrieved from http://www.eurogamer.net/articles/2012-11-30-who-spilled-hot-coffee

Salen, K. and Zimmerman, E. (2006) *The Game Design Reader*. Cambridge, MA: MIT Press.

Sterling, J. (2012) "*Mass Effect 3* makes over $200 million in sales." Destructoid. Retrieved from http://www.destructoid.com/mass-effect-3-makes-over-200-million-in-sales-227119.phtml

Stratford, L. (2011) "Jack Thompson targets Gabe Newell over School Shooter mod." BeefJack. Retrieved from http://beefjack.com/news/jack-thompson-targets-gabe-newell-over-school-shooter-mod

Taylor, T. L. (2006) "Beyond management: Considering participatory design and governance in player culture." First Monday. Retrievedc from http://firstmonday.org/ojs/index.php/fm/article/view/1611/1526

Tito, G. (2011) "Inside the sick mind of a School Shooter mod." *The Escapist*. Retrieved from http://www.escapistmagazine.com/news/view/108065-Inside-the-Sick-Mind-of-a-School-Shooter-Mod

Toms, K. (1982) *Football Manager* [computer program] UK: Addictive Games.

Vanderhoef, J. (2009) "Cease and desist: Games culture and copyright laws." Press Start to Drink. Retrieved from http://pressstarttodrink.blogspot.co.uk/2009/11/cease-and-desist-games-culture-and.html

White, S. and Sutherland, A. (1983) *Ant Attack* [computer program] UK: Quicksilva.

Yin-Poole, W. (2012a) "BioWare announces *Mass Effect 3: Extended Cut*." Eurogamer.net. Retrieved from http://www.eurogamer.net/articles/2012-04-05-bioware-announces-mass-effect-3-extended-cut

——(2012b) "Standalone DayZ confirmed." Eurogamer.net. Retrieved from http://www.eurogamer.net/articles/2012-08-07-standalone-dayz-confirmed

Your Computer (1983, April) Virgin Games Ltd, p. 154. [advert]

49
From letters to tweeters
Media communities of opinion

Karin Wahl-Jorgensen

Mass media have always served as central institutions of the public sphere, providing opportunities for public debate and opinion formation. This chapter addresses the historical development of mediated forums for public participation, paying particular attention to the relationship between technological change and transformations in the role of media professionals as gatekeepers in mediated communities of opinion. It argues that successive waves of technological change have had profound consequences in terms of broadening access as well as diversifying forms, platforms and genres through which communities of opinion have taken shape. In the process, journalists and media organizations have been compelled to loosen their grip on editorial control over the mediated expression of public opinion. This shift has taken place alongside – and in part as a result of – developments through which the ideal of interactivity and the valorization of participation have gained ever more purchase.

The early history of communities of opinion: Tracing the development of letters to the editor

Early print publications, by most measures the first mass media, made little distinction between opinion and news content, or, correspondingly, between opinion pieces in the form of letters to the editor and reports on current events. In the prominent account of Jürgen Habermas in *The Structural Transformation of the Public Sphere* (1989), for example, the first newspapers emerged as the organic continuation of private newsletters. Before the advent of the steam train and the telegraph, printers relied on news arriving by postal coach or ship, and stories published in the early British and American press were often several months old. In this information-poor environment, printers and editors welcomed any publishable material. The Philadelphia printer Andrew Bradford, writing in the early eighteenth century, justified his printing of a personal letter in terms of the lack of other suitable news: "Having but few remarkable occurrences to fill up our paper at present, we believe it will not be unacceptable to our readers, to incert [sic] the following letter from a Gentleman to his Friend upon the loss of his only Daughter" (Hart, 2001: 113). This dynamic encouraged the inclusion of correspondence from members of the public, sowing the seeds of the creation of communities of opinion within the pages of the newspaper.

Furthermore, it was opinion writing, rather than news content, which served as the main selling point of the printing press. This was perhaps as a result of the dearth of fresh and relevant local news in print publications and the fact that news could, for many people, be more reliably gathered through conversations and gossip in local communities as well as private letters. The emerging British political press of the early eighteenth century made the critical opinion essay, in the form of a letter to the editor, a centerpiece of the newspaper. For example, the *Daily Spectator* quickly became popular for its political essays, written by professional authors, including the novelist Daniel Defoe, whose contributions came in the form of anonymous letters. Early periodicals also drew on letter-writing from members of the public. "The periodical fostered [a] sense of engagement by incorporating readers' writing [...], establishing the appearance of dialogue between editors and readers and sometimes among readers themselves, and representing readers writing about a variety of public and private concerns" (Shevelow, 1989: 44). In the United States, after an initial period of relatively bland print publications that were generally supportive of the colonial government, solicited letters quickly came to be used as a vehicle for the generation of critical debate. When Thomas Fleet took over the *Boston Weekly Rehearsal* in the 1730s, he "solicited opinion writers by inviting 'all Gentlemen of Leisure and Capacity ... to write anything of a political nature, that tends to enlighten and serve the Publick, to communicate their productions, provided they are not overlong'" (Hart, 2001: 111). Letter writers to the colonial press contributed their opinions about political matters large and small, having their say on everything from the icy streets of Philadelphia to the need for more watchmen, firemen and street lights (ibid.: 117). As such, letters in the early newspapers generated a sense of a broader debate on topics of common concern, even if it was not premised on the strict separation between the contributions of professional writers and correspondents and 'ordinary' citizens.

The separation of news and opinion, and therefore of stories from letters, was integral to the slow but steady professionalization of journalism. One indication of this separation can be seen in the demarcation of letters to the editor as a distinctive genre and forum within the newspaper. The *New York Times* published its first letter to the editor five days after its first issue came out, on 18 September 1851 (Rosenthal, 1971: 135). The paper sought to make its letters section "a forum for the consideration of all questions of public importance, and to that end to invite intelligent discussion from all shades of opinion" (Seigel, 1972: 3–4). Since the emergence of newspaper sections specifically devoted to letters from readers, they have served as important forums for debate about issues that touch on the lives of people in local, national and global communities. Although newspaper editors are quick to point out that narrowly local topics such as potholes and dog fouling in city parks top the agenda of debates on letters pages (e.g. Wahl-Jorgensen, 2007), they have also functioned as important forums for debating and crystallizing the positions of key social movements, from abolitionists to women's rights (e.g. Chambers, Steiner and Fleming, 2004).

From print to broadcast: Talk radio and audience participation on television

Letters sections have always served as a *constructed* community of mediated public opinion, where decisions about which letters to include and which to reject have been made on the basis of distinctive and institutionalized rules of selection, implemented by newsworkers who have served as gatekeepers to guarantee the quality of contributions (Wahl-Jorgensen, 2002). However, even if letters were, for a long time, the most prominent site for the creation of communities of opinion, other traditional mass media, particularly radio and television, have given birth to a much wider range of forums for mediated discussion. Audience participation in radio genres has been around as long as the medium itself, and has consistently offered a space for the representation of the public, claiming to speak for 'the people' (Loviglio, 2002). For instance, the network radio program *Vox Pop*, broadcast between 1932 and 1948, searched for the voice of the American people by interviewing individuals in the streets, with the stated intention of "posing questions of 'spectacular unimportance'" (Loviglio, 2002: 91). Community and shortwave radio stations have provided an important way for otherwise disenfranchised groups to gain a foothold in the public sphere (Fairchild, 2001: 89; Riismandel, 2002). Talk radio has been a key venue for 'populist deliberation', through which citizens may bypass the mainstream media to make their opinions heard and hold politicians to account (Page and Tannenbaum, 1996; Thornborrow and Fitzgerald, 2013), even if many observers have raised concerns over the incivility and intolerance often characterizing the genre, as well as for its domination by people with extreme and polarized political positions (Sobieraj and Berry, 2011).

A significant and related innovation in participatory programing was that of the audience participation talk show which rose to prominence in the late 1980s with programs such as Kilroy in the UK and the Oprah Winfrey show in the US, both broadcasting their first season in 1986. One of the first major studies of such shows, Livingstone and Lunt's (1994) *Talk on Television*, looked at the opportunities for regular citizens to contribute to public debate, and how program makers encourage and discourage particular forms of participation. Their work demonstrated that talk shows carve out a space to "attempt to confront established power with the lived experience of ordinary people" (Livingstone and Lunt, 1994: 160). They proposed that television talk shows, by combining opportunities for personal story-telling and public debate, may "support an emancipatory public sphere" (ibid.). Talk shows have provided a voice for marginalized groups, including women, ethnic minorities and lesbians and gays (Gamson, 1998). They have provided audiences with both a language and an awareness "about how their personal experiences intertwine with politics on issues such as abortion and welfare" (Shattuc, 1997: 195). As such, talk shows may challenge conventional understandings of 'proper' public debate. Laura Grindstaff (2002) has suggested that the power of talk shows comes from how they engage their audiences emotionally, in moments of "joy, sorrow, rage or remorse expressed in visible, bodily terms that are the hallmark of the genre" (ibid.: 19–20). Nonetheless, because of the fact that the genre is frequently, and increasingly, focused on personal story-telling and on the public display of spectacular and sometimes violent emotion, critics of television talk shows have long worried about their cultural effects, asserting that they erode "social barriers, inhibitions and cultural distinctions" (Abt and Seesholtz, 1994: 171) and could be seen as part of a trend towards a "rude, nasty stubborn politics" (Shea and Fiorina, 2012). Such criticisms take issue with the irrational and often uncivil tone of discussion which may violate basic norms of conduct and tend to focus on personal problems over matters of common concern.

These worries have only intensified with the proliferation of genres based on the experiences of 'ordinary people' and with a distinct emphasis on 'lifestyle' issues since the late 1990s, including a greater variety of talk shows, as well as reality-based programing. As Lunt (2009) has pointed out, such programs might also be seen to contribute to a normative social order based on their articulation of the politics of identity or the 'project of the self' central to reflexive modernity, even if this does not conform to conventional understandings of the political. Indeed, the increasing presence of ordinary people in the media has been theorized as a 'demotic turn' which, while involving the cultivation of 'ordinary celebrity' does not necessarily equate to an enhancement of broader empowerment and political participation (Turner, 2010).

What talk shows, radio phone-ins and letters share, then, is the formation of *mediated* communities of opinion which generate debate on the large and small, public and private matters which preoccupy us all and, in the process of doing so, also foster larger "imagined communities" (Anderson, 1991) of audiences who orient themselves towards these discussions and may continue them in interpersonal contexts. Platforms for opinion expressed in conventional print and broadcast media, including letters to the editor, television and radio talk shows, and audience participation programs, have allowed editors, journalists and program makers to shape the tone and content of mediated public debate. They have functioned as an integral part of media content, whether as a section in the newspaper, or incorporated into programing in the form of television news vox pops or audience participation shows. This mode of incorporation into conventional media operations and professional practices has, however, been challenged by technological change. This, in turn, complicates the relationship between access, mediation and professional intervention in and contribution to communities of opinion.

Online communities of opinion, social media and public participation: Challenging the role of news organizations as gatekeepers?

The emergence of the internet and, subsequently, convergent forms of news content which enable greater interactivity in a proliferation of forums, genres and forms, ranging from blogs, comments and user-generated content to social media, has had profound consequences. First of all, the technological advances of the internet have enabled greater interactivity (e.g. Kammer, 2013). Starting with the earliest experiments in the 1990s and early 2000s, media organizations enabled users to comment on online stories, while the introduction of blogs also enabled further instantaneous dialogue, for the first time generating communities of opinion that could respond in real time to unfolding news events (see Steensen, 2011). The internet was welcomed with much fanfare by observers who saw it as an opportunity to "produce virtual public spheres" (Papacharissi, 2002) and hence revolutionize mediated public participation. For example, proponents of radical democracy viewed the new communicative opportunities in terms of how they might be "constitutive of alternative political communities, new subject positions, new possibilities for acting in concern, and ultimately radical new democratic cultures that challenge dominant political assumptions" (Dahlberg and Siapera, 2007: 11–12). These were valued for their potential to give voice to otherwise marginalized, oppressed or alternative groups in society (ibid.). As discussed in further detail below, however, questions of inequality in access, or the so-called 'digital divide', have always been salient among those more skeptical about the transformative possibilities of new technologies and the communities of opinion created by them.

Nonetheless, new technologies have certainly contributed to destabilizing power relations in the public sphere, particularly with respect to the production and distribution of content and opinion. These trends began with the emergence of citizen journalism and user-generated content. User-generated content – the views, images and videos contributed by members of the public – first gained prominence after the 2004 Indian Ocean tsunami, where eyewitnesses were able to film the disaster as it unfolded, providing news organizations with unprecedented immediacy in their coverage (Allan, 2009). In the UK, the 7/7 bombings in July 2005 represented the watershed for "accidental journalism" carried out by ordinary citizens (Boaden, 2008; Allan, 2013). The use of audience materials in the context of major breaking news events, particularly natural disasters, was focused on information provision, rather than the sharing of opinion, even if such 'citizen witnessing' has always taken place from a particular subject position, which implies, at the very least, an investment and an interest in current affairs (Allan, 2013; see also Andén-Papadopoulos and Pantti, 2011). News organizations' heady embrace of opinion-based user-generated content over the next few years heralded the increasing prominence and centrality ascribed to such audience participation, which was seen as a useful venue for generating public debate on major news stories in ways that might enhance public participation, bolster relationships with audiences and generate sources for follow-ups and future stories. At the same time, critics have also suggested that the rise of user-generated content represents the nefarious outsourcing of newswork to members of the public (e.g. Jenkins and Deuze, 2008).

The increasing use of audience materials in the conventional media worked in tandem with the creation of new platforms and forums where audiences could participate by contributing news and opinion, leading to the rise of 'citizen journalism' (e.g. Allan and Thorsen, 2009). In a keynote speech and subsequent blog post on the phenomenon published in 2008, the BBC's then director of news, Helen Boaden, framed the growing awareness of citizen journalism within the corporation in terms of audience relations and a subsequent shift of resources in its direction:

> The biggest challenge for us is about our relationship to the people who matter most – our audiences. It's about capturing and keeping their hearts and minds. And for audiences who want to join in, that means including

them in the process of making the news. Our journalism is now fully embracing the experiences of our audiences, sharing their stories, using their knowledge and hosting their opinions; we're acting as a conduit between different parts of our audience; and we're being more open and transparent than we have ever been [...] [W]ith blogs in particular – but also podcasts and videoblogs – the ability of the public to express opinion in public has exploded – especially in the USA – and they no longer need to be 'hosted' by broadcasters.

(Boaden, 2008)

Boaden's position illustrates journalists' complex orientation towards the proliferation of forums for the sharing of content and opinion: the promise of new platforms as an unprecedented opportunity to connect with audiences has often been a key driver for both commercial and public service media, but at the same time, news media hosting such spaces and therefore taking responsibility for them also need to exercise extensive vigilance. Concerns about the monitoring, moderation and quality control of online forums have remained central for news organizations and have, over time, led to more considered constraints and limitations on the spaces for discussion, with the closing down of discussion boards and comments originally hosted by broadcasters and newspapers (Wahl-Jorgensen, Williams and Wardle, 2010).[1] Such concerns highlight a contemporary twist on an apparent paradox that has always plagued sites for public debate and opinion formation. They are viewed as central to democratic practice and the formation of a public sphere for discussion of matters of common concern, and as such represent a key responsibility for media organisations. But their management requires extensive resources, and individuals participating in discussion through such venues are not necessarily reflective of the demographics or views of a broader public.

On the other hand, the shift also challenges the conventional power relations of the public sphere, where participation in the form of opinion expression is no longer the preserve of mainstream media. Instead, participants have been granted a greater autonomy over the production and distribution of opinion, and the associated creation of communities of opinion. Media organizations, which have tended to function as the 'gatekeepers', have now become 'gatewatchers' or curators, sorting through and publicizing information available elsewhere on the internet (Bruns, 2005: 2). This gradual shift has taken away control from the media organizations which previously served as the loci of public debate and participation. This has worried observers for several reasons. First, some suggest that the quality of participation suffers from the conditions of anonymity and lack of face-to-face interaction, which has meant that social norms of civility are more easily violated online. Furthermore, there is concern that the sheer proliferation of sites for public discussion has led to the fragmentation and individualization of debate (e.g. Papacharissi, 2002). Relatedly, this proliferation raises questions about a potential trade-off between the quantity and quality of opinion expression.

The past few years have also seen the rise of hyperlocal blogs which often include both opinion-based content alongside local news content as further opportunities for debate. Though the emergence of such hyperlocal news sites has been broadly welcomed in the context of a crisis in local news provision, "where local newspapers are operating on skeleton staffs, where they've already been closed down, or where there was never much mainstream media to speak of in the first place" (Williams et al., 2012), it also represents a deprofessionalization of journalism and, relatedly, highlights the emerging curatorial role of news media in communities of opinion.

The shift in the locus of control over communities of opinion has been further consolidated with the birth of social media. Since the mid 2000s, social media or Web 2.0 venues such as Twitter, YouTube and Facebook have enabled users to share their own content independently of the intervention of media organizations. This development has been seen to offer the promise of a "networked citizen-centred perspective providing opportunities to connect the private sphere of autonomous political identity to a multitude of chosen political spaces" (Loader and Mercea, 2012: 2; see also Benkler, 2006). Yet there has been considerable debate about whether the interactivity of the online world, from the first wave of blogs and discussion boards to the second wave of social media, has transformed the nature of democratic debate. If early observers of the online world expressed great hopes for the emancipatory potential of new technologies, these hopes have been echoed by the later wave of social media enthusiasts, who have pointed to the radically decentering and distributive nature of Web 2.0 forums dedicated to the sharing of opinion and information by 'ordinary people' (Loader and Mercea, 2012). But utopian dreams have been tempered by evidence that consecutive innovations in participatory forums have not actually transformed democratic practice for a variety of reasons. First of all, the persistent digital divide, which means that some groups and individuals are systematically underrepresented in online debates due to lack of access or the cultural capital, time and interest required to participate, stands in the way of egalitarian deliberation. In the contemporary ecology of communities of opinion, there is evidence instead of an "unequal spread of social ties with a few giant nodes" and a limited number of influential voices (Loader and Mercea, 2012: 4). As Loader and Mercea have observed:

> Instead of facilitating an increasing host of active citizen-users, social media perhaps more typically facilitates [sic] online shopping, gossip and file-sharing between friends already known to each other.
>
> (ibid.)

This analysis points to two concerns. First, that much of the discussion which takes place in social media is not about political matters but is instead based on consumption and the sharing of personal information. This is consistent with longer-standing concerns about the tension between the discussion of matters of common concern in communities of opinion and the actual practice of discussions focused on the 'project of the self', emerging through personal experience and story-telling (Lunt 2009). Second, the observation that discussion in social media takes place "between friends already known to each other" taps into broader issues around the selective communities of opinion fostered by online communities in general and social media in particular. The preference for interacting and carrying out discussion with like-minded individuals is not a new development brought about by technological change. As Diana Mutz has demonstrated, people, if given any choice, will systematically opt for political discussion with others of a similar ideological inclination, "secure in the knowledge that their basic values and political goals [a]re shared" (Mutz, 2006: 16). Nonetheless, these trends might be strengthened by technological change. As Pariser (2011) has warned, the selective communities of social media combine with the sophisticated personalization algorithms of the big industry players, including Facebook, Google and Yahoo, to generate a "filter bubble" which constitutes our own unique information universe, through which we "receive mainly news that is pleasant, familiar and confirms our beliefs" (ibid.) He demonstrates how our "past interests will determine what we are exposed to in the future, leaving less room for the unexpected encounters that spark creativity, innovation and the democratic exchange of ideas" (ibid.: Kindle edition location 12). Put differently, the increasingly personalized, targeted and tailored nature of interactions in today's media ecology may mean that there is, in fact, limited opportunity to participate in a broader debate involving all stakeholders, regardless of specific personal interests or political views.

In terms of conventional understandings of political activity, it appears that pre-existing groups, including activists, social movements and political parties, have benefited from and made great use of social media (Bengtsson and Christensen, 2012). Though the jury is still out on whether they are "replicating or challenging existing imbalances" (Mascheroni, 2012: 222), most research has found "at best a limited effect on the propensity to be actively involved in political affairs" (Bengtsson and Christensen, 2012: 133), though some evidence suggests that otherwise disengaged citizens may be mobilized by new opportunities (ibid.).

Conclusion

This chapter has argued that mass media have always played a key role in the formation of communities of opinion, but that successive waves of technological change, particularly the invention of the internet and social media, have taken away some of the control over such spaces from conventional news organizations. The proliferation of expressive opportunities has resulted in the fragmentation of public debate and the increasing personalization of participation; trends which generate both opportunities and challenges. Some evidence suggests that emerging forums have empowered marginalized and previously disengaged groups and citizens. Nonetheless, social inequalities continue to be reflected in such communities of opinion. But journalists are no longer acting as the main gatekeepers of the public sphere, and the power to determine which topics should be on the agenda, and how they should be discussed, has been radically redistributed.

Further reading

Stuart Allan and Einar Thorsen's (2009) edited volume *Citizen Journalism: Global Perspectives* contains a variety of useful contributions on the phenomenon of citizen journalism. Axel Bruns' 2005 work, *Gatewatching: Collaborative Online News Production*, contributes a further exploration of changes in news production and related transformations in the role of journalists. Sonia Livingstone and Peter Lunt (1994) offer a pioneering study of television talk shows in their *Talk on Television: Audience Participation and Public Debate*. In Zizi Papacharissi's (2010) *A Private Sphere: Democracy in a Digital Age*, readers can find a sophisticated analysis of the consequences of technological change for the nature of the public sphere. Finally, Karin Wahl-Jorgensen's (2007) *Journalists and the Public: Newsroom Culture, Letters to the Editor, and Democracy* presents an in-depth study of letters to the editor.

Note

1 For example, the BBC closed down a range of sports and music-related discussion boards following the Graf Report into the corporation's online activities in 2004 (see http://news.bbc.co.uk/1/hi/entertainment/3866355.stm). This move reflected a broader view of such discussion boards as difficult to moderate and relatively peripheral to the public service mission of the corporation.

References

Abt, V. and Seesholtz, M. (1994) "The shameless world of Phil, Sally and Oprah: Television talk shows and the deconstructing of society." *Journal of Popular Culture*, 28(1), 171–101.

Allan, S. (2009) "Histories of citizen journalism." In S. Allan and E. Thorsen (eds.) *Citizen Journalism: Global Perspectives*. New York: Peter Lang (pp. 17–32).

——(2013) *Citizen Witnessing*. Cambridge: Polity.

Allan, S. and Thorsen, E. (2009) "Introduction." In S. Allan and E. Thorsen (eds.) *Citizen Journalism: Global Perspectives*. New York: Peter Lang (pp. 1–16).

Andén-Papadopoulos, K. and Pantti, M. (eds.) (2011) *Amateur Images and Global News*. Bristol: Intellect Books.

Anderson, B. (1991) *Imagined Communities: Reflections on the Origin and Spread of Nationalism*. London: Verso.

Bengtsson, Å. and Christensen, H. S. (2012) "The political competence of internet participants: Evidence from Finland." In B. D. Loader and D. Mercea (eds.) *Social Media and Democracy: Innovations in Participatory Politics*. London and New York: Routledge (pp. 131–49).

Benkler, Y. (2006) *The Wealth of Networks: How Social Production Transforms Markets and Freedom*. New Haven, CT: Yale University Press.

Boaden, H. (2008) "The role of citizen journalism in modern democracy." BBC News: Editors' blog, Thursday, 13 November. Retrieved from http://www.bbc.co.uk/blogs/theeditors/2008/11/the_role_of_citizen_journalism.html

Bruns, A. (2005) *Gatewatching: Collaborative Online News Production*. New York: Peter Lang.

Chambers, D., Steiner, L. and Fleming, C. (2004) *Women and Journalism*. London and New York: Routledge.

Dahlberg, L. and Siapera, E. (2007) "Introduction: Tracing radical democracy and the internet." In L. Dahlberg and E. Siapera (eds.) *Radical Democracy and the Internet: Interrogating Theory and Practice*. London: Palgrave Macmillan (pp. 1–16).

Fairchild, C. (2001) *Community Radio and Public Culture*. Cresskill, NJ: Hampton Press.

Gamson, J. (1998) *Freaks Talk Back: Tabloid Talk Shows and Sexual Nonconformity*. Chicago, IL: University of Chicago Press.

Grindstaff, L. (2002) *The Money Shot: Trash, Class, and the Making of TV Talk Shows*. Chicago, IL: University of Chicago Press.

Habermas, J. (1989) *The Structural Transformation of the Public Sphere*. Cambridge, MA: MIT Press.

Hart, R. (2001) "Citizen discourse and political participation: A survey." In W. L. Bennett and R. M. Entman (eds.) *Mediated Politics: Communication in the Future of Democracy*. Cambridge and New York: Cambridge University Press (pp. 407–32).

Jenkins, H. and Deuze, M. (2008) "Editorial: Convergence culture." *Convergence: The International Journal of Research into New Media Technologies*, 14(1), 5–12.

Kammer, A. (2013) *News on the Web: Instantaneity, Multimodality, Interactivity, and Hypertextuality on Danish News Website*. PhD thesis, Faculty of Humanities, University of Copenhagen.

Livingstone, S. and Lunt, P. (1994) *Talk on Television: Audience Participation and Public Debate*. New York: Routledge.

Loader, B. D. and Mercea, D. (2012) "Networking democracy? Social media innovations in participatory politics." In B. D. Loader and D. Mercea (eds.) *Social Media and Democracy: Innovations in Participatory Politics*. London and New York: Routledge (pp. 1–10).

Loviglio, J. (2002) "Vox pop: Network radio and the voice of the people." In M. Hilmes and J. Loviglio (eds.) *Radio Reader: Essays in the Cultural History of Radio*. New York and London: Routledge (pp. 89–112).

Lunt, P. (2009) "Television, public participation, and public service: From value consensus to the politics of identity." *The Annals of the American Academy of Political and Social Science*, 625(1), 128–38.

Mascheroni, G. (2012) "Online participation: New forms of civic and political engagement or just new opportunities for networked individualism." In B. D. Loader and D. Mercea (eds.) *Social Media and Democracy: Innovations in Participatory Politics*. London and New York: Routledge (pp. 207–23).

Mutz, D. (2006) *Hearing the Other Side: Deliberative Versus Participatory Democracy*. Cambridge and New York: Cambridge University Press.

Page, B. and Tannenbaum, J. (1996) "Populist deliberation and talk radio." *Journal of Communication*, 14, 371–88.

Papacharissi, Z. (2002) "The virtual sphere: The internet as a public sphere." *New Media & Society*, 4(1), 9–27.

——(2010) *A Private Sphere: Democracy in a Digital Age*. Cambridge: Polity.

Pariser, E. (2011) *The Filter Bubble: What the Internet is Hiding from You*. London: Penguin UK.

Riismandel, P. (2002) "Radio by and for the public: The death and resurrection of low-power radio." In M. Hilmes and J. Loviglio (eds.) *Radio Reader: Essays in the Cultural History of Radio*. New York and London: Routledge (pp. 423–51).

Rosenthal, I. (1971) "Who writes the 'letters to the editor'?" In A. Kirschner and L. Kirschner (eds.) *Journalism: Readings in Mass Media*. New York: Odyssey Press (pp. 135–42).

Seigel, K. (1972) *Talking Back to the New York Times: Letters to the Editor, 1951–1971*, New York: Quadrangle Books.

Shattuc, J. M. (1997) *The Talking Cure: TV Talk Shows and Women*. New York and London: Routledge.

Shea, D. M. and Fiorina, M. P. (2012) *Can We Talk? The Rise of Rude, Nasty Stubborn Politics*. New York: Pearson Higher Ed.

Shevelow, K. (1989) *Women and Print Culture*. London and New York: Routledge.

Sobieraj, S. and Berry, J. M. (2011) "From incivility to outrage: Political discourse in blogs, talk radio, and cable news." *Political Communication*, 28(1), 19–41.

Steensen, S. (2011) "Online journalism and the promises of new technology: A critical review and look ahead." *Journalism Studies*, 12(3), 311–27.

Thornborrow, J. and Fitzgerald, R. (2013) "Grab a pen and paper: Interaction v. interactivity in a political radio phone-in." *Journal of Language and Politics*, 12(1), 1–28.

Turner, G. (2010) *Ordinary People and the Media: The Demotic Turn*. London and Thousand Oaks, CA: Sage.

Wahl-Jorgensen, K. (2002) "Understanding the conditions for public discourse: Four rules for selecting letters-to-the-editor." *Journalism Studies*, 3, 69–81.

——(2007) *Journalists and the Public: Newsroom Culture, Letters to the Editor, and Democracy*. Creskill, NJ: Hampton Press.

Wahl-Jorgensen, K., Williams, A. and Wardle, C. (2010) "Audience views on user-generated content: Exploring the value of news from the bottom up." *Northern Lights*, 8, 177–94.

Williams, A., Turner, J., Harte, D., Dewey, S. and Mottershead, G. (2012) "The value of online hyperlocal news in the UK: Interim findings from a content analysis." Paper presented at the ECREA conference, Istanbul, October 24–27.

50
Digital memories and media of the future

Joanne Garde-Hansen

Pierre Nora (2002) has argued that "[u]nlike history, which has always been in the hands of the public authorities, of scholars and specialised peer groups, memory has acquired all the new privileges and prestige of a popular protest movement." It is not surprising, then, that the emergence of memory studies has coincided with a period of increasingly democratized media. For example, *The Collective Memory Reader* (2011) edited by Olick, Vinitzky-Seroussi and Levy devotes a whole section to Media and Modes of Transmission. They recognize the "material and technological substrata of individual and social memory" and that "there is an important interaction between brains and cultures and that brains are not the only or even the most important technologies of memory" (Olick, Vinitzky-Seroussi and Levy, 2011: 311). Technologies of memory have been commonplace for centuries and now there is a desire to organize and connect them. In a 2011 public lecture for the UK Arts Council, Jake Berger, Program Manager of the BBC's Digital Public Space, suggested:

> I would like you to imagine that every museum, archive, gallery, library, theatre and studio in the country could all be found next to each other and they each had each item in their collection on display. And imagine if the smallest organisations, archives and objects had the same level of visibility and accessibility as the big nationals. And imagine that all of this material and information were linked together. Now hold that thought for a minute.
> (Berger, 2011)

The imagined digital repository of the future (pan-BBC, pan-cultural, pan-organizational) drives digital enthusiasm. Yet media archive repurposing needs to forget a great deal to imagine such a project. As Assmann notes, the "continuous process of forgetting is part of social normality"; for "much must be continually forgotten to make place for new information, new challenges, and new ideas to face the present and future" (2011: 97). Media researchers have begun exploring how digital technologies produce a surfeit of memory (see Hoskins, 2009; Mayer-Schönberger, 2010; Reading 2011) as new ways of doing things remake old information (see Parikka, 2012, on media archaeology). For the BBC, remembering and forgetting are part of its cultural production and its production of culture. The case study in this chapter is localized to BBC archives management discourse where, during a working day, digital enthusiasm is squared with all that needs to be remembered: history of preservation criteria, rights management, commerciality, governance, increasing costs, degradation, format obsolescence, storage issues, policy changes, partnerships, staff changes and value for the licence fee payer. Here, to preserve, make accessible and repurpose in a digital economy requires that one remains mindful that the underlying economics of remembering are in danger of being forgotten.[1]

Memory boom

In the UK, 'new information technologies' have been characterized by equal amounts of celebration and fear and were singled out by Andreas Huyssen as producing a "boom in memory [...] inevitably accompanied by a boom in forgetting" (2003: 17). In *Save As ... : Digital Memories*, Garde-Hansen, Hoskins and Reading stated that "[k]eeping track, recording, retrieving, stockpiling, archiving, backing-up and saving are deferring one of our greatest fears of this century: information loss" (2009: 5). What if that loss is also the forgetting of a concept of a single medium upon which distinct media histories and archives have been built? What if, in the light of Google CEO Eric Schmidt's (2011) MacTaggart address to broadcasters, media organizations are compelled to think mnemonically: as recording and recordable (big) data, remembering preferences, predicting desires, catching up, while on demand? Such new mnemonic technologies may well be absorbed into media working practices but media of the future need to also serve media of the past: as heritage, archive and memory.

For Snickars, Schmidt's address promotes "new ways of looking" and a "shift in perspective, accentuating a web-centric view of the televisual landscape" (2012). There is implicit in Schmidt's address a concomitant demand for new ways of remembering; digital remembering connected to personal memory that is predictive and serendipitous. How far such digital remembering fossilizes media history into the examination of distinct forms and practices or re-energizes media heritage into 'born digital' content and metadata will determine the media (studies) of the future. While some may celebrate the death of a concept of a single medium, others, whose professional and academic careers depend upon it, may need to engage in a good deal of collective memory work and detailed periodization in order to keep the concept of a single medium separate from techno-cultural convergence. One way of doing this is to go back: historically, archaeologically and mnemonically.

Managing media archives

In the light of these techno-cultural issues, this chapter takes the argument presented in my book *Media and Memory* (2011), in chapter four: "Digital memories: The democratisation of archives", and examines production memories as archivists' reflections through a grounded theory approach. Here, I explore the 'production cultures' and 'industrial reflexivity', to borrow John Thornton Caldwell's (2008) terms, that position 'value' as what drives and is driven by remembering. My main focus is the BBC because the written and broadcast archives

> cover everything the BBC does [...] programmes about everything under the sun [...] as well as the functions of the BBC, which is one of the biggest commissioners of music and drama in the country. It runs choirs and orchestras, it runs the promenades concerts, it's a big newsgathering organization, that has monitoring as well as news dissemination [...]. It's an engineering organization, it has its own patents [...]. It's a major education body [...]. It deals with the government on all kinds of subjects [...]. It writes to all kinds of people about making programmes. Anybody you care to name in the twentieth century may have dealt with the BBC.
> (Written Archives Interview, Caversham 21-11-12)

BBC archive managers see technologies as re-mediating cultural heritage as a clear demonstration of their performance of corporate memory. On the one hand, mediated memory practices have commercial drivers (consider BBC Worldwide or the success of BBC online in the USA), highlighting the underlying economies at work in future-proofing institutional memory and global reach. On the other hand, for audiences (and in particular British audiences) the digital remediation of past media forms is an accessible, marketable and participatory heritage, connecting present and future users with deeply felt, lived and practiced popular cultures. Still framed by "technological logics and futurist projections" (Born, 2003: 775), the archive managers show cultural memory production in action and challenge researchers to accept the digital as endemic to media past, present and future. Yet they also remind us that financial feasibility is a key driver to what is archived and repurposed. Thus, while digital media archives can be said to provide a hub of 'globital' heritage and creativity (as Reading [2011] neologises the 'global' with 'bits' of information), such archives require a media policy that would secure their future as national memory (as much as corporate memory). Thus, the licence fee could be presented as the only way to secure such a valuable heritage, with the BBC's passionate industrial reflexivity, self-remembering and public memory work as the ultimate safeguard.

In what follows, I draw on a range of scholarship from Halbwachs (2011), van Dijck (2007), Caldwell (2008), Garde-Hansen (2011) and Ellis (2012) to reflect upon how BBC senior archive managers perceive their roles. The research relied on gaining the cooperation of individuals who are quite difficult to meet. The chapter uses industry research undertaken from September–December 2012 with the BBC Archives' senior team at Broadcasting House, London, and Caversham Park, Reading. Based upon face-to-face interviews, I focused on their 'trade talk' (as Caldwell [2008] defines it). That is, their critical and self-reflexive understanding of working in the BBC and their roles within their respective areas. They offered non-controversial, internal literature that I could review in order to understand how the corporation presents its own history to its staff. Between them, the managers had accumulated over 50 years of working experience of managing both analogue and digital content/records. The interviews offer a microanalysis of production research and contribute to an ongoing exploration of the ideas, themes and theory that evolve when researchers interact with participants.

Corporate memory of the BBC

In *Media and Memory* (2011), I defined the relationship between digital media, memory and archiving in four integrated ways. First, "through *digital media producing an archive* of history, heritage and memories"; second, "through *digital media as an archiving tool*, power and technology"; third, "through *digital media as a self-archiving phenomenon*"; and fourth, with "*digital media as a creative archive*" (Garde-Hansen, 2011: 72). In Information and Archives or in the Written Archives we have the discursive performance of a centralized, 'intellectual capital' of the BBC, drawing upon its 'institutionalized authority' as 'a custodian of the past' in the UK. These features are, as Cameron and Kenderine highlight in *Theorizing Digital Cultural Heritage: A Critical Discourse* (2007: 1) fundamental to heritage management in a digital age.

Thus, archive managers at the BBC are keen to promote the many types of archives the BBC holds, partially owns or employs: sound and moving image, correspondence, production notes, scripts, research material, documents, photography, fine art, sculpture and artefacts, maps, costumes, design materials, interview scripts and music as well as living archives of employees, retirees, producers, technicians, location scouts, extras, witnesses and fans. Reconnecting media archives with all these other forms of records, memories and artefacts has coincided with what van Dijck has termed the increase in 'mediated memory'. Here, ordinary "people decide what to record or what to remember without records, often being unaware of the cultural frameworks that inform their intentions and prefigure their decisions" (van Dijck, 2007: 6–7). On the one hand, the democratization of media means that the corporate memory of the BBC can be challenged to take account of competing personal and collective memories of those outside the organization. On the other hand, the BBC is keen to incorporate audience memories into its own cultural value frameworks (for example, BBC Radio 4/The British Library's The Listening Project since 2012; BFI's Missing Believed Wiped campaigns since 1993; the BBC's Missing Presumed Wiped 2008, 2011).

The Popular Memory Group of the 1980s had characterized the BBC as one of those institutions "linked to the national or local state" who operate "with high-cultural, educational, preservational or archival purposes" (1998: 255). Previously, Halbwachs had argued that collective memory is "a current of continuous thought" that "retains from the past only what still lives or is capable of living in the consciousness of the groups keeping the memory alive" (2011: 142–43). The BBC Written Archives at Caversham Park have had a significant role to play in preserving the BBC as an institution that produces heritage inside and outside of itself. Covering approximately 14,000 square feet of paper records, the archives offer controlled access to written material up until 1980 (paper records of the last decade or so are likely to be still in offices and increasingly on computers). In fact, a Freedom of Information request for a 1986 production archive I was working on for another project only generated two of the four files, with the other two suggested as lost, in a solicitor's office or in a producer's collection, suggesting that the notion of a centralized, complete and well-preserved archive is a discursive function of corporate memory.

Defined by the Written Archive Manager as offering "something unique and important", the BBC was mindful as early as 1927 that it "should take care of its own history" (Written Archives Interview, Caversham 21-11-12). Like many bureaucratic UK organizations of the early twentieth century, it began centralized filing registries that were then rolled out to the regions. Thus, "the arrangement of the [written] archives naturally follows the arrangement of the organisation" with the critical aspect being continuity in filing systems through radio, television, the World Service and the Regions and across activities from engineering and transmitters to program making and staff polices (Written Archives Interview, Caversham 21-11-12). Continuity was critical, and it can be suggested that digital technologies offer new articulations of that continuity rather than simplified departures from it. The broadcast archives offer a different experience. Stored at Perivale, they represent an archive policy that only began for television in 1978 as programs were broadcast live in the early years of the BBC or recorded over due to the high cost of tape in the 1960s/1970s. Hence, the written archives serve as the corporate memory that fills in the gaps, with audience collections, potentially, offering up lost treasures.

The BBC uses its archive – and allows access to it by approved researchers for approved purposes – in order to produce its organizational history. Scholars have contributed to its collective memory through histories of media reputations (see Briggs, 1961–70), histories of media genres (see Holmes, 2008) and histories of media policies (see Curran and Seaton, 2010). In part, this has been assisted by the BBC's arrangement of its internal history based on 'whose papers they are', rather than subject or theme. "Provenance is everything, it is more like archaeology or art", states the senior archivist (Written Archives Interview, Caversham 21-11-12). While the Written Archives have operated archivally, driven by provenance, the broadcast archives have been produced thematically and selectively, driven by future use value. They are the 'nuts and bolts' of the 'factory', so to speak, with some nuts and bolts more valuable than others. Yet as tangible artefacts they have been treasured or forgotten by audiences in ways that do not always accord with the official histories produced by the BBC or by academics.

For audiences, BBC programing is a form of collective memory that digital technology has, in part, repurposed – not simply in making old programing available online, which in itself has allowed fans and researchers access to past treasures, but also in creating new audiences for old media as the analogue is remade as digitized content. Ellis (2012) has argued that there is potential for a wide use of data from archival TV: changes to language for language learning, reminiscence therapy for ageing populations, audiovisual data on bodies and performance in the long careers of celebrities, and data on physical spaces and lost buildings. All of which "could then be used for envisioning new uses as well as tracing historical ones" (ibid.). What is critical, states Ellis, is that bigger data and data mining, which does not yet exist for archival media, emanate from ordinary media outputs rather than exceptional ones. Thus, it, "does not depend on any belief in TV as a series of cultural objects that might endure" and we could extend this to other forms of popular mediation (ibid.). That is, while focusing on 'quality' and 'the canon', archivists and scholars have contributed to an analogization of media; preserving and reiterating, judging and valuing with little sense that digital memories may be far more ordinary than they anticipate.

Inheriting British media

The idea that British media are a form of popular cultural inheritance is an important one for thinking through the different business models that now operate around media archives. The BBC mines previous output and tries to meet the demands of a proliferating set of organizations that see cultural/commercial value in past content from museums, libraries, heritage centres, NGOs, community projects and Heritage Lottery Funded initiatives. Again, this is all benchmarked by notions of 'value' for the British public as mediations of ordinary life at local, regional and national levels that become digitally accessible through cultural policy initiatives. From a production perspective, this cultural inheritance is shot through with underlying corporate memories. Having interviewed BBC workers from a range of areas of production, television, radio and digital media over the years, what is striking is that they all, in one form or another, produce a collective memory as per Halbwachs's definition: "When it considers its own past, the group feels strongly that it has remained the same and become conscious of its identity through time" (2011: 146). While historians focus on changes, ruptures, discontinuities, challenges and differences, as this volume may highlight, collective memory produces life 'essentially unaltered'. For the group, "living first and foremost for its own sake aims to perpetuate the feelings and images forming the substance of its thought" (Halbwachs, 2011: 146). Likewise, BBC archive managers who were interviewed stressed a self-portrait of the BBC and the individual BBC worker as able to maintain their institution's values throughout the technological changes.[2]

Nevertheless, the 'field of cultural production' (see Bourdieu, 1993) inhabited by BBC archivists is one where all the hybridity, ambiguity and messiness of British media history converge. Here culture and economics are not separated as digital technology has expanded the amount of recorded material. As the Multi-Media Archivist of BBC's Information and Archives noted:

> In terms of unpublished material, the rushes and stuff that didn't make it into the final cut […]. In the scale of things, it's like your own digital camera, when you used to have 24 or 36 shots on a roll of film and now we just shoot away like anything and that is exactly what productions do as well, and the shooting ratio is enormous, so they produce an enormous amount of material, and it has to be managed or should be managed in some form or another, and the challenge for us is to ensure we are managing the right amount of material for the right time; and in terms of long-term retention, are selecting the right kind of stuff of value.
>
> (Information and Archives Interview, London 27-9-12)

When I asked what criteria are being used in 'selecting the right kind of stuff of value', he responded:

> Those values are short-term production values, longer-term, you know, historical, research value. There's material that's of commercial interest to our BBC Worldwide, which is our commercial company owned by the BBC. So, there are various aspects that influence selection decisions.
> (Information and Archives Interview, London 27-9-12)

This professional assessment shows that the BBC archivist has moved from a position at the end of the process of production (backward engineering value) to the 'heart' of it. Passionate about archives, archivists see themselves as 'barbarians' deselecting or 'angels' in selecting for preservation. Their risk management strategy may deselect *Cash in the Attic* rushes because they do not tick the boxes of 'value': little commercial value to rest of BBC, does not take high quality stock material for reuse, not dealing with important issues, unlikely to have a wonderful interview or reminiscence, not needed for litigious reasons and not historic (Information and Archives Interview, London 27-9-12). The archive managers are 'working through' uncertainty in order to create what is to be treasured. Even if fans and researchers view media 'rubbish' as valuable evidence of lives lived (see Ellis, 2006), the economics of memory for archive managers creates scarcity from plenty. As they were keen to emphasize, "if your building is full you can't just run out and build another one" and "digital storage is starting to create those kinds of problems" as the "management of a digital service requires the same infrastructures and people around it" (Information and Archives Interview, London 27-9-12).

The archive managers state that their primary purpose is to provide governance over an increasingly diffuse media landscape in the UK. In Information and Archives, the department consists of 400 people split into operational areas that reflect the functions of an archive: access, metadata enhancement and preservation. "At the heart of it all is the team of archivists, of which there are four, we call them multi-media archivists because nobody has a direct specialization in any one media or platform output" (Information and Archives Interview, London 27-9-12). Reflecting a move away from the notion of a single medium, the multi-media archivist works on the connections between, and connectedness of, media forms and media content. This is critical for media researchers and practitioners to understand for their distinct, creative practice (film, TV, radio, journalism), which was once archived and developed separately, in different buildings, with distinct teams, and distributed in a single media form, is now imagined and increasingly practiced as converged and cross-platform. "We have a hand in everyone else's pie basically: storage, access [...] standards of cataloguing and metadata management [...] research and people doing stuff on the ground" (Information and Archives Interview, London 27-9-12).

The team's taxonomy manager has a pivotal role in the digital economy, dealing with the 'metadata strategy'. Tellingly, the team found that 'metadata' has become so 'endemic' to what the BBC does that the taxonomy manager is "being pulled into all sorts of projects about the wider aspects of metadata than just taxonomies" (Interview with Information and Archives 27-9-12). This 'trade-talk' about 'metadata' represents both continuity and a discursive shift. It is characterized by change through recollection: "What is the right thing to do? And that changes all the time with production techniques and volumes of material being produced and we have to continually review and revise and reconsider. Are we doing the right thing here?" (Information and Archives Interview, London 27-9-12). Their 'critical industrial practices', how they talk about media archivability in a digital age and how they understand and interpret the history of archive policy at the BBC "informs and governs [their] production work worlds" (Caldwell, 2008: 7).

These archive managers were pleased to have got media producers talking about 'metadata' themselves. They are critically aware of their own dynamic position as providing governance on preservation values that shift and change over time and over which they do not have total control. Hence, they do not chastise their predecessors for wiping clean thousands of hours of programing or for recording over tape. They recognize that while they have different governance, storage and format issues, their criteria for selection have to be subject to change. More importantly, they freely admit to using the terms 'assets' and 'content' rather than genres or programs, a shift in nomenclature that has also permeated the teaching of and research into media.

The corporate memory of the BBC and all the recordings of its broadcast and written material have been separated from the memories of the people who produced that content, worked in those buildings and consumed the output. As a hierarchical institution that is often difficult to access for researchers, students and the general public, the BBC is compelled to engage in 'industrial reflexivity' on a scale not comparable to a commercial media company. Hence, it tells a story of itself to itself and this can be clearly seen in its publication *Guide to the BBC's Archives 2012: What's in The Archives and How to Use Them*, edited by Jake Berger (2012), a key digital enthusiast who was quoted at the beginning of this chapter. A copy of this 213-page book was given by the archive managers as an example of the extent and ambition of the BBC archive strategy. Acknowledging that only "a small proportion of the archive has been digitised, and even less is available to be seen online or outside BBC premises" (Berger, 2012: 4), the book draws together in uneditable[3] hard copy key information about the Central Archive Collections (Art, Artefacts, Music Library, Photo Library, Pronunciation Unit, Sound Archive, Sports Library, TV Archive, Written Archives), the National Archive Collections (Northern Ireland, Scotland, Wales), the Regional Archive Collections (covering 13 British regions), alongside the other half of the book devoted to General Rights Guidance, with a final A-Z of terms and acronyms.

What is most insightful about the staff guide is that all the holdings of the BBC are defined and described with a glossary of historical terms of old technologies. Recognizing that future staff will be born digital, the BBC has to ensure that its collective memory is passed down as a coherent set of working practices.

> But first, we need to tell everyone what we've got and what we are doing with it. […] and to offer some straightforward advice to BBC staff who might want to use material from the archive for their own purposes or to advise external organisations who wish to work with the Archive.
>
> (Berger, 2012: 5)

What the book conveys is the complexity, cost and multiple rights issues that confront a member of staff who wants to reuse BBC archival material.

The complexity, the cost and the rights issues do not disappear in a digital age. Multimedia archivization is directed toward the selection of assets, 360 degree programing, digital storage, devolved first line selection of material to production communities outside the BBC, the attractiveness of rights-free content for commercial reuse, playing catch up with multi-platform versions and new applications, negotiating with fans who keep everything, appeasing producers whose work has been lost, format obsolescence, and increasing responsibility toward the licence-fee paying audience. What is vital to note is the keenness to move forward not as archivists, that is, not as postproduction BBC workers as per the Written Archive, but rather, alongside the senior media managers who have accompanied production teams since 2005, they present themselves as sitting above, below, behind, in front of and around media creativity.

Conclusion

It is important that as researchers we continue to ask questions about the history of production cultures, the collective memories that media archives contribute to and the cultural performance of the media archivist in a digital age. What are they choosing to forget and what do they try to remember? To turn our attention to archive production is to grapple with the messy economics that underlie digital media and memory research; that is, an approach to media that explores the 'value' ascribed to memory and seeks to measure it. If media historians do not tackle the thorny issue of what is valuable to media producers and researchers to remember and forget, they are in danger of a circuitous celebration of all that is popularly remembered as good, with a knee-jerk skepticism towards industrial reflexivity as cynical public relations.

Inevitably, media history is no longer a trusted 'academic' painstakingly appraising archives to which he or she has been granted privileged access. History from below, popular memory research, the growth of the heritage industry and the migration of millions to the internet mean that citizens demand access to archives and expect media's past to be accessible, mobile, context-specific and personalized. They may even challenge the collective memories of media institutions themselves and make public their past experiences of media (as consumers, fans, extras, below-the-line production workers, or even as victims of abuse by media celebrities). It became clear in my interviews that the BBC's archives are being pushed and pulled in multiple directions (cultural, ideological, commercial, legal, personal, technological, local, global and political) and they are also expected to be complete, open and ready for digital re-purposing as a nation's creative seam to be mined in an economic downturn.

The challenges are unlikely to weaken as more research projects seek out those whose memories have been forgotten or ignored (for example, the AHRC-funded A History of Television for Women 1947–1989 Project). As custodian of a nation's history, the BBC is perceived to control, house, document, preserve and re-use its audio-visual archive, written archive and even its living archive if we include retired

BBC staff. Since the broadcast and written archives are incomplete, not always well organized, unwieldy, closed, in legal hold, selective, copyrighted to multiple stakeholders, distributed across the country or simply far too expensive to make digitally accessible, this means that digital enthusiasm is actually produced by a strong thread of living corporate memory work, strongly inscribed with marketing discourses. It is within BBC workers that analogue and digital media meet as experienced and converged practices. It is within audience members that mediated memories have a cultural value that may conflict with official versions of media history. The sense of opportunity at researching the media's past should not belie the fact that open, online access to institutional media archives is at present more an illusion than a reality. One only has to refer to the BBC's industry literature to its staff:

> Material is made available on bbc.co.uk as an on-demand stream only. Material will be 'Geo-IP' restricted to block access to users outside the UK. There will be no ability for users to download or manipulate content. There will be no ability for users to share the content with other users on other devices (apart from those permitted under the BBC's Syndication Policy as approved by the BBC Trust).
>
> (Berger, 2012: 130)

Thus, digital memories and media of the future are matters of piecing together 'media heritage' from bits of archives, everyday cultural artifacts, audience memories and production culture research. This methodological approach may be considered less about history in the epistemological sense. That is, the production of a history as "a certain kind of organized and inferential knowledge" that is distinct from memory seen as "not organized, not inferential at all" (Collingwood, 1999 [1946]: 8). Focusing on audiences, because they are easier to access, easier to get copyright clearance from and have licensed their memories for worldwide use when already online, should not detract us from the underlying economies of memory at work in the self-reflexive production of archival content by media organizations. The migration of broadcast media to the internet, alongside every other cultural/creative form and practice, suggests that remembering media is also about preserving the memory of a concept of the single medium[4] in an increasingly converged media landscape.

In a global media economy, the UK is highly valued for its media heritage. Archival media content has become a commodity privatized by both producers and users, with an increase in asset experts standing between people and their pasts (see Lowenthal, 2007). At the same time, audience memories of media online offer a "flood of electronic data as heterogeneous, multivocal, instantly accessible, infinitely reproducible, and readily disposable" without "the social framework grounded in an abundance of shared cultural references" (ibid.: 201). The BBC has staked out a territory for curating those cultural references and providing that social framework. It has also, through its Rights Business Development unit, determined a commercial value for those archival references. For the media researcher and digital practitioner of the future, it is tempting to forget the BBC in order to remember the vast majority of ordinary memories and media ephemera that seem more easily accessible. That is, to "make place for new information, new challenges, and new ideas to face the present and future", as noted at the beginning of this chapter (Assman, 2011: 97). Yet to do so is to forget the 'rights' of the many cultural producers who have contributed to the commercial and public value of British media heritage; rights the BBC itself cannot forget in its role as national caretaker.

Further reading

Garde-Hansen's (2011) *Media and Memory* is a useful introduction to the theory and practice of media and memory, drawing upon radio, popular music, television, film, mobile camera phones and online video. Olick, Vinitzky-Seroussi and Daniel Levy's (2011) edited *The Collective Memory Reader* is the 'go to' reader for memory studies from the late eighteenth century to current scholarship, covering media and modes of transmission. Van Dijck's (2007) *Mediated Memories in the Digital Age* is the first extended key study on the theory and cultural practice of mediated memories, exploring digital culture and its impact on remembering.

Notes

1 In May 2013, the BBC admitted to wasting £98.4m on the Digital Media Initiative, a five-year project that sought to create tapeless, streamlined access to its vast audio-visual archive. The project did not deliver the pan-BBC tapeless environment that its future-focused strategy had invested in.
2 To focus on what *stays the same* (the collective memory) is of no interest to policymakers, media creatives and digital enthusiasts, and yet the BBC was forced to revert to transporting video tape by taxi across London after the death of Margaret Thatcher in April 2013.
3 The book has *Jim'll Fix It* as a highlight of the TV Archive Collection (Berger, 2012: 49), while some months later the programs of Jimmy Savile were being systematically removed from online archive material in the light of sexual abuse allegations. With the BBC no longer promoting this previously treasured past content, corporate memory was challenged by personal memory resulting in the criteria of what was valuable changing overnight.
4 With thanks to Andrew Hoskins for this valuable suggestion about the death of the concept of a single medium in a digital media ecology.

References

Assmann, A. (2011) "Canon and Archive." In J. K. Olick, V. Vinitzky-Seroussi and D. Levy (eds.) *The Collective Memory Reader*. Oxford: Oxford University Press (pp. 334–37).
Berger, J. (2011) "Digital archive opportunities and BBC Digital Public Space." Building Digital Capacity for the Arts, 15th October. Retrieved from http://www.youtube.com/watch?v=4d6KhsB5A_0
——(ed.) (2012) *Guide to the BBC's Archives 2012: What's in the Archives, and How to Use Them*. Produced by BBC Archive Development © BBC. Available to BBC staff only.
Born, G. (2003) "Strategy, positioning and projection in digital television: Channel Four and the commercialization of public service broadcasting in the UK." *Media, Culture and Society*, 25, 773–99.
Bourdieu, P. (1993) *The Field of Cultural Production: Essays on Art and Literature*. Cambridge: Polity Press.

Briggs, A. (1961–70) *The History of Broadcasting in the United Kingdom, Volumes I–III.* Oxford: Oxford University Press.

Caldwell, J. T. (2008) *Production Culture: Industrial Reflexivity and Critical Practice in Film and Television.* Durham: Duke University Press.

Cameron, F. and Kenderdine, S. (eds.) (2007) *Theorizing Digital Cultural Heritage: A Critical Discourse.* Cambridge, MA: MIT Press.

Collingwood, R. G. (1999 [1946]) *The Idea of History.* Oxford: Clarendon.

Curran, J. and Seaton, J. (2010) *Power Without Responsibility: Press, Broadcasting and the Internet in Britain* (Seventh Edition). Oxford: Routledge.

Ellis, J. (2006) "The past as television: Are television programmes more that nostalgic ephemera?" In J. Ellis and A. Grasso (eds.) *Fare Storia con la Televisione.* Milano: Vita e Pensiero (pp. 167–72).

——(2012) "Why digitise historical television?" *Journal of European History and Culture*, 1(1). Retrieved from http://journal.euscreen.eu/index.php/view/issue/view/1

Garde-Hansen, J. (2011) *Media and Memory.* Edinburgh: Edinburgh University Press.

Garde-Hansen, J., Hoskins, A. and Reading, A. (eds.) (2009) *Save As ... : Digital Memories.* Basingstoke: Palgrave Macmillan.

Halbwachs, M. (2011) "The collective memory." In J. K. Olick, V. Vinitzky-Seroussi and D. Levy (eds.) *The Collective Memory Reader.* Oxford: Oxford University Press (pp. 139–49).

Holmes, S. (2008) *Entertaining Television: The BBC and Popular Television Cultures in the 1950s.* Manchester: Manchester University Press.

Hoskins, A. (2009) "The diffusion of media/memory: The new complexity." Warwick Writing/Complexity. Retrieved from http://www2.warwick.ac.uk/newsandevents/warwickbooks/complexity/andrew_hoskins

Huyssen, A. (2003) *Present Pasts: Urban Palimpsests and the Politics of Memory.* Palo Alto, CA: Stanford University Press.

Lowenthal, D. (2007) "Archives, heritage and history." In F. X. Blouin Jr and W. G. Rosenberg (eds.) *Archives, Documentation and Institutions of Social Memory: Essays from the Sawyer Seminar.* Ann Arbour, MI: University of Michigan Press (pp. 193–206).

Mayer-Schönberger, V. (2010) *Delete: The Virtue of Forgetting in the Digital Age.* Princeton, NJ: Princeton University Press.

Nora, P. (2002) "Reasons for the current upsurge on memory." *Transit–Europäische Revue*, 22. Retrieved from http://www.eurozine.com/articles/2002-04-19-nora-en.html

Olick, J. K., Vinitzky-Seroussi, V. and Daniel Levy, D. (eds.) (2011) *The Collective Memory Reader.* Oxford: Oxford University Press.

Parikka, J. (2012) *What is Media Archaeology?* Cambridge: Polity Press.

Popular Memory Group (1998) "Popular memory: Theory, politics, method." In R. Perks and A. Thompson (eds.) *Oral History Reader.* New York: Routledge (pp. 43–53).

Reading, A. (2011) "Six dynamics of the globital memory field." In M. Neiger, O. Meyers and E. Zandberg (eds.) *On Media Memory: Collective Memory in a New Media Age.* Basingstoke: Palgrave Macmillan (pp. 241–52).

Schmidt, E. (2011) "Television and the Internet: Shared opportunity." MacTaggart Lecture at the MediaGuardian Edinburgh International Television Festival, 26 August. Retrieved from http://www.guardian.co.uk/media/interactive/2011/aug/26/eric-schmidt-mactaggart-lecture-full-text

Snickars, P. (2012) "If content is king, context is its crown." *Journal of European History and Culture*, 1(1). Retrieved from http://journal.euscreen.eu/index.php/view/issue/view/1

van Dijck, J. (2007) *Mediated Memories in the Digital Age.* Paolo Alto, CA: Stanford University Press.

Index

Abbey Road studios 64–65
Abdication crisis (1936) 32–33
Abraham, Andy 501
Abrahamson, David 274
Absolutely Fabulous 456
Absurdism 360
Abt, V. 574
Abu Ghraib prison 177
'accidental journalism' 575
Adams, Douglas 362
Adamthwaite, A. 257
Addams, J. 86
Adorno, Theodor 544, 546
advertising: market for 76; in newspapers 81–82, 201, 206, 211, 218, 230, 255–56, 521, 530–31, 534; on television 553–54; of tobacco products 234; on the web 554
Afghanistan, war in 175–76
'ages' in the development of British television 461
aggression, testing for 94
Albury, K. 136
Alcott, Louisa May 462
Allen, Peter 367
Allison, George 370
'alternative comedy' 454–55
'alternative press' 523
'alternative publications' 124
Althusser, Louis 45, 290
Altman, Rick 416
Amanpour, Christiane 175
American culture 102
Americanization 218, 223, 335, 505, 545
Amis, Martin 250, 564
Anderson, Benedict 23, 153, 198–99, 276, 416, 546, 574
Anderson, Billy 280
Anderson, Craig 91–92, 96
Anderson, Lindsay 394, 428
Anderson, R. 107
Anderton, William 202

Andrews, Eamonn 370
Andrews, M. 456
Ang, I. 104
Anglia TV 479
Answers to Correspondents 210, 218
appeasement policy 257, 446
Appleyard, B. 480–81
Apted, Michael 431
The Archers 356, 359
archives *see* media archives
Arden, John 362
Ardis, Ann 268
Arena (magazine) 297, 302–6
Ariès, Philippe 16
Armchair Theatre 464
armed conflict 171–79
Armstrong, Archie 192
Armstrong, Lance 152
Armstrong-Jones, Antony 313
Arnett, Peter 174
Arnold, Matthew 266, 325
ARPANET (Advanced Research Project Agency Network) 534
Arts Councils 269–70, 401
Asquith, Anthony 395–97
Assmann, A. 582
Associated Newspapers 211
Astute Radio 349
Attenborough, David 479–81
Attlee, Clement 289
Attwood, Feona 306
Auden, W.H. 428
audience participation 573
Austen, Jane 462

Back, L. 113
Badenoch, A. 352
Bagehot, Walter 264
Bailey, M. 3, 128
Baker, Danny 375
Bakewell, Joan 134–35

Balcon, Michael 396
Baldasty, G. 211
Baldwin, Stanley 32, 102, 253–54
ballads, topical 184–93
Ballaster, Ros 291
Bandura, A. 94
Bangs, Lester 317
Barclays Bank 157
Barker, H. 197, 199, 229–32
Barker, M. 93, 96, 137, 422
Barlow, D. 455
Barnes, Thomas 530
Barnett, S. 251, 442, 507, 555–56
Barnhurst, K.G. 240
Barr, Charles 394–95
Barrett, Syd 66, 70
Barthes, Roland 13, 45, 290, 426
Baudrillard, Jean 63, 106
Baxendale, John 31, 36
Bazin, André 398
Beaverbrook, Lord 446
Beck, Ulrich 10
Becker, H.S. 161
Beckett, Samuel 356, 360
Beerling, Johnny 340
behaviorist models of media effects 92–93
Bell, Alan 529
Bell, Alexander Graham 540
Bell, Andy 510
Bell, Martin 174–75
Benet, J. 290
Bengry, Justin 139
Benn, Tony 311, 334, 477
Bennett, Arnold 287
Bennett, Hollie 567
Bennett, Russell 567–68
Bentham, Jeremy 258
Berelowitz, Sue 137
Berger, Jake 582, 589, 591
Bergonzi, Bernard 35
Berland, Jody 542, 544
Bernasconi, R. 113
Bernstein, Sidney 464
Best, George 221
Betting and Lotteries Act (1934) 233
Big Brother 433, 498
Bill of Rights 197
Billig, M. 451
bin Laden, Osama 177
Bingham, Adrian 34, 230–31, 253
BioWare 561
Birch, Philip 337, 341
Biressi, A. 501
Birmingham Centre for Contemporary Cultural Studies 20, 44–45

Birt, John 328, 466
Black, J. 199, 239–40
Blackburn, Tony 335, 340
Blackstone, William 197
Blair, Tony 103, 175, 252
Blake, John 222
Bland, Lucy 141
Bleasdale, Alan 465
Blumenfeld, R.D. 218
Blumler, Jay 44, 47, 54
Bly, Nellie 217
Boaden, Helen 575–76
Bolter, J.D. 11–12
'bonk journalism' 222
Booth, D. 157
borderless products, online media treated as 536
Born, G. 329, 584
Botham, Ian 151
Bourdieu, Pierre 106, 273, 281–82, 293
Bourke, Joanna 36
Bourne, Nicholas 185
Boxer, Mark 312–13
Boyce, G. 250
boycotts 155–57
Boyd-Barrett, Oliver 46
Boyle, Karen 91–92, 96
Boys from the Blackstuff 465–66
Bradford, Andrew 571
breakfast television 223
'breaking news' 509, 511, 556–57, 575
Breazeale, Kenon 299
Breivik, Anders 91
Breward, Christopher 298
Brewer, J. 196
bribery 201–2
Bridson, D.G. 358
Briggs, Asa 3, 356, 529, 533
Briggs, Mark 520, 525
Bristol Post Boy 240
British Board of Film Censors/Classification (BBFC) 32, 54, 88, 406, 418, 422, 437–41
British Broadcasting Company 324, 383
British Broadcasting Corporation (BBC) 21, 24, 31, 33, 44–45, 60, 77, 81, 100, 104–5, 126, 142, 149, 323–31, 383, 467; Agreement with the government 441–43; archives management 583–92; BBC Trust 441, 508; BBC Worldwide 278, 489; censorship of 442–44; Charter 441; critiques of 325–27; current affairs programing 504–9; effect of pirate radio on 334–35, 340–42; engagement with women 345–47, 350–52; Features Department 358–61; General Advisory

Council 472; government hostility towards 442; History Unit and history programing 484–86; Natural History Unit (NHU) 471–75, 479–80; News Channel 509; as a pivotal institution 553; radio drama output 356–64; Radio 5 Live 366–68, 376; Radiophonic Workshop 360, 362; Science Consultative Committee 474; sports journalism 366–69, 374–77; Third Programme 360; use made of online media 534–35; website 328
British Film Institute 43, 401, 431
British Satellite Broadcasting (BSkyB) 221, 375, 466, 507
Britten, Benjamin 358–59, 428
Broadcasting Acts 445, 461, 466, 507, 521
Broadcasting Act (1996) 521
broadcasting technology 532
Bromley, M. 223, 244
Bromley, Peter 373
Bronowski, Jacob 432, 476
Brooke, R.E.J. 462
Brookes, R. 152–55
Brookside 465
Brougham, Lord 78
Brown, Gordon 430
Brown, James 304
Brownlee, Jonny and Ali 154–55
Bruce, Toni 154
Brundson, C. 128
Bryant, J. 94–95
Buckingham, D. 87, 92
Buijzen, M. 106
Bulger, James 88, 440
Bull, Michael 540–46
Bunnage, Mick 304
Burdsey, D. 114
Burke, Edmund 198–99
Burke, P. 3, 529
Burnat, Emad 427
Burns, Ken 485–86
Burns, Tom 44, 441
Burton, Richard 359
Burton's (men's clothing chain) 301
Bush, George Sr. 176
Bush, George W. 177
Butler, Judith 297
Buxton, Aubrey 479
Byrne, Mary 501

Calcutt Report (1990) 222–1
Calder, Iain 223
Caldwell, John Thornton 584
The Cambridge Intelligencer 200, 202
Cameron, F. 585

Campaign for Nuclear Disarmament 164
Candid Camera 496
Canter, L. 247
Capote, Truman 317
car radios 541–44
Cardiff, A. 377
Cardiff, D. 533
Carey, J. 150, 219
Carleton Greene, Hugh *see* Greene, Hugh
Carnegie, Andrew 241
Carpenter, Harry 374
Carpenter, J.R. 69
Carry On films 220–21, 399, 408
Carter, C. 347
Carter, S. 347–48
Cash, Dave 341–42
Cashmore, E. 155
Caughie, John 460
Cave, Edward 298
Cavendish, Thomas 113
celebrity culture 221, 293
censorship 32, 172–73, 233–36, 257–58, 437–46, 521; of the BBC 442–44; of home videos 439–41; by market forces 444–45; *moral* and *social* 233–34; political 234–35
Chadwick, Edwin 78–79
Chalaby, J. 211
Chambers, Ephraim 263
Channel Four 429, 433, 445, 457, 465–66, 484, 487–88, 506, 511
Channel Five 507, 510–11
Chapman, Rowena 303
Charles I 189, 191
Charters, W.W. 87
Children and Young Persons Act (1933) 233
Childs, P. 113–14
Chudacoff, Howard 298
Churchill, Winston 22, 253–54, 289
cinéma vérité and *ciné véristes* 425, 427
Cinematograph Acts 396, 401, 438–39
circulation figures 76, 82, 254–56, 519–20
'citizen-consumer' concept 101–2, 107–8
'citizen journalism' 556, 575
Citizen Khan 117
citizens' band radio 382
citizenship, traditional model of 101
The Civil War (American television series) 486
Clapp, Susannah 270
Clark, Arthur C. 477
class 100–106; changing attitudes to 103–4; definition of 100
class mobility 501
'Clerks of the Road' 78
Cleverdon, Douglas 359

Clinton, Bill 175
Clough, Brian 221
Club (magazine) 302
Clubman (magazine) 301–2
CNN and the 'CNN effect' 174, 178, 507–9
Cobbett, William 78
Cockett, Richard 446
coffee-house culture 195
Cohen, Stanley 44, 160–61
Cohen, W.A. 140
Cold War, ending of 171, 176
Coleman, David 374–75
Colley, Linda 418
Collingwood, R.G. 591
Collins, R. 229
color television 464, 479
comedy, nature of 451–55
commercial radio *see* pirate radio
commercial television 326–29, 385; *see also* independent television
commercialization of the press 211, 216, 242
Committee for Imperial Defence 32
commodification of information 211
common culture, emergence of 36, 224–25
Communications Acts 89, 443, 521, 554
communications technologies 11, 16, 75, 478, 517–18, 528–29
communities of opinion 571–78
communities of taste 219, 278–82; virtual 280–82
community radio 345, 348–50
competition: between newspapers 75–76, 82, 216, 255; between newspapers and other media 76–77; in broadcasting 466; in markets 75–77
Conboy, M. 102–4, 123, 142, 150, 209, 231, 241, 247, 531, 533
Connolly, Cyril 269
Constable, Archibald 264
consumer sovereignty 106–7
consumerism 101–2, 106–7
Coogan, Steve 457
Cook, C. 311
Cook, Pam 408
Cooper, Giles 356, 360–61
Cooper, Thomas 78
copyright 207, 232
Corner, John 9, 497–98
Coronation of The Queen (1953) 384–85, 485, 505
Coronation Street 464
Corthorn, P. 156
Cosmopolitan (magazine) 290–91, 294
costume dramas 467
Cottenham, Earl of 409

Couldry, N. 164
Council for National Academic Awards (CNAA) 47–48
Coutts, Graham 88
Cranfield, G.A. 229
Crawford, Lord 325
creative industries 53
Crewe, Ben 302–3
Crimean War 531
Crimewatch 496–97
Criminal Justice and Immigration Act (2008) 88–89, 96
Criminal Libel Act (1819) 233
Crisell, Andrew 382
Cross, N. 266
Crouch, John 191
crowdfunding for video game development 567–68
cultural industries, expansion of 51
cultural studies 15–16, 20, 45, 153
'cultural turn' in the humanities 1, 20, 25, 34
Cumberbatch, G. 94
Curran, James 3, 9, 20, 24, 26, 29, 48, 129, 137, 148, 222, 230–31, 250
current affairs programing 445, 504–11
Curry and Chips 117
Customs Consolidation Act (1876) 233

D-Day 6.6.1944 489–90
'D' Notice Committee 234
Dahl, H.-F. 5
Dahlberg, L. 575
Dahlgren, P. 224
Daily Express 210, 218, 255
Daily Mail 90, 114, 135, 210, 218–19, 222–23, 256, 422, 535
Daily Mirror 45, 102–3, 123, 156, 177, 210, 219–22, 289
Daily News 531–32
Daily Sketch 222
Daily Sport 222
Daily Star 222
Daily Telegraph 76, 116, 208–9
Dale, Henry 472
Daly, Phil 476
Darfur 178
Darwin, Charles 114
Daubney, Martin 135–36
Davidson, Martin 486
Davies, Gavyn 443–44
Davies, Walford 359
Dawson, Geoffrey 446
de Botton, Alain 41
Debord, Guy-Ernest 426
Debrett, M. 329

Defoe, Daniel 201, 572
Delane, John T. 207
Deloney, Thomas 187
DeLuca, K.M. 166–67
Dennis, Felix 278, 304
deregulation of broadcasting 442, 466, 506
desensitization of media viewers 94–95
DiCenzo, M. 127
'digital divide' 575, 577
digital technology 26, 245–47, 363–64, 387, 517, 520
Dines, Gail 135
disc jockeys (DJs) 335–42, 350–51, 545
Dixon of Dock Green 463
Dobell, Byron 309
Docherty, D. 400
Docherty, T. 53
Doctor Who 464, 468
documentaries 425–35, 498, 500; technology used for 434–35; on television 430–35
docu-soaps 431–32, 497–500
Donnerstein, E. 95
Doom (video game) 565–66
Douglas, Jahmene 501
Dovey, Jon 497
Dowler, Millie 252
drama on radio 356–64
drama on television 361, 460–68;
    first 'age' of (1936–55) 461–63;
    second 'age' of (1955–90) 463–66;
    third 'age' of (1990–present) 466–68
Drazin, Charles 397
du Garde Peach, L. 357
Du Gay, P. 542, 546
'dumbing down' 223, 497
Dunne, T. 178
Durbridge, Francis 462
Durgnat, Raymond 394
Durkin, Martin 429
Dyer, R. 112, 117
Dyke, Greg 328, 443–45

'earthquake journalism' 220
Ebert, Roger 431
The Economist 275
Edensor, Tim 416–17
Edge of Darkness 466
Edgerton, David 14
The Edinburgh Review 263–66
Edison, Thomas 11
Education Act (1870) 208
Edward VIII 32, 446
Edwards, Tim 303–6
Egan, Kate 422
The Egoist 268

Ehrenreich, Barbara 301
Ehrick, C. 346
Elderton, William 185, 188
Eldridge, John 44
Eliot, T.S. 22, 268–69
Elizabeth I 187, 409
Elle (magazine) 292–93
Elliott, Phillip 43
Ellis, J. 128, 461, 586
'embedding' of reporters 171, 173, 430
Emergency Powers Act (1920) 234
Emerson, M. 105–7
Emmett, B.P. 104
emotional environment 36–37
Empire Marketing Board 32
Encounter 269
Enders Analysis 256
The English Review (founded 1783) 263–64
The English Review (founded 1908) 268
English Woman's Domestic Magazine 287
English Woman's Journal 287–88
Enron Corporation 430
entry barriers in the media 77, 80, 82
Erskine, Thomas 77
Esquire (magazine) 298–303, 309–10, 313
L'Estrange, Sir Roger 438
Esslin, Martin 360
ethnic minorities 118
ethnographic research work 96
European Directive on Audiovisual and Media Services (2007) 89
evening newspapers 208
Everett, Kenny 338, 341
exclusivity of news 80–81
Express Newspapers 222
extra-mural departments of universities 47

Fabian of the Yard 463
The Face (magazine) 302
factual programing 494, 497–98
Faithfull, Emily 288
Falklands conflict (1982) 171, 178–79, 222
The Family (television serial) 433, 496–97
'family audiences' 124–28, 456–57, 552
Fanon, F. 119
Fekete, L. 118–19
Feldman, Sally 347
Fem FM 346, 349–51
feminism 25, 124–29, 274, 314, 290–91, 345–48; backlash against 305
Fenwick-Miller, Florence 267
Ferguson, C.J. 92
Ferguson, Marjorie 286, 288
Ferguson, Niall 429, 487
Fernández-Vara, C. 563

Fessenden, Reginald 382
FHM (magazine) 304–7
film, British 393–402; era of silent movies 394–96; golden age of 396–98; post-war decline 398–400; revival since the 1980s 400–402; *see also* historical films; horror films
'filter bubble' phenomenon 578
Financial Times 46, 76
Fiorina, M.P. 574
Fire 86
Forster, E.M. 409–10
The Forsyte Saga (television adaptation) 464
Foucault, Michel 62
Fowler, Neil 524
Fox, A. 184
Fox, Charles James 200
Fox News 330, 511
fragmentation of media audiences 387–88, 467, 520
franchise system for commercial television 444–45, 466
Franco-Prussian War 531–32
Franklin, B. 239, 244–46
Fraser, S. 123
Fraterrigo, Elizabeth 301
free market economy 251, 521
free newspapers 245
free radio 338
free trade 78; in news 79
Freedman, J.L. 91
Freedom of Information Act (2000) 235
freedom of the press 77–78, 196–98, 202–3, 229, 231, 244, 254, 258, 522
Freeman, A.J. 86
Freidan, Betty 290
French Revolution 197, 202
Freud, S. 452
Friedman, James 495
The Frost Report 103
FTI Consulting 239
Funt, Alan 496
future prospects for television 550–59
Future Publishing 280–81

Gaber, Ivor 222, 251, 442, 507
Gaiman, Neil 363
Gales, Joseph 202
Gallagher, M. 345–47
Gamson, J. 141
Gamson, W.A. 164–65
Garde-Hansen, J. 583
Gardham, Tim 487
Garnett, Tony 465
Garnham, Nicholas 9, 45, 47, 54

Gascoigne, Paul 152
Gauntlett, D. 91, 93, 96
gender inequality 128–29
General Strike (1926) 441, 505, 533
The Gentleman's Magazine 263, 273, 298
The Gentleman's Quarterly 301, 303, 305
Gibney, Alex 430
Gibson, Thomas Milner 80
Gielgud, Val 356–59
Gieryn, Thomas 479
Gill, R. 304–5, 350
Gillette Soccer Saturday 375
Gingrich, Arnold 299
Gitelman, Lisa 11–12
Gitlin, Todd 165, 273
Glasgow University Media Group 44, 164, 172–73
Gledhill, Christine 116, 396
Glendenning, Raymond 369–70
Global Justice Movement 165–67
Goddard, P. 453
Golding, Peter 9, 45–46, 243
Good Housekeeping (magazine) 290
Goodhart, D. 245
Goodrich, Louis 462
Goody, Jade 501
Gordon, J. 140
Gordon, James Alexander 371–72, 376
Gore, Al 429
Gorringe, H. 166–67
Gough-Yates, Anna 286, 292–93
Gove, Michael 49
Gowing, Nik 175
Grade, Michael 442
Graf Report (2004) 535
Graham, Alex 488
Graham, G. 53
Gramsci, Antonio 45, 290–91
Granada Television 464
Grandstand 374
Grant, Hugh 257
Gray, A. 128
Gray, Frances 360–62
Greaves, Jimmy 221
Greeley, Horace 80
Green, Charlotte 376–77
Green, Michael 328
Greene, Hugh 327, 464
Greenfield, Jill 300
Greenham Common protest 164
Grierson, John 32, 393, 396, 425, 428
Griffiths, D.W. 427
Griffiths, Ralph 263
Grindstaff, Laura 573
Gripsrud, Jostein 558

Grossberg, Lawrence 14
grounded theory 583–84
The Grove Family 463
Grusin, R. 11–12
The Guardian 76, 168, 256, 276, 535
Guccioni, Bob 302
Gulf War (1990–91) 63, 173–74, 176, 509
Gunning, Tom 395
Guthrie, Tyrone 357
Guttmann, Allen 155–56

Habermas, Jürgen 23, 45, 101, 147–48, 195, 200, 455, 571
Hacked Off (not-for-profit company) 251
Hackett, Dennis 313
hacking: definition of 563; of video games 563–65
Hackluyt, John 190
Hadlow, Janice 486–87
Hajkowski, Thomas 358
Halbwachs, Maurice 585, 587
Haley, Sir William 326, 373
Hall, Stuart 43–45, 116–17, 161–62, 291, 334–35
Hallin, Daniel 172, 177
Halliwell, Leslie 404
Halloran, J. 43, 46–47, 163, 166
Hamilton, Archibald 263
Hammer Films 415, 419–20
Hampton, M. 215, 241–42, 251, 253
Hancock's Half-Hour 361, 453
Hanson, S. 400
Haralovich, M.B. 453
Harcup, T. 253
Hardwicke, Lord 197
Hare, David 363
Hargreaves, I. 518
Harley, Robert 201
harm arising from the media, legal definition of 90
Harmsworth, Alfred 80, 114, 210–11, 218–19, 265
Harmsworth, Esmond 446
Harper, S. 398, 408
Harrington, S. 223
Harris, Bob 197
Harris, Michael 201
Harris, R. 230
Harrison, J. 507
Hartley, J. 215
Hartman, P. 112
Harvey, Sylvia 554
Hawkings, Kate 279
Hawkins, Desmond 471–75, 478–79
Hayes, N. 244

Hayward, Tim 279
headphones, use of 540–43, 546
Hearst, William Randolph 209, 216–19
Hefner, Hugh 300
Hemingway, Ernest 299
Hendrix, Jimi 313
Hendy, David 36–37, 324, 331, 357, 362
Henry, Wendy 222
Henry VIII 231, 409
Her Majesty's Inspectorate of Constabulary (HMIC) 168
Herbert, George 22
Herbert, J. 52
Herbert, Sir Thomas 112
heritage cinema 409–10
Hermes, Joke 293
Heseltine, Michael 313
Hess, Alison 69
'hierarchy of credibility' (Becker) 161
Higson, Andrew 396, 410
Hill, Annette 499
Hill, Christopher 411
Hilmes, Michele 126, 346
Hilmmelweit, Hilde 43
Hilton, M. 101–2
Hinerman, S. 140–41
Hirsch, Seymour 172
historical films 404–11
history on television 484–90; co-productions and international programing 489–90; significance for public service broadcasting 485–87
Hitchcock, Alfred 395–97
The Hitchhiker's Guide to the Galaxy 362
Hobbs, Andrew 241
Hoggart, Richard 20, 44–45, 105, 334–35, 471
Holmes, T. 277–78
Holt, Richard 148–49, 156
homosexuality 139–40
Horizon (magazine) 269
Horizon (television series) 470–71, 476–78, 481
Horne, J. 155
Horrie, C. 224
horror films 414–23
Hoskins, A. 583
Hosokawa, S. 546
The Hour 506–8, 511
Houseman, Rupert 434
Hubbard, Louisa 288
Hudson, Robert 374
Hughes, K. 294
Hughes, Richard 357
Huhtamo, Erkki 61

Human Rights Act (1998) 235
humanitarian interventions 176, 178
Hume, M. 176
Humphrys, John 53
Hunt, Frederick Knightley 23
Husband, Charles 45, 112
Husni, Samir 277
Hussein, Saddam 174, 177
Hutchings, Peter 414, 417, 420–23
Huyssen, Andreas 583

id Software 565–66
identity: formation of 25–26; and sport 153–55
Illustrated Daily News 219
'imagined communities' 198–99, 276, 416, 546, 574
immigration 114–16, 119
imperialism 114
Incitement to Disaffection Act (1934) 234
Indecent Advertisements Act (1889) 233
independent television (ITV) 104–5, 128, 385, 463–64, 487, 505, 553–54
Independent Television News (ITN) 505–7
Inside The Story (online magazine) 279
Institute of Journalists 52, 243–44
interconnectedness of the media 29–38
International Criminal Court 178
internet communities 566–68
internet technology and usage 24, 77, 108, 518, 522, 534; and social conflict 167–68
'inverted pyramid' of news reporting 242
iPod devices 540–46
Iraq War (2003) 173–78
Irish Republican Army (IRA) 173
Isaacs, Jeremy 429
Ivory, James 409

Jack the Ripper 209
Jackson, Jack 338
Jackson, Michael 486–87
Jackson, Peter 305
Jacob, Sir Ian 473
Jacobs, Jason 460
Jallov, B. 347–48
James, Robert 35
James I 185
Jancovich, Mark 415, 423
Jebb, John 199
Jeffrey, Francis 264
Jenkins, Henry 12, 136, 518
Jenkins, R. 452
Jewell, J. 241
Jewish humour 453–54
Johnson, C. 105

Johnston Press 246, 256
Jones, Darryl 417–20
Jones, Kennedy 212
Jones, Peter 362
Jones, S.E. 565
journalism: 'contextual' 536; critiques of 21; and current affairs 504–11; democratization of 211; de-professionalization of 577; education for and training in 52–53; link with democracy 521; 'long-form' 535; 'new' 123, 208–10, 218, 242, 266, 309–11; professionalism in 530; 'public' 523; and sport 152–53; on television 555–57
'journalism in action' 217
'journalism of attachment' 174–75
'journalism of opinion' 207
journalistic culture 510
Joyce, James 317
Judicial Proceedings (Regulation of Reports) Act (1926) 233
J. Walter Thompson (advertising agency) 220

Kaplan Daniels, A. 290
Kaul, C. 113
Kavka, Misha 493, 499
Kemsley, Lord 446
Kemsley Newspapers 243
Kenderdine, S. 585
Kendrick, W. 136
Kennedy Martin, Troy 466
Kent, Nick 315–18
Kershaw, Ian 486–87
Kidd, A. 101
Kilburn, J. 92
Kinnock, Neil 157
Kipnis, L. 136
Kirkham, William 188
Kittler, Friedrich A. 61–66, 70
Klein, N. 166
Klein, Richard 432
Klingender, F.D. 43, 405
Kneale, Nigel 462–63
Kolkowski, Aleks 68–69
Konzack, L. 567
Korda, Alexander 396, 405–7
Kosovo conflict (1999) 175
Koss, S. 230
Krutnik, F. 451–52
Kuhn, A. 86

laboratory-based research on the media 94–96
Lacey, Kate 345

'laddism' 126
The Ladies' Mercury 273, 286
'lads' mags' 304–6
Laity, Mark 175
Lamb, Larry 220, 222
Lambert, Olly 430
Lane, Carla 456
Lang, Andrew 266–67
Langer, J. 223
Langhamer, C. 34
Lannon, J. 105–7
Lanza, Adam 91
The Late Show 486
Law, Graham 265
Layton, Sir Walter 446
Leach, Gerald 476
Leary, Patrick 266
Leavis, F.R. 42, 253–54, 269
Leavis, Q.D. 269
Leblanc, Warren 89–90
Lee, A. 243, 255
Lehmann, John 269
Leicester Centre for Mass Communication Research 43–47, 54
leisure time 34
Lejeune, C.A. 409
Le Mahieu, Daniel 36
Lenin, V.I. 426
letters to the editor 571–73
Levene, Harry 373–74
Leveson, Sir Brian (and Leveson Report, 2012) 251–53, 257–58, 487
Levy, Daniel 582
Levy, S. 563
Lewis, Cecil A. 357
Lewis, J. 509
Lewis, P. 359
Lewisohn, M. 453–55
Libel Act (1792) 233
licence fee system for broadcasting 324, 327–29, 381, 442, 505, 553, 584
licensing: of broadcasting 441; of films 438–39; of home videos 440; of the press 195–96, 229–32, 437–38; of television 444
Liddle, D. 207
'life-world' concept 148, 157
'lifestyle' programing 499
Lilliput (magazine) 300
Lincoln, Abraham 531–32
Link, David 69–70
Linz, D. 95
'listening in' to the radio 381–84
listening to music, personal 539–47
literary periodicals 263–70
Littlejohn, Richard 134

Littlewood, J. 455
Livingstone, S. 89, 573
Loach, Ken 465
Loaded (magazine) 304–5
Loader, B.D. 577
Lobato, Ramon 416
local newspapers 518–24, 576–77
local radio 341–42, 386–87
Local World Limited 246
Logan, Nick 302, 315
Lois, George 313
London bombings (7 July 2005) 575
The London Magazine 269
London Review of Books (LRB) 270
Longhurst, Jane 88
Look (magazine) 278–79
Look (television series) 478–79
Lorant, Stefan 300
The Lord of the Rings (radio adaptation) 362
Lotbinière, Seymour Joly de 368, 372
Love Thy Neighbour 117
Lovelace, Richard 192
Lovell, Alan 394, 404
Lovett, William 78
Low, Rachael 395
Lowe, K. 254
Lull, J. 140–41
Lumby, C. 136
Lumière Brothers 426
Lunt, P. 573–74
Lynam, Desmond 372
Lynch, Jessica 176–77

McBride, Sean 46
McCarthy, Desmond 268
McCarthy, Tom 67
McCartney, Paul and Linda 316
McChesney, R. 511, 524
McClendon, Gordon 336
McCloy, James 473–75
McCracken, Ellen 291
McCulloch, D. 127
MacDonald, I. 316
McDonald, Jane 497
MacDonald, M. 116, 118
McDonough, F. 257
McElligott, J. 189
McGuigan, J. 106
Mackay, Angus 368–77
McKee, A. 136
McKee, Robert 481
MacKenzie, Kelvin 53, 222
McKibbin, R. 30
McKie, D. 311
MacKinnon, R. 108

McLean, Bethany 430
MacLeish, Archibald 358
McLuhan, Marshall 62–64, 426
McNair, B. 223
MacNeice, Louis 358–61
MacPherson, Stewart 373
McQuail, Denis 44, 48
McRobbie, Angela 45, 293
McWhinnie, Donald 360
Madison, James 258
magazine pioneers 309–18
magazines see literary periodicals; men's magazines; specialist magazines; women's magazines
Maggs, Dirk 363
'making of documentaries' (MODs) genre 481
Malik, K. 113
Malone, David 477
Man About Town (magazine) 302, 313
Mandeville, Bernard 77–78
Manhunt (video game) 89–90
Mann, Arthur 33
Mansfield, F.J. 52
Maras, S. 532
Marconi, Guglielmo 382–83
Marie Claire (magazine) 292–93
market segmentation 76–77
Marr, Andrew 223, 225, 531–32
Marshall, Penny 135
Martin-Jones, David 421
Marvin, Carolyn 12, 62
Marxism 45
Mascheroni, G. 578
masculinity, concepts of 297–307
Mason, Michael 362
Mason, T. 149, 156
mass circulation press 206–9, 213
Mass Effect 3 (video game) 561–62, 568
Mass Observation 35, 43
Matheson, D. 242
Matheson, Hilda 346–47
Maud, Ralph 359
Maxim (magazine) 304–7
Mayer, J.P. 43
Mäyrä, F. 562
Medhurst, Andy 410, 452, 454
media archaeology 60–70; definition of 61–62
media archives 583–92
media effects 85–96; in the popular press 87–89; and the rise of mass consumption 85–87
media heritage 591–92

media history, 'liberal' and 'radical' narratives of 24
media industries, employment in 51
media studies 2, 9–16, 20, 41–55; degrees in 47; early development of 44–46; historical approach to 12–16; weekend and evening classes in 47
Melody Maker 316
memory: collective or corporate 584–91; surfeit of 582
Men Only (magazine) 300
men's magazines 125–26, 277–307; early development of 298–300; future prospects for 306–7; 'lifestyle' titles 302–3; and the *Playboy* ethic 300–302
Mercea, D. 577
Merchant, Ismail 409
Mercurius Aulicus 190
Mercurius Demoncritus 191
Mercurius Fumigosus 191
Mercurius Melancholicus 190–91
Mercurius Politicus 183, 193
Mercurius Pragmaticus 184, 190–93
Merret, C. 156
Messner, M. 152
metadata 588–89
Meyer, D.S. 164–65
Meynell, Alice 267
middle-class identity and consumption 101–2, 105–7
Middleton, Sue 9
Midland Daily Telegraph 243
Miles, R. 112–13, 119
Millaud, Moïse 218
Miller, Jonathan 476
Miller, Karl 270
Miller, Toby 400–401, 557
Milligan, Spike 117
Mills, B. 451, 455–56
Millwood Hargrave, A. 89, 92–93
Milne, M. 241
Milosevic, Slobodan 175
miners' strike (1984–85) 163–64, 179
Minic, D. 347
Mist, Nathaniel 202
Mittell, J. 451, 495
Mitting J 90
Mjøs, O.J. 489
M'Millan, John 369–70
'modding' 565–66
Modern Man (magazine) 300
modernism 312–18; definition of 268; in journalism 215
Mollie Makes (magazine) 280–81
Monbiot, George 429

Monkey (digital magazine) 306–7
monopolistic competition 76
Montagu, A. 111
Montague, Lord 140
Montgomery, David 246
Montgomery, James 202
monthly periodicals 264–65
Moore, Michael 427–29
Mora, Philippe 314
moral panics 44–45, 87–88, 116, 119, 138–39, 160–61, 421–22, 546
Morgan, Carolyn 280
Morisset, T. 561
Morley, D. 128
Morris, Desmond 479
Morris, Errol 427
Morrison, D.E. 92–93, 400
Mort, Frank 26, 301, 303
Mortimer, John 363
Moss, Kate 225
Mott, F.L. 219
MUD (video game) 566
multimedia environment 535
multiplex cinemas 400, 402
Münsterberg, Hugo 86
Murdoch, James 324, 329
Murdoch, Rupert 220–23, 256, 327–28, 441–42, 466
Murdock, Graham 45, 87, 162–63, 243
Murphy, D. 244–45
Murphy, Kate 347
Murphy, Robert 399
Murray, Andy 151
Murray, Colin 367
Murroni, C. 229
Murry, John Middleton 269
music *see* listening to music, personal
music hall 382, 452
Muslim communities in Britain 118–19
Mutiny Act (1797) 233
Mutz, Diana 578

Nash, Andew 266
National Council for the Training of Journalists (NCTJ) 52
National Enquirer and *National Star* 223
national identity 153
National Lottery 401
National Union of Journalists (NUJ) 243–45
natural disasters, reporting of 575
natural history television 471, 475, 478–81, 489
Nazi regime 32, 257
Neale, S. 451–52
Nedham, Marchamont 183–84, 189–93

Nel, F. 246
Nerone, J. 240
Neville, Richard 314
The New Age (weekly periodical) 268
'new man', the 303–5
new media studies 14–15
New Musical Express (NME) 315–16
New Statesman 268
'new woman', the 292–93
New York Journal 217
New York Times 86, 572
New York World 218
Newman, G.F. 466
Newman, Kim 421
Newman, Sydney 464
Newnes, George 210, 218, 265–66
News at Ten 223
news reporting 504–11, 555–56; radio once seen as a threat to the press 255, 533; use of new technologies in 528, 534–36
News of the World 220–24, 252
newsbooks in the seventeenth century 189–91
Newspaper Publishers Association 244
Newspaper Regulation Act (1798) 202
Newspaper Society 81–82, 244
newspapers: competition between 75–76, 82; distribution systems for 518–21; early development of 195–96; function of 219; future prospects for 517, 524; political economy of 520; political role of 23; production costs of 80, 208, 211, 230, 530; profits made by 524; readership of 198–200, 519–22; systems for distribution of 78–79; uniqueness of 198; used as sources 21–22; websites of 523; and women 123–24
Nice, L. 277–78
Nicholas, Sian 29–30, 35–36, 255
Nicholls, D. 101
Nichols, Bill 425, 434
Nichols, J. 524
Nicholson, B. 253
Nietzsche, Friedrich 62
Nineteen Eighty-Four (television adaptation) 462
1930s period 30–31, 34–36
Nintendo 564
Nixon, Sean 303, 305
Nora, Pierre 582
North, R.D. 324
Northcliffe Newspapers 243
Northern Ireland 443
Norway 510
Nott, James 34

Nova (magazine) 313
Nunn, H. 501
Nuts (magazine) 306

objectivity in the media 21, 532
Obscene Publications Acts 233, 422
O'Connor, Thomas P. 209–12
O'Conor Eccles, Charlotte 267
Office of Communications (Ofcom) 443–44, 508
Official Secrets Acts (1911 and 1989) 234
Ohmann, R. 273
O'Kane, Maggie 175
Olick, J.K. 582
Oliphant, Marcus 472
Oliver, Jamie 429
Olympic Games, boycotts of 155–56
online media 528–36
Open University 47–48
opinion, written expression of 571–78
opinion leaders 531
Orage, A.R. 268
O'Rahilly, Ronan 336
Oram, Alison 138
Oram, Daphne (and Oramics) 60–61, 67–68
Orchard, Rob 275
Orwell, George 258, 269, 463
'otherness' in the media 112–13, 119
Outram, D. 480
outside broadcasts (OBs) 367–73, 476
Owen, David 157
Oz (magazine) 314

Pacifica Radio 349
Paine, Thomas 77, 202
Pakeerah, Stefan 89–90
Pall Mall Gazette 209, 218
Panahi, Jafar 427
Pariser, E. 578
Park, Richard 375
Parker, Martin 185–86, 189–90
parliamentary lobby system 230
parliamentary reform 202
parliamentary reporting 200, 233
Parmar, Belinda 278, 281
Parsons, Christopher 175
Parsons, Tony 318
participation by the public in media organizations and programs 523–25, 573
patriarchy 127–28
Patten, John 49
Patten, Robert L. 265
Pattison, Mark 266
Paulussen, S. 517
Pawling, Chris 31–36

Payne, Philip 219
Payne Fund studies 86–87
paywalls 279–80, 535
Peacock, Sir Alan 327, 507
Pearson, Cyril Arthur 210–11, 218
Pearson, G. 87
Pebody, C. 212
Peccinotti, Harri 312
Peel, John 337, 340
Peenemünde 66
Peeples, J. 166–67
Peg's Paper 288
Pennell, Elizabeth 267
Pennies from Heaven 465
Penrod, S. 95
Penthouse (magazine) 302
The People 139
Peoples' Charter Union 522
personal computers, use of 563–64
Petley, Julian 89, 93, 96, 222, 251, 408, 422
Phelps, Guy 54
Phillips, J. 163
Phillips, Richard 202
Phin, Christopher 276
Pickering, Lionel 245
Pickering, M. 455
Picture Post 311–12
Piepe, A. 105–7
Pilger, John 172
Pilkington, A. 113
Pilkington Report (1962) 327, 506
Pink Floyd 66, 313
Pinter, Harold 360, 464
pirate radio 334–42, 386; aims and aspirations of 338–39
Pirie, David 418–19
Pitt-Rivers, Michael 140
Pitzulo, Carrie 300
Place, Francis 78
Play for Today 464–65
Playboy (magazine) 300–302
Poliakoff, Stephen 468
Police and Criminal Evidence Act (1984) 234
police series on television 463, 465, 467
political economy of the media 75–82, 215, 225, 520
political news 510
Polytechnic of Central London 47
Pope, Alexander 78
Pope, Generoso 223
popular culture 151, 221–25
popular history 404, 411
popular press 210–12, 215, 218, 221–22
populism 104–5, 221, 223, 507
pornography 88–89, 94–95, 133–37, 302

Porter, L. 455–56
Porter, Roy 78
Porter, V. 398
Post Office 78–79, 324, 428, 532
Poster, Mark 11, 14
postmodernism 9, 15
post-structuralism 297
Potter, Dennis 465
Pöttker, H. 242
Pound, Ezra 268
Powell, Colin 173
Powell, Enoch 115, 117, 156
Powell, Jonathan 430
Poynor, R. 312
Prendergast, Tom 298–300
present-centredness 10–14
press, the, definition of 228–29
Press Association (PA) 79–81, 212, 241, 519
Press Council and Press Complaints Commission 235
Preston, P. 223
Prevention of Corruption Act (1889) 34
Price, Katy 68–69
Priessnitz, H. 356
Priestley, J.B. 22, 36, 462
Printing Act (1663) 521
'producer choice' system 466–67
professionalism 371, 530
Project CARS (racing simulation) 567
propaganda 173, 176, 289, 428
Protection of Children Act (1978) 234
protest movements 161–67
provincial media 33–34, 198–200, 208, 239–47, 519–24
Provincial Newspaper Society 232, 241
psychedelic style 313–14
Public Interest Disclosure Act (1998) 235
public opinion 195–203; definition of 197; and newspaper content 200–201; and politicians 201–3; and press liberty 196–98
public service broadcasting (PSB) 21, 45, 105, 126, 323–31, 445, 461, 464, 466, 532–35, 544, 553–55, 558; characteristics of 323–24; consolidation of 326–27; critiques of 327; on current affairs 504–11; international profile of 328; original vision of 324–26; significance of history programs for 485–87; threats to and durability of 328–31, 336, 341–42
public sphere 23, 45, 101, 103, 147–48, 157, 167, 211, 324, 327, 329, 455, 493, 521–22, 546, 571–76; *strong* and *weak* 195
publication bias 92
Pulitzer, Joseph 209, 216–18

Putterman, B. 452
Pynchon, Thomas 65

Quandt, T. 562
Quatermass 419, 462–63
Queen (magazine) 313

race: concept of 111–19; as represented on television 116–18
Race Relations Act (1965) 234
Racial and Religious Hatred Act (2006) 234
racism: cultural 119; 'external' and 'internal' 114; 'new' 115; in sport 155
radio audiences 380–88; measurement of 387
Radio Clyde 375
Radio Luxembourg 104, 325, 336, 385–86
radio sports news 366–77
radio technology 381–82, 541
radio time 544
Radiorakel 348
Rank, Leopold von 258
Ratcliffe, P. 113
Raymond, J. 189
Reading, A. 583–84
reality television 105–6, 493–501; definition of 494–95; histories of 495–98
Reed International Ltd 244–45
Rees, Laurence 486–87
Rees-Mogg, William 443
regional identity in television 467
Regulation of Investigatory Powers Act (2000) 234–35
regulation of the press 228–36, 253; economic 231–32; history of 229–36; meaning of 229
Reid, C. 200
Reid, Robert 480
Reith, John 33, 105, 126, 323–26, 335, 359, 383, 385, 464; definition of the BBC's role 325, 380, 505, 533; legacy of 328–31
Representation of the People Act (2000) 428
Reuters news agency 81, 212, 531–32
reviews, literary 263–66
Reynolds, Gillian 363
Reynolds, J. 126
Richards, Jeffrey 410
Richards, Julian 421
Richmond, Bruce 267
Riefenstahl, Leni 427
Rigby, Jonathan 418–19
riots in England (summer 2011) 160
Riposte (magazine) 279
Roberts, K. 106
Robertson, Geoffrey 439

Robinson, Piers 178
Rockstar North (company) 566
Rodger, Ian 357
'rolling news' channels 509–11
Rooney, D. 103
Root, Alan 480
Rose, David 465
Rosengard, P. 455
Rosenstone, Robert 411
Rosie, M. 166–67
Ross, D. and S.A. 94
Ross, K. 124, 305, 347
Rotha, Paul 475
Rotundo, E. Anthony 298
Routledge, P. 164
Royal Family 222
Rucht, D. 165
Rudkin, David 362
Runnymede Trust 118
Rusbridger, A. 523
Ruskin, John 325
Russell, Jason 434
Russell, Samantha 567
Russell, William H. 172, 207
Rutter, Alan 277

St John, Bridget 315
St John, Ian 221
Saintsbury, George 266
Sala, George W. 209
Sandel, Michael 101, 107–8
Sarner, Moya 281–82
satellite television 466–67
Satz, Aura 67–68
Savigny, H. 108
Savile, Jimmy 142
Scammell, M. 100–101, 107–8
scandals 140–41
Scannell, P. 331, 335, 377, 533
Scargill, Arthur 164
Schafer, Tim 567
Schama, Simon 484–87
Schiller, Herbert 46
Schlesinger, James 174
Schmidt, Eric 583
Schönhammer, R. 543, 546
Schuchard, Ronald 22
Schuman, Howard 465
Schwarzkopf, Norman 173
Schweizer, K. 230
Science Museum 60–61, 67–69
science on television 470–81; aim of 474, 476
scoops 80, 212
Scorsese, Martin 418

Scott, Peter 478–79
Scrutiny (periodical) 269
Scudamore, Frank Ives 79
Seaton, Jean 3, 24, 48, 230
Seattle protests (December 1999) 166
Second World War 81, 234, 269, 288, 310, 312, 336, 380, 384, 397, 407, 428, 505, 529, 533
Sector Skills Councils 53–55
seditious libel, law of 232–33
Seesholtz, M. 574
self-censorship in television 445–46
self-regulation by the press 235–36, 252, 257
sex and sexuality in the media 133–43
Seymour, E. 507
Shaaber, M. 185
Shaar Murray, Charles 315
Shafer, R. Murray 346
Shah, Eddie 245
Sharp, Martin 314
Shattuc, J.M. 573
Shaw, George Bernard 266
Shea, D.M. 574
Shea, Jamie 175
Shevelow, K. 572
Shirky, Clay 434
Short, Ramsay 476
Short, William H. 86
Shrubsole, G. 103
Siapera, E. 575
Sieveking, Lance 357
Silverstone, Roger 47, 477
Simpson, D.H. 245
Simpson, Mark 303
Simpson, Wallis 32, 437, 446
Singer, Aubrey 470–77, 481
situation comedies ('sitcoms') 116–17, 451–57; British and American types compared 453–54; definition of 451, 456
skinheads 314–15
Skoog, K. 347, 352
Sky News 507–9
Sky TV 327–28, 466
Slightly Mad Studios 567
Slimbridge Wildfowl Trust 478
Smart, David 299
Smith, A.C.H. 142
Smith, C. 143
Smith, G.A. 395
Smith, O. 221
Smollett, Tobias 263
Smythe, T.C. 216
Snickars, P. 583
soap operas 221, 359, 431, 497, 545
social conflict, media coverage of 160–69

social democracy 310–15
social media 167, 224, 520, 577–78
Society for the Diffusion of Useful Knowledge 78
Solomons, Jack 373
Solomos, J. 112–13, 118
Sony *Walkman* 540–41, 544–46
South Africa 156–57
Southern Daily Echo 520
Southwell, Tim 304
Spacewar! (video game) 563
Spake, Jeremy 497
Spare Rib (magazine) 270, 291–92, 315
spare time 34
specialist magazines 273–82; as 'experience makers' 277–78
The Spectator 263–65
Speight, Bernard 66
Speight, Johnny 117
Spence, Bob 427
Spencer, D.R. 216, 219
Spender, Stephen 269
Spigel, L. 128
sport 147–57; and identity 153–55; and journalism 152–53, 366–77; and popular culture 150–52; marginalization of women in 154–55; politicization of 155–56; role in social and cultural history 148–50
Sports Report 367–77
Spurlock, Morgan 429
Squire, J.C. 268
stage plays, television adaptations of 462
Stankievech, C. 540
Starkey, David 116, 484, 487
Stationers' Company 229–32, 437–38
Stead, William T. 209, 212
steam press technology 241, 529–33
Steinberg, Michael 13
Steiner, G. 1
Steiner, L. 347
Stelling, Jeff 375
stereotyping 117, 119, 155, 222
Stevens, Jocelyn 313
Stockhausen, Karlheinz 65
Stopes, Marie 138
Strand Magazine 266
Street, Sarah 410
Street, Sean 360
subscription channels 554–55
The Sun (newspaper) 103, 118, 142, 220–24
Sunday Pictorial 139–40
Sunday Sport 222
Sunday Times 221, 312
Swallow, Norman 475
'Swampy' 165

Swiencicki, Mark 298
Swift, Jonathan 201
Swinnerton, Frank 267
Sykes Committee (1923) 324, 505

tabloid press 211, 215–25; in Britain 217–20; decline of 224; milestones in development of 216–17; profitability of 221
talk shows on television 573–74
'talking stories' 220
'taxes on knowledge' 78–79, 199, 208, 241, 265, 438, 522, 530
Taylor, Gordon Rattray 470, 476
Taylor, S.J. 225
Team Rock 280
technological progress, impact of 456–57, 528–29, 536, 558
technology transfer 65
telegraphy, development of 79, 212, 519, 529–35
telephones, use of 212
television technology 384
television viewing time 554–55
Temple, M. 531
Terrorism Acts 118–19, 235
Terrot, Charles 462
'text-mining' 26
Thacker, Andrew 15
That Was The Week That Was 506
Thatcher, Margaret (and Thatcherism) 103, 107, 115, 163–64, 244, 327, 431, 441–42, 466, 506
Thomas, Dylan 359
Thompson, Denys 42
Thompson, E.P. 20
Thompson, Hunter 314
Thompson, J.B. 140
Thompson, Roy 104, 463
Thorburn, D. 12
Thorpe, Andrew 31
Thumim, J. 128
Till Death Us Do Part 117, 454
'time shifting' 551, 554
The Times 31, 34, 207, 221, 529–30
Times Literary Supplement 267
Tindle, Sir Ray 246
Tinsley, William 265
Tit-Bits 210, 218, 265–68
'toddlers' truce' 126
Tolkien, J.R.R. 362
Tolson, A. 335
Tomlinson, Ian 168
Tosh, John 298
Tracey, M. 323–24, 327, 400
trade union legislation 244–45

trade unions in printing 244
Traill, H.D. 267
transistor radios 385–88, 541, 543
travel writing 112–13
Treason Felony Act (1848) 233
Trenaman, Joseph 44
Tribune 532
trivialization of the media 34–35
True (magazine) 300
Tuchman, G. 290
Tunstall, Jeremy 44, 46
Turing, Alan 63–66, 69–70
Turner, Graham 490
Turnock, R. 105
Twain, Mark 239
typewriters, use of 212

Uimonen, H. 543
'umbrella competition' between newspapers 75
Under Milk Wood 359
Unger, S. 103–4
universities, role of 53
Upstairs Downstairs 464–65
user-generated content 388, 575
'uses and gratifications' approach 44

Valkenburg, P.M. 106
Van Dijck, J. 585
Van Dijk, T. 116
Van Loo, J. 562
Van Zoonen, L. 128
vernacularization 221–22
Verne, Jules 217
Video Appeals Committee 90
video games 89–92, 561–69; customization of 565; links between players and developers 567–68; nature of 562–63
'video nasties' 87–88, 415, 421–22, 440–41
Video Recordings Act (1984) 88–90, 422–23, 440
Vietnam War: protest against (London, 1968) 162–63, 166; reporting of 171–72, 177
Vinitzky-Seroussi, V. 582
violence: causes of 91, 96, definition of 92–93; effects of 93; on screen 89
Virgin Games 564
Virilio, Paul 63
Viva Radio 348
Vox Pop (radio program) 573
Vujnovic, M. 524

Wade, David 361
Wagg, S. 453

Wagner, P. 14
Wahl-Jorgensen, K. 167
Walker, A. 240, 242, 521
Walker, Johnnie 338–42
Wall, D. 165
Wall to Wall Television 487–88
Walpole, Robert 201
Walsh, Louise 501
Walton, William 358
war: media coverage of 171–73, 176; technologization stemming from 63; *see also* armed conflict
'war on terror' 175–76, 178
Warner, John 190–92
Watney, Simon 139
Watson, Paul 433, 495–96
Watson, Robert Spence 241
Web 2.0 technology 247, 523–25, 577
Webb, Sydney and Beatrice 268
Webster, John 371
Wedgwood Benn, Anthony *see* Benn, Tony
The Wednesday Play 464
Weintraub, William 299
Weissmann, Elke 417
Wellington, Chrissie 154
Wells, H.G. 69, 113–14
West, Amy 493
Westbrook, Adam 279
Whannel, Garry 151–52
Whannel, Paddy 43
Wheelan, Imelda 305
Wheeler, N.J. 178
WHER-FM (radio station) 348
White, Cynthia 285
'white man's burden' 113–14
Whitehead, Kate 360
Whitehouse, Mary 127, 134, 422, 440
Whiteley, N. 102, 106
Who Do You Think You Are? 488
W.H. Smith (retailer) 292
Wickberg, D. 452
Wickham, P. 105
Wickwar, W. 229
Wiener, J. H. 531–32
Wife Swap 432, 495, 500
Wilbur, Jay 566
Wildeblood, Peter 140
Wiles, R.M. 240
Wilkes, John 197, 200
Williams, A. 577
Williams, Christopher 394
Williams, K. 141, 210
Williams, Leonard 137–38
Williams, M. 350
Williams, Raymond 10, 45–47, 105, 550

Willis, John 484, 487
Willock, Collin 479
Wilmes, Mary Kay 270
Wilmut, R. 455
Wilson, B. 433
Wilson, Brian 316–17
Wilson, Harold 311–12, 334, 441
Wilson Report (2012) 53
Winship, Janice 286, 290–91
Winston, Brian 47, 252, 540
Winthrop-Young, Geoffrey 63
Wintour, P. 245
'wireless', use of term 380–81
Witty Report (2013) 53
Wolfe, Tom 309–13, 317
Wolfenstein 3D (video game) 565–66
Wolsey, Tom 312–13
Woman and Home (magazine) 290
Woman's Hour 345, 347, 349
women: and literary periodicals 267; and newspapers 123–24; in sitcoms 55–56; and sports broadcasting 376–77
women's magazines 125, 273, 278, 285–94; early examples of 286–88; in the inter-war and post-war years 288–89; and the 'new woman' 292–93; in the second half of the twentieth century 289–91
women's radio 345–52
Women's Realm 289
Wood, Linda 397
Wood, Michael 487
Woods, F. 400
working-class values and consumption 102–7
Working Woman (magazine) 292
The World About Us (TWAU) 479–80
World Trade Organization (WTO) 166–67
Worth, Katharine 360
Würzbach, N. 186

Xavier, F. 431
The X Factor 501

'yellow press' 216
The Yorkshire Post 33

Z Cars 464
Zielinski, Siegfried 12
Zillman, D. 94–95
Zoo Weekly (magazine) 306